Marxist-Leninist 'Scientific Atheism'

Religion and Reason 25

Method and Theory
in the Study and Interpretation of Religion

Mouton Publishers
Berlin • New York • Amsterdam

Marxist-Leninist 'Scientific Atheism' and the Study of Religion and Atheism in the USSR

JAMES THROWER
University of Aberdeen

Mouton Publisher
Berlin • New York • Amsterdam

Library of Congress Cataloging in Publication Data

Thrower, James, 1936-
   Marxist-Leninist "scientific atheism" and the study of religion and atheism in the USSR.

   (Religion and reason; 25)
   Bibliography: p.
   Includes index.
   1. Atheism—Soviet Union. 2. Atheism—Study and teaching—Soviet Union. 3. Religion—Study and teaching—Soviet Union. 4. Communism and religion.
I. Title. II. Series.
BL2747.3.T495 1983   207'.047   82-22423
ISBN 90-279-3060-0

Typesetting: Asian Research Service, Hong Kong. - Printing: Druckerei Hildebrand, Berlin. - Binding: Lüderitz & Bauer Buchgewerbe GmbH, Berlin.   **Printed in Germany.**

For Penelope, Charlotte
and Annabel, my other,
and more important, offspring.
And to:
ANDREW FINLAY WALLS
Most generous of scholars

Marx's whole manner of conceiving things is not a doctrine, but a method. It offers no finished dogmas, but rather points of reference for further research, and the method of that research...
(Engels, *Letter to Werner Sombart*)

The Russians have displayed a quite peculiar disposition to take up and transform Western ideas. What in the West was a scientific theory which could be criticised as a hypothesis or as a relative or partial truth with no pretence to universal validity, *that* was put forward by the Russian intelligentsia as an ultimately valid affirmation bordering on religious revelation. The Russian always seeks for the absolute. (Berdyaev, *Les sources et le sens du communisme russe*)

Foreword

The book by James Thrower which I have been asked to present to the public — and which I had the good fortune to read before publication — fills an obvious gap. It is not for nothing that this gap existed, for, in general, the subject did not seem to deserve serious treatment, and certainly not treatment by the specialists of what one may call (not without reservation) the science of religion, *Religionswissenschaft*. Even today, the publication of this book and its inclusion in the series "Religion and Reason" will no doubt appear to many astonishing, superfluous, and perhaps even unsuitable.

In his Preface, which follows this Foreword, James Thrower well defends the stance he has taken, but I would like to add just a few remarks from my own point of view, which coincides in part with that of the author. I do not think it entirely unnecessary to point out here, in passing, that, having conscientiously begun reading the book at the beginning, I conceived and openly expressed my great appreciation of the work long before I discovered that Thrower had thought fit to end with a quotation from one of my own works, with which he enthusiastically concurred.

Naturally, specialists in the study of religion and even the public at large, except for those who totally adhere to communism (indeed, even certain communists), cannot help but feel repelled by the formulations found in Soviet scholarly or popularizing works on religion or religions. They can only see in such works base political polemics of a prejudiced nature resulting in a fundamental, staggering incomprehension of the nature of the religious. The most they can suppose is that genuine scholars dissimulate their ideas privately and perhaps publish some of them in disguised form under the debased cover of official theses. This is also the opinion of Soviet dissidents and it certainly contains a large measure of truth. But it is not the whole truth.

An ideology imposed by the state is not an isolated phenomenon, nor something new or exceptional in the history of
societies (rather the contrary is the case), even if our era has seen
the model taken to hitherto unattained extremes of domination
over individuals. Intellectuals educated, like others, in the bosom
of such a state ideology and, moreover, charged with the task of
defending and propagating it, may well conceive doubts about it
at a given moment. They may even start to revolt, either passively
and silently in the intimacy of their conscience, or, if the circumstances are favorable, coming out into the open and expressing
their rebellion publicly. But only rarely can this rebellion efface
all traces of the conditioning they have undergone since childhood.
It is possible for someone to remain attached to basic conceptions
whose link with conclusions he violently rejects is not at first
glance clear. Some of these conceptions are unconscious and
some he deems sound, rightly or wrongly, after examination, even
though he repudiates the system of which they form a part. Thus,
even critics of the ideology may, in all sincerity, at times diffuse
its dogma.

All this is correct, but it should be added immediately that
some of these ideas which we put forward in the framework of an
ideological system with a political aim really are acceptable. The
fact that conclusions or ideas are imposed by a state does not
necessarily imply, in good logic, that they are false. This is evidently true of the past. In particular, it will be evident to believers,
Christians for example, who cannot reject the divinity of Christ
for the sole reason that, for fifteen centuries, at least a superficial
belief in it was imposed on pain of the most cruel punishments.

The acceptability of ideas put forward within a politically
orientated ideological framework seems less clear where dogmas
imposed by communist states are concerned. Yet, to take just one
example, is not the idea that the class struggle has played at least
a large part in history admitted, explicitly or implicitly, by many
non-communists? If the churches now denounce, parallel with
Marxist materialism, the materialist conceptions and practices of
capitalist societies, do they not thus assume — rightly or wrongly

— a background of ideas diffused by the state in communist countries which are also believed in — "freely" — by many people not subject to this pressure?

Everyone will readily concede that specific theses enunciated by Soviet scholars working in the social and human sciences (in the natural sciences the question does not even arise) can well be valid. But, when the level of ideas most directly linked to the realm of philosophical concepts is reached, doubts increase.

Even at that level, however, much can be retained by minds that do not subscribe to the communist political options or share the really fundamental dogmas of the Marxist ideological system. In advancing such a bold proposition, it is perhaps wise to invoke some unimpeachable authorities, in addition to the conclusions which follow from Thrower's arguments. I will choose two Catholic clergymen of high intellectual attainments, the Jesuit Gustav Andreas Wetter and the Dominican I.M. Bochenski, who agree essentially in their analyses and who are both militantly, zealously anti-communist and, so to speak, officially recognized as such.[1] They pronounce very harsh judgments on official Soviet philosophy; but, nevertheless, also think that the system contains very important positive elements with which they are manifestly in agreement, even if they consider the way in which these theses are expressed is technically hardly satisfactory and marked by distortions and contradictions. They refer, among other things, to "a healthy epistemological realism" which vigorously safeguards the possibility of knowledge of the real. They see this as a happily preserved legacy of Aristotle and Thomism. Like others, these authors point hopefully to the development after the death of Stalin of more original analyses by certain Soviet philosophers. I.M. Bochenski has thus judged it useful to undertake (with T.J. Blakeley) a remarkable enterprise, the compilation of a bibliographical inventory of Soviet philosophical publications. He introduces the work with the following noteworthy remarks, which will no doubt astonish more than one reader: "Certain of these works [of Soviet philosophers] are not without interest for the philosophers of the free world too — especially for those among them who, like the editor of this series, share with Soviet philosophers objectivism, epistemological realism, recognition of the legitimacy of ontology and formal logic as well as, finally, a universalizing conception (*einen ganzheitlichen Begriff*) of man. But, by the same token, philosophers who think otherwise might similarly see their interest develop for Soviet philosophy as its evolution continues."[2]

If I invoke the opinion of such highly competent figures, who are also at the same time ferociously hostile to the communist movement, it is to disarm the prejudices that may assail those who approach James Thrower's book and dissuade them from even undertaking the reading of it. In the course of it, the reader will see that the author defends the interest of his object of study in convincing fashion and with most pertinent arguments. He has conducted his study very well, scrutinizing conscientiously the Soviet texts. Basing himself on extensive documentation, he has succeeded in revealing the main lines of the principal tendencies in the practical and theoretical attitude of Soviet authors to religion. He has succeeded in addressing, in an intelligent, open, and sympathetic way, ideas he does not share. Without the slightest complacency, he nonetheless shows their positive elements and highlights their valid motivations. Likewise, he has succeeded in situating these ideas within the total world view (*Weltanschauung, mirovozzrenye*) adopted by the Soviet regime, yet less as a guide for its leaders than as a norm recommended — in a very imperative manner — for the thoughts of those who are subjugated to it.

The Western reader and especially those interested in the study of religion, the usual readership of "Religion and Reason", will learn much from this book. It will suggest to them that a religion should — though the specialists do not always do so — be studied *not only* as a coherent body of dogmas and rites, *but also* as one phenomenon (among others) of mobilizing energy for tasks assigned by a particular society. Consequently, the critique of religion practiced in the West since the Enlightenment — the Marxist and Soviet theses are no more than an extreme form, more or less crude or refined — does *not* appear *only* as a selfish political exercise, a vulgar manoeuvre. It is *also* an effort to replace the traditional religions by a new ideology endowed with the same functions. Seen in this way, the Soviet *Weltanschauung* requires an analysis of the same type as those which strive to investigate the religious ideologies of the past and present.

By pondering the ideas and facts presented by Thrower, specialists of religion may convince themselves that the phenomena habitually associated with religions *stricto sensu* also manifest themselves outside of this framework. We may mention just a few rapidly in passing: ardent faith, predisposition toward martyrdom, as well as dogmatic intolerance and heretic-hunting. Must that not lead to the conclusion that I have been advocating for some years already, that this framework should be enlarged?

From that perspective, should not their use of the category of "the sacred" (in Otto's sense of *mysterium tremendum*) for explication have its scope — which I in no way deny is very large — limited, unless the category of the "sacred" itself is considerably expanded?

Equally, it might lead to the notion that ideas, feelings and rites — i.e. the privileged (and often exclusive) domains of the study and reflections of specialists in religion — fail to account for the whole of their field of study. Such specialists often tend, in their practice if not in their theory, to presuppose that they do. To be sure, it is understandable that when a person devotes his life to the study of such profound doctrines, to which he has a deep emotional attachment, and of rites looked upon as assuring contact with a higher world, he has nothing but impatience and disdain for phenomena which are clearly limited to this sublunary world—to talk as the Ancients did. But, in fact, on the one hand there exist the organizational structures for the mobilization of individuals, the relations they establish between ideas and rites, and on the other hand there are the norms to which the constraints of concrete reality submit everyday life. Do not these structures, relations and norms weigh much more heavily on the conceptions and manifestations of the sacred than the specialists in question are inclined to admit?

It is with these queries that I will close these few pages, stressing once again that readers will find in James Thrower's book a well-informed, intelligent and honest study from which they will be able to derive material for much reflexion enriching for their work and thought, and perhaps even discover an appeal to examine critically their existential choices.

Maxime Rodinson

Preface

The Marxist-Leninist critique of religion claims to be the most fundamental, the most thorough, the most widespread and the most sustained critique to which the religions of the world have, as yet, been subjected. Where governments have come into being inspired by the world-outlook of Marxism-Leninism, the educational and administrative offensive which they have launched against religion has been one of their most characteristic features. Church-State relations in the Communist world have, however, been amply documented and analysed and it is not my intention to duplicate such studies as already exist;[1] nor is it my intention to deal in detail with popular Communist anti-religious propaganda, for again such studies already exist.[2] My intention is, rather, to look at the way in which Soviet Marxism-Leninism has developed its own distinctive *Problematik* and methodology for the study of religion and atheism, for I believe that this has important implications for the study of religion as a whole.

The study which I present is, therefore, neither a political, nor a sociological, still less a theological, study of Marxism and religion,[3] but an attempt from within the discipline of religious studies — *Religionswissenschaft* — to articulate and assess the Soviet contribution to that discipline and to examine the Soviet claim that the Marxist-Leninist approach to the study of religion is the only valid one, in that it, and it alone, constitutes the true 'science of religion'.[4]

No such study, so far as I am aware, yet exists. Soviet work in religious studies has, for sixty years, been carried out in virtual isolation from Western scholarship, and Western scholarship has been content to remain in almost total ignorance of Soviet work in this field.[5] It is my hope that this present study will go some way towards mitigating this lamentable state of affairs.

I do not, however, seek to minimise the very real differences which exist with regard to the study of religion between Marxist-Leninists and scholars in the Western world. The differences in basic presuppositions are fundamental and, I shall argue, ultimately irreconcilable — although I believe that both approaches offer valuable insights into the complex phenomenon of religion. In the conclusion I put forward my own views regarding the way in which I think 'the science of religions' should develop.

Marxism-Leninism is an outlook on life which seeks to combine theory with practice. In my attempt to formulate the *Problematik* and methodology of Soviet study of religion I begin, therefore, with theory, as this is found in the writings of Marx, Engels and Lenin. To some extent this involves my going over ground that will be familiar to those acquainted with Marxism, but not so familiar, I think, to those whose interest lies primarily in religious studies. In any case, with the exception of a book by Delos McKown (1975), little serious attempt has yet been made to look at Marxism-Leninism explicitly from within the discipline of *Religionswissenschaft*.[6]

From theory, as it is found in the classics of Marxism-Leninism, I move to delineate the main outlines of Soviet studies of religion and atheism from the Revolution of 1917 to the present day. Here again I seek to break new ground for, so far as I am aware, no serious study has yet been made of what Soviet Marxism-Leninism today refers to as 'scientific atheism' (*nauchnyy ateizm*) — that aspect of the Marxist-Leninist world-view which deals explicitly with religion and atheism. Here I draw on original Soviet sources and work from a basis of personal discussions with Soviet scholars engaged in this field. I quote at length — at what some may consider inordinate length — from these, I must confess, at times somewhat banal and even turgid sources, not only because they are inaccessible to Western scholars who do not read Russian — and are often hard to get hold of when they do — but also because it is the only way of showing that I have not misrepresented Soviet scholarship in this field. Soviet scholars do, I assure the reader, say what I quote them as saying; naïve and dogmatic as much of it must appear to be to those trained within the Western tradition of scholarship. I have, however, limited the amount of the Soviet material referred to, both in the interests of convenience and because in the Soviet Union anything which gets into print in this highly sensitive area has gone through such a severe process of editorial redaction, that what is finally published — the approval of sub-editors, chief-editors, and editorial boards having been secured — can be taken not only to be representative of the official view but, as a consequence of this process, bears a remarkable similarity — in both style and content — to other works in the same field. I have sought, therefore, to cull, from the extremely vast literature of 'scientific atheism', only such material as Soviet scholars themselves regard as being important and by which they would wish to be judged. In this enterprise I have been helped enormously by my conversations — in Leningrad and Moscow — with scholars actively engaged in this field and in particularly by conversations with Professor M.I. Shakhnovich of Leningrad University and by scholars working in the Museum of the History of Religion and Atheism, also in Leningrad.

Three bibliographical surveys relating to Soviet studies of Buddhism, Christianity and Islam are given as appendices to this present work. A full analysis of the material contained in these would be beyond the competence of all but experts in these fields. Any comments I make, therefore, are but the comments of a general historian of religions with only a passing acquaintance with specialised work pursued in these fields. Their inclusion will have been justified, however, if Western historians of religion take up and pursue the studies referred to from within their own disciplines.

Finally, I seek to assess the Marxist-Leninist understanding of religion and the Marxist-Leninist claim that theirs is the only true 'science of religion'. This is the most difficult part of my enterprise, for I believe that anyone who writes seriously about religion, or the study of religion, discloses — whether he recognises it or not — his own answer to the fundamental question of *Religionswissenschaft*, which is whether religion is to be regarded as a primary or secondary datum; that is, whether religion is to be studied in and for itself, or whether it must be reduced to the data of some other, and more amenable, discipline; whether religion is to be encouraged or whether it is to be rejected. The nature of the claims inherent in the religions of the world are, I believe, such that continued and sustained neutrality with regard to these claims betrays a lack of serious engagement with the material one is studying. An author's basic ontological commitment must come out. It is for this reason that this study closes with the personal conclusion that it does.

The translations from Russian are my own, although I have been helped by Mrs. Josephine Forsyth of the department of Russian Studies in the University of Aberdeen, and by Mrs. Masha Fergus, a former teaching assistant in the same department. Any errors of translation that remain are, however, solely my responsibility. I must also admit that, on occasion, my translations from Russian are somewhat more 'free' than some professional translators would, quite rightly, allow; but I have not, I believe, altered the sense, only the style.

In my exposition of Marx's and Engels' own thinking about religion I have made considerable use of their early writings, but it must be pointed out that these were not, in fact, available to early Marxists or to Lenin, nor to Soviet scholars working in religious studies until well into the 1930's; indeed, it is only, in fact, today that they are beginning to be taken seriously in Soviet study of religion. The unwillingness of Marx and Engels themselves to re-publish their early writing; the story of their suppression in the Soviet Union until 1927 — when an incomplete edition was produced — and of their eventual publication in Germany in 1932 as the third volume of Marx and Engels, *Historisch-Kritische Gesamtausgabe*, edited by Rjazanoy and Adoratski (*MEGA*), makes fascinating reading and can be found in Chapter XI of Robert Tucker's *Philosophy and Myth in Karl Marx* (1961). They are now, however, freely available in a variety of editions and it is for this reason that I have made full use of them in attempting to get at Marx and Engels' own views on religion. The fact of the lateness of their publication must be borne in mind, however, when considering early Soviet work on religion.

I must thank the Carnegie Trust for the Universities of Scotland, the University of Aberdeen, and the British Council, for making it financially and administratively possible for me to have spent one month in 1976 and three months in 1979 working — under the auspices of the Anglo-Soviet Cultural Agreement — at the University of Leningrad and at the Museum of the History of Religions and Atheism, also in Leningrad. A grant from the Sir Edward Cassell Education Trust enabled me to spend a month in Moscow at the end of 1976. Without such assistance this study would not have been possible. The Carnegie Trust and the University of Aberdeen have also given generous financial help towards the publication of this book, and for this too I would like to express my gratitude.

Finally, I must thank Mr. James Forsyth, Reader in Russian Studies in the University of Aberdeen, as well as Sir John Lawrence and Professor Trevor Ling of Manchester University for reading through the entire manuscript and for making numerous suggestions for improving both its style and content. Mrs. Jeanette Thorn, with rare patience and remarkable ingenuity, working from a very untidy manuscript of my own, produced the final typescript, and to her my thanks are also extended, as they are to John Gauss and my wife, Judith, who gave invaluable help with the proofs.

Balgownie Lodge,   James Thrower
Aberdeen, October 1982

Contents

Abbreviations

Further details of publications can be found in the Select Bibliography

AR	*Antirelioznik*
FN	*Filosofskiye nauki*
IiTA	*Istoriya i teoriya ateizma*
KNAS	*Kratkiy nauchno-ateisticheskiy slovar'*
KPSS v resolyutsiyakh	*Kommunisticheskaya Partiya Sovetskogo Soyuza v resolyutsiyakh i resheniyakh s"ezdov, konferentsii i plenumov Tsk*
LCW	*Lenin: Collected Works*
MEBW	*Marx and Engels: Basic Writings*
MECW	*Marx and Engels: Collected Works*
MEGA	*Karl Marx, Friendrich Engels: Historisch-Kritische Gesamtausgabe. Werke*
MEOC	*Marx and Engels: On Colonialism*
MEOR	*Marx and Engels: On Religion*
MSW	*Marx: Selected Works*
MEW	*Karl Marx, Friedrich Engels: Werke*
NA	*Nauchnyy ateizm*
NiR	*Nauka i religiya*
NKA	*Nastol'naya kniga ateista*
OMLF	*Osnovy marksistko-leninskoy filosofii*
ONA	*Osnovy nauchnogo-ateizma*
PZM	*Pod znamenem marksizma*
RADU	*Religion und Ateismus in der UdSSR: Monatlicher*
RCL	*Religion in Communist Lands*
SE	*Sovetskaya etnografiya*
SCW	*Stalin: Collected Works*
VDI	*Vestnik drevney istorii*
VF	*Voprosy filosofii*
VI	*Voprosy istorii*

VIRA   *Voprosy istorii religii i ateizma*
VNA   *Voprosy nauchnogo ateizma*
YMIRA   *Yezhegodnik muzeya istorii religii i ateizma*

A Note on Transliteration

There is unfortunately no universally accepted system of transliterating the Cyrillic alphabet. The system used in this book is presented below. It is based on that used by the American Library of Congress with the difference that Ц is transliterated here by 'ts' (and not t͡s), Щ by 'shch' (and not sh͡ch), Ю by 'yu' (and not i͡u) and Я by 'ya' (and not i͡a). Final unaccented Ий and ый have been transliterated by 'iy' and 'yy' respectively, except when they occur at the end of commonly recognised surnames where, in accordance with now well established convention, I have written 'y' (e.g., as in Dostoyevsky [not Dostoyevskiy]).

Cyrillic		Used in Present Book
А	а	a
Б	б	b
В	в	v
Г	г	g
Д	д	d
Е	е	ye, e*
Ё	ё	ye
Ж	ж	zh
З	з	z
И	и	i
Й	й	y
К	к	k
Л	л	l
М	м	m
Н	н	n
О	о	o
П	п	p
Р	р	r
С	с	s
Т	т	t

Cyrillic		Used in Present Book
У	у	u
Ф	ф	f
Х	х	kh
Ц	ц	ts
Ч	ч	ch
Ш	ш	sh
Щ	щ	shch
Ъ	ъ	"
Ы	ы	y
Ь	ь	'
Э	э	e
Ю	ю	yu
Я	я	ya

* Transliterated as 'ye' at the beginning of a word, after vowels, and after ъ and б, elsewhere as 'e'.

PART ONE

The Theoretical Basis of the Marxist-Leninist
Approach to the Study of Religion

The Classical Marxist Critique of Religion

1.1   MARX, ENGELS, AND THE GERMAN CRITICISM OF RELIGION

For Germany the criticism of religion is in the main complete, and the criticism of religion is the premise of all criticism.

With this opening sentence of his *Contribution to a Critique of Hegel's Philosophy of Law*, published in 1844 when he was twenty-six years old, Marx's historical standpoint in the criticism of religion was clearly determined. In seeking to establish the burden of Marx's critique of religion our first task, therefore, must be to outline the substance of that criticism which Marx, at the outset of his career, regarded as 'in the main complete'.[1]

As is well-known, the beginnings of Marx's thought are closely bound up with the controversies surrounding the philosophical legacy of Hegel who had died in 1831. These controversies centred upon two areas of Hegel's thought – his philosophy of the state and his philosophy of religion. This, of course, is not surprising, given the political situation in Germany at the time of Hegel's demise, for there had arisen in Germany a strongly authoritarian regime, the twin pillars of which were Throne and Altar. The Prussian monarchy, in alliance with the Prussian church, was more and more claiming that the existing socio-political structure of German Society embodied the structure of the ideal Christian state.[2] Before his death, Hegel, from his chair at the University of Berlin, had become the great exponent of this system, the cultural interpreter of Prussian *Realpolitik*.

There were some of his pupils, however, who remembered that the great conservative, as Hegel had become towards the end of his life, had also been the great dialectician, and that his philosophy had taught not only reconciliation with the given, but the destruction of outworn forms. It was here that issue was joined; church and state roundly supporting the conservative interpretation of Hegel's somewhat ambiguous philosophical legacy, and a group of young, 'left' Hegelians expounding the more revolutionary side of his thinking. In particular, the young 'left' Hegelians wished to explore the way in which the religious and political ideas of their own age were destined to give way to a more satisfactory view of the world. As Engels wrote late in his life:

The doctrine of Hegel, taken as a whole, left plenty of room for giving shelter to the most diverse practical party views. And in the theoretical Germany of that time two things above all were practical: religion and politics. Whoever placed chief emphasis on the Hegelian *system* could be fairly conservative in both spheres; whoever regarded the dialectical *method* as the main thing could belong to the most extreme opposition, both in politics and religion. (Engels, *Feuerbach; MEBW:* p. 224)

The young, 'left' Hegelians, who concentrated on the *method* rather than on the *system* of Hegel, included such men as Heinrich Heine, David Friedrich Strauss, Bruno Bauer, Max Stirner and, most important of all, Ludwig Feuerbach. It was these men who brought to fruition the tradition of German criticism of religion which Marx, though not without reservation, accepted as 'in the main complete'.

Marx began his critique of religion, therefore, in conscious continuity with the philosophical critique of his time and we must, if we are to understand him right, outline the development of the philosophical criticism of religion in Germany and say something about the point that it has reached when he entered into the criticism of the religion and the society of his day.

The history of the German criticism of religion can be taken to begin with Kant, the founder of 'the critical philosophy', and with Kant's development of Descartes' emphasis on subjectivity towards an unequivocal affirmation of the autonomy of man. Whereas, for Descartes, man merely discovers truth as something divinely pre-established, according to Kant he constitutes it in virtue of his own resources. Seeking to refute what he considered the inadequate views of both post-Cartesian rationalists and post-Cartesian empiricists, Kant developed a defence of truth and value in which these were grounded, not in the Being of a transcendent God, but in the transcendental dimensions of the human spirit itself. The universality and seeming necessity of scientific statements about the world, together with the seeming absoluteness of moral values, were located, for Kant, not in the mind and will of God, but in the *a priori* forms of man's own understanding and in the autonomy of the practical reason.

The autonomy of man, proclaimed by Kant, was greatly enriched by Fichte who, more than any previous philosopher, integrated man into the world. Man, he believed, could achieve full self-consciousness only in the process of building the future. Fichte's philosophy stressed three great themes: freedom, subjectivity and *'Praxis'*.[3] Even more than had Kant, Fichte laid stress on the sovereignty of man as the creator of his own destiny. Ethics, he maintained, were based on the autonomy of the human will — religion on its heteronomy. There was thus a contradiction in principle between ethics and religion. Fichte founded his entire humanistic philosophy on the notion of man as creator, upon the notion that a man is what he does. The absolute, for Fichte, is thus within history. The man of theory must also be the man of action but — and here Fichte went beyond Kant — man's activity in history is not the activity of the individual alone, for the individual is a man among men. He wrote:

The man who isolates himself renounces his destiny and detaches himself from ethical progress. Morally speaking, to think only of self is not even to think of self, since the absolute goal of the individual is not within himself — it is in all mankind. The sense of duty is not statisfied, as some believe, and actually turn into a merit, by sequestering oneself on the heights of abstraction and pure speculation, by leading the life of an anchorite; it is satisfied not in dreams but in acts, acts accomplished in society and for it. (Fichte, *Sittenlehre:* IV, para. 8)

The most profound attempt, prior to Marx, to solve the enduring problem of German philosophy — that of the relationship of the finite to the infinite — was undoubtedly that of Hegel. Hegel did not, however, at the outset of his career, see the problem in such general terms. It was brought to his attention by his early attempt to understand the true significance of the primary object of his concern – the Christian religion. In an early essay, *The Positivity of the Christian Religion* (1876), Hegel had criticised the authoritarian, dogmatic religion of his day as a corruption of the original 'moral' religion of Jesus – the religion of all free men. Such authoritarian forms as the Christian religion had assumed could be nothing other than a source of alienation, a religion for servile men, and a far cry indeed from that willing obedience to the moral law preached, so Hegel believed, by Jesus. All contingent, historical forms of religion must be measured against the yardstick of their effectiveness in mediating to man the divine reality in the depth of his being – a reality whose lifegiving power is made effective through free and reverent commitment to the moral law. In a slightly later work, *The Spirit of Christianity and its Fate* (1800), the influence of Kant, so obvious in Hegel's earlier understanding of the Christian gospel, waned, and the moral law of the pure practical reason was replaced by a pantheism of love as constituting the true meaning of the Christian religion. Authoritarian religion was still the object of Hegel's criticism, and such religion was now accused of radically de-humanising man. The interiorisation of the master – slave relationship in the Kantian conflict of duty and inclination simply makes man, according to Hegel, his own slave. The morality of duty, therefore, must give way to a morality of love, understood as an inner harmony of reason and inclination – a fundamental disposition of life which transcends the order of duty and commands and thus overcomes alienation by uniting the finite and the infinite. Through love we come to an awareness of the unity of our life with infinite life and thus with all life.[4]

During his early years Hegel believed that philosophy – the reflective, analytical discipline *par excellence* – could not comprehend this loving union of finite and infinite; only religion could do this by means of symbols. His later career, however, can be seen as an attempt to work out, at the level of philosophical reflection, the unified conception of reality inherent in his earlier vision. What he was searching for was a style of philosophising which would render intelligible to the rational mind that which religion expresses only in symbols, and which would overcome the duality inherent in all forms of rational thought hitherto, and in particular the duality of man and God, philosophy and religion. For Hegel, this philosophical rationality took the form of a philosophy of Spirit (*Geist*). In his mature philosophy Spirit was disclosed as the active unification of all oppositions, and all oppositions were known as ultimately reconciled self-determinations of Spirit. This is the inner living truth of reality.

From the outset Hegel repudiated any ultimate opposition of finite and infinite. He wrote: 'We must rid ourselves of this opposition of finite and infinite, and do it by getting an insight into the real state of the case'. (Hegel, *Lectures on the Philosophy of Religion:* Vol. I, p. 174). And the 'real state of the case', for Hegel, was that the traditional understanding of the relationship between finite and infinite was sadly amiss. The order of finite being is not, as had traditionally been maintained, causally dependent upon the infinite; rather the order of finite being is the theatre whereby the infinite accomplishes its full and true reality as infinite. This it does through a process of self-differentiation and mediation whereby, in the order of finite being, it negates the abstract affirmation of itself as sheer identity and comes to a concrete affirmation of itself through the negation of this negation. He wrote:

The finite is therefore an essential moment of the infinite in the nature of God, and thus it may be said that it is God Himself who renders Himself finite, who produces determinations within Himself. (ibid., p. 198)

The finite is an objectification of the infinite, and the whole finite order is, therefore, seen to be necessary if God is to achieve that correct knowledge of His limitless virtuality which constitutes His true infinite actuality. All the vicissitudes and alienations of finite existence must be seen as necessary accompaniments of the process whereby Absolute Spirit returns to a realisation of Itself through the self-transcending finite consciousness. The mode of thought necessary for comprehending this dynamic process was, according to Hegel, dialectical. It was this insight which was to have so decisive an influence on Marx.

In the Introduction to his *Lectures on the Philosophy of History,* Hegel described world history as it appears at first sight. He wrote:

> . . . we see a vast picture of changes and transactions; of . . . manifold forms of peoples, states, individuals, in unresting succession . . . On every hand aims are adopted and pursued. . . In all these occurrences and changes we behold human action and suffering predominant; everywhere something akin to ourselves, and therefore everywhere something that excites our interest for and against . . . Sometimes we see the more comprehensive mass of some general interest advancing with comparative slowness, and subsequently sacrificed to an infinite complication of trifling circumstances, and so dissipated into atoms. Then, again, with a vast expenditure of power a trivial result is produced; while from what appears unimportant a tremendous issue proceeds . . . and when one combination vanishes another immediately appears in its place. The general thought — the category which first presents itself in this restless mutation of individuals and peoples existing for a time and then vanishing — is that of change at large. The sight of the ruins of some ancient sovereignty directly leads us to contemplate this thought of change in its negative aspect. . . But the next consideration which allies itself with that of change, is that change, while it imports dissolution, involves at the same time the rise of new life, that while death is the issue of life, life is also the issue of death. (Sibree, 1900: p. 75f)

For Hegel the most obvious springs of historical action are, *prima facie*, human interests and passions and the satisfaction of selfish desires to the disregard of law, justice and morality (Sibree, 1900: p. 21f). Yet it is interesting that Hegel felt compelled to put the question: To what final purpose are these enormous sacrifices offered time and time again? — a question which, as he himself said, arises 'necessarily' to our way of thinking. Thus, after describing history in the way referred to above, Hegel went on to distinguish this 'oriental' conception of history, as he called it, symbolised as it was, for him, by the life of nature, from the occidential conception of history which is a history of Spirit and which, although it is also self-consuming, does not merely return to the same form but comes forth 'exalted and glorified', with each successive phase becoming in turn material on which the spiritual history of man proceeds to new levels of fulfilment.

This occidental conception of history, implying, as it does, irreversible direction toward a future goal, is not merely occidental for, aware as we are today of the very different conceptions of history abroad in world cultures, we can recognise it for what it is – namely, the Judeo-Christian assumption that history is providentially directed towards the fulfilment of an ultimate purpose – a notion which Hegel partially secularised by translating the religious symbol of providential care into the philosophical counter of 'Spirit' or 'Reason' as the 'absolutely powerful essence'. The conception of 'providence', which in its religious mode Hegel found profoundly unsatisfactory, must, he argued, be brought to bear upon the details of the historical process and 'the ultimate design of the world perceived'. He wrote:

Our intellectual striving aims at realising the conviction that what was intended by eternal wisdom is actually accomplished in the domain of existent, active Spirit, as well as in that of mere Nature. Our mode of treating the subject is, in this aspect, a theodicy, a justification of the ways of God... so that the ill that is found in the world may be comprehended, and the thinking Spirit reconciled with the fact of the existence of evil. Indeed, nowhere is such a harmonising view more pressingly demanded than in Universal History.[5] (Sibree, 1900: p. 16)

In order to harmonise the view of history as it appears at first sight with an ultimate design of the world, Hegel introduced the notion of 'the cunning of reason' which, he held, works through the passions of men, using them as its agent (Sibree, 1900: p. 34). It is not by chance, but of the very essence of history, that the ultimate outcome of historical events is always something unintended. The apparent freedom of human action is the ambiguous freedom of passions pursuing, with an almost animal faith, a particular purpose, but in such a way that the pursuit of individual interests

is prompted and driven by an anonymous impulse: universal purpose and individual intent meet in a dialectic of passionate
activity. Men act historically, argued Hegel, by being acted upon
by the power and cunning of reason. This is the true import of
that which is symbolically expressed in the religious conception of
divine providence. Looked at with the eye of reason, world history
is no longer meaningless, but meaningful because purposeful – the
purpose being nothing less than the total liberation and fulfilment
of man. 'The process displayed in history', Hegel wrote, 'is only
the manifestation of religion as human reason, the production of
the religious principle under the form of secular freedom' (Sibree,
1900: p. 35).

Marx, who, in the words of Karl Löwith, was 'a philosopher
with an immense sense of history' (1949: p. 33), was to think, to
a greater extent than he himself always realised, from within this
occidental, Judeo-Christian conception of history – something
of which Marxists are only today beginning to take cognisance
(cf. below, pp. 369ff.). Marx, however, was to secularise the
symbol of 'divine providence' even more radically than had Hegel,
by transforming it, according to his own estimation, into the
language of a 'scientific' materialist understanding of history.

Although Marx had read Fichte and Hegel as a student and was
to utilise much of what they had said in his own philogospy, it was
with the controversies surrounding Hegel's philosophical legacy
that his thinking began in earnest. The most important figure in
the immediate post-Hegelian period in Germany, for Marx, was
undoubtedly Ludwig Feuerbach.[6] Of him Marx wrote:

I advise you, you theologians and speculative philosophers, to rid your-
selves of the concepts and prejudices of the old speculative philosophy, if
you want to deal with things as they are in reality, that is, in truth. And
there is no other road for you toward truth and freedom than this 'stream
of fire' (*Feuer-bach*). Feuerbach is the purgatory of our time. (MEGA: I,
i(1) 175)

Feuerbach was an erstwhile theologian who had been converted to
philosophy by Hegel, but he had retained sufficient interest in

religion to seek to get behind its outward and outworn forms in order to penetrate to what he took to be its essence – an enterprise which involved his discarding both traditional theology and Hegel's own philosophy of religion. As Karl Barth remarked in an introduction to Feuerbach's *The Essence of Christianity*: 'Having proceeded far beyond Hegel as well as Kant, Feuerbach belongs to the Berlin master's disciples who scented the theological residue in his teaching and stripped it off' (Barth, 1957: p. xii). Like Strauss, who had in *The Life of Jesus* (1835) sought to explode that aspect of Hegel's philosophy which posited God, Nature and History as being at the heart of the dialectical process of coming to a true understanding of the world, Feuerbach also dissociated philosophy from religion and sought to render to history its own autonomy and reality. The dialectical process, Feuerbach further maintained, was not limited to the understanding of history, but was to be extended into the future. Philosophy should no longer be seen as supportive of the *status quo* but as rebellion against it. The decisive step in this rebellion was, for Feuerbach, the rejection of traditional religion and its replacement by a truer religion of humanity.[7] What Feuerbach offered was an anti-theological interpretation of religion, an interpretation which would get at the truth behind the appearance – and the truth was that, at bottom, religion believed in and worshipped not God, but human nature conceived as being itself divine or the supreme perfection. Seeking his own solution to the problem of duality Feuerbach came to the conclusion that:

The antithesis of divine and human is altogether illusory, that it is nothing else that the antithesis between human nature in general and the human individual; that, consequently, the object and content of the Christian religion is altogether human. (*Essence of Christianity*: pp. 13-14)

The origin of religion, for Feuerbach, is to be found in man's consciousness of himself – not, however, of himself as an individual, but as a species. It is because man's 'species nature' can become the object of thought that man can transcend his own individual

limitations and attain to 'consciousness of the infinite' — Feuerbach's synonym for religion. Religion is the consciousness man
has of his own infinite nature. This consciousness is, furthermore,
'nothing else than the consciousness of the infinity of consciousness' (ibid., pp. 23). The proper constituent elements of the nature
of man are the absolute, self-authenticating attributes of reason,
will and love. Feuerbach wrote:

> That alone is true, perfect, divine, which exists for its own sake. But such is
> love, such is reason, such is will. Reason, will and love are not powers which
> man possesses, for he is nothing without them, he is what he is only by them;
> for they are the constituent elements of his nature, which he neither has nor
> makes, the animating, determining, governing powers — divine absolute
> powers — to which he can oppose no resistance. (ibid., p. 3)

Whatever our individual limitations, we recognise reason, will and
love as in themselves infinite, unqualified perfections — objects of
absolute worth. 'The absolute to man is his own nature' (ibid.,
p. 5). But man as an individual does not properly comprehend his
infinity and is all too prone to ascribe his own individual limitations to the species as such and to project the infinite possibilities
of his own nature onto an external object — that is, onto God.
Feuerbach wrote:

> All divine attributes, all the attributes which make God God, are attributes
> of the species — attributes which in the individual are limited, but the limits
> of which are abolished in the essence of the species. . . My knowledge, my
> will, is limited; but my limit is not the limit of another man, to say nothing
> of mankind; what is difficult to me is easy to another; what is impossible,
> inconceivable, to one age, is to the coming age conceivable and possible. My
> life is bound to a limited time, not so the life of humanity. (ibid., p. 152)

Religion is thus man's earliest, if mistaken, form of self-know-
ledge, in which he contemplates his own nature as though extrinsic
to himself. Religious man is alienated man, for religious man, the
true creator, makes that which is his own creation — God — into
an authority over himself, thus throwing away his natural
sovereignty and reducing himself thereby into a servile and miserable being. As Feuerbach expressed it:

Religion is the disuniting of man from himself; he sets God before him as the antithesis of himself. God is not what man is — man is not what God is. God is the infinite, man the finite being; God is perfect, man imperfect; God eternal, man temporal; God almighty, man weak; God holy, man sinful. God and man are extremes: God is the absolutely positive, the sum of all realities; man the absolutely negative, comprehending all negations. (ibid., p. 33)

If we are to achieve an integral humanism — such as Feuerbach hoped — this false antithesis must be resolved, and resolved in a way which allows man to realise for himself the infinite possibilities inherent in his nature. Hegel's philosophy of Spirit, Feuerbach contends, failed to do this, in that the self-alienation of man of which it speaks is, in the last resort, but the realisation of Absolute Spirit working through him. Man must begin, therefore, by rejecting both Hegel and traditional religion, or rather he must see religion for what it is, then the truth will become clear — theology is anthropology and God simply a projection on the part of unenlightened men. In a concluding appraisal of his own achievement in the *Essence of Christianity*, Feuerbach wrote:

We have reduced the superhuman, supernatural nature of God to the elements of human nature as its fundamental elements. Our process of analysis has brought us again to the position with which we set out. The beginning, middle and end of religion is MAN. (ibid., p. 184)

The significance, and limitation, of Feuerbach's position, as viewed by Marx, we shall discuss shortly.

From the outset of his career Marx was a convinced atheist, although there is some evidence that in adolescence he had moments of fervent, if somewhat sentimental, religious fervour; but by the time he was a student in Berlin, to whose university he had transferred from Bonn in 1836, such early religious beliefs as he might have held had been abandoned.[8] In a letter written to his father in November, 1837, in which he describes his early spiritual Odyssey, he wrote:

From the idealism which, by the way, I had compared and nourished with the idealism of Kant and Fichte, I arrived at the point of seeking the idea in reality itself. If previously the Gods dwelt above the earth, now they became its very center. (*MECW:* 1;18)

And in the introduction to his doctoral thesis, *On the Difference between the Natural Philosophy of Democritus and the Natural Philosophy of Epicurus*, written in 1841, he wrote:

Philosophy makes no secret of it. The confession of Prometheus: 'In simple words I hate the pack of gods' is its own confession, its own aphorism against all gods who do not acknowledge human self-consciousness as the highest divinity. It will have none other besides. (*MECW:* 1;30)

This, then, the position reached by the philosophy of his day, was the point at which Marx began his own critique of religion. The autonomy of man, proclaimed by Feuerbach, was for him axiomatic. His atheism was not, as some have maintained, accidental, but integral to his entire vision of the revolutionary transformation of man and society upon which, in the early years of the 1840's, he was beginning to embark. Feuerbach had placed at the centre of his philosophy neither God not Spirit, but man, and Marx was to begin his own thinking at this point. Hegel's story of the progress of Spirit, overcoming alienation in order to achieve liberation, was for Feuerbach a rather mystifying way of describing the progress of human beings overcoming the alienation of both religion and philosophy. Marx seized on this idea of bringing Hegel down to earth by using Hegel's methods to attack the present condition of human beings in the Germany of his day.[9] His ideas at this stage of his development, however, were liberal rather than socialist, for he still thought — with Feuerbach and the 'left' Hegelians — that a change in consciousness is essentially what is needed to transform both man and society. As he wrote to his collaborator on the *Deutsch-Französische Jahrbücher,* Arnold Ruge, in 1843:

The self-confidence of the human being, freedom, has first of all to be aroused again in the hearts of these people. Only this feeling, which vanished from the world with the Greeks, and under Christianity disappeared into the blue mists of the heavens, can again transform society into a community of human beings united for their highest aims, into a democratic state. (*MECW:* 3;137)

The centre of Marx's concern, as of Feuerbach's, was man – his freedom and his fulfilment; and this, as many contemporary Marxists are recognising, was not only Marx's starting point, but the central concern of his life. As the Austrian Marxist, Ernst Fischer, has put it:

Marx's thought underwent many variations in the course of his life, but what had served as his starting point remained intact: the possibility of the whole, total man. . . Religion, atheism, communism were, for Marx, stages or features of development rather than its goal. The goal was positive humanism, the real life of man. . . The starting point of religion is God. Hegel's starting point was the State. Marx's was man. (Fischer, 1973: pp. 20-21)

And the Polish Marxist, Adam Schaff, has written that:

Economics, for Marx, although he devoted his entire life to it, is not an end in itself. Marx was and remained the philosopher and sociologist for whom man is the central concern. . . His researches in economics are not the end in itself. . . but only a means of achieving the main goal which is the *liberation of man*. (Quoted, Skolimowski, 1967: p. 260)

Marx's earliest concern with man, however, was, like that of Feuerbach, one which concentrated on the activities of thought and consciousness. The first sign of the shift to the later emphasis on the material and economic conditions of life came in an essay written in 1843 entitled 'on the Jewish Question' – an essay in which Marx reviewed two publications by his friend, Bruno Bauer, on the issue of civil and political rights for Jews. In this essay Marx rejected Bauer's treating of this question as if it were a religious question. It is not the 'Sabbath Jew', he writes, that we should consider, but the everyday Jew. Working from the common stereotype of the Jew as obsessed with money, Marx describes the Jew as simply a special manifestation of what he calls the 'Judaism of civil society'— that is, the dominance in civil society of financial interests generally, and he suggests that the way to abolish 'the Jewish problem' would be to reorganise society so as to abolish the dominance of financial interests (*MECW:* 3; 146-174).

The importance of this essay, from the point of view of Marx's understanding of religion, is that, in it, Marx sees economic life and not religion, as the chief form of human alienation. Whilst the rejection of religion was, as the 'left' Hegelians maintained, a prerequisite of the liberation of man, religion, Marx now maintained, was not the real enemy; it was but the symptom of a deeper malaise. Friedrich Engels, Marx's life-long friend and collaborator, had come to a similar conclusion via the same route as had Marx.

Engels came from a family renowned for its Protestant fundamentalism and from a part of Germany — Barmen in the Rhineland — in which pietism and evangelical religion were held in high regard. During the first seventeen years of his life Engels was steeped in authoritarian faith and intolerance and broke with Christianity only after a period of considerable mental turmoil. The story of Engels' loss of faith can be traced in his letters of the late 1830's to the Graeber brothers. Instrumental in this loss of faith was his reading of such radical theologians as Schleiermacher and David Friedrich Strauss. His reading of the latter's *Life of Jesus* led him to take an interest in speculative philosophy and in the Absolute Idealism of Hegel. In a letter to Friedrich Graeber, written in June 1839, he wrote: 'I have come to the conclusion only to treat a teaching as divine if it can defend itself before the bar of reason.' (*MECW*: 2;454).

Later in the same year he wrote the *Letters from Wuppertal,* in which the fanatical religiosity of the environment of his early years was mercilessly criticised. A period of military service in Berlin in 1841 brought him into contact with the Young Hegelians and in a series of three articles attacking Schelling's philosophical theology, Engels became the first of the Young Hegelians to proclaim atheism openly. In 1842 his father sent him to work in one of his factories in Manchester in England, where he continued to take an active interest in theological discussion and in a review of Thomas Carlyle's *Past and Present*, which he published within two years of arriving in England, he exhibited a critique of religion which bore a remarkable similarity to that which Marx was also developing (*MECW:* 3;444-468). The German critique, and that of Feuerbach in particular, was for Engels, as for Marx, decisive. Both thinkers picked up that critique at the point where Feuerbach and the Young Hegelians had left it, but both developed it in a way uniquely their own by setting it within a radically new understanding of the world and of man.

This is clear, as we have seen, as early as Marx's 'On the Jewish Question' and in his *Contribution to a Critique of Hegel's Philosophy of Law* — both of which were written in 1844. In the latter of these essays Marx begins by stating the position of the 'left' Hegelians:

The basis of irreligious criticism is: Man makes religion, religion does not make man. . . religion is the self-consciousness and self-esteem of man who has either not yet found himself or has already lost himself again.

But he adds immediately:

Man is no abstract being encamped outside the world, Man is the world of man, the state, society. This state, this society produce religion, an inverted world-consciousness because they are an inverted world. (*MECW:* 3;175)

Here we meet for the first time with Marx's insistence that man is no monadic individual, but a social being living at a certain period of history — something which had important consequences for the way in which Marx understood human alienation. Alienation, for Marx, does not originate, nor does it operate in the restricted areas of the spiritual life — in religion and philosophy — but in the total world of man and above all in the social and economic spheres. Under existing socio-economic and political conditions, robbed of the fruit of their labour, the majority of

men have become the root of a universal perversion.[10] What
Feuerbach saw as rooted in religious perversion – the oppression
of man, the real creator, by God, his own creation – Marx now
saw in existing socio-economic and political relationships. It was
here that man was enslaved by his product and thus alienated on
every side. The religious form of alienation was secondary for
Marx, for it was only a symptom of the far more important form
of alienation which produced it. He wrote:

Religion is the general theory of that world, its encyclopaedic compendium,
its logic in a popular form, its spiritualistic *point d'honneur*, its enthusiasm,
its moral sanction, its solemn complement, its universal source of consolation
and justification. It is the fantastic realisation of the human essence because
the human essence has no true reality. The struggle against religion is therefore indirectly the fight against the world of which religion is the spiritual
aroma. Religious distress is at the same time the expression of real distress
and also a protest against real distress. Relgion is the sigh of the oppressed
creature, the heart of a heartless world, just as it is the spirit of spiritless
conditions. It is the opium of the people. (*MECW:* 3;175)

Religion, for Marx, as we see from the above quotation, plays a
two-fold role: it is an expression of and a protest against real
distress and it is also a means whereby those who are distressed
find consolation. It is, however, for Marx, a false consolation. The
consequence that he drew from his understanding of religion was
that the real struggle is not against religion, but with the world
which produces religion:

To abolish religion as the illusory happiness of the people is to demand their
real happiness. The demand to give up illusions about the existing state of
affairs is the demand to give up a state of affairs that needs illusions. The
criticism of religion is therefore in embryo the criticism of the vale of tears,
the halo of which is religion. (*MECW:* 3;176)

One cannot make a complete scapegoat for the ills of the time out
of religion – as Feuerbach and the Young Hegelians were inclined
to do – for religion is only a symptom and the struggle against
religion is but a prelude to the more fundamental struggle with the
world which produces it. Marx wrote:

The task of history, therefore, once the world beyond the truth has disappeared, is to establish the truth of this world. The immediate task of philosophy, which is at the service of history, once the holy form of human self-alienation has been unmasked, is to unmask self-alienation in its unholy forms. Thus the critique of heaven turns into the critique of earth. (*MECW:* 3;176)

The critique of religion is but a step in a wider struggle, but in certain situations — as Soviet Marxists argue — it might well be an important first step to take, for the trouble with religion, as Marx saw it, is that it distracts men from their true goal and — as he argued later in his life — is often used as such by those whose interests are best served by such distraction. He wrote:

Criticism has plucked the imaginary flowers from the chain not so that man will wear the chain without any fantasy or consolation but so that he will shake off the chain and cull the living flower. The criticism of religion disillusions man to make him think and act and shape his reality like a man who has been disillusioned and has come to reason, so that he will revolve around himself and therefore round his true sun. . . The criticism of religion ends with the doctrine that man is the highest being for man, hence with the categorical imperative to overthrow all conditions in which man is a degraded, enslaved, neglected, contemptible being. (*MECW:* 3;176, 179)

In placing the struggle against religion within the wider context of the struggle for the total liberation of mankind, Marx and Engels showed that their outlook was positive throughout. The negative denial of religion is not enough, and Marx and Engels were far from ascribing to the struggle against religion the importance that it tended to assume in the writings of the 'left' Hegelians. They were, in fact, continually surprised, and on occasion not a little annoyed, by the persistent attacks on religion of Feuerbach and Bauer. As they saw it, religion in general, and the Christian religion in particular, were already *in extremis*, and the attacks on religion by the 'left' Hegelians reminded them, as Marx said, of Sancho Panza in Cervantes' novel, *Don Quixote*, who mercilessly beat the harmless attendants at a funeral procession. The attack on religion, for Marx and Engels, was as unnecessary as it was misplaced – unnecessary, because religion was a spent force; misplaced, because the real enemy was not religion but the society which produced religion.[11] To criticise religion without criticising its secular basis advanced the liberation of man not one whit. As they wrote in *The German Ideology:*

The 'liberation' of 'man' is not advanced a single step by reducing philosophy, theology, substance and all the trash to 'self-consciousness' and by liberating 'man' from the domination of these phases. . . it is only possible to achieve real liberation in the real world and by employing real means. . . liberation is an historical and not a mental act. (*MECW:* 5;38)

Further, to criticise religion without criticising its secular basis is to persist in a standpoint which is as theological as the religious standpoint itself, for an atheism which takes itself as an end in itself is only the negation of religion and does not succeed in transcending the religious level. As Marx wrote in his *Economic and Philosophic Manuscripts of 1844*:

But since for the socialist man the entire so-called history of the world is nothing but the creation of man through human labour, nothing but the emergence of nature for man, so he has visible, irrefutable proof of his birth through himself, of his genesis. Since the real existence of man and nature has become evident in practice, through sense experience, because man has thus become evident for man as the being of nature, and nature for the being of man, the question about an alien being above nature and man a question which implies the admission of the unreality of nature and man – has become impossible in practice. Atheism, as the denial of this unreality, has no longer any meaning, for atheism is a negation of God, and postulates the existence of man through this negation; but socialism as socialism no longer stands in need of such mediation. (*MECW:* 3; 305-306)

Thus did Marx and Engels see themselves 'bringing to fruition' the process begun by the German critical philosophy. In the resolution of that process, philosophy itself was transformed and became, what it had not been either in Hegel or in Feuerbach – revolutionary *Praxis*. As Marx put it in the last of his *Theses on Feuerbach:*'The philosophers have only *interpreted* the world, in various ways; the point, however, is to *change* it.' (*MECW:* 5;9).

1.2   MARX AND ENGELS ON THE ORIGIN, ESSENCE AND SOCIAL FUNCTION
      OF RELIGION

Marx's criticism of Feuerbach was that, although he had seen
rightly that religion is an alienation of the human essence, he had
failed to see that the real cause of this act of self-alienation, and
hence the true source of religion, lies in the fact that men are compelled to create the fantasy world of religion by the very nature of
the society in which they live and had thought, therefore, that it
would be sufficient for men to get rid of the illusions of religion
for them to come to themselves. This for Marx was not so. As he
wrote in the fourth of his *Theses on Feuerbach:*

Feuerbach starts out from the fact of religious self-estrangement, of the
duplication of the world into a religious, imaginary world and a real one.
His work consists in resolving the religious world into its secular basis. He
overlooks the fact that after completing his work, the chief thing remains to
be done. For the fact that the secular basis lifts off from itself and establishes
itself in the clouds as an independent realm can only be explained by the
inner strife and intrinsic contradictoriness of this secular basis. The latter
must itself, therefore, first be understood in its contradictoriness and then,
by the removal of the contradiction, revolutionised in practice. (*MECW:*
5;7)

Feuerbach had also, in Marx's opinion, ignored the fact that man
himself is a social product and that, as a consequence, religion is
also a social product.

Feuerbach resolves the essence of religion into the essence of man. But the
essence of man is no abstraction inherent in each single individual. In its
reality it is the ensemble of social relations. Feuerbach, who does not enter
upon a criticism of this real essence, is hence obliged. . . to abstract from
the historical process and to define the religious sentiment (*Gemüt*) regarded
by itself, and to presuppose an abstract − isolated − individual. . . Feuerbach,
consequently does not see that the 'religious sentiment' is itself a social
product, and that the abstract individual that he analyses belongs to a particular society. (*MECW:* 5;8)

Although Marx and Engels accepted the basic insight of Feuerbach that religion is an illusory form of human fulfilment, they took his analysis much further by searching out the roots of religion — its secular basis — not only in human nature but in society. For Feuerbach, man makes religion by setting up an illusory world onto which he projects what the real world denies him. Marx and Engels accepted this analysis of religion but posed the further question, why does man create such an illusory world? — and they thought that the answer was to be found in the fact that society hitherto has been and still is a society in which man is not truly himself. Henceforth their search for the sources of religion and their efforts to eradicate it, were to be subsumed under what was, for them, the more important question of humanity's self-inflicted imprisonment in its own world — that is, on the problem of alienation.

1.2.1 RELIGION AS A FANTASY OF ALIENATED MAN

Marx took over the notion of 'alienation' (*Entfremdung*) from Hegel, but changed its meaning in a number of important respects. The role of 'alienation' in the philosophy of Marx is, however, difficult to determine, for the concept functions in a variety of ways in his early writings and then disappears to re-emerge only in the manuscripts upon which he was working when he died (e.g., *Capital*, III: p. 259). Until quite recently Soviet scholars virtually ignored it in their expositions of classical Marxism — despite the publication in the Soviet Union in 1932 of the *1844 Manuscripts* of Marx in which the concept is especially predominant — and it is only in the last decade or so that they have given serious attention to it (cf. Mitin, 1963 and 1968; Fedoseyev, 1963; Kon, 1969).[12] All Western commentators, however, are agreed that the use of the concept in the early writings of Marx is vague, ambiguous and confused (cf. Gregor, 1974; Plamenatz, 1975: pp. 87-146). It is also agreed that the concept underwent considerable modification as Marx's thought about the state of affairs which it indicates developed.

As a concept 'alienation' is, of course, rooted in German Idealism, although the mood which it sometimes appears to indicate is one which is as old as universal as humanity itself. As John Plamenatz wrote, at the outset of his own discussion of the concept, in his book *Karl Marx's Philosophy of Man:*

Theologians, poets, and ordinary men in reflective mood have spoken of man as if he were lost in the world, or as if he were oppressed by it, or have said of him that he is his own enemy, the victim of his own actions. Man at odds with himself and man a stranger in a hostile world are themes as old as poetry and myth. A human condition which is part of what Hegel and Marx refer to when they speak of alienation has long been familiar to the introspective who see that condition revealed in themselves. (Plamenatz, 1975: p. 87)

The word itself has been used in a variety of ways throughout history. In the European Middle Ages it was used of a certain degree of mystical ecstasy in man's communion with God. Later, Protestants, beginning with Calvin, understood by it a condition of spiritual death resulting from man's estrangement from God by virtue of original sin. Rousseau spoke of the alienation of the individual's natural rights in favour of the community as a whole, which results from the 'social contract', and showed, particularly in his *Discourse on Inequality*, in parts of *Émile* and in some of the letters in *La Nouvelle Héloïse*, that he was not unaware of the ways in which society can oppress and bewilder the spirit of man. It was Hegel, however, who gave the term those distinctive emphases which it bears in the early philosophy of Marx, and it was Hegel who saw the connection between a condition of alienation and religion.[13]

Hegel believed that the spiritual condition which he called alienation (*Entfremdung*) is one which is revealed in several religions, but in none more powerfully than in Christianity, in which he saw not only the symptoms of alienation, but the condition of alienated man symbolically expressed. Hegel, however, as we have seen, sought to translate the symbols of religion into the language of rational understanding and nowhere was this more in evidence than when he was discussing the condition represented by the religious symbols of alienation.

No part of Marx's thought owes as much to Hegel as his conception of man. In the third of his *Economic and Philosophical Manuscripts of 1844* Marx acknowledged his debt to Hegel in this respect as follows. He wrote:

The outstanding achievement of Hegel's *Phenomenology* is, first, that Hegel grasps the self-creation of man as a process. . . and that he, therefore, grasps the nature of *labour*, and conceives objective man (true, because real man) as the result of his *own labour*. The real, active orientation of man to himself as a species-being, or the affirmation of himself as a real species-being (i.e. as a human being), is only possible in so far as he really brings forth all his species-powers (which is possible only through the co-operative endeavours of mankind and as an outcome of history). (*MECW:* 3;333)

Marx also acknowledged that Hegel understood what it is for man to suffer alienation – an understanding that takes us to the root of most social and psychological ills. He wrote:

The *Phenomenology* is a concealed, unclear and mystifying criticism but in so far as it grasps the alienation of man. . .all the elements of criticism are contained in it, and are often presented and worked out in a manner which goes far beyond Hegel's point of view. The sections devoted to the 'unhappy consciousness', the 'honest consciousness', the struggle between the 'noble' and 'base' consciousness, etc., etc., contain the critical elements (though still in an alienated form) of whole areas such as religion, the state, civil life, etc. (*MECW:* 3;332)

Hegel, said Marx, understood what alienation is and how it is related to religion, the state and other areas of social life – though his understanding was vitiated by his desire to go beyond man to talk about Infinite Spirit. For Marx, two facts about man stood out in Hegel's philosophy: that man is 'self-creative' and that he suffers 'alienation'. Man is the product of his own labour and becomes properly human only as a result of his own activities. This he does in the course of history. Hegel, Marx tells us, 'grasps the self-creation of man as a process' – not of man as an individual, but of mankind as a whole.

Yet Hegel's conception of man forms part of an outlook which Marx rejected, for Marx, like Feuerbach, wanted nothing to do with Hegel's metaphysical speculations regarding Infinite Spirit or Consciousness. Man himself, and not the Absolute, Infinite Spirit or Consciousness, was, for him, the true subject of the historical process. This, in Marx's own eyes, was the essence of his reform of the Hegelian dialectic. Feuerbach had argued that Hegel had succeeded in projecting human qualities, determinate predicates, into some metaphysical realm, thus elevating them to the status of 'moving subjects', so that predicates had been transformed into substantives, self-moving 'mystical subjects' and man's determinate traits reduced thereby to the status of predicates of the Absolute Spirit. In Hegel's philosophy men were nothing other than by-products in the life-history of the self-moving Spirit, and in rejecting this view Marx agreed with Feuerbach (cf. *The Poverty of Philosophy* and *Letter to P.V. Annenkov, MECW:* 6;163-167; *MECW:* II; 400-410). But if, as Feuerbach had perceived, man and not Spirit is the true subject of history, then the cosmic objectifications of Spirit, as they were to Hegel's way of looking at things, the alienations in the metaphysical realm, must be translated into their real counters and ascribed to the true subject of history – that is to man. This was the task which Marx set himself when he claimed to have found Hegel standing on his head and to have set him the right way up (Preface to second edition of *Capital*, I, 102-103). Much in Hegel's understanding of man and of alienation was, however, to survive this process.

Man, the self-creative being is, Marx claimed, the product of nature, even though in many crucial respects he differs from the rest of nature. For Marx, mental activities were inconceivable apart from the bodily behaviour in which they were manifest, and inconceivable except within the context of an evvironment external to man. But man is unique, for Marx, not only because he is self-creative, but also because he is self-conscious in ways that other animals are not, and his self-consciousness and his self-creativity are intimately connected. As Marx wrote:

The animal is one with its life-activity. It does not distinguish the activity from itself. It is its *activity*. But man makes his life activity itself an object of his will and consciousness. . . Conscious life activity distinguishes man from the life activity of animals. Only for this reason is he a species-being. Only for this reason is his activity free activity. (*1844 Manuscripts, MECW:* 3;276)

The conclusion which Marx drew from this was that man has, over and above his biological needs, needs peculiar to himself as a self-conscious and self-creative being — in particular the need for self-affirmation and recognition — needs which depend on the quality of his relations with others and with himself. Man is a social being, produced by, yet at the same time producing, society. He also acts on and humanises nature. Thus he produces his world. When man does so recognise himself as self-creative he attains his majority. He sees that, as a rational, moral and creative being, he is the product of his own activities, of a long course of social and cultural change, which consists of what he has himself done and its effects upon him, and in thus understanding himself he no longer needs to postulate a creator external to himself. There are in the world no higher purposes than his own; 'Man is the highest being for man' (*1844 Manuscripts, MECW:* 3;304-306). His aspirations and ideas must be kept within the bounds of his powers, though he has at times grossly underestimated and under-valued these, but when he comes to see himself as he truly is he will be satisfied and secure in a godless world, for his idea of the world will then be congenial to him. He will be, as John Plamenatz has expressed it, 'fully human in a humanised world' (Plamenatz, 1975: p. 77).

We shall return to Marx's conception of man when we come to look at his 'materialist' conception of history, but for the moment we must notice that in the process of thus coming to himself man suffers alienation. Here again, Marx's understanding of the human condition owes much to Hegel, even though Marx rejected Hegel's notion of a self-creative, transcendent Spirit, and thus understood alienation as something wholly human. But Hegel had grasped what appeared to Marx to be an important truth — that man develops his powers through activities which involve alienation and the overcoming of alienation. In the passage already referred to, in which Marx paid tribute to Hegel for grasping the self-creation of man as a process, Marx went on to claim, with Hegel, that:

Man's affirmation of himself as a real species—being (i.e. as a human being) is only possible in so far as he brings forth all his species-powers. . .*which can only* [says Marx] *be done at first in the form of alienation.* (*1844 Manuscripts, MECW:* 3;333) (my italics)

As he works together with other men, man adapts his natural environment to his needs, and in the process of doing so produces a social environment, though without realising what he has done. Society, therefore, which man himself has created, appears as something external to him and he feels towards it as he would to a thing alien to himself which has him in its thrall. He feels oppressed by it, despite the fact that he has created it by his own activity. When men fully understood this they will, Marx believed, be in position to do something about it.

But although Marx took much of his early understanding of alienation from Hegel, he believed that Hegel had not fully appreciated the full range of human activity, nor had he understood the most fundamental human activity of all, as it was for Marx, of material human labour. 'Hegel', he wrote, 'understands labour as abstract and mental labour' (*1844 Manuscripts, MECW:* 3;333). Whether this was, in fact, so, is open to question (cf. Plamenatz, 1975: pp. 92-93), but Marx certainly believed that both Hegel and Feuerbach had underestimated the role of productive relations — that is socio-economic relationships — in human life, and had therefore, not seen the true cause of human alienation. Hegel had rightly seen mankind as passing from stage to stage in a historical process in which men developed their specifically human powers. But this, for Marx, is only part of the truth about man. There is indeed a movement, intellectual, moral and aesthetic, from less to more adequate views of the world, from less to more satisfying attitudes to it, but this movement is not autonomous. It depends, in ways which Marx never, unfortunately, made wholly clear, on more fundamental movements in the socio-economic sphere. Hegel had seen man as subject to needs peculiar to a self-conscious being, but in Marx's opinion, he had never fully appreciated the earthy, material basis of these needs – had never, in fact, taken fully into account the whole range of man's needs, and certainly never appreciated the material substratum upon which all the higher needs were based. He had passed too quickly, so Marx thought, to what he regarded as the fundamental human need – the need for recognition. Marx did not ignore this need; he fully appreciated that man has a sense of what is due to him as a human being and that when the fulfilment of this need is denied him, he feels diminished in his own eyes (cf. *Capital*: I; pp. 303-304), but he was aware – as perhaps few before him were aware – of the importance of the equally fundamental human needs for clothing, shelter, food, etc. He agreed with Hegel, however, that progress is related to need, and that it was in the course of history that men became aware of their needs and developed new ones. History, for both Marx and Hegel, is a process of self-discovery.

But Marx, like Hegel, was also aware that men are often dissatisfied, often unfulfilled, and that the unsatisfied, the essentially human needs (for material well-being, for self-affirmation and for recognition) persist. It is out of this alienated condition, for Marx, that the illusions of religion are born. Alienated in this world, men come to believe in another world in which they will be at home. Religion is a fantasy of alienated man.

Unless we see that for Marx, as for Hegel, men's needs are more than biological, that they are what may, indeed, be called spiritual, we shall not, I think, fully appreciate the depth of his analysis of religion as a fantasy of alienated man, although Marx himself obscured this analysis of the human condition by writing, at times, as if man's needs were wholly material, and there are passages in his writings where he wrote as if 'material production was the reproduction of life', in contexts which suggest that 'reproduction' consists only in the making, growing, or getting of that which preserves the species. But that he recognised, overall, that the needs of a self-conscious rational creature are wider than these basic needs, his writings taken as a whole leave us in no doubt. As he expressed it in his early writings:

Man is not merely a natural being. He is a being for himself (i.e., he is self-conscious) and therefore a species-being; and as such has to express and authenticate himself in being as well as in thought. (*MECW:* 3;337)

Thus, to explain how man becomes alienated, we must look to how, in society, man is denied his all-round development as a human being, how he is thwarted in his attempt to express, affirm and authenticate himself, and how, in religion above all else, he seeks a substitute satisfaction for the authenticity denied to him in reality.

In the philosophy of Hegel there are two distinct but related ideas — externalisation (*Entäusserung*) and estrangement or alienation (*Entfremdung*). Externalisation is the process whereby Spirit (and man as that in which Spirit is manifested) brings into being a world — especially a social world, a culture — through which it seeks to come to full self-realisation. Estrangement, or alienation, on the other hand, is the sense which the majority of human beings have of being restricted or oppressed in this world, or at odds with it and with themselves, without which the onward dialectical process of the self-realisation of Spirit might not take place. Much confusion has been caused by a number of Hegel's (and Marx's) interpreters who have used 'alienation' to cover both the process of externalisation and the condition of alienation. Yet the two must be kept logically distinct, for there can, as a matter of logic, be externalisation without alienation — indeed, there must be in Hegel's Rational State or in Marx's Communist Society, where alienation is overcome without man ceasing to be man. Thus, for Hegel, as for Marx, while self-externalisation (*Selbstentäusserung*) is integral to the human condition, alienation is not — or at least need not be so. Only where these two aspects of the total historical process are confused can alienation be described, as by one recent writer, as 'a logical necessity if there is to be any progress at all' (A. James Gregor, 1974: p. 292; Cf. also Gollwitzer, 1970: p. 74). As a matter of historical fact, however, all societies hitherto have been characterised by varying degrees of alienation and hence have been dominated by a religious outlook on life. But this for Marx is a contingent fact and not a logical or a metaphysical necessity. Alienation can and will be transcended, with the consequence that for Marx, if not for Hegel, religion, as a mistaken spiritual response to the condition of alienation, will disappear.

Awareness of this distinction between 'externalisation' and 'alienation' provides the answer, I think, to those who, in criticism of Marx and of his vision of the future Communist society, ask whether in a society where alienation has been overcome, development and progress will cease. This, as should be clear, need not be so for man, just because he is man, will still need to externalise himself in activity — will still seek for self-affirmation and recognition.

A necessary step in the process of transcending the alienated world, for Marx, is Communism, but Communism is not conceived as the end of the process. Communism, Marx wrote: '. . . is the necessary pattern and the dynamic principle of the immediate future, but Communism as such is not the goal of human development.' (*1844 Manuscripts; MECW:* 3;306). The goal of human development, for Marx, is that man should be truly and fully fulfilled. Communism, however, is a necessary pre-requisite for this to be so. Marx wrote:

Communism, as fully developed naturalism, equals humanism, and fully developed humanism equals naturalism; it is the genuine resolution of the conflict between man and nature and between man and man — the true resolution of the strife between man and man — the true resolution of the strife between *existence* and *essence*, between *objectification* and *self-confirmation*, between freedom and necessity, between the individual and the species. (*ibid., MECW:* 3;296)

The reason why Communism is a necessary prerequisite for overcoming alienated existence is that alienation is, for Marx, essentially a social phenomenon, in that it arises out of the perverse social relationships existing in all forms of society hitherto, but which are exacerbated in capitalist society. Marx's mature analysis of the phenomenon of alienation is thus concentrated almost exclusively on the socio-economic aspects of that phenomenon. After settling their account, as Engels was later to express it, with the Hegelian tradition by the writing of *The German Ideology* in 1845-46, Marx and Engels turned more and more to the analysis of the socio-economic structure of society and to the laws governing its development, and had less and less to say about other forms of alienation, although they did not lose sight entirely of their earlier concerns. Rather did they presuppose them. As Academician, M.B. Mitin of Moscow State University has said:

A consistent line runs from Marx's early works, where he philosophically substantiated communism as real humanism, to his profound economic substantiation of the fact that communism would inevitably replace bourgeois social relations. (Mitin, 1968: pp. 52-53)

For Marxism-Leninism, Marx's abandoning of his earlier and excessive concern with Hegel — or as others would say, his translation of the language of Hegelian metaphysics into the language of political economy (cf. Tucker, 1961) — marks the transition within Marx's own thought from philosophy, even philosophy conceived as revolutionary *Praxis,* to science. From this period onwards, Marxists maintain, 'scientific communism' was born, and from this period onwards 'alienation' — where it is referred to at all — is thought of almost exclusively in terms of alienated labour and as arising out of what, for Marx, were the most perverse aspects of capitalist society — the division of labour and private property. Whether in this transposition much of what was of value in Marx's earlier analysis of religion was lost is a question to which we shall return in Part III of this study.

The process of breaking with the Hegelian way of looking at history began with the writing of *The German Ideology* in 1845, in which Marx, working now in combination with Engels, sought to establish the revolutionary world-view on the surer foundations of empirical assessment rather than, as had been the case hitherto, from abstract derivation. In this work he and Engels sought to provide what they called 'an earthly basis' for human history, to trace man's history empirically without recourse to the metaphysical concepts and categories of the old or reformed Hegelians.

The 'materialist conception of history', as Marx now began to call it, starts from the 'real' premises that men produce in order to live and that, as production increases, division of labour occurs on the basis of natural distinctions among men and that classes begin to take shape. It is out of these empirical conditions that Marx and Engels now conceived 'alienation' as arising, and in the *Communist Manifesto* of 1848 they went so far as to mock those socialists who conceived the 'real' activity of political economy in terms of the *abstract* concept 'alienation of humanity'. Marx's notebooks of the time contain a fragment which clearly records the transition from the somewhat abstract treatment of his early years to the empirical conception of his later treatment of the subject. 'How is it possible?', he asks:

. . . that man's relations become relations standing opposed to him, that the powers of his own life threaten to overpower him? In one word: the *division of labour*, the level of which depends upon the correlative development of the productive forces. (L. Feuerbach: *MEW*: 3;540)

What happened between 1844 and 1847 was that Marx, perhaps under the influence of Engels, systematically reduced the scope of 'alienation' to what he considered to be 'real' or empirical alienation and began to see this as a consequence of the division of labour, private property and the class structure of society. By the time *The German Ideology* was completed in 1846, Marx was convinced that political economy constituted the study of the real basis of society. Henceforth his critique of other forms of alienated life — where they were not abandoned altogether — became subservient to this more fundamental critique.

The key to human nature, to its alienation and to the way in which alienation can be overcome, is to be found, Marx and Engels now maintained, in human labour and in the relations of labour. It is here that human beings are constricted and denied their full and true development as human beings. What they now claimed to have seen was that certain historical forms of the labour process have inevitably resulted in false or distorted communities, in which the relationships of production become relationships of subjugation rather than truly communal ones. The 'self-contradiction of the secular basis' of religion, of which Marx had spoken in the fourth of his *Theses on Feuerbach* — that is the antagonistic character of bourgeois political economy — was examined in detail by Marx later in his life in *Capital* and in *Theories of Surplus Value.*

The first section of *Capital* (1867), contains a section on the mystery of the fetishistic character of commodities in which the problem of religious alienation is dealt with directly. It is an idea which, as the émigré Russian philosopher, N.N. Alexeiev, claimed as early as 1938: 'provides the key to the understanding of the philosophical basis of the whole Marxian anthropology' (1938: p. 96). In capitalist manufacturing society, Marx argued, the conditions of the individual seem to depend on things, on commodities and the laws of their development — that is, on the market. A mysterious power transforms the results of human labour, which have definite characteristics making possible their use, into 'commodities', endows them with 'value', and makes them exchangeable for other commodities of equal value. This mystery Marx elucidated as follows:

The mystery of the commodity form is simply this, that it reflects the social characteristics of men's own labour as objective characteristics of the products of labour themselves, as the socio-natural properties of these things. Hence it also reflects the social relation of the producers to the sum total of labour as a social relation between objects, a relation which exists apart from and outside the producers. Through this substitution, the products of labour become commodities, sensuous things which are at the same time supra-sensible or social . . .

We are concerned only with a definite social relationship between human beings which, in their eyes, has assumed the semblance of a relation between things. To find an analogy we must take flight into the misty realm of religion. There the products of the human brain appear as autonomous figures endowed with a life of their own, which enter into relations both with each other and with the human race. So it is in the world of commodities, with the products of men's hands. (*Capital,* I:pp. 164-65)

The fetishistic character of commodities, and the fact that the world of commodities develops an independence from the individual, who is nonetheless a partner in work and production, not only presents, according to Marx, an analogy with religious alienation, but also forms the basis for the latter's continuance, for so long as men's social relations are seen by them as relationships between alien goods (commodities), so long as their own society confronts them as a complex of objective relations with its own inflexible laws, they will not stop inventing a transcendental divine being beyond this society to control and regulate it.

Further, for Marx, in capitalist society, truly human relationships, and therefore truly human beings, have little or no chance of developing. In capitalist society alienation is total, although in a society structured in terms of class, alienation will affect different classes in different ways. As the Soviet philosopher, M.B. Mitin, has written.

Naturally, Marx and Engels did not deny that in bourgeois society alienation (as the domination of people by the results of their own activity) was total; it left an indelible imprint on the life and work of each individual irrespective of the class to which he belonged. But as distinct from petty-bourgeois ideologists, they proved that in this system of total alienation the different classes nonetheless occupy different positions. They explained this key truth, which is one of the major points of Marxist, revolutionary-critical, real humanism, as follows: 'The propertied class and the class of the proletariat present the same human self-alienation. But the former class finds in this self-alienation its confirmation and its good, *its own power*: it has in it a *semblance* of human existence. The class of the proletariat feels annihilated in its self-alienation; it sees in it its own powerlessness and the reality of an inhuman existence, (Marx and Engels, *The Holy Family*). (Mitin, 1968: p. 57)

Alienation reduces all men to a less than truly human existence, but in society structured into classes alienation relates to different classes in different ways. Religion, as expressive of this condition of alienation is, therefore, for Marx and Engels, not just a response to a general condition of alienation, it is also a form of what they term 'ideology'.

1.2.2 RELIGION AS A FORM OF IDEOLOGY

What Marx and Engels understood by 'ideology' is almost as difficult to establish as what they understood by the term 'alienation'. Like 'alienation', 'ideology' is a word much in evidence in Marx and Engel's early works, but one which we come across only infrequently in their later writings and, like 'alienation', 'ideology' has been susceptible to a variety of interpretation by later commentators on their work.

The word 'ideology' itself was not used in European thinking until the end of the eighteenth century although, as Jorge Larrain has demonstrated in a recent study of the concept, preoccupation with the problems covered by it and, particularly, with the relationship of religion to what was later to be called 'ideology', can be discerned in European thought from the beginning of the modern era (Larrain, 1979: pp. 17-34). Machiavelli, for example, at the beginning of the sixteenth century, anticipated one of the recurrent themes of nineteenth century usage of the concept in his critique of the reactionary social functions of religious ideas, and Francis Bacon, in urging in *Novum Organum* (1620) that knowledge of nature could not advance unless certain irrational factors which beset the human mind derived, for the most part, from religion – the 'idols' or false notions which obstruct the human understanding and prevent it from reaching truth – are jettisoned,[14] can be said to have anticipated another – namely, the opposition between science and ideology which is so prominent a feature of Marx and Engels' writing on the subject.

Also pertinent to nineteenth century usage of the term 'ideology' is the critique of religion put forward by the philosophers of the French Enlightenment — particularly by Helvetius and the Baron d'Holbach — a critique which saw religion as being kept alive by the machinations of priests seeking to preserve their power, influence and riches by keeping people in ignorance of the true nature of things. D'Holbach had written that man was unhappy

. . . because he misunderstands nature. His mind is so infected by prejudices that one may think him as forever condemned to error. . . Reason, guided by experience, must attack at their source the prejudices of which mankind has been the victim for so long. . . Truth is one and necessary for man. . .it is necessary to unveil it to mortals. . . The chains which tyrants and priests forge are due to error. . . Ignorance and uncertainty are due to errors consecrated by religion. . . (D'Holbach, *Système de la Nature:* quoted Larrain, 1979: p. 24)

Religion, argued d'Holbach and the philosophers of the French Enlightenment, is kept in being by those whose worldly interests are best served by its teachings but, prior to Marx, little or no attempt was made to establish any meaningful connection between religion and social relations. The opposition put forward by the philosophers of the Enlightenment between religious prejudices, on the one hand, and science and education on the other, advances but little on Bacon's opposition between 'idols' and science.

When the term 'ideology' itself was first used — by Destutt de Tracy in his book *Elements d'ideologie* published in 1801 — it was used in a positive sense of a system of ideas to be founded on surer foundations than those hitherto derived from metaphysics and religion. Destutt de Tracy's model was the work of the English philosopher, John Locke. The first pejorative use of 'ideology' was when Napoleon, who had originally shared the ideals of the *ideologues*, as de Tracy's disciples at the Institute de France were called, became disillusioned with them and labelled them *'ideologistes'*, in the derogatory sense that they were unrealistic and doctrinaire. The nineteenth century was to complete the convergence of 'ideology' and this sense of negative content.

Finally, Hegel and Feuerbach had, as we have seen, argued that religion is not what it appears to be, not what it claims for itself, but is a disguised way of talking about something else: for Hegel, a less than satisfactory way of talking about the self-realisation of Spirit, and for Feuerbach a way of talking about the possibilities inherent in the 'species-nature' of man.

From the point of view of contemporary empirical study of religion, it should be noted that the understanding of religion which we find in the writings of Hegel and Feuerbach marks a considerable advance in the understanding of religion prevalent in the eighteenth century, for no longer is religion understood as something externally imposed upon man, but is now understood as arising out of his very essence; no longer is religion conceived as an arbitrary and independent phenomenon, for it is now seen as having a real basis in human nature and in society. But not only does the critique of religion which we come upon in the writings of Hegel and Feuerbach mark a considerable advance in the empirical understanding of religion, it also marks the real beginning of the Marxian understanding of the concept of 'ideology', for Feuerbach's understanding of religion as an alienation of the human essence is the mediating link between the older critique of religion and the newly emerging one, which sees religion not simply as ignorance but as ideology, that is as subserving purposes other than those which the religions of the world themselves profess.

Religion, according to Marx and Engels, as we saw in the previous section, expresses man's sense that he is not yet his own master, that he has not yet learned to adapt his environment to his needs, that he is the victim of circumstances beyond his control and yet, at the same time, it expresses his desire to be his own master and to order his affairs for his ultimate good. Where religion restricts the fulfilment of this desire, either by legitimating conditions in which man remains unfulfilled, or by offering a substitute (and deferred) fulfilment in a hereafter, that is, where religion presents the truth about man and his self-creation through his own practice, as other than indeed it is, then religion is also, for Marx and Engels, a form of what they term 'false-conscious-ness', and more often than not it can be found to subserve inter-ests which they also term 'ideological'. Religion is not, therefore, the effect of mere ignorance, it does not consist — or at least not entirely — of explanations which the ignorant make do with for want of something better, it does more than simply reinforce morality by promising rewards and threatening punishments in an after-life — as many of its critics in the past had maintained — it consists of more than attempts to propitiate malevolent spirits and to invoke the help of benevolent ones — as many anthropologists in the nineteenth century were to maintain — for it reflects, in fact, the human condition at a stage in the historical process when man was still incapable of understanding that condition and used religion — consciously and unconsciously — both as means of expressing that condition and as a means of seeking to overcome it.

Thus conceived, religion is a fantasy that compensates men for their failure to be what they aspire to be, but for Marx and Engels it is more than that, for though religion is born of impotence, it is the creation of men who, as social beings, reflect in their think-ing the precise conditions of their impotence and frustration.

Men's practice, as we saw in the previous section, produces, for Marx and Engels, social conditions which are more often than not thought of as independent of their will — a fact which determines the constitution of social reality as a 'contradictory reality', a reality in which the division of labour and the development of classes produce situations fraught with tensions and with conflicts of interests. As Marx and Engels' thinking about this state of affairs and its historical evolution developed they came to see that much of it appeared as so many different forms of ownership and consequently as a division between capital and labour — an opposi-tion between private (class) interest and communal interest. The conditions under which men carry out their practice are the conditions of the rule of a definite class which holds 'contradic-tory' relationships with other classes. This is the basis upon which Marx and Engels approached the concept of 'ideology'.

Reviewing, in 1839, the results of his investigations to date, Marx asserted that consciousness must be explained by the 'contradictions' (*Widerspruchen*) of material life and that, as he put it:

Mankind always sets itself only such tasks as it can solve; since, looking at the matter more closely, we will always find that the task itself arises only when the material conditions for its solution already exist or are at least in the   process of formation. (*Preface to a Contribution to the Critique of Political Economy: MSW:* Vol. I, p. 301)

From this, Marx drew the conclusion that men cannot solve in consciousness those 'contradictions' that they are unable to solve in practice.

But as 'contradictions' arise and reach consciousness before men can, in fact, solve them in practice, they are given, in the opinion of Marx and Engels, a distorted solution in the mind. 'The phantoms formed in the human brain', they wrote, 'are also, necessarily, sublimates of their material life-process' (*The German Ideology, MECW:* 5;36). Men project the 'contradictions' of their life in ideological forms of consciousness. Ideology is, therefore, for Marx and Engels, a solution in the mind to contradictions which have not been solved in practice; it is the necessary projection in consciousness of man's practical inabilities.

By attempting to solve in consciousness 'contradictions' which are not overcome in practice, ideology necessarily negates and conceals them. Marx and Engels repeatedly describe this negation of 'real contradictions' as an 'inversion' (*Umkehrung*) of reality, but they did not mean an arbitrary 'inversion' produced by consciousness. They wrote:

If the conscious expression of the real relations of these individuals is illusory, if in their imagination they turn reality upside-down, then this in its turn is the result of their limited material mode of activity. (*The German Ideology, MECW:* 5;36)

Ideology, therefore, appears as a sublimation in consciousness of the limitations of human practice which leads to the negation of social 'contradictions'. But ideology, for Marx and Engels, does not arise as a pure invention of consciousness, nor as the result of an objectively opaque reality which deceived a passive consciousness; ideology arises from 'the limited material model of activity' which produces both 'contradictory' social relations and, as a consequence, distorted representations about them. Ideology cannot, therefore, be overcome by theoretical criticism, but only by revolutionary *Praxis* designed to severe it at its roots in the 'contradictory' social world in which it has its origin.

As the conditions under which productive practice is carried out are always the conditions of the rule of a definite class, the ideological hiding of the contradictions in society necessarily serves the interests of that class. Ideology, therefore, is not only the result of the division of labour and of the rise of 'contradictory' classes; it is also a condition for the functioning and reproduction of the system of class domination. It plays this role precisely by hiding the true relations between classes and by explaining away the relations of domination and subordination. In this sense ideology legitimates the class structure, and indeed the social structure in general, and thus becomes indispensible in its reproduction. For this reason it necessarily subserves the interests of the dominant class. Thus, for Marx and Engels, each new class is compelled

. . .to present its interest as the common interest of all the members of society, that is, expressed in ideal form: it has to give its ideas the form of universality, and represent them as the only rational, universally valid ones. (*The German Ideology, MECW:* 5;60)

Initially the class making a revolution represents the common interests of all the non-ruling classes, but as soon as it develops its own particular class interests, contradictions appear between it and other classes. By concealing these, ideology allows the now dominant class to continue to appear 'not as a class but as the representative of the whole of society' (ibid; *MECW:* 5;60).

To summarise the argument thus far: ideology, for Marx and Engels, as a distorted consciousnsss, has a particular negative connotation whose two specific and related features are 1. that it conceals social 'contradictions' and 2. that it does so in the interests of the dominant class or classes. Hence ideology is a restricted kind of distortion which does not exhaust the range of possible errors of consciousness. The relationship between ideological and non-ideological consciousness cannot be conceived simply as the relationship between truth and falsehood. Non-ideological consciousness can still be erroneous for reasons other than the concealing of contradiction in the interest of the dominant class.

Marx examined the concept of ideology, at this stage in his thinking, in conjunction with the related, but separate problem of the determination of all forms of consciousness by material reality, in terms of the now famous distinction between the material 'base' (*Basis*) of society and the ideational 'superstructure' (*Oberbau*), and this has proved a source of considerable confusion for subsequent discussion of Marx's understanding of ideology – if indeed it was not a source of confusion to Marx himself. That it probably was a source of confusion to Marx is shown by the fact that he wrote, at times, as if the term 'ideological' referred to all forms of consciousness, theory and intellectual representation corresponding to a certain economic base, and some interpreters of Marx follow him in this and use the term 'ideological superstructure' to refer to all forms of intellectual representation. Marx himself, however, never used this term and, overall in his writings, ideology refers to a particular, distorted kind of consciousness which conceals social 'contradictions'. If we are to understand fully what Marx meant when he described religion as a form of ideology – indeed if ideology as understood by Marx is to have any distinctive meaning at all – then these two notions must not be confused. Not all forms of consciousness are, for Marx, ideological in the sense in which, overall, he himself used this term, in which such forms are class-based, although the later Engelisian tradition, as it has been called (cf. Larrain, 1979: pp. 69-77), and Lenin in particular, tended to interpret Marx in this way.[15]

When, however, Marx, refers to consciousness at a structured level, one may say that he is including all forms of consciousness, but not all of them have an ideological character in the sense of being a distortian which conceals 'contradictions'; certainly all of them are socially determined, but not all of them are ideological. Thus, consciousness necessarily survives the eventual ending of social 'contradictions', but ideology, in the sense in which Marx and Engels understood the term, does not. Ideology only arises and only persists in antagonistic kinds of society.

Further, although in the ideational superstructure of society, the ruling ideas are, according to Marx, the ideas of the ruling class, this of itself does not make them necessarily ideological for the 'class character' of certain ideas is not sufficient in itself to characterise them as ideological for Marx. Only where they serve to justify or conceal social 'contradictions' are they, for him, also ideological.

However, the distinction between ideational superstructure and ideology does not solve the problems stemming from the attribution of superstructural character to all forms of consciousness, and to this problem we shall be returning at various points in the ensuing discussion. Suffice it for the moment to note that, for Marx and Engels, religious conceptions are both ideational and ideological and so socially determined by 'contradictions' inherent in all forms of society hitherto. Thus, all the functions which are served by ideology, and which have been outlined above, apply to what Marx and Engels have to say about religion. Though in the original Marxian analysis of the essence of religion, as found in the early writings of Marx in particular, religion is more than a class-ideology, it has a good deal in common with class-ideology as Marx and Engels were later to understand class-ideology, for just as religion expresses man's attitude to his own species in the form of a system of beliefs about society, or indeed about the world as a whole, so bourgeois ideology, for instance, is more than a set of beliefs that promote the interests of a class by justifying its claims; it is also an image of society that expresses the bourgeois attitude to man, and can take the form of a legal system, a philosophy, a religion. It has thus been extremely tempting for the later Marxian tradition, and particularly for Marxism-Leninism, to speak as if religion was *nothing but* the ideology of a class and to forget the wider aspects of religion of which Marx and Engels wrote – at least in their early writings.

Marx spoke of religion as a fantasy of alienated man and as a form of ideology. He did not exempt from this verdict the religions of primitive peoples, even though what he took to be the major cause of alienation and a pre-requisite of ideology – the division of labour – is not found among such peoples. His ideas about religion and alienation – or at least the ideas expressed in his later socio-economic understanding of alienation – do not therefore fit easily together to form a consistent whole, for there were for Marx (and Engels), as we shall see shortly, elements in the religious response to the world which are outwith the division of labour and the development of the class-system, although Marx and Engels did not say as much about these as the historian of religion seeking to trace their opinion on this matter might wish. These elements have, however, of late, been of considerable concern to Soviet students of religion, in as much as religion in Soviet society has not disappeared as rapidly as might have been expected in a society in which the major socio-economic sources of alienation have – so it is claimed – all but been eliminated.

Marx and Engels' views regarding the sources of religion lying outside the socio-economic sphere are found in what they surmise about the origin of religion in pre-class society – itself, as we shall see in Part II of this study, an important area of study for Soviet ethnographers and archaeologists.

In *The German Ideology*, in the context of a discussion of the inter-related phenomena of human language and consciousness, Marx and Engels put forward a theory of the two-fold aetiology of religion to explain what they termed 'natural religion' and 'religion in civil society'. (op. cit., pp. 29f).

The question whether 'natural religion' continues to exist as a constituent element in the religion of civil society, and so as an element in religion at the present time was, unfortunately, not a question which Marx and Engels discussed although Engels, in some of his later writings, did hint that this might be so. The question has, however, proved to be important in discussion of the Marxist critique of religion, for if we broaden the sources of 'natural religion', in the way some contemporary anthropologists suggest, to include such uncertain areas of man's truck with the world as accident, certain diseases, and death — areas which lie beyond the competence of science to alleviate — then it may well be that religion is more broadly based and more persistent, than classical Marxism was prepared to admit.[16]

Immediately after identifying 'natural religion' as an instinctual response to the awe-inspiring phenomena of nature Marx later added, as a marginal note, that the behaviour which 'natural religion' signified was 'determined by the form of society and vice-versa'. He wrote:

We see here immediately: this natural religion or this particular attitude to nature is determined by the form of society and vice-versa. Here, as every-where, the identity of nature and man also appears in such a way that the restricted attitude of men to nature determines their restricted attitude to one another, and their restricted attitude to one another determines men's restricted attitude to nature. (*MECW:* 5 ;44)

Nature is, as yet, hardly altered by history, but:

It is man's consciousness of the necessity of associating with the individuals around him, the beginning of the consciousness that he is living in society at all. This beginning is as animal as social life itself at this stage. It is mere herd consciousness. . . (ibid.)

This herd consciousness, which Marx and Engels identified with tribal consciousness, is developed and extended in history through productivity, increased needs and the growth of the population. With these developments division of labour occurs and evolves through differences in strength, abilities, needs, etc., leading to the all-important division between mental and physical labour. Within the Marxian scheme of things, the division of labour, leading as it does to the breakdown of the original organic unity which characterised primitive society in the thought of Marx and Engels, plays a very similar part to that played by the doctrine of The Fall in the Christian scheme of things. From this moment on society is characterised not by unity but by conflicts of interests. For the development of ideology the important step, of course, was the division between mental and physical labour. As Marx and Engels wrote:

From this moment onward, consciousness can really flatter itself that it is something other than consciousness of existing practice, that it really represents something real; from now on consciousness is in a position to emancipate itself from the world and to proceed to the formation of 'pure' theory, theology, philosophy, morality, etc. But even if this theory, theology, philosophy, morality, etc. come into contradiction with the existing social relations, this can only occur because existing social relations have come into contradiction with existing social forces. (*MECW:* 5;45)

But although the realm of ideology can be thought to exist independently of the social realm, ultimately, as Marx and Engels saw it:

It is self-evident. . .that 'spectres', 'bonds', the 'higher being', 'concept', 'scruple', are merely idealist, speculative, mental expressions, the concepts of apparently isolated individuals, the mere images of very empirical fetters and limitations, within which move the mode of production of life, and the form of intercourse coupled with it. (ibid.)

From these passages we see that, for Marx and Engels, the basis of 'natural religion' and the basis of 'religion in civil society' are very different. The one — 'natural religion' — is an animal, instinctual response to natural forces, the other — 'religion in civil society' — is a reflection in consciousness of the 'contradictions' of socio-economic life. 'Natural religion' and the highly articulate, theologically construed 'religion of civil society' are discontinuous, but not necessarily opposed; both could co-exist in any living religion. Marx and Engels do not, however, explicitly say that this is so, though Soviet scholars have tended to see it in this way.

But whatever might or might not be the case with regard to the historical origins of religion, religion as it now exists is, as we have seen, for Marx and Engels, a form of ideology arising out of and kept in being by conditions of social alienation. This is their answer to the question of the essence and function of religion.

Although in his later works Marx had certain things to say about religion and society on the basis of the theoretical position we have outlined, he never again returned to theoretical matters with regard to religion except to summarise what he had already said,[17] but as Delos B. McKown has shown in his book, *The Classical Marxist Critiques of Religion,* whatever might be the case with Marx's views on other things, the position which he had taken up with regard to religion in his early writings never changed. With the single exception of the consolatory function of religion, to which Marx had referred in his *Contribution Towards a Critique of Hegel's Philosophy of Law,* every point which Marx made *vis-à-vis* religion in his early works can be documented exclusively from works published after 1847 (op. cit., pp. 10-13).

Engels, on the other hand, who was always more interested in religion and in religious controversies than was Marx, did, in a number of works which he published independently of Marx, and in particular in *Socialism: Utopian and Scientific* (1877), *Anti-Dühring* (1878) and *Ludwig Feuerbach and the End of Classical German Philosophy* (1886), seek to amplify the position which he and Marx had set forth in *The German Ideology.*

In *Anti-Dühring*, Engels dealt with the origin of religion much as he and Marx had dealt with it in *The German Ideology.* Although he does not re-employ the term 'natural religion', it is clear that he had the substance of what he and Marx had earlier so described in mind. He wrote:

When men made their way into history they were still half-animal, brutal, still helpless in the face of the forces of nature, still ignorant of their strength. . . All religion is nothing but the fantastic reflection in men's minds of those forces which control their daily life, a reflection in which terrestial forces assume the form of supernatural forces.

But Engels now widened the basis of 'natural religion' to include threatening social forces.

It is not long before, side by side with the forces of nature, social forces begin to be active – forces which confront man as equally inexplicable, dominating him with the same apparent necessity as the forces of nature themselves. The fantastic figures, which at first only reflected the mysterious forces of nature, at this point acquire social attributes, become representative of the forces of history.

And he added:

In this convenient, handy, and universally adaptable form, religion can continue to exist, that is, the sentimental form of men's relation to the alien natural and social forces which dominate them, so long as men remain under the control of these forces. (*Anti-Dühring:* p. 438)

Engels thus answers in the affirmative the question left open in *The German Ideology* as to whether the springs of 'natural religion' continue to operate in the 'religion of civil society', although later, in *Anti-Dühring*, he so plays down the continued existence of uncontrollable forces – natural as well as social – that he can look forward to the day when they and religion will vanish from the society of the future altogether. He wrote:

When therefore man no longer merely proposes, but also disposes – only then will the last alien force which is still reflected in religion vanish; and with it will vanish the religious reflection itself, for the simple reason that there will be nothing left to reflect. (ibid: p. 440)

Eight years later, in *Ludwig Feuerbach*, Engels had more definite things to say about the origin of religion; things which marked a fairly radical departure from the theory which he and Marx had earlier put forward and which he himself had repeated in *Anti-Dühring*. Interested as he had become in the anthropoligical writings of his day, Engels now utilised views put forward by the leading anthropologist of the time, Sir Edward Tylor, and offered an 'animistic' aetiology of such conceptions as 'the soul' and

'God'. He did not cite Tylor by name, but there is evidence from his correspondence that he was not unacquainted with Tylor's writings, and in particular with Tylor's *Primitive Culture* which had been published in 1871.[18] The following passage from Engels' *Ludwig Feuerbach* is, in fact, a summary of what Tylor says in Chapters Eleven to Seventeen of the second volume of *Primitive Culture*:

From the very early times when men, still completely ignorant of the structure of their own bodies, under the stimulus of dream apparitions, came to believe that their thinking and sensation were not activities of their bodies, but of a distinct soul which inhabits the body and leaves it at death — from this time men have been driven to reflect about the relation between this soul and the outside world. If upon death it took leave of the body and lived on, there was no occasion to invent yet another distinct death for it. Thus arose the idea of immortality, which at that stage of development appeared not at all a consolation but as a fate against which it was no use fighting, and often enough, among the Greeks, as a positive misfortune. Not religious desire for consolation, but the quandary arising from the common universal ignorance of what to do with this soul, once its existence had been accepted, after the death of the body, led in a general way to the tedious notion of personal immortality. In an exactly similar manner the first gods arose through the personification of natural forces. And these gods in the further development of religions assumed more and more an extra-mundane form, until finally by a process of abstraction, I might almost say of distillation, occurring naturally in the course of man's intellectual development, out of the many more or less limited and mutually limiting gods there arose in the minds of men the idea of the one exclusive god of the monotheistic religions. (*MEBW*: p. 247)

This highly intellectualistic theory marks a quite considerable departure from the view that religion arose from instinctual fear of the forces of nature and developed as a 'reflex echo' of man's real life process, for here religion is grounded in primitive man's intellectual reflections — as reconstructed by nineteenth century anthropologists.[19] Engels, unfortunately, did not relate his new theory to his earlier theory and we can only guess that he saw the two theories as complementary — religion arising out of both instinctual fear and out of primitive intellectual speculation. Neither did Engels attempt to bring this new theory into relationship with the theory of the social origin of religion which had been such a distinctive element in his and Marx's earlier writings on religion, and again, in the absence of evidence, we can only surmise that Engels thought of developed religion as arising from all of these things.

We must, therefore, conclude that Engels espoused no single theory of religion, though, overall, his explanation of the persistence of religion would appear to be that religion continually draws sustenance from the 'contradictions' inherent in all existing societies. That the various causes which initially gave rise to religion continue to operate in developed society, Engels would seem to have allowed when he wrote to his friend, Schmidt, in 1890 that:

As to the realms of ideology which soar still higher in the air – religion, philosophy, etc., – these have a prehistoric stock, found already in existence by and taken over in the historical period, of what we should today call bunk. These various false conceptions of nature, of man's own being, magic forces, etc., have for the most part only a negative economic element as their basis; the low economic development of the pre-historic period is supplemented and also partially conditioned and even caused by the false conceptions of nature. And even though economic necessity was the main driving force of the progressive knowledge of nature and has become even more so, it would surely be pedantic to try to find economic causes for all this primitive nonsense. (*MEBW:* pp. 443-444)

Much in religion was, for Engels, no more than a 'hangover' from the primitive period, having little, if any, socio-economic basis and no doubt destined to disappear as man's understanding of the world, and of himself, progressed. Such a 'hangover' does, however, as Engels had pointed out in *Anti-Dühring*, take on more and more of a determined social form:

The fantastic figures, which at first only reflect the mysterious forces of nature. . . acquire social attributes, become representative of the forces of history. At a still further stage of evolution, all the natural and social attributes of the numerous gods are transferred to one almighty god, who is but the reflection of abstract man. (*MEBW:* p. 439)

Thus, towards the end of his life, did Engels broaden the basis of religion, whilst seeking to keep intact the theory he and Marx had put forward in *The German Ideology*.

We have now completed our survey of what Marx and Engels have to say about the essence, the origin, and the social role of religion. Five points have emerged, and may be summarised as follows:

1. Religion is a human product and must be analysed as such.
2. Religion must be understood wholly in material terms.
3. Religion arises out of fear before the awesome phenomena of nature and out of ignorance of the workings of the world and of human society.
4. Religion in developed societies 'reflects' existing forms of social relations and the human self-alienation inherent in them.
5. Religion has served, within all hitherto existing forms of society, as
   (a) a disguised means of protest against existing conditions;
   (b) a false means of consolation for the lack of human fulfilment inherent in all hitherto existing forms of society;
   (c) a means whereby one class — the ruling class — has sought to maintain and legitimate the *status quo* and so sought to keep other classes in subjection to itself. Religion is a form of ideology.

To this it must be added that, for Marx and Engels, religion, as the 'illusory happiness of the people', must be abolished if people are to achieve real happiness; that criticism of religion is but part of the wider and more important criticism of society, and that the criticism of religion is part of that practical criticism of society which is revolutionary activity.

These are the guiding principles which govern all Marxist study of religion. Their adequacy is, of course, another matter and one to which we shall be returning towards the close of our study.

1.3 TOWARDS A MARXIST METHODOLOGY FOR THE STUDY OF RELIGION

With the exception of the general remarks appertaining to the materialist conception of history, and the consequent impossibility of writing any history of religion independently of a history of society and the material development of society, at the outset of *The Germany Ideology* (*MECW:* 5;36-37), and a remark in a footnote to the first volume of *Capital*, to the effect that even a history of religion written in abstraction from the material basis of society would be uncritical (*Capital:* I, pp. 493-494), neither Marx nor Engels had anything to say about the study of religion as such. It should be clear, however, both from their own approach to the phenomenon of religion, and from what they have to say — particularly in *The German Ideology* — about the materialist conception of history, that there is in their writings material for constructing a methodology for the study of religion. Whilst Marx and Engels rejected out of hand the claims which religion makes for itself, they did not believe that such claims could be lightly and summarily dismissed for, for them, religion is one of the profoundest, if ultimately mistaken, forms of human self-expression. In seeking to get from their writings a methodology for the study of religion three considerations must be borne in mind. These concern what Marx and Engels have to say about (1) the essence of religion, (2) the role of religion in all human history hitherto, and (3) the subjective attitude of the scholar engaged in religious studies.

(1) What Marx and Engels say about the essence of religion provides the theoretical foundation for Marxist methodology for the study of religion. Unlike contemporary Western phenomenological study of religion, which places in parenthesis the validity of the claims made by the religions which are under scrutiny, Marx and Engels, as avowed materialists, were quite explicit in their denial of the validity of any attempt to ground the manifestations of religious realities.[20] What they had to say about religion was explicitly reductive. The student of Marx and Engels' writings on religion has, thus, the advantage that, from the outset, he knows

what to expect. In this he is in a better position than is the student of so many non-Marxist nineteenth and twentieth century studies of religion, where the presuppositions underlying such studies are rarely so overtly expressed.

For Marx and Engels, religion arose out of fear, ignorance and impotence in the face of the awesome phenomena of nature and, at a later stage in man's development, out of frustration at the non-fulfilment of himself as a truly *human* being. Religion is, therefore, as Marx expressed it in his early essay *Contribution Towards a Critique of Hegel's Philosophy of Law*, 'the fantastic realisation of the human essence in a world where the human essence has no true reality'. This, in its way, can be taken as Marx's answer to the quest for the essence of religion which dominated late nineteenth century and early twentieth century studies of religious phenomena. The scholars who founded the autonomous discipline of *Religionswissenschaft*, however, without exception, identified the essence of religion in a transcendental reality which manifests itself, to a greater or lesser extent as the case may be, in the religions of the world.[21] Thus, for example, Friedrich Max Müller, in his book *Natural Religion* (1888) defined religion as: '. . . the perception of the infinite under such manifestations as are able to influence the moral character of man. (ibid: p. 188). And Cornelis P. Tiele in his *Elements of the Science of Religion* (1899) wrote: Our religion is ourselves, in so far as we raise ourselves above the finite and transient (ibid, Vol. II, p. 24). Tiele was in no doubt that in so far as man raised himself above the finite and transient he was in touch with a Reality external to himself, although for him, as he made clear in the first volume of *Elements of the Science of Religion,* the subject matter of the empirical study of religion was not 'The Transcendent' as such but

. . .the aggregate of all those phenomena which are invariably termed religious, in contradistinction to ethical, aesthetical, political, and others. . . those manifestations of the human mind in words, deeds, customs, and institutions which testify to man's belief in the superhuman, and serve to bring him into relationship with it. . .the object of our science is not the super-human itself, but religion based on belief in the superhuman; and the task of investigating religion as a historical-psychological, social, and wholly human phenomenon undoubtedly belongs to the domain of science. (ibid, Vol. I, p. 5)

Thus far Marx and Engels would have agreed, but they would not have agreed with Tiele's leaving open the question whether the ultimate essence of religion was 'a transcendent' reality which manifested itself through religious phenomena, a question which for Tiele, as for all the early protagonists of the empirical science of religion, was only to be considered at the end, and certainly not at the beginning, of their enquiry (Tiele, ibid, Vol. I, p. 4). Marx and Engels, however, asserted at the outset of their investigations, that religion is nothing but a socio-psychological function of man considered as a social being. In and of itself religion corresponds to nothing outwith the psycho-sociological areas of man's collective life, and it is thus exhaustively explicable in terms of the pathology of man in society as hitherto constituted. As such it is destined to disappear from the truly humanistically organised society of the future. In this respect religion is the exception within the realm which Marx and Engels designated 'ideology', for whereas in the society of the future there will exist correct forms of philosophy, art, literature, law, etc., there can be no correct form of religion — unless, of course, it be the future communist society itself as the ultimately realised eschatology. By thus grounding religion in the social realities of history as they saw them, Marx and Engels prepared the way for the methodological approach to the understanding of the role of religion in history which we meet with in the materialist conception of history.

(2) Neither Marx nor Engels — the attempt of Engels' later years to produce a 'scientific Marxism' notwithstanding — were systematic thinkers, and we do not find in their writings anything approaching a definitive system: rather were they explorers, charting areas as then little approached by the major intellectual disciplines of their day. This is nowhere more evident than in their understanding of history. Marx himself never, and Engels only towards the end of his life, used the expression 'historical materialism' — so popular in later Marxist writing — to describe his

approach to the understanding of history; still less did either Marx or Engels write of 'dialectical materialism', which was the invention of the German Social Democrat, Dietzgen and popularised by Marx and Engels' Russian disciple Plekhanov. Marx's own preferred way of describing his approach to history was 'the materialist conception of history' -- an indication, as David McLellan has said, of the open-ended nature of his approach (1975: p. 38).

The assumption which lies behind the materialist conception of history is that all human activities can be described by the same naturalistic method, which applies equally to the world of nature and to the world of mind. To describe man's activity, his spiritual and cultural achievements, in naturalistic terms, we must consider human beings primarily as social beings, living and acting in ongoing relationships with others. In this process, which lies at the root of historical development, material production, for Marx and Engels, is fundamental, for labour, as we have seen, is the instrument of man's self-creation. As Marx expressed it in *Capital:*

Labour is . . . a process between man and nature, a process by which man through his own actions, mediates, regulates and controls the metabolism between himself and nature. . . Through this movement he acts upon external nature and changes it, and in this way simultaneously changes his own nature. He develops the potentialities within his nature and subjects the play of its forces to his own sovereign power. (Capital, 1, p. 283)

This act of self-creation through labour is, for Marx, the prime mover in history and ideas — political, philosophical, religious, etc., — are secondary. In opposition to all idealist notions of determination from without man and the world, Marx and Engels insisted that history is made by man. As they wrote in *The Holy Family:*

History does nothing; it does not possess immense riches, it does not fight battles. It is real men, living men, who do all this, who possess things and fight battles. It is not 'history' which uses men as a means of achieving. . . its own ends. History is nothing but the activity of men in pursuit of their own ends. (*MECW'* 4;93)

But if men are the subject of history they are also, in a sense, its object, for although it is true that men make their own history

They do not make it just as they please; they do not make it under circumstances chosen by themselves, but under circumstances directly encountered, given and transmitted from the past. (*Eighteenth Brumaire of Louis Bonaparte; MEBW:* p. 360)

History, for Marx and Engels, is an objective natural development, in which nothing is derived from extra-social or extra-historical factors, still less from the autonomous development of ideological forms. 'The real profane history of men' has to present them 'as both the authors and actors in their own drama' wrote Marx in *The Poverty of Philosophy* (*MECW:* 6;170). It is in the recognition of this constant, ongoing interaction between man and his environment, between what is given and what man does with what is given, between productive relations which tend to conserve what has already been achieved and human productive forces which press inexorably forward, that we find the essence of the materialist interpretation of history.

In this process of self-creation — which is the true dialectic of history — material production in satisfaction of material needs is, for Marx and Engels, of overriding importance. It is in this sense that Marx avowed himself a materialist.

To arrive at the materialist conception of history, therefore, the naturalistic assumption must be supplemented by the principle of investigating all the facts of history and social life in their relation to material production. Marx and Engels wrote:

Our conception of history depends on our ability to expound the real life process of production, starting out from the simple material production of life, and to comprehend the form of intercourse connected with this and created by this (i.e., civil society in its various stages), as the basis of all history; further, to show it in its action as state, and so, from this starting point, to explain the whole mass of different theoretical products and forms of consciousness, religion, philosophy, ethics, etc., and to trace their origins and growth, by means of which, of course, the whole thing can be shown in its totality (and, therefore, too, the reciprocal action of these various sides of one another). (*The German Ideology: MECW:* 5;53)

Such is the task which Marx and Engels lay on the would-be Marxist historian, including, of course, the would-be Marxist historian of religions.

For the historian of religion, this task is made all the more difficult by the remoteness of religion, as a form of ideology, from its basis in the socio-economic structure of society — as Engels recognised later in his life when he wrote that:

Still higher ideologies, that is, such as are still further removed from the material, economic basis, take the form of philosophy and religion. Hence the interconnection between conceptions and their material conditions of existence becomes more and more complicated, more and more obscured by intermediate links. But [he adds immediately] the interconnection exists. (*Feuerbach: MEBW*: p. 277)

The relationship between material production and ideas has been a source of continuing controversy within the Marxist tradition since its inception. It has also proved one of the more vulnerable points for adverse criticism of the Marxist understanding of history. Its importance, however, for the Marxist analysis of the role of religion in history cannot be over-estimated, for it lies at the heart of the distinctive Marxist claim with regard to the role which religion and religious ideas have subserved in the historical development of society hitherto.

The relationship between material activity and ideas is expressed as follows in *The German Ideology:*

The production of ideas, of conceptions, of consciousness, is at first directly interwoven with the material activity and material intercourses of men, the language of real life. Conceiving, thinking, the mental intercourse of men, appear. . .as the direct efflux of their material behaviour. The same applies to mental production as expressed in the language of politics, laws, morality, religion, metaphysics, etc., of a people. Men are the producers of their conceptions, ideas, etc., real, active men, as they are conditioned by a definite development of their productive forces and of the intercourse corresponding to these, up to its furthest forms. (*MECW:* 5;36)

This, and like passages in Marx and Engels' early writings, needs to

be read not only against the background of the German philosophical tradition's obsession with the history of *ideas*, but against
the background of what Marx, in the *1844 Manuscripts* had called
'a consistent naturalism or humanism' (*MECW:* 3;336), and which
he was concerned then, and afterwards, to distinguish from the
materialism of both the eighteenth century and of his own day.

The problem with the German philosophical tradition – as with
its greatest representative, Hegel – was that it had never left the
realm of ideas to examine the possibility that ideas might not be
the primary motivating determinants in history that the German
tradition had taken them to be. Ideas, so Marx and Engels suggested, might, instead of being the cause of change in the world, be
themselves the result of change, of development in the world –
that is, in what Marx and Engels regarded as the 'real' world, the
world of material production and material relationships between
people engaged in the business of production. For Marx and
Engels the real motivating forces behind the dialectical movement
of world history are the changing productive forces and the
changing productive (class) relationships that men enter into in the
course of their history, and not, as for Hegel, Ideas, or Absolute
Spirit. Thus, Marx and Engels began their interpretation of
historical development not with ideas, but with the material conditions under which men live – with the material conditions which
they find and with the material conditions which they create in
the course of their history. Above all else they were concerned
with the various forms of relationship which men enter into in
history, forms of relationship to the productive process which, for
Marx and Engels, conform to a definite series of development.
These they termed 'primitive/communal', 'slave', 'feudal' and
'bourgeois/capitalist' (cf. Marx, *Critique of Political Economy;
MEBW:* p. 85). History is thus a process of development under
very definite material conditions, and this is as true of the history
of religions as it is true of all history. To try to understand any
period of history wholly in terms of ideas – without reference to
underlying socio-economic conditions – is, said Marx and Engels,
to share in the 'illusion' of that period. They wrote:

For instance, if an epoch imagines itself to be actuated by purely 'political' or 'religious' motives, although 'religion' and 'politics' are only forms of its true motives, the (idealist) historian accepts this opinion. The 'idea', the 'conception' of the people in question about their real practice, is transformed into the sole, determining force, which controls and determines their practice. (*The German Ideology; MECW:* 5;55)

The Marxist historian of religions must, in contrast, seek to dig beneath the surface of overt and seemingly 'religious' motivations for actions to the underlying socio-economic realities. For the Marxist there can be no such thing as a history of religion which is not at the same time a history of the society in which it is found. Such a study Marx and Engels now sought to establish as a science. They wrote:

Where speculation ends — in real life — there real positive science begins. Empty talk about consciousness ceases, and real knowledge has to take its place. When reality is depicted, philosophy as an independent branch of knowledge loses its medium of existence. At best its place can only be taken by a summing-up of the most general results, abstractions which arise from the observations of the historical development of men. Viewed apart from real history, these abstractions have in themselves no value whatsoever. (*The German Ideology, MECW:* 5;37)

The contrast between the 'speculations of the ideologists' and 'real, positive science', which Marx and Engels set forth in *The German Ideology,* and which Marx repeated in the preface to *A Contribution to a Critique of Political Economy* a decade or so later in 1859, was based, as was Comte's contrast between positive science and theologico-metaphysical thinking by which it was influenced, upon a distinction between what is held to be verifiable in experience and what is unverifiable. What Marx and Engels sought to provide was a scientific account of the development of human society *and* of the human propensity to indulge in theological and metaphysical speculation. The fact that Marx and Engels thought it sufficient to give a secular account of how men come to have the religious beliefs they have in order to refute them, shows just how influenced they were by Positivist philosophy, for, for them, as for the Positivists, nothing can be known but what sense perception and the methods of science reveal. As H.B. Acton has written:

The theory of Historical Materialism is held to unmask the deception of theology, but it can only do so on the basis of the positive theory of science. (1973: p. 109)

Marx and Engels wrote in *The German Ideology* of 'real history', and by 'real history', as will now be evident, they meant the onward development of the socio-economic structures of society — what they also refer to as the 'substructure' (*Unterbau*) or 'base' (*Basis*) of society — and which they contrasted with the 'superstructure' (*Oberbau*) — the realms of philosophy, political theory, law, morality, art and religion; realms which they claimed to be in some way dependent on the activity which takes place in the more fundamental realm of the 'base' of society.

On the precise nature of the base — superstructure relationship Marx and Engels were, in *The German Ideology* as elsewhere in their writings, somewhat more than vague, and yet clarity is essential if what they say about 'the materialist conception of history' is to make sense. It is also crucial to any attempt to relate the overtly *religious* beliefs, practices and institutions in a society to the material structures of that society out of which -- in the ongoing course of history — for Marx and Engels, they arise.

In *The German Ideology,* whilst the primacy of the material base is unequivocally asserted, the precise way in which it 'determines' the superstructure is spoken of only in the most general way. Thus, the socio-economic structure of a society is said to 'determine consciousness', to 'condition' the production of ideas; the superstructure is said to be an 'efflux' of man's material conditions, to be a 'reflex and echo' of his material life process. Marx's oft quoted *Preface to the Critique of Political Economy,* written in 1859, which attempts to set forth the materialist conception of history in a series of propositions, but repeats the language of *The German Ideology*. Marx wrote:

In the social production of their life, men enter into definite relations that are indispensable and independent of their will, relations of production which correspond to a definite state of development of their material productive forces. The sum total of these relations of production constitutes the economic structure of society, the real foundation, on which rises a legal and political superstructure and to which correspond definite forms of social consciousness. The mode of production of material life conditions (*Beding*) the social, political and intellectual life process in general. It is not the consciousness of men that determines (*Bestiment*) thier being, but, on the contrary, their social being that determines their consciousness. (*MEBW:* p. 84)

How the socio-economic structures 'determine' or 'condition' consciousness in any particular society we are not told, nor is any precise meaning given to these terms. (It is for this reason that I have put them in inverted commas, preferring simply to repeat what Marx says rather than to try to interpret it.) Yet this passage is regarded by the entire Marxian tradition as the classic formulation of the materialist conception of history and neither Marx nor Engels ever repudiated it – although Engels, as we shall see, did seek to modify it later in his life.

The confusion inherent in both *The German Ideology* and in *The Preface* is deeper, however, than the imprecision inherent in the use of terms such as 'determine', 'condition' and 'reflect', and the consequent lack of anything meaningful being said about the relationship of 'base' to 'superstructure', for the materialist conception of history is also held to explain the political struggle between classes as the effect of 'contradictions' within the 'material, economic, base'. In fact, as Plamenatz has point out, it does neither; it leaves both the struggle and the 'contradictions' unexplained, for if we look at what Marx says other than in *The Preface* we find that the 'contradictions' within the 'economic base' are never accounted for except as *consequences* of the struggle between classes. Our conclusion must be, therefore, with Plamenatz, that neither Marx nor Engels had any clear idea what they were about, and that, as a consequence, their theory, taken as a whole, is simply unintelligible (Plamenatz, 1954: pp. 19f; cf.

Acton, 1973: pp. 151-179). We shall be returning to this point, via Soviet study of religion, later.

Writing after Marx's death, in a letter to Bloch, written in 1890, Engels said that both he and Marx tended in their early years to deliberately over-emphasise the economic 'determining' of consciousness on account of its previous neglect. But he added that:

If someone twists this into saying that the economic element is the *only* determining one, he transforms that proposition into a meaningless, abstract, senseless phrase. The economic situation is the basis, but the various elements of the superstructure – political forms. . .political, juristic, philosophical theories, religious views and their further development into systems of dogmas – also exercise their influence upon the course of historical struggles and in many cases preponderate in determining their *form*. (*MEBW:* pp. 436-37)

This still unclear qualification notwithstanding, the decisive motivating factors in history, as Engels made quite plain elsewhere in the letter, are men's material interests. At all times and in all places these are the real motivating forces underlying all men's activities, and unless the historian recognises this and comes to a true understanding of the dialectical laws governing the development of society, he cannot at all arrive at a true understanding of the course of history. This, as Engels stated in his famous speech at Marx's graveside in 1883, is the essence of the materialist understanding of history:

Just as Darwin discovered the law of evolution in organic nature, so Marx discovered the law of evolution in human history; he discovered the simple fact, hitherto concealed by an overgrowth of ideology, that mankind must first of all eat and drink, have shelter and clothing, before it can pursue politics, religion, science, art, etc., and that therefore the production of the immediate material means of subsistence, and consequently the degree of economic development attained by a people or during a given epoch, form the foundation upon which State institutions, legal conceptions, the art, and even the religious ideas of the people concerned, have been evolved, and in the light of which these things must be explained, instead of vice versa as had hitherto been the case. (*MESW:* II, p. 153)

Interpretations of the relationship between the socio-economic structure of any given society and its ideological conceptions have varied widely within the Marxist tradition, ranging from the truism expressed in Engels' speech quoted above, to doctrines of the rigid 'determining' of the ideological superstructure by the economic base. Whilst there certainly are statements in the writings of Marx and Engels which would appear, on the surface at least, to support a fully determinist view, the balance of their writing on the materialist conception of history, as is now widely recognised, tells against such an interpretation.[22] Two points need to be borne in mind. The first is, as we have mentioned above, that what Marx and Engels said about the materialist conception of history needs to be understood against their conception of materialism as such; and secondly, we must remember that their conception of the relationship between man and his environment was dialectical, and not one of simple cause and effect.

Marx's materialism must be understood against the background of what he said in the *1844 Manuscripts* about what he termed 'a consistent naturalism and humanism', for on this he never wavered, and he was extremely concerned, throughout his life, to distinguish this from 'materialism' as this was understood at the time at which he was writing. Here he followed Feuerbach, who had declared his indifference to all previous philosophical schools, claiming that, since his own philosophy was concerned exclusively with man, it was neither idealist nor materialist: 'Nature', he claimed, was a more comprehensive concept than 'matter',[23] So Marx, in his doctorial dissertation *On the Difference Between the Natural Philosophy of Democritus and the Natural Philosophy of Epicurus*, declared his preference for Epicurus' natural philosophy on the grounds that it contained 'an invigorating principle' lacking in the natural philosophy of Democritus. This principle, as Marx made plain, was that Epicurus formulated his naturalistic conception of the world in terms appropriate to the description of *human* activities in the world. The 'natural', as used by Epicurus, includes matter and life, body and mind, the movement of physical objects and flights of the imagination. This was also how Feuerbach had used the term in his now little known writings, *Vorläufige Thesen zur Reform der Philosophie* (1842) and *Grundsatze der Philosophie der Zukunft* (1843), works in which he sought to formulate his 'true materialism and real science', and which Marx described as having profound and enduring significance (*MECW*: 3; 232). Feuerbach's materialism was neither the reductive mechanical materialism of the eighteenth century, nor the rigid 'dialectical materialism' of the later Marxist tradition. It is described by Z.A. Jordan, in his study of *The Evolution of Dialectical Materialism,* as an 'anthropological materialism', because it makes man the chief object of philosophy and declares that consciousness and personality without nature is an empty abstraction (Jordan, 1967: p. 19) – a position that Feuerbach defended against Hegel's transcendental conception of the 'ego'. The philosopher's starting point, Feuerbach asserted in *Vorläufige Thesen zur Reform der Philosophie,* is 'the man who knows himself as the self-conscious being of nature, as the being of history, as the being of the state, as the being of religion' (ibid: p. 264). It was with this that Engels identified the materialism of Marx in his *Ludwig Feuerbach and the End of Classical German Philosophy* (*MEBW:* pp. 251-56). To assert that mind is dependent on the material activity of the brain is not, for Marx, to assert their identity, but simply to deny that mind has the kind of autonomous, disembodied existence that it had been thought to have in the Idealist tradition in philosophy from the time of Plato. Man is the product of material conditions, but if it be asserted, as it had been asserted by the mechanical materialists of the eighteenth century and was asserted by those whom Engels dubbed 'vulgar' materialists in his own day, that man is wholly and entirely the product of determining material conditions, such a view is undoubtedly false, in that it leaves out of account the subjective, creative side of man's interaction with nature. As Marx expressed it in his critique of Feuerbach's materialism:

The chief defect of all hitherto existing materialism – that of Feuerbach included – is that the thing, reality, sensuousness, is conceived only in the form of the object or of *contemplation,* but not as *human sensuous activity, practice,* not subjectively . . . The materialist doctrine that men are the products of circumstances and upbringing, and that, therefore, changed men are the products of other circumstances and upbringing, forgets that it is men that change circumstances and that the educator himself needs educating . . . The coincidence of the changing of circumstances and of human activity can be conceived and rationally understood only as revolutionary practice. (*Theses on Feuerbach, MECW: 4;8*)

Revolutionary practice changes circumstances and changes man himself. It presumes that man is not only the object of history but also its subject. Here we have the core of the Marxist dialectic. In the recognition of this constant, ongoing interaction between man and his environment, between what is given to man and what he does with what is given, we have the essence of the materialist conception of history, not only as something which aids our understanding of the past, but and more important, as something which can be guide to our actions in seeking to change the present. To this task all theoretical knowledge, for Marx and Engels, should be subservient.

The most important concept which, for Marx and Engels, mediated the objective and subjective sides of the dialectic of history was that of class. For them, classes were the basic social groups by means of whose conflicts society develops and progressed: 'The history of all hitherto existing societies is the history of class struggles. . .' wrote Marx and Engels at the outset of *The Communist Manifesto* of 1848, and whilst neither of them offered a systematic analysis of the concept of 'class' anywhere in their writings, it is clear from what they said about class that the class struggle was for them a compound of objective and subjective factors. Objectively there is the undoubted existence of classes mutually opposed to each other throughout history — although Marx and Engels varied in the identification of such classes.[24] Subjectively, a class only comes into being when it becomes conscious of itself as such — something which necessitates its becoming conscious of its conflict of interests with another social class. This is not, of course, to deny that class interests can be pursued unconsciously. Class interests, for Marx and Engels, are often so pursued, and the role of religion as an, often unconscious, ideological weapon in the class struggle is one that Marx and Engels repeatedly emphasise. It is a weapon which has been used in history by both the oppressed and by the oppressors. Whilst, as Marx recognised in his early writings, religion has sometimes served as a disguised means of protest on the part of the exploited classes against their exploiters, it has, more often than not, been used as an ideological weapon by the exploiting classes seeking to preserve the *status quo* by legitimating it in the name of religion. Both of these ideological functions are exemplified in the writings of Marx and Engels. Two examples will suffice. Marx, criticising a leading article in the newspaper *Deutsche-Brusseler Zeitung* in 1847, took up the claim which it made, that if Christians would only seek to develop the social principles of their Faith, then Communists would be put to silence, by pointing to the inherently conservative, not to say reactionary, role which the Christian religion has played in the history of Europe. He wrote:

> The social principles of Christianity have now had eighteen hundred years to develop. . . The social principles of Christianity justified the slavery of Antiquity, glorified the serfdom of the Middle Ages and equally, when necessary, know how to defend the oppression of the proletariat, although they make a pitiful face of it. The social principles of Christianity preach the necessity of a ruling and oppressed class, and all they have for the latter is the pious wish the former will be charitable. . . The social principles of Christianity declare all vile acts of the oppressors against the oppressed to be either the just punishment for original sin and other sins or trials which the lord in his infinite wisdom imposes on those redeemed. The social principles of Christianity preach cowardice, self-contempt, abasement, submission. . . (*Rheinische Beobachter; MECW:* 6;231)

Engels took up the notion of religion as a disguised form of social protest in his writings on early Christianity, as well as in what he had to say about the Peasant War in Germany. In *Anti-Dühring,* for example, he wrote:

In Catholicism there was first the negative equality of all human beings before God as sinners, and, more narrowly construed, the equality of all children of God redeemed by the grace and blood of Christ. Both versions are grounded in the role of Christianity as the religion of the slaves, the banished, the dispossessed, the persecuted, the oppressed. With the victory of Christianity this circumstance was relegated to the rear and prime importance attached next to the antithesis between believers and pagans, orthodox and heretics. . . With the rise of cities and thereby of the more or less developed elements of the bourgeoisie, as well as of the proletariat, the demand for equality as a condition of bourgeois existence was bound gradually to resurge, interlinked with the proletariat's drawing of the conclusion to proceed form political to social equality. This naturally assumed a religious form, sharply expressed for the first time in the Peasant War. (*Anti-Dühring:* p. 476)

Marx and Engels thought in broad historical categories and in terms of the basic factors governing historical change. They believed that the class structure of a society was bound sooner or later to manifest itself in basic institutional forms – including the institutions of religion – but that the course of events which brought this about would depend on a multitude of chance circumstances. Reviewing Marx's *Critique of Political Economy* in 1859 Engels wrote:

History often proceeds by leaps and zigzags and it would this way have to be followed everywhere, whereby not only would much material of minor importance have to be incorporated, but there would be much interruption of the chain of thought. . . (*MSW:* Vol. I, p. 311)

The materialist conception of history, therefore, does not profess to be the key to the interpretation of particular historical events, but only of the broad general sweep of historical development, and in this development, as Engels put it in his letter to Joseph Bloch in 1890: '. . . amid all the endless hosts of accidents. . . the economic movement finally asserts itself as necessary.' (*MEBW:* p. 437). Thus, for example, great individuals who appear to shape the course of history can only do so if society is ready for such shaping as they appear to accomplish. Jesus, Mohammed, Cromwell and Napoleon are instruments of the historical process, the unconscious agents of a great impersonal historical force which they in no wise created themselves. Leszek Kołakowski, in his monumental study of the history of Marxism, reconstructs the views of Marx and Engels as follows:

All human acts are governed by specific intentions — personal feelings or private interests, religious ideals or concern for the public welfare. But the result of all these multifarious acts does not reflect the intentions of any one person; it is subject to a kind of statistical regularity, which can be traced in the evolution of large social units but does not tell us what happens to their components as individuals. Historical materialism does not state that personal motives are necessarily perverse or selfish, or that they are all of a kind; it is not concerned with such motives at all, and does not attempt to predict individual behaviour. It is only concerned with mass phenomena which are not consciously willed by anyone but which obey social laws that are as regular and impersonal as the laws of physical nature. Human beings and their relations are, nevertheless, the sole reality of the historical process, which ultimately consists of the conscious behaviour of individuals. The sum total of their acts forms a pattern of diachronic historical laws, describing the transition from one social system to the next and also functional laws showing the interrelation of such features as technology, forms of property, class barriers, state institutions, and ideology. (Kołakowski, 1978: Vol. I, p. 341)

In this process religion, along with all forms of ideology, cannot but, in the last resort, serve class interests. It is at this point that the interpretative possibilities of the materialist conception of history begins to show certain limitations. In explaining, for example, the history of a particular religion it can account not so much for the genesis of an idea as for the fact of its becoming widespread — which is what Engels sought to do in his *On the Early History of Christianity*. Neither can the theory account for every doctrinal dispute that has arisen in the history of the Christian, or indeed of any other, religion. All that it can do is to explain the main tendencies of religious sectarianism in terms of the social classes to which their adherents belonged, and set those within the context of the general development of history. Ideologies can and do, once they have arisen, have a life of their own, and, as Engels certainly recognised, can reverberate back on the material base (cf. his letter to Joseph Bloch; *MEBW:* p. 437).

But even the attempt to show the broad sweep of the religious 'reflection' of socio-economic material realities and struggles lays upon the would-be Marxist historian of religion the obligation to acquaint himself as thoroughly as he can – as a pre-requisite to his task – with the socio-economic structure and its development in the society whose religion he proposes to study, for only thus will he be able to uncover the real motivating forces underlying religious development and demonstrate the social role of religion in that society. When this role has been demonstrated the Marxist historian of religion will have fulfilled his task, for religion as a subject for empirical, scientific research will have been exhausted. Any further interest that the Marxist historian might display in religion will be at best a purely personal matter, at worst an aberration. So far as concerns the subject matter of religious studies, the Marxist historian of religion is limited, by the methodological presuppositions we have outlined, to the study of religion solely as a social phenomenon. He can have little, if any, interest in individual, personal religion, except in so far as this reflects the interest of an individual as a member of a social class. As Marx and Engels themselves wrote:

Religious questions today have only a *social* significance. There can be no more talk of religious interests as such. Only theologicians can believe that religion is a matter of concern. (*The Holy Family, MECW:* 4;108)

By directing attention away from 'the religious' as such, and by concentrating on the material social realities of which it is, for Marxists, but a 'reflection', Marxism offered – and still offers – a distinctive outlook on the history of religion. Much of this has now become commonplace in the study of religion in the Western world – but Marxism remains the most extreme example of sociological reductionism that we shall find anywhere in the study of religion today. What distinguishes the Marxist approach from other forms of sociological reductionism is the use which it makes of its evolutionary and dialectical understanding of the development of history and the role which it sees religion as having played in this. It is here that the distinctive insights of Marxism are to be found.

(3) But perhaps the greatest difference between Marxist and non-Marxist approaches to the study of religion lies in the differing attitudes to the study of religion on the part of Marxist and non-Marxist students of religion. The academic ideal of objectivity and neutrality – of value-free study – which is still the predominate ideal in Western study of religion, is not an ideal which Marxist students of religion espouse. All study of religion by Marxists is essentially and avowedly partisan. The *locus classicus* for the Marxist position is Marx's *Theses on Feuerbach*, although the partisan nature of Marx and Engels' own writings on religion does not need the explicit statements of *The Theses on Feuerbach* to make this plain: it underlines all their work in whatever sphere they operated. What they were concerned to deny was the validity of any views which claimed to give an objective, neutral, static account of the world from an uninvolved position. As Marx put it in the second of his *Theses on Feuerbach:* 'The question whether objective truth can be attributed to human thinking is not a question of theory but a practical question' (*MECW:* 5;6). In order for a scholar to obtain to a neutral position he would need to be outwith all class society. Since, at the present, this is clearly impossible, the eleventh of the *Theses on Feuerbach* is mandatory on all who would obtain to a truer vision of things: 'Philosophers have only interpreted the world, in various ways; the point is to change it.' This is as true for the scholar as it is for the professional revolutionary. It is the premise from which, as we shall see in Part II, all Soviet study of religion begins.

The clearly partisan nature of Marxist writing on religion can be disconcerting to those educated into a very different scholarly tradition – although there are, of course, parallels in Western theological writing on religion. But for those engaged in Western *Religionswissenschaft*, where the ideal is that of value-free study, it can be particularly disconcerting to have an evaluation of religion so nakedly, and often so stridently proclaimed. This is what makes Soviet studies of religion appear to many Western scholars just so much propaganda. But from a Marxist point of view, so long as class society exists, there can, in the nature of things, be no such thing as a point of view relating to social phenomena which is not – either explicitly or implicitly – partisan. All that we can hope for is to be possessed of the 'correct' view, and the 'correct' view is that which is in accord with the 'progressive' forces at work in society at that stage of development to which society has attained in the scholar's own day. For Soviet Marxists, the 'correct' view must, therefore, be that enshrined in their own 'scientific' world-view – the outlook of the victorious proletariat living in an advanced socialist society rapidly approaching the classless society of Communism – the outlook known as 'dialectical materialism'. But before looking at the origins of dialectical materialism in the later writings of Engels, and at its development in the writings of Russian and Soviet Marxists, it behoves us to look at the application of the methodology for the study of religion that we have outlined to the actual history of religion – and to the history of the Christian religion in Western Europe in particular – as we have it in the writings of Marx and Engels themselves.

1.4   THE MATERIALIST CONCEPTION OF HISTORY AND HISTORY OF RELIGIONS

The evolutionary schema for the historical development of society, which Marx outlined in the *Preface to the Critique of Political Economy*, and according to which society is held to have passed through the stages of primitive/communal, slave-owning, and feudal forms of social orgainsation before reaching the bourgeois/capitalist society of his own day, lies at the basis, as we have said, of what Marx and Engels have to say about the history of religion.

On the religion of primitive/communal society, and on religion in slave-owning (Ancient) society – the societies of Greece and Rome – neither Marx nor Engels had much to say. In these societies the social organisation was much simpler than in bourgeois society, more transparent, more comprehensible. Why then, we may ask, did not men reach self-consciousness and social integration? Why did they have need of the illusions of religion? Marx wrote:

Those ancient social organisms of production are much more simple and transparent than those of bourgeois society. But they are founded either on the immaturity of man as an individual, when he has not yet torn himself loose from the umbilical cord of his natural species-connection with other men, or on direct relations of dominance and servitude. They are conditioned by a low stage of development of the productive powers of labour and correspondingly limited relations between men within the process of creating and producing their material life, hence also limited relations between man and nature. The real limitations are reflected in the ancient worship of nature, and in other elements of tribal religions. (*Capital,* Vol. I, pp. 172-73)

Marx's own answer to the question of the origin of religion, therefore, is that religious consciousness in primitive/communal and in slave-owning societies results from the fact that individuals are still at one with the natural community and have not as yet developed any individual consciousness, or else live in direct master-slave relationships; both phenomena being finally conditioned by the low stage of development of man's means of work (tools, machines, etc.,). For Marx, the religion of these societies is the worship of nature, although he had also, in one of his early writings, stated that as far as the Ancients were concerned, their real religion was the cult of their nationality — something which he also believed to be true of the traditional religion of the ancient Slavs and of the ancient Germanic peoples. Such religions disappear with the downfall of the states whose religions they are, and not vice versa, as had so often been maintained. He wrote:

If with the downfall of the old states the religions of the old states disappear, this needs no further explanation than that the 'true religion' of the peoples of antiquity was the cult of 'their nationality', of their 'state'. It was not the downfall of the old religions that brought about the downfall of the old states, but the downfall of the old states that brought about the downfall of the old religions. (Art. 179 in *Kölnische Zeitung,* 1842; *MECW:* I;189)

Engels made the same point in *Ludwig Feuerbach* (*MEBW:* pp. 258-59 and p. 263). On ancient Hinduism, Marx was at his most vituperative. Hinduism, for Marx, represented the very nadir of human degradation (cf. 'The British Rule in India', *MEOC:* pp. 31-32 and pp. 36-37).[25]

It is, however, in what Marx and Engels have to say about the various forms which the Christian religion has assumed in Western Europe that we can best see the application of the materialist conception of history to the history of religion. Whilst Marx himself had little to say about the origin of the Christian religion, Engels had a great deal to say, for he believed that if he could explain the origins of Christianity — or at least if not its actual origins, the reason for its triumph in the ancient world — then he would be some way towards undermining the authority of that religion in the present. He wrote:

A religion like the Christian cannot be destroyed through ridicule and invective alone. It has to be overpowered scientifically, i.e. historically explained and that cannot be done even by the natural sciences. (*The Peasant War in Germany:* p. 232)

Engels' first attempt at explaining the origins of Christianity was in a short obituary article entitled 'Bruno Bauer and Early Christianity', which he published in the newspaper *Der Social-demokrat* in May 1882 on the occasion of Bauer's death. Engels used that occasion to put forward his own explanation for the rise of Christianity — an explanation couched, of course, in predominately materialistic terms. Bauer had maintained that Christianity had been a necessary stage in the evolution of human consciousness. The origins of Christianity were, for Engels, much more mundane.

Dismissing the rather crude view, as he held it to be, but much canvassed in the eighteenth century, that Christianity had originated as the work of deceivers, as being inadequate to explain a religion which 'had brought the Roman Empire into subjection' and which had dominated 'by far the larger part of civilised humanity for 1,800 years', Engels went on to maintain that at a time when the imposition of Roman social, legal, political and economic structures on the subject peoples of the Empire had destroyed the efficacy of the previously worshipped local gods, Christianity alone had possessed the necessary assets to satisfy the still felt need for the consolations of religion and to provide that unity of outlook that the late Empire so desperately needed to survive. Christianity alone among its rivals in late Antiquity combined Eastern and Western ideological elements. It also put forward the notion of a single god at a time when the most popular philosophies of the ancient world were moving in a similar direction, and a conception of universal sin which did much to explain the currently felt decadence and depravity. It further possessed doctrines which gave hope to the wretched of the earth. The Christian religion, in fact, explicitly sought, at first, its converts from the poor, the miserable, the slaves and despised the rich, the powerful and the privileged. Summarising the material and moral situation at the time when Christianity made its debut on the Mediterranean stage, Engels described that situation as one in which 'the present was unbearable, the future still more menacing'. In this situation, wrote Engels:

In all classes there was necessarily a number of people who, despairing of material salvation, sought in its stead a spiritual salvation, a consolation in their consciousness to save them from utter despair. This consolation could not be provided by the Stoics any more than by the Epicurean school, for the very reason that these philosophies were not intended for the common consciousness and, secondly, because the conduct of the disciples of the schools cast discredit on their doctrines. The consolation was to be a substitute, not for the lost philosophy, but for the lost religion; it had to take a religious form, the same as anything which had to grip the masses both then and as late as the seventeenth century. (*MEOR:* p. 180)

It is interesting to note that, whilst Engels here revived Marx's view of the consolatory function of religion, he did not analyse the origin of Christianity wholly in terms of class. In fact he explicitly says that there were those 'in all classes' who sought comfort in religion — a tacit admission that the factors making for religion are wider than class and other than those related to material interests. It was unfortunate for the later Marxist tradition that Engels did not develop this insight further, for this might have gone some way towards explaining the continued existence of religion in a (supposedly) classless society — a problem with which Marxist-Leninist theoreticians are struggling to deal in the Soviet Union today. Instead, in his later writings on religion, he was to rest content with repeating that religion simply serves class interests — a view which persisted in the writings of Soviet theoreticians until quite recently. Thus, when he came to a more sustained treatment of early Christianity, in what were virtually the last writings of his life, Engels concentrated almost entirely on the theme of the Christian religion as a movement of protest on the part of the oppressed — an analysis which allowed him to see in early Christianity a prefiguration of the working-class movement of the late nineteenth century. He wrote:

The history of early Christianity has notable points of resemblance with the modern working-class movement. Like the latter, Christianity was originally a movement of oppressed people: it first appeared as the religion of slaves and emancipated slaves, of poor people deprived of all rights, of peoples subjugated by Rome. Both Christianity and the workers' socialism preach forthcoming salvation from bondage and misery; Christianity places salvation in a life beyond, after death, in heaven; socialism places it in this world, in a transformation of society. . . If, therefore, Professor Anton Meger wonders in his *Right to the Full Product of Labour* why, with the enormous concentration of land-ownership under the Roman emperors and the boundless sufferings of the working class of the time. . . 'socialism did not follow the overthrow of the Roman Empire in the West', it is because he cannot see that this socialism did in fact, as far as was possible at the time, exist and even become dominant — in Christianity. Only this Christianity, as was bound to be the case in the historic conditions, did not want to accomplish the social transformation in this world, but beyond it, in heaven, in the eternal life after death, in the impending 'millennium'. (On the Early History of Christianity', in *Die Neue Zeit,* 1894-1895; *MEOR:* pp. 281-282)

With the establishment of the Christian religion as the official religion of the late Empire, that religion quickly dropped any revolutionary pretensions which it may have harboured and quietly settled down to the legitimisation of the *status quo* as that *status quo* became enshrined in feudalism. Revolutionary movements, however, persisted, and more often than not took a religious form, as Engels demonstrated in what is, perhaps, his most insightful piece of writing on the history of religion – *The Peasant War in Germany*. Engels also took note of religiously disguised social protest movements in Islam.[26]

From about the ninth century of the Christian era we meet with a new mode of productive relations in Europe and with a new religious ideology associated with it. This is feudalism, and the religious ideology which reflects this change in productive relations is, of course, Catholicism. Marx and Engels, however, had little to say about Catholicism for, for them, it was an anachronism, a relic of an era of history already doomed and as such destined to disappear. Long before the actual demise of feudalism its executioners and grave-diggers had already been called forth and had, from the sixteenth century, gone about their task with relish and with industry. These were the rising bourgeoisie – their mode of production and of productive relations was capitalism, their religion Protestant.

The world-outlook of the feudal period – that is, of the Middle Ages in Europe – was, as Engels noted, predominantly religious and theological. The unity of Western Europe, which did not exist internally, was established, so Engels claimed, externally during this period against a common foe – Islam – by the Christian religion. The unity of Europe, which in reality consisted of a group of independent nations in continual intercourse, was welded into Christendom by the Catholic Church. This unity, as Engels noted, was not simply a unity of belief, but had a very substantial material basis in that the Catholic Church owned about a third of the land in every country in Europe – something which gave it a considerable political position in the national and supra-national organisation of Europe. The Church was the real link between countries and the feudal organisation of the Catholic

Church itself gave, in Engels' words 'a religious consecration to the feudal state system' (*MEOR*: p. 240).

But, as Engels put it:

Within the womb of feudalism the power of the bourgeoise was developing. A new class appeared in opposition to the big landowners. The city burghers were first and foremost and exclusively producers of and traders in commodities, while the feudal mode of production was based substantially on self-consumption of the product within a limited circle. . . The Catholic world outlook, fashioned on the pattern of feudalism, was no longer adequate for this new class and its conditions of production and exchange. Nevertheless, this new class remained for a long time a captive in the bonds of an almighty theology. (*MEOR:* pp. 240-241)

Thus from the thirteenth to the seventeenth century all the reformations and struggles carried out ostensibly in the name of religion were, in reality, but repeated attempts on the part of the burghers and plebeans of the towns, and of peasants in the country-side, to adapt the old theological outlook to changing economic conditions and the way of life associated with them.

In the seventeenth century the inevitable eruption took place, and we can discern, said Engels, the beginnings of the gradual secularisation of the theological outlook (*MEOR:* p. 241). Human right took the place of divine right and the State the place of the Church. But before profane feudalism could successfully be attacked, its sacred central organisation and legitimating agency – the Catholic Church – had to be destroyed. This was wrought by the Reformation in close alliance with the growing scientific movement. 'Science rebelled against the Church; the bourgeoisie could not do without science, and therefore had to join in the rebellion', as Engels put it in the introduction to his *Socialism: Utopian and Scientific* (*MEOR:* p. 267).

On Protestantism, as the fitting ideology of the bourgeoisie, both Marx and Engels had a great deal to say. It was, for them, the supreme example of religion's propensity to 'reflect' the real world of material production. As Marx wrote in *Capital*:

The religious world is but the reflex of the real world. And for a society based upon the production of commodities, in which the producers in general enter into social relations with one another by treating their products as commodities and values, whereby they reduce their individual private labour to the standard of homogeneous human labour — for such a society Christianity, with its cultus of abstract man, more especially in its bourgeois developments, Protestantism, Deism, etc., is the most fitting form of religion. (*Capital:* I, 79)

Of the two major forms that Protestantism was to take — Lutheranism and Calvinism — it was Calvinism which, for Marx and Engels, best reflected the new bourgeois spirit that was abroad. As Engels wrote:

Its predestination doctrine was the religious expression of the fact that in the commercial world of competition success or failure does not depend upon a man's activity or cleverness, but upon circumstances uncontrollable by him. It is not of him that willeth or of him that runneth, but of the mercy of unknown superior economic powers. (*Socialism: Utopian and Scientific; MEOR:* p. 268)

Despite the intellectual vacuity of Protestantism and its justification of exploitive economies, to Marx and Engels it was a progressive step forward from feudalism and the Catholic form of Christianity associated with it. The strength of Protestantism lay in the autonomy it claimed and promoted for man. When shorn of its religious guise, religious autonomy would, so they believed, give way to human autonomy — thus freeing man to determine for himself a purely human destiny.

The progressive element in Protestantism was recognised by Marx as early as his essay *Contribution to a Critique of Hegel's Philosophy of Law*, where he wrote:

Luther overcame the bondage of piety by replacing it by the bondage of conviction. He shattered faith in authority because he restored the authority of faith. He turned priests into laymen because he turned laymen into priests. He freed man from outer religious authority because he made religiosity the inner man. . . But if Protestantism was not the true solution it was at least the true setting of the problem. It was no longer a case of the layman's struggle against the priests outside himself, but of his struggle against his own priest inside himself, his priestly nature. . . Secularisation will not stop at the pillaging of churches. (*MECW:* 3;182)

But whatever the benefits that Protestantism had conferred in the past, it, along with all forms of religion, was destined to disappear, for just as the bourgeois destruction of feudalism had eclipsed Catholicism in the major states of Western Europe, so would the forthcoming proletarian revolution overthrow capitalism and doom Protestantism. In this Engels believed that they would be aided, as had the bourgeoisie in their overthrow of Catholicism, by the most advanced scientific thought of the time. The new proletarian, Socialist order would be securely grounded in the newly emerging scientific, materialistic outlook and, unlike religion, a socialism so grounded would offer not only the possibility, but the realisation of hope. Engels wrote:

When this act has been accomplished, when society, by taking possession of all the means of production and using them on a planned basis, has freed itself and all its members from the bondage in which they are now held by these means of production which they themselves have produced but which confront them as an irresistible alien force; when therefore man no longer merely proposes, but also disposes — only then will the last alien force which is still reflected in religion vanish; and with it will also vanish the religious reflection itself, for the simple reason that then there will be nothing left to reflect. (*Anti-Dühring:* pp. 439-440)

Such is the denouement in store for religion according to the materialist conception of history. The *Problematik* of Marxist study of religion is both to demonstrate the truth of this thesis, and to bring it to fruition.

We thus see that the study of religion for Marx and Engels is not a discipline which can have an interest in religion in and of itself. The study of religion — and, in particular, the study of the history of religion — is part of the wider study of the history of society — a study which is carried on on the basis of the belief that the history of society is the history of man's struggle to achieve social, economic and political liberation, — a liberation which is, in fact, no more and no less than the fulfilment of man as a truly human being. In this struggle ideas — whether literary or artistic, juristic or political, philosophical or religious — are secondary, and the student of the history of these ideas must show how this has been so. But whilst the history of art, literature and the like is a history of the distortion of what — given different social, economic and political circumstances — they might truly have been, the history of religion is the history of an illusion. In the society of the future the true expression of religion will have no place. What man in the past sought in religion will have come to pass — for religion can have no object which transcends man, nature or human society and no motivation other than the desire for a harmonious relationship with these and with himself. In Communist society man will be truly fulfilled. The study of religion is part of the revolutionary struggle to bring about this state of affairs.

1.5   TOWARDS THE DIALECTICAL MATERIALIST WORLD–VIEW

We have mentioned the fact that neither Marx nor Engels were systematic thinkers who structured their work as a coherent and definitive whole; much of it was written, in fact, to provide imme- diate guidance for the growing working-class movement whose theoreticians Marx and Engel sought to be, and a consequence of this is that much in their writing is polemical and lacking technical precision. Problems and solutions were formulated under the pressure of controversy, with the result that the task of clarifica- tion and interpretation of their work has become a major part of their intellectual legacy.

Engels, however, did, towards the end of his life, in *Anti-Dühring, Ludwig Feuerbach and the End of Classical German Philosophy,* and in the posthumously published *Dialectics of Nature,* attempt to formulate a would-be 'scientific Marxism' and so, as David McLellan maintains, 'took the initial steps along the path that was to end with the portrayal of Marxism as a dogmatic metaphysical system embodied in Soviet (and other) text-books on dialectical materialism' (1979: p. 9). Two factors influenced Engels' attempt to develop a world-view strongly orientated towards natural science: the need felt within the growing socialist movement – particularly in Germany – for clear theoretical guidance, and the growing prestige of natural science among members of the public in general and among members of the international Socialist movement in particular (McLellan, 1975: pp. 56-57; 1979: pp. 10-11).

Marx and Engels had often written about the need to develop a historical 'science of man' and they believed that they had, in their materialist conception of history, laid the foundations for just such a science. It is, perhaps, worth considering what the term 'science' – in Marx and Engels' German, *Wissenschaft* – might have meant to them. As Quentin Lauer, on the basis of Jacob and Wilhelm Grimm's *Deutsches Wörterbuch*, notes, the term *Wissenschaft*, which originally had signified no more than 'information', had, by the end of the eighteenth century, begun to take on the meaning of the sum total of what is objectively known in the strictest sense of the term 'know' (*wissen*). In Hegel – who, of course, had a strong influence on Marx and Engels, *Wissenschaft* became the whole process of coming to know in the strictest sense, so that any stage in the process was knowing in a relative sense and was thus, in connection with the whole process, 'scientific'. Human knowledge, for Hegel, progresses; to be 'scientific' is to be in line with the direction that progress is taking. What Marx took from this was the belief that truth reveals itself only gradually – that is to say, historically – because it is constantly in the making. Lauer also points out that in the thought of the Enlightenment – which in this respect influenced not only Marx, but the whole of cultured Europe – the concept of 'scientific' was largely negative, in the sense that stressing the autonomy of human reason in 'scientific' thinking largely involved denying the validity of authority, tradition and the supernatural. He writes:

Thus, a natural explanation of what had been previously explained supernaturally, even though it might be on our terms only plausible, was in the eyes of the 'enlightened' a scientific explanation. (Lauer, 1974: p. 144)

It is against this background that we must read Marx and Engels' attempt to study man, society and history 'scientifically'. From the Enlightenment they inherited the demand that reality be explained on the basis of human reason and of objectively discovered 'laws'; from Kant, Fichte and Hegel, the realisation that these 'laws' are not contained in nature, but are the products of human thinking – and especially of dialectical thinking – and from Feuerbach they had inherited the belief that there is no going beyond the evidence presented to the senses. Their achievement – and according to Engels' own admission, this was to a great extent Marx's achievement alone – was to weld all three elements into a synthesis based on the notion that man is only truly human in the context of society, society itself being constantly the product of human material activity governed by dialectical laws intrinsic to the process itself. Engels, towards the end of his life – and for the most part after Marx's death – sought to take this development further, both by grounding the materialist conception of history in an absolute metaphysical materialism, and by seeking to subsume under one set of universally operative laws, the process of nature and the process of history. This attempt to formulate a monistic vision of reality marks the beginning of what was to become known in Soviet Marxism-Leninism as 'dialectical materialism'.

After his retirement from business in 1869, Engels devoted the better part of the next eight years to obtaining as thorough an acquaintance as he could with recent developments in natural science. In particular, he was greatly interested in the discovery of the law of the conservation and transformation of energy, which he felt came near to providing a complete explanation for the multiplicity of phenomena; in the discovery of the cell as the basic unit of biological change, which gave promise of the further discovery of a single system of laws applicable to all organic phenomena; in the evolutionary hypothesis of Darwin which, for him as for so many of his contemporaries, provided a general historical schema of the development of living creatures, including man; and in Fechner's studies which opened up the way to the quantitative measurement of mental phenomena. To Engels the day seemed not far off when the unity of nature, so far hidden beneath seeming multiplicity, would be accessible to the human mind. These developments in natural science were to influence heavily Engels' presentation of Marxism as *the scientific* world-view. It was a presentation which – mediated through the philosophical thinking of Plekhanov and Lenin – was to have a decisive influence on the Russian and Soviet Marxist tradition, and was to become the corner-stone of the Marxist-Leninist critique of religion.

The most systematic attempt to formulate a specifically Marxist world-view is found in *Anti-Dühring*, written by Engels in 1877. Dühring, a lecturer at the University of Berlin, had propounded a reformed socialist philosophy which had had considerable influence in German socialist circles and which, because of its divergence on a number of fundamental issues from the views of Marx, had threatened to split the German Social Democratic Party. Dühring's views had the advantage that they were presented as a complete system of philosophy. Engels was called upon by those loyal to Marx – who could not himself reply owing to failing health and other pressing concerns – to reply. Although Engels agreed to do so only reluctantly, he later came to realise that the systematic comprehensiveness of Dühring's own philosophy had given him the opportunity of developing, in opposition to Dühring, in a more connected way than had previously been done, the views which Marx and he held on a variety of topics. Despite his contempt for Dühring's system-building, Engels confessed in the Preface to the second edition of *Anti-Dühring* that his own polemic was transformed into 'a more or less connected exposition of the dialectical method and the Communist world outlook' (p. 14). The result was a book which was destined to become the authoritative statement of Marxist philosophy for generations to come.

Underpinning Dühring's self-proclaimed 'revolutionary scientific socialism' were what Engels regarded as rather naïve materialistic and evolutionary views; views which were also popularised at the time by contemporary materialists such as Büchner, Vogt and Haeckel, and which were beginning to take root among the working classes of Europe. Engels, as he himself recognised, was so far tempted to outbid such views as to end by producing a superior form of materialistic monism (Preface to the first edition of *Anti-Dühring*).

According to Engels, the whole history of philosophy has turned on the opposition of idealism and materialism – an opposition which is, at bottom, an opposition of differing views with regard to the creation of the world, but which is also an opposition between differing views with regard to the relationship of mind and matter. Idealists regard mind or spirit as primary and matter as secondary, whilst materialists regard matter as primary and mind as either dependent on matter or in some cases as identical with it. Engels' views on the relationship of mind and matter are difficult to ascertain for he seems to oscillate between a substantial, metaphysical materialism on the one hand, and a phenomenological, methodological materialism on the other.

In so far as Engels held that the essential opposition in philosophy is between opposing views with regard to the relationship which exists between nature and spirit, we might think that he saw both idealism and materialism as expressing a kind of dualism – with materialism maintaining that whilst mind or spirit is genetically secondary to matter, it is separate and different. In fact Engels did not take this view, but maintained that the opposition between nature and spirit is not an opposition between two different substances – with the dispute between materialism and idealism being about the relationship which exists between them – for there is, for Engels, in reality only one substance – matter, and consciousness is no more than an attribute of matter organised in a particular way. His standpoint was, therefore, monistic in that ultimately, for him, only matter exists. He wrote:

The real unity of the world consists in its materiality, and this is proved not by a few juggled phrases, but by a long and wearisome development of philosophy and natural science. (*Anti-Dühring:* pp. 65-66)

And in *The Dialectics of Nature* he expressed the belief that the greater the advance of science

. . . the more impossible will become the senseless and anti-natural idea of a contradiction between mind and matter, man and nature, soul and body. . . (*Dialectics of Nature:* p. 293)

There are, however, passages in both *Anti-Dühring* and in *The Dialectics of Nature* where Engels would seem to espouse a methodological and phenomenological materialism rather than an ontological one. Thus, for example, in *The Dialectics of Nature*, he wrote that:

The materialistic outlook on nature means nothing more than the simple conception of nature just as it is, without alien addition. (ibid: p. 322)

And again:

Matter as such is a pure creation of thought and an abstraction. We leave out of account the qualitative difference of things in comprehending them as corporeally existing things under the concept matter. Hence matter as such, as distinct from definite existing pieces of matter, is not anything sensuously. (ibid: pp. 322-323)

From these and like passages it would appear that Engels' materialism was not, in fact, an ontological but an anti-philosophical materialism, which was content to put on one side questions relating to 'substance' and simply to accept the bare facts of natural science without any speculative additions. This would also be consistent with what Engels said elsewhere about philosophy coming to an end in the nineteenth century with the advent of sound natural science (cf. *Ludwig Feuerbach: MECW:* pp. 240-243). In *Anti-Dühring*, he wrote:

Modern materialism. . . . is not a philosophy but a simple conception of the world which has to establish its validity and be applied not in a science of sciences standing apart, but within the actual sciences. Philosophy is, therefore, 'sublated' here, that is, 'both overcome and preserved'; overcome as regards its form, and preserved as regards its real content. (ibid: p. 192)

And again:

As soon as each special science is bound to make clear its position in the great totality of things, a special science dealing with this totality is superfluous (or unnecessary). That which survives, independently, of all earlier philosophy is the science of thought and its laws — formal logic and dialectic. Everything else is subsumed in the positive science of nature and history. (ibid: p. 40)

But although Engels was inclined at times to temper his materialistic outlook in the way described above, there is no doubt that, overall, his views imply not simply a methodological materialism, but a philosophical materialism as well. As he wrote: 'the real unity of the world consists in its materiality'. For him there exists no behind-the-scenes world different in kind from the world observed by the natural scientist; there exists only matter in motion. Were this not so we would have to look for the source of change outside of matter, in something like the *primum mobile* of the Deists. The world, however, for Engels, is its own final cause (ibid: p. 521).

Whether Engels' transformation of Marx's naturalism into a metaphysical monism of absolute materialism goes beyond Marx, or whether it is only a logical extension of a position that is, to all intents and purposes, inherent in Marx, but which Marx, being himself singularly uninterested in metaphysics, never articulated, is a question vigorously discussed by contemporary Marxian scholars.[27] All that need concern us, however, is that the Marxist-Leninist tradition sees no difference here between Marx and Engels — absolute materialistic monism being, from its point of view, the position taken up by both thinkers.[28]

This metaphysical position was to harden the anti-religious stance of Marxism-Leninism by taking the argument with religion into the deeper area of ontology. Engels himself, in fact, had made this clear, for the crux of his argument with 'mechanical' material-

ism was that it necessarily led to theism. Only the new materialism, with its dynamic conception of matter could, in his opinion,
escape the conclusion that the world needs a creator. If matter
were not perpetually in motion but could exist at rest, if motion
was not an integral property of matter and if matter without motion was not as inconceivable as motion without matter, we would
not be able to get from immobile matter to matter in motion without an impulse from outside, i.e., − as Newton well saw − without
God. Once, however, we accept the dynamic theory of matter inherent in both modern science and in dialectics, with its asscump-
tion of the invariability of natural forces and the idea of the
transformation of energy, then, Engels contended, 'the last vestiges
of the extra-mundane creator is obliterated' (*Anti-Dühring*: p. 20).
Engels' argument against Dühring was that his materialism involved
just such an assumption of an extra-mundane creator (ibid: pp.
87-88).

Engels' belief that the laws governing nature and history were
essentially the same rested on his belief that mind had emerged
from matter. Only dialectics, however, could truly comprehend
the processes of both and in this belief Engels was convinced that
he had the support of the most recent developments in natural
science − something which helped to establish Engels' 'modern
materialism' as the only possible scientific outlook in the eyes of
his supporters in the international socialist movement. It is a
position that Marxist-Leninists vigorously defend to this day. It
was also thought by Engels to lend additional support to the view
that society behaves in as law-like a way as do the processes of
nature. 'Nature', he contended, 'is the proof of dialectics' (ibid:
p. 36). The essential insight of dialectics is that everything moves,
changes, comes into being and passes away − an insight which
Hegel, the founder of modern dialectics, had salvaged from the
Greeks. The details of the dialectical process in nature and in
society remains, however, to be explained. Engels believed that
Marx and himself had made a beginning, but they bequeathed the
working out of the details to their successors.

Integral to Engels' materialistic conception of the world was his epistemology, in which man's knowledge of the external world consisted of what he called 'reflections' or 'more or less abstract pictures of actual things and processes' and in which concepts were 'merely the conscious reflex of the dialectical motion of the real world'. He wrote:

Dialectics, so-called *objective* dialectics, prevails throughout nature, and so-called *subjective* dialectics, dialectical thought, is only the reflex of the movement in opposites which asserts itself everywhere in nature. (*Dialectics of Nature:* p. 206)

If the world is in flux, and if knowledge is a reflection of the world, then knowledge can come only through dialectics, for dialectics alone can follow the motion actually taking place in nature and society. *The Dialectics of Nature* was Engels' tentative attempt to show that this was so.

The laws which, for Engels, governed the dialectical development of both nature and society were three: (1) the law of the transformation of quantity into quality, (2) the law of the interpenetration of opposites, and (3) the law of the negation of the negation. Their exposition, reformulation and application will take up much of the time and much of the ingenuity, of philosophers within the Marxist-Leninist tradition for decades to come.

What is lacking in Engels' account of man, nature and society, as David McLellan has noted, is the subjective side of man's interaction with nature which had been so prominent a feature of Marx's understanding of the dialectical process and to which we ourselves earlier called attention (cf. above, pp. 62-64). As McLellan says:

What Engels aimed at was the construction of a systematic materialism as all-embracing as Hegel's own system; and it is scarcely an over-simplification to say that this centrally involved the replacement of 'spirit' by 'matter' as the Absolute. (1977: p. 63)

A consequence of this is that Engels' later argument with religion lacks both the subtlety and the profoundity of Marx's earlier, more humanistic critique of that phenomenon. It is, however, Engels' later argument with religion which – as transmitted by Plekhanov and Lenin – dominates Soviet approaches to religion today.

Engels himself, however, was aware of the tentative nature of his proposals. As he wrote in *Anti-Dühring:*

How young the whole of human history still is, and how ridiculous it would be to attempt to ascribe any absolute validity to our present views. . . (*Anti-Dühring:* p. 159)

His philosophical heirs have, unfortunately, but rarely expressed such caution – or such self-irony – and in Soviet Marxism-Leninism, Engels' attempt to produce an all-embracing 'scientific Marxism' has taken on all the characteristics of a final revelation – a revelation which, in many respects, is presented as an alternative to any and all forms of religion. To the beginnings of this, almost exclusively Soviet, development of Marxism we now turn.

The Marxist-Leninist Critique of Religion

2.1. THE RUSSIAN BACKGROUND

Soviet thought is not based simply on the writings of Marx and Engels but also on the work of Lenin, and although Lenin's chief source of inspiration was undoubtedly the thought of Marx and Engels, he was also influenced by nineteenth century Russian thinkers and by the social, political, economic and religious situation obtaining in the Russia of his day. It will, therefore, be necessary to devote some attention to the peculiarly Russian background to Marxism — Leninism, particularly as this bears on Lenin's attitude to religion.[1]

Russia received the Christian religion from Byzantium towards the end of the tenth century and there developed in its western provinces, centred on Kiev, and later on Novgorod, a high form of culture which was not without contact with Western, Latin civilization. In the middle of the thirteenth century this culture was overthrown by invading nomads from central Asia and for two centuries Russia was subject to 'the Tatar Yoke'. The Mongol invaders imposed their own cultural patterns on Russia to such an extent that it can be argued that even today the Soviet Union, as Russia has become, is as Asiatic as it is European in its outlook on life.

The fact that Russia received the Christian religion from Byzantium, rather than from the West, had the most profound consequences for the subsequent development of that country for, by accepting the Eastern Orthodox form of Christianity, Russia cut herself off from the mainstream of Western cultural development. This, together with the added severance from Western influences consequent upon the Mongol invasions, meant that Russia developed in virtual isolation from the West until at least the eighteenth century — if not beyond, up to and including our own day. The 'Europeanisation' of Russia, traditionally considered to have been begun by Peter the Great in the eighteenth century, was, until the late nineteenth century, well nigh exclusively confined to the aristocratic élite. Some of the consequences of this isolation were that Russia participated in neither the European Renaissance nor in the 'Scientific Revolution' of the West, nor did there arise in Russia, as there did in the West, a more or less independent church, middle class, nor even a fully independent aristocracy. The entire country was ruled by a single, autocratic authority to which all were subject. Nowhere was this more evident than in the life of the church.

The basic element in Orthodoxy, it has been said, is that of resignation (Pipes, 1977: p. 221). Orthodox spitituality considers all earthly existence an abomination and it, therefore, preaches, retirement from, rather than involvement with, the world. It also preaches, to a greater extent than has Western Christendom, the patient acceptance of one's fate and the redemptive value of silent suffering. Yet, despite this, the Russian church has always been deeply involved with society and with the state. Lacking, however, practical rules of conduct for such intercourse, it not only compromised its fundamental spiritual values, but, as Richard Pipes has claimed, it 'placed itself more docilely than any other church at the disposal of the state, helping it to exploit and repress' (1977: p. 222). Russian Christianity was also syncretistic. As James H. Billington has pointed out in his classic study of Russian culture, *The Icon and the Axe:* 'for the primitive peasant imagination of pre-industrial Russia, the world was saturated with religious meaning. God came to man not just through the icons and holy men of the Church but also through the spirit-hosts of mountains, rivers, and, above all, the forests. . . belief in the magic power of words and names persisted; the fear of *naklikanie*, or bringing something upon oneself merely by mentioning its name, was widespread . . . Christianity had melted into and enriched this world of primitive nature worship without supplanting it. Religious rites, particularly the ever-repeated sign of the cross and the 'Christ have mercy' prayer in the Orthodox liturgy, were often little more than an animistic effort at *naklikanie* – at summoning up God's power and force by endless repetitions of His name', (1970: p. 403). Among the older generation and in the country-side such attitudes persist to this day.

The organisation of the Eastern Orthodox Chruch into auto-cephalous units with no centralised authority, as in the Roman Church, weakened the position of Orthodoxy to stand up to secular authority in any individual state. It has, therefore, had little choice but to adapt itself to whatever temporal power it has had to live under, although during the period 1613-50 it was itself, for a time, the supreme authority in the Russian state.[2] As a French observer, Anatole Leroy-Beaulieu, put it in his book *L'Empire des Tsars et les Russes* in 1889:

In Eastern Orthodoxy, the ecclesiastical constitution tends to model itself on the political, while the boundaries of the churches tend to reproduce the boundaries of states. These are two correlative facts, inherent in the national form of the Orthodox churches. Confined within the frontiers of the state, deprived of a common head and religious centre abroad, independent of one another, these churches are more susceptible to the influence of temporal power, more vulnerable to the backlash of revolutions of lay society. With their everywhere identical hierarchy of identical priests and bishops, the Orthodox churches adapt themselves, depending on the time and place, to the most diverse regimes: the mode of the internal administration always ends up harmonizing with the mode of the political organization. (Vol. III, p. 167. Quoted Pipes, 177: p. 224)

Such symbiotic identification, of course, has its roots deep in Orthodox doctrine and history, for in Byzantium the Emperor had been head of the church and the church part of the state organisa-tion – a fate which, after the expropriation of church lands by Peter the Third in 1762, was to overtake the Russian church. It was, in fact, that church itself, in seeking the help of the 'secular arm' to help it maintain the vast lands which it had acquired during the Mongol domination, in the face of criticism from those within it who were urging it to dispossess itself, which had, in the sixteenth century, persuaded Ivan the Fourth to crown himself Emperor and had supplied him with a theology of absolutism.[3]

Integral to this theology was the conception of Moscow as the third Rome, the true heir to Byzantium, and the notion that the Russian Tsars were universal Christian sovereigns with a mission to the whole of Christendom — Eastern and Western; a notion which was to re-emerge in Russian 'Messianism' in the nineteenth century and yet again, some would say, in Soviet domination of the international Communist movement today. By throwing its weight behind the autocracy, the church achieved its immediate objectives, but at the price of complete subservience to the state; a subservience which Peter the Great and his successors were to make all the more complete. After Peter's reforms the Russian Orthodox Church became little more than a branch of the Imperial civil service and the holy Synod little more than a ministry of religious affairs. Priests were turned into informers and had, upon their appointment by the state, to take an oath of allegiance to it which over-ruled the secrecy of the confessional itself. They were charged that:

If during confession someone discloses an unfulfilled but still intended criminal act, especially one of treason or rebellion against the Sovereign or the State, or an evil design against the honour or health of the Sovereign and the family of his Majesty. . . the confessor must not only not give him absolution of his openly confessed sins . . . but must promptly report him. . . such villains are commanded to be apprehended with all despatch and brought to the designated places (i.e., the Tsar's Privy Chancellery and *Preobrazhenskii Prikas*). (Quoted, James Cracraft, 1971: pp. 238-239.)

To the taking of this oath the clergy of the Orthodox church offered no resistance.

By the end of the nineteenth century the church was almost completely out of touch with large sections of the people of Russia, and especially with the intellectuals who, on account of its anti-intellectual conservatism — the Russian church had never developed anything like the intellectual theology of the Western churches — despised it. 'Impoverished, isolated, and identified with the autocracy, the clergy commanded neither love nor respect', says Richard Pipes, and he continues: 'No branch of

Christianity has shown such callous indifference to social and political injustice' (1977: pp. 244-245). Identified with the hated autocracy to the extent that it was, it is not surprising that when the autocracy fell the Russian Orthodox Church fell with it. It is against the background of such a national church that Lenin's attitude to religion was formed.

Within the state bureaucracy, consequent upon Peter the Great's reform of the aristocracy, there originated in the nineteenth century a distinctive social layer which became known by the word which it itself gave to the world – the *intelligentsia.*[4] The intelligentsia was a loosely connected group of people who strove for reform but which, lacking any possibility for action in the Russia of its day, confined itself, for the most part, to theoretical activity. One of the essential features of the intelligentsia was *printsipialnost'* – love for the abstract, combined with an obsession with principles and a distrust of the concrete – a frame of mind which made for excessive dogmatism and in which the critical, sceptical spirit, so characteristic of the Western intellectual's approach to life, was lacking.

The basis of the intelligentsia's desire for reform lay in its profound dissatisfaction with prevailing social conditions in Russia; poverty, serfdom, corporal punishment, compulsory military service, and forced marriages were just some of the evils of Russian society which the intelligentsia wanted to eradicate. Many members of the intelligentsia also suffered from a feeling of inferiority *vis-à-vis* Western Europe and were averse to spiritual values – particularly the spiritual values enshrined in Orthodoxy. Yet, paradoxically, their own views for a reformed Russia were enshrouded in a deeply religious and near messianic atmosphere.

The rebellion of the intelligentsia began in 1825 with the December revolt of a group of aristocratic army officers protesting against the unlimited powers of the autocracy. The brutal suppression of this revolt and the consequent repressive measures designed to stifle all future expression of dissent – which continued throughout the century – drove many intellectuals not only to lives of sterile theorising, but often to self-imposed exile in Western Europe.

With the exception of the Slavophiles, a group which emerged in the 1840's in Russia and who believed that the seeds of the new Russia must be found in Russia itself — in the traditional values the Russian people and in the Orthodox church — almost all the intelligentsia were opposed to religion in any form. This was certainly the case with Aleksander Herzen, an aristocratic landowner, who can be regarded, along with Belinsky, as the founder of the radical tradition in Russia. Although Herzen can be classified as a Westerniser, that is a member of the group which also emerged in the 1840's — the 'remarkable decade', as the late nineteenth century Russian writer F.V. Annenkov called it — in opposition to the Slavophiles, and for whom reform implied 'Europeanization', and although he advocated the cultivation of science and was hostile to all forms of religion, he was no uncritical enthusiast of Western ideas. In fact in his critique of capitalism he was very close indeed to Slavophile ideas — not least after his self-imposed exile in the West in 1847. Herzen's criticism of capitalism was not so much that it bred poverty and exploitation, as that it degraded people by its exclusive cult of material values, thus impoverishing society spiritually and reducing it to a general mediocrity. His critique was, as Leszek Kołakowski has said, 'an attack on capitalism from the standpoint of aristocracy rather than socialism' (1978: Vol. II., p. 312). Like most intellectuals of his generation in Russia, Herzen had passed through an Hegelian phase in which he, like the Young Hegelians in Germany, had criticised conservative interpretations of the rationality of the real and had upheld the dialectic as the principle of the permanent negation and criticism of the existing order of things. Whilst Russian radicalism had its indigenous roots in traditions of peasant rebellion, the influence of left wing Hegelianism in Russia, as in Western Europe, was strong. Under its influence Herzen wrote a number of philosophical essays which propagated naturalistic and anti-religious attitudes in Russia.

Vassarion Belinsky was primarily a literary critic, but one who sought to create a new kind of literary criticism — a criticism which reflected not only his own tortuous ideological evolution, but the general 'civic aggressiveness', as it has been called, of the intelligentsia as well (cf. Pomper, 1970: p. 44). Belinsky taught a whole generation of Russian intellectuals to look for social truths in art and to seek not only for aesthetic values but, more importantly, for the moral implications of a writer's work. His own later criticism was itself increasingly didactic in tone, and his concerns are nowhere better expressed than in his famous letter to Gogol on the occasion of the publication, in 1847, of Gogol's *Selected Passages from Correspondence with Friends*, which, overtly at least, seemed to side with the reactionary creed of the Tsar Nicholas I, and his minister of Education, Count Uvarov. In this letter Belinsky's attitude to the official religion of Russia is made clear. He wrote:

Advocate of the knout, apostle of ignorance, champion of obscurantism and reactionary mysticism, eulogist of Tatar customs — what are you doing? That you should tie your ideas to the Orthodox Church I can understand— it has ever been the support of the knout and the toady of despotism; but why do you bring in Christ: What do you think He has in common with any church, and particularly the Orthodox Church? He was the first to teach men the ideals of liberty, equality and fraternity, and He illustrated and proved the truth of his teaching by his martyrdom. And it was man's salvation only until the Church was organised around it, based on the principle of orthodoxy. The Church was a hierarchy, and hence a champion of inequality, a toady to power, an enemy and persecutor of brotherhood among men, and so continues to be to this day. The true meaning of Christ's teaching was revealed by the philosophical movement of the last century. That is why Voltaire, who used the weapon of mockery to put out the bonfires of fanaticism and ignorance in Europe, is certainly far more a son of Christ . . . than all your bishops, metropolitans, and patriarchs . . . When a European, especially a Catholic becomes possessed by the religious spirit, he turns to denouncing authority, like the Hebrew prophets, who denounced the great of the earth for flouting the law. In Russia, on the other hand, if a man (even a decent man) develops the illness known as *religiosa mania*, he at once proceeds to burn more incense to the earthly God than to God in heaven. What scoundrels we Russians are! (Belinsky, *Letter to Gogol*, Raeff, 1966: pp. 256-257).

The letter is further illustrative of Belinsky's affiliation with the French revolutionary tradition. The exact trend of his radicalism is, however, difficult to determine, but his authentic rendering of the spirit of the French and German radical ideologies made him the idol of the coming revolutionary generation.

The writings of Nikolai Chernyshevsky had much more influence on the radical intellengentsia of the latter part of the nineteenth century than has those of Herzen or Belinsky. Chernyshevsky was one of the forerunners of the outlook on life which Turgenev dubbed 'nihilism', and which Dostoyevsky devoted much of his writing to combatting.[5] More of a Westerniser than Herzen, Chernyshevsky was deeply influenced by Jeremy Bentham and the English Utilitarians. He also adopted the naturalistic philosophy of Feuerbach and presented this to the Russian public in 1860 in his *The Anthropological Principle in Philosophy*. He was a consistent exponent of enlightened, materialistic self-interest, or 'rational egoism' as he himself preferred to call it. Arrested in 1862 and exiled to Siberia he wrote, during two years of imprisonment prior to exile, what was to become the text-book of the revolutionaries of the latter part of the century – the novel *What is to be Done?*. Though somewhat pedantic, not to say boring in parts, it succeeded in instilling into revolutionary youth, among whom must be numbered the young Lenin, a spirit of dedicated asceticism, high seriousness, and devotion to the cause of the people. In this respect Chernyshevsky can also be considered a forerunner of the *narodniki* or populists, from whose circles Russia's early Marxists were to emerge. Chernyshevsky was also extremely critical of the moral conventions of the older generation of his day; conversion to revolutionary views involved, for him and for those influenced by him, the rejection of all values advocated by the privileged classes. The cultivation of spiritual, aesthetic or even intellectual values was, for Chernyshevsky, a betrayal of the revolutionary mission. Materialistic utilitarianism was, therefore, the perfect expression of this attitude. Its advocacy was to be furthered by two of Chernyshevsky's younger disciples, N.A. Dobrolyubov and D.I. Pisarev.

In the writings of Chernyshevsky and his disciples, materialism in Russia began to take on a clear political sense and it involved, of course, virulent opposition to both the Orthodox church and to any and all forms of religion. This was nowhere more evident than in the figure of Mikhail Bakunin, an anarchist propagandist who was at first a follower and then later an opponent of Marx. Bakunin was notorious for his hatred of God. 'If God exists', he is reported to have said, 'then man is a slave'. Religion was the main pillar of the state which Bakunin was pledged to abolish.[6]

The radical movement which developed in Russia in the 1860's bore the general title of *narodnichestvo* or populism. This movement, of which the representative figures were A.I. Zhelyabov — hanged for the murder of Tsar Alexander II in 1881 — , the anarchist P.A. Kropotkin, Mikhail Bakunin, P.L. Lavrov, N.K. Mikhailovsky, and P.N. Tkachev were, for the most part, agrarian socialists who saw in the Russian *mir obshchina* — the village commune — the natural foundation for a new social order. They aimed to 'go to the people' — hence their name, which is derived from the Russian *narod,* meaning people. As they were the sons of landowners and priests, with only a highly romanticised knowledge of 'the people', they were more often than not misunderstood by 'the people' and denounced to the police as atheists and subversives. In the light of this searing experience Lavrov — the most influential of the populist writers — was led to change his tactics, and to hold that, whilst the intellegentsia were the front of the revolutionary consciousness, so long as 'the people' were not ready for socialism and revolution, the mission of the intelligentsia must be to propagate the enlightenment necessary for the emergence of a truly revolutionary consciousness. Lavrov and his friend Nikolai Mikhailovsky held that this task was a necessary pre-requisite to a successful revolution. In this they were to be opposed by the early Marxists in Russia and by Lenin in particular. Yet Lavrov's views, which included an attack on religion as arising out of ignorance, on law as the instrument of coercion by privileged classes, on property as a form of theft, an insistence on the moral motivation of revolution and a call for revolutionary asceticism and the enlightenment of the people, did much to form the ethos out of which the more radical social democratic Marxists in Russia were to emerge.

Given the revolutionary ferment in Russia from the 1860's onwards, it is not surprising that many Russian revolutionaries were attracted to Marxism.[7] As J.M. Bocheński has remarked, here was a doctrine which suited their 'doctrinaire, revolutionary, atheistic and messianic character' (1963: p. 26). Most of the populist writers knew of Marxism and accepted some, though by no means all, of its doctrines. Marx's economic doctrines had been taught and discussed in Russian universities by, among others, Z. Ziber, from 1870 onwards, but the only populist writer to actually style himself a Marxist was N.F. Danielson who, in 1872, had brought out the first Russian translation of Marx's *Capital*. The real founder of Russian Marxism, however, was the erstwhile populist Georgi Plekhanov, and it was via Plekhanov's codification and popularisation of Marxism, as a complete world-view, that Marxism became established in Russian revolutionary circles towards the turn of the century.

2.2   PLEKHANOV AND THE BEGINNINGS OF RUSSIAN MARXISM

Plekhanov, the son of a landowner in Tambov province, had, in 1875 at the age of eighteen, embraced atheism and joined the revolutionary *narodnik* movement. By 1880 he had become so involved in revolutionary activities that he had had to flee Russia in order to escape arrest. He settled in Switzerland where he began to study the works of Marx and Engels and was immediately converted to Marxism. One of the founders of the first Russian Marxist organisation, *Gruppa 'Osvobozhdeniye Truda* — the Emancipation of Labour Group — Plekhanov translated much of the Marxist literature into Russian and in his own writings gave Russian Marxism many of its distinctive emphases. His early polemical writings after his conversion to Marxism were directed against his erstwhile populist friends, although he also took it upon himself to defend what he regarded as orthodox Marxism against the revisionist tendencies of the Russian empirio-critics and of the German, Eduard Bernstein. Plekhanov's major works were

The Development of the Monist View of History: A Defence of Materialism (1895); *Essays in the History of Materialism* (1896); *The Role of the Individual in History* (1898); and *Fundamental Problems of Marxism* (1910). Lenin was to say of these works — with the exception of the last — that it was impossible to come to a true understanding of Marxism without having read them, and of *The Development of the Monist View of History,* in particular, that: 'it educated a whole generation of Russian Marxists' (*Philosophical Notebooks: LCW: 38;162* and 'On the Significance of Militant Materialism'; *LCW: 33;227-228*).

Along with Chernyshevsky, Lenin recognised Plekhanov as the chief architect of the materialist tradition in Russian thought, and he praised Plekhanov's determined struggle against political and philosophical revisionism which, in Lenin's words, 'he carried on from the point of view of a consistent dialectical materialism' ('Marxism and Revisionism'; *LCW:* 15;33). It was Plekhanov also, who, as Lenin confessed in a letter to Maxim Gorky, had opened his eyes to the importance of philosophy for the ordinary Marxist (*LCW:* 13; 448-449). With such credentials, Plekhanov's place in the pantheon of Soviet Marxism is assured, despite his often bitter disagreements with Lenin over Bolshevik policies. For an understanding of the world-view of Soviet Marxism, which he did so much to help articulate, a study of the outlines of Plekhanov's thought is essential.

Plekhanov considered the dissociation of historical from philosophical materialism a grave error. Engels, he maintained, fully represented Marx's views on materialism, particularly as he had articulated these in *Anti-Dühring* and in *Ludwig Feuerbach.* It is to Plekhanov that we must trace the now well-established Soviet view that the writings of Marx and Engels form a unified and indissoluble whole — a view which was to be reinforced by Lenin. The most important legacy of Marx/Engels — as we should, perhaps, designate the composite personality of Plekhanov's reading of those two authors — was, in Plekhanov's opinion, what he termed 'dialectical materialism' — an outlook which he was inclined to identify with the Marxist philosophy as a whole.

He wrote: 'The philosophy of Marx and Engels is not only a materialist philosophy; it is dialectical materialism.' (*Fundamental Problems of Marxism:* p. 40).

If, however, we look carefully at his references to the writings of Marx and Engels, we see that by 'the philosophy of Marx and Engels' Plekhanov meant the philosophical materialism of Engels' later years. With Engels, Plekhanov insisted that 'Marxism is a materialist world outlook' and that it cannot be reduced to its historical and economic aspects alone. The laws of dialectics reflect natural as well as social processes. 'Marx and Engels', he wrote, 'were conscious materialists not only in the field of history but in natural science as well' (ibid: p. 22). Plekhanov's object was not, however, to put forward a philosophy of nature – in which he had little, if any, interest – but to secure for historical material-ism a cosmological foundation. Marx, in Plekhanov's opinion, laid the foundations of social science by introducing the notion of necessity – which lies at the basis of all scientific thinking – into the study of social phenomena and into the study of history. The dynamism which Plekhanov, following Engels, believed to be inherent in matter, when taken together with the principle of evolution and the laws of dialectics was, he believed, sufficient to establish dialectical materialism as an integral and consistent world-view and one which would explain all contingencies. Marx had transformed the idealist world-view by showing that the necessities of history are rooted in material conditions and that freedom consists in understanding the laws of history and of acting effectively on the basis of them.

Plekhanov, as do Soviet theoreticians today, began his exposi-tion of the Marxist world outlook by drawing a distinction between materialism and idealism, both of which, he claimed, were monisms in that both sought to explain reality by means of a single principle. Marxism not only explains everything in terms of matter, but finds therein the historical factor which produces both society and ideas. Marxism differs from both idealism, and from previous forms of materialism, by admitting the importance of both environment and ideas. Ultimately, though, both environment and ideas need to be explained and Marxism seeks to uncover the factor in history which explains both. For Plekhanov, neither the French historians of the Restoration, who had sought to explain legal, moral, political and economic questions in terms of 'human nature', nor the utopian socialists, whose focus of attention was society as it ought to be and not society as it is or has been, nor the German idealists, had been able to do this. Only Marxism had done so by seeing that the correct answer lay neither in human nature, nor in ideas, but in external nature and in the material conditions in which men live and work, in their means of production and in productive forces. Plekhanov then presents historical materialism as the way in which the development of society is to be accounted for; extending this into areas which neither Marx nor Engels had touched upon. He maintains, for example, that

. . . the influence of the literature of one country on the literature of another is directly proportional to the similarity of the social relations of these countries. (*The Development of the Monist View of History*: p. 226)

It is, in fact, in the field of aesthetics that Plekhanov's most interesting and most original contriburions to Marxist theory are to be found.

But although Plekhanov sought to apply the insights of historical materialism to as wide an area of social and cultural life as he could, he virtually ignored it when he came to discuss religion. In fact, as the Russian emigré philosopher Berdyaev has noted, Plekhanov's attitude to religion is essentially that of a man of the Enlightenment. Berdyaev wrote:

His struggle against religion is intellectual, scholarly in character. He still thinks that religious beliefs will die out as a result of the growth of enlightenment among the masses. (1933: p. 246)

And Berdyaev noted that Plekhanov's 'good-natured and mocking attitude' neglected what was central to Marx and Engels, and what was later to become important for Lenin — namely, the class character of religion and the necessity for a class struggle against it. Plekhanov did, however, note the soporific effect of religion on the class struggle when he wrote that religious beliefs impaired the development of the self-consciousness of the working class and that it acted as an opiate, lulling it to sleep. (*'Svyashchennik G. Gapon'*; *Socheneniya:* 17;232). But such views were marginal to his overall view that religion was simply the outcome of lamentable ignorance. Religious beliefs were, for Plekhanov, at bottom, animistic. When purged of their animistic elements what is left is not religion but morality, and morality, he insisted, pre-dates religion and has no need of a religious foundation. That religion was for him almost entirely a matter of a mistaken understanding of the world can be seen from the reply which he gave in a questionnaire sent to him by the French journal *Mercure de France* in 1907: 'As for religious feeling or conviction, it will disappear with the dissolution of the religious idea.' (*Soch.* 6;619).

From this it would appear that, for Plekhanov, the sole root of religion is false belief. The remedy, therefore, is, according to Plekhanov – and Lenin and the Soviet tradition were to agree with him to a great extent – education in atheism through public lectures, particularly lectures on the incompatibility of religion and modern science, and huge printings in cheap editions of the works of Lucretius, Rabelais, Voltaire, Diderot, and, of course, Feuerbach, Marx and Engels, in readable Russian translations. Any emotional substitute for religion could be adequately provided by art and music. Taking his cue from Schiller's *Letters on the Aesthetic Education of Mankind*, Plekhanov suggested that churches should be turned into theatres; thus would religion, a product of the human imagination which masquerades as knowledge, become what in fact it was – namely art. The correct way with religion, said Plekhanov, was 'not to abuse, nor upbraid, but to enlighten' (*Soch.* 13;199). As Lenin's collaborator, Lyubov Akselrod, commented, Plekhanov's attitude to religion was an urbane lift of the Marxist eyebrow in incredulity that such intelligent people as Lev Tolstoy could find satisfaction in the worldviews of old peasant women (L.I. Akselrod, *Etyudy i vospominan-*

iya: p. 39). Such an attitude did not bode well for the serious study of religion among Soviet Marxists.

2.3. LENIN: THE PARTY AND THE PROBLEM OF RELIGION

Vladimir Ilyich Ulyanov — Lenin — was born in April 1870 in Simbirsk on the Volga, the son of a school inspector. By the time that he began his university studies at the University of Kazan in 1887 he had not only become an atheist, but was also deeply involved in revolutionary activities. His elder brother Alexander had been executed that same year for his part in a plot to kill the Tsar, Alexander III, and Lenin himself was exiled for a short time to a small village some thirty miles away from Simbirsk, where he lived, under police surveillance, with his mother. His father had died the year before. In 1888 the family moved to Samara, where Lenin, who had already begun to read Marx, organised a small Marxist study circle. After a period of home-study Lenin finally took his examinations at the University of St. Petersburg and received his law degree in 1891. Henceforth, his life, both in Russian and in exile abroad, was to be entirely at the service of the forthcoming revolution, for that the revolution was coming Lenin was in no doubt. He, in fact, would make it come.

One of Lenin's major contributions to Marxism was his theory of the Party — its organisation and its role in revolutionary struggle. It was this Party — the Party of Lenin — which, in 1917, spearheaded the Russian Revolution, seized power, and has held on to it ever since. The Party, as the self-appointed vanguard of the proletariat, is the guide and guardian of every aspect of life in the Soviet Union today. The world-outlook of the Party is Marxism-Leninism and its philosophy is dialectical materialism. The Party claims to be the sole interpreter of the legacy of Marx, Engels and Lenin; it is the arbiter in all doctrinal disputes, and it is the maker of all policy. In this latter task it claims to unite theory with practice. It is thus inextricably linked to all developments in Soviet thought — including, of course, all Soviet thought about religion and the study of religion – and without some knowledge of its theoretical basis the overt subservience of Soviet scholars to it will be incomprehensible.

It was in *What is to be Done?* (1902) and in *One Step Forward, Two Steps Back* (1904) that Lenin first developed his views regarding the Party. The former opens with a vigorous discussion of 'freedom of criticism' within the Party. Such criticism, Lenin argues – particularly if it implies that Marx or Engels might have been wrong in any way – no truly revolutionary Party can tolerate. Within a revolutionary Party there can be no concessions to theory for

. . . without a revolutionary theory, there can be no revolutionary movement . . . The role or the vanguard can be fulfilled only by a party that is guided by advanced theory. (*LCW:* 5;369)

The truth of Marxism must be kept free from even the germ of criticism lest the revolutionary movement become infected and crippled. The strength of the revolutionary movement, Lenin argued, lies in the awakening of the masses, but the masses stand in dire need of consciousness and leadership which must be brought to them from without. This is the duty of the Party; but to play this role the Party needs strong organisation and firm principles. The Party must learn

. . . to apply practically the materialist analysis and the materialist estimate of *all* aspects of life and activity of *all* classes, strata and groups of the population. (*LCW:* 5;412)

The basis of the Party, Lenin argued in *One Step Forward, Two Steps Back*, must be a democratic centralism, (cf. *LCW:* 7;205-425 *passim;* and especially pp. 368-379). As a long standing commentator on the Soviet Union, Richard T. De George, has said:

The importance of the Party in Lenin's theory can scarcely be over-emphasised. The Party is the vanguard of the proletariat and the proletariat is the most progressive element of the masses. The Party is thus in the forefront of all humanity and the leader of the progressive elements. The Party sees most clearly what is needed by all of society, brings these needs to the consciousness of people, and leads the way in social development. (1970: p. 127)

De George was writing about Lenin's views on the Party prior to that Party's assuming the government of Russia during the Revolution of 1917, but his words are still relevant to the role which the Party plays in the Soviet Union today.

The notion of *partiinost'* — party mindedness — follows logically for Soviet scholars from the Party's claim to represent mankind. Marx and Engels had held that the superstructure in any society reflects the material base, and that law, morality, philosophy, religion and the like were, therefore, always expressive of the ideas of the dominant classes in any society. The Party, however, represents no class but the proletariat and eventually, therefore, all mankind. Thus is it enabled to rise above particular class interests and because of this, its laws, its morality, its philosophy — with the single exception of religion which is destined to disappear altogether —reflect not class interests but the interests of humanity as a whole. The Party, therefore, as the representative of the most progressive elements in society, is alone in a position — without class bias — to determine what is true and what is false, what is right and what is wrong, what is better or what is worse, for society as a whole. The Party must, therefore, be obeyed: anything less would be perverse individualism.

Lenin was first and foremost a man of action and not a theorectician, but he was a man of action who was also heir not only to the practically orientated philosophy of Marx and Engels, but to the indigenous Russian revolutionary tradition. He recognised, therefore, the importance of the theoretical idea not, however, in and for itself, because, for Lenin, philosophical questions had no meaning in themselves, but were simply weapons in the political struggle — as also were art, literature, law, and, as we shall see, religion. On this point Lenin applied the materialist conception of history rather more thoroughly than did Marx and Engels themselves. Lenin was also a tactician who, being singularly unfettered by traditional moral values, could never see what connection morality might have with social and political action, which, for him, were purely technical fields. J.M. Bocheński, in fact, has hazarded the guess that just as Lenin regarded individuals – including the members of his own Party – as so much material to be moulded and used, so his denial of God was in large measure due to his seeing in God a rival impeding his, Lenin's, freedom of action (Bocheński, 1963: p. 29).

This is as may be, but Lenin was also a man of principle, and one of his principles was the materiality of all existence – a materiality which excluded the supernatural *in toto*. His atheism, which was uncompromising, was rooted in his materialistic understanding of the world and of man. His first incursion into philosophy, in fact, was occasioned by disputes within international Marxism and by positions taken up by some Marxists which, he felt, led directly to idealism and religion. These disputes arose out of the need felt by some Marxists for a Marxist theory of knowledge. Since neither Marx nor Engels had had much to say about this, some Marxists sought to make good this deficiency by various forms of neo-Kantianism. Such Marxists – who called themselves 'empirio-critics' and who included such leading Bolsheviks as Bogdanov, Lunacharsky and Bazarov – were threatening Marxism, in Lenin's eyes, every whit as much as were the outright idealists and Machian philosophers of science. What, for Lenin, was at stake was nothing less than the consistency and integrity of Marxist materialism. In attacking empirio-criticism Lenin's object was to show that it compromised the basic division of all philosophy into idealism or materialism and was, therefore, calculated to uphold religion and the interests of the exploiting classes.

Lenin's attitude in this dispute is as good an example as we shall find of the close unity, which, for him, existed between theory and practice for, as Leszek Kołakowski has pointed out, Lenin's argument with the Empiriocritics is based on the principle of '*partiinost*', understood here as simple partisanship (ibid., 1978: Vol. II, pp. 451-452). For Lenin, philosophical theories could never be neutral in the class struggle because they are the instruments of it. As he wrote: 'Non-partisans in philosophy are just as hopelessly thick-headed as they are in politics.' And again: 'Non-partisanship in philosophy is only wretchedly masked servility to idealism and fideism.' (*Materialism and Empirio-criticism LCW*: 14; 286 and 355).

Lenin's reply to Bogdanov and the Empirio-critics can be found in his book *Materialism and Empirio-criticism*, which he wrote in the early months of 1908, and which he urged should be published as soon as possible as this was necessitated 'not only by literary, but also by serious political considerations' (*LCW*: 14; 366). The position which Lenin put forward in this work is so important for later Soviet Marxist materialism, and hence of considerable importance for Soviet attitudes to religion, that we must describe it in some detail.

Before setting forward on his own – and, therefore, the future Soviet – understanding of materialism, Lenin first sought to refute the idealist argument against materialism which he traced back to the eighteenth century British philosopher, Berkeley. Berkeley, taking what he took to be Locke's position to its logical conclusion, had held that all the human subject is ever aware of is sensations – of matter as such he knows nothing. Matter, for Berkeley, was, therefore, a fiction. The reason, for Berkeley, why things continued to exist when neither we, nor anyone else, was actually perceiving them, was that they are constantly perceived by God. It is this which gives things continuity. Thus, for Berkeley, 'matter' was unnecessary and materialism was nonsense. Lenin claimed that all idealist criticism of materialism could be reduced to this argument of Berkeley and it was this argument which he sought to refute.

His own reply is somewhat confused and he seems, as did Engels before him, to confuse realism with materialism in philosophy, but the general outlines of his argument are clear enough. In opposition to all forms of idealism Lenin maintained that:

. . . materialism, in full agreement with natural science, takes matter as primary and regards consciousness, thought, sensation as secondary, because

in its well-defined form sensation is associated only with the higher forms of
matter (organic matter) . . . (ibid; *LCW:* 14;46)

Sensation was defined by Lenin as 'the direct connection between
consciousness and the external world; it is the transformation of
the energy of external excitation into a state of consciousness'
(ibid; *LCW:* 14;51). How this transformation takes place Lenin
did not say, but he did maintain that both parts of it are given in
experience. Sensation, we are told 'depends on the brain, nerves,
retina etc.', that is on matter organised in a definite way (ibid;
LCW: 14;49). It is the result of actions on the part of objects
which exist outside of and independently of ourselves, and is thus
the 'subjective image of the objective world' (ibid., *LCW:* 14;119).
Sensations thus give information about the objective world — the
only world there is. As Lenin wrote: 'Sensation reveals objective
truth to man.' And, quoting from Feuerbach: 'My sensation is
subjective, but its foundation [or ground — *Grund*] is objective.'
(ibid., *LCW:* 14; 130-131).
    Lenin puts forward five further arguments against idealism.
1. He claimed that the world and other people exist independently
of ourselves; that sensations and our consciousness are an image of
the external world and since the image cannot exist without the
thing imagined, the external world must exist. 2. He pointed out
that according to modern science the world existed long before
man came into being, with the consequence that matter existed
before man or sensations: matter, therefore, is primary. 3. Lenin's
third argument against idealism was based on the fact that some
of the things which we now know about matter were not always
known — from which he draws the inference that things must
exist independently of our consciousness of them; that there
is not difference in principle between 'appearances' and 'things—
in—themselves', and that we must think dialectically because
knowledge emerges out of ignorance as history progresses. 4. His
fourth argument was a variation on his second argument —
namely, that the world existed before society and that consequently it does not need man to organise it into an intelligible

whole – as he understood Kant to have maintained. 5. Lastly, Lenin claimed that there must be objects which our knowledge reflects if the notion of 'objective truth' was to have meaning – only materialists, he claimed, could, therefore, be in possession of anything which could properly be called 'objective truth'.

Lenin's arguments – whilst stated with great vigour – are, to say the least, imprecise, and much philosophical work in the Soviet Union is taken up with refining, developing and defending them. Put simply, what Lenin argued in *Materialism and Empirio-criticism* was that idealism (and philosophical agnosticism, which he equated with idealism) contradicted the most elementary scientific and common-sense knowledge that we have of the world and is thus contrary to all progress, whether social or intellectual.

Having thus, to his own satisfaction, refuted idealism, Lenin concluded his book by setting forth, in opposition to idealism, the philosophy of the 'militant proletariat' – dialectical materialism. Basic to his explication of this philosophy was his 'copy theory' of knowledge, in which sensations, abstract ideas, and all other aspects of cognition are held to be reflections in our minds of actual realities in the material world which exist in complete independence of ourselves. He wrote:

Matter is a philosophical category denoting the objective reality which is given to man by his sensations, and which is copied, reflected and photographed by our sensations whilst existing independently of them. (*LCW:* 14; 130)

Dialectical materialism does not, of course, attempt to solve the scientific problems concerning the structure of matter – that is not its task. It can accept all that science tells us

For the sole property of matter with whose recognition philosophical materialism is bound up is the property of being an objective reality, of existing outside the mind. (*LCW:* 14; 206-201)

A corollary of this, for Lenin, is the rejection of relativism, and the espousal of a correspondence theory of truth in which the

truth of any statement is in direct proportion to its correspondence with reality. The most effective way, however, to find out
whether this is the case, said Lenin – and here he follows Engels
– is the test of practice. Marxist theory, for example, has, for
Marxists, been shown to be true by the success of the workers'
movement based upon it.

Whilst *Materialism and Empirio-criticism* had little success upon
its first publication – those whom it attacked, such as Bogdanov,
Bazarov and Yushkevich, despised it and thought it hardly worthy
of a reply – it became, after Stalin had proclaimed it the epitome
of Marxist philosophy, the foundation of the dialectical materialist approach to the understanding of reality, and the cornerstone
of the philosophical critique of religion. For all its obvious failings
it did, however, as Kołakowski has said, represent 'one of the last
points of contact between orthodox Leninist Marxism and European philosophy' (1978: Vol. II, p. 458).

The importance of the book, as we have indicated earlier, lay
for Lenin himself, not in any enrichment of Marxism that it might
or might not be said to contain, but as a political work, giving to
the revolutionary movement that clear-cut, uniform, materialist
world-outlook which Lenin believed it essential that it possess.
Any kind of idealism – even the slightest concession to idealism
– was, for Lenin, a concession to religion and hence to those who
sought to delude and exploit the masses, and indeed, quite often
in argument, Lenin would try to show that an opponent's position
lead to idealism and hence to religion – at which point he would
terminate the discussion.

Lenin's rejection of religion was more than a consequence of his
materialism – though it was that – for, as Bocheński has pointed
out, it was 'one of the logical bases of his philosophy – perhaps
the most important one' (1963: p. 31). Similarly, Kołakowski has
reminded us that 'Lenin regarded religion as a key issue in the
party's ideological activity' (1978: Vol. II, p. 459), and Bohdan
Bociurkiw has written that 'while it may appear from the paucity
of his writings on the problem that Lenin took only a secondary
interest in religion, it would be far from correct to minimise either

the importance of atheism in Leninist theory or the political significance ascribed by him to the role of religion in Russian society'
(in Shapiro and Reddaway, 1967: pp. 107-108). In fact Bociurkiw
has claimed that whilst Lenin echoes the notion of religion as an
ideological weapon of the exploiting classes of Marx's early
polemics over the social principles of Christianity, and draws
heavily on Engel's discussion of the evolution of the social function of religion in the context of class relations, he so modifies the
classical Marxian formula which derives religious alienation from
more basic forms of economic and social alienation, as to upgrade
the importance of the active struggle against religious ideology to
an extent where it becomes a means, if not indeed a condition, of
a successful struggle against political and economic oppression. If
this is so, and we shall see later that this is the way in which
contemporary Marxist-Leninist theoreticians appear to read Lenin,
then we cannot fail to detect here the influence on Lenin of the
indigenous Russian tradition of political atheism of Belinsky,
Herzen, Pisarev and Bakunin (cf. Bocuirkiw, 1967: p. 109).

Lenin's writings on religion consist of articles, speeches, letters
and notes evoked in response to immediate and pressing political
concerns. They are thus written – as are almost all of Lenin's
writings – in a robust polemical, partisan and dogmatic style.
They can be divided into three periods: (1) those made before the
first Russian Revolution of 1905; (2) those made between 1905
and the Second Russian Revolution of 1917, and (3) those made
after the Revolution, where Lenin was in a position of power and
up to his death in 1924.

1. In the first period religious questions attracted Lenin's attention only in so far as they provided him with the opportunity for
expanding his political agitation.

2. In the second, and most important period, Lenin set forth
the distinctive Bolshevik position (theoretical and tactical) on
religion, whilst taking issue with those within the Social Democratic Party who sought to invest Marxism itself with a religious aura.
This group, the most important single figure of which was Anatoly
Vasilyevich Lunacharsky – the man who after 1917 was to

become Lenin's commissar for education — but which also attracted the writer Maxim Gorky, sought to counteract the interest in religion which had developed in Russian society after the Revolution of 1905 by offering a religion of its own — a 'socialist religion'. Their programme, which drew heavily on 'the religion of humanity' expounded by Comte and Feuerbach, was known as *bogostroitel'stvo* — god building. It was conceived not only as an answer to the god-seeking (*bogoiskatel'stvo*) movement of some Russian Christian philosophers, but also as a move beyond the arid and old-fashioned atheism of Plekhanov and other orthodox Marxists, for whom the history of religion was but the history of the conflict between it and science.

In his book *Religion and Socialism*, which he published in 1908, Lunacharsky argued that there was more to historical religion than superstition and misuse. Although religions were ideologically false, they were, Lunacharsky argued, expressions of desires and feelings that socialism should take over and ennoble, not destroy. As a religion of immanence — in it there was no God, no supernatural world and no personal immortality — and stressing as it did man's need for community, his yearning to transcend himself, and his unity with nature and all mankind, socialism, as presented by Lunacharsky, can, in some ways, be held to foreshadow the position of those who today hold that Marxism is the legitimate secular successor to the Christian religion in Western Europe, (see pp. 370ff below). Certainly, Lunacharsky's insight into some of the functions which the historic religions have fulfilled can be said, from the point of view of Western sociology of religion, to be an advance on the somewhat narrow analysis of function put forward by Marx and Engels. Religion, for Lunacharsky, had sought to reconcile men with their lives and to give them a sense of meaning and purpose. This, and not the offering of a metaphysical explanation of reality, was, for him, its primary function. Thus, although the old myths had collapsed, men still yearned for meaning in life and this socialism ought to provide. In Lunacharsky's religion God was replaced by humanity — a fitting object for man's love and worship and one in devotion to which he could rise above his own ego and experience the joy of sacrificing his own interests to the whole. Such identification with humanity as a whole would, Lunacharsky believed, free man from the fear of suffering and death, restore his dignity and develop his creative energies. The true creator of God, he held, was the proletariat, and the proletariat's coming revolution would, in Lunacharsky's opinion, be the fundamental act of god-building.

Whilst such views added nothing of substance to Marxism, they did lend it an emotional colour which had been missing since the days of Marx's earliest writings although these, of course, were not known to them. They also, perhaps, articulated the appeal of Marxism to many of its adherents — both then as now.[8] Plekhanov and Lenin, however, roundly condemned such views as a dangerous flirtation with religious obscurantism (cf. Lenin's correspondence with Gorky; *LCW:* 35; 121-124 and 127-129), and their influence on the subsequent development of Marxism in the Soviet Union has, therefore, been negligible. In fact, Lunacharsky himself quickly dropped his advocacy of this way of presenting Marxist atheism. Henceforth in the Soviet Union it would be the philosophical and political — some would say even personal — atheism of Lenin which would provide the context for all dealings with religion, although outwith the Soviet Union views not unlike those of Lunacharsky and the 'god-builders' would re-emerge in the 'open' Marxism of the Post–Stalinist period in Eastern Europe and the West (See below pp. 369ff)

Atheism, and an optimism with regard to science's ability to dispel all mystery from the world, had early become an article of faith with Lenin — certainly before his acquaintance with Marxism.[9] In the virulence of his opposition to religion it is possible, as we have said, to trace the influence of the political atheism of the Russian radical tradition — an atheism which sprang from the rejection of the historic interdependence of the autocracy and the Orthodox church. Lenin's earliest pronouncements on religion were, in fact, concerned to expose and unmask the Orthodox church as the servant of the State.[10] Later, Lenin's opposition to religion and the church — whilst still vigorious — took a more intellectual turn. As he came to view the matter, the mundane origin of the idea of the God in whom he had long ceased to believe – he himself dated this as having occurred at the age of sixteen – had been revealed for what it was by Feuerbach, and its class nature and harmful social role in history definitively established by Marx and Engels. Lenin was thus singularly un-interested in probing further into the theory of religion and throughout his life was impatient of any who sought to re-open the issue. It is not surprising, therefore, that in what is his most important single piece of writing on religion – the article entitled 'Socialism and Religion' which he published in the journal *Novaya Zhizn* in 1905 – he devoted but a single paragraph to the origin and social function of religion. He wrote:

Religion is one of the forms of spiritual oppression which everywhere weighs down heavily upon the masses of the people, overburdened by their perpetual work for others, by want and isolation. Impotence of the exploited classes in their struggle against the exploiters just as inevitably gives rise to the belief in a better life after death as impotence of the savage in his battle with nature gives rise to belief in gods, devils, miracles and the like. Those who toil and live in want all their lives are taught by religion to be submissive and patient while here on earth, and to take comfort in the hope of a heavenly reward. But those who live by the labour of others are taught by religion to practice charity whilst on earth, thus offering them a very cheap way of justifying their existence as exploiters and selling them at a very modest price tickets to well-being in heaven. Religion is opium for the people. Religion is a sort of spiritual booze (*sivukha*), in which the slaves of capital drown their human image, their demand for a life more or less worthy of man. (*LCW:* 10; 83-84)

Thus far Lenin repeats – in somewhat more vivid, if atrophied, form – the aetiology of religion found in Marx and Engels. Equal-ly, Lenin had Marx's aversion to probing into the sources of natural religion, preferring to explain religious phenomena in terms of class structure and exploitation. For him, as for the later Marx, socio-economic slavery was ultimately 'the true source of the religious humbugging of mankind' (*LCW:* 10; 87). He thus ignores completely Engel's later evocation of the animistic theory of the origin of religion. Similarly, Lenin – like Marx and Engels –

ignored completely those feelings of dependency and contingency upon which Feuerbach had laid stress in his theory of the aetiology of religion and which he saw as one of the major factors making for the persistence of religion (cf. Feuerbach, *Lectures on Religion*: pp. 33-36). In fact, as Delos B. McKown has noted, Lenin ignored completely in his comments on Feuerbach's *Lectures on Religion*, found in his *Philosophical Notebooks*, all reference to the origin of religion other than that which fitted into the predominately social theory of Marx and Engels (1975: pp. 95-103). Lenin did, however, comment favourably on those passages in Feuerbach where he layed stress on human ignorance and superstition as factors making for the origin and persistence of religion (*LCW:* 38; 78), although in an article entitled 'The Attitude of the Workers' Party to Religion', written for the journal *Proletarii* in 1909, he explicitly rejected, as superficial, the view that ignorance alone was the cause of religion among the more backward sections of the population – a view which he attributed to bourgeois materialists. To him, this view failed to take cognisance of the fact that the roots of religion in capitalist countries were almost wholly social. He wrote:

The deepest root of religion today is the socially down-trodden condition of the working masses and their apparently complete helplessness in the face of the blind forces of capitalism, which every day and every hour inflicts upon the ordinary working people the most horrible suffering and the most savage torment, a thousand times more severe than those inflicted by extraordinary events, such as wars, earthquakes, etc. 'Fear made the gods'. Fear of the blind force of capital – blind because it cannot be foreseen by the masses of the people – a force which at every step in the life of the proletarian and small proprietor threatens to inflict, and does inflict 'sudden', 'unexpected', 'accidental' ruin, destruction, pauperism, prostitution, death from starvation – such is the root of modern religion. . . (*LCW:* 15; 405-406)

The accuracy of this judgement must await our assessment of the Marxist-Leninist critique of religion at the close of our study, but we must note that Lenin, following Marx and Engels, refused to recognise that some of the causes of what Marx and Engels had

termed 'natural religion' might persist into contemporary religion
— although, as we saw, Marx and Engels, unlike Lenin, were slightly ambiguous on this point. The effect of this on Soviet studies
was to make Soviet scholars wary for a long time of exploring the
possible non-social factors which have brought religion into being
both among primitive peoples and among the men and women of
today.

Lenin paid even less attention to the development of religion
than he had done to its aetiology. With the exception of a few,
almost throw-away, remarks on the evolution of Christianity (cf.
LCW: 38; 73) he had nothing whatever to say about the history of
religion. The reason, of course, is obvious — for if one accepts as
Lenin did, that the factors which make for religion are to be
found in social and economic deprivation, and if one believes
further that these causes are destined to disappear quickly in the
new political and socio-economic order of Communism, then little
is to be gained from writing the history of a well-nigh obsolete
phenomenon. It was only when it was realised that religion was
not disappearing as quickly as had once been believed that Soviet
scholars turned in earnest to the science of religion.

Whilst recognising that at its inception the Christian religion had
been possessed of 'a democratic revolutionary spirit' ('The State
and Revolution'; *LCW:* 25; 420), Lenin contended, with the
French socialist Paul Golay, that 'Christianity had lost value on
the day when Constantine promised it revenue and a place at
court' (*LCW:* 21; 353). Henceforth, for Lenin, its history was
wholly that of its placing itself at the service of the ruling classes.
There is no echo in Lenin of Engels' positive assessment of
plebeian religious radicalism — for Lenin, religion 'always put to
sleep and blunted the 'social feelings', (Letter to Gorky; *LCW;* 35;
129).

We thus see that Lenin added little, if anything, to the classical
Marxist analysis of religion. For him, Marx and Engels had
exhaustively explored what there was to be said on the subject and
he was content to repeat — in an attenuated way — their conclusions. Among these he concentrated exclusively on the oft-

repeated contention that religion was a reflection of socio-economic conditions, a set of mental projections corresponding to no realities in the external world, and thus nothing but an extreme and pernicious form of false-consciousness. In one of his less vulgar comments on religion, Lenin characterised the epipheno-menal nature of modern religion as so much 'medieval mildew' ('Socialism and Religion'; *LCW:* 10; 87) – a view which in no way modified his assessment of it as a major instrument of spiritual and social oppression.

To conclude: the essence of Lenin's position *vis-à-vis* religion during the period 1905-1917 – a position which he in no way modified upon his assuming the government of Russia in 1917 – can best be expressed in his own words as these are found in his article 'The Attitude of the Workers' Party to Religion', written in May, 1909:

Marxism is materialism. As such it is as relentlessly hostile to religion as was the materialism of the eighteenth-century Encyclopaedists or the materialism of Feuerbach. This is beyond doubt. But the dialectical materialism of Marx and Engels goes further than the Encyclopaedists and Feuerbach, for it applies the materialist philosophy to the domain of history, to the domain of the social sciences. We must combat religion – that is the ABC of *all* material-ism, and consequently of Marxism. But Marxism is not a materialism which has stopped at the ABC. Marxism goes further and says: We must *know how* to combat religion; and in order to do so we must explain the source of faith and religion among the masses in a materialist way. The combatting of religion cannot be confined to abstract ideological preaching . . . It must be linked up with the concrete practice of the class movement, which aims at eliminating the social roots of religion. . . It means that Social-Democracy's atheist propaganda must be *subordinated* to its basic task – the development of the class struggle of the exploited *masses* against the exploiters. (*LCW:* 15; 405-406)

3. After coming to power in the Bolshevik *coup d'etat* which overthrew the Revolution of 1917, Lenin was faced with the task of coming to terms with the openly hostile Orthodox church. In the ensuing battle, in which Soviet decrees were answered with sweeping ecclesiastical anathemas calling for resistance

to 'the enemies of Christ', ideological niceties were quickly forgotten. The passions aroused during this immediate post–revolutionary period left their mark on all subsequent Soviet policy with regard to religion – which went far beyond the provisions of the pre-revolutionary Bokshevik programme with regard to religion.[11] Further, many of these provisions, which were designed for some form of social democracy, became obsolete as the Party's monolithic structure developed under the exigencies of the struggle with counter-revolutionary factions, ofter centred upon the church. Many of the previous – and often tactical – restraints upon the Party's anti-religious stance disappeared and, as time went by, the distinction which Lenin had earlier drawn, between the attitude of the Party and the attitude of the State toward religion, became meaningless as the structures of the Party and the structures of the State increasingly began to coincide. Whilst the original constitution of the Russian Federal Republic of 1918 guaranteed freedom of conscience and included the right to both religious and anti-religious propaganda, this in reality meant freedom from religion – as was evident when the decree proclaiming the new constitution forbade all private religious instruction for children under the age of eighteen, and when, shortly afterwards, Lenin ordered all religious literature which had previously been published – along with all pornographic literature – to be seized and destroyed.[12] Eventually – in the Stalin constitution of 1936. – the provision for religious propaganda, other than religious worship, was withdrawn.[13] The consequence for the serious study of religion in the Soviet Union was that the Soviet understanding of religion – in the absence of any real intellectual opposition or criticism – became ossified, remaining, overall, content with the simple, almost incantational repetition of the stereotyped phrases of the classical Marxist critique as set forth by Lenin.

But if Lenin did little to forward the serious study of religion in the Soviet Union, he did much to develop one branch of the study of the history of ideas which was, until recently, grossly undeveloped in Western scholarship – the history of the rejection of religion: a branch of the study of the history of culture not without some bearing on the history of religion (cf. Thrower, 1976). Not only had Lenin much to say himself about the history of atheism, but in various articles and speeches he encouraged others to study the topic more deeply (cf. M.I. Shakhnovich, *Lenin i problemy ateizma:* Ch. 2). In an article in the journal *Pod znamenem marksizma* – Under the Banner of Marxism – in 1922, entitled 'On the Significance of Militant Atheism', Lenin urged Soviet intellectuals to continue the philosophical struggle with religion by researching deeper into the materialist tradition – particularly the materialist tradition of the European Enlightenment – and by studying the writings of contemporary, but non-Marxist, materialists. He wrote:

Without an alliance with non-Communists in the most diverse spheres of activity there can be no question of any successful communist construction. This also applies to the defence of materialism. . .

And after castigating Soviet intellectuals for their extreme apathy in this respect to date, he urged that:

. . . a journal which sets out to propagandise militant materialism (namely, *Under the Banner of Marxism*) must carry on untiring atheist propaganda and an untiring atheist fight. The literature on the subject in all languages should be carefully followed and everything at all valuable in this sphere should be translated, or at least reviewed. (*LCW:* 33; 232)

Taking up the suggestion made by Engels and Plekhanov, that the contemporary leaders of the working class should arrange for the translation of the literature of the militant materialism of the late eighteenth century, Lenin, after again castigating Soviet intellectuals for being remiss in this respect, took up their excuse that the old literature on atheism is antiquated, unscientific and naïve. He wrote:

There is nothing worse than such pseudo-scientific sophistry, which serves as a screen either for pedantry or for a complete misunderstanding of Marxism. There is, of course, much that is unscientific and naive in the atheist writings of the eighteenth-century revolutionaries. But nobody prevents the publishers of these writings from abridging them and providing them with brief postscripts pointing out the progress made by mankind in the scientific criticism of religions since the end of the eighteenth century, mentioning the latest writings on the subject and so forth. It would be the biggest and most grevious mistake a Marxist could make to think that the millions of people (especially the peasants and artisans), who have been condemned by all modern society to darkness, ignorance and superstition, can extricate themselves from this darkness along only the straight line of a purely Marxist education. . . The keen, vivacious and talented writings of the old eighteenth-century atheists wittily and openly attacked the prevailing clericalism and will often prove a thousand times more suitable for arousing people from their religious torpor than the dull and dry paraphrases of Marxism. . . The most important thing. . . is to know how to awaken in the still undeveloped masses an intelligent attitude towards religious questions and an intelligent criticism of religions. (*LCW:* 33; 229-230)

In the years following this plea of Lenin's Soviet scholars were to respond with a wide variety of studies in the history of atheism concentrated on, but by no means exclusively confined to, the eighteenth century. Lenin himself, as M.I. Shakhnovich has shown in the second chapter of the book, *Lenin i problemy ateizma* (Lenin and the Problem of Atheism), was wont to quote from an atheistic tradition which he took to stretch from the pre-Socratic philosophers of ancient Greece to his own time (Shakhnovich, 1961: pp. 85-151). Soviet scholars were not slow to respond to exploring this tradition (cf. below: Section 6).

There is óne further aspect of Lenin's contribution to the development of Marxism which bears directly on both the study of religion in the Soviet Union, and on the wider relationships of Marxism-Leninism with religion today, which we must perforce consider, and that is Lenin's development of the attempts on the part of Engels and Plekhanov to present Marxism as a complete *Weltanschauung.* Marxism, for Lenin, was a complete and harmonious world-view — a world-view which continued and completed the best thinking of the most advanced countries in the world: classical German philosophy, classical British political economy and French socialism (cf. 'The Three Sources. . . of Marxism'; *LCW;* 19; 23-28). Though its completeness as a world-view is open to question – and has been questioned by Marxists as well as non-Marxists – there is no doubt that Lenin himself saw Marxism as fulfilling this function. As a complete *Weltanschauung* Marxism was, according to Lenin, incompatible with other world-views and more particularly with world-views in religious and idealist philosophies. 'All-powerful because true', as he put it, Marxism must not be compromised in any way. Fundamental to the Marxist world-view, for Lenin, was materialism, but a materialism which differed from all other forms of materialism – past and present – in that it was dialectical and concrete. Historical materialism was the extension of philosophical materialism to human society. Lenin also repudiated traditional bourgeois, religious, absolute ethics. He wrote:

Our morality is entirely subordinated to the interests of the proletariats' class struggle. Our morality stems from the interests of the class struggle of the proletariat. . . morality is what serves to destroy the old exploiting society and to untie all the working people around the proletariat, which is building up a new, communist society. ('The Tasks of the Youth Leagues' *LCW:* 31; 291-293)

The only moral ideal, for Lenin, was Communism – all else was subordinate to its achievement. He unfortunately pre-supposed rather than articulated this ideal and it was left to his successors – often on the basis of the model provided by the person and life of Lenin himself – to work out its application in terms of personal and social morality for the Soviet citizen.

Lenin died in 1924, and from the moment of his death – if, indeed, not before – his authority was considered by the Soviets to be on a par with that of Marx and Engels; in fact his authority in the Soviet Union is somewhat greater than theirs because it is only Lenin's interpretation of their writings that is considered orthodox. It is his works, rather than those of Marx and Engels, which are the most frequently cited in all philosophical and political discussion. It is with good reason, therefore, that Soviet philosophers refer to their outlook on life, not simply as Marxism, but as Marxism-Leninism.

The nature of Lenin's contribution to Marxism is difficult to assess. Some see it as no more than a difference of theory and practice, others as no more than the adaptation of Marxism to the particular circumstances obtaining in Russia. Some even see it as the negation of Marxism. Preobrazhensky distinguished within Marxism between those elements which were unchanging and those which have to be developed and completed. Marxist methodology, however, that is, dialectical materialism, was one of the unchanging elements, and the identification of this in Marx, Engels and Lenin constitutes the basic theoretical identity of Marxism and Leninism.

Bukharin made a similar distinction between the aggregate of specific ideas and the methodology whereby this aggregate is built up. If the term 'Marxism' is taken to denote, not the corpus of ideas to be found in Marx and Engels, but the methodology peculiar to Marxism, it follows, argued Bukharin, that Leninism is not something which alters or disturbs the methodology of Marxism; rather is it something which represents a return to the Marxism formulated by Marx and Engels themselves.

Thus for orthodox Bolshevism in the years immediately following upon Lenin's death, Leninism was in no way regarded as a correction of the teachings of Marx and Engels. It was, therefore, necessary that a formula be found which would both safeguard Lenin's Marxist orthodoxy, and yet allow for his creative development of it. This, for Soviet Marxists, was finally produced by Stalin who, in *Problems of Leninism* (1926) put forward a definition of Leninism in which due regard was paid to Lenin's development of Marxism in all its constituent elements — philosophic, economic and so on. Stalin wrote:

Leninism is the Marxism of the era of imperialism and of the proletarian revolution. To be more exact, Leninism is the theory and tactics of the proletarian revolution in general, the theory and tactics of the dictatorship of the proletariat in particular . . . that is why Leninism is the further development of Marxism. (*SCW:* VI; 73)

In Stalin's view, however, such a development of historical materialism would not have been possible without Lenin's further enlargement of Marxist methodology – that is, of dialectical materialism. Thus the standard Soviet view is that Lenin's contribution to the further development of Marxist philosophy – dialectical materialism – lies in his deepening of the concept of matter, his development of a Marxist epistemology, and in his emphasis on the unity of theory and practice and of partisanship in philosophy (cf. M.B. Mitin, *Dialekticheskyy materializm*: p. 311 f.).

Apart from his presentation of Marxism as a competing, alternative world-view to any and all religious understandings of man and of the world, Lenin's only contribution to the Marxist critique of religion – beyond reinforcing what Marx and Engels have said about religion as the ideology of the ruling classes – lay in the suggestions found in his posthumously published *Philosophical Notebooks* with regard to the epistemological roots of religion (1st edit. 1929-30; *LCW:* 38). Lenin there expands upon Engels' observation that there is a close connection between religion and idealism in philosophy, and suggests that religion is but the emotional expression of idealism and that idealism is but a refined expression of religious ideology. This suggestion was one, however, that was not to be developed to any great extent in the Soviet critique of religion until the 1960's. (cf. below, pp. 201ff.)

To detail the development of Soviet thought after Lenin's death – and the eventual triumph of Lenin's understanding of dialectical materialism over its rivals would take us far beyond the task that we have set ourselves in this present work, but the seal upon the outlook which eventually triumphed came in 1931 when the Central Committee of the Communist Party of the Soviet Union officially condemned all views opposed to those of Lenin as being linked to various forms of political deviationism. Henceforth in the Soviet Union, Marxism-Leninism and the philosophy of dialectical materialsim was to be the only officially sanctioned outlook on life, though the tension between dialectics and materialism, positivism and philosophy, which lay at the heart of the controversies of the 1920's, together with the ambiguous and never resolved question of the relation of science to philosophy, were to re-emerge — though in a subdued form — after Stalin's death in 1953. But for the next quarter of a century the dominant, indeed the only, outlook on life, was to be that of dialectical materialism as interpreted by Stalin.

2.4   MARXISM-LENINISM: THE OFFICIAL IDEOLOGY OF THE SOVIET STATE: DIALECTICAL AND HISTORICAL MATERIALISM

Dialectical materialism is the world outlook of the Marxist-Leninist Party. It is called dialectical materialism because its approach to the phenomena of nature, its method of studying and apprehending them, is *dialectical*, while its interpretation of the phenomena of nature, its conception of these phenomena, its theory, is *materialistic*. Historical materialism is the extension of the principles of dialectical materialism to the study of social life, an application of the principles of dialectical materialism to the phenomena of the life of society, to the study of society and of its history. (Stalin, *Dialectical and Historical Materialism: MSW:* I; 69)

Dialectical Materialism is the theoretical foundation of Marxism-Leninism. This ideology or conception of the world reflects a universal law of development in Nature, society and human thought. This conception applies to the past, present and future. Dialectical Materialism is opposed by metaphysics and idealism. If a Marxist political party does not base its analysis on dialectics and materialism, the inevitable result will be the rise of one-sidedness and subjectivism and the ossification of all thought. (*Pravda*, November 22, 1957)

As H.B. Acton has pointed out in his philosophical study of Marxism-Leninism, *The Illusion of the Epoch*, there has been a tendency, particularly in Great Britian, to consider Marxism-Leninism primarily as a body of economic and social doctrine and to ignore its claims to be a total outlook on life (1973: p. 1). In the Soviet Union this would be impossible, for in that country

Marxism-Leninism has established itself as a system of thought and conduct which comprises not only a system of economics but which contains views about the most general or significant features of the universe and about the principle purposes of human life.

From the time of its intervention in 1931 into the controversy surrounding the Marxist conception of 'matter' the Communist Party of the Soviet Union has been the final arbiter, not only in philosophy, but over all aspects of life in the Union of Soviet Socialist Republics – including, of course, the highly sensitive area of the study of religion. Until 1956, when Nikita Khrushchev denounced Stalin – his crimes and 'the cult of his personality' – the Twentieth Congress of the Communist Party of the Soviet Union, Stalin himself was regarded as the supreme embodiment of the Party, and it was during the period of his ascendency that the monolithic structure of the ideology of the Party and hence of the Soviet State – Marxism-Leninism – was established under his general supervision. Although Stalin is no longer openly revered in the way that he was, his influential formulation of Marxism-Leninism is still that which directs the lives and thoughts of Soviet citizens and – at least in their official *personae* – of Soviet scholars today.

Stalin's formulation of dialectical and historical materialism – the theoretical foundation of the Marxist-Leninist world-outlook – can be found in the section under that title which he is held to have contributed to the highly influential *History of the Communist Party of the Soviet Union (Bolsheviks): Short Course* which was published in 1938. Of this work Leszek Kołakowski has written:

Published in millions of copies in the Soviet Union, it served for fifteen years as a manual of ideology completely binding on all citizens. . . It was published and taught everywhere without ceasing. In the upper forms of secondary schools, in all places of higher learning, party courses etc., wherever anything was taught, the *Short Course* was the Soviet citizen's main intellectual pabulum.[14] (1978: Vol. III, pp. 93-94)

It thus helped, to a degree which it is hard to over-estimate, to form the consciousness of Soviet intellectuals, including the consciousness of those intellectuals who are in the forefront of intellectual endeavour – including the study of religion – today.

Briefly, the *Short Course* set forth the role of the masses in the making of history and, in particular, the role of the 'vanguard of the masses' – the Communist Party of the Soviet Union – during the present era of the building of Communism. In an earlier work, *Concerning Questions of Leninism* (1926), Stalin had pointed out that

In the proletarian revolution the seizure of power is only the *beginning* and power is used as a lever for transforming the old economy and organising a new one. (op. cit., p. 256)

The five-year plans, initiated in 1927, were intended to do just that. If the development of society according to plan seemed to contradict the economic determinism of Marx and Engels, the *Short Course* provided the justification, for it emphasised the influence of the superstructure in society and introduced the notion of a 'revolution from above' – that is, of a revolution initiated by the state, but directly supported from below by the masses (*Short Course:* p. 467). Later, this conception of a 'revolution from above' was interpreted as covering all aspects of life in the Soviet Union, including the consciousness of its citizens. It was, under Khrushchev, to provide the justification for the intellectual and administrative offensive which he launched against religion in 1959, and which continued until he was dismissed from power in 1964. In Khrushchev's view, the influence of the superstructure of religion on Soviet society was so great, and so detrimental, that he felt justified in moving against it, rather than waiting for its natural 'withering away' according to the classical Marxist analysis of the fate in store for religion in socialist society.

Stalin, though an erstwhile theological student, had nothing whatever to say publicly about religion – his persecution of it being but part of his wider policy of eliminating all sources of possible opposition to his rule – real and imaginary, within the

Party and without. But among the conceptions found in the *Short Course*, one in particular — 'the relics of capitalism' (*perezhitka kapitalizma*) was to be much used in later Soviet writing on religion (*ibid:* p. 492). Since production and social relationships in the Soviet Union are socialistic, the only 'relics of capitalism' that can be openly avowed must be confined to the realm of ideas. Their continued existence in Soviet society was accounted for by the view that consciousness lags behind social being. Of these 'relics', the most insidious was held to be religion.

It is in the famous 'fourth chapter' (of the *Short Course*), as it is familiarly known in the Soviet Union, that the essential outline of the official Marxist-Leninist world-outlook is to be found. As in Stalin's earlier *Anarchism or Socialism* (1907), the discussion of dialectical materialism is divided into a presentation of the Marxist dialectial method followed by a presentation of Marxist philosophical materialism. This method of presentation was perpetuated by Soviet philosophers until Stalin's death, when they reverted to the more traditional presentation of Engels — in which the exposition of philosophical materialism precedes the exposition of the dialectic and its three laws, and of the dialectic as a method of enquiry.

Stalin outlined four major features of the dialectical method:

1. All of nature forms an interconnected whole, and thus any given phenomena should be considered in its interrelations.

2. Nature is in a state of continuous movement and change, and thus any given phenomenon should be looked upon as developing and changing.

3. There is an onward and upward movement in nature; quantitative changes lead to abrupt qualitative changes and all phenomena should be looked at in this light.

4. Internal contradictions, positive and negative sides, and a struggle between old and new, are inherent in all phenomena, form the basis of all development, and should be sought in the analysis of all phenomena and of social phenomena in particular.

A glaring omission in this presentation of the dialectic was the absence — for which no explanation was offered — of the law of the negation of the negation; nor was there any discussion of categories such as 'freedom and necessity', 'causality', 'space and time' and the like.[15]

The principal features of Marxist philosophical materialism according to Stalin are:

1. The world is by its very nature material.
2. Matter is primary, and is an objective reality existing outside of and independent of our minds, whilst mind is secondary, being but a reflection of matter.
3. The world and its laws of operation are fully knowable — knowledge of it being tested by experience and practice.

The cognitive value of such baldly asserted general principles will be discussed in part III of our study.

Stalin's discussion of historical materialism — the application of the dialectical method to the understanding of the past and future development of society — introduced an innovation in theory which Stalin and the Party were introducing into Soviet life in practice. This was the emphasis we have noted on the influence of the superstructure of society on the material base. Following Marx and Engels, Stalin explained how social ideas, political views and so on, 'reflect' the material conditions of society, but this, he contended, holds only for the *origin* of the ideas which we find in the superstructure, not for their *significance*. He wrote:

New social ideas and theories arise only after the development of the material life in society has set new tasks before society. But once they have arisen they become a most potent force which facilitates the carrying out of the new tasks set by the development of the material life of society, a force which facilitates the progress of society. (*MSW:* 1; 81)

The emphasis on the potent force of ideas, whilst representing something of a retreat from the way in which Marx and Engels had regarded the role of ideas in history was, in fact, in line with the quasi-voluntaristic view of the determination of history which we find in the writings of Lenin, and in particular in *What is to be Done?* and *Materialism and Empirio-criticism*. The immediate consequence of this emphasis on the role of the superstructure was a renewed emphasis on the importance of theory, and on the necessity for indoctrinating the masses with a 'correct conscious-ness' so as to fit them for their revolutionary tasks. The negative side of this was, of course, the necessity that was seen for the forceful elimination of ideas thought to be detrimental to the achievement of Communism, especially of those enshrined in a religious outlook on life.

This, Stalin's lasting contribution to Marxism-Leninism, was reinforced by the terms of his intervention in 1950 into the controversy surrounding the attempt of the Soviet linguist N.Y. Marr to create a specifically Marxist linguistics. Stalin's inter-vention – originally in the form of a letter to the Party newspaper *Pravda* – clarified, among other things, some of the points he had made in his earlier contribution to the *Short Course*. He reiterated, for instance, his view of the active role of the superstructure in the development of society, adding that the superstructure is only indirectly connected with production and that it therefore does not reflect changes in the development of the productive forces immediately and directly (*Marxism and Linguistics*: p. 13). Stalin also clarified the Marxist-Leninist position with regard to the relationship of the superstructure to the base – and contributed thereby a significant addition of his own to Marxist-Leninist theory.

Stalin began by stating the traditional Marxist view that:

The base is the economic structure of society at a given stage of its develop-ment. The superstructure consists of the political, legal, religious, artistic, and philosophical views of society and the political, legal and other institutions corresponding to them. Every base has its own superstructure corresponding to it. (*ibid:* p. 9)

The question at issue was where linguistics fitted into this model. Marr had argued that as language is based on thought, and that as thought is secondary and dependent on matter, it followed that language must be secondary and so part of the superstructure. But if language is part of the superstructure, then language must, in part, be class-determined. This was the argument that Stalin unequivocally condemned. He wrote:

Briefly, language cannot be ranked either among bases or among superstructures. Neither can it be ranked among 'intermediate' phenomena between the base and the superstructure, as such 'intermediate' phenomena do not exist. (*ibid:* p. 34)

In rejecting this argument of Marr's, Stalin formally dissociated the categories of base-superstructure from the categories of matter-mind on which they had previously been modelled. He thus freed linguistics from the superstructure, and in stating that not every discipline is contained in the base-superstructure dichotomy, raised the question as to what else might not be so contained and hence not be class-determined. Mathematics was an obvious case in point as, perhaps, was formal logic; but in no way was it suggested that religion might be so excluded and religion has remained, in fact, the supreme example of an ideology held to be wholly determined by its social base. The relative freeing of the superstructure from being in all cases a direct reflection of the social base, and Stalin's emphasis on its active role in the formation of social consciousness, did, however, as Richard T. De George has shown (1963: pp. 83-103), produce a rash of works on ethics and on education. It was, under Khrushchev, to have repercussions in the field of the study of religion.

On the basis of the model provided by Stalin, Soviet theoreticians have continued their codification of Marxism-Leninism and the development of what they term its 'component parts' (*sostavnye chasti*), among which must now be included 'scientific atheism' (*nauchnyy ateizm*), so that today in the Soviet Union, Marxism-Leninism is presented as a unitary and total world-view; a world-view which in breadth and, so it is claimed, in depth also, offers as comprehensive an understanding of life as that traditionally offered by the great world religions, giving point to the claim made by the Western social philosopher Alasdair Macintyre, when he wrote that:

Only one secular doctrine in the modern world retains the scope of traditional religion in offering an interpretation of human existence by means of
which men may situate themselves in the world and direct their actions to
ends which transcend those offered by their immediate situation: Marxism.
(Macintyre, 1971: p. 9)

The fundamental difference, of course, between Marxism and
the religions of the world is that Marxism from its inception was,
and has remained, wholly committed to a naturalistic understanding of man and the world, to the extent that Marxism-Leninism
continues to this day to define itself in explicit opposition to
religion. This, in the Soviet Union, is the task of 'scientific
atheism'. 'Scientific atheism' further provides the *Problematik*,
and defines the methodology, of all official study of religion in
the Soviet Union and to the development of this now vital aspect
of Marxism-Leninism we now turn.

PART TWO

'Scientific Atheism' and the Study of Religion and
Atheism in the USSR

Prolegomena: The Programme of 'Scientific Atheism'

3.1 THE POLICY OF THE COMMUNIST PARTY OF THE SOVIET UNION AND THE GROWTH OF 'SCIENTIFIC ATHEISM'

As we have seen, atheism has, from the very inception of Marxism, been an integral feature of its understanding of man and the world. Marx, Engels and Lenin were at one in their total rejection of any and all forms of religion, and the Communist Party of the Soviet Union, whilst varying the intensity of its administrative and ideological offensive against religion, has continued steadfast in that rejection to the present day. But it is only since the renewal of the offensive against religion following upon the decrees of the Party's Central Committee of 1954,[1] and reinforced by Khrushchev's vigorous administrative offensive against religion in the period 1959-1964,[2] that 'scientific atheism' has been proclaimed a formal component of the Marxist-Leninist *Weltanschauung* and developed accordingly.

Although some serious work in religious studies was produced prior to the outbreak of war in 1941, it was not until after the war that the study of religion and atheism began in earnest. In the pre-war period the emphasis was on 'practical atheism' – the more so as Stalin, the sole arbiter in such matters, had made not a single theoretical pronouncement on religion or the study of religion – and 'practical atheism' meant schools for the propagation of atheism, the administrative elimination of the clergy, atheist museums housed where churches had once stood, and a continuous stream of hate-propaganda designed to terrorise the faithful into submission. This, of course, was in line with Lenin's policy of militant atheism, as was the emphasis on education as means of eliminating religious beliefs and practices – a policy pursued in the early period of Soviet Power by Lenin's widow Krupskaya, as well as by Lunacharsky, Kalinin and Skvortsov-Stepanov. This policy depended, for the most part, on a series of agitational slogans – such as that religion is an impediment to the revolution and to social progress, that it is unscientific, that the churches are corrupt and anti-Soviet and, where evangelical Christianity was concerned, even anti-Russian – slogans which had little beyond their constant repetition to commend them.[3]

Some serious study of religion during this period there undoubtedly was, although it has been ignored by almost all Western commentators on religion in the USSR during the early period of Soviet power, but a search through the journals of the period, such as *Revolyutsiya i tserkov*, (The Revolution and the Church), *Bezbozhnik* (The Godless), *Ateist*, known after 1931 as *Voinstvuyushchiy ateist* (Militant Atheist), and *Antireligioznik* (The Antireligionist), reveals a number of articles and discussions on religion from the pens of scholars of repute, as does a search through such serious Party journals as *Pod znamenem marksizma* (Under the Banner of Marxism). Thus, for example, a serious discussion on the history and nature of Islam took place in the journal *Ateist* during the year 1930; during 1938-1939 M. Baskin contributed a series of extremely well researched articles on atheism in ancient Greece and Rome to *Antireligioznik*; in 1940 A.N. Kochetov wrote on materialism and atheism in Ancient India for the same journal; and in the pages of *Pod znamenem marksizma*, in 1922-1923, a famous exchange between Skvortsov-Stepanov and M.N. Pokrovsky on the historical origin of religion took place (see below p. 240). Overall, however, the journals of this period are characterised by the crudity and vituperativeness of their antireligious propaganda and serious study of religion is rare.[4]

The possibility of a serious dialogue with religion, and hence of a serious understanding of it, was also vitiated by the closing, in the period immediately following the revolution, of all religious publishing houses and by the forbidding of religious propaganda of any kind, other than acts of worship – prohibitions which are still in force. The dismissal of the religious philosopher Nikolai Berdyaev and other non-Marxist philosophy teachers from the universities in 1922 marked the end of any serious criticism of

Marxism-Leninism from within the Soviet Union, and Marxism-Leninism has thus developed immune from any critical challenge. The consequence is that Soviet scholarship today is characterised by a dogmatic conservatism unknown in the West or, indeed, in any other part of Eastern Europe. Lack of access to Western writings and meagre participation in (Western organised) international conferences has also served to isolate Soviet scholarship – particularly in the arts and social sciences – still further from the West and, of course, vice versa.

There was, however, one area of study related to religion which was quickly developed in the earliest period of Soviet power, and that was the history of atheism.

Impetus for the study of atheism came from the publication in the journal *Pod znamenem marksizma* (Vol. 3, 1922) of Lenin's article '*O znachenii voinstvuyushchego materializma*' (On the Importance of Militant Materialism), an article in which Lenin urged Soviet scholars to study both the history of materialism and the history of atheism, and to make themselves acquainted with the best expositions of materialistic philosophy in the contemporary bourgeois world. Thus there developed an interest among Soviet historians in the history of atheism – and in particular in the atheism of the eighteenth century which Lenin had especially commended – which has continued to this day (see Ch. 6 below). This early period – the 1920's and the early 1930's – was also characterised by internal disputes within the Party itself between rival interpretations of Marxist materialism. By comparison with the situation today – where a grey uniformity of opinion prevails – this early period appears positively exciting.[5]

It was in the early 1930's that the guidelines for Soviet study of religion were laid down. Two authors in particular dominated Soviet study of religion during this period: Emiliyan Yaroslavsky and A.T. Lukachevsky. Yaroslavsky's article '*Kommunisty i religiya*' (Communists and Religion) (1934) and Lukachevsky's '*Marksizm-Leninizm kak voinstvuyushchiy ateizm*' (Marxism-Leninism as Militant Materialism) (1932) are especially looked back to today by Soviet 'scientific atheists' as having aided the development of their discipline (cf. Gubanov, 1967: p. 196). In these articles Yaroslavsky and Lukachevsky argued that, whilst Marxism-Leninism was uncompromisingly anti-religious, only patient, attractive, and intellectually respectable anti-religious propaganda would succeed in creating an'atheist mentality' among the populace, views which were reinforced by a Central Committee Plenum in the Spring of 1936.[6]

Little, however, was achieved, and soon the anti-religious campaign, and with it the study of religion, were both overtaken by the onslaught of war. Once the war had begun, anti-religious propaganda became less virulent and soon ceased altogether. However, as the war drew to an end, the Party once again began to move against religion. In September 1944, the Central Committee adopted a decree calling for renewed anti-religious efforts through 'scientific-educational propaganda' and Party workers were reminded of the need to combat 'survivals of ignorance, superstition and prejudice among the people' (*Sputnik ateista:* pp. 457-458). Less than a year later the Central Committee repeated this call and the mass media took up the cry. Yet little was done, and the opinion of David E. Powell, who has made a special study of anti-religious propaganda in the Soviet Union, is that these exhortations were 'routine, almost perfunctory' (Powell 1975: p. 38).

Similarly the study of religion resumed but slowly in the aftermath of war. Of 211 dissertations in philosophy (including 15 doctoral dissertations) presented to the Academy of Social Sciences of the USSR in the period 1943-1951, only three, and these at *kandidat* level, were concerned with religion and atheism (Gubanov, 1967: p. 196) and of books published during the same period only one – M.I. Shakhnovich's *Ot suyeveriya k nauke* (From Superstition to Science) (1948) is today thought worthy of mention by scholars reviewing the development of 'scientific atheism' (cf. Gubanov, 1967: p. 196).

The Museum of the History of Religion and Atheism in Leningrad, with its massive library built up in the 1930's by V.G. Bogoraz and D.D. Bonch-Bruyevich, re-opened in 1946 – with

Bonch-Bruyevich as its director – and this and the Institute of History of the Moscow Academy of Sciences – of which Bonch-Bruyevich was also the head – were for many years the chief centres for research into religion and atheism. In 1950 Bonch-Bruyevich initiated publication of the Institute's yearbook *Voprosy istorii religii i ateizma* (Problems of the History of Religion and Atheism) and twelve volumes were published between 1950 and 1964, when it ceased publication. In the same year he also initiated publication of an occasional monograph series, *Nauchnoateisticheskaya biblioteka* (Scientific-Atheist Library). In 1957 the Museum of the History of Religion and Atheism in Leningrad started publication of its Yearbook, *Yezhegodnik muzeya istorii religii i ateizma* (Yearbook of the Museum of the History of Religion and Atheism), which included, among other things, an extremely valuable annual bibliographical survey of leading Soviet work in the study of religion and atheism. Seven volumes were published between 1957 and 1964 before this series too ceased publication. Both this series, and the series *Voprosy istorii religii i ateizma*, were superseded in 1964 by a new series, *Voprosy nauchnogo ateizma* (Problems of Scientific Atheism).[7]

When in the early 1950's, immediately upon the demise of Stalin, the Central Committee of the Communist Party of the Soviet Union renewed the Party's commitment to atheism and to an ongoing anti-religious offensive it was, in its own eyes, simply calling the Party back to Leninist policies with regard to religion which had been pursued by the Party up to the outbreak of the war with Germany in 1941 when, in the interests of national unity, the anti-religious campaign had been suspended. In the immense task of rebuilding the nation after victory in the war with Germany, this period of *détente* between the Party and religious believers had continued. The result was that, despite the progress towards Communism which, so it was maintained, had continued despite the war and the aberration of Stalinism, such religion as had survived the onslaught of the pre-war offensive against religion showed little, if any, signs of 'withering away' – a fact which by the mid-1950's was explained by Party theoreticians as being due to 'ideological lag', 'external capitalist influences', 'the war' and, and – here the Leninist view begins to reassert itself – 'the neglect and inadequacy of anti-religious propaganda' (cf. Lane, 1975: pp. 236-242).

It had also become obvious in the immediate post-war period that the older style atheist propaganda must give way to propaganda more in keeping with the changed times in which Soviet citizens were now living. This came to light in 1954 when the Central Committee of the Communist Party published – only five months apart – two decrees on mistakes made in this field. These two decrees are the foundation documents of contemporary Soviet 'scientific atheism' and they must, therefore, be looked at in some detail.[8]

The first, '*O krupnykh nedostatkakh v nauchno-ateisticheskoy propagande i merakh yeyo uluchsheniya*' (On Great Insufficiencies in the Propagating of Scientific Atheism and On Measures for its Improvement), of July 7, 1954, began by pointing out that, while scientific atheists had been sleeping, religion had gained ground, with the consequence – and this is important as revealing something of the official understanding of religion – that there had been an increase in the observance of religious holidays and in pilgrimages to religious shrines. This had resulted in a loss of man-hours in agriculture and in industry, a decrease in worker-discipline and a lack of interest in the building of Communism. Atheists, the decree continued, have fallen prey to passivity, thinking that, just because the Soviet Union is now a classless society (*sic*), religion will automatically disappear. Moreover, publications on religion and atheism are little read, the decree adds, because they are of such low intellectual calibre and lack the militant, partisan spirit of true 'scientific atheism'.

Having drawn this rather bleak picture of the current state of 'scientific atheism', the decree then specified the means for correcting the situation: increased propaganda at all levels – including person to person contact – in favour of atheism and against religion. Such propaganda was to be based on the spread of scientific knowledge, that is of rational positions on the structure of the universe, the origin of life etc. The All-Union Society for the Propagation of Political and Scientific Knowledge (The *Znaniye* Society) was to publish a popular 'scientific atheist' monthly, *Nauka i religiya* (Science and Religion). The State publishing company, *Gospolitizdat*, was to organise, during 1954-1955, the publication of a selection from the Marxist classics on religion and atheism, and the publishing house of the Academy of Sciences was to publish the works of both the ancient and of the French atheists. The Foreign Languages Publishing House was to publish translations of the best works on atheism by foreign scholars. *Gospolitizdat* was also to publish massive editions of atheistic literature of an artistic character. The editors of national and local journals were to publish popular materials on atheism. The Ministry of Public Education was to see that atheistic propaganda be included in the school syllabus and must hold conferences on this theme. Trade unions and youth organisations were to see to the atheistic education of their members. The decree concludes by recognising that this is an ambitious programme, but it says that it simply represents what should have been the case before the decree was published.

The second decree, *'Ob oshibkakh v provedenii nauchno-ateisticheskoy propagandy sredi naseleniya'* (On Mistakes in Carrying out Scientific-Atheist Propaganda Among the People) of November 10, 1954, was less detailed, but it has proved much more important for the subsequent study of religion and atheism, for in it can be discerned, for the first time, a shift from an ideological to a philosophical presentation of atheism. The decree also went out of its way to point out that, although the Party is against religion, it cannot countenance personal attacks on, and administrative discrimination against, believers who are, on the whole, loyal Soviet citizens. This did not mean that propaganda for atheism is out of place, but it does mean that such propaganda must become more refined, so as to be more in tune with the sensitivity of loyal, and often not unintelligent, believers. The basic factor working in favour of atheism, so the decree contended, is that atheism is based on science whilst religion is basically anti-scientific. It is, therefore, through sound education in science that religion will ultimately be abolished.

These two decrees have continued to be the guidelines for the development of 'scientific atheism' in the period since 1954, and are often referred to in current scholarly writing on religion and atheism. The naïve faith in the value of theoretical education in atheism, which they exhibit, is only today being questioned in the Soviet Union (cf. Section 3.2 below).

This renewed initiative against religion was given further impetus when, in the period 1959-1964, the then First Secretary of the Communist Party of the Soviet Union, Nikita Khrushchev, gave his personal support to the anti-religious campaign.

Khrushchev had given a hint of what he was later to express openly when, in his report from the Central Committee to the Twentieth Congress of the Communist Party of the Soviet Union (CPSU) in 1956, he had stated that 'it would be wrong to think that the survivals of capitalism in the minds of people had already been wiped out' (cf. Gruliow, 1962: Vol. 2, p. 54). In the 'Building of Communism' discussions at the Twenty-First Party Congress in 1959 the attack on the 'survivals of capitalism' was renewed, and it was rumoured that a secret resolution calling for the total abolition of religion in the Soviet Union during the seven-year plan then under discussion had been approved (cf. Donald A. Lowrie, 1961: p. 69). Two years later, at the Twenty-Second Party Congress in 1961, Khrushchev lent his overt support to the anti-religious campaign which was then vigorously under way. The Party newspaper *Pravda* reported that part of his speech dealing with religion as follows:

The battle with the survivals of capitalism in the consciousness of the people, the changing by our revolution of the habits and customs of millions of people built up over the centuries, is a prolonged and not a simple matter. Survivals of the past are a dreadful power, which, like a nightmare, hold sway over the minds of living creatures. They are rooted in the modes of life and in the consciousness of millions of people long after the economic conditions which gave them birth have vanished. . . Communist education presupposes emancipation from religious prejudices and superstitions, which hinder individual Soviet people from fully developing their creative powers. A well thought-out and well-proportioned system of scientific-atheist propaganda is necessary, which will embrace all strata and groups of society, to prevent the spread of religious attitudes, especially among children and young people. . . The interests of building Communism require that such questions of Communist education stand at the centre of the attention and activity of each Party organisation, of all communities. (*Pravda*, October 18, 1962)

The Party organisations, of course, were not slow to respond to this prompting from above.

In 1959 the Praesidium of the Soviet Academy of Sciences adopted a resolution, 'On the Intensification of Scientific Work in the Realm of Atheism', which led to the setting up of a learned council for co-ordinating work on atheism and religion within the Division of Economic, Philosophical and Legal Sciences of the Academy. A sector on atheism was also set up in the Academy's Institute of Philosophy and subsequently groups studying the history of the critique of religion were established in the Academy's Institutes of History, of Ethnography, and in the Institute for the Study of The Peoples of the East. At the same time chairs in the History and Theory of Atheism were established in many of the country's leading universities and institutes of higher education, and courses on 'scientific atheism' were introduced in the curriculum of higher education. Prior to 1959, Soviet higher academic institutions had provided only small doses of anti-religious propaganda, primarily in history and social science courses, and the obligatory course 'Dialectical and Historical Materialism', the subject most concerned with questions of religion and atheism, had devoted only six hours of lectures and seminars – out of a total of a hundred and forty hours – to these problems (cf. *Administration of Teaching in Social Sciences in the USSR*, 1960: pp. 1-35, especially pp. 23-24).

In 1959, a new course, entitled *Osnovy nauchnogo ateizma* (Fundamentals of Scientific Atheism) was introduced into the curriculum of all higher educational institutions, including the universities. The course was originally voluntary, but owing to the paucity of student response it has, from 1964, been compulsory for all students. At present, the course calls for twenty-four hours of instruction — twelve lectures a term for two terms (cf. Moiseyev, 1966: p. 2).

Also in 1959, The Central Committee of the CPSU augmented its two earlier decrees by issuing two further directives directly concerned with 'scientific atheism'. The first, 'On the Journal *Science and Religion*' of May 5, 1959, reiterated the earlier demand, contained in the decree of July, 1954, for publication of a popular journal to propagate 'scientific atheism' (cf. *Voprosy ideologicheskoy raboty* (Problems of Ideological Work), (1961: p. 271) and the journal *Nauka i religiya* eventually appeared in 1960. The second decree 'On a Popular Textbook, *Questions of Atheism*' of February 15, 1960, ordered the preparation and publication of a popular textbook on 'scientific atheism' (ibid., pp. 169), and this was produced almost immediately in 1961. It was entitled *Osnovy nauchnogo ateizma* (The Fundamentals of Scientific Atheism).

There were also two semi-official texts — both of them editorials in the journal of the Institute of Philosophy, *Voprosy filosofii* (Problems of Philosophy) — produced in response to the decrees of the Central Committee which have had far-reaching influence on the study of religion and atheism in universities and institutes of higher learning.

On January 9, 1960, the Central Committee promulgated a decree 'On the Tasks of Party Propaganda Today' (cf. *KPSS o kul'ture, prosveshchenii i nauke:* pp. 106-122). Shortly afterwards, the editors of *Voprosy filosofii* published a *peredovaya* (lead-article) entitled 'For a Creative Elaboration of Problems of Scientific Atheism' (*VF* 1960, 3, pp. 3-7), the main theme of which was that, although scientific-atheist work was now going well, there was not enough collaboration in this respect between the various academic disciplines. Thus, for example, the sociologist and the psychologist should be able to assist work on religion and atheism by providing an analysis of the mentality of the Soviet citizen who is still a believer. The editorial also pointed out that religion was changing its face, especially by trying to show that it could co-exist with modern science and that it could co-operate loyally with socialism. These false claims – as the editors of *Voprosy filosofii* believed them to be – must be shown for what they are, but this could only be done, the editorial argued, by carefully studying the dogmas and the tactics of existing religions. Help must also be sought from experts in ethics, epistemology, aesthetics and the other philosophical disciplines.

A later decree of the Central Committee, 'On Immediate Tasks of the Ideological Work of the Party' of June 21, 1963, elicited a further editorial in the journal *Voprosy filosofii*: 'A Theory of Scientific Atheism for Today' (*VF*, 1964, 5: pp. 3-12). The first part of this editorial specified the inadequacies of 'scientific atheism' to date, while the second explained in detail how the discipline should henceforth be developed.

In listing the deficiencies of current work, the editorial frankly acknowledged that the provisions of the decree of November 1954 had not been carried out. There had been some good books published, but the introduction of 'scientific atheism' into the curriculum of the universities meant that more and better books were now needed. Better and more qualified teachers were also needed for, at the time of writing, the editorial claimed, authors and lecturers were writing and speaking more out of ignorance than of knowledge, little effort having as yet been made to understand religion and the complex mentality behind it. Further, there are no basic works on the different varieties of religion and religious experience; too many writers and lecturers were one-sided and vague in their treatment of religious questions.

The editorial then passed to specify areas where immediate development in 'scientific atheism' was imperative: the emotional side of religion must be carefully examined; the activities of religious organisations must be catalogued; special attention must be paid to the changes currently taking place in religions; atheism must show that no 'adaptation' to science or modern society can ultimately save religion from its fate – its duplicity, one-sidedness and contradictory character have to be scientifically exposed for all to see. Efforts at 'cleansing' religion must also be shown to be in vain; atheists must know how to present their own system (Maxism-Leninism) and its values – truth, honour, humanism, etc., – as superior to that of any religion. By epistemological and logical analysis the atheist must show that religion's use of science is fraudulent, and that on the contrary, modern science confirms the philosophical, i.e., dialectical materialistic, basis of 'scientific atheism'. Further, extensive sociological investigations are necessary to find the explanation for the vestiges of religion surviving in the USSR today. Such investigations to date into the causes of the persistence of religion have been few and of little scientific value. Since the object of the investigation, i.e., religion, is universal, all domains of scientific and philosophical activity must co-operate in the development of a sound 'scientific atheism'. Further, students must be encouraged to pursue research into 'scientific atheism'; at the time of writing, the editorial asserts, out of some 10,000 dissertations defended in philosophy, history, law, pedagogy and art from 1955-1962, only 50 dealt with problems connected with 'scientific atheism' and the greater part of these were historical – and badly written!

The attitude of the Party to the study of religion and atheism should now be clear. The Party wanted more and better from those engaged in the business of 'scientific atheism' and it wanted more co-operation from those engaged in cognate disciplines. More particularly, it wanted greater emphasis laid on the philosophical refutation of religion and urged those engaged in expounding dialectical and historical materialism, aided by those working in psychology and sociology, to provide detailed and more positive analyses of religion, emphasising, particularly, contemporary religion. The Party also wanted those engaged in propagating atheism to present it attractively in richness and in depth.

The culmination of this renewed commitment to atheism was the decision of the Party's Ideological Commission in November 1963 to establish a specific institute within the Academy of Social Sciences of the USSR to oversee and co-ordinate all work in the field of 'scientific atheism' — a decision which was approved by the Central Committee of the Communist Party in January 1964 (*'Aktivno vesti ateisticheskoye vospitaniye'* (Atheistic Education Must be Carried Out in an Active Manner), *Pravda*, March 2, 1964, p. 2). This meant the wholesale re-organisation of research into religion and atheism. The task of the new Institute of Scientific Atheism (*Institut Nauchnogo Ateizma*) was described by the Central Committee decree as 'the supervision and co-ordination of all scientific work in the field of religion and atheism', including work which was, at the time of the setting up of the new institute, being pursued in the various institutes of the Academy of Sciences, the institutes of the Ministry of Higher and Special Education (including the universities) and the establishments of the Ministry of Culture. The new institute was also charged with the task of co-ordinating inter-disciplinary research and with organising, on an ongoing basis, all-union scientific seminars and congresses on 'scientific atheism'.[9] It was to have two divisions: one for the study of the theory of 'scientific atheism' and the criticicm of modern religious ideology, and another for organising education or upbringing in atheism (*ateisticheskoye vospitaniye*). Its council of management consisted of representatives of the Academy of Social Sciences, the Ministry of Higher and Special Education, the Ideological Commission and other Party Organisations, and the *Znaniye* Society (cf. *'Aktivno vesti ateisticheskoye vospitaniye'*, *Pravda*, March 2, 1964; *'V dobry chas'*; *Nauka i religiya*, September 1964; *'V institute nauchnogo ateizma'; Izvestia*, February 19, 1967, p. 6; R.A. Lopatkin, *'Na opornykh punktakh instituta nauchnogo ateizma'*, *VNA*, Vol. 5 (1968), pp. 336-342).

A further decision of the Central Committee was that the editorial boards of the journals *Voprosy istorii religii i ateizma* and of the *Yezhegodnik* of the Leningrad Museum were to be disbanded and replaced by a new editorial board and a new journal, *Voprosy nauchnogo ateizma* (Problems of Scientific Atheism), which was to be published under the auspices of the new institute.[10] A.F. Okulov was appointed to head the new institute and to be the editor-in-chief of the new journal — positions which he held until 1978, when he was succeeded by P.K. Kurochkin.

The consequence of these fundamental changes in the organisation of research into religion and atheism was that this was more
strictly than before brought under the control of the Party – a
measure of just how seriously the Party took work in this field.
This brought mixed blessings for scholars; on the one hand, their
work was now given high priority and funds allocated accordingly;
on the other, their work suffered from the demand that it have
immediate and obvious propaganda effect, though after the fall
of Khrushchev in October 1964 pressures in this latter aspect were
eased. But the fall of Khrushchev did not mean an end to the
importance assigned by the Party to work in 'scientific atheism'
– that has continued to this day; in fact, if anything, Soviet
research into religion and atheism has increased in both volume
and quality since 1964.

In addition to work done under the direct supervision of the
Institute of Scientific Atheism, it must be borne in mind that
much valuable work relating to the study of religion is still being
pursued – as it has always been pursued – by scholars working
in the numerous specialised institutions for the study of history
and ethnography, and in institutes and faculties of Oriental and
Middle Eastern studies. Some would say that it is here that the
most important Soviet work in the study of religion is to be
found, although since 1954 this work, too, has become increasingly politicised.

3.2 'SCIENTIFIC ATHEISM' AN INTEGRAL, YET RELATIVELY INDEPENDENT, PART OF MARXIST-LENINIST IDEOLOGY: THE NATURE AND SCOPE OF 'SCIENTIFIC ATHEISM'

Consequent upon the decrees of the Communist Party of the
Soviet Union outlined in the previous section, 'scientific atheism'
is today an integral component part of the Marxist-Leninist world-
view and Soviet theoreticians have, since 1954, sought to develop
it accordingly. As the officially approved text-book used for the
teaching of the subject in all Soviet institutions of higher education expresses it:

Scientific atheism is an integral part (*neot"emlemaya chast'*) of the Marxist-Leninist world-view. As a complete system, Marxism-Leninism comprises dialectical and historical materialism, scientific atheism, ethics, aesthetics, etc. The peculiarity of all the parts of this system is that, together, they form an integral materialist world-view, which provides the methodological foundation for the cognition and re-organisation of the world. (*Nauchnyy ateizm:* p. 4)

As an integral part of the Marxist-Leninist world-view, 'scientific atheism' is grounded in the view of the world and of man enshrined in dialectical and historical materialism:

The study of scientific atheism brings to light an integral side of the Marxist world-view. Being a philosophical science, scientific atheism emanates from the basic tenets of dialectical and historical materialism, both in explaining the origin of religion and in its scientific criticism of it. (ibid., p. 272)[11]

Thus the text-book *Istoriya i teoriya ateizma* (The History and Theory of Atheism) produced for use in university departments of 'scientific atheism' by the Department of the History and Theory of Atheism at Moscow State University under the editorship of M.P. Novikov, I.G. Ivanov and D.M. Ugrinovich, and published in 1974, defines 'scientific atheism' as follows:

A system of views which submits religion to a critical analysis . . . and which reveals the philosophical, natural-scientific and historical implausibility of religion from a materialist point of view. The philosophical criticism of religion reveals the origin and nature of religious illusions, their social and epistemological roots; scientific criticism confirms the implausibility of the religious picture of the world and historical criticism reveals the origin and evolution of religion, shows its reactionary role in the historical process, its transitory character, and the certainty of its dying out. A scientific criticism of religion is possible only on the basis of a materialistic analysis of its nature its social base and its social role. (ibid., pp. 5-6)

But although 'scientific atheism' is grounded in dialectical and historical materialism, and as such can be said to be a philosophical science, it is also held by its professional exponents to be relatively independent of dialectical and historical materialism, in that it is held to be a subject in its own right with a range of problems peculiar to itself — problems which take it well beyond the scope of philosophy. This is argued with considerable vigour, for example, in an article by N.A. Gorbachev entitled, 'K voprosu o predmete teorii nauchnogo ateizma' (On the Problem of Subject of the Theory of Scientific Atheism) in the first volume of the journal Voprosy nauchnogo ateizma (Vol. i, 1966, pp. 68-87).

Gorbachev opens his paper by stating that 'scientific atheism' is not, of course, in any sense wholly independent of Marxist-Leninist philosophical materialism. He writes:

Scientific atheism does not present itself as a totally independent world-view for, in Marxist philosophy, materialism and atheism are united in a single, monolithic (monolitnoye) unity, are organically connected.

What he does argue is that:

This unity does not exclude the fact that, within the framework of the dialectical-materialist world-view, the theory of scientific atheism has relative independence, in that it has acquired its own specific problems. (Gorbachev, 1966: p. 70)

The 'specific problems', peculiar to 'scientific atheism', arise out of the fact that, as experience has shown, the philosophical criticism of religion is not enough when confronted by the practical task of seeking to eliminate all vestiges of the religious outlook on life from the consciousness of the people. As Gorbachev writes:

The peculiar nature of these problems stands out when we look at the criticism of philosophical idealism and compare it with the criticism of religion, for in the criticism of idealism we get away from the particular features of religion, from the substantial religious consciousness, with its belief in supernatural forces, and blind faith. But unlike philosophical idealism, religion is not only a matter of ideology, but a matter of psychology, in that it includes feelings and emotions. Moreover, the emotional experiences of believers possess certain specific features and in this connection it is possible to say very definite things about religious feelings. If in the criticism of idealism it is sufficient to pay attention to its social and epistemological roots, in the criticism of religion the atheist must also offer an analysis of the psychological (the emotional) roots of religion. (ibid., p. 70)

Whilst Gorbachev does not, perhaps express himself as clearly as he might have done here — as we shall see in a later section, Soviet philosophers have of late been concerned with the analysis of the emotional and psychological roots of both philosophical idealism and religion (see below, pp. 201f) — the gist of what he is saying is clear enough, and it is that, as those engaged in anti-religious education will testify, theoretical arguments are insufficient to eradicate religion from the consciousness of the people, in that they do not come to terms with the part played in religious belief by emotional and aesthetic factors, by the belief that morality requires a religious backing, etc. Such factors require a special department of Marxist-Leninist philosophy to fully and adequately investigate them and this, argues Gorbachev, is the peculiar concern of the theory of 'scientific atheism' (ibid., p. 71). Further, in the formulation of the theoretical structure of 'scientific atheism', not only philosophers, but historians, social scientists, psychologists and others must play their part.

A.F. Okulov, the director of the Institute of Scientific Atheism and editor of *Voprosy nauchnogo ateizma* came to a similar conclusion in his inaugural address to the Academy of Social Sciences upon the occasion of his taking up these important offices (*'Za glubokuyu nauchnuyu razrabotku sovremennykh problem ateizma'*) (Towards a Thorough Scientific Formulation of the Contemporary Problems of Atheism) *VNA*, Vol. I, 1966, pp. 7-35).

Okulov, like Gorbachev, begins by immediately identifying the *practical* problem, which is that of imbuing the masses with the atheistic outlook necessary for the building of Communism — a problem which is compounded by the persistence among Soviet citizens of long-standing traditions and habits of mind derived from a religious culture. The struggle with religion, therefore, is not just a struggle with wrong views about the world, but a struggle against 'everything that has to do with the old order' (*protiv vsego starogo mira*), (op. cit., p. 7). This, says Okulov, the 'scientific atheist' must continually bear in mind, for it is the fundamental premise of the Marxist attitude to religion. The task upon which the 'scientific atheist' is engaged is no armchair debate with religion; it is nothing less than the building of the new post-revolutionary order in which all men will find their true fulfilment. 'The struggle against the religious world view', he writes, is: '. . . an integral part of the Communist education of Soviet people, to which the Party attaches enormous importance'. (ibid., pp. 7-8).

And in the task of communist education the practitioners of many disciplines are called upon to play their part – particularly sociologists and psychologists. Okulov is as aware as was Gorbachev, of the situation to which the decrees of the Party in 1954 had called attention; a situation in which religion, despite the fundamental changes which had taken place in the socio-economic structure of society in the Soviet Union, not only continues to exist, but shows few signs of 'withering away'. In the face of this situation Okulov urges that sociologists should be employed to carry out concrete (*konkretnye*) sociological research into the extent of religiosity in the Soviet Union, and that psychologists deploy their expertise to enquire into the intricacies of the religious mentality (ibid., p. 10). The upsurge of interest in both the sociology and psychology of religion in Soviet study of religion, consequent upon the decrees of 1954, and the changes in the organisation of research into religion set in motion thereby, has been one of the more interesting features of Soviet study of religion in the last two decades.

But it is not only sociology and psychology which have been remiss in the lack of attention which they have paid to religion in the past. Okulov also calls the philosophers to account, for not only is much current philosophical criticism of religion out of touch with contemporary developments in religion, it has also failed to pay sufficient attention to the philosophical problems of atheism and Okulov instances the ethical problems involved in atheism as a way of life as one area which he feels merits more serious philosophical attention. For the present he concentrates on the need for renewed philosophical analysis of the essence of religion and of the part which it has hitherto played in the life of man. The tenacity of the religious way of looking at the world must not be underestimated.

In this pertinent reminder of the difficulties of the practical task of inculcating atheism into the masses, Okulov echoes the experience of those *antireligiozniki* who, after the fall of Khrushchev, contributed to the post-mortem on the anti-religious campaign conducted by the country's leading newspapers and journals.[12] Thus, for example, G. Kelt, writing in the newspaper, *Komsomol'skaya Pravda* in 1965, had pointed out that:

It was foolish to suppose that religion could be abolished in a day, for it represents a historical phenomenon which has existed for thousands of years.

And he went on:

Today, we are again lulling ourselves by the thought that many believers in our country have left the church and religion. This is self-deception. It is true that in the greater part of the territory of the Soviet Union there are no churches and no servants of the cult. But believers there are; if not Orthodox, then all shades of sectarians . . . The closing of a parish does not make atheists out of believers. On the contrary, it attracts people all the more to religion and in addition embitters their hearts.

In the course of his article he had attacked what he termed 'a bare, negative, bookish-orientated atheism' and had stated that such cannot succeed, in that it does not reach the level of the aesthetic and emotional needs that turn the people to religion. What is needed, he had argued, in language reminiscent of Lunacharsky and the *bogostroiteli* (the god-builders) was 'a new shrine dedicated to the apotheosis of the genius of man', new liturgies which would replace the liturgy of the church (*Komsomol'skaya Pravda*, August 15, 1965). At the practical level, the 'new Soviet rites', which were increasingly coming into being at this time, were designed to meet just this need (cf. Powell, 1975: pp. 66-84; Binns, 1978).

It was, I suspect, the experience of Kelt, and of thousands of other *antireligiozniki* during the period 1959-1964, that led the academic exponents of 'scientific atheism', such as Gorbachev and Okulov, to call for a reassessment of the role of religion in the lives of the people, and to search for a more sophisticated approach to the understanding of religion (and of atheism) than had characterised Soviet propaganda hitherto. It had become increasingly obvious over the years since 1917 that religion was fulfilling needs with which the Party had not, as yet, come to terms — particularly in the field of ethics, aesthetics and in *'rites de passage'*. Thus Okulov, writing of the general problem facing 'scientific atheism', and striking a more positive note than had Gorbachev, could write:

Scientific research work into the depth, further enrichment and into the *Problematik* of atheism depends on a whole series of facts. But the general problem has to do with the contribution which atheism can make to the spiritual life (*dukhovnaya zhizn'*) of society, the growth of culture, social consciousness, its form and standard, the all-round development of the personality, to questions of work, of being, of the family, of tradition, etc. (ibid., p. 15)

This, as Okulov does not shrink from recognising, the religions of the world have, to their advantage, hitherto provided. Communism, therefore, if it is to win the hearts and minds of the masses, will have to do likewise. He writes:

All this commits us to carrying the struggle with religion into the area of personal questions, and before all else, into fundamental questions of world-view . . . for religion, as is well known, gives people answers to all the fundamental existential questions: gives them a picture of the world, a conceptual understanding of the universal historical process, a code of morality, etc. (ibid., p. 15)

But having recognised this, Okulov, unlike Gorbachev, throws the problem back at the philosophers for – and here, of course, he is following Lenin – religion is closely allied with idealist philosophy. If the masses now have a more sophisticated, and less anthropomorphic, conception of God, for example, as 'a Higher Power', 'a Creative Force', etc., it is because of developments in idealist philosophy. Marxist philosophers must counteract this.

But the most important philosophical problem for atheism, says Okulov – and here he takes advantage of Soviet philosophy's belated recognition of the significance of the early writings of Marx – is the problem of getting at the roots of religion and of showing the connection between religion and alienation (*otchuzhdenie*). Soviet philosophers, he says, have, unfortunately, preserved the myth that the problem of alienation is a problem foisted on Marxism by bourgeois philosophy, and he refers in support of this contention to an article by I. Bikkenin, S. Oduyev, A. Pozner and G. Smirnov in the authoritative Party journal *Kommunist* where it was stated that:

Among Soviet philosophers there is still a prejudice against the problem of alienation. . . partly . . . because they consider it only in evidence in the early works of Marx, whereas there is more than sufficient evidence for it in *Kapital* and other of Marx's writings. But it would evidently be useful to look again at the ideas of Marx on the unity of man, of man and work, man and society, and man and man, and for contemporary Marxists to develop these on the foundation of contemporary materialism. (*Kommunist*, No. 5, 1965: p. 65)

Nowhere, however, does Okulov suggest, as some bold Soviet philosophers have suggested, that one of the reasons for the persistence of religion in Soviet society is because the conditions of alienation are still in existence in that society (cf. P.P. Cherkashin, '*O sotsial'nykh kornyakh religii*' (On the Social Roots of Religion), *Voprosy filosofii*, No. 6, 1958, pp. 29-41).[13] Okulov considers the problem of alienation in more general terms. It is, he says, 'a problem which, from time immemorial, has engaged the attention of philosophers and theologians' and is one to which Soviet philosophers must give more thought. More work, therefore, is called for on problems connected with the spiritual life of man, for the problem of man is the paramount problem of philosophy, as evidence by the renewed interest in the West in 'axiology' and by the rise of Existentialism. No doubt with Existentialism in mind, Okulov asserts that:

Marxism-Leninism is itself a humanistic philosophy which rejects the abstract speculations of religious and idealistic philosophy á propos human personality, its laws and its freedom, and which sets the problem of man on a concrete-historical footing, and seeks to solve it by connecting it with the problem of the revolutionary transformation of society. (op. cit., p. 17)

Further, as Okulov points out, the problem of man is a problem which has come increasingly to the force in recent international philosophy. It was the theme, for example, of the XIIIth International Congress of Philosophers held in Mexico in 1963, and it has been the subject of many books and articles by Soviet philosophers since.[14]

Continuing this theme, Okulov identifies yet another area where Marxist philosophers have fallen sadly behind theologians and idealist philosophers, and that it is in the area concerned with life and death (*zhizn' i smert*). He writes:

Fear of death, and the attempt to find a way out of the organic conditions of human life, gives rise to the illusions about a future life which we find in philosophy and theology and to arguments about the relationship of soul and body. (ibid., p. 18)

These views, Okulov argues, must be counteracted by Marxist philosophers, but the problem of the fear of death is a problem to which Soviet psychologists must also turn their attention, for it is major factor contributing to religious belief at the present time, l oth in the Soviet Union and elsewhere in the world, and he ς otes from William James' book, *The Varieties of Religious Experience*, to the effect that: 'They who entertain religious beliefs live peacefully and happily', and that 'religion helps people to die happily' (James, 1901: p. 472). In fact, Soviet philosophers have not totally ignored this problem and Okulov cites a book by the Leningrad philosopher V.P. Tugarinov, *O tsennostyakh zhizni i kul'tury* (On the Values of Life and Culture), which deals with just this problem, although Tugarinov, in fact, had argued 'that either these problems do not exist or they are answerable by science'. He wrote that:

> These problems disturb everybody. . . Contemporary man reflects deeply and in secret about the problems of being (*bytie*). Who but philosophers can answer them? We must not refer him to religion, but give him feasible, scientific answers to these questions; not let him languish in depression, or decadence, or in subjectivity, but give him Marxist answers to these questions, which are the real problems of social thought. (op. cit., p. 92)

Okulov agrees, but is not above quoting approvingly from the American Humanist Corlis Lamont's book, *The Illusion of Immortality* (1961) in answer to this question. Lenin's call for an anti-idealist alliance – despite the isolation of Soviet philosophy over the past half-century or so – occasionally bears fruit!

Finally, Okulov turns his attention to moral problems as constituting another area of concern to 'scientific atheism', an area where, yet again, the Marxist must accept the challenge posed by contemporary developments in religious thinking – as, for instance, by Richard Niebuhr's book *An Interpretation of Christian Ethics* which he cites. Here the 'scientific atheist' must not only criticise religious morality, in theory and in practice, but also put forward a positive morality of his own, based upon the materialistic and atheistic outlook of Marxism-Leninism. This, says Okulov, in his concluding remarks, is one of the most important tasks of education in atheism (*ateisticheskoye vospitanie*) today.[15]

Okulov's address to the Academy of Social Sciences is the most thorough statement to date of the problems confronting the newly established discipline of 'scientific atheism'. As will be evident, the range of problems is vast and it is an understatement to say that the discipline is as yet in its infancy. But the problems had been identified, and this represents a considerable advance on the situation which prevailed before the Party decrees of 1954 and before the fomal recognition of 'scientific atheism' as an integral and vital part of the Marxist-Leninist world-view. The adequacy of the answer which 'scientific atheism' offers to these problems is, of course, another matter.

That many of the issues discussed by Gorbachev and Okulov were still matters of contention six years later, can be seen from a paper delivered by M.P. Novikov to a special, all-union conference, called by the Ministry of Higher and Special Education in 1972, to discuss the state of academic teaching in 'scientific atheism' and to suggest ways of improving it. A selection of the papers delivered to this conference, which covered both the theoretical and the practical aspects of 'scientific atheism', were published in the journal *Voprosy nauchnogo ateisma* (Vol. 15, 1973) and Novikov's paper *'O predmete nauchnogo ateizma'* (On the Subject of Scientific Atheism) was one of them.

Novikov began by reasserting the importance of 'scientific atheism' as an academic discipline in a socialist society. That 'scientific atheism' has an important place to play in Soviet society Novikov does not doubt; his concern, as was that of Gorbachev and Okulov, was with the relationship of 'scientific atheism' to the system of Marxist philosophy as a whole, with the full range of the problems peculiar to it, and with the constructive role it should be playing in the building of a socialist society, and in the formation of the spiritual world-view (*dukhovnoye mirovozzreniye*) of contemporary man.

With regard to the relationship of 'scientific atheism' to Marxist-Leninism philosophy as a whole, Novikov gives the impression that there was still some dispute over this. He writes:

If we get away from details, we can discern two fundamentally different positions with regard to the relationship of scientific atheism to Marxist philosophy as a whole: one holds that scientific atheism is part of dialectical materialist philosophy; the other, that it is a separate science, utterly (*polnost'yu*) divorced from philosophy, and having its own area of research. (Novikov, 1973: p. 26)

I take it that Novikov is setting up possible positions, rather than describing an actual debate, for he makes no reference to anyone who has actually taken up the position that 'scientific atheism' is 'utterly divorced' from dialectical materialism and, certainly, it would be a very surprising position for anyone in the Soviet Union to take up publicly. But by polarising things in this way, Novikov can pass on to discuss what he sees as the 'delicate and complicated' relationship obtaining between these two aspects of the Marxist-Leninist world-view. He puts it like this:

From philosophy [he says] have come all the specialised sciences of nature and society. At the present time logic, psychology, ethics, aesthetics, and latterly, atheism, are seeking to establish themselves independently of the parent discipline. Scientific atheism [he continues] certainly bears all the marks of a particular science: it is systematic, offers proofs of its conclusions, has its own specific categories, concepts and laws of operation; its truths issue in practice. It studies problems which do not, and cannot, engage the attention of other philosophical sciences — the problem of the origin and essence of religion, and especially of religion as a reflection of reality. It also plays a unique part in the formation of the scientific-atheistic world-view and shows the way to overcoming religion. All these problems are dealt with, at a fundamental level, only in scientific atheism. (ibid., p. 26)

But having put the case for the autonomy of 'scientific atheism' as an academic discipline — and Novikov has more to say later in his paper about the specific problems of 'scientific atheism' — he now feels compelled to point out that it is impossible to separate 'scientific atheism' from dialectical materialism for, as Lenin argued, dialectical materialism is the heart of kernel (*sut'*) of militant atheism. Novikov expresses the problem of the autonomy of 'scientific atheism' as a discipline as follows:

It is common to differentiate philosophical sciences in terms of the varied and complex problems presented in human life and in terms of the expansion of human knowledge. But it is impossible to differentiate atheism from materialism, for materialism is the basis of atheism. The difficulty is establishing atheism as a subject of study (in its own right) is due to the different approaches to the understanding of Marxism-Leninism. Any attempt to limit dialectical materialism to the sphere of the laws of being and to exclude the sciences from the sphere of philosophy would naturally also exclude scientific atheism from philosophy. Similarly, an abstract epistemology which separates the theoretical aspects of science from social-production and social-political practice would also exclude scientific atheism from being part of the philosophical sciences, as would the views of those philosophers who have doubted the view that social consciousness lags behind social relations, and who have declared this notion 'unworkable' (*nerabotayushchii*) as a means for explaining religious survivals, thus limiting the problem of religion to that of empirical analysis. . . (Novikov, 1973: p. 27)

Novikov's own opinion is that more attention should be devoted to questions concerning 'the relative independence of the development of social consciousness', and that as this includes 'the study of the development of religion, and the study of the contradictions in its development', that this constitutes the philosophical side of 'scientific atheism'. 'Scientific atheism' is, he asserts, part of Marxist-Leninist philosophy, yet at the same time, like ethics and aesthetics, it is an autonomous field of study with problems specific to itself — problems which he broadly identifies as 'the struggle with religion and the formation of an atheistic outlook' (ibid., p. 28).

Having settled the general problem of the status of 'scientific atheism' *vis-à-vis* Marxist-Leninist philosophy as a whole, Novikov then passes to look more closely at some of the specific problems involved in defining the area of study of 'scientific atheism'. Past and current Soviet atheistic literature does not, he claims, distinguish at all clearly between atheism and materialism, between the history of philosophy and the history of atheism, and it is also unclear whether the scientific study of religion and the sociology of religion are to be considered independent sciences. In the absence of any unified view from within current atheistic literature, Novikov contents himself with pointing out the weaknesses of some of the views which have been put forward. Thus, he comments that where atheism is regarded wholly as a philosophical science, it is often held to be identical to materialism. But such a view, he contends, ignores the specific problems of atheism and also its practical significance. Further, where the history of atheism is regarded as simply part of the general history of philosophy this leads, he says, to a too narrow view of atheism and thus impoverishes the history of the subject. Similarly, if one separates Marxist study of religion from 'scientific atheism', and considers it a separate science, this would mean, he argues, that 'scientific atheism' will be left only with general methodological principles. On such a view the science of religion would deal with all the major problems of religion and atheism would simply be an addition to materialism. Novikov's own view, like those of Okulov and Gorbachev whom we considered earlier, is that it is 'scientific atheism' which is the discipline which has the remit to fully and completely study religion in all its aspects – its origin, structure, social nature, etc., – and which has, in addition, the practical task of overcoming it. Should the study of religion be separated from 'scientific atheism' – as some have advocated – then atheism would lose all that makes it significant.

Similarly, to separate either the history of religion or the sociology of religion from 'scientific atheism' would also, Novikov argues, be a very grave mistake.

'Scientific atheism' (he writes) does not deny sociology of religions' right to exist. Marxist sociology of religion is now making an all-round scientific analysis of modern religion and for this scientific atheism is grateful. But it is only possible to make such an analysis with the help of the basic principles of scientific atheism. Thus, it is more correct to consider the sociology of religion as a branch of scientific atheism and the same can be said of the history of religion. The history of religion should be fully explained in works on scientific atheism with the help of the laws governing Marxist atheism. Without this any history of religion cannot be scientific. (ibid., p. 29)

Thus, for Novikov, as for Okulov and Gorbachev, 'scientific atheism' is the all-encompassing discipline for the study of religion. It has its own specific problems, and it is further charged with the important revolutionary task of overcoming the survivals of religion in the consciousness of the masses and of replacing these with a positive atheistic consciousness. Marxist-Leninist atheism, as Novikov now passes to assert, differs from all previous forms of atheism in that it does not seek simply to overcome religion but to replace it with a positive atheistic mentality. He writes:

Marxist atheism, unlike the atheism of the French materialists of the eighteenth century, does not simply fight against religion. In his letter to Bernstein, Engels wrote that 'atheism as the naked rejection of religion is in itself nothing and is still religion', and Lunacharsky used to say that 'the destruction of religion without establishing Marxism in its place is a slogan of the liberal bourgeoisie. . .' (ibid., pp. 29-30)

Novikov, again like Okulov and Gorbachev, ends his paper by reasserting Marxist atheism in the face of attempts on the part of 'revisionists' such as Garaudy and Fischer, to either reject it completely or to mitigate its force. Any accommodation to religion, he asserts – particularly views which would make Marxist atheism a matter of what he terms 'doctrinal subjectivism' – must be resisted as likely to undermine the ideology of the working masses. On the writings of Garaudy and Fischer, Novikov comments:

They try to criticise Marxist-Leninist atheism for what they claim is its unhistorical evaluation of religion, for its failure to recognise the positive role which religion has played in the development of human culture and for its contribution to humanism, as well as for not recognising that contemporary religious modernism is a progressive event which has drastically changed religious ideology. (ibid., p. 33)

His reply is to ignore the specific charges of Garaudy and Fischer and simply to assert that Garaudy and Fischer seek to present a form of Marxism which is divorced from life, for life, he asserts

. . . shows that modern revisionists base their arguments on theological and bourgeois propaganda which more far-sighted churchmen have themselves rejected. In lending support to religion revisionism lends support to imperialist propaganda and so takes the wrong side in the contemporary ideological struggle (ibid., pp. 33-34)

– an indication of just how deeply antagonistic Marxism-Leninism's emotional reaction to religion is.

Finally, in seeking to rebut what he regards as contemporary falsifications of Marxist-Leninist atheism, Novikov comes to what he terms the 'immanent criticism' (*immanentnaya kritika*) of atheism. By this he means the criticism that Marxist atheism is incapable of supporting the spiritual life of a people. This criticism he holds to have originated with the Second Vatican Council's report 'On the Church in the Modern World', in which it was maintained that atheism encourages indifference to the real problems facing the world, in that whilst atheists have stopped believing in God, they have not acquired any real spiritual values to take its place. Atheism, so such criticism maintains, encourages crass materialism and ignores the spiritual needs of man. It further maintains that atheism is a pseudo-science, since it rejects not religion, but 'misinterpreted' religion which has little to do with religion in real life. Atheism must, so such criticism contends, be understood psychologically and as being without 'deep roots and convictions'.

Such criticism, Novikov claims, fails to understand Marxist atheism, seeing in it only the absence of belief, whilst remaining blind to its positive values. To counter such criticism 'scientific atheism' must, therefore, show forth clearly its positive side and not rest content with simply exposing religious ideas about the origin of the world and the destiny of man. 'Scientific atheism' must show how it is fighting for nothing less than the spiritual freedom of man from all forms of superstition as enshrined in religion – a freedom which goes hand in hand with the development of science (ibid., p. 35).

Novikov summarises the basic principles of 'scientific atheism' as follows:

a. the evaluation of religion as a complex of fantastic ideas created by human dependences on nature and by the social conditions of life hitherto;
b. the exposing of the connections between religion and the interests of the reactionary classes;

c.   the acknowledgement that fighting against religion means fighting the
     socio-economic order which religion reflects;
d.   the conviction that doing away with religion 'as an opium of the peo-
     ple' is the most important condition for the liberation of the creative
     forces in mankind in their struggle for a better life here on earth. (ibid.,
     p. 35)

And he concludes his paper by asserting that apart from studying
religion as a social phenomenon, 'scientific atheism' has the further task of studying religious psychology and the peculiarities of
mass religious consciousness, of criticising the main tendencies of
contemporary theology, religious philosophy, bourgeois religious
studies and philosophy of religion. It is also the job of 'scientific
atheism' to organise sociological surveys of the differing religious
groups still functioning in the USSR. A further task of 'scientific
atheism', Novikov contends, is the study of the origins and
development of atheism and of showing the connection between
atheism and movements of liberation among peoples. The 'scientific atheist' must, he says, make full use of the atheistic heritage of
the past and show how Marxism-Leninism brings it to fruition. He
concludes:

Exposing the religious consciousness for what it is, scientific atheism thus
becomes an important means of orientation in social life. Rejecting the world
of fantasy, it helps one to separate the real from the illusory in the realm of
values. It liberates the human consciousness from all forms of superstition.
Exposing the reactionary nature of religious ideology, Marxist atheism helps
to establish progressive ideas and thus fulfils an important ideological function. The task of scientific atheism is not only to expose the reactionary
nature of religious ideology and to overcome religion, but to form a scientific
materialist ideology to take its place. This is one of the most important
means in the formation of a communist consciousness. Thus the subject of
scientific atheism is the criticism of religion as a fantastic reflection of reality
in the human mind, the formulation of a scientific account of the origin of
religion and of its evolution and decline and, by studying the objective and
subjective factors of its persistence to help towards overcoming it and sub-
stituting for it the principles of the common and specific formation of an
atheist outlook. (ibid., p. 36)

As will be evident, in identifying the particular range of problems we have outlined as the problems confronting 'scientific atheism', Okulov, Gorbachev and Novikov show themselves conscious of the fact that Marxism-Leninism must compete, as a world-view, with the views put forward by the religions of the world, and this not only in the Soviet Union — where, as a matter of fact, almost all the major religious world-views are indeed represented — but on the wider international scene. Soviet 'scientific atheists' are continually reminding both themselves and others that the struggle with religion is part of the wider, contemporary, international ideological struggle (cf. *Nauchnyy ateizm*: pp. 161-169). To this task, therefore, must be brought to bear the resources not only of professional 'scientific atheists', but of philosophers, sociologist, psychologists, historians, historians of religion and of culture and ethnographers, for only by such inter-disciplinary co-operation can the immense task facing 'scientific atheism' be fulfilled (Okulov, op. cit., sect. 5 *'O koordinatsii raboty i rasstanovke nauchnykh kadrov'* (On the Co-ordination of Work and the Development of Scientific Personnel) pp. 31-45). The organising of this task is the concern of the Institute of Scientific Atheism.

There are thus two sides to Soviet 'scientific atheism': (1) the criticism of religion, and (2) the formation of a positive atheistic outlook on the world (cf. *Nauchnyy ateizm*: pp. 9-11). Unfortunately, as the discipline has progressed, it is the former which has engaged far more of the attention of professional 'scientific atheists' than the latter. Thus, for example, the textbook *Istoriya i teoriya ateizma*, published in 1974, enunciates the following five principles as being of the essence of 'scientific atheism'. 'Scientific Atheism', it asserts:

1. sees religion as a collection of fantastic ideas, born of man's dependence on the elements and on social forms alien to his true being;
2. shows the link between religion and the interests of the reactionary classes;
3. shows that the struggle against religion is, in reality, a struggle against a reactionary social order;

4.   shows how combatting religion is a pre-requisite of the liberation of the masses and of improving social conditions;
5.   shows that systematic ideological education is necessary to overcome religion. (op. cit., p. 9)

Of these five, for the most part negative, principles, it will be clear, from our earlier discussion of the theoretical basis of the Marxist-Leninist critique, that whilst the first three echo, in a somewhat simplified form, the classical Marxist critique of religion, the last two are pure Leninist, giving substance to Bohdan Bociurkiw's remarks that Lenin so modified the classical Marxist position, in which religion would disappear upon the successful completion of the struggle against reactionary social orders which give rise to the religious illusion, as to upgrade the struggle against religion into a pre-requisite, if not a necessary condition, of the success of that struggle (Bociurkiw, 1967: pp. 109-110). Stalin's emphasis on the importance of the formation of a 'correct consciousness' in the masses, if they were to fulfil their revolutionary role in the building of Communism, is also in evidence here.

Thus it is that the authors of this important and widely used textbook can argue that 'scientific atheism' is a militant, revolutionary force with an important part to play in forming Communist society. This claim is more than an attempt to bolster the 'scientific atheist's, own importance in the scheme of things — though it is no doubt partly that — it is also a correct reading of the fundamental principles of Leninist Marxism.

Istoriya i teoriya ateizma does, however, conclude its summary of the subject of 'scientific atheism' by formally recognising both of the aspects of the discipline to which we have called attention, for it states that:

The subject of scientific atheism is the criticism of religion as a false reflection of reality (*kak lozhnogo otrazheniya deystvitel'nosti*) which studies the origin, rise and fall of religion, the objective and subjective conditions of overcoming it, and the formation of an atheistic world-view. (op. cit., p. 10)

— which is as good a definition as we shall find of the nature and the task of Soviet 'scientific atheism'.

Before passing to consider in greater detail the execution of this task there are three points with regard to 'scientific atheism' which I would like to emphasise. The first concerns the description of Marxism-Leninist atheism as 'scientific', the second, that unity of theory and practice which, as we saw in Part I of this study, has been so essential a feature of Marxist methodology from the beginning, and the third, the uncompromising nature of the Soviet attitude to religion.

1. Whatever the specific problems which 'scientific atheism' has abrogated to itself, all the exponents of it are agreed that it rests logically on the basis of Marxist-Leninist philosophical materialism — that it is grounded in the view of the world and of man enshrined in dialectical and historial materialism (Okulov, 1966: p. 7; Gorbachev, 1966: pp. 69-70; Novikov, 1973: pp. 25-28; *Nauchnyy ateizm:* pp. 4-8; *Istoriya i teoriya ateizma*: p. 41). As *Istoriya i teoriya ateizma* puts it:

Only on the foundations of a scientific analysis of religion and its social nature and social role is it possible to arrive at a scientific atheist theory. By revealing the causes of the origin and existence of religious beliefs, by determining the manner and means of overcoming them, scientific atheism puts forward a critical analysis of the whole complex of religious conceptions and claims . . . From a consistent materialist position, scientific atheism provides a well-founded philosophical, natural-scientific, historical and psychological critique of the untenability of religion. (op. cit., pp. 4-5)

Dialectical and historial materialism, so Marxist-Leninists believe, constitutes the only truly 'scientific' understanding of the world and of man, and thus the understanding of religion's role in human history, which is an intrinsic element in that view, must also be 'scientific' — must, in fact, be the only possible 'scientific' view, and Marxist-Leninist 'scientific atheism', therefore, be the only true 'science of religion', the only valid *Religionswissenschaft.*

The consequence of thus grounding 'scientific atheism' is, of course, that such atheism is only 'scientific', in so far as dialectical and historical materialism is itself 'scientific' — and this claim we will be examining in Part III of this study.

2. The second point which I wish to emphasise is that we have, in the views with regard to the nature and task of 'scientific atheism' outlined above, a good illustration of that unity of theory and practice — of that 'cognition and reorganisation of the world' — which is an essential feature of Marxist-Leninist methodology, for not only does what is claimed to be a 'scientific' understanding of religion demonstrate the untenability of religion, it also issues in the practical imperative to overcome it and replace it with a more tenable, 'progressive' world-view. Historical materialism provides additional impetus to this task by seeking to show that such anti-religious activity is in accordance with that progressive development of the human race which Marxists claim to discern in world history. This practical, revolutionary vision is never far from the minds of those writing on the nature and history of religion in the Soviet Union, and, it adds, in their own estimation, point, purpose and even grandeur to their task.

3. Lastly, I would like to say something at this point about the uncompromising nature of the Soviet attitude to religion. This comes to the fore, more often than not, when Soviet scholars are discussing the 'falsifications', as they believe them to be, of 'scientific atheism' produced by (bourgeois) philosophers, theologians and Marxist 'revisionists' in the West (cf. *Nauchnyy ateizm:* pp. 11-14; *Istoriya i teoriya ateizma:* pp. 14-16; Novikov, 1973: pp. 33-34). Thus, *Istoriya i teoriya ateizma*, whilst citing no particular philosopher or theologian by name, singles out four specific criticisms of 'scientific atheism' for attention: (1) that 'scientific atheism' ignores the innate nature of religious feelings, with the consequence that atheism is incapable of developing the spiritual life of man; (2) that 'scientific atheism' is not scientific but political, i.e. that it is not an essential ingredient of Marxism, but simply a tool in a political struggle; (3) that Marxist atheism is itself a kind of *ersatz* religion, in which belief in a supernatural being is replaced by belief in the 'laws of history' or in the classless society of the future; and (4) what is termed 'immanent criticism', designed to show that such atheism is false and unscientific (op. cit., pp. 14-15).

It is to the credit of this new phase of Soviet criticism of religion — which emphasises the philosophical rather than the ideological criticism of religion — that these criticisms of Marxist-Leninist 'scientific atheism' are, in fact, mentioned at all, and it is, perhaps, an indication that the possibility of a renewed dialogue between Soviet Marxism and religion cannot be dismissed entirely out of hand. However, these criticisms are given an extremely cursory dismissal — such 'distortions', it is simply asserted, can in no way halt the growth of atheism nor its spread among the masses. Marxist 'revisionists' — the Austrian, Ernst Fischer and the French Marxist, Roger Garaudy, are here mentioned by name — who have sought to come to terms with what they regard as the beneficial effects of religion in the life of the peoples of the world, are taken rather more seriously. These, it is said, not only distort Marxism but ignore the historical record of religion (cf. Novikov 1976: pp. 33-35). They point to the so-called positive aspects of the Christian religion in aiding the development of the revolutionary movements but forget the role that religion has played as a weapon in the hands of the exploiting classes. Further, the 'revisionist' thesis about the positive role which Christianity has played in the creation of European culture ignores the 'scientific' insight of Marxism that religion alone is incapable of directing cultural development, in that this is entirely dependent on developments in the material life of society. Modern 'revisionists' also try to show that the Christian religion has played a positive part in the formation of Marxist humanism, to the extent of warning Marxists that if they ignore this legacy then Marxist humanism will itself be limited. In reply, it is simply asserted that such 'revisionists' ignore the reactionary nature of religion. Finally, revisionists who argue that, as modern religion has freed itself from past social structures, it can now become the ally of Marxsim, forget that Lenin has shown that this view is false, that religion remains inexorably linked to bourgeois ideology.

Soviet students, for whom the text-book to which we are referring is intended, are thus made aware at the outset of their study of 'scientific atheism' of the uncompromising character of Marxist-

Leninist atheism. The *rapprochement* between religion and Marxism that has come about in parts of Western Europe and in Latin America is something which Soviet 'scientific atheists' roundly condemn, and Soviet Marxists have, in fact, been conspicuously absent from such Marxist-Christian dialogues as have taken place in Europe.[16] Soviet Marxism remains to this day vehemently opposed to any suggestion of a compromise with religion and such, it might be said, is its Leninist legacy. But to condemn this attitude would, I think, be too easy, for the question can be raised whether, in rejecting out of hand the suggestion that Marxist humanism owes anything specific to the Christian tradition, whether in fact either the Christian, or indeed any other religion, could, in any long term, *non-tactical*, sense, become an ally of Marxism, and Marxism (or religion) remain true to itself, and in rejecting the suggestion that Marxism itself is in some sense religious, Soviet Marxism is not being truer to both the European tradition which it claims to bring to fruition, and to its own materialist principles, than are those European and Latin American Marxists who search for some, as yet to be identified, middle ground between two *prima facie* fundamentally opposed ways of looking at the world. Although I raise this question now, I shall leave discussion of it until I have looked in greater detail at Soviet 'scientific atheism'. The point I wish to make at the moment is that it may not, as might appear, be the case that the Soviets, in rejecting anything other than a tactical *rapprochement* with religion, are simply being churlish.

3.3   THE PARTISAN NATURE OF SOVIET STUDY OF RELIGION

The struggle against religion is not a campaign, not an isolated phenomenon, not a self-contained entity; it is an inseparable component part of the entire ideological activity of Party organisations, an essential link and necessary element in the complex of communist education. (*Pravda*, January 12, 1967)

As should be clear from the discussion of the theoretical basis of the Marxist-Leninist understanding of religion in Part I of this study and, from what we have said about 'scientific atheism' above, there can, from the point of view of Marxism-Leninism, be no neutral, value-free study of religion. The study of religion in the Soviet Union subserves, and is explicitly intended to subserve, the overall objectives of the Soviet state, one of which has been, from the beginning, the total secularisation not only of the institutions of the state but of the consciousness of its citizens as well. Nowhere has Aristotle's dictum that 'the citizen should be moulded to suit the form of government under which he lives' (*Politics*, VIII, 1) been taken with greater seriousness.

As Marxist, the leadership of the Communist Party of the Soviet Union has always expected secularisation to follow naturally from scientific progress and socio-economic change, but as Leninist, it has also been very aware of the necessity of accelerating this process by an active policy of secularisation. Within this active policy of secularisation, and in particular within the area of the secularisation of consciousness, the study of religion as we saw in the previous section, is called upon to play its part. As one of the Soviet Union's leading historians of religion acknowledges at the outset of a recent book on the history of religion:

The education of the people in the spirit of scientific, materialist understanding of the world is one of the most important tasks of ideological work in the contemporary period of the building of communism in the Soviet Union today. The programme of the Communist Party of the Soviet Union points to the necessity of conducting 'broad, systematic scientific-atheist propaganda and of thus making clear the ill-founded nature of religious beliefs. (S.A. Tokarev, 1974: p. 5)

Such a task will be impossible, Tokarev contends, unless those carrying it out have an acquaintance in depth with the role which religion has played in world history. He continues:

It is necessary to be clear to oneself when and how religious fantasies originated, of what they were in the beginning and how they developed, of how there came into being isolated, exclusive groups of professional ministers of religion – sorcerers, shamans, priests and others – and of how churches are organised. In short, it is necessary to know the history of religion. (ibid., p. 5)

— although a leading Soviet ethnographer, B.F. Porshnev, has criticised the excessive reliance, as it seems to him, of Soviet anti-religious propaganda on 'parallels resting solely on the history of religion' at a time when religion is building defences against the advance of scientific and realistic thought. In such a situation he writes:

The development in the individual of an integrated and unified dialectical materialist world-view comes to be the principal weapon in the propaganda of scientific atheism. Nevertheless (he concludes) it must be emphasised that the significance of a thoroughgoing and rigorously scientific knowledge of the world history of religion for the development of the new man, the man of communist society, is very great. (Porshnev, 1965: p. 136)

Similarly, another historian of religion, I.A. Kryvelev, openly acknowledges his adherence to the general objectives of the Marxist-Leninist approach to religion at the outset of his recently published two-volume study of the history of religion. He writes:

As in general philosophical work, so also in dealing with historico-religious problems, the author is guided by Marxist-Leninist doctrine. The guidelines are laid down by Lenin in a letter to I.I. Skvortsov-Stepanov: to write 'volumes on the history of religion and *against every sort of religion* (including Kantian and other refined forms of idealism and agnosticism), with surveys of material from the history of atheism and to show the connection of the churches with the bourgeoisie.

But having thus declared his position, Kryvelev hastens to add that:

. . . the fact that a work on the history of religion must be directed 'against all religion' does not signify a one-sided approach to the selection and interpretation of facts, for the author is convinced that the objective elucidation of historico-religious problems leads to the revealing of those aspects of religion which characterise it as the opium of the people, as a reactionary ideology acting against the interests of mankind. (1975: Vol. I, p. 9)

Finally, an example from a leading Soviet Islamist, who, after summarising recent Soviet work in the study of Islam, and of the collecting of material for this task, concludes:

These materials will have not merely theoretical significance, but will be of inestimable help in the important task of overcoming the relics of religion in the consciousness and life of Soviet people. The Study of Islam is a complex and many-sided process of scientific growth, which answers vital requirements in our social life, and creates broad possibilities for the formation of a scientific world-view. (Smirnov, 1967: pp. 425-427)[17]

The committed nature of the Soviet approach to the study of religion could not be more clearly expressed. The objectives which these leading Soviet historians of religion acknowledge are, of course, no more and no less than the objectives which we have seen to be those of 'scientific atheism' in general. In the Soviet Union the study of religion is under an explicit obligation to demonstrate the mundane origins of religion, the harmful role which it has played in the history of the peoples of the world, and to show the incompatibility of its view of man and the world with that enshrined in contemporary science as explicated by Marxism-Leninism and hence, the inevitability of its passing away as society progresses towards Communism. It is also part of the practical struggle to bring this situation about.

Thus, the Soviet scholar must write to a theme and to a theme laid down, as, the abundance of references to the writings of Marx, Engels and Lenin found in all Soviet writing on religion testifies, by those authors. Both Tokarev and Kryvelev renew their ritual acquaintance with the sacred texts at the outset of their studies as inevitably as do all Soviet writers beginning a study of religion. The results of Soviet scholarship are, therefore, a foregone conclusion and interest must focus on the detailed working out of the thesis. I shall be returning to this point later, but I would like to note here that avowed commitment is not new in the history of religion – it was, indeed, the norm in nineteenth century *theological* writing on the history of religion – and I would also like to suggest that a commitment openly avowed might well be illuminating in the way Kryvelev contends. I shall, in fact, argue in Part III of this study that this is so.

It is in terms of the *Problematik* set out above that all study of religion and atheism in the Soviet Union takes place. Whilst it may appear to some to be a strange hermaneutical principle that insists that religion be studied in such a seemingly negative way, it should now be clear that it makes perfectly good sense, given the basic premises and the practical intent of Soviet 'scientific atheism'. Religion must not only be shown to be false, but must also be shown to be but a mask for those more fundamental material forces which, from a Marxist point of view, are the real determinants of the historical process and which will lead eventually to the disappearance of religion as a phenomenon of human culture. Soviet writing on religion is designed to show that this is so, although Soviet 'scientific atheism' must also deal with the positive problems of atheism outlined above.

Thus it is that, in the Soviet Union, the subject matter of 'scientific atheism' includes all and more of what in Western scholarship would come under the rubric of the History and Phenomenology of Religion. The following brief, formal outline of the compulsory course followed by all students in higher education gives graphic illustration of this:

Section I: *Religion as a Social Phenomenon*
1. The Essence, Fundamental Elements and Social Function of Religion
2. The Historical Forms of Religion
3. World Religions:
   (a) Christianity:
       Orthodoxy
       Catholicism
       Protestantism
   (b) Islam
   (c) Buddhism
   (d) International Religious Organisations and Societies
4. National Religions
   (a) Judaism
   (b) Hinduism, Jainism, Sikhism
   (c) Confucianism and Taoism

(d) Shintoism
(e) The Parochial Religions of Class Society
(f) Tribal Religions
5. The Crisis of Religion at the Present Time

Section II: *Atheism and Social Progress*
6. The Evolution of Atheism as Conforming to the Natural Law of the Spiritual Progress of Mankind
7. Pre-Marxist Atheism
8. Marxist-Leninist Atheism as the Highest Form of Atheism
9. Atheism and the Contemporary Ideological Struggle

Section III: *The Philosophical Basis of Atheism*
10. The Opposition Between Religion and the Scientific Outlook
11. The Natural Scientific Foundations of Atheism
12. The Materialist Conception of History and Atheism
13. The Moral Content of Atheism

Section IV: *Atheism and Religion in Socialist Society*
14. The Evolution of Mass Atheism in Socialist Society
15. The Grounds and Causes of the Survival of Religion in Socialist Society
16. Marxism-Leninism on Freedom of Conscience

Section V: *Scientific-Atheist Education*
17. The Scientific Foundations of the Policy of the Communist Party Towards Religion and the Churches
18. A System of Scientific Atheist Education
(*Nauchnyy ateizm*: pp. 287-288)

A fuller account of the content of courses in 'scientific atheism' is given in Appendix II of this present work.

It will be clear from the above outline that the two aspects of 'scientific atheism' — the refutation of religion, on the one hand, and the positive affirmation of atheism as the foundation of the Soviet way of life, on the other — are intimately connected; the latter, in fact, can only proceed on the basis of the former, for this is the way history itself proceeds, and Soviet 'scientific atheism', in which the history of atheism is taught alongside of the history of religion, tells what is, in effect, the story of man's journey from darkness to light.[18]

The Contemporary Soviet 'Scientific Atheist' Critique of Religion

Although 'scientific atheism' is concerned to criticise all aspects of religion its criticism, in effect, is confined to (1) philosophical criticism designed to undermine the foundations of the religious world-view from the point of view of dialectical and historical materialism; (2) natural scientific criticism designed to show the incompatibility of religious views about the world with that established by the natural sciences, particularly with regard to such things as the origin of life on earth, the origin of man, his essence, psychology, destiny, etc.; and (3) historical criticism designed to show that, from the point of view of history, archaeology and ethnography, the origin and development of religion is susceptible to naturalistic explanation.

But, as a contemporary Soviet 'scientific atheist' writes:

Each of these aspects of the criticism of religion in scientific atheism does not just deny the validity of religious views but opens up positive scientific insights into the nature of religion. Marxist atheism not only rejects belief in God and the supernatural, but seeks to give a scientific explanation of the essence of religion, of its social, historical and epistemological roots and to show the ways and means to freeing the workers from religious prejudices. (N.I. Gubanov, 1967: p. 183)

Further, Gubanov insists that these three aspects of the critique of religion form an organic unity and must not be taken in isolation from one another. The critique of religion in contemporary 'scientific atheism' is a cumulative one, although as I hope to show in the third and final part of this study, it rests on the validity or otherwise of one or two fundamental premises.

Before looking in detail at contemporary Soviet study and/or critique of religion under the three headings outlined above, although I shall deal with the third — the naturalistic understanding of the development of religion — in a separate chapter on

Soviet history of religion, it will be necessary, as a prelude to this, to say something about the way in which Soviet 'scientific atheism' understands 'religion', that is, to look at the answer which it gives to the question 'What is religion?', for the Soviet understanding of 'religion' differs, in some important respects, from that found in Western studies.

4.1   SOVIET 'SCIENTIFIC ATHEISM' AND 'THE ESSENCE OF THE RELIGIOUS CONSCIOUSNESS'

Although the basic criticism of religion in the Soviet Union has always been that its beliefs are incompatible with a scientific-materialist understanding of the world, and although, in the early years of Soviet power it was felt sufficient simply to point this out for the masses to be converted to atheism, in recent years, and arising directly out of a recognition of the failure of an anti-religious campaign conducted along just such lines, Soviet 'scientific atheism' has sought to penetrate rather more deeply than hitherto into what it terms 'the essence of the religious consciousness', and has, as a consequence, somewhat revised the conception of 'religion' implicit in its earlier approach, in which religion was seen as being little more than a complex of false beliefs about the world — though it is also, for 'scientific atheism', that as well.

Thus, since the early 1960's, a great deal of research in the Soviet Union has been devoted to studying the specific features (*spetsifika*) and structure of the religious consciousness and, in particular, to studying the emotional roots of religion (cf. V.R. Bukin and I.I. Bukina, 1962, 1964; V.K. Tancher and E.K. Dulman, 1964; I.N. Yablokov, 1965a, 1965b). That this represents an advance on earlier Soviet study of religion is recognised by no less a figure in contemporary 'scientific atheism' than Professor D.M. Ugrinovich of Moscow State University who, in an article published in 1961, wrote that:

Until quite recently in the greater part of our anti-religious books, brochures and articles, religion was regarded only as an ideology, that is, as an anti-scientific, perverse theory, put forward and expounded by professional theologians and churchmen.

And thus, as he points out:

The struggle to overcome religion has been concerned only with the theoretical refutation of religious dogma. (Ugrinovich, 1961: pp. 36-37)

But there is more to religion, Ugrinovich contends, than dogma, and consequently more to the overcoming of it than the refutation of its beliefs (cf. Okulov's paper referred to in Section 3.2 above). Religion has deep emotional roots in the consciousness of ordinary believers and these must be understood before the task of overcoming and replacing them can take place. Ugrinovich's own analysis of the religious consciousness — based as it is on recent Soviet research in this area — is worth looking at in detail, for it represents the conclusions of one who is regarded within the Soviet Union itself as the leading exponent of the 'scientific atheist' critique of religion.

Before turning to an analysis of the structure of the religious consciousness, Ugrinovich first looks at its specific features, seeking an answer, thereby, to the question 'What is religion?'. Religion, he argues, like all forms of social consciousness, can be considered under three fundamental aspects: It can be considered from the point of view of the *subject matter which is reflected in the religious consciousness*: that is, by looking at the forms of social life which it reflects — at its social roots. Secondly, it can be looked at from the point of view of *the form of the reflection itself*; that is, from the point of view of the 'specific features' of the religious consciousness, and lastly, it can be looked at from the point of view of its *social function and social role*. A complete account of religion for Ugrinovich, and for 'scientific atheism', will combine all three ways of looking at religion, but in the paper which we shall consider, Ugrinovich looks only at the second of these ways of regarding religion — that is, at the religious con-

sciousness itself, which, from a religious point of view, says Ugrinovich, is the 'chief element in the religious complex' (ibid., p. 27).

Here, then, according to religious people themselves, we have
the core (*sterzhen'*) of religion. Of what does it consist? Ugrinovich
writes:

Social phenomena and human activities become religious and acquire specific
social orientation if they are connected with religious beliefs, or in one way
or another are attached to the religious consciousness. So, for example, the
ordinary actions of men become part of the ritual of a cult and take on a religious orientation if they are directed towards an invented supernatural goal,
created by the imagination of a religious person. Therefore, a religious cult is
impossible without religious consciousness or outside of religious consciousness. So far as the religious organisations are concerned, they are created by
people for the propagation of a religious doctrine and for the performance of
religious rituals. These organisations are formed in conformity with religious
consciousness with the aim of consolidating it, preaching and disseminating
it. (Ugrinovich, 1966: pp. 37-38)

Having stated these near platitudes, Ugrinovich begins his analysis of the essence of the religious consciousness by looking at its
particular content (*soderzhaniye*) — that is, at that which makes
religion religion. Naturally, as he points out, this is something to
which religious people have also devoted some attention, and
about which they have put forward a number of interesting views.
In particular, Ugrinovich notes that they have often sought to
distinguish between 'superstition' (*suyeveriye*) and 'authentic religion' (*podilinnaya religiya*), and have sought to minimise the
connection between 'authentic religion' and primitive forms of
religion. One way in which they have sought to do this has been to
distinguish between primitive religions and 'religions of revelation'
(*religii otkroveniya*), by which they have meant to indicate the
great monotheistic religions. As an example of the kind of distinction he has in mind Ugrinovich cites the work of the German
theologian Mensching, who sought to define 'authentic religion' in
terms of the quality of some 'interior experience' in relation to
religion. According to Mensching, any study of religion which fails

to take account of this misses its object (Mensching, 1959: p. 11). Similarly, according to another theologian, Adolf Richter, it is impossible to offer a rational scientific analysis of the essence of religion from any standpoint other than that of belief. True religion can be known only from the standpoint of faith (Richter, 1961: pp. 969-970). From these two examples Ugrinovich concludes that 'bourgeois' religious studies is hopelessly in the grip of what he terms 'fideism'.[1] For an objective, scientific understanding of religion we must, therefore, he concludes, look elsewhere.

It is indicative of the state of Soviet acquaintance with Western scholarship that Ugrinovich makes no reference to Wittgenstein's writings on religion, nor to those writers on religion, such as D.Z. Philipps, whom a Canadian critic, Kai Nielson, has dubbed 'Wittgensteinian fideists' – reference to which would have greatly strengthened his case.[2] But neither does he make reference to a whole host of contemporary Western students of religion who do *not* define religion in terms of internal criteria and who have sought for objective, universally valid, criteria for identifying religion.[3] Soviet scholars, it must be noted, can be highly selective in their use of Western sources.

Having dismissed Western scholarship as 'fideistic' – an approach to the understanding of religion which he traces back to Schleiermacher – Ugrinovich then puts forward what he takes to be the Marxist answer to the problem of the essence of religion. Drawing on an older tradition of Western scholarship, many Marxist students of religion have been heavily influenced in their search for an answer to this problem, Ugrinovich points out, by Tylor's 'minimum definition' of religion as 'animism'. However, in the light of both Soviet and foreign ethnographic and archaeological study of the wide variety of religious expression, this definition, he claims, must today be regarded as too narrow; not all expressions of religious consciousness are animistic: fetishism being a case in point. Here Ugrinovich refers to the research of the Soviet scholar, Y.P. Frantsov, which we will be considering in our next chapter. Suffice it to say, at the moment, that Ugrinovich regards Frantsov as having shown that fetishism is an earlier stage in the growth of religion than animism. Additional support for the case against 'animism' as a minimal definition of religion, Ugrinovich contends, can be found in the writings of the Soviet ethnographer, A.F. Anisimov who, on the basis of his study of the beliefs of the Evenk people of Siberia, has shown that, in the hunting magic of this people, what is termed *shingken'* — that is, the use of parts of the carcases of wild animals, teeth, skin, bones, etc., — is one to which no animistic notions are attached. Anisimov wrote:

The conceptions surrounding *shingken'* introduce us to an area of belief where supernatural attributes inhere in things themselves. These fetish-objects are not connected with any abstract conception of a soul which inheres in them. (Anisimov, 1958: p. 25)

The research of the earlier Soviet ethnographer, L.Y. Sternberg, Ugrinovich further contends, also lends additional support to this view. Sternberg had written:

We have only by virtue of a long historical evolution arrived at the intellectual conception of a soul which is completely separate from nature, and from the body. Among primitive people the soul is always associated with the body, or even with the blood. (Sternberg, 1936: p. 318)

On the basis of these remarks, Ugrinovich concludes that animistic conceptions do not exhaust primitive religious responses to the world, and he holds also that where we do come across undoubtedly animistic conceptions in primitive world-views, they are a development out of more concrete, visual and corporeal conceptions of the supernatural — that is, out of views in which material objects, or supposed connections between material objects, are themselves regarded as being supernatural.

Ugrinovich anticipates the objection that, whilst in the past there may have been religious beliefs which did not involve animism, in that these have now disappeared, animism might well serve as a minimum definition of religion as it is at the present time. However, ethnographical research, he replies, tells against this, for ethnographical research shows that 'fetishism' — the term which Ugrinovich, and Soviet 'scientific atheism' uses to designate the pre-animistic stage in the development of religion — is still prevalent today among many peoples in Africa, Asia and Australia and so must be considered in any attempted minimum definition of religion, even of religion today.

It is difficult for a Western student of religion to know quite what to make of this, so different is Western (and indigenous) understanding of the religions of these areas of the world, but as we shall be discussing Soviet views of early and primitive forms of religion in a later section (Section 4.4) we will forego comment here and simply note (a) the speculative nature of Ugrinovich's remarks — he offers few, if any, examples to support his argument — and (b) the rather simplistic understanding he has — from a Western point of view — of the traditional religions of Africa, Asia and Australia. No reference to recent Western and indigenous African study of these religions is made at all, studies which show the absurdity of describing these religions as 'fetishistic'.

Before Ugrinovich essays his own characterisation of religion, he takes up another topic with which Soviet study of religion has been greatly concerned — that is, the relationship of magic to religion. For him, as for many Western scholars today, magic and religion are inseparable in primitive religion, and he is thus led to a critique of the views of the British anthropologist Sir James Frazer, who has drawn a rigid distinction between the two.[4] Frazer failed to see, he contends, that magic, like religion, involves belief in the supernatural; that like religion, it is founded not on fact but on fiction, and that like religion it is born of illusion, in that it believes that human beings can, by the performance of certain rites and rituals, by the mere utterance of certain words, affect the processes of nature. The magician believes that that which exists only in his own consciousness can alter the course of nature. By concentrating only on the differences between magic and religion, Frazer ignored completely the most important thing about magic — namely, that it is an essential part of all religious activity. This is confirmed by the fact that even today magic is an essential ingredient in much religious activity, especially in the rituals of Catholicism and of the Russian Orthodox Church: in rituals designed to produce rain, avert natural disasters, bring about healing, and in the proclamation of anathemas.

Here, I think, Ugrinovich is on much safer ground, and I have myself argued elsewhere (Thrower, 1980: pp. 15-33) that the term 'magico-religious' is a better, because more apt, description of both archaic and of much modern religion than either 'magic' or 'religion' taken separately. To this point I shall be returning later in this study (Section 8.l).

Having shown, as he believes, that animism fails as a minimum definition of religion, Ugrinovich now raises the obvious question — what then does constitute a minimum definition of religion, without which, as he points out, the 'scientific' study of religion cannot get underway? And his answer is — and this is no individual opinion, for all Soviet writers on the history of religions support him in this (cf. Kryvelev, 1975 and Tokarev, 1976b: p. 15) — that the only definition of religion which will hold for all religions — past and present — is that religion is 'belief in the supernatural' ('vera v sverkh', yestestvennoye'). Only such a substantial definition can, he claims, incorporate the facts which he has previously adduced, and which he believes establish the fact that both 'fetishism' and 'magic', as well as 'animism', from which they must be distinguished, are an essential part of the religious world-view. It is 'belief in the supernatural' which, for Ugrinovich as for Soviet 'scientific atheism' in general, distinguishes a religious understanding of the world from a non-religious one. In seeking to explicate his use of the term 'supernatural', Ugrinovich points out that by 'belief in the supernatural' he understands 'not only belief in supernatural beings — gods, spirits, the soul, devils, etc., — but also belief in supernatural properties appertaining to certain physical objects (fetishism) and belief in supernatural connections obtaining between physical objects (magic, totemism)' (op. cit., p. 46). This, I shall argue in Part III of this study, is an important point.

Whilst 'belief in the supernatural' constitutes a *minimum* definition of religion for Soviet 'scientific atheism' it is not by any means thought of as constituting an exhaustive characterisation of

the religious outlook on the world. Equally important in charac-
terising the religious consciousness is the attitude (*otnosheniye*)
which religious believers take up towards the supernatural. It is
motivation, in fact, which distinguishes the religious from other
forms of consciousness which in the past, and indeed in the present, can be said to involve an awareness of the supernatural – as
in some forms of art and philosophy, for example: for religious
people it is not sufficient simply to believe in the supernatural,
they must also respond actively to it. There is, as Soviet scholars
now generally recognise, an emotional affective side to religion
which must not be underestimated. Any characterisation of the
religious consciousness must take due account of this – as indeed
must those engaged in the business of education in atheism.

But although Ugrinovich recognises that emotion plays a large
part in religion, he is careful to distinguish the kind of emotions
that he will be concerned to analyse from the emotions and feelings which some Western students of religion have seen as being of
the essence of the religious consciousness – and in particular he is
concerned to distance his own analysis from the views of both
Lévi-Bruhl and Rudolf Otto.

Lévi-Bruhl had maintained that religion arose out of an attitude
to the world which he called 'pre-logical', and which he took to
be one in which feelings of mystical participation predominated
(Lévi-Bruhl, 1935, 1938). Rudolf Otto had also maintained that
religion arose out of a specifically 'religious' emotional response to
the world – which he characterised in his now famous book *Das
Heilige* (1916) as consisting in feelings of both dread and fascination before a reality which he called the 'Numinous'. Ugrinovich's
criticism of both of these views is to deny that there are, or could
be, feelings which were specifically 'religious'. The emotional side
of religion can be understood, he contends, without resorting to
the postulation of such feelings. What, for him, differentiates the
feelings found in religion from feelings found in other activities is
not to be sought in the feelings themselves, but in the differing
objects to which they are directed, and the particularity of the
religious consciousness lies in its being directed, as he has argued

earlier, towards the supernatural. It is upon this that Ugrinovich now directs his attention, for there is one important aspect of man's relationship with the supernatural of which he intends to take note. He puts it as follows:

Religious man not only believes in the reality of the supernatural, not only postulates it, not only enters into an emotional relationship with it — he finds in his relation with the supernatural, practices which we can only call 'illusory' (*illyuzorno-prakticheskimi*). (Ugrinovich, 1966: p. 51)

By 'illusory practice' Ugrinovich means that religious people believe that supernatural beings are able to help them in their daily lives. Without this 'illusion' there would, Ugrinovich contends, be no religion. This is why magic plays such an important part in the majority of religions and it is also, he adds, why phenomena such as Deism failed to get a mass following. Every religion which has become a 'mass phenomenon', he claims, has always offered this 'illusion' of practical, utilitarian concourse with the supernatural — in the past and in the present. It is for this reason that all the great world religions are characterised by a cultus. A religion without a cultus would not be a religion but a form of philosophical idealism.

This latter point again seems to me an important one, and one grossly neglected in much Western study of religion, and I shall be returning to it in my discussion of the understanding of religion which we find in Soviet 'scientific atheism' in part III of this present study (Section 8.1).

Having now identified the distinguishing features of the religious consciousness, Ugrinovich turns next to what he terms its 'structure' (op. cit., pp. 53-57). He begins by making, what I myself think is an important point, and one which again is under-stressed in Western study of religion, and that is that in religion, as in other forms of social consciousness (including, I would myself add, Marxism-Leninism) we must distinguish between two broad levels of consciousness: between the ordinary, everyday consciousness of the vast mass of believers on the one hand, and official, institutional ideology on the other. A complete understanding of the phenomenon of religion, and certainly any attempt to influence the mass of religious believers must take this distinction into account. Those engaged in education in atheism must take particular note of this, for it is not sufficient simply to criticise religious dogma, or to criticise contemporary theology or philosophical idealism; progress in atheistic education will only come about when the peculiarities of the religious consciousness of the vast mass of believers – and especially of their emotional attachment to religion – is fully understood. This is the task, as we have seen earlier, which Soviet 'scientific atheism' sets before Soviet psychologists and Ugrinovich adds his voice to this.

Marxism, however, has, he claims, some distinctive insights to offer at this point. In particular, as Marx himself pointed out, religion, as a form of ideology, is class-based and it is for this reason that there exists, in fact, the distinction between the two levels of relationship to religious doctrine that Ugrinovich has already noted. Bearing in mind the fundamental distinction between mental and physical labour, the Marxist theoretician can well expect that the common religious consciousness of the masses, on account of the masses' closer relationship to the economic base, will be more affected by changes in that base than will be the consciousness of theologians and philosophers. The religion of the masses is more susceptible, Ugrinovich contends, to direct or immediate (*neposredstvennyy*) 'reflection' of the economic base. He writes:

The common religious consciousness is the totality of religious beliefs, feelings and moods, which to a considerable extent, is born as an elemental response reflecting the distress of people in the face of the social conditions of their life. In this respect it is possible to say that the ordinary religious consciousness is nearer to the economic base than is religious ideology (theology). It reflects the objective conditions of people more directly and more sensitively. (Ugrinovich, 1966: p. 54)

Pursuing this further, Ugrinovich, drawing on the work of the Soviet psychologist, A.I. Goryacheva, points out that Soviet social psychology has shown that the psyche is made up of two components – the one more stable, more conservative, the other more mobile, more sensitive to changes in the economic base (cf. Goryacheva, 1963: p. 61). In the light of its different relationships to the economic base, and mindful of the two aspects of the psyche to which Goryacheva has called attention, we can see that certain elements of the ordinary religious consciousness seek to conserve habits of life, making people set in their ways and more reluctant to accept change. It is chiefly these elements in the ordinary religious consciousness which are directly involved in the functioning of the religious cult. Other components, chiefly connected with the emotions, the so-called religious moods, are, on the other hand, highly volatile. Changes in social conditions are thus able, in this sphere of the social psyche to give rise very quickly to quite violent changes in religious consciousness. Thus Lenin noticed that the horror and despair of the 1914-1918 War served but to strengthen the religious feelings of the masses. Similarly, the plagues and epidemics of the Middle Ages in Europe were not without their effect on the religious life of the masses.

The difference between the religion of the masses and the official doctrines of the churches is nowhere more clearly to be found than in the early period in the growth of religions, before official doctrine had been clearly formulated and the masses brought under its influence, and Ugrinovich cites the early history of Christianity as a case in point. Soviet scholars are unanimous, he claims, in noting the vagueness, bordering on chaos, of early Christian ideology and he quotes from Y.P. Frantsov, who has described the early period of Christian history as one in which:

. . . there was still no stable outline of myth and no established dogma. In the different communities which were springing up, chaos, legend and variety of traditions were rife. (Frantsov, 1959: p. 468)

It is important to see, Ugrinovich continues, that whilst early Christianity consisted of a motley of traditions and was composed of a variety of beliefs, certain common themes, derived from the experience of the exploited masses in the Roman Empire, predominated — eschatology, messianism, etc. Here we can identify the sensitive reflection of the social conditions of the masses who yearned for release from bondage. Within the framework of the general social determination of ideas, a complicated dialectical interaction took place between the religious consciousness of ordinary people and religious ideology. The situation in which the masses found themselves laid them open to almost any religion which promised them release. Thus, if the masses did not actually produce the dogmas of Christianity, they gravitated towards them as answering to their need, and attached to them their feelings and hopes. Thus were the masses open to influences emanating from the churches and the churches placed in a position to develop their doctrines. Not that the churches did not pay attention to the beliefs that the masses brought with them, for we can trace in early Christianity a variety of beliefs drawn from traditions which predate the Christian religion.[5]

But religious ideology, argues Ugrinovich, is not just passive. Unlike the ordinary religious consciousness of the broad mass of people, religious ideology develops, as a rule, on the initiative of the ruling classes. It is they — or rather their intellectual representatives — who formulate and systematise doctrines; it is they who, in their own interests, bring order to the chaotic religious expression of the masses. This is not, of course, an entirely smooth process, as is seen, for example, in the conflict of interests between the prophets of Israel in the sixth century B.C. and the representatives of the established religion, and by the conflict within early Christianity between charismatic movements and the episcopacy. Similarly, in the Middle Ages, the Catholic church was continually plagued by reforming, schismatic movements which reflected the volatile religious consciousness of the masses. Luther and other leading Protestants who, in opposing the authority of the Catholic church were aided by the masses, seized on this form of religious expression as an aid to their own desire to break with Catholic doctrines and ceremony as 'reflective' of the feudal order with which they wished to have done. Not, Ugrinovich hastens to add, but that Protestantism did not quickly superimpose its own authority and order on the religious consciousness of the masses.

The difference between the common religious consciousness and religious ideology is seen not only in the differing relationship which each has to the economic base of society; it can also be seen in the differing structures which characterise the common religious consciousness and religious ideology. The common religious consciousness differs from religious ideology, that is, from theology, in that it is, above all else, unsystematic. The religious conceptions of the masses do not, as a rule, possess shape, agreement or consistency. The majority of ordinary believers do not carry around with them a formal theological system. The religious conception of the ordinary believer is, Ugrinovich contends, a jumble of separate ideas, images, mythological tales and such like. It does, however, in his opinion, possess one outstanding feature which he expresses as follows:

So far in our examination of the religious consciousness we have made much use of the terms 'belief' and 'conception'. In the sphere of the common religious consciousness there is little doubt that the abstract understanding implied by such terms has little place. What we have to do with here is rather concrete conceptions derived from the imagination. The 'sensual-concrete' (chuvstvennokonkretnyy), graphic character of the mass religious consciousness does not happen by chance, but flows from the specific peculiarities of religion. As we have said earlier, one of the peculiarities of the common religious consciousness is the spontaneity of its emotional relationship with religion. Out of this emotional attitude to the objects of religious belief it necessarily follows that the object of religious belief must be presented to the ordinary believer in concrete, visual form. (Ugrinovich, 1966: pp. 57-58)

This figurative (obraznyy) character of the common religious consciousness is particularly, but by no means exclusively, evident in primitive religion, for it is by means of myth that primitive men seek to present their awareness of the world. Mythology, however, as Ugrinovich recognises, is far from being wholly understood, and he therefore contents himself with remarking that mythology has to do with graphic narration of the doings of supernatural beings and entities. Myth is, in fact. as was recognised by Plekhanov, an essential element in all religion.[6] It is also closely related to art, and Ugrinovich's view is that when people cease to believe in the truth of events recounted in myth, myth then becomes art.

That primitive religion had this graphic character Ugrinovich proceeds to illustrate from the Bible, whose style and structure of presentation bears little resemblance to philosophical or theological writings. He writes:

Being, in its original form, a fusion of ancient mythology, ritual, political and moral prescriptions and of the artistry of its time, the Bible is a heterogeneous and complex work. But overall, despite its variety of content, the Bible presents its ideas in concrete, graphic, mythological form. In this respect the Bible is to be distinguished from Christian dogmatics as formulated by the Churches of a later time. The decrees of the Bible in particular can be understood if we take into account the conditions of their origin. The individual parts of the Old Testament came into being at a time when men were still living in primitive conditions on the threshold of class society. Many myths were borrowed by the Jews from other peoples and thus appertain to an even earlier period. The New Testament, which was created in the period of the growth of slave-owning society, is extremely interesting in that the attitudes which we find in many parts of it are the product of the mythological creations of the lower classes who formed the majority in early Christian society. In this respect the New Testament is to a large degree the product of the common religious consciousness. It was of and for the masses and this explains the peculiarly graphic nature of the greater part of its mythology. (Ugrinovich, 1966: pp. 58-59)

This elemental upsurge of the common religious consciousness was soon, however, to be submerged in the official theology of what was to become the established church.

There remains one further important difference which Ugrinovich wishes to note between the common religious consciousness and the theological doctrines of the churches, and that is the tremendous role played by emotional processes in the consciousness of ordinary believers. We should notice, he says, not simply the feelings which pave the way for religion and which assist its origin, but those which are characteristic of believers at all times. Only these latter can strictly be called 'religious feelings'. These are, as we should now realise, highly complex, and we show our ignorance of them if we concentrate on one simple feeling, such as fear. Ugrinovich is not alone in this implied criticism of earlier Marxist-Leninist criticism of religion which saw religion as arising almost wholly out of fear. Another 'scientific atheist', V. Bukin, has similarly criticised earlier Marxist accounts of religion on just this account (cf. V. Bukin, 1963: p. 69).

This, we should note, represents a considerable advance in the Soviet understanding of religion and one not always recognised in Western writing on the Soviet understanding of religion (cf. Bocheński, 1974: pp. 1-16). A Marxist understanding of religion will seek, Ugrinovich argues, to relate the various feelings involved in upholding a religious view of the world to particular religions and to particular periods. It is on that account wise not to try to be too general when we speak of the emotional side of religion. This will be found to be relative to different historical periods.

It soon becomes clear why Ugrinovich emphasises this point, for when he passes, finally, to confront what is the all-important question for Soviet 'scientific atheism' – why does religion persist in Soviet society? – he can answer this question – in the light of the approach to religion which he has adopted – by changing it into the question – what are the specific emotions which keep religion in being in the period of socialist society? These must – by the very nature of the Marxist analysis of religion as a 'reflection' of the socio-economic base of society – be very different from the emotions which keep religion in being in capitalist society. 'The Marxist historian of religion must', Ugrinovich writes, 'study the particularity of the mass religious consciousness at any given time and in any given country and in any given class'. However, as he adds, 'this work has hardly begun' (1966: p. 60). It is to Ugrinovich's credit, however, that he recognises this task as the logical outcome of the Marxist-Leninist analysis of religion. Further, he says that Marxists must study especially the religious consciousness of the different classes which make up contemporary capitalist society and must also show how different is the consciousness of believers who are workers from that of those who belong to the peasantry and to the petty bourgeoisie, and this as a matter of practical policy to be pursued on behalf of the Party.

A more urgent task, however, is the study of the ordinary, everyday religious consciousness of believers who live in socialist societies, that is in societies where the socio-economic base is very different to that which characterises capitalist societies. In socialist society the social roots of religion — reflected in the religious consciousness of the classes in capitalist society — no longer exist, and thus it cannot be what Ugrinovich terms 'objective social attitudes' (*ob''yektivnyye obshchestvennyye otnosheniya*) which make for the persistence of religion in that society. But if this is the case, what then is the cause of religion's persistence in socialist society? Only research into the religiosity of Soviet people, and in particular research into the psychology of the religious consciousness of workers who are believers, will provide the answer to this important question, says Ugrinovich, and there he leaves the matter. Not a very satisfactory state of affairs, but one which must be recognised before it can be remedied. 'Scientific atheism' has work to do. We shall be looking at some of the results of 'concrete' sociological research in this area later (Section 7.1).

Before concluding his article, Ugrinovich looks at one other principle aspect of the religious consciousness, and that is at theology and particularly at the claim made by theology to be a science. This, as we would expect, he dismisses. Theology and science, he says, look at the working of the world in different ways: Science is naturalistic and materialistic, theology supernaturalistic, in that it holds that God and other supernatural beings can alter the processes of nature. Further, historically considered, theology has impeded the advance of scientific understanding and has, at times, been avowedly anti-rationalist, if not indeed positively irrationalist — Tertullian and Bernard of Clairvaux being cases in point. To illustrate his case Ugrinovich cites a battery of references from recent articles in the *Journal of the Moscow Patriarchate*, before concluding that theology professes a 'knowledge' which it does not have. It can appeal only to the ignorant, for the 'objects' which it introduces into its discourse are illusory.

Such is the understanding of what is involved in religious belief put forward by a scholar who is regarded as being among the foremost of Soviet 'sceintific atheists'. It is for this reason that I have made the extensive reference to it that I have. It is not a particularly deep analysis and there is little in it, other perhaps than the recognition of a range of problems that we might call 'emotional', that takes us beyond the earlier Soviet conception of religion as a complex of false beliefs about the workings of the world. Ugrinovich's acquaintance with Western study of religion – and in particular with the disciplines of *Religionswissenschaft* and socio-anthropology – is limited and dated. It is also, as are his references to theology, selective – culled to support a case, rather than chosen with any attempt to seriously come to terms with religion. And yet, as I shall argue in Part III of this study, much to which Ugrinovich calls attention is important and, for whatever reason, is given little space in Western study of religion. The study of the 'common religious consciousness' is important, and Ugrinovich is right to attempt to delineate it, and to point to the differences between it and a theological understanding of religion, which so often in Western writing on Christianity, and on religions other than Christianity, is presented as if it was the whole of religion. His emphasis on religion as cult, and his insistence that so far as the majority of believers are concerned religion is what religion does, is one that Western students are now themselves beginning to emphasise.

From the point of view of Soviet study of religion, however, the importance of Ugrinovich's remarks lies in the range of problems which he identifies as the problems with which Marxist-Leninist historians, sociologists and psychologists should be concerned. Soviet historians, he says, must seek to show the connection, in any given period, between the socio-economic base of society and the religious attitudes to which it gives rise, and Soviet sociologists and psychologists must explore the religiosity of contemporary Soviet believers in an attempt to discover the *non-social sources* of their belief. In recognising that religion can be the outcome of attitudes which are not a reflection of the socio-economic base, Ugrinovich gives tacit expression to what has become *the* problem in Soviet study of religion. It is a problem which, as we saw earlier, was also stressed by Okulov and Gorbachev (Section 3.2). It is here that, to succeed, Soviet 'scientific atheism' must go beyond what it finds in the writings of Marx, Engels and Lenin. At the present time, however, it has done little beyond identifying the problem. How far 'scientific atheism' will eventually go in its analysis of the non-social sources of contemporary religion only the future will show. How far a satisfactory analysis of religion must go beyond the almost exclusively social understanding of the sources of religion as set forth in the classical sources of Marxism-Leninism I shall argue later in Part III of this study.

4.2   THE PHILOSOPHICAL CRITIQUE OF RELIGION

Marx and Engels assumed, rather than argued, the falsity of religious claims and Lenin, whilst he did, in the course of his more general criticism of philosophical idealism, have certain things to say about the untenability of religious beliefs, was on the whole more concerned to oppose the influence of religious institutions than to refute their claims. Until quite recently Soviet 'scientific atheism' also believed it sufficient to oppose religion by exposing its social and psychological roots, as these had been revealed in the classics of Marxism-Leninism, and to show the incompatibility of religion with natural science. Experience of the tenacity of religion and the renewal of theology and religious apologetic in the West has, however, of late, led some Soviet philosophers to a more sustained philosophical critique of religion and of religious beliefs. This has issued in renewed criticism of belief in God and criticism of the contemporary religious claim that religion alone can answer the fundamental needs of man.

With regard to belief in God, the arguments which contemporary Soviet 'scientific atheism' adduces against this belief seek to demonstrate that the properties and functions traditionally attributed to God conflict with the most assured results of modern science.[7] For example: the God of traditional theism is presented as being immaterial or spiritual; 'scientific atheism' asserts that such a Being cannot possibly exist since contemporary science has shown that all that exists is material. The assumptions underlying this argument are (1) that the science in question is what is usually referred to as 'hard science' (physics, chemistry, biology), and (2) that this science has found no evidence (i.e., sense-verifiable proof) for the existence of any immaterial beings; a conclusion of course, which is in accord with the basic priniciple of the only truly 'scientific' philosophy – the philosophy of dialectical materialism, according to which all is matter or a function of matter. Where contemporary science – or, to be more precise, some contemporary *scientists* – appear to question this assumption, this aberration, as it is believed to be, is accounted for, not as arising from any new insights into the objective world, but as explicable in terms of the *social* commitment of the scientists in question. As a contemporary classic of Marxism-Leninism in the Soviet Union proclaims:

The victory of socialism in the Soviet Union, and subsequently in the other countries that now form the world system of socialism, has sharply intensified the ideological commitment of bourgeois philosophy, making it an inseparable element in the incessant war that imperialist propaganda wages against the world of socialism. Modern bourgeois philosophy provides a unique reflection of the contradictions of capitalist society at the present stage of its development. . . (*The Fundamentals of Marxist-Leninist Philosophy:* p. 599)

And one important aspect of this crisis in bourgeois philosophy – of which Existentialism as the philosophy of despair is another – is, for Marxist-Leninism, the 'fundamental change in the bourgeois attitude to science' (ibid., p. 601). Whereas, says Marxism-Leninism, the ideologists of the revolutionary bourgeoisie in the seventeenth and eithteenth centuries proceeded from scientific philosophy and believed in the power of human reason, many contemporary bourgeois philosophers propose the rejection of both reason and science, or at least seek to impose severe restrictions on their sphere of competence.

Whilst this is, of course, an exaggeration, what Marxist-Leninist philosophers mean to indicate by such statements is either the position taken by a number of scientists in the West to the effect that science itself is ultimately neutral with regard to world views, or else they mean to refer to the reticence which some scientists have expressed about the possibility of a 'science of society' - a reticence which Marxism-Leninism believes to be based on a reluctance to face the fact that Communism will eventually (and inevitably) replace bourgeois society (ibid., p. 602).

Further, and more relevant to the Marxism-Leninism's immediate task of refuting bourgeois science's flirtation with the supernatural, the crisis brought about in modern science by the overthrow of the nineteenth century picture of the world by the revolution associated with the rise of relativity and quantum mechanics, far from casting doubt on science, is held, by Marxist-Leninists, to be a confirmation of dialectical materialism. Marxism-Leninism puts this as follows:

Any knowledge, including concrete scientific knowledge, is relative truth, and this is something that metaphysically thinking natural scientists cannot admit. The revolution in the natural sciences, as a result of which the physical picture of the 19th-century world yielded place to a new picture based on the theory of relativity and quantum mechanics, confirms the truth of dialectical materialism. But the speed and unexpectedness with which one picture of the world was superseded by another evoked the rejection of materialist epistemology by quite a number of scientists. . . The denial of science's right to objective truth, and the sceptical underestimation of the significance of science in building a world outlook, have continued to dominate bourgeois philosophy to this day, determining the character of its propositions in many respects. (*FMLP:* pp. 602-603)

Thus bourgeois intellectuals, bereft of the insights of dialectical materialism, have reacted to the changed outlook of science by either reducing philosophy to epistemology, and by seeing the function of philosophy as that of analysing the language of science (the Logical Positivists), or by espousing some form of irrationalism (Existentialism or religion). Either way bourgeois intellectuals proclaim the bankruptcy of bourgeois philosophy and of bourgeois society which it 'reflects'.

Having thus dismissed the claimed neutrality of bourgeois philosophy and science with regard to a religious understanding of the world, Marxism-Leninism can return to its own self-proclaimed 'scientific' refutation of religion, which is based, as in the later writings of Engels and with Lenin on the materiality of the world.

Among the more Marxist arguments for the non-existence of God found in contemporary Soviet 'scientific atheism' is the argument from man's self-sufficiency. Here it is held that God is not the real creator of man because man makes himself through his own labour. Man creates both himself and his world by his own effort. As the culmination of the evolutionary process man shares in matter's self-sufficiency and auto-dynamism. The 'achievements' of the Soviet Union itself and of the 'Socialist Countries' are often adduced in support of this point.

By the same token it is also unnecessary to postulate God as the creator and guarantor of values. The fundamental value is man and his aspirations, as expressed in the goals of the proletariat and its Marxist-Leninist Party. Only the bourgeois world of metaphysically fixed values, which serve to perpetuate the position of the exploiters in class society, has need of a creator.

Finally, proclaims 'scientific atheism', the God of traditional theism is shrouded in mystery; even those theologians and philosophers who have offered proofs of his existence have not pretended to prove more than his existence, agreeing that nothing positive can be affirmed about his nature or activities — unless, of course, he chooses to reveal it. Believers, therefore, so Soviet 'scientific atheism' contends, wallow in what amounts to openly admitted irrationalism, maintaining that nothing can be known about the object of their devotion until the beatific vision in the hereafter. Such a being, so 'scientific atheism' maintains, cannot exist, for all that exists is knowable or at least intelligible. If the God of religious belief existed he would, after so many centuries of religion and theology, be known. As he is not, he does not exist.

These are the major arguments which Soviet 'scientific atheism' brings against belief in God. They can be summarised as follows: God is traditionally held to be immaterial, to be the creator of the world, of man and of values and to be shrouded in mystery. But science and dialectical materialism have demonstrated that a being with such properties is both superfluous and impossible. Therefore, God does not exist. All, therefore, that remains is to show why people have believed in God for the matter to be closed. This is done, overall, by an appeal to what Marx and Engels had to say about religion as a response to a condition of alienation. As put forward by Soviet 'scientific atheism' this is, for the most part, attenuated to the view that religion is simply an escape mechanism from the burdens of class society, although, as we have indicated, there has been some attempt, of late, to deepen this analysis, both by renewed attention of the original Marxist analysis of alienation and by study of the psychology of religious believers.

But, for 'scientific atheism', it is not sufficient simply to demonstrate — in the ways we have outlined — the non-existence of God; the ongoing struggle with bourgeois ideology also demands that the arguments put forward by theologians and religiously-minded philosophers for the existence of God also be refuted. These arguments 'scientific atheism' reduces to five: (1) the ontological proof of Anselm, Descartes and Leibnitz; (2) the cosmological argument of Aquinas and contemporary neo-Thomists; (3) the teleological argument; (4) what is termed the 'historical or psychological' argument developed by Descartes — more commonly known in the West as the argument from the general consent of mankind; and (5) the ethical argument, associated in the history of philosophy with the name of Kant.

The ontological proof, as understood by 'scientific atheism', maintains that God is conceived as the absolutely perfect concept. If this concept lacked a feature (*priznak*) as essential as 'being', then it would not be perfect. Therefore, God must exist. This, 'scientific atheism' maintains, is simply 'scholasticism'. At bottom, the ontological argument argues from the existence of a concept to the existence of a real being corresponding to this idea. This is illegitimate. All that the ontological argument can establish is the existence of the concept of God — which none would wish to deny (*KNAS:* p. 177).

The cosmological argument, which seeks to argue from the contingency of the world to a creator who is an unconditionally necessary being, fails, according to 'scientific atheism', to ask about the cause of this cause of all things. Besides, if there is something which is eternal and uncaused then it is material nature, the existence of which is completely evident, rather than a God whose existence has to be proved. But the untenability of the cosmological argument only became fully evident, so 'scientific atheism' maintains, with the advent of dialectical materialism, which demonstrates the falsity of the view that a cause is simply external to its effect (*KNAS*: p. 176).

The teleological argument, which seeks to argue from purposiveness in nature to an intelligent designer of the world, not only ignores disteleology, that is the purposelessness which we observe in much of nature, but also ignores the facts of suffering and injustice. It was Darwin, however, who, for 'scientific atheism', finally disproved the teleological argument by showing that the so-called purposiveness of nature is due to natural and not supernatural causes, and it was Marx and Engels who gave a scientific explanation of the course of history and, by getting at the true causes of social phenomena, removed any basis that the teleological argument might have been thought to have (*KNAS:* pp. 176-177).

'Scientific atheism' seeks to refute the historical or psychological argument which holds that belief in God is universal among men, by pointing out that, as a matter of fact, not all people have believed in God, that even where they have, their ideas about God have differed widely, and that often what people have worshipped has not been the God of traditional theism, but a series of anthropomorphic and zoomorphic supernatural beings, whose existence cannot be proved in the way that the historical or psychological argument seeks to prove the existence of the God i.e., by arguing that as our knowledge is imperfect and limited, the conception of a God who is perfect and unlimited can only have been implanted in our minds by such a perfect and unlimited Being (*KNAS:* p. 177).

The ethical argument, which seeks to argue to God on the basis of man's claimed knowledge of an immutable and universal ethical law and, in its Kantian version, on the supposed ultimate reconciliation of duty and happiness in a *Summum Bonum* after death, 'scientific atheism' seeks to refute by denying that there is such a universally recognised moral law. Morality, it claims, is class-determined and ethical norms come into being on the basis of the social conditions in which social groups and classes live. They are dictated by the interests of these social groups and they vary in the course of history. Society itself is the source of morality, and it does not require a supernatural being to explain its existence (*KNAS:* p. 177).

Analogous arguments are used by Soviet 'scientific atheists' to disprove the existence of an immortal soul — nothing but what is material exists; of religious mysteries — all is knowable; of angels and saints and to demonstrate the inanity of religious rites — they are offered to a non-entity. In general the futility of all religion is considered to have been established when it has been shown that it has no objective referent.

Whilst arguments along the lines portrayed above are repeated in almost all standard expositions of 'scientific atheism' in the Soviet Union today, there have been attempts recently to offer a somewhat more sophisticated philosophical analysis of the roots of religion; the most interesting attempt, in my opinion, being that put forward by P. Cherkashin in a book entitled *Gnoseologicheskiye korni idealizma* (The Epistemological Roots of Idealism) published in 1964. This book deals, in fact, with the roots of both idealism and religion, in that, for Marxism-Leninism, idealism is conceived (*pace* Lenin) as but a refined philosophical expression of religion. For Cherkashin there are two major 'roots' of religion — the epistemological and the social, although in this present work he deals only with the former.

The epistemological roots of idealism and religion fall within the purview of Marxism-Leninism's theory of knowledge where, following Engels, all the basic categories are defined in terms of 'the basic question of all philosophy' – whether matter or spirit is primary. Materialists maintain that matter is primary and that spirit is secondary. Thought is both a reflection and a function of matter, and as such is the natural operation of the most complex and highly developed of all matter – the brain. As a reflection of material processes thought also involves a subjective dialectic, that is, a dialectical reproduction of the dialectic that operates in the objective world of material reality. Knowledge, therefore, is either sense-knowledge or logical knowledge. (Thus far Marxism-Leninism would appear to agree with Logical Positivism, which also divides meaningful propositions into matters of fact and matters of logic, but there, of course, the similarity ends.) Sense-knowledge is basically concrete, logical knowledge abstract. Truth is either relative or absolute. Practice is both the basis of know-ledge and the criterion of its truth.

Granted this framework, the epistemological roots of idealism and religion are, Cherkashin maintains, those aberrations of thought which arise from an illegitimate prolongation of an otherwise normal cognitive function. Idealism and religion arise, he contends, not because of a basic malfunctioning of the process whereby we reach knowledge of reality, but because of the non-observance of the limits of a perfectly normal function. Cherka-shin isolates three such areas of non-observance of this limit: (1) those dealing with sense-knowledge; (2) those dealing with logical knowledge and (3) those involving an opposition between the metaphysical and the dialectical ways of looking at reality.

With regard to sense-knowledge, Marxist-Leninists adhere strictly to the old empirical principle *nihil in intellectu nisi prius fuerit in sensibus*, though they recognise also a certain subjectivity in sensation and admit that the subject exercises a synthesising function in the formation of perceptions. It is extremism in the interpretation of both of these functions that leads to a peculiar type of opening for idealism and religion, the commonest cause being the absolutisation of sensation as the primary and unique cognitive given. The argument for idealism and religion Cherkashin reconstructs as follows: sense-perceived things are ideas; ideas exist only in minds; therefore sense-perceived things exist only in minds. By absolutising sensation idealist philosophers arrive at the denial of the existence of anything outwith sensation, and it is thus senseless to talk of matter which we can never know. Dialectical materialism, on the other hand, whilst it holds to sensation as the unique and primary cognitive given, maintains that sensation is the sensation of something, and that, consequently, its primacy and uniqueness are relative to the matter which it reflects. Idealism, however, by denying the existence of matter, gives primacy to the subject and thus clears the way for the postulates of religion.

The mistake of idealism is that, in absolutizing the subjective element of sensation, it forgets that alongside the subjective element there is the objective aspect of sensation, that is, the fact that it is the reflection of objective, material reality. Dialectical materialism, however, holds, on the contrary, that the subjective moment in sensation is but the necessary correlate of the more fundamental, objective moment which is its reflection of the material world. The subjective moment is necessary, since sense-knowledge is the work of the individual knower whose personal traits and situation influence the way in which he receives external stimuli, but this subjective moment is, by its very nature, secondary to that material objectivity which makes up the fundamental aspect of sensation and saves it from solipsism. Idealist stress on subjectivity leads to the engulfing of the object by the subject, and so surrenders cognition to religious obscurantism.

Similar consequences result, for Cherkashin, from the idealist absolutisation of the subject's synthesising function in the formation of perceptions. Once again, by ignoring the material source of the data involved in this analytic process, which necessarily precedes the synthesising function, idealists maintain that the essence of the percept is produced by the subject and that the subject is, therefore, the creator of perception. Again, dialectical materialism, whilst recognising the synthesising role of the subject in the production of perceptions, insists that this has significane only within the total context of the formation of percepts where one must take into account the preliminary analytic function which, in turn, can only be based on data from the objective, material world, of which all knowledge is but a reflection. Thus we see that idealism, by attributing to the subject the sole responsibility for the creation of all that is contained in sensation, paves the way for the notion of a God, who is brought in to guarantee the veracity of our intra-personal experience, rather in the manner in which Berkeley, according to common misrepresentations of Berkeley, introduced him into his theory of knowledge.

The most familiar path to idealism and religion, says Cherkashin, is when philosophers absolutise the distinction between sense-knowledge and logical thought. The dialectically contradictory character of the cognitive process makes it easy for the undiscerning to lay stress on one type of knowledge to the exclusion or depreciation of the other. Dialectical materialism, however, teaches that the 'sense-particular' and the 'abstract-general' are mutually complementary dialectical contradictories. In addition to real, individual, material things there also exists, in objective, material reality, the universal, in the form of universal laws and bonds which connect all real things into a harmonious whole. On the other hand, in addition to the abstract-general, there exists in thought, in the subjective dialectic, that is, the concrete-singular, which is a representation in the subjective dialectic of the objective dialectic in all its ontological and historical detail. The one interpenetrates the other, and must do so, since any separation would destroy both, and overemphasis of either leads to religion. Overemphasis on the sense-particular (nominalism) forces those who do so to attribute to sensation qualities only proper to logical thought and, thereby, to fall into one of the absolutisations of the functions of sensation described earlier; overemphasis on the abstract-general (idealism) produces the view whereby the abstract-general is given an existence apart from its material source and matter is made dependent on thought. This paves the way to a religious outlook, Cherkashin maintains.

The absolutisation of the creativity of logical knowledge is the

counterpart, on the level of logical knowledge, of the absolutisation of the subject's synthesising function in the formation of
perceptions, although the former is the more serious and leads
more quickly to idealism and religion owing to the distance which
separates logical knowledge from material reality. Dialectical
materialism, whilst recognising the creative role of the subject of
such knowledge, emphasises also that, however abstract such
thought, it still reflects material realities, and that human practice
is the basis of all knowledge and the ultimate criterion of truth.
This means that logical knowledge is creative only because of the
needs of practice and that the results of its creativity are legitimate
only in terms of practice. Idealism, on the other hand, by giving
free range to abstract creative thought, gives respectability to the
most fantastic creations of religion – God, angels, spirits and so on.

The fundamental error in metaphysical thinking – by which
Marxism-Leninism means all non-dialectical thinking – is, for
Cherkashin, that it ignores motion, isolates aspects which should
not be isolated, and is generally one-sided and fixed in its view of
things. The epistemological roots of idealism and religion, which
result from this wrong methodological approach to the understanding of reality, are the artificial separation of the universal
from the particular, of the ideal from the real, and of the absolute
from the relative. These are, however, best viewed as possible
aberrations in the operation of man's cognitive apparatus, as pro-
pensities which need to be activated before they lead to idealism
and religion, and their activation is explained by Cherkashin in
terms of historical materialism's interpretation of the structure
and development of society. The activating elements are known
as the social roots of religion – fear of nature, fear of the blind
forces of social development and of class-pressure, class-interest
and so on. As we have dealt with these earlier we need not go over
what we then said, except to say that, for the philosophical
critique of religion, it is these social roots which serve as occasions
for the development of the epistemological roots which are
essential in determining the origin and character of religion as a
false ideology. There has, however, been no attempt on the part

of Marxist-Leninist 'scientific atheists' to correlate the ideological and the social roots of religion more closely, yet this would seem imperative if this thesis regarding the origin of religion is to be sustained.

In this doctrine of the epistemological and social roots of religion we are, I think, confronted by something very specific to Marxism-Leninism; few other philosophies discuss these matters and none do so in quite this way. There are, however, a number of questions that will occur immediately to the student of religion irrespective of the truth or otherwise of Marxist-Leninist claims. The student of religion cannot deny, of course, that religious doctrines are influenced by the society in which they occur. On the other hand, the student of religion will also be aware that religion is not just a cognitive operation, as well as of the fact that religion is not exclusively a social phenomenon. Religion relates to the whole of man's being and the student of religion may well ask why Marxism-Leninism isolates the epistemological and social aspects for special analysis? The best explanation is in terms of the nature of Marxism-Leninism itself which is – essentially – an epistemology. All of its terms are defined with reference (direct or indirect) to thought, and all of its enemies it invariably condemns for epistemological aberrations. Further, Marxism-Leninism is peculiar in having a doctrine of society as an integral part of its total philosophical outlook. Philosophy is for it 'the science of the most general laws of nature, society and human thought' (*FMLP:* p. 33). It is thus natural that Marxism-Leninism should view religion – its counterpart, as we have seen – as essentially constituted by these same two factors. We shall have more to say on this matter in our critical assessment of the Marxist-Leninist understanding of religion at the outset of Part III of this study. For the moment, we must again point out that the epistemological factors which contemporary 'scientific atheism' lists as lying at the roots of religion are as valid as Marxist-Leninist epistemology is valid and this also we shall be discussing in Part III of this study.

There is, however, one weakness in the general Marxist-Leninist analysis of the epistemological roots of religion which we should mention at this point. It is this: each of the roots we have seen Marxist-Leninism identifying as lying at the basis of the religious understanding of the world is a breach, so it maintains, of one or other 'dialectical unity' in the operation of man's cognitive process, and can be reduced, therefore, to the opposition between 'the dialectical' and 'the metaphysical' — as contemporary Marxist-Leninist philosophers conceive this. The 'metaphysician' views reality, Marxist-Leninists maintain, in terms of fixed concepts, without motion, without seeing the essential connections between things. If this means anything — which many Western philosophers doubt — then all it means is that the metaphysician is thinking — and can he, in fact, think otherwise? — in terms of fixed concepts. Western philosophers have found it exceedingly difficult to get Marxist-Leninist philosophers to provide examples of unfixed, moving concepts and some would say that it is impossible to do so. What many Western philosophers deny is that the ebb and flow of reality can be described without using fixed and relatively motionless concepts, for, as one Western metaphysician has said:

All the mystical annointment of dialectic cannot change the brute fact that when one thinks one must use relatively stable concepts or (to keep the anti-concept group happy) univocally defined terms. If the dialectical materialists have discovered a new way in which to think, all we can say about it at present is that it is incommunicable and, therefore, irrelevant to science. (Blakely, 1967: p. 77)

With regard to the philosophical refutation of religious claims that a religious sense is innate in man and that only religion can, therefore, fully satisfy human aspirations, Soviet 'scientific atheism', as we have seen from our discussion of the early part of Ugrinovich's paper in 'The Essence of the Religious Consciousness', meets this claim with the counter claim of absolute denial (Section 4.1). Such feelings as are involved in religion are — so Soviet psychologists claim — no different to feelings devoted to other and non-supernatural entities (cf. Bukin and Bukina 1962, 1964). What 'scientific atheism' must do is to seek to re-direct such feelings towards natural objects and objectives, such as the

Party, mankind, Communism, etc. Whether such objects and objectives will ultimately bear the emotional weight thus thrust upon them is, I would have thought, very much an open question and it is a question to which I shall return in a rather different context in Part III (Section 9.2). Certainly, it is on this issue that Western critics of 'scientific atheism' have, above all else, focussed their attention.

4.3   THE INCOMPATIBILITY OF NATURAL SCIENCE WITH RELIGION

Criticism of religion on the score of its claimed incompatibility with natural science lies at the heart of popular Soviet anti-religious apologetic.[8] It also, as we have seen, underlies the standard philosophical critique of religion of 'scientific atheism'. Yet, despite the centrality of this claimed incompatibility between science and religion, little serious study of this has actually taken place, and Soviet 'scientific atheism' has tended to rest content with what is essentially, for it, an assumption, supporting this, where possible, with illustration taken either from the history of religion, or from some of the more bizarre practices and beliefs of the more backward sections of its own population. This was the staple diet of the anti-religious journals of the 1930's (particularly of the journal *Bezbozhnik* − The Godless) and it can still be found today in the milder and, on the whole, more sophisticated journal, *Nauka i religiya* (Science and Religion). Where some Western and, indeed, some Soviet scientists of repute, such as Sakharov, seem to flirt with a religious understanding of the world this, as we have also seen, is summarily dismissed as arising from causes unrelated to the scientific understanding of the world. Here we touch on what is, in my opinion, the most 'closed' area in Soviet thought today, an area where even to discuss the possibility of a *rapprochement* between science and religion is seen as striking at the most fundamental (and, therefore, unfortunately, unexaminable) assumptions of the Soviet world-view. In this area open discussion is impossible and Marxist-Leninist dialectical materialism is, therefore, presented rather than argued.

So far as concerns the materiality of the world, many Western philosophers of science would, of course, agree with Marxist-Leninists. As the well-known American philosopher of science, Herbert Feigl wrote in a paper on the 'Critique of Dialectical Materialism:

Most scientific empiricists consider theological or speculative metaphysical doctrines at least fruitless, if not (in some of their claims) simply false, and, in some of their formulations, even factually meaningless. Hence there is also a positive agreement regarding man's place in nature and society (with Marxist-Leninists). The dialectical materialists discredit theological supernaturalism primarily by pointing to its plausible origins in anthropomorphic and wishful thinking, and its perpetuation by religious institutions in the light of their socio-economic settings and functions. They prepare the ground for and supplement the logic-analytic critique offered by the scientific empiricists; a critique which rests on distinctions any honest thinker must make between the cognitive and the non-cognitive types of meaning, or the corresponding functions of language. As soon as one grasps the difference between *information* on the one hand, and *exhortation* (consolation, edification, fortification) on the other, it becomes clear that religious language (whether or not within the frame of a theology) at best conveys a moral message, but is devoid of informational content. . . many scientific empiricists would join forces with the dialectical materialists in maintaining that there is no good reason whatever for accepting the truth-claims of the theologians. (Feigl, 1974: pp. 108-109)

The point I want to make is that, whilst there are many philosophers (and non-philosophers) in the West who would agree with Feigl — and so, so far as concerns philosophical materialism, with Marxist-Leninists also — the issue between them and philosophers who think differently is still an open one, to the extent that controversy between intellectually equal opponents still takes place at all levels of society — in the serious journals, in the lecture hall, in the debating chamber, and in 'the media' and argument, refutation and reformulation of argument goes on. In the Soviet Union, this is not so, and the consequence, so far as concerns the critique or religion, is that dialectical materialism is presented as if any rational alternative not only does not but *could not* exist. The religious believer is, therefore, not only regarded as wrong in his views, he is represented as an ignorant fool, whose ignorance must be socially accounted for. Thus, L.N. Mitrokhin can write:

Religion is not simply an error of the mind, not some incorrect conception of this or that law of nature and society. It is a world-view, reflecting and embodying a certain attitude of man towards society, a certain understanding of his place in it. Education (if, of course, we take it not from a formal point of view but as a means of assimilating socio-cultural values) — is one of the features of the given person's connection with society. *Of course, religion and semi-literacy accompany each other.* But the effect of religious ideas on a person is determined not by the fact that he is semi-literate, but by the fact that in this case we are dealing with a man who finds himself in a certain relationship to society, and semi-literacy itself appears as one of the signs of this relationship. (Mitrokhin, 1967: p. 49 (my italics))

It is perhaps not beside the point in this respect to note that Feigl, despite his agreement with Marxist-Leninist philosophical materialism, is merciless in his criticism of the further formulation of it as 'dialectical', concluding that:

Once one replaces the dialectical formulae (the Hegelian triad, the interpenetration of the opposites, the 'negation of the negation') by straightforward modern scientific language, nothing of their intended scientific significance would be lost, and an enormous gain in conceptual clarity would be achieved.

In sum, it seems to me (he continues) that the leftovers of Hegelian verbiage in current dialectical materialism have tended to petrify and fossilise their doctrines. This is something that should not have happened to a radical and revolutionary movement that prides itself on its forward-looking philosophy. One can only hope that once the fossils are removed, the thus enlightened representatives of dialectical materialism will get ready for one more revolution in their thought and join forces with the defenders of the *critical* approach, of the policy of the open mind, and of the open society! (op. cit., p. 115)

Two extremely typical examples of the dogmatic presentation of dialectical materialism as the only possible phisosophy of science are, in fact, found in the papers presented to the international symposium, from which Feigl's remarks are taken, by the two Soviet participants P.V. Kopnin and V.V. Mshvenieradze (cf.

Somerville and Parsons, edit., 1974: pp. 5-30). Their replies to Fiegl's and others' extremely severe criticism of their views is, unfortunately, not recorded.

It is not, however, the uncritical nature of Soviet self-confidence in the 'scientific' character of dialectical materialism that concerns me at the moment, but the consequent lack of any but the most superficial, and to some extent, outmoded, understanding of religious views about the world displayed in Soviet writing on this issue. Unacquainted, as Soviet 'scientific atheism' appears to be, with contemporary Western presentations of religious claims in the face of science, and confining itself, on the whole, to the claims of the Orthodox Church of the past, Soviet writing on the relationship of religion and science constitutes one of the most depressing areas in the whole of the literature of 'scientific atheism'; nowhere is the nineteenth century legacy of Soviet Marxism-Leninism and the influence of Orthodoxy's lack of a developed natural theology more in evidence and nowhere is Soviet 'scientific atheism' at its most dogmatically naïve.

To give but one example: writing of the relationship between science and religion, the official Soviet text book of Marxism-Leninism, *The Fundamentals of Marxist-Leninist Philosophy* puts this as follows:

These (science and religion) are essentially opposed phenomena. Religion gives a false and distorted reflection of reality, whereas science, taken as a whole, provides a true reflection of nature and society. The mistaken hypotheses and theories that arise in the process of the development of science do not alter the substance of the question, because error in science is either the result of the pressure of reactionary ideology or a by-product of the quest for truth. Religion is hostile to reason, whereas science is the highest achievement of human reason, the embodiment of its strength and effectiveness. Religion appeared before science, at an extremely low level of practical achievement, when man was totally dominated by natural and social forces and was unable to understand and bend them to his will. The birth of science, on the other hand, is a direct result of man's increased practical power. . . Thus, taking into consideration the opposition between science and religion, we can define science as *a system of objectively true knowledge generalising practice, from which it is acquired and by which it is tested.* (*FMLP:* p. 508)

This, variously expanded and re-worded, is the substance of the 'natural scientific' criticism of religion. Where Soviet writing on science and religion moves beyond these generalities, it is to confront a 'scientific' account of some phenomena (the origin of life, of man, of the earth) with some supposed 'religious' account, or *vice versa*. An extended account of the 'victories' of Soviet science in this respect can be found in an article entitled (*Ateisticheskoye znacheniye trudov sovetskikh yestestvoispytateley*' (The Atheistic Significance of the Work of Soviet Natural Scientists), contributed by I.G. Ivanov to a volume in the series *Voprosy nauchnogo ateizma* commemorating 'The Victory of the Scientific Atheist World View in the USSR' (vol. 4, 1967: pp. 205-241). The gist of Ivanov's panegyric is two-fold: on the one hand, Soviet natural scientists have, he holds, exposed the untenability of the old religious view of the world and have replaced it by a cosmology and an understanding of natural processes more in accord with the way things are; on the other, in that they have played a large part in alleviating the conditions under which men live and work in the Soviet Union – Soviet advances in medicine are cited at this point – they have helped to get rid of the social roots of religion and so undermined it at its source. Ivanov concludes:

Soviet natural scientists, by replacing the religious picture of the world in which man is presented as 'the crown of creation' and subject to the providential care of his creator, by a picture of an infinite universe, where life and its highest flowering – mankind – represent only links in the chain of the various transformations of matter developing according to natural laws, by no means diminishes the lofty mission of man in the world. Human cognition is penetrating ever more deeply into the secrets of nature, and man's ever increasing power to transform reality bears witness to the unlimited possibilities open to mankind. (op. cit., p. 241)

In no other country in the world is so unqualified a faith in science, and in the inevitability of scientific progress, so fervently asserted as in the Soviet Union. Many find this attractive; to others – and certainly to many religious people – such a faith ignores so much that they hold to be true about the human condition, that it is the Soviet vision of the world – rather than the religious – to which, for them, the term 'fantasy' is more truly applicable. We shall be returning to this point later in our study (Section 9.2).

The History of Religion

5.1   RELIGION IN WORLD HISTORY

Marxism is nothing if not a philosophy of history and it is not, therefore, surprising that Soviet 'scientific atheism' has sought, above all else, for a historical understanding of religion. From a Marxist point of view, the history of religion, as we saw in the first part of our study (Section 1.3 above), can never be an autonomous science, but must be part of that wider and more fundamental history of the material development of the society which, for Marxism, it 'reflects'. Setting the history of religion within such a context is held by most Soviet historians of religion to provide a sufficient empirical explanation of religious phenomena. Thus the Soviet Union's leading historian of religion, S.A. Tokarev, writes:

The systematisation of the subject matter of research is a primary problem in any science. It would be impossible to study any aspect of our environment without at least attempting to reduce it to order, to establish — if only in an elementary way, — some classification of the subject matter. But if in the treatment of natural phenomena a simple, formal classification is sufficient, *the classification of the facts of social life has value only in so far as it helps us to understand the historical causes of phenomena.* (Tokarev, 1976: p. 62) (my italics)

Whether the particular classification which Tokarev offers, or indeed whether any system of classification can, as such, help us to understand causes, may well be doubted, and certainly a number of Soviet ethnographers are today seriously worried about the sufficiency of this approach. We shall be looking at their (implicit) criticism of the traditional Marxist-Leninist approach to the study of religion shortly (pp; 263 ff. below); for the moment we shall continue to explore the way in which Soviet history of religion still, despite such criticism, goes about its task.

In the light of what Marxism says about the essence and function of religion we would expect Marxist-Leninist historians to seek to show how — across world cultures — certain historical forms of material relations have given rise to, and have been 'reflected' in, certain historical forms of religion — and Marxist-Leninist historians do, on the whole, claim to do this. Indeed, it is in Marxism's claimed ability to do just this that, so it is asserted, Marxist history of religion succeeds where previous attempts at a scientific history of religion have failed (Tokarev, 1976: pp. 63-69), for the problem, as Tokarev describes it, is not simply that of dividing the development of religion into periods — a problem which he terms *periodizatsiya* (periodisation) — it is also a problem of understanding the real 'determination' (*obuslovlennost'*) of each stage in the development of religion and of connecting this with specific levels of social and economic growth. It is, further, a problem of locating the qualitative originality of each separate stage in the growth of religion in the socio-economic and political life of any given period.

This Tokarev had himself sought to do in two major works, both published in 1964: *Ranniye formy religii i ikh razvitiye* (Early Forms of Religion and Their Development) and *Religiya v istorii narodov mira* (Religion in the History of the Peoples of the World) — works which in the opinion of one of the Soviet Union's leading ethnographers marks an 'upswing' in Soviet history of religion after three decades of neglect (Porshnev, 1965: p. 135). We shall look shortly at Tokarev's understanding of the history of religion, both in relation to these important works — which are now standard works of reference for all Soviet historians of religion — as well as at what he says in a later, reflective, theoretical paper *'Problemy periodizatsii istorii religii'* (Problems of Periodisation in the History of Religion) published in 1976, and from which the quotations given above were taken.

The history of religion being, for Marxism, but a 'reflex' of the material historical development of the society in which it occurs, we would expect that the 'periodisation' of the history of religion in 'scientific atheism' would follow closely the schema laid down for the development of society by Marx and Engels themselves, but this, as we shall see, is rarely the case.[1] The most important qualitative division in the history of society for contemporary Marxism-Leninism is that between pre-class society (*doklassovoye obshchestvo*) and class society (*klassovoye obshchestvo*), and following this, 'scientific atheism' today divides the history of religion similarly into (1) the religion of pre-class society and (2) the religion of class society.

Although this division of the history of religion is today firmly established in Soviet 'scientific atheism', it has not gone unchallenged, and a number of Soviet historians have criticised it on the grounds that since, according to the classical Marxist analysis of religion,[2] religion is a response to 'social contradictions', the phenomenon of religion could not have existed in pre-class society where no such 'contradictions' existed – any more than there can be religion in the classless society of the future (Popov, 1958); and although, today, this is regarded as a purely terminological dispute, in that it is argued that the beliefs of man in pre-class societies bear sufficient resemblance to the undeniably religious beliefs of man in class society as to be designated by the same name (Tokarev, 1976: pp. 70-71), one important Soviet ethnographer, B.F. Porshnev, has continued to express concern over the use of the term 'religion' to designate the beliefs found in primitive, pre-class society – a concern which must, I think, be worrying, not only to Soviet historians of religion, but to historians of religion in general. It is not, in fact, a specifically Marxist concern, although it does presuppose a naturalistic understanding of religion. Porshnev puts his point as follows:

Is it really true (he asks) that the great variety of phenomena described in Tokarev's books – including say, the beliefs and practices of hunters, maleficent rites, or healing rituals – should be incorporated under the umbrella of religion? Or, contrariwise, should it not also be extended to many other customs or omens not dealt with in Tokarev's books – the entire enormous sphere of false connections that the human mind has established in the course of its history? Tokarev has vouchsafed in his works only a brief footnote rejoinder to the repeatedly expressed opinion that the term 'religion' should be reserved only to class society, inasmuch as the erroneous ideas about nature and men that existed in the period of communal and clan society do not possess the earmarks of religion. The author offers no critique of that opinion, in the belief that the entire content of his book [*Ranniye formy religii i ikh razvitiye*] serves to refute it.

. . .

Terminology [Porshnev continues] is, of course, always a somewhat arbitrary thing, and sometimes it is even possible to set forth good truths in bad terms. But that footnote cannot persuade me. . . The abundant data on religions in pre-class society adduced in Tokarev's books convince one only of the fact that the question of the state would have been interpreted in identical fashion. In pre-class society there are many institutions and social phenomena on the basis of which the state, as found in antagonistic societies with some-times absolute classes, subsequently comes into being. These include the authority of the elders, the tribal chieftains, and the council of chiefs. One also finds judicial assemblies, laws, wars, and military techniques. By not calling all this 'state' or governmental authority, we do not in any way impoverish science. On the contrary, we make the concept 'state' theore-tically richer. It seems to me that it would be entirely rational to apply the term 'religion' only to faiths and cults of class society, in which they perform a fundamentally different socio-historical function than in societies not yet divided into antagonistic classes. This limitation promotes a more fully historical approach to the use of the concepts 'state' and 'religion' and opens the field for the introduction of new terms, not having such a tradition behind them, into investigation of the superstructure of the primitive com-munal system. The practical value of this would lie in the fact that anti-religious propagandists would do less talking to the religious about exotic barbarians who do not even know the concept 'god' and more about the central concept of contemporary religion. The very words 'godless' and 'atheist' presume a struggle against belief in God or in gods and against the clergy and the churches as the carriers of the idea of God or gods.

. . .

What is most important, however, is not the dispute over terms. Let us call all these things 'religions'. The basic thing is to understand that 'religions' serve as an expression of a given stage in the historical development of the human mind. (Porshnev, 1965: pp. 137-138) (my italics)

This, as we shall see, is precisely what, in Porshnev's opinion the current, well nigh exclusively historical, approach of Soviet study of religion does not bring out (pp. 263ff. below).

Yet Tokarev's approach, in which little, if any, distinction is drawn between the religious beliefs of man in pre-class society and man in class society, and which is still, despite Porshnev's important criticism, the prevailing one in Soviet history of religion (cf. Kryvelev, 1975: pp. 16-51), does have its merits. It resolves positively, for instance, the ambiguity which we found in Marx and Engels' early writings on religion, in which it was not clear whether the sources of what Marx termed 'natural religion' continued into the period of civil society (cf. p. 44f above) and this enriches, in a way in which Porshnev's restrictive suggestion would not (despite his own claim to the contrary) the Soviet understanding of religion, for in terms of this usage religion can no longer be considered as arising wholly out of the antagonisms and contradictions of class society.

But to divide the history of religion into religion in pre-class society and religion in class society is, for Soviet historians of religion, only the first stage in the search for detailed knowledge of the development of religion. We need, says 'scientific atheism', a more detailed understanding of the development of religion during these two important epochs in the history of man, and the search to provide such an understanding for religion in pre-class society has led Soviet history of religion into a remarkable labyrinth, in which attempt after attempt has been made, as we shall see (in Ch. 5.2), to establish some chronological sequence between such aspects of primitive religion as 'animism', 'totemism', 'fetishism', 'magic', 'cults of ancestors', 'cults of the dead', etc., etc. These attempts continue, despite a tendency on the part of some historians of religion – such as Tokarev himself – to argue that, in the light of such evidence as is available, we can only say that in early society all these varied aspects of early religion co-existed alongside each other, so that to establish a historical sequence is impossible (cf. Tokarev, 1976: pp. 73-74) – a view with which many contemporary Western historians of ancient cultures would agree (cf. Sanders, 1979: p. 103).

But whatever the interest which the religion of pre-class societies retains for Soviet scholars, it is on the religious development in class society itself that attention is concentrated and the problem here, as seen by Soviet historians of religion, is how to bring order into the multitudinous variety of religions – from the religions of ancient Egypt and ancient Babylon, to the religions of the present day – which class society has thrown up. Here also, as with religion in the pre-class society, the initial problem is considered to be one of 'periodisation' – and whilst in class society the problem of the comparative dating of the great world religious is now firmly established, social development in the world has occurred and is still occurring, unevenly at different times and places. Each religion, therefore, must be looked at in terms of the internal social development of the region in which it is located. Any 'absolute' chronology will have meaning only in relationship to the 'concrete' history of each separate country and people, and is thus of little help in writing a universal history of religion (Tokarev, 1976: p. 76).

Surprisingly, although it looks attractive at first sight to Marxist-Leninist historians, the traditional Marxist schema for the development of society, in which society is held to pass from 'slave-owning' relationships through feudal and capitalist to socialist and eventually, Communist relationships, is dismissed by contemporary Soviet scholars as offering little help to historians of religion – indeed, Tokarev goes out of his way to criticise the Italian Marxist, Ambrosio Donini, for seeking to utilise just such a schema. In fact, it is now maintained, that we possess, as yet, insufficient evidence about the pre-capitalistic stages of development of society, and especially about the prevailing means of production in many societies – particularly in the East – during certain periods, for anything significant to be said about the relationship between material conditions and the ruling ideas; although it is true, as Tokarev argues, that in certain specific instances it is easy to see the connection – as the founders of Marxism themselves pointed out. That Puritanism, for example, was 'the product' of the epoch of early capitalist accumulation and that Catholicism clearly 'mirrored' the feudal ordering of society is plain for all to see. But such clear examples, Tokarev admits, are few and far between, and at present we cannot utilise this Marxist insight to write a general history of religion. The situation is further complicated, says Tokarev, when we recognise, as we must, the inertia of religious belief in the face of the changing conditions of life in all societies, just as, in the West it has lagged behind material developments in feudal and capitalist societies. This, of itself, would make for difficulties in writing the history of religion wholly in terms of developments in the material conditions of life. The issue is further complicated by the fact that religions have their own peculiar ways of keeping themselves in being, ways, which bear little relation to the socio-economic base (ibid., pp. 76-77).

Another leading Soviet 'scientific atheist', Y.I. Semenov, displays a similar hesitation at using the traditional Marxist schema and, incidentally, reinforces Tokarev's usage of the term 'religion' as being applicable to beliefs in pre-class as well as in class society, in a methodological paper entitled *'Razvitiye obshchestvenno-ekonomiycheskikh formatsiy i ob''ektivnaya logika evolyutsii religii'* (The Development of the Socio-Economic Stages of Society and the Objective Logic of the Evolution of Religion) (1976). Beginning, like all Soviet 'scientific atheists' discussing the history of religion, by stating that, according to the materialist understanding of history, the evolution of social consciousness 'is determined' (*opredelyaetsya*) by the development of social conditions, Semenov passes immediately to qualify this by stating that, according to Engels, historical materialism not only does not deny, but positively emphasises, the 'relative independence' (*otnositel'naya samostoyatel'nost'*) attaching to the development of any form of social consciousness, and so to the development of religion. Indeed, religion, just because it stands (as was pointed out by Engels) at the furthest remove of all forms of social consciousness from the socio-economic base of society, has rather more scope for independent development than have other forms of social consciousness more closely allied to the material base. It, therefore, follows, he says, its own internal logic.

This is not as surprising an admission on the part of a Marxist as might at first sight appear for, according to Semenov, this is again but to recognise what Engels said – and Semenov proceeds to refer to what, to many, has proved a quite unintelligible passage in Engels, to support this. Engels, he says, revealed the relationship between the 'historical' and the 'logical' when he pointed out that the 'logical' is none other than the 'historical' freed from historical stages of development and from chance occurrences (Engels, *Anti-Dühring:* p. 54). The task which Semenov sets himself, therefore, is, in his own words, that of 'freeing (*osvobodit'*) the process of the evolution of religion from the historical stages of development and from chance occurrences, so as to present it in a logical, i.e., abstract and theoretically consistent form' (Semenov, 1976: pp. 43-44).

What this amounts to is that Semenov, like Tokarev, eschews any attempt to link empirically, in any precise way, the development of religion and the development of the material base of society. 'Socio-economic conditions', he says, 'determine' religious ideas only in the most general way – and he tells the story of the development of religion according to a schema which, whilst it sees religion as developing from an initial division of the world into 'natural' and 'supernatural', and proceeding via magic and a belief in supernatural forces and spirits, and polytheism, to eventually issue in monotheism, says little that is meaningful about any *empirical* relationship between this development and that of society as a whole.

Of religion in general, Semenov writes:

A characteristic feature of every religion possessing any degree of development is the acknowledgement of the existence of a supernatural world together with the natural world. It is quite obvious that the concept of the existence of two qualitatively different worlds could not emerge at once, ready-made. It could arise and be formed only gradually. The inner objective logic of the establishment and development of religion was first of all the logic of the duality of the world in man's consciousness.

. . .

Any attempt to demonstrate the objective logic of the development of religion can be successful only if it recognises that the independence of this process is only relative. The basic moving forces of the evolution of religion are found beyond its frontiers, beyond the limits of consciousness in general. Therefore, one cannot understand the development of religion without looking at those objective factors, which gave birth to it and nourished it, and without paying attention to changes which have been taken place in it. (Semenov, 1976: p. 44)

How or why the initial 'bifurcation' of the world into 'natural' and 'supernatural' took place, Semenov does not say, but it is this which, for him, eventually, under the 'determination' of objective social forces, is the underlying *leitmotiv* of all religion. He writes:

If we approach the evolution of religion from the point of view of form, then the evolution of religion in class society appears to us, basically, only as a natural continuation of its previous development – as the completion of a movement along the line of an ever greater division of the world in the consciousness of man. The stratification of society – the development out of a previously equitable tribal society (sic) of a powerful aristocracy, finds its illusory reflection in the stratification of the supernatural world, in the separation from previously equal supernatural powers of a new class – the gods. . . Polytheism becomes definitely established, however, only in fully developed class society where the gods acquire the characteristics of terrible sovereigns, ruling over both people and the world. The character of the cult alters accordingly: pacification of the gods becomes the aim of ritual. Finally, the coming into being of large, centralised states finds its reflection in the division which occurs in religion between the gods and a 'high god' (*verkhovnyy bog*). The logical conclusion of this process is the appearance of monotheism. The emergence of first polytheism, and then monotheism, is accompanied by a greater separation of the supernatural world from the natural world. If demons most often live with people, then gods are all the more often apart from them. Their habitation becomes heaven. (Semenov, 1976: p. 53)

This certainly does have a sort of inner logic about it. Whether the history of any religion actually occurred in this way is, of course, another matter, and one for which more empirical evidence than either Semenov, or any other 'scientific atheist', has yet provided, is needed before it can be regarded as having been substantiated.

Semenov, like most Marxists, is also an unconscious Eurocentric Hegelian, and he thus feels obliged to point out that the Christian religion is the 'highest stage' in the development of religion in class society before its final demise and, therefore, the highest form that religion as such can assume. This he does by arguing that Christianity is the most ideological of all religions — religion as ideology being itself, for Semenov, a new element in the development of religion which occurs only in class society — and Christianity therefore 'reflects' the most advanced stage in the development of society prior to the advent of socialism. Only Christianity could have fulfilled this role. He writes:

All the fundamental characteristics of religion in class society are fully manifested only in the so-called world religions — Buddhism, Christianity and Islam — and, out of these, they are fully embodied only in Christianity. This is explained by the fact that Christianity, in the first place, owed its origin to the helplessness of people before the forces making for the development of society; secondly, because it arose only as a religious teaching; and thirdly, because it was born as an ideology, not of the ruling class, but of the exploited masses, as an ideological current opposed to the existing social order. (op. cit., p. 59)

Semenov elaborates on this as follows:

The roots of Christianity are found in the existence of an insoluble contradiction between the passionate desire of the exploited masses to do away with the hated slave-owning social order and to create a very different, new and equitable social order on the one hand, and the laws of social growth based on the exploitation of man by man on the other. (op. cit., pp. 59-60)

The latter, of course, prevails, although something of the old protest can be seen in some of the heresies which arose to challenge, from time to time, established Christian orthodoxy. Where such heresies succeeded in overthrowing the established order they themselves, says Semenov, quickly became a new orthodoxy exploiting the masses.

There are two comments that I would like to make at this point. The first is that Semenov's account of the rise of polytheism and its development into monotheism, and even more so what he says about the rise of the Christian religion, seems to me a good illustration of both the general vagueness and the general dogmatism which characterises 'scientific atheism's' assertions about social relationships and the development of religion. Much evidence indeed would be required to substantiate – what many historians of religion deny – that the emergence of a 'high-god' is a late development in polytheistic societies, that it only occurs in highly centralised states, that monotheism is always a later phenomenon than polytheism and is a 'logical' development from it, that Christianity was but a protest on the part of the oppressed, and that Protestantism, either at its inception or since, always legitimates capitalism, and neither Semenov nor any Soviet historian that I have read provides such evidence. All make do with general assertions of the kind illustrated in the passages from Semenov's paper that I have quoted and all ignore the sort of counter arguments that appear so obvious to Western historians – for instance, that both Judeo-Christian and Islamic monotheism arose in social circumstances very different from those which a Marxist-Leninist understanding of the development of society and religion requires; that the origins of Buddhism and the development of certain aspects of Hinduism appear to be utterly at variance with the schema Marxism-Leninism offers for the development of religion; that much of the more interesting aspects of religious development are left completely untouched, etc. Thus the impression is left that 'scientific atheist' accounts of the development – 'the objective logic' in Semenov's terminology – of religion, which differ but little from those put forward by Marxism's nineteenth century founders, are not the outcome of any empirical investigation into the phenomena of religion, but are superimposed on it from without. History is but rarely as 'logical' as Semenov makes out.

The second comment that I wish to make relates to what both Tokarev and Semenov say about the 'relative independence' of religion from the material base. Neither scholar, we must note, is at all concerned to define the limits of this autonomy – beyond the bare assertion that this takes place within the wider context of the social 'determination' of religious ideas – or to offer a criterion which would allow us to know when religion is developing of its own volition and when it's under the 'determination' of social forces. We can but conclude, in the absence of such a criterion, that the invocation of 'relative independence' is, like Engels' own mention of it in his letter to Bloch of September 1890, simply a way of escaping from some very awkward questions.

But way of escape or not, the recognition that religion often develops relatively independently of socio-economic conditions allows for the possibility, at least, that something of what Soviet scholars say about religion will go beyond demonstrating the 'truth' of Marxist themes. To date, however, this remains no more than a possibility, and I believe that a genuine interest in the 'superstructural' ideas of religion, in and of themselves, will have to develop among Soviet scholars for this to become a reality in Soviet study of religion.[3]

But to return to our theme, which is the attempt of Soviet 'scientific atheism' (and of one of its leading representatives – S.A. Tokarev), to offer guidelines for a Marxist-Leninist history of religion. Tokarev, having abandoned any attempt at writing this history in terms of the general Marxist schema of the evolution of the material base of society, offers in place of this a rather simple classification of religions in class society into national or state religions on the one hand, and international or world religions on the other – a division which corresponds, he says, to two epochs in the general development of religion (op. cit., p. 77). The criterion for this division lies, to a great extent, as we shall see, in religion itself.

In writing about national religions, Tokarev feels on much safer ground, for the founders of Marxism themselves wrote on this, and 'concrete' historical research has confirmed, he claims, what they said. The religions of antiquity – of Egypt, Babylon, Syria, Greece and Rome – although they were extremely unlike one another in their substantial beliefs – a point which Tokarev illustrates with examples – were united in one important respect: they all arose, as Engels noted, out of similar social and political conditions, and all served as the ideological 'reflection' of these conditions. All served to unite people in one social organism defined by race. Tokarev writes:

Egyptians living in Egypt, speaking the Egyptian language, subject to the Pharoah, simultaneously worshipped Osiris, Ammon and the other state gods of Egypt. The religious community was not in any way independent of the more general community of people. (Tokarev, 1976: p. 78)

Surprisingly, he nowhere suggests that religion in Egypt might have related differently to different social classes — another indication of the general abandonment by contemporary Marxist-Leninist historians of religion of the opinions of earlier years. He also seeks to guard against a possible criticism from his fellow Marxists, by pointing out that Marxist writing on religion has never had any objection to putting the religions of antiquity into a special category and to seeing them as constituting a special type (or form) of religion. What he seems to be guarding against is the objection, that many Soviet scholars have, to calling these religions 'national', as, for example, had the authors of a standard work of reference in Soviet 'scientific atheism', *Nastol'naya kniga ateizma* (Reference Book of Atheism) (cf. p. 58), and Tokarev himself is not wholly enamoured of the term, a term which he holds to be something of an anachronism when applied to the past. With Marx, he prefers the term 'folk religions', on the grounds that the cultures of the states of the past were often wider than the boundaries of nation-states, or at least transcended race: many of the sacred centres of antiquity, he notes, served others besides their own people — as did Delphi, for instance. However, Tokarev fails to follow through the full implications of what he has said, for there would surely appear to be something requiring comment in asserting, on the one hand, that the social function of the religions of antiquity was to bind people together according to race, and then asserting, on the other, that these religions served peoples other than those whose religions they were. We would at least expect Tokarev to tell us something about these additional

functions. Unfortunately he does not — in fact he seems completely unaware of anything odd in what he has said, so firmly is his
mind concentrated on the terminological problem of whether to
call the religions of antiquity 'national' or 'folk', and restricted by
the methodological presupposition that the only function that
religion can fulfil is a social one.

But whatever we call the religions of antiquity, Tokarev is in no
doubt that they represent a definite stage in the development of
religion — a stage which began in the fourth or even the fifth
century BC and which, in parts of the world, continues to this
day; a fact which, incidentally, shows the irrelevance of any
absolute chronology. 'national' or 'folk' religion (*narodnaya
religiya*), for Tokarev, is a definite stage in the development of
religion, which comes into being at a definite stage of the development of society — the period of the formation of class society.
Unfortunately, the little that we know about the majority of
religions at this stage of development is derived almost entirely
from the literary and physical remains they have left behind.
Some, however, have become entwined in later and more complex
cults, where remnants of the ancient gods survive under other
names, and ancient forms have been given new meaning, and a
very few have survived into the present, although in a considerably
modified form. Such, for example, are Shintoism, Taoism, Confucianism, Hinduism and, of course, Judaism.

The second and last stage of the development of religion in class
society, for Tokarev, is the development of Buddhism, Christianity
and Islam into world religions. The important question here, as
Soviet 'scientific atheists' recognise, is why these religions, and
no others, should have developed in this highly significant direction. Rejecting, on the gounds of the very substantial differences
in belief that actually exists between these three religions, that it
could be anything intrinsic to them as religions which brought
about their ecumenical status, Soviet 'scientific atheists' look, as
we would expect, to the socio-economic base of the societies
from within which these three religions expanded and, again as
we would expect, they see similar, if not identical, socio-economic

conditions in the 'earthly foundation' (*zemnaya osnova*) of all three religions. What were these conditions?

Before offering his own Marxist-Leninist answer to this question, Tokarev points out that this is not the first time that scientific students of religion have sought to answer this kind of question. The Italian scholar Raffael Pettazzoni, for example, has written of the 'great problem' of historical science, namely, why, within the space of a century or so, major and far-reaching religious developments took place in Judaea (the Prophetic Movement), in Iran (Zarathrustra), in Greece (Orphism), in India (The Buddha) and in China (Lao-tze and Confucius)?[4] Were these developments, Pettazzoni asks, autonomous and coincidental, or were they, perhaps, the outcome of diffusion from some centre? The Marxist historian Donini, in a critical study of Pettazzoni's work (Donini, 1961), put forward his own materialist answer to this question, and with it Tokarev has much sympathy.

The epoch, Donini claims, in which these important religious developments took place was that in which 'slave-owning societies' were coming into being and in which, as a consequence, vast masses of people were plunged into conditions of hopeless slavery. Out of eight million people alive in these countries, Donini estimates — on what basis we are not told — only three or four million were free men. The upsurge of religion to which Pettazzoni calls attention was, Donini asserts, a response to this situation. The gods of these ancient religions were the gods of the rulers, the masters, and simple people were not allowed to take part in their worship. Therefore, as he puts it:

In this epoch was born a different type of religion: folk religions, religions of secret cults, religions of the cult of poverty, of the unprivileged masses who yearned for a better life — if only in another world. (Donini, 1961: p. 64)

Unable to contemplate changing life in this world, Donini contends that the masses sought their salvation outwith this world. This explains the fact that, according to Donini, simultaneously in various countries, religious life was split asunder into religions of the ruling classes and religions of the poor.

Once again we are confronted with a Marxian analysis which moves at a breath-taking level of generality, with a minimum of substantial argument, and which leaves a multitude of unanswered questions. This is not the place, however, to look at criticisms which historians of Judaism, Buddhism, and Confucianism might bring against Donini's rather simple generalisations. All I want to do here is to call attention to the kind of 'argument' on which Soviet 'scientific atheism' relies for its serious analysis of religion. It is for this reason that I have summarised Tokarev's paper at the length and in the way that I have. It is all too characteristic of the vast majority of Soviet writings on this matter.[5]

Whilst Tokarev thinks that Donini's explanation of religious phenomena during the period we have referred to is right – he himself will utilise a similar analysis in his discussion of the reasons for the expansion of some 'national/folk' religions into world religions – he sees more urgent questions. What, he asks, is the historical connection between the sources of the 'national/folk' religions of the period of 'slave-owning society' and contemporary world religions? Why, out of all the so-called 'higher religions', do only three develop into world religions? Why did Buddhism, why did Christianity, and why did Islam – in very different socio-political circumstances than had characterised the origin of Buddhism and Christianity – become world religions?

These, by any criterion, are important questions for the historian of religion, and many historians have sought to answer them, although, on the whole, they have sought answers to particular questions relating to the expansion of particular religions. Tokarev, however, whilst he is very aware of the particularity of each of the three religions under consideration, and of some of the ways in which they differ from each other – which he spells out at length – assumes that a single, unifying, explanation can be found, which will apply equally to all three religions.

Different from each other as these three religions are – in their beliefs about the world and that which lies beyond the world, in the socio-economic and political systems with which they became entwined – what, for Tokarev, unites them, and allowed them to break free from 'national' boundaries, was that they each in their own way were a protest against the *status quo*. Unlike other 'national/folk' religions, which simply supported, by legitimatising, established social orders, Buddhism, Christianity and Islam – at least in their early periods – opposed them. Buddhism, it is contended, arose as a protest against the caste system of traditional (and religiously legitimated) Indian society, Christianity as a protest against the unjust social order both of Judaea and later of the Roman Empire – and, like Buddhism, it originally turned its back on earthly power and sought a 'kingdom' elsewhere – and Islam as a protest against the small-scale, fragmented, tribal aristocracies of its time.

This is Tokarev's answer to the problem of the rise of the great world religions – as it is the answer given, over-all, by all Soviet 'scientific atheists' (cf. Zhukov, 1976). Tokarev writes:

It was general condemnation of all that formerly had been justified and consecrated by religion that allowed these new religions to break away from their native soil. . . and to become world i.e., supernatural religions. (Tokarev, 1976: p. 83)

This answer – to which certainly, so far as Buddhism and Christianity are concerned, no one could deny an element of truth – is important from the point of view of the development of Soviet 'scientific antheism's' understanding of religion, marking as it does a return to the original Marxist analysis of religion as both a 'reflection' of existing socio-economic and political conditions and a protest against them. The dynamic underlying the great world religions is not sought for in religion itself, but in the material base of society. This makes it imperative for Soviet historians of early Buddhism, Christianity and Islam to concentrate their attention on the social evils of the time, and to show how these religions drew their support from – if they were not actually originated by – the lower classes. Soviet historians, therefore, virtually ignore many of the questions which have fascinated Western historians of religion – for example, questions concerning the provenance of particular religious ideas – the notion of *samsara*, and the identity of atman-Brahman, in the Indian tradition, and of the Trinity in the Christian, for example. In and of themselves, the details of the ideological superstructure are of little interest to 'scientific atheism'. What matters is the function which religious ideas subserve.

But although it is easy to see why certain ideas – the promise of 'salvation', either in the near future here on earth or in the hereafter, the equality of all men before their Maker, etc., – can be regarded as subserving ideological purposes, it is difficult to see how others could do so – the notion of spiritual 'perfection', the ideas found in Christological and Trinitarian controversies in early Christendom, etc. At what point does the superstructure of religion, philosophy, etc., develop a life of its own? Marxists do not tell us. Religion, it is said, is a protest, but why it takes the particular form that it does, and issues in certain beliefs and no others, we are not told.

But although, for 'scientific atheism', the three world religions have their origin in a protest against the established order of society they soon become reconciled to it and take their place amongst its foremost supporters. This began to happen to the Christian religion with the Constantinian settlement and a similar reconciliation with the establishment can be traced in Buddhism which, claims Tokarev, soon became reconciled to the caste system in Northern India and, at a later stage in its development, with the social systems of many of the countries of the East. Similarly, Islam quickly became reconciled to the tribal aristocracies of Arabia and with the class systems of the Near and Middle Eastern states – systems which, in fact, it actively supported.

Thus, at various times and places, world religions have fulfilled exactly the same function as 'national/folk' religions. Religion, Tokarev concludes, is ultimately a conservative institution, and although world religions begin as, and owe much of their initial success to, their having been movements of protest on the part of the oppressed, in the light of these later, conservative functions, it cannot be said that this is what distinguishes them from 'national' or 'folk' religions (See also Zhukov, 1976: p. 20). All that can be said is that world religions represent a later stage in the development of religion. In fact, for Soviet historians of religion, they are not only the latest, but also the last historical stage in the development of religion (Semenov, 1976: p. 45).

This said, there are, Tokarev contends, differences in structure, and in belief, by means of which it is possible to distinguish between 'national/folk' religions and world religions: for instance, 'national/folk' religions consist strictly only of a priesthood, who serve the temples of the cult, and of other professionals — various diviners, shamans, prophets, soothsayers, etc. In 'national/folk' religions there are no churches nor a general congregation of believers. The masses play a passive role and are able to approach God only through priests or other intermediaries; they have no choice whether to believe or disbelieve. In world religions things are different: membership is determined by 'theoretical considerations' (i.e., by belief) and not by birth or citizenship. People accept membership 'voluntarily', as they think fit, as believers, and are given answers, says Tokarev, perhaps with the Christian catechism in mind, 'as children are given answers by parents or godparents'. At least this was the way in the beginning, before world religions took on the characteristics of 'national/folk' religions and the term 'voluntary' took on less and less meaning.

The absence of ethnocentrism in world religions has consequences also in the realm of belief. In particular it affects the development of religious cosmology and of the conception of God, who becomes the Creator and Ruler — in Buddhism, says Tokarev, only the Ruler — of the whole world, so that the entire universe comes to be thought of as a single whole, and mankind as one 'collective', whose destiny does not depend on their belonging to any particular nation. It is true, Tokarev admits, that notions not dissimilar to these are found in some 'national' religions, but in them, he contends — though without argument — 'it is a foreign element' (ibid., p. 85).

Other distinguishing features of world religions flow from their 'universalism' and two in particular should be noted: (1) the soteriological character of world religions: notions of 'salvation' (*spaseniya*) dominate all three world religions, arising out of notions of evil (*zlo*) unknown in 'national/folk' religions; and (2) the missionary element in world religions, which flows directly from the former of these two characteristics, in that if salvation is necessary for all people, and if salvation is thought possible only through true belief, then this truth must be preached to all peoples. This, argues Tokarev, is the motivating factor behind the missionary activity of all three world religions, although the actual missionary activity of each religion has taken very different forms – from forced 'baptism' and the physical destruction of 'paganism', to preaching and teaching in the wake of colonial expansion.[6]

But just as there is no sharp edge in history between tribal and 'national/folk' religions, so also there is no sharp dividing line between 'national' and world religions. In fact, several of the 'national/folk' religions of antiquity developed tendencies to universalism, in that they put forward vague protests against the evil in the world, and entertained notions of salvation from it which they sought to propagate: for example, in ancient Greece, Orphism, Pythagorianism and the Eleusinian mysteries; in ancient Egypt, the reforming movement associated with the Pharoah Iknaton; and in Judaism the prophet movement and some of the later sects, for instance the Essenes, had this character. In the Roman world Mithraism, the great rival to Christianity, also displayed tendencies towards universalism, and parallel movements can be identified in other parts of the world.

Finally, we must note a process within world religions which Tokarev terms 'involution' (*involyutsiya*), by which he means a tendency, once world religions become established in certain countries, for them to take on characteristics peculiar to that country and so to revert to being, to all intents and purposes, 'national/folk' religions – Anglicanism in England, Presbyterianism in Scotland, and Catholicism in Ireland, are instanced as examples from within the Christian religion, Shï'ism in Saudi Arabia as an example from within Islam, and though Buddhism has never become as established, in the sense that it has ever become a 'national church', as Christianity and Islam have, it has without doubt, says Tokarev, given to certain countries a distinctly 'national' hue.

Tokarev concludes his paper by noting that, overall, we see two contrary tendencies at work in the history of religion in 'class society': one which makes for internationalism and another which makes for nationalism – two tendencies particularly associated with religion during the epoch of capitalism, but discernible much earlier. These tendencies, he says, can be seen at work in all spheres of social and cultural life, and are not limited to one religion. Corresponding to these two tendencies we should note two contrary functions of religion, which again affect all areas of cultural life – a 'segregating function' (*funktsiya segregatsii*) and an 'integrating function' (*funktsiya integratsii*). For Soviet 'scientific atheism', the dialectical interplay of these two functions constitutes the larger part of their understanding of the history of religion (cf. Tokarev, 1976b; Kryvelev, 1976).

Such is Tokarev's schema for the writing of the history of religion – a schema to which almost all Soviet historians of religion now adhere. It is, alas, as should now be evident, vague, general, arbitrarily selective of evidence, evasive and dogmatic. It is to illustrate these aspects of the 'scientific atheist' writing of history of religions that I have referred to it in detail and quoted, often verbatim, from it.[7] Western historians of religion will wish to question many of the statements made about particular religions and many more will be doubtful of the possibility of ever writing the kind of overall history of religion – as opposed to writing histories of particular religious traditions – to which Soviet 'scientific atheism' aspires – although Eliade's recent attempt at a general, chronological *History of Religious Ideas* shows that such attempts are not wholly eschewed among Western practitioners of *Religionswissenschaft* (Eliade, 1979-); Others, of course, will doubt the value of the particular schema which Tokarev suggests. Certainly, apart from the original Marxian insight into the role of religion *vis-à-vis* nationality, it seems to have little to commend it in the face of a variety of other ways in which religions might be categorised. The divisions of religions into 'religions of pre-class society' and 'religions of class society' – to which almost all Soviet historians subscribe – is particularly artificial and not a division that those who are not Marxists will see much sense in. The evidence for there having ever been any pre-class societies as such is dubious in the extreme.

What is particularly interesting, from the point of view of Marxist-Leninist methodology, however, is the way in which both Tokarev and Semenov abandon any attempt to relate the history of religion to the evolution of social relations in society as these are found in the classical Marxist tradition. The reasons which Tokarev gives for the development of certain 'nation/folk' religions into world religions have little to do with developing social relations and much to do with ideas endemic to religions themselves – though Tokarev himself does not overtly avow this – but in citing ideas concerning 'evil' and notions of 'salvation' – said, albeit in a vague way to 'reflect' dissatisfaction with the world – as the motivating factors for the extra-territorial expansion of Buddhism, Christianity and Islam, Tokarev comes at least close to admitting an inner dynamism to religion itself – which marks a considerable advance on earlier Soviet writing on the history of religion in which religion was seen as little more than an ideological tool in the machinations of the ruling classes. This, as we shall see, is in line with a general tendency in Soviet study of religion today to return to the analysis of religion found in the classical sources of Marxism, and in particular in the early writings of Marx and the later writings of Engels, where the 'protest' role of religion is emphasised, as well as a recognition of religion's tendency to draw inspiration from sources other than exclusively socio-economic ones. How this will effect future attempts at writing the history of religion only time will tell, but I suspect myself that, as religion persists and, perhaps, thrives in Soviet socialist society, this will result in more attention than has been devoted hitherto being given to those aspects of religion which Soviet scholars today refer to as 'relatively independent' of the material base of society. It is, as we would expect, in the exploration of the religion of pre-class society (natural religion) that Soviet tendencies in this direction are most noticeable.

5.2 RELIGION IN PRE-CLASS SOCIETY:
THE ORIGIN AND EARLY FORMS OF RELIGION

As men of the nineteenth century, Marx and Engels were not without opinions — derived, for the most part, as we have seen, from the anthropology of their day — about the origin and early forms of religion. The British anthropologist, Sir Edward Evans-Pritchard, in his celebrated account of *Theories of Primitive Religion,* has described the motive behind the interest of nineteenth century anthropologists in primitive religion as follows:

They sought, and found, in primitive religions, a weapon which could, they thought, be used with deadly effect against Christianity. If primitive religion could be explained away as an intellectual aberration, as a mirage induced by emotional stress, or by its social function, it was implied that the higher religions could be discredited and disposed of in the same way. (Evans-Pritchard, 1965: p. 15)

Marx and Engels were no exception to this generally held belief, and their authority has ensured that this, essentially nineteenth century, attempt to discredit religion by revealing its mundane origins, believed to be disclosed in archaic and in contemporary 'primitive' forms of religion, is one which, to this day, is taken extremely seriously by Soviet 'scientific atheism'.

As early as 1923, a resolution of the XIIth Congress of the Communist Party of the Soviet Union, relating to anti-religious agitation and propaganda, had urged those engaged in anti-religious work to pay particular attention to the study of the origin of religion as a sure way of combatting 'the religious illusion', and as recently as 1967 the Professor of the History and Theory of Atheism at the University of Leningrad wrote that:

The classics of Marxism-Leninism repeatedly point out that in the criticism of religion it is necessary to reveal the origins of religion, to make clear its material foundations. In Soviet work on religion, therefore, questions concerning the origin and early forms of religion have an important place. (M.I. Shakhnovich, 1967: p. 242)

Interest in the chronological origin of religion goes back to the earliest days of Russian Marxism. A.A. Bogdanov (1873-1928) in his writings on social psychology, put forward a theory known in Soviet history of religion as the 'authoritarian' theory (*avtoritarnaya*) of the origin of religion. According to Bogdanov, the earliest known form of thought was 'animism' and he deduced its origin from the social relationships obtaining in 'authoritarian' or patriarchal society, relationships which turned primitive savages (*dikari*) into proto-philosophers who saw personal intent behind every phenomenon and who thus attributed 'soul' (*dusha*) to all things. The distinction between 'soul' and 'body', Bogdanov argued, arose from the interiorisation of the external relationship obtaining in the society of the time between administrative (*organizatorskiy*) and executive (*ispolnitel'nyy*) persons (Bogdanov, 1914: p. 67; 1924: p. 20). For Bogdanov, therefore, religion – the earliest form of which was 'animism' – came into being only with the advent of patriarchal society, that is, only after the division between 'administrative' and 'executive' persons in society had come about. It originated, he thought, from the feelings aroused in cults in which the first 'ancestor-administrators' (*predkiorganizatory*) were venerated (Bogdanov, 1920: pp. 29-30).

Though ridiculed by Lenin and Plekhanov (cf. *LCW*: 38;487), Bogdanov's theory was extremely popular during the early period of Soviet writing on the history of religion and exercised some influence on N.Y. Marr, whose own theory of the origin of religion continued to attract supporters until about 1950 when his linguistic theories were attacked by Stalin and his influence waned. For Marr, primitive religion arose out of the 'religio-economic' (*kul'tovo-khozyaystvennyy*) interests of the class of magicians (Marr, 1937: IV; 41). These magicians, according to Marr, also created language as a 'working-magical' (*trudmagicheskoye*) activity for the sake of intercourse with a totem (Marr, 1937: II;204) – a view which some Soviet anthropologists were inclined to compare with Lévi-Bruhl's views concerning a primitive 'pre-logicial' mentality (cf. Lévi-Bruhl, 1910; 1922). Whilst Marr's theories have now passed into oblivion – no mention is made of them, for instance, in the article on the origin of religion in the *Kratkiy nauchno-ateisticheskiy slovar'* (Short Scientific-Atheist Dictionary) published in 1964 — it is the opinion of M.I. Shakhnovich that his writings on totemism and magic are not entirely without merit (Shakhnovich, 1967: p. 244) and B.F. Porshnev, as we shall see, has sought recently to revive both Lévi-Bruhl and Marr's notion of a pre-logical mentality (see pp 266f. below).

But although now neglected in Soviet studies of religion, theories not dissimilar to those of Marr and Bogdanov have been put forward of late by the British anthropologist Mary Douglas in her book *Natural Symbols*. For instance, she writes:

The social body constrains the way the physical body is perceived. The physical experience of the body, always modified by the social categories through which it is known, sustains a particular view of society. There is a continual exchange of meanings between the two kinds of bodily experience so that each reinforces the categories of the other. (Douglas, 1978: p. 93)

and again, and drawing support from the French anthropologist, Marcel Mauss, she writes:

The scope of the body as a medium of expression is limited by controls exerted from the social system. . . the human body is always treated as an image of society and there can be no natural way of considering the body that does not involve at the same time a social dimension. . . The relation of head to feet, of brain and sexual organs, of mouth and anus are commonly treated so that they express the relevant patterns of hierarchy. Consequently I now advance the hypothesis that bodily control is an expression of social control. . . furthermore, there is little prospect of successfully improving bodily control without the corresponding social forms. And lastly, the same drive that seeks harmoniously to relate the experience of physical and social, must affect ideology. Consequently, when once the correspondence between bodily and social controls is traced, the basis will be laid for considering co-varying attitudes in political thought and in theology. (ibid., pp. 98-99)

A more popular view of the origin of religion in the early years of Soviet power was that associated with the name of Skvortsov-Stepanov — a view which also drew on the views of Bogdanov.

Stepanov held that the earliest form of religion was the cult of the ancestors, and thus religion only began to take shape in the era of patriarchal-tribal organisations of society, i.e., after the division of administrative and executive functions in society had given rise to 'the cult of the souls of the administrators' (*kul't dushi organizatorov*) or 'the cult of the primal ancestors' (*kul't samikh predkovstarikov*) who had been converted into 'totemic divinities' (*totemnye bozhestva*). Belief in the soul, Stepanov argued, arose by analogy: just as hands direct immobile instruments, so the soul was thought to direct the body (Skvortsov-Stepanov, 1925: p. 20). He also thought that the religion of the ancient states had been the form of the organisation of productive relationships, and thus 'reflected' the working experience of the people, and he thought he found some support for his views in the writings of the German ethnographer and sociologist Henry Cunow, whose book *On the Origins of Religion and Belief in God* he had translated into Russian in 1919. Stepanov also attacked 'nature theories' of the origin of religion which attempted to derive belief in God from early man's contemplation of the sun and the moon or from his fear of thunder and lightning.

Stepanov's theories did not go uncontested in the Soviet Union, as is shown in the lively exchange of opinion which he had with the Moscow historian M.N. Pokrovsky in the journal *Pod znamenem marksizma* (Under the Banner of Marxism) in 1922-23 (op. cit., 1922; nos. 11-12; 1923; nos. 1, 2-3; cf. also V.F. Zubkovets, '*Ob odnoy diskussii*' ('About a Certain Discussion') in *Voprosy istorii religii i ateizma*, VII, 1959, pp. 303-312). The exchange closed with both participants agreeing that the question of the origin of religion must await further concrete, material evidence – Pokrovsky being rather more emphatic on this point than Stepanov. Pokrovsky's last contribution to the discussion was significantly entitled '*Istoriya religii na kholostom khodu*' (The History of Religion Freewheeling) – a view with regard to the search for the chronological origins of religion echoed by not a few historians of religion and anthropologists in the West (cf. Brandon, 1970: pp. 535-536).

Three other well-known Soviet theoreticians turned their attention to the problem of the origin of religion in the early years of Soviet history of religions – A.V. Lunacharsky, E.M. Yaroslavsky and A.T. Lukachevsky. Lunacharsky – probably under the influence of the British anthropologist Sir James Frazer – separated magic from religion, but held that the latter arose not from the fear of dead corpses, but from animism (Lunacharsky, 1924: pp. 7-9). In 1924, Yaroslavsky published the first edition of his *Kak rodyatsya, zhivut i umirayut bogi i bogini* (How Gods and Goddesses are Born, Live and Die), a book in which there can be found traces of Bogdanov's 'authoritarian', as well as of 'nature theories' of the origin of religion. These were not, in fact, removed until the fourth edition in 1938. Lukachevsky also shared the then widespread view that religion arose from animism (1930: p. 3), but in 1932, in the course of an article in the journal *Antireligionznik*, he wrote:

My book on *The Origin of Religion* (2nd edit., 1930) lacks foundation in that it gives a review of a series of theories (on the origin of religion) without placing them within the context of Marxism-Leninism. (op. cit., 1932: no. 2, p. 14)

This was a significant admission, for it was to mark the beginnings of a wholly new approach to the question of the origins of religion in the Soviet Union.

The theories which we have looked at so far are not dissimilar to the many other speculative theories regarding the origin of religion found on the international scene during the latter part of the nineteenth and the early years of the twentieth centuries. As such theories go, they are no better, and not much worse, than the theories of Herbert Spencer, Sir James Frazer or Sir Edward Tylor. The problem with such theories, as the Soviet historian, Pokrovsky had pointed out in his exchange of opinion with Skvortsov-Stepanov, is that we lack any evidence that might confirm, or indeed refute, them – a point which the British anthropologist Sir Edward Evans-Pritchard was also to make in his book *Theories of Primitive Religion* (1965: p. 29).

A more important criticism, from the Soviet point of view, was that there was nothing specifically Marxist about them. This is what Lukachevsky realised in 1932, although he did little to rectify the situation, and his *Vvedeniye v istoriyu religii* (Introduction to the History of Religion), published in 1934, is in much the same vein as his earlier work: animism is still the initial and most ancient form of thought, and whilst magic may be earlier than religion when its objects are considered animistically, and when the notion of 'soul' has developed. Further, a single animistic notion, he contends, does not add up to religion. Religion occurs only when notions such as 'soul', and 'mana' are conjoined with a cult. Animism, said Lukachevsky, is a symptom of religion, but must not be identified with it (1934: pp. 62-63).

Between 1933 and 1939, P.N. Fedoseyev – who was destined to become one of the Soviet Union's leading philosophers of religion – published a series of articles in the journals *Pod znamenem marksizma* and *Antireligioznik* in which he sought to analyse the problem of the origin of religion from the point of view of Marx, Engels and Lenin (cf. *'Lenin o sotsial'nykh i gnoseologicheskikh kornyakh religii'* ('Lenin on the Social and Epistemological Roots of Religion')). *PZM*: 1933, no. 4, pp. 159-178); *Gnoseologicheskiye korni religioznykh verovaniy'* ('The Epistemological Roots of Religious Beliefs), *AR*: 1939, no. 9)). After this it was impossible for Soviet scholars to continue as before, for it now became imperative that they work out a distinctly Marxist approach to this most intractable of problems. It was only, however, after the war, and the death of Stalin, and in the shadow of the new offensive against religion launched by the decrees of the CPSU in 1954, that work in this area began in earnest.

Side by side with the pre-war theoretical search for the origins of religion Soviet archaeologists and ethnographers strove to provide historians of religion with the factual material necessary for their task. The latter did particular valuable service, not only by making available to Soviet historians of religion the work of such Western scholars as Frazer, Tylor and Lévi-Bruhl, but also by their study of some of the less developed peoples of the USSR itself.

V.K. Nikol'sky was particularly active in the former enterprise. Between 1930 and 1939 many of the writings of Western anthropologists were published in Russian translation under his editorship (cf. also his earlier article '*Novyye inostrannyye raboty o pervobytnykh verovaniyakh*' ('New Foreign Work on Primitive World-Views'), *AR,* 1926: nos. 3, 5). In his own early works, *Ocherki pervobytnoy kul'tury* (Outline of Primitive Culture) and *Ot kamnya k metallu* (From Stone to Metal), both published in the 1920's, Nikol'sky championed the then fashionable 'pre-animistic' theory, although in the 1950's we find him writing that: 'Primitive religion originated in clan society, possibly during the period of Neanderthal man, in the form of totemism' (Nikol'sky, 1954: xiv). But in his posthumously published works he is found reasserting the view that while religion begins with 'animism', 'animism' is not, in itself, religion until it is enshrined in a cult (*Uchenyye zapiski Moskovskogo oblastnogo pedagogicheskogo instituta*) (Study Notes of the Moscow Region Pedagogical Institute), Vol. XXVIII, part 2). In Soviet writing 'religion' and 'cult' go together.

The Soviet ethnographic school was founded by L.Y. Sternberg and V.G. Bogoraz, both of whose scholarly lives had begun well before the Revolution of 1917. Sternberg's writings had in fact, been favourably noticed by Engels. One of the first Soviet historians of religion, Sternberg had been exiled by Tsar Nicholas II to the Far Eastern part of the Empire on account of youthful political activity and whilst in exile there, in a manner reminiscent of Malinowski in similar circumstances some forty years later, he occupied his time studying the local inhabitants – in Sternberg's case the peoples of the Amur region and Siberia (cf. S.A. Ratner-Sternberg, 1928). During 1893-1916 he published a series of articles on the religious beliefs of the Gilyak, Oroch, Gol'd and Ainu peoples, and between 1910-1911 he produced for the *Brokhaus-Efron Encyclopaedia* a series of articles on early forms of religion based on this material. In 1925-1927 he delivered, at the University of Leningrad, a course of lectures on the evolution of religious belief, and these formed the basis of his most well known book *Pervobytnaya religiya v svete etnografii* (Primitive

Religion in the Light of Ethnography), a book which covered such topics as 'The Cult of the Eagle Among the Siberian Peoples', 'The Cult of Twins in China and India' and 'The Notion of "Election" in Religion'. This work, which runs to nigh on 600 pages, also shows Sternberg's wide acquaintance with Western anthropological writing on religion. He had written earlier, in his articles for the *Brokhaus-Efron Encyclopaedia*, of the poor state of Russian scholarship in this respect (op. cit., p. 185), and not until after the 1941-45 War was this state of affairs to be rectified. Sternberg's own view with regard to primitive religion was that it must be seen as having evolved in three stages — from animism to a belief in spirits, to belief in a 'soul' (1936: p. 217).

V.S. Bogoraz, the other founder of the Soviet Ethnographic School, had also been banished in his youth to the East, where he had also studied the beliefs of the indigenous population of outer Siberia. In the second volume of his massive study of the Chukchi, published in 1939, he not only charted their 'animistic' beliefs, as he called them, but offered one of the earliest studies of Siberian shamanism, building in this respect on the one study which, incidentally, Sternberg had exempted from his general indictment of Russian socio-anthropological study: V.M. Mikhailovsky's *Shamanstvo* (Shamanism), published in 1892. The conceptual apparatus which Bogoraz brought to bear on his study of these peoples was heavily indebted to Frazer, Lévi-Bruhl, and Friedrich Boas. It was Frazer, in fact, who inspired his superb study of the myth of the dying and rising 'beast' (*zver'*) found in many parts of Siberia (*khudozhestvennyy fol'klor*, 1926, no. 1). Almost all of the future leaders of the Soviet ethnographic school — B.L. Bogayevsky, A.M. Pokrovsky, G.P. Frantsov, V.O. Vasilenko, A.I. Novikov, A.F. Anisimov and L.N. Manuylova — were his pupils. It was also he who, in 1932, in collaboration with D.D. Bonch-Bruyevich, established the Museum for the History of Religion and Atheism in Leningrad.

Once again we are struck, in looking over early Soviet ethnographical study, at how little its conceptual apparatus owes to Marxism. Although the work which these scholars produced was utilised – often crudely – in the anti-religious cause, it had, in itself, very little that was specifically Marxist. One reason, of course, was that most of these early scholars, though they worked in the Soviet period and were, on the whole, loyal Soviet citizens – some of them with impeccable revolutionary backgrounds – had received their early academic training well before the advent of Soviet power. Further, and more important, these scholars of the early Soviet period were unaware – for reasons we have already stated – of the early writings of Marx and Engels on religion and the origin of religion. They knew, of course, and indeed made reference to, the later writings of Engels, but as we have seen, Engels' later writing owes much to the same, non-Marxian, anthropological sources as were utilised by these scholars themselves. This, however, was soon to change, and one of the things that we see in the writings on religion of the ethnographers of the post-war period is a concerted attempted to work within a much more self-conscious and explicitly Marxist-Leninist framework. At the forefront of this endeavour stands the work of Bogoraz's pupil, G.P. Frantsov, in the opinion of the majority of Soviet scholars with whom I have spoken on these matters, the single most important scholar in the entire field of 'scientific atheism'.

G.P. Frantsov (1903-1969) – who published much of his work in 'scientific atheism' under the name Y.P. Frantsev – first made his name in 1940 with the publication of his doctoral thesis *Fetishizm i problema proiskhozhdeniya religii* (Fetishism and the Problem of the Origin of Religion). In this work Frantsov argued that 'fetishism', 'magic', 'animism', and 'totemism', as studied by ethnographers, are the products of a long historical development, from which he concluded that the earliest form of religion could not be identified with any one of these much later phenomena. However, in all of these later phenomena he held, but especially in 'fetishism', it is possible to discern earlier forms of consciousness which give us at least some idea of where to look for the earliest form of religion. At this stage Frantsov was not prepared to say, however, what that form was.

In 1959, Frantsov published a work which is now regarded in

the Soviet Union as a classic of 'scientific atheism', *U istokov religii i svobodomysliya* (The Sources of Religion and Freethinking), recently revised and re-issued under the title *Nauchnyy ateizm* (1972). In this work, Frantsov put forward what he regarded as the Marxist-Leninist, materialist solution to the problem of the origin of religion – a solution which he claimed was in accordance with all known ethnographic facts. He also analysed what he took to be the essence of ancient religious views and looked at their relationship to myth, rite and ceremony, at the rise of Christianity and at the beginnings of the materialist tradition in the ancient world and at its development in Western Europe up to the time of Marx.

Working with an explicitly Marxist-Leninist methodology meant that when Frantsov came to look at the origin of religion and at its earliest forms, he did so in the light of the materialist conception of history. Man is what man does; look, therefore, argues Frantsov, to the artifacts of ancient cultures and look particularly at what he calls 'sensual-supersensual' (*chuvstvenno-sverkhchuvstvennyye*) things – that is, at the articles used in 'fetishism', which are at the same time 'sensual' and yet 'supersensual', in that they are held to be more than what they, at first sight, appear to be (Frantsov, 1972: pp. 104-144; and esp. pp. 158-159)

For Frantsov and, we must add, for all Soviet historians of religion writing after him, 'fetishism' is the most important single phenomenon in the whole of primitive religion, and one which lingers on in the so-called 'higher' religions as well. Although not present to the same degree in all religions, no religion, for Frantsov, is without it. (One wonders what he made of some of the more sophisticated forms of Hinduism and Buddhism – of the *advaita vedanta*, for example, in which not a trace of 'fetishism' remains. Unfortunately, he does not tell us.) It is, however, in the religions of black Africa, and of West Africa in particular, that 'fetishism' can best be stuided. Here, says Frantsov, it exists alongside of a cult of the 'tribal ancestors', *kak kul't lichnykh fetishey-pokroviteley* – as a cult of personal-fetish-cum protectors. But in the course of history 'fetishism' changes. Whereas among the very primitive, 'fetish' beliefs are not associated with 'animistic' beliefs – the 'fetish' being the object of veneration in and of itself – at a later stage it becomes associated with animistic beliefs, that is, with the belief in the presence of a 'soul'. Thus in studying more highly developed cultures we meet quite often with a distinction between the material object – 'the fetish' – and that which resides in it – namely 'the soul' or 'spirit'. Whilst originally 'fetishes' were made of stone, of wood, of parts of wild animals, in fact out of anything, says Frantsov, that struck the imagination of early man, in the 'higher' religions these have become more sophisticated – thus, in Christianity, for example, we find the veneration of 'the Host', of relics and of icons, in Islam of the 'Black Stone' of Mecca, and in Buddhism the worship of relics of the Buddha (so also Mary Douglas, 1979: p. 69). Frantsov does not, of course, claim that this is all that there is to the 'higher' religions, but he does claim to have called attention to an essential element which cannot be ignored (Frantsov, 1972: pp. 144-157; 245).

It is hard to know quite what to make of these assertions, so counter do they run to the way in which contemporary Western socio-anthropologists and historians of religion seek to understand 'primitive' cultures. Frantsov, for instance, makes no attempt to explicate the meaning which the 'fetish' had for those who use it, in the way that, for example, Mirčea Eliade has sought to do (cf. Eliade, 1958; p.11 and *passim*), nor does he attempt to uncover the, often quite complex, logic of 'primitive' beliefs in the way that Evans-Pritchard, Mary Douglas and other Western scholars have sought to do (cf. Evans-Pritchard, 1956; Mary Douglas 1956, 1978). Example after example is cited, but apart from the intrinsic interest of the examples themselves, little seems to be accomplished, and one has the impression that the examples are given simply to illustrate a theme – that of the evolution of 'primitive' religion mentioned earlier – which is already pre-established. Frantsov is not alone, of course, in using examples in this way – it is a criticism which in Western scholarship is often brought against the views of Sir James Frazer and occasionally against Eliade as well.[8] The only difference, it could be said, is that Frantsov's conceptual scheme is a good deal less complicated than some of those put forward in Western scholarship.

The major criticism, however, that can be made of Frantsov's work concerns the distinction that he draws between an earlier 'fetishistic' phase in the development of human culture and a later 'animistic' phase, for it is difficult to conceive of any empirical evidence that might support such a thesis. Part of the difficulty is that Frantsov nowhere clearly defines what he means by 'fetishism', that is beyond his description of its objects as 'sensual and super-sensual' and the negative assertion that 'fetishism' must be distinguished from 'animism'. As it stands, it is difficult to see how Frantsov's use of 'fetish' differs from the views of those such as R.R. Marret in Great Britain and K.T. Preuss in Germany who postulated an earlier pre-animistic stage in human response to the world to that in which, according to Tylor — the author of the 'animistic' theory — all things are possessed of 'soul' (Marret, 1909; Preuss, 1904-05), or how 'fetishism' is to be distinguished from 'magic'. How the 'fetishist' conceived of his 'fetish' Frantsov does not say. Thus the problem has remained to trouble Soviet ethnographers, to an extent where a great deal of Soviet writing on 'primitive' religion revolves around the exchange of the counters of 'magic', 'fetish', 'soul' and so on. In Western history of religions, the overall view seems to be that the entire question is one that is misconceived, in that there is no evidence which could resolve it (cf. Evans-Pritchard, 1965); certainly it would be difficult to find many Western scholars who would today support the assumption which underlines so much Soviet research into the origin and early forms of religion — namely that the so-called 'primitive' religions still flourishing in the world today can provide us with evidence towards the resolution of this question. 'Primitive' religion, it is now realised, is much more complex than was once thought, and what is more, it too has a history. Soviet ethnography, however, has continued to pursue research into 'primitive' religion on the assumption that this will cast light on the early forms of religion (cf. Shakhnovich, 1967: pp. 258-259), and so on the origin and essence of all religion.

The questions raised by Frantsov, and the answer which he gave about the earliest forms and evolutionary development of religion, have continued to dominate much Soviet writing on religion. Thus, for example, A.F. Losev, in a book *Antichnaya mifologiya v ee istoricheskom razvitii* (Ancient Mythology in its Historical Development) published in 1957, wrote: 'we begin the study of mythology not with animism, but with fetishism' (Losev, 1957: p. 595).

A more thorough discussion of the earliest forms of religion can be found in the work of A.F. Anisimov — work which began in 1929 when he went to found the first elementary school in the Podkamen — Tungus district of Siberia and in his spare time pursued research there into the beliefs of the Evenk people. In 1936 he published the results of this work in a book entitled *Rodovoye obshchestvo evenkov (tungus)* (The Tribal Society of the Evenks [Tungus]), in which he sought to reconstruct the religious outlook and rites of the Evenk, on the assumption that this would cast valuable light on early forms of religion; for Anisimov believed that the Evenks had preserved, in their religious rites, conceptions which were among the earliest in human history. He was particularly interested in the cult of animals, known as '*shingkeny*', in which the skins, teeth and other parts of wild animals were used in the hunting magic of the Evenk as, he says, a 'fetish'. Anisimov, however, makes no attempt to distinguish between 'magic', 'fetish' and 'religion'. All, to him, appear as part and parcel of a single 'primitive' outlook on life — a view which is now fairly generally accepted by Soviet historians of religion (see below p. 253).

In a later book, *Religiya evenkov v istorikogeneticheskom izuchenii i problemy proiskhozhdeniya pervobytnikh verovaniy* (The Religion of the Evenk People in Historico-Genetic Studies and the Problems of the Origin of Primitive Beliefs), published in 1958, Anisimov looked at a wide range of problems connected with the early forms of religion. Basing what he had to say on his own researches among the Evenks, he sought to portray the religion of pre-class society. He returned to this problem in two of his later books, *Kosmologicheskie predstavleniya narodov sibiri* (Cosmological Beliefs of the Peoples of Siberia) (1959) and *Dukhovnaya zhizn' pervobytnogo obshchestva* (The Spiritual Life of Primitive Society) (1966). Taking to heart a suggestion of the writer Maxim Gorky that the study of folk-lore reflected the rudiments of primitive man's understanding of nature, Anisimov tried to show — from a study of Siberian beliefs and art-forms, that a religious outlook on life was preceded by an earlier naïve-materialism with regard to the natural world — a conclusion, of course, in accord with the then prevalent belief in Soviet study of religion that the true origins of religion were to be found only in class-society. The Indian Marxist D.P. Chattopadhyaya has tried to show a similar stage in early Indian cultural development (Chattopadhyaya, 1959).

In 1967, Anisimov put forward a general schema for the development of religion in pre-class society; a schema directly related to developments, as Anisimov saw them, in the social relations of primitive society. Thus, for Anisimov, the most common religious representation in pre-class society was totemism. In the epoch which he designates the epoch of 'the growth of the matriarchal family' and which he, along with the majority of Soviet anthropologists today believes to have preceded the advent of 'patriarchal-tribal society', the predominant religious expression, he claims, was 'the anthropomorphic cult of nature and of the elements', together with cults of animals. Patriarchal-tribal society itself is characterised by the anthropomorphisation of spirits which were formerly represented in animal form, an anthropomorphisation in which not only is nature personified, but social forces as well. The transition from female to male personifications of spirits during this period mirrors the changes which he holds to have taken place in society, as does the structuring of the primitive pantheon along hierarchical lines. It is during this period also, he contends, that the cult of the ancestors originated. Pantheism itself, however, does not arise until the period which Anisimov calls the period of 'military democracy' (*voennaya demokratiya*). We thus, according to Anisimov, have the following development of primitive religion in pre-class society: totemism, worship of the female Spirit or Spirits, worship of male spirits culminating in the worship of ancestors, polytheism. The transition to monotheism takes place only in class society (Anisimov, 1967).

An alternative account of the development of religion in pre-class society had been put forward earlier than that of Anisimov, by M.I. Shakhnovich in a book entitled *Ot suyeveriy k nauke* (From Superstition to Science). Shakhnovich postulated three stages in the evolution of religion during this epoch: (1) the worship of nature; (2) a period in which witchcraft, sorcery and magic were predominant; and (3) a later period in which belief in souls and spirits began to emerge (Shakhnovich, 1948: p. 370).

Both these schemes have been criticised by S.A. Tokarev, on the grounds that neither takes into account many of the now generally accepted features of early religion; and he instances 'the cult of the erotic', cults of the dead, rites of passage, and secret societies, not considered by either Anisimov or Shakhnovich (Tokarev, 1976: pp. 74-76).

By the 1950's, in the wake of the newly felt need within Soviet science of religion for a specifically Marxist approach to the problem of the early history of religion, the view that religion arose only on the threshold of what, in Marxist terminology, is known as 'class-society' (*klassovoye obshchestvo*), or indeed that religion arose only within 'class-society', was becoming widespread in Soviet history of religion. Prior to the advent of religion, it was maintained, there existed only rudimentary opinions about nature and natural processes. This view can be found, for example, in the writings of the Soviet ethnographer A.A. Popov, and in particular in his article *'Perezhitki drevnikh doreligioznykh vozzreniy dolganov na prirodu'* ('Survivals of Ancient Pre-Religious Views of the Dolgans on Nature') which he published in *Sovetskaya etnografiya* (Soviet Ethnography), 1958, issue no. 2); a publication which evoked an immediate critical response from both M.I. Shakhnovich (*SE*, no. 5, 1958) and B.I. Sharevskaya (*SE*, no. 6, 1958). The gist of their criticism was that both archaeology and ethnography told otherwise and Sharevskaya, in particular, pointed out that neither Marx nor Engels had suggested that religion was to be accounted for *wholly* in terms of its social roots. We have already noted Tokarev's criticism of Popov's views (p. 217 above).

The issues involved in this discussion were not, however, destined to be at the storm centre of Soviet ethnography for very long, for as Soviet ethnographers and historians of religion were soon to admit, the question of the early forms of religion was one about which we know, in fact, very little. Thus the prestigious *Issledovaniya i materialy po voprosam pervobytnykh religioznykh verovaniy* (Reasearch and Materials on Problems of Primitive Religious Beliefs) published by the Institute of Ethnography of the Academy of Social Sciences in 1959, pronounced that:

We may never be in a position to know precisely and reliably how religion began in the times of our remote ancestors and what were the earliest forms that it took. (op. cit., vol. IX, p. 5)

This did not stop speculation into the question, but it had the effect of making it cease to be an ideological issue, and thus allowed for the diversity of opinion which we find in Soviet writing on early religion today.

The hesitant note with reference to precise statement regarding the earliest forms of religion, sounded by Soviet ethnographers in this work, was one which has been heard increasingly in the period since 1959, to an extent where B.P. Porshnev, writing in 1965, could, as we have seen above, complain that Soviet historians and ethnographers were inclined to use the one term 'religion' to describe anything and everything that was strange or nonsensical in the spiritual world of primitive man (Porshnev, 1965: p. 138). The truth in Porshnev's criticism was that Soviet historians of religion – like their counterparts in the West – were less inclined than were the anthropologists and historians of the early years of the century to distinguish at all precisely between 'magic', 'religion', 'fetishism', 'totemism', etc., although substantial monographs on these individual aspects of 'primitive' religion continued to be produced. Thus, for example, S.A. Tokarev writes – as do a number of scholars in the West – of what he calls the '*religiozno-magicheskoe verovanie*' – the religio-magical worldview (1976b: p. 540 and *passim*).[9]

Tokarev holds that the forms of religious conceptions among 'primitive' peoples are diverse, and depend on the differing 'concrete' conditions of life obtaining among them. For Tokarev, 'fetishism', 'magic' and 'animism' are all 'aspects' of early religion but are not to be identified with it, for also part of early religion were 'totemism', 'black' and 'white' magic, agricultural rites, burial rites, cults of the dead, etc. Only at a later stage did religion reflect the appearance of more complex forms of social life and material production – as in the cult of the primal ancestors, what Tokarev calls '*initsiatsiya*' (initiation) (shades of Durkheim?), the hunter's cult, family-tribal cults of ancestors, the cult of the personal soul of the 'protectors', of tribal gods and agricultural cults. But with regard to the very early forms of religion, at the present stage of our knowledge, he concludes, all that ethnographers can do is to describe as fully as they can the forms as they find them (1956: pp. 125-138; 1962: pp. 338-375). This he himself sought to do in the early part of his work *Religiya v istorii narodov mira* (Religion in the History of the Peoples of the World), published in 1964 – the first attempt made in the Soviet Union at a complete history of religion from a Marxist point of view. We shall be returning to discuss this work in greater detail shortly.

The attempt to develop a specifically Marxist perspective on the history of religions, and on the problem of the origin of religion in particular, was due in large measure to the increased self-awareness of Marxism-Leninism as a distinctive outlook on life, with a distinctive view of history, which had been developing outwith religious studies. Impetus for the renewal of a distinctive Marxist view of religion had also been given by the publication in 1955 of the collected writings of Marx and Engels on religion. The impact of this renewed awareness of what Marx and Engels themselves had had to say on the essence and origins of religion

– particularly in their early writings which were now freely available in the Soviet Union for the first time – together with a renewed emphasis on what Lenin had said about the epistemological roots of religion and idealism, was soon to be felt in all areas of the study of religion.

The seminal work in this respect is D.M. Ugrinovich's *Filosofskiye problemy kritiki religii* (Philosophical Problems in the Criticism of Religion) published in 1965, although A. Levada's *Sotsial'naya priroda religii* (The Social Nature of Religion), published in the same year, is almost equally influential. Both these works are today extensively quoted in Soviet writing on the early history of religion. Levada's is, in many ways, the more theoretical critique, as the titles of his early chapters indicate: 'The History of the Posing of the Problem', 'Religion as a Social Phenomenon' and 'Religious Ideology as a Form of Social Consciousness'. The burden of his critique – and Ugrinovich makes essentially the same point – is that both Western (bourgeois) anthropologists, and Soviet ethnographers when they have posed the problem of the early forms of religion in a similar way, have been misled in assuming that primitive religion was a philosophical reading of the world. What both have ignored is its deep, social roots – and Ugrinovich adds its deep emotional roots as well – a point with which many Western social anthropologists, who are not Marxists, would agree (cf. Beattie, 1966: pp. 202-239). But although early religion is not philosophy, Ugrinovich makes a point which is not dissimilar to that made by Francis Cornforth, in his book *From Religion to Philosophy* (1912), to the effect that religion and much early philosophy spring from the same epistemological and emotional roots. We have looked earlier at how Soviet philosophers are now seeking to develop this suggestion (Section 4.2).

There is still one further area of Soviet study which we must mention, and that is what Soviet scholars call the 'pre-religious epoch' (*doreligioznaya epokha*). This, as they recognise, is not an area of study to which Western scholars devote much attention (mistakenly, in fact, cf. Brandon, 1970: pp. 535-536; James,

1949: pp. 22-23), but for them it is extremely important. Zybkovets, in his book on the subject, *Doreligioznaya epokha: k istorii formirovaniya obshchestvennogo soznaniya* (The Prereligious Epoch: Towards the Formation of Social Consciousness), published in 1958, puts it like this: according to contemporary science man appeared on earth about a million years ago, but religion in any definite form began only in tribal society, that is, according to archaeology – here he cites a number of Soviet archaeological sources – during the Palaeolithic period about 30-40,000 years ago. Therefore, for something like 900,000 years man knew no religion. This is the 'epoch before religion', and its importance for Soviet scholars is that it shows, so they believe, that man could get along very well without religion, that it was not, as Durkheim claimed, essential to man; for during this period, Zybkovets claims that man clothed himself, built dwelling places, fashioned weapons with which to kill wild animals, etc. The pre-religious history of man also shows us that a religious sense is not, as many theologians maintain, innate (cf. Tokarev, 1976b: p. 27).

All this, of course, is pure speculation and is based on the negative fact that before the Palaeolithic period no religious remains have, as yet, been found. The argument given above is, therefore, limited, to say the least, but it is one that is taken seriously by Soviet 'scientific atheism' and is repeated as an established fact in all standard expositions of the history of religion (Krivelev, 1975: vol. I, pp. 17-20; Tokarev, 1976b: pp. 27-28).

To bring my survey of Soviet study of the origin and early forms of religion to a close I propose, on the basis of the accounts given in the authorative text book *Istoriya i teoriya ateizma* (1974) and in the two general histories of religion produced up to the present time in the Soviet Union (Kryvelev, 1975 and Tokarev, 1976 (3rd ed.)) to give a summary of the origin and early history of religion as it now appears to Soviet 'scientific atheism'. It is an account, so Soviet scholars claim, which is based upon the present state of scientific knowledge in archaeology, linguistics, ethnography and psychology (*IiTA*: p. 43), and it represents the substance of their naturalistic, 'scientific' account and critique of the origin of religion. It runs as follows:

For many hundreds of thousands of years after his first appearance in the evolutionary time scale *homo sapiens* had no religion. Archaeology shows that religion is unknown before the middle of the Palaeolithic period – the attempts of some Western historians of religion, such as E.O. James and G. Koenigswald, to argue that Sinanthropus had a religion are false.[10] By the late Palaeolithic period, however, the existence of some form of religion and of magic rituals is beyond doubt. Religion appears at different times and in different places, and thus one cannot postulate a 'cradle of religion', though some ideas may have spread from group to group. Religion appeared spontaneously in human cultures owing to a variety of objective and subjective factors, but what is certain is that the rise of religion was a collective and not an individual occurrence. Durkheim, therefore, tells us nothing new, for Marxism has always maintained that consciousness is formed in the mutual relationships of people and not in isolation. Before religion arose, man was a materialist, working by means of trial and error, but he could, and did, think logically and the attempt of Lévi-Bruhl to argue for a primitive 'pre-logical mentality' is mistaken.[11] At some stage in his development, however, man acquired 'fantastic' notions about the operation of the world and 'fetishism', and later 'animism', was born. All that we can say about this is that it arose from a division in consciousness which gave rise to the notions of 'soul' and 'body'. This dualism is rooted in the conditions of the social life of primitive man, but there is no mention now of Bogdanov's theory as to how this happened; in fact, no account at all is now given of the social conditions which gave rise to this important distinction in human thought. What is usually asserted at this point is that Lenin's (*sic*) theory of man's helplessness in the struggle with nature, as being the ultimate cause of primitive religious beliefs, is illuminating, and that it is, therefore, essential that Soviet ethnographers and historians of religion 'reveal the wealth of its content in the light of what they

can find out about the life and consciousness of primitive man'
(Kryvelev, 1976: p. 19). But man cannot have been totally helpless or he would not have survived, and this raises the question
why religion was not existent in the times of the earliest men
who were more, or at least as, helpless as the men of the middle
Palaeolithic period? The answer given is that, before religion
could develop, man had to develop a sense of dissatisfaction with
his lot and so begin to fantasise an alleviation of his present
condition. Man's consciousness had also to develop to a degree
where he could break free from empirical reality and form concepts and ideas, and this took place only in the course of the
struggle for the elementary technical and economic knowledge
necessary for him to develop and progress. But the development
of man's imaginative powers in the course of this struggle had
negative, as well as positive, consequences, in that it allowed
men to dream, and so develop a fantasy relationship to reality.
Thus, man came to believe that the impossible was possible. The
positive side of man's imaginative development was, however,
the stronger and more important, as is proven by the fact that
man continued to develop and progress in spite of his religious
fantasies. Primitive men – and here such psychological evidence as
is believed to be relevant is adduced – had a naïvely realistic
relationship to the world, including the world of their own imagination, believing that all their feelings and impressions were
equally valid. Turning away from empirical reality, man, helped
by these abstractions, began to construct a view of the world
which bore only a tenuous relationship to reality. In particular,
primitive man sought to explain the workings of the world by
analogy with himself and with his society. Did intellectual
curiosity lead man to this view of the world or did it arise instinc-
tually? The answer is that neither of these popular views are
correct. The development of a religious understanding of the
world arose neither from the desire for an explanation of nature
as a whole, nor from instinct, but from the desire for a correct
orientation to the immediate environment. Man's curiosity was
only roused by that which had an immediate bearing on his

struggle for survival, and by that which interfered with it. Kryvelev suggests, however, that primitive man's response to the world was more 'impulsive-emotional' (*emotsional'no-impul'sivnyy*), as he calls it, than that of men of later times, because of the greater number of dangers and uncertainties that he faced, and he even hazards the guess that there were more psychological disorders among primitive man than there are among men today![12] Fear, despair and a sense of helplessness all make for religion, which is, of course, from a Marxist-Leninist point of view, the greatest psychological disorder of all.

Man seeks comfort and security above all else and, according to Soviet 'scientific atheism' other ways of achieving these being denied to him, primitive man found them in a religious 'fantasy' world of his own imagination. Further, 'scientific atheism' claims that religion can also arise as an imaginative response to positive emotions of gratitude and joy.[13]

Thus the Soviet 'scientific atheist' account of the origin of religion concludes that religion arose when it was inevitable that it did so and possible for it to do so. It was inevitable, early man being what he was, that it should arise as a 'fantasy' response to the hard and unacceptable conditions of life under which he laboured, as a fantasy of hope containing the promise of future bliss. But it was possible only when human consciousness had reached a stage of social and imaginative development where the fantasy world of religion could be formulated.

With regard to the earliest forms of religion, the standard 'scientific atheist' account claims that certain common features can be noted from various parts of the world, linked, firstly, to social and geographic conditions and secondly, to common stages in the development of thought. If we examine the language of primitive peoples, it claims, we find that, in comparison with the language of developed peoples, the language of primitives is characterised by fewer concepts for the expression of abstract thought, although it is rich in terms that describe particular features of the world. Thus, theories which imply that primitive religion was complex and abstract — as does the theory of Codrington regarding 'mana'

– are wrong. Primitive man could not have conceived of an 'impersonal force'. Whilst 'animism' is indeed a feature of later primitive thought, its explanatory value with regard to primitive religion is limited. A more important notion for establishing the earliest form of religion is 'fetishism', and in its original form 'fetishism' was not connected with 'animism', nor with anything else. In the beginning man had only a special attitude to certain objects which had a mysterious significance for him. Only when these mysterious objects were regarded as supernatural do we find the beginning of religion. This, of course, is in comformity with the now generally accepted view in the Soviet Union that man was originally non-religious.

'Fetishism' is defined as:

Veneration (*pochitaniye*) for various objects of reality, to which people attach supernatural qualities – the power to heal and to ward off danger. (*Istoriya i teoriya ateizma:* p. 45)

These objects may be natural – an oddly shaped stone or piece of wood – or, at a later stage of development, man-made; at which point 'fetishism' merges into 'magic' defined as:

. . .an aggregate of representation and action, connected with the belief in the possibility of influencing objects by supernatural means, i.e., by performing symbolic actions and by incantation. (ibid., p. 46)

And in 'magic' itself,

. . .we can clearly discern the sources of religious belief. The weakness, the inability to achieve, by realistic means, the desired goal, forces primitive people to turn to false, to illusory means. (ibid.)

Religion, says Soviet 'scientific atheism', arose out of, and continues to draw sustenance from, ignorance and impotence, for this is of its essence, and thus 'magic' continues to be an important aspect of the immature response to the world which religion enshrines.

A further feature of primitive religion to which 'scientific atheism' draws attention is 'totemism'. This is defined as:

. . .the belief in a supernatural connection, or kinship, between a group of people and some particular species of wild animal or plant. (ibid.)

'Totemism' comes to the fore, Soviet scholars argue, as the ideology of early tribal society, when man had still not separated himself off from the kingdom of nature. Totemism is closely connected with the agricultural realities of primitive man — with food gathering and hunting:

Wild animals and plants, which provide man with the means of existing, become an object of veneration. In totemism, there is also reflected, especially, the social relationships of the primitive collective, which is founded on the principle of blood relationship. The awareness of this relationship is carried over into surrounding nature. The 'totem' — the wild animal or plant — is thought of as the ancestor of the tribe — its progenitor. With it there is connected a series of myths describing its life and peregrinations, its instructions regarding what it is prohibited to kill etc. (ibid., pp. 45-46)

Finally, when describing the earliest forms of religion, Soviet scholars turn to 'animism' — the belief that 'souls' inhabit certain natural objects, including animals. This belief arose, argues 'scientific atheism', from man's tendency to interpret natural occurences by analogy with himself, and so to see behind certain phenomena the doings of a personal will. In the animistic view of the world we find 'reflected' those aspects of reality which struck the imagination of primitive man, which caused him fear and which affected his immediate interests. 'Animism' also arises from primitive man's conception of his own psyche — from dreams, swoons, hallucinations, which are apprehended as the activity of a 'soul' detached from a body — a conception which primitive man reads into animals and other natural phenomena. The notion of a 'soul' also gives rise to the belief in immortality, in a life beyond the grave. The 'animistic' way of looking at the world is yet another feature of the earliest form of religion which continues into the present. It is, in fact, for Soviet scholars (as for many Western Humanists) the most universally recognisable characteristic of religion.

These four distinguishable, yet related, features of early religion — fetishism, magic, totemism and animism — exhaust Soviet descriptions of the beginnings of religion. All spring from the same psychological and social roots and all, with the possible exception of totemism, are held to continue into developed religion. No one form is today identified as positively more fundamental than any other, but there is a tendency to see 'fetishism' as the earliest of the four — though no concerted attempt is made to distinguish it from magic — and 'animism', as a somewhat later development (cf. *KNAS:* pp. 22-23). No empirical reasons are given for this preference and it would seem to appeal to Soviet scholars on the purely *a priori* ground that 'fetishism' appears to have a less overtly 'religious' content than 'animism', and thus to be nearer to the pre-religious period of man's development of Soviet 'scientific atheism's' speculation.

Taken together, it is claimed that these four forms of early religion 'reflect' the specific conditions of the material and spiritual life of early man; the low level of material production, and the consequent low level of social relations, giving rise to the particularities of the fantasy world of the early religious imagination. As tribal life developed and diversified, so religious belief changed to 'reflect' changed conditions. As individuals acquired wealth and a social hierarchy developed, so a hierarchy of gods developed. Polytheism emerged after individual tribes were forced through circumstances to forge alliances with each other. As national states arose, so there arose state religions and with them the conception of a single all-powerful supreme god, out of which monotheism arose. Thus we reach the era of the beginnings of the great world religions.

In this somewhat simplistic account of the origin and early forms of religion there is much that is interesting, much that is speculative and tendentious and much that is just plain non-sensical — such as, for example, that primitive man suffered a greater degree of mental illness than ourselves. What is interesting is the shift which has taken place since the late 1950's from an intellectualistic approach, which saw religion as a primitive and mistaken philosophical response on the part of early man to the mystery that surrounds him. By rooting the origin of religion in the realities of life, as they see them, Soviet 'scientific atheism' has followed much the same path as has social anthropology in the West, although the Soviet understanding of these realities is a good deal less complicated – the unkind will say more naïve – than those propounded in the West. Drawing upon the classical Marxist account of religion as 'the fantastic realisation of the human essence in a world where the human essence has no true reality', Soviet 'scientific atheism' uses this insight as virtually its sole metholdological device for unlocking the mystery of the origin of religion.[14] There is thus little in its account of the earliest forms of religion that cannot be found in the writings of Marx and Engels – as the wealth of quotation from the writings of these authors, which abounds in all Soviet writing on the origin of religion, testifies.

Our conclusion must be, therefore, that, except for its usefulness for apologetic purposes, Soviet 'scientific atheists' are but little interested in the historical origin of religion as an empirical problem. For 'scientific atheism', the origin and early development of religion is but a function of its essence, as this was defined by Marx and Engels, and the conclusions of Soviet study of this problem have, therefore, about them an air of inevitability. The account of the origin and early development of religion which we find in Soviet study – in which what is earliest in time must be simplest in structure – *must* be the way in which religion arose and developed. This is particularly evident in Frantsov's claim that 'fetishism' must be the earliest form of religion. The most that we can say about this is that religion may have developed like this, but that there is no evidence – and perhaps could be no evidence – to show that it did so (cf. Evans-Pritchard, 1965: p. 29; N.K. Sanders, 1979: pp. 103-104). In telling the story of the rise of religion as they do, Soviet historians of religion differ but little from those Western nineteenth century anthropologists who were their mentors.

How Marxist-Leninist 'scientific atheism' tells the story of the continued development of religion, as this is found in the great world religions, will be the subject of our next section.

But before turning to this, I would like to look at a criticism of this approach to the history of religion put forward by the Soviet ethnographer, B.F. Porshnev, and referred to at the outset of this chapter, for it is a criticism which is, I think, relevant, not only to Soviet study of religion, but to any study which seeks to give a naturalistic account of the origin and early development of religion. Its immediate target, however, was the approach to the history of religion exemplified in Tokarev's books, *Early Forms of Religion and Their Development* and *Religion in the History of the Peoples of the World*, which, as mentioned earlier, Tokarev published in 1964.

Tokarev's book, *Religion in the History of the Peoples of the World*, like many Western books on the same topic, is constructed on the historical and geographical principle. It is divided, as we would expect, into three parts: (1) the religion of pre-class society and of the transition to class society; (2) the national-state religions of class society, and (3) the world religions of class society. Within each section, Tokarev describes the religions of the ancient and modern peoples of all continents and arranges the data, as far as possible, in ascending order, from the more primitive to the more complex and highly developed social orders and their corresponding religions.

Tokarev's other book, *Early Forms of Religion and Their Development*, is somewhat different, for in this work Tokarev presents his material, not in ethnographical or historical sequence, but as a *classification* of primitive forms of religion. Yet Tokarev does make an attempt at arranging the various forms of religion which he identifies in a sequence, which, in his opinion, corresponds, to an ascent from lower to higher forms of religion.[15] Thus he begins by describing the forms of religion observed, as he believes, at the lowest stages of social development – totemism, maleficient rites, sorcery, erotic rites and cults, funerary cults — and then passes to describe the cults of the early tribal stage of social development — rites of passage, hunters' cults, cults of the matriarchal clan structure and patriarchal family and clan ancestor worship. Lastly he describes the forms of religions associated with the tribal structure of society — shamanism, the cult of personal protector spirits, the cult of secret societies, the cults of leaders, the cult of the tribal god and agrarian cults. It is Tokarev's book *Early Forms of Religion and Their Development*, dealing as it does with primitive forms of religion, which raises most pertinently the question which Porshnev wishes to put to the discipline of the history of religions.

Porshnev lays great stress on the importance of the history of religion as a discipline: 'it constitutes', he says, 'a chapter in the science of the human mind and the paths by which it came into being' (op. cit., p. 136). And he continues:

For the fact is that the sciences of 'the true' - such as logic and information theory, mathematical logic and semiotics — which underlie the remarkable achievements of cybernetic technology, remain incomplete. . .until they are supplemented by the sciences of 'the untrue'. The capacity of the human mind for confusion, absurdity and contradiction — i.e., for distorting reality — cannot be explained solely as mechanical breakdowns in the thinking machine. (Porshnev, 1965: pp. 136-137)

The facts recorded in Tokarev's book — or, indeed, in any book on primitive religion — compel us, says Porshnev, to face this fact. They also, he contends, raise important questions regarding the relationship between the socio-historical sciences and the rest of the complex of contemporary sciences, and at this point he refers to recent criticism of the historical disciplines by prominent Soviet scientists in the influential journal *Voprosy filosofii* (Problems of Philosophy) (*VF*, 1964, no. 5); criticism which reveals, incidentally, just how influential natural science remains today in the Soviet Union as a model for all science. Castigating the historical sciences for their lack of progress, the journal asks 'whence will these 'obsolete' disciplines be fertilised?' and it answers, 'from the sciences termed fundamental — that is, from mathematics, cybernetics, physics, chemistry, biology' (*VF,* 1964, no. 5, p. 76). In another article in the same issue, the point is put even more forcibly. The authors write:

The development of thought in the sciences in recent years has by-passed the field of history, hardly touching it at all. As a consequence, it continues to rest content with general scientific concepts typical of a level of scientific thought long since past. (op. cit., p. 83)

But far from being disheartened by such criticism, Porshnev argues that historians should seek to meet this challenge by developing new methods for analysing their material. This applies particularly to historians of religion. He writes:

The headlong advance of the front of the sciences has already become widely separated. . .from the idea that one must always take an historical approach, from evolution, and from the idea of development. Many fundamental concepts with respect to the possibility of formalization, logical modelling, and structural analysis of any and all processes and phenomena, and one might say, many fundamental notions of theoretical or abstract cybernetics, are based on a sort of timeless phenomenology. (op. cit., p. 137)

What is needed, argues Porshnev, 'is a way of writing differential equations describing the behaviour of evolving systems', for without this all hope of building logical and technical models of all that is, including the human mind itself, will remain mere daydreams,[16] and he refers at this point to a conversation which he once had with a leading Soviet cybernetician, who said to him: 'in order to advance further with my generalisations, it is absolutely necessary for me to understand the nature of what is called religion' (op. cit., p. 137). Expanding on this remark, Porshnev calls attention to Academician A.N. Kolmogorov's point that, in cybernetics, analysis of higher nervous activity has so far, in Soviet science, concentrated on two opposite poles: on the one hand, cyberneticians study the conditioned reflexes of animals and, on the basis of this most elementary and simplest activity of the brain, they develop models known as mathematical theories of instruction; on the other hand, computer science is successfully employing mathematical methods to investigate the highest functions of the human brain – its operations in formal logic. But Kolmogorov notes, with amazement, that the vast area between these two poles – the most primitive and the most complex mental acts – is unfortunately not the subject of cybernetic analysis (Kolmogorov, 1964: pp. 25-26). It is in this grey area that Porshnev locates the beliefs and activities of religion.

We have seen earlier in this chapter how Porshnev is critical of the rather blanket use of the term 'religion' to cover all that is strange in the outlook and behaviour of 'primitive man', but even if we restrict 'religion' in the way Porshnev suggests – in which it would apply only to the faiths and cults of class society to which the notion of belief in god is central – we are left, he says, with a very interesting 'expression of a given stage in the historical development of the human mind' – even if, today, it serves more as an example of the malfunctioning of the human organism than as a stage in its historical development. This is, in fact, why religion is of such interest to Soviet cyberneticians.

Having said this, it is not, therefore, surprising that Porshnev seeks to re-open one of the classic *cause célèbres* in the whole history of anthropology and religion (of what, in the Soviet Union is called ethnology) – the view put forward by Marr, on the basis of his reading of Lévi-Bruhl, regarding a primitive pre-logical mentality. Both Lévi-Bruhl and Marr, in Porshnev's opinion, attempted very radical solutions to the problem of the history of human thought, and of language which is so intimately connected with it. The matter at issue, argues Porshnev, was not the historical accumulation of knowledge, not change in the content of thought; what was at stake was the claim made by Lévi-Bruhl and Marr, who had grown up with the heritage of prior generations of ethnologists and ethno-psychologists, to have demonstrated that the mental operations performed by primitive men were qualitatively different in structure – if not in all cases, then in some – from those admitted by contemporary logic. It is a claim which today is dismissed out of hand in both Soviet and Western history of religion (cf. Evans-Pritchard, 1934, 1940 and 1965: pp. 78-99; Sharevskaya, 1959), but Porshnev does not believe that such a cursory dismissal is justified. 'Were these scholars criticised from the right direction?', he asks (op. cit., p. 138) and his reply is that they were not. He writes:

Lévi-Bruhl, who had a tremendous influence on Marr, defined primitive ideation not only as pre-logical, but also as magical and mystical. He was on the one hand, an observant empirical ethnologist and, on the other, an idealist in philosophy. The extremely abundant concrete facts collected by both himself and by other scholars, such as Durkheim and Frazer, brought Lévi-Bruhl to the threshold of major discoveries and syntheses, but his idealist philosophy led him farther from the fruitful path of the science of the historical development of the human mind. His ultimate conclusion was that it was not two stages that were involved, but two unchanging, opposed aspects of the human spirit — faith and reason. The logic of idealism brought Lévi-Bruhl, towards the end of his life, to abandon the concept of 'pre-logical thought' and to retain only that of 'mystical thought'. Science, however, required exactly the opposite. It was necessary to discard definitions such as 'mystical' and 'magical' because they themselves are truly mystical and explain nothing. . . Marr too did not escape — despite his attempt to place the problem on a Marxist footing — from this 'magism'. Yet the Soviet ethnographers [Sharevskaya is mentioned by name] who offered critiques of Lévi-Bruhl and Marr, in rejecting the notion of the pre-logical character of primitive thought, rejected what was most valuable (and progressive) in their thinking. (op. cit., pp. 138-139)

Porshnev recognises that the term 'pre-logical' is just as inadequate as, for example, the terms 'pre-feudal' or 'pre-capitalistic' and science, in order to advance, will, he says, have to fill the negative concept with a positive scientific content. To this end he says:

It is necessary to overcome altogether that timidity in the face of theoretical thought that has, in recent decades, been characteristic of a number of branches of the humanities in our country. Previously Soviet scholars have stated with justice that the description and systematization of ethnographic facts is not an end in itself but a means towards the creative treatment of various theoretical problems in the development of culture, society, and man. (op. cit., p. 139)

Unfortunately – and this as we shall see is Porshnev's basic criticism of Tokarev and the discipline which he represents – ethnography has not progressed very far in the direction of theory; that is, beyond the collection and systematization of facts. This is the root of Porshnev's dissatisfaction, not so much with Tokarev himself, as with the discipline which he represents. Yet both Tokarev's books vividly represent, for Porshnev, the situation as it exists at present in Soviet ethnography and history of religion. It is not accidental, Porshnev points out, that they are organised as surveys, although it cannot be said that we have simply a 'facto-graphy', for Tokarev sets himself the task, as we saw in the quota-tion given from one of his later papers at the outset of this chapter, not only of describing, but of explaining. Porshnev finds great interest in the theoretical conclusions which Tokarev draws at the close of his book, *Religion in the History of the Peoples of the World* – and because it is representative of the current outlook of Soviet history of religion I have translated it verbatim as an appendix to this present work. But interesting as it is, for Porsh-nev, it only reveals the more clearly 'the conscious abandonment of theory that permeates the entire book' (op. cit., p. 139). The reader will be able to judge for himself (cf. Appendix III).

But Tokarev does not wholly evade theoretical issues. As his conclusion makes clear, he eagerly and, in Porshnev's opinion, most convincingly, criticises – both in the body of his book and in the conclusion – earlier concepts and theories in the fields of both primitive beliefs and the history of religion as a whole. But the result is wholly destructive, in that the subject under discussion, according to Porshnev,

. . .dissolves into a great multiplicity of individual subjects, even though they are often 'contaminated' (to use a favourite word of Tokarev's) i.e., mutually connected and intersecting, and a motley sequence of cults and beliefs of diverse peoples of the pre-class epoch parades before the reader. (op. cit., p. 139)

The Western student of the history of religion will, I am sure, recognise a similar state of affairs when reading many of the introductory surveys written by historians of religion within his own academic tradition![17]

By introducing the notion of 'forms of religion', Tokarev, like his counterparts in Western Europe and America, seeks to shift the centre of gravity of synthesising thought from theory to classification. In *Religion in the History of the Peoples of the World* this task is performed fairly easily for the material is arranged, as we have noted, on the historical-geographical principle. The classification of the factual data among clan-tribal cults, national-state religions, and world religions (Buddhism, Christianity and Islam) is quite clear-cut and indisputable. All the other concepts, including totemism, fetishism, sorcery, shamanism, funerary cults, mythology, and the like, are introduced by Tokarev in the course of his presentation. But in *Early Forms of Religion and Their Development,* it is logical systematics that is involved. Here, under the rubric of each of the identified forms of religious, examples are cited from the beliefs and rituals of the most diverse peoples. (The Western reader will be reminded of the writings of Frazer and Eliade at this point).[18] The impression created is that what Tokarev regards as most important in his book is, on the one hand, his critique of previous classifications of religions; and on the other hand, his own new 'morphological' classification of religion. But, as Porshnev points out, no new rigorously logical system of classification emerges; no uniform basis of classification is adhered to and, instead, the model offered cannot itself incorporate all phenomena. Thus, Tokarev divides the most ancient and primitive forms into totemism, sorcery (in the sense of maleficent rites), witch-doctoring (the health cult), erotic customs, and funerary rites. This, argues Porshnev, is not a classification but an empirical grouping and something has been left out; in particular, divination, prediction of the future, and soothsaying. Among later forms of religion, which already, for Tokarev, reflect the process of breakdown of the clan-communal structure, we find cults based on hunting and gathering isolated as a special form of religion, but military cults are omitted, although they have been equally well described in ethnographic literature. In classifying family-clan

cults into two groups – sacred things and protectors, and ancestors – which Tokarev associates with matriarchal and patriarchal
clans respectively, he omits, for example, beliefs and rituals
associated with childbirth. In short, for Porshnev, Tokarev's
'forms of religion' are not so much 'logical-synthetic' as descriptive, not so much a classification as a list.

Again the Western student will be conscious that this criticism
applies equally to much Western writing of the history of religion
and to the writings of Mirčea Eliade in particular. What, in Porshnev's opinion, such an approach lacks is a synthesising theory.
Tokarev, he admits, places before us a number of guiding methodological principles for the study of the history of religion –
principles which include the proposition that all forms of religion
are 'determined' by earthly, socio-historical factors, and the
proposition that they are at the same time relatively independent
of such factors – principles which, as we have seen, govern all
'scientific atheist' study of the history of religion. Tokarev also
holds that there is a historical sequence and 'contamination' of
the various forms of religion. His dominant idea, however, his
basic task, as we saw earlier, is to reveal the material foundation
of each separate form of religion, to find its real roots (Tokarev,
1976b: p. 43) and, as a Marxist, he sees them in the various forms
and spheres of practical life. It is on this basis that he classifies the
early forms of religion. Thus, the roots of totemism are located in
the utterly real organisation of the life relationships of consan-
guinity, the phratry system, etc. These real, earthly relationships
of human beings, distortedly 'reflected' in their minds, are transferred by them to external nature and become personified in
imagined mythological images. The earthly roots of sorcery lie
in emnity among primitive communities and tribes, later clothed
in magical and animistic techniques for injuring enemies when it
was not possible to do this in reality. The terrestrial root of 'witch-
doctoring' is the struggle against diseases and death, which was
clothed in superstitions, magic, and notions of the soul. Erotic
rituals are, again, for Tokarev, a 'reflection' in fantastic form of
an important sphere of human life – the relation between the

sexes. The funerary cult is a superstitious superstructure of ritual and fantastic notions over how to handle the corpse of a dead fellow clansman. Rites of passage are a religious and superstitious 'reflection' of ancient divisions of society by age and sex and, indeed, the same goes for any 'form of religion'; it is a distorted, superstitious 'reflection' of men's life practice in their social and natural environment, although Tokarev warns against our thinking that each individual religious notion or ritual can be taken in isolation and related directly to material practice (1964a: p. 532) and he recognises that it is not always possible to relate such 'forms' at all to material practice (ibid., p. 534).

In accordance with this principle of explanation and classification of the 'forms of religion' Tokarev ascribes great significance, in the totality of each cult, not only to beliefs, but, above all, to ritual practices. He emphasises, in all his writings, that religion is not merely ideas in the minds of men, but also customs, rituals, the magic of techniques, behavioural prescriptions and taboos. Rituals, as for the English anthropologist Marrett are, for Tokarev, of earlier origin than concepts or ideas, and this 'practical' aspect of religion emerges, for Tokarev, as a transitional or connecting link between the practice of people in their material lives and the world of false notions about a fantastic, supernatural life. First, in Tokarev's opinion, there arose a belief in the supernatural power of human action itself, and gradually this took on the form of images, souls and spirits – that is, it underwent animistic and mythological personification.

What emerges from Tokarev's study, *The Early Forms of Religion and Their Development,* is that there is no internal law of development in the religion of primitive peoples. The mythological, fetishistic, animistic, pre-animistic, magical, and all other theories about the most ancient stage in the evolution of religion are discarded and, on the ruins of these scholarly structures, Tokarev erects a new structure with, so he believes, a firmer material foundation and one infinitely simpler in appearance. It is this very simplicity that worries Porshnev. He writes:

Tokarev demonstrates again and again how a distorted reflection of some terrestial, everyday practice arises with the passage of time, in the form of supernatural acts and supernatural images. Tokarev frequently says that 'superstitions' arose from earthly roots, as though that word, of which he is very fond, could answer the basic questions: *why* and *how* does this happen? Why, in fact, has the human mind, so inventively, so liberally in a sense, distorted the objective world? (op. cit., p. 141)

This, it will be recalled, is precisely the question that we ourselves would have wished to have put to the founders of Marxism (cf. above, p. 60) and we can only assume that Porshnev, through the medium of his sustained critique of Tokarev, would have liked to have put it too. To say so openly would, of course, be quite out of the question in the Soviet Union, but it is, as Porshnev insists, the question which any attempted naturalistic explanation of the origin and early development of religion has to answer.

Tokarev's own answer is, as we would expect, the classical Marxist one that religion, as a distorted reflection of the real world, is an expression of the helplessness of man in the face of his environment, both natural and human. But this, says Porshnev, 'requires deep-reaching explanations' (ibid., p. 141), for why, to use Feuerbach's phrase, did man, in responding to the world religiously, 'turn the world inside out'?

This, for Porshnev, is the question with which the history of religion – drawing on the other specialised sciences wherever possible – should be concerned. 'Will science', he asks, 'really not discover the logical, psychological, or physiological laws of this mental activity?' Reading Tokarev's books, saturated as they are with learning, leads one inevitably to ask, says Porshnev, whether all this infinite variety of ritual and belief really is not amenable to synthesis? He himself thinks that it is. He writes:

The greater the variety of the forms and manifestations of religion revealed to us, the more the spirit of contemporary scientific thought insists that general laws or formulae descriptive of a particular type of mental operation can be identified in it. (op. cit., p. 142)

And he continues:

Cybernetics has created the category of 'stochastic' machines, which carry out the type of linkage or identification that is not determinated by the objective conditions among the elements, but is of random origin and consequently infinitely more diverse. In short, can all the operations of the mind referrable to the field of the history of religion be generalised and formalised? More broadly, is it possible to generalise, to formalise all the operations called fantasies? (ibid.)

Porshnev does not profess to know the answer to this question, but what he does contend is that to make the attempt is the only way forward for the science of religion. His final criticism of Tokarev is, in fact, that he fails even to attempt to utilise the findings of contemporary psychology in his account of the rise of the religious consciousness – particularly findings relating to the emotions. Porshnev writes:

Today, in order to write books in the realm of psychology (and the history of religion, I repeat, penetrates deeply into that sphere and rests on it), one cannot be satisfied with commonplace, uncritical, vague notions about mental phenomenon and processes. (ibid.)

It will not do, for example, to say of shamans simply that they are 'nervous' people, or to (groundlessly) connect hysteria with epilepsy, nor to use what Porshnev calls 'do-it-yourself' concepts, such as 'a consciously controlled nervous-hysterical attack' or 'self-hypnosis' – concepts which appear in no reputable psychological text-book. The numerous mental acts which seem to Tokarev – and indeed to many other historians of religion, both Soviet and Western – to require no explanation, and to be 'natural', actually, says Porshnev, call for the application of the rather complex techniques of modern scientific psychological analysis. As yet, as Porshnev also makes clear, this is as much a call to historians of religion to take part in a creative enterprise as it is to apply assured results. Scientific materialist psychology still has a long way to go. But that this is the way forward in the science of religion, again, Porshnev has no doubt, and he closes his paper with some positive suggestions as to how this might be done.

In presenting Porshnev's criticism of Tokarev and contemporary Soviet history of religion, I have, I trust, not only shown that Soviet study of religion can, at times, be envigorating, but what is more important, self-critical, and self-critical in ways that Western *Religionswissenschaft* has rarely been. Soviet study of religion can indeed be positive and creative. This much comes through in Porshnev's paper. Whether the actual suggestions that he makes for positive advance in the study of religion, which owe more to materialist psychology than to Marxism, have any future, only time will tell. But important or not, they at least mark an advance upon the trite reiteration of what Marx, Engels and Lenin had to say about religion, and in terms of Soviet study of religion this is something that all concerned with that study cannot but welcome. This will become the more obvious when we turn, as we do now, to look at what Soviet 'scientific atheism' says about the development of religion in class society.

5.3 RELIGIONS OF CLASS SOCIETY: THE WORLD RELIGIONS OF BUDDHISM, CHRISTIANITY AND ISLAM

As we saw earlier, of the many religions of class-society, only three are held by Soviet 'scientific atheism' to be truly universal and to have played any appreciable role in the 'world historical process'. These are Buddhism, Chritianity and Islam. As such these three religions are accorded a special place in Soviet writing on religion (Tokarev, 1976: p. 79; Zhukov, 1976: p. 19). All three religions, of course, are still active within the Soviet Union today.

What distinguishes Buddhism, Chritianity and Islam from the other, and largely 'national', religions of class society is, in the words of Academician Zhukov, that:

They have displayed maximum adaptability to changes in social relations far beyond the countries of their origin — thus showing their ability to subserve different and antagonistic stages of social development. (Zhukov, 1976: p. 19)

Any analysis of the universal historical process which ignored the vitality of these three religions must, therefore, he says, be incomplete. Above all other forms of religion, Buddhism, Christianity and Islam clearly demonstrate religion's role of 'reflecting in the ideological realm' the ongoing socio-economic and political conflicts which take place in the base of society. It would, therefore, be a mistake to write the history of these religions, says Zhukov, as if it were a history of independent, autonomous belief-systems which influenced, but were themselves uninfluenced by, the real life situation of the peoples whose religions they are: not that religion does not influence people; Zhukov, like all 'scientific atheists', insists that:

It is impossible not to take account of the aptitude of religion to exert some influence on the conduct of people. . .

But he adds immediately, as we would now expect:

It is, however, an influence wholly and completely determined by the social class content, by the ideological direction, corresponding to the religious system. It is not religion itself, in itself, but the real social relations which it reflects or presents that represent the true source of its influence. Specific forms of religious ideology act as a veil for social content giving rise to its distinctive historical aberration. The very duration of the existence of world religion sometimes creates mistaken views about the absence of a straight connection between them and the changing social milieu. But, in reality, world religions are able to preserve their significance just in so far as they have adapted to changes in social relations. (Zhukov, 1976: pp. 19-20)

Zhukov does allow that there is a certain organic consistency about religious systems, but he says that this must not be taken to imply that religions are static — or, at least, not world religions, for the very fact of their being world religions shows their ability to adapt themselves, if reluctantly, to changing social conditions;

although a more correct way of putting it would be to say that changes in social relations 'produce' changes in these religions. Religions of themselves, asserts Zhukov, are rarely revolutionary. In fact, more often than not, once they are established, they take up a conservative position – at least initially – to social change. But crises in the developing class struggle – the ultimate *leitmotiv* of all history – produce changes in religion; first and foremost in the growth of heresy and schism, and then eventually in the established religions themselves. The problem, therefore, for the Marxist historian of world religions is to observe and analyse, bearing in mind the principles of historical materialism, the origin of this internal change and so to explain the vitality (*zhivuchest'*) in world religions.

I would suggest that no historian of religion who has puzzled over the failure or success of religions can regard this as an unimportant question. Whether the Marxist-Leninist answer is an adequate one is, of course, another matter. Zhukov puts it like this: all the great world religions arose in the era of 'slave-owning' societies – in India, in the Roman Empire, in Arabia. Buddhism and Christianity arose as movements of protest on the part of the enslaved masses against their condition. (The origins of Islam, however, as we shall see, were somewhat different). Buddhism, writes Zhukov:

. . .arose among the enslaved strata of the population of India in the sixth to the fifth centuries B.C. It was characterised by the striving of people to find a way out from unbearable conditions through a recognition of 'spiritual equality' and ostensibly offered the possibility of salvation to all, irrespective of their social position. Its thesis that suffering makes everyone equal, that it is the 'natural condition' of man, is grounded in an appeal to passivity and of reconciliation to reality. Such opinions were in keeping with the interests of the ruling class and were willingly encouraged by them. Buddhist teaching about reincarnation opened up to slaves the possibility of recompense in a future life for the suffering of the present one, as well as the possibility of an eventual retribution in the future for cruel rulers. It thus helped slave-owners to keep the oppressed masses in spiritual subjection. (Zhukov, 1976: pp. 21-22)

Tokarev tells a similar, if more detailed, story. He writes:

Buddhism arose out of the conditions of a bitter class struggle which flared up in the north Indian kingdoms, and in particular in the kingdom of Magadha, in the fifth-sixth centuries B.C. Here, class contradictions reached an extreme degree: the luxurious, coddled life of the rich slave-owners, brahmins, kshatriyas, princes; the poverty of the enslaved lower castes, the rivalry and the struggle for power between the highest castes (the brahmins and kshatriyas), the emergence of military dynasties. . .from out of the ranks of the kshatriyas, which pushed aside the brahmins — all of these things produced a crisis in the traditional world view. The belief in an unalterable caste-system, led by the brahmins, was shaken. The phenomena of retreat from the world, of asceticism, of wandering holy men — in all of which a discontent with existence as given was displayed — arose in the higher castes. In this situation there sprang up heretical teachings, sects and even atheistic philosophical systems, such as that of Carvaka. One of these belief-systems, and one in which the general mood of dissatisfaction, uncertainty and despair is found to a high degree, was Buddhism. (Tokarev, 1976b: p. 451)

'Scientific atheism' gives a similar account of the rise of Christianity. Thus Zhukov writes that:

Christianity arose in analogous social conditions (to Buddhism) in the slave-owning societies of the Roman Empire in the first century of our era. As Engels pointed out, Christianity 'appeared, at first, as the religion of slaves and emancipated slaves, of poor people deprived of all rights, of people subjugated or dispersed by Rome'. Thus, just as Buddhism consoled the unfortunate by offering them the possibility of a future recompense, so Christianity appealed for patience in the light of an expected divine salvation. (op. cit., p. 22)

The origins of Islam, however, whilst still a 'reflection' of social forces, are somewhat different, for Islam, argues 'scientific atheism', was imposed on the masses by their rulers. Unlike Buddhism and Christianity it was not a movement of protest. Thus Zhukov writes that:

Islam arose in different social circumstances to Buddhism and Christianity. The feudal Arabian chieftains, concerned to unite their forces with a view to territorial expansion and trade, proclaimed a monotheistic religion as a way of overcoming the resistance of tribal, small-scale, fragmented groups, and as a way of liquidating localised cults so as to replace them with a centralised authority. Thus Islam was different in origin from Buddhism and Christianity, in that it was not a spontaneous movement but was the result of intentional activity on the part of the ruling social circles. (ibid., p. 22)

But although differing in origin, the further history of all three world religions is, says Zhukov, the history of the *rapprochement* and coincidence of their social role, which, for Zhukov, is that of legitimatising established social systems.

However, before looking at what Zhukov – and 'scientific atheism' generally – has to say about this, some comment is, I feel, called for on what has been said so far about the origins of Buddhism, Christianity and Islam, and although I have referred primarily to Academician Zhukov, the account which he gives differs in no way from those given in other and more detailed Soviet accounts about the origins of these three world religions (cf. Tokarev, 1976b: pp. 447-458, 471-493, 520-526; Kryvelev, 1976: vol. 2, pp. 196-301, 305-311, vol. 1, pp. 126-16., vol. 2. pp. 140-149).

Soviet accounts of the beginnings of Buddhism, Christianity and Islam are open to a variety of criticism, both general and particular. In general, it might be said that, in ignoring any appeal in Buddhism, Christianity or Islam other than an appeal to what are really frustrated material interests, Soviet study of the origin – and indeed of the later history – of these religions is limited in the extreme. This limitation is, however, a limitation arising out of the entire Marxist-Leninist understanding of religion, and of the motivation underlying adherence to a religious view of the world, and I shall be discussing this at length in Part III of this study. This is not to say that material factors are unimportant in accounting for the rise of Buddhism, Christianity and Islam; it is – as adherents of these religious themselves testify – simply to say that factors other than material ones are equally to be taken into consideration. It is here – in the role assigned to religious ideas themselves – that one of the major differences between Soviet and Western historians of religion must be located, for Western historians of religion do, by and large, allow that religious ideas, in and of themselves — even in cases where a scholar's own personal judgement might well be that such ideas are false — play some part in the overall appeal of Buddhism, Christianity and Islam, and some, certainly, would argue that the decline in religious adherence today is due not simply to changing social conditions, but to the decline in the inherent credibility of certain religious beliefs in the light of an ever increasing naturalistic understanding of man and of the world.

With regard to particular criticisms that might be brought against Soviet 'scientific atheist' accounts of the rise of the three great world religions, whilst this belongs properly to historians of the particular religions concerned, there are one or two comments that I would like to make.

To take the case of the rise of Buddhism first. It is interesting, in this connection, to note that Trevor Ling, a foremost Western historian of Buddhism, who in his recent study of early Buddhism (1976) goes as far as any previous Western historian has ever gone in seeking to understand the social and political situation in which Buddhism arose, nowhere contemplates that the appeal of Buddhism was as a surrogate for frustrated social and political hopes of the kind on which Zhukov, Tokarev, and Soviet 'scientific atheism' in general, lay so much stress. Emphasising the humanity, rationality and near irreligiousness — in terms of the traditionally accepted conception of religion in Indian culture — of the Buddha's original message, Ling severely criticises those interpreters of early Buddhism who see in it no more than 'an answer to personal spiritual *malaise*, a doctrine of personal salvation' (Ling, 1976: p. 113). Far from being, as Ling claims many Westerners have imagined, 'a private cult of escape from the real world', early Buddhism, both in its denial of the notion of an individual soul and in the emphasis which it places on the communal life of the *Sangha* or monastery, shows a concern for social and political matters to a high degree. Much in it is, in fact, for Ling, a response not to political oppression but to the growing 'disease of individualism', as he calls it, and which he sees as having flourished in the rapidly developing urban centres of sixth century Aryan civilization in India (ibid., pp. 149-150). Buddhism, as Ling and other Western commentators point out, is a diagnosis of and a therapy for *the human condition as such*, irrespective of the social class to which human beings might belong, although Ling also stresses the hope that early Buddhists had that the democratic *Sangha* might serve as an example to society as a whole, showing it how to so order its life that the *spiritual* quest, which lies at the centre of Buddhist concern, might the better be pursued – although it was at the same time extremely sanguine about the possibility of realising this hope (ibid., pp. 150-163). For Buddhism, the vast mass of mankind – the *punthujjana* – were too addicted to pleasure, and too much at the mercy of the senses, to be over-interested in the goal which the Buddha set before them. 'The Buddhist *Sangha*', writes Ling, following the Indian historian J.P. Sharma, 'like the Greek oligarchies, was based on a belief in the 'unwisdom of the multitude' (ibid., p. 165). In its early years Buddhism appealed only to the few, and was certainly not a movement of mass proletarian protest of the kind envisaged by Zhukov and other Soviet 'scientific atheists'. It should also be noted that not only the Buddha himself, but also his immediate disciples, came not from the lower castes in society, but from the *Kshatriya* caste – a caste which in power and influence was equal, if not superior, to the highest caste, the *Brahmins*. That the original organisation of the *Sangha* ignored distinctions of caste is perfectly explicable in terms of the Buddha's diagnosis of the human condition as common to all, as well as by his view that progress towards the goal of *nibbana* depends not on social status but on mental and spiritual effort.

This is as may be. The point I want to make here is that the story of the rise of Buddhism which we find in 'scientific atheism', in that it fails to take into account the actual, detailed, substantial beliefs of Buddhism, fails to answer the question why people should have responded to the social, economic and political crisis which it diagnoses as having occurred in Northern India in the fifth-sixth centuries B.C., with the views peculiar to Buddhism and not with some other view. The same criticism, of course, can be brought against 'scientific atheist' accounts of the rise of Christianity and Islam, or indeed of any religion, and it is a point to which I shall be returning in the final part of this study.

As with Buddhism, a full critical assessment of what 'scientific atheism' says about the rise of Christianity and Islam is properly the task of historians of those religions and I will confine myself here to one critical comment only.

The point I would like to make is that, once again, as in their accounts of the rise of Buddhism, Western historians of Christianity and Islam see the situation as a good deal more complex than that described by 'scientific atheism'. That the Christian religion drew its early converts on the whole — but by no means exclusively — from the lower orders of society is beyond doubt, but that the reasons for its rapid expansion into all classes of late Roman society had much — if anything — to do with its being a disguised, or even a transmuted, form of socio-political protest against the slave-owning society of Rome seems, in the light of the entirely secular reasons put forward by such Western historians as E.R. Dodds and Peter Brown, to be pretty far off the mark. Without going at all deeply into what these and other secular historians of early Christianity say about the rise of Christianity — something which would take us well beyond the scope of this study — the points to which they call attention have to do with the areas of human concern which, whilst they include the social dimension, pass well beyond it. Dodds, for instance, describes the age of the expansion of the Christian religion as being, like our own, an 'age of anxiety'. Yet the 'anxiety' of which he speaks, and to which he sees the Christian religion as offering an answer, is an anxiety which falls entirely outwith the purview of 'scientific atheism's' understanding of man — although it has, perhaps, a good deal in common with the basic human need for self-affirmation and self-recognition of which Marx had written in his early writings. It is also an anxiety which pre-dates the crisis in the material base of Roman society which set in in the third century AD and of which Soviet 'scientific atheism' makes so much in its account of the rise of Christianity (Dodds, 1965: Ch. I).

Another Western secular historian, Peter Brown, also writes of the 'vast and anxious activity in religion' which set in in the Roman Empire towards the end of the second century AD, and whilst he links it closely to political and social change, the changes which he describes have little to do with the almost wholly economic crisis on which Soviet 'scientific atheism' lays so much of the burden of explaining the rise of Christianity. Rather has it to do with the breakdown of traditional belief amidst the new social mobility and expanding world-view of the late Empire. As Brown writes:

Traditional belief in the activity of the gods in the universe presented a singularly unified and unbroken surface. The thoughts and anxieties of the 'new mood' after 170 drove fissures across it. It is by examining some of the new preoccupations of sensitive men that we can appreciate the nature of the spiritual revolution that makes Late Antiquity such a distinct and fertile period in the history of the ancient Mediterranean. (Brown, 1971: p. 51)

Among these preoccupations Brown lays emphasis on the growing sense that many individuals had of possessing, in themselves, something that was 'infinitely valuable and yet painfully unrelated to the outside world'. 'After generations of apparently satisfying public activity', he writes, 'it was as if a current that had passed smoothly from men's inner experience into the outside world had been cut. The warmth drained from the familiar environment' (ibid., p. 51). Traditional concerns began to seem trivial. 'Finding a sudden reserve of perfection or inspiration inside oneself', Brown writes, 'went hand in hand with a need for a God with whom one could be alone' (ibid., pp. 51-52).

To expand on either Dodds' or Brown's sensitive recording of the mood of the second, third and fourth centuries AD would take us far from our present concerns. I mention their work simply to contrast it with the somewhat superficial understanding of the period, and of human motivation, which one finds in the writings of Soviet 'scientific atheism'. A similar superficiality characterises Soviet writing on the rise of Islam where, again, little attempt is made to pass from an analysis of the socio-economic, and political situation to a sympathetic understanding and appreciation of the human hopes, fears and anxieties out of which – as the two greatest contemporary Western historians of the rise of Islam, W. Montgomery Watt and Maxime Rodinson – the one a Christian and the other a Marxist – show Islam to have arisen. Soviet scholarship – of which the remarks which we have quoted from Academician Zhukov are typical – ignores, as irrelevant, the kind of motivating factors upon which Western historians of religion have laid stress in seeking to account for the rise of Buddhism, Christianity and Islam. But to return to Zhukov's account of the further development of these three world religions. He writes:

We must stress the fact that the rise of world religions is connected with the establishment of feudalism. This connection is not accidental. In Antiquity, when Buddhism and Christianity originated, the ruling classes did not consider the spiritual suppression of slaves important, for the slave was not considered human. His obedience was achieved by force and the idea of controlling slaves by influencing their consciousness was foreign to the ways of slave-owners. (op. cit., p. 22)

With feudalism all this was to change, for under feudalism, argues Zhukov, the more complex structure of class relations made it necessary to control the lower classes ideologically. Thus, he says, the ruling classes needed religion to enslave people 'spiritually', so as to sanctify feudal privileges. To this task Buddhism, Christianity and Islam were particularly suited. All three religions, in fact, rapidly assimilated to feudal social structures. In Europe, for instance, the hierarchical organisation of the Christian church was an exact replica of the social relations existing in society. In Japan, Buddhist monasteries with their vast estates competed for power with their secular counterparts. Further, as the Christian religion spread throughout Europe, and eventually beyond, this was, says Zhukov, 'connected with the development and strengthening of feudal laws', and it is thus not surprising that the Christian church was originally hostile to the growth of capitalism in Europe. Feudal and ecclesiastical interests were too closely identified to allow any encroachment on them, and he adds:

The middle classes presented a greater danger to feudalism than did the lower classes because the middle classes tended to form their own opinions — particularly with regard to religion — and these were often quite different from the views of the church. This was inevitable since even the most progressive views in the Middle Ages had to be expressed religiously. Such views were quickly pronounced heretical. (op. cit., p. 23)

Islam, Zhukov claims, was also used by feudal lords for political ends and, in fact, was used to suppress the masses in much cruder ways than was Christianity. Islam spread by force of arms and such — wherever possible — has remained an essential feature of the propagation of that faith to this day. Islam was forcibly introduced by the Arabs during the period from the seventh to the eighth centuries into the Near East, Central Asia, the Caucasus, Northern Hindustan and North Africa. It was typical of Islam, under feudalism, to have a supreme ruler who was at the same time the spiritual ruler of the religion — the *Khalīfah*. Further, the foundation and development of the Ottoman Empire did much to strengthen Islam by guaranteeing feudal rights and by justifying the cruel despotism of the conquerors.

Zhukov continues his account of the general development of religion as follows:

The period of the 16th to the 17th century in Europe marked the beginning of the crisis of feudalism and the growth of capitalist relations. It was also the beginning of the Reformation of the Christian Church. Social relations in those days had to have religious expressions and religion was quick to adapt itself to the changes which were taking place in society. New Protestant churches became extremely active and the occurence of religious wars showed that great socio-economic changes were happening and that some form of revolution was coming. The revolution in the Netherlands in the 16th century, the English revolution of the 17th century, and the French bourgeois revolution of the 18th century, marked a new epoch in world history — the decline of feudalism and the rise of capitalism. In the great peasant wars in Europe and later, during the first revolutions, the revolutionary element was very predominant. Christianity and society were divided into antagonistic groups, all of which sought to legitimate their aims in the name of religion. Only the French revolution of the 18th century was free from a religious element and sought to expose the reactionary role of religion. (op. cit., pp. 24-25)

France was thus, in Soviet eyes, the most politically advanced nation in Europe at this time, but the class that eventually came to power – the bourgeoisie – soon realised the usefulness of religion, says Zhukov. After achieving power, the bourgeoisie quickly lost its revolutionary spirit and its main concern became the preservation of its own power and security. Thus it had to keep the masses in their place both materially and spiritually. Even Napoleon espoused a religious ideology, as had the leaders of the revolution – Robespierre in particular. Although they were suspicious of the Roman Catholic Church – in view of its still continuing support for feudalism – they sought to find a substitute religion in the various forms of deism imported from England.

With the growth of antagonistic classes in capitalist society, the bourgeoisie assumed its reactionary role with a vengeance and religion once again became a means of distracting the masses from revolutionary aspirations. Protestant Christianity soon began defending bourgeois productive relations, and eventually the feudal structure of the Roman Church found itself able to come to terms with the bourgeoisie and to find a new role for itself as the defender and upholder of bourgeois rights, since the 'democracy' of which the bourgeoisie spoke, and which on the surface appeared to run counter to feudal structures, was seen to appertain only to themselves. The old and new ruling classes, quickly recognising the coincidence of their mutual interest against the masses, became reconciled.

We mentioned earlier in this chapter Zhukov's remark that the development of the three world religions was 'the coincidence of their social role' and this, Zhukov now seeks to justify with reference to Buddhism and Islam. 'The fate of Buddhism in this period', he writes, 'is very similar to that of Christianity'. The difference, as he sees it, lies in the fact that Buddhism is practised in under-developed countries and – with the exception of modern Japan – has, on that account, taken longer to modernise. But, he adds:

Its ability to adapt is well demonstrated by the variety of its forms. Here it did better than Christianity for it has proved itself capable of expression both in primitive cults, which are not far removed from witchcraft, and in refined philosophical systems claiming to be scientific. That is why it can cater for such a variety of people, regardless of their nationality, sex, age, social position and education. Its most important feature, however, is its ability to unite with other religions — in India with Hinduism, with Confucianism in China and with Shintoism in Japan. (op. cit., p. 26)

Turning to Islam, Zhukov points out that Islam is practised mainly in agricultural areas, where capitalism has not yet become established. Islam, therefore, still supports the most conservative and reactionary social forces in the world, and can be said to have hardly moved beyond the feudal period. This is certainly so, so far as Islamic Law (the *shari'a*) is concerned. However, with the rapid growth of a local bourgeoisie in many countries, Islam is at last beginning to adapt itself to their interests. The only positive thing that Zhukov can find to say about Islam is that it has often supported national independence movements and helped fight colonialism — though it is doubtful if he would still find this a 'positive' aspect of Islam today!

Finally, Zhukov comes to our own time. The new epoch, he says, which was ushered in by the Great October Socialist Revolution, tolled the death knell for capitalism, and the development of new socialist societies have not been without impact on the great world religions. Although these religions still continue to fulfil their primary function of legitimating the exploiting sections of societies, they have not remained immune to the influence of the socio-economic changes taking place in socialist societies. This influence, Zhukov claims, is two fold:

Firstly, many believers became personally involved in this struggle (for a socialist society), though the side they chose depended on their class interests. Also, as a result of this struggle, many people acquired political views diametrically opposed to those of the churches and this, not infrequently, led them to reject all forms of religion as reactionary. . . Secondly, since religion was never independent of the state, it reacted strongly to the weakening of the last antagonistic society it had supported. The victory of socialism, and the changes in the correlation of forces in favour of socialism, endangers capitalism and thus makes it more difficult for religion to defend capitalism. Christianity, in particular, has been quick to see the necessity to adapt itself yet again to a changed situation. Originally violently hostile to communism. . .once the socialist system had become established, 'peaceful co-existence' became the fashionable idea. . . Thus has a world religion proven itself, yet again, capable of adapting to circumstances to maintain its position. (ibid., pp. 28-29)

Yet Communists should not be deceived, concludes Zhukov: the Christian churches, whilst leaving themselves room to manoeuvre by pretending that they serve the cause of progress, in reality serve only capitalism and imperialism. Thus, the effect of this stance is to slow down progress, and Zhukov draws a final and, for Soviet 'scientific atheism', an important practical conclusion.

History shows [he writes] that religion in its manoeuvres simply uses progressive movements, in which believers participate, for its own ends, to strengthen its position and influence. Religious organisations taking part in anti-war and anti-imperialistic movements have a positive role only in so far as they attract masses of believers to these movements. But it is also obvious [he concludes], that believers are attracted to these movements because of their class position and class-consciousness, and not because of their religious beliefs. Religious organisations can take no credit here. (ibid., pp. 27-28)

Such then is Academician Zhukov's account of the origin and development of religion and of the role which it has played in world history. It has one simple theme — religion has always and everywhere served class interests and, in particular, the interest of the ruling class. Whilst Marx himself did, at times, write as if religion was a direct expression of class interest, religion was certainly, for him, much more than that. Indeed, Norman Birnbaum has gone so far as to state that 'the notion of religion as directly derived from class interests. . .is not compatible with the central tenets of the original Marxist analysis of religion' (1973: p. 21) and, in the light of our earlier discussion of Marx's views, we cannot but agree. The origins of this reduced thesis — that is, of the view that religion is a reflection of class interests as a direct means of class domination — which is now firmly established in

Soviet 'scientific atheism' - it is, for instance, central to Tokarev's conclusion given in Appendix III to this present work — Birnbaum traces to the writings of the German Marxists Kautsky (1910) and Bernstein (1895). There the distinction — found in practice if not always in theory in the original Marxist writings — between religion and ideology, was obliterated, and nothing of the substance of human spirituality, which had been an essential aspect of Marx and Engels own understanding of religion, remained. The reasons why this should have been so need not concern us,[19] but Birnbaum argues that a line may be traced — downwards — from Bernstein and Kautsky to Lenin, whose views on religion, in Birnbaum's opinion, mark 'a low point in the history of modern Marxist thought' (op. cit., p. 23), for it is to Lenin that the simple thesis that religion is but a tool in the ongoing class struggle — which was, as we have just seen, the burden of what Academician Zhukov had to say about its role in world history — must be traced. From this simplistic thesis, Soviet thought about religion, and about the history of religion, is still struggling to recover.

The History of Atheism, Free-Thinking and Humanism

An integral aspect of Soviet 'scientific atheism' is the study of the atheistic tradition itself; that is, for 'scientific atheism', the study of the role which atheism, including also today free-thinking and humanism, is held to have played in the progressive enlightenment of mankind. Thus all courses in 'scientific atheism' in the USSR follow what has been said about religion – about its origin, growth, social function, differing traditions and ultimate falsity – with a section on the origin and growth of atheism and humanism. So, for example, the text book for the course 'The Fundamentals of Scientific Atheism' used in all institutions of higher education, follows its survey of the religious beliefs of mankind with a section entitled 'Atheism and Social Progress', which contains sub-sections on topics such as 'The Growth of Atheism as the Law of the Spiritual Progress of Mankind', 'Pre-Marxist Atheism', and 'Marxist-Leninist Atheism as the Highest Form of Atheism' (*Nauchnyy ateizm:* pp. 127-160; cf. also *IiTA*, part IV, *'Istoricheskeye formy ateizma'* [The Historical Forms of Atheism] pp. 228-308).

If the history of religion is, for Soviet 'scientific atheism', the history of an illusion, the history of atheism and, to varying degrees, of free-thinking and humanism also, is the history of man's struggle to overcome that illusion and to arrive at a true understanding of the world, of society and of human destiny – a struggle which has its denouement in Marxism-Leninism, a world-outlook and a form of society in which both religion, and all previous forms of its rejection, are finally, in theory and in practice, transcended. Eventually, of course, as Marx suggested in his *Manuscripts of 1844*, atheism itself – or at least atheism understood as the denial of religion – will be transcended by the positive humanism of socialism (see p. 20 above). Nowhere, however, in the writings of Soviet 'scientific atheism' is this state of affairs seen as imminent − 'scientific atheists' will be needed for some time to come!

The history of atheism, which until quite recently in the Soviet Union meant the history of materialism, was early the concern of Soviet historians of philosophy and culture. Lenin, in his article 'On the Significance of Militant Materialism' of 1922, had urged Soviet philosophers and historians to study the history of material- ism and to make common cause with contemporary materialists, whether Marxist or not (*LCW:* 33;228-230), and Soviet scholars responded, first with articles in the more serious Party journals on topics such as 'Outline of the History of Atheism' (Lukachevsky, 1929, 1930), 'Atheism in Ancient Greece and Rome' (Baskin, 1938, 1939), 'On Materialism and Atheism in Ancient India' (Kochetov, 1940) and later with lengthier articles and books on these themes, and more particularly on the development of the European Materialistic tradition of Hobbes, Spinoza, the English Deists, the French *philosophes,* and the left wing Hegelians which, they argued, came to fruition in the writings of Marx, Engels and Lenin.[1] Native Russian revolutionary thinkers are today also held to have played a not inconsiderable part in the development of this tradition and serious studies of their contribu- tion to the development of materialism have been produced.[2] The study of the history of progressive thinking has continued un- abated to the present day and some extremely fine studies − not least on the English free-thinking tradition − have been published.[3]

But the study of the history of atheism, free-thinking and, more recently, of humanism has, like the cognate study of religion, its vital, practical side as well, for an essential aspect of such study is the necessity of showing the superiority of Marxist-Leninist atheism − in that it, and it alone, is 'scientific atheism' − over all previous and all contemporary forms of atheism. The same has been true for the study of humanism since that term began to come to the fore in Western philosophy and theology in the period since 1945. Marxist humanism must now be shown to be the only true humanism (so Petrosyan, 1972; Popov, 1977).

Soviet study of atheism, free-thinking and humanism − that is, the study of the 'progressive' tradition in human history, as 'scientific atheism' understands it – divides the history of this tradition, with the exception of the anomaly of free-thinking which is usually in Soviet study linked to pre-scientific atheism, into two major 'epochs': the pre-scientific; that is, the epoch before the advent of Marxism, and the scientific; the epoch of Marxism-Leninism.

6.1   PRE-SCIENTIFIC ATHEISM AND HUMANISM

The beginnings of materialism and atheism can be found early in the history of human culture – in ancient India and China and in ancient Egypt, Greece and Rome.[4] But with the exception of India, the study of the atheism of Antiquity is, in Soviet study, the study of the ideas of 'progressive' individuals, rather than of anything that can be seen as expressive of underlying social forces. Indeed, it is quite explicitly recognised by a number of Soviet historians of atheism that the materialism and atheism of Classical Antiquity but 'expresses the world view of sections of the slave-owning classes of ancient Greece and Rome in their struggle with religion' (Grigor'yan, 1974: p. 40). Why they should have struggled against religion is not stated and no analysis is attempted of any material socio-economic forces by which such views can be said to have been 'determined'. In fact, G.P. Frantsov – one of the most influential of Soviet 'scientific atheists' – goes so far as to write of the 'spontaneous' materialism of Classical Antiquity (Frantsov, 1975: p. 28). Thus, the Soviet view is that whilst the materialism and atheism of thinkers such as Democritus, Epicurus, Lucretius and Lucian dealt a blow at the religious (and socially conservative) ideas of the ruling classes of their time, in that they lacked any real insight into (or concern with) the true nature of human society – a lack of insight which they shared, of course, with the enslaved masses – and as they were unsupported by any 'progressive' social forces, their views came to nought, and the vacuum was filled by the popular religious cults (and by Christianity in particular) and their fantasy fulfilment of human aspirations.[5]

The same is true of such materialism as was thrown up from time to time in Indian and Chinese culture, although following the lead of the Bengali Marxist historian of Indian philosophy, Debiprasad Chattopadhyaya, Soviet Indiologists have paid considerable attention to such popular movements in Indian thought as *Lokāyāta* – a philosophy which, Chattopadhyaya claims, represented – as his own, but disputed, understanding of the meaning of the term *lokāyatā* as 'the philosophy of the people' indicates – the common outlook of the masses at an early stage in the development of Indian culture (Chattopadhyaya, 1959).[6] The most that such materialism could achieve, say Soviet 'scientific atheists', was to criticise such current religious notions as that the existing social order was divinely ordained, and to voice certain material human hopes, but this without offering any constructive way forward for the furtherance of human happiness on earth (cf. Grigor'yan, 1974: lectures 2 and 3; Frantsov, 1975: pp. 28-33).

The failure of Soviet historians to offer any serious socio-economic analysis of the rise of ancient materialism – outwith Lokāyāta in India – seems to me to have implications for Marxist-Leninist theory which Soviet historians of ancient materialism totally ignore, for to call such materialism 'spontaneous' is, I would have thought, a tacit admission of the fact that philosophical thinking about religion can, at times, have little or nothing to do with those general underlying socio-economic forces upon which Marxist-Leninism lays so much emphasis in its historical analysis of religion, and of other forms of ideology. This is not, however, a conclusion that is drawn by Marxist-Leninists.

Soviet historians feel on safer ground when they come to tell of the rise of materialism, atheism, free-thinking and humanism in mediaeval Europe and in Russia. Here, the connection of such thought with 'progressive' social forces is clearly indicated.[7] Thus, for example, a Soviet historian of humanism, Maria Petrosyan, writing on the late Middle Ages, says:

In the West during the 13th and 14th centuries there was questioning and open denial of the justice of social inequality, the criticism of division of people into those who must work and those who have the right to idleness, the division between rich and poor. In the ideology of the oppressed masses there was an increasing tendency to reject the idea that man was put on this earth to suffer. (Petrosyan, 1972: p. 21)

And she cites in support of this contention the mediaeval sect of the *Behards*, which arose in Flanders in the thirteenth century, and which advocated the idea of communal property and sought to set up a kingdom of justice and beatitude on earth. The more radical members of the Lollards were to espouse similar ideals in fourteenth century England, but in that they recognised the need for the use of force to overthrow the feudal barons, they are regarded by Marxist historians as somewhat more 'progressive' than the *Behards*.

The necessity for the use of force was also recognised by the followers of Fra Dolcino, whose plebian revolt in fourteenth century Italy is regarded, along with the later revolts of the Taborite wing of the Hussite movement in Bohemia in the fifteenth century, and of Thomas Münzer and the Anabaptists in Germany at the beginning of the sixteenth century, as the high point of peasant revolt in the Middle Ages (cf. Petrosyan, 1972: pp. 22-23; Frantsov, 1975: p. 35).

Yet these spontaneous, mass revolutionary movements were doomed to failure for, as Engels pointed out, they were the 'uprisings of a class not yet developed', (*Anti-Dühring*: p. 30). Consequently, we find that not only were their aspirations clouded by being cast in a religious mould but that, as Frantsov puts it, 'the more spontaneous the mass revolutionary movement, the less evidence we find in it of any positive programme, of any clearcut notions of the goals of the struggle, of the possibility of social reform' (op. cit., p. 35). Even Münzer's programme, which was much more realistic in Frantsov's eyes than Dolcino's, was characterised by the ideal of the establishment of the kingdom of God on earth – an ideal which was vague, and at times 'mystical', in that all that it seemed to involve was the abolition of private property and power for all to be well. As Frantsov writes:

Indeed, the leader of this peasant uprising (Münzer) seems to have had only a vague notion of a social system without estate or class distinctions and private property, or a government alien to the people. Subsequently, this vague urge and their general ideas, were to be unfolded in various versions of utopia in the form of more or less detailed scenes of human life to which the working people aspired. (op. cit., p. 35)

And as he later comments:

Social thought has its beginnings, and a powerful impetus for its development, in the emergent awakening of consciousness in spontaneous popular revolts, an awakening which is expressed in the fact that the working people begin to see that the oppressive order is not immutable. This takes the form of visions about a social system free from such oppressive elements. In the minds of masses of people this vision does not at first acquire any definite contours or elaborate forms, which first appear in the early utopias. But these too boil down to the announcement of what their ideal society is free of; namely, oppression, money, and private property. Social thought had to travel a long way before it produced the systematic answer to the question of what the ideal and rationally structured society should be free from, including the social order which had but recently appeared to be quite solid. (ibid., p. 36)

But although the peasant revolts of the Middle Ages did not produce a coherent social theory, they did suggest that a social order other than the present one could exist, and in this their contribution to the development of European thinking was considerable, as were the social theories found later in the utopian thinkers of the sixteenth and seventeenth centuries to whom Marxist-Leninist historians also devote a great deal of attention.[8]

Much work of late has also been pursued into indigenous Russian reforming movements in the Middle Ages – particularly by A.I. Klibanov[9] – and into the humanistic values, supposedly disclosed in the early folk-law of the Transcaucasian peoples of the now Soviet Union and which surfaced in the twelfth and thirteenth centuries during the period when craft industries and trade, the growth of towns, and the deepening of 'contradictions' between the ruling feudal aristocracy and the anti-feudal masses, produced a new secular culture in these regions (Petrosyan, 1972:

pp. 23-24).[10] The work of the Azerbaijani poet Nizami, for instance, in which the strength and beauty of the common people and their superiority over rulers and despots is extolled, is a case in point, as is the work of the Georgian poet Rustaveli whose poem *The Knight in the Tiger's Skin* is seen by contemporary Soviet historians to extol, not an abstract Christian love of man for man and man for God, but the real love of real people. Rustaveli, it is claimed, praises friendship and courage and exults in man, his intellect, his strong, harmoniously developed body; his heroes are inspired by a profound patriotism, and are ready to defend their homeland, relying only on their own strength, courage and will and are all in all, a prototype of the 'New Soviet Man' of much current Soviet 'scientific atheist' literature and are often presented as such. A similar secularisation of the human ideal can, of course, be traced in Western Europe from the twelfth century onwards.[11]

But it is on developments in philosophy that Soviet historians of the development of culture in the Middle Ages lay the greatest stress for it is here, so they claim — in thinkers such as Abelard, Roger Bacon, Averroës, Siger de Brabant, Avicenna, Duns Scotus and William of Ockham — that we can discern the true beginnings of the modern world, in that it is in the work of such thinkers that they locate the beginnings of that conflict between science and religion which, in their reading of the situation, was to sound the death knell for religion in the centuries to come.[12] The thought of these 'progressive' mediaeval thinkers is seen as part of a wider struggle to free both philosophy and man from the dictates of dogmatic theology, and from the authority of religious institutions (Christian or Islamic), so that man could explore and change the natural world in terms of philosophy's own autonomous principles (*IiTA:* pp. 246-247). In this struggle Soviet historians lay great stress on the 'rationalism' of Abelard, on the development of the theory of 'double truth' by the Averroists and Siger de Brabant, on the 'materialistic pantheism' of the school of Chartres, and on the radical separation of theology and philosophy, faith and reason, which we find in the work of Duns Scotus and William of Ockham (cf. Livshits, 1973: pp. 185-206). All are seen as harbingers of the development of science, and of the 'bourgeois' humanism and atheism which develops along with it, in the sixteenth and seventeenth centuries. In the Middle Ages itself − in the development of 'progressive' philosophies and in 'progressive' peasant revolts − Soviet 'scientific atheism' also discerns the beginnings of the break-up of the religiously legitimated feudal order. As the university text book *Istoriya i teoriya ateizma* sums it up:

The peculiarity of mediaeval freethinking consists in the fact that the atheistic world view is expressed very inconsistently. This was a result of pressure from the Church at a time when most people were satisfied by false conceptions of the world. The social classes which attacked the ruling order clothed ideas hostile to religion in a religious form, because they could not break its fetters. Monotheistic religions by their nature required new methods to oppose them which were only hinted at by mediaeval freethinkers.

The contribution of mediaeval free thought was that, in difficult conditions, it began to undermine the dogmas of world religions which had seemed eternal. In the works of the freethinkers man was gradually freeing himself from the power of supernatural forces. Reason asserted its rights, accumulating arguments against religion. Mediaeval free-thought cleared the way for the critique of Christianity by representatives of bourgeois atheism. (*IiTA:* pp. 255-256)

The development of capitalist relations within the feudal system found expression in all spheres of cultural life, and not least in philosophy, literature and art. As Soviet historians see the matter, the ideology of the rising bourgeoisie made common cause with the anti-feudal ideology of the masses. This was natural enough, they argue, in that both were directed against feudal relations and the 'feudal-clerical' view of the world. Developing capitalism needed unrestricted manpower, a workman who was not bound by personal allegiance. It was eager, therefore, to shake off the social hierarchy of feudalism. Its development also implied a rapid development of the productive forces and this in turn required a rapid increase in scientific knowledge. This is the material base which 'determined' according to Marxist-Leninist historians, the characteristic features of bourgeois humanism and free-thinking. Knowingly, or unknowingly, its representatives upheld, from the bourgeois point of view, the ideals of freedom and equality and the liberation of the intellect from the control of the Church. The earliest works of bourgeois humanism – the works of Petrarch, Boccaccio, Leonardo Bruni, Poggio Bracciolini, Lorenzo Valla, Leonardo da Vinci – to name but a few of those singled out for detailed study by G.M. Livshits towards the close of his monumental study, *Svobodomysliye i ateizm v drevnosti i sredniye veka* (Free-thinking and Atheism in Antiquity and the Middle Ages) published in 1973 – extol man, stress his essential worth, and proclaim his inalienable rights as an individual. As one 'scientific atheist' puts it:

The bourgeois humanism of the Renaissance grew exceedingly bold in the defence of human values from religious tutelage and was soon heading towards total denial of the supernatural. It proclaimed the cult of man and of human reason, expressed invincible faith in man's creative potential and gradually evolved its own philosophical, sociological and ethical conceptions in its war against theology and scholasticism. Step by step the advanced thinkers of the fourteenth, fifteenth and sixteenth centuries undermined the foundations of religious teaching, ever seeking to narrow the 'domain of the divine' and to extend the 'domain of man'. They tried to explain all phenomena without resorting to traditional religious mystification to the arguments of the pitifully diminished scholasticism that was out of touch with man and nature and entirely committed to upholding all the 'divine' truths. (Petrosyan, 1972: p. 27)

This simplified, and by no means exclusively Marxist, account of the development of humanism – the British humanist, H.J. Blackham tells a similar story in a chapter of his book *Humanism* (Blackham, 1968: pp. 112-116) – is repeated in all Soviet accounts of this period and is the guiding principle for all detailed study of individuals and movements.[13] But the underlying teleological *motif* which is peculiar to Marxism, is aptly – if unconsciously – brought out in some words of G.P. Frantsov, when he wrote that:

The feudal order was being eroded *by time*, which carried society closer to the *inevitable* victory of bourgeois relations. Ultimately this determined the great changes in world outlook which were characteristic of the 16th and 17th century. (Frantsov, 1975: p. 36) (my italics)

The cultural atmosphere was determined by the Copernican revolution and by the revolutionary advances in the natural sciences — advances which heralded a new society and new requirements. As the hitherto 'motionless' earth was now seen to revolve around its sun, the idea that all things were immutable began to lose ground. The solidity of the seemingly age-old social order in the form of a hierarchy of ranks and powers — 'degrees', as Shakespeare had called them in *Troilus and Cressida* (Act I, Scene iii) — running from the intricate hierarchy of feudal lords to the intricate hierarchy of the angels in heaven — all this was shaken and new views about social progress were in a position to develop.

It is with the 'bourgeois' free-thinking of the sixteenth and seventeenth centuries that Soviet study of the anti-religious tradition in European culture begins in earnest. It has been the subject of an extremely large number of studies, of which by far the best is G.M. Livshits' *Svobodomysliye i materialisticheskaya filosofiya v zapadnoy yevrope: vtoraya polovina XVII v* (Free-thinking and Materialistic Philosophy in Western Europe: The Second Half of the XVII century), published in 1975.[14]

The ideologists of the Dutch and English 'bourgeois' revolutions championed the rights of the individual, democratic freedoms, and humanity among men. With varying degrees of consistency, every one of them upheld the need to destroy the absolute monarchies of feudalism, despotic forms of government, and the privileges of the feudal estates. From Spinoza to Locke, 'progressive' thinkers opposed the imposition of reactionary, anti-scientific beliefs, attacked religious fanaticism and intolerance, and defended the principles of religious freedom and freedom of thought and speech. As Livshits says:

The social-political and philosophical outlook of Winstanley, Hobbes, Locke, Newton, Bayle and Spinoza reflected the social and political struggle which originated in Western Europe in the second half of the seventeenth century. (Livshits, 1975: p. 4)

The ideologists of the rising bourgeoisie were particularly interested in the proper relationship of the individual to society and were thus led to reject the older conception of the state which had been a weapon in the hands of the old feudal nobility and had hindered the development of the bourgeoisie, preventing them from expanding their economic, political and even their spiritual abilities. The new ideal, as set forth by Hobbes, and later by Locke, saw the state, not as something God-given, but as embodying the 'common interest' — in effect, say Soviet historians, the interests of the rising bourgeoisie. Thus they sought to offer rational, as opposed to theological, accounts of how the state had come into being, and of how it might be improved so as to serve the interests of (bourgeois) man. Hobbes had also rejected absolute and immutable moral standards and developed the idea that the morality of an action must be judged, not according to supernatural principles, but by its contribution to the common good and made, according to Soviet historians, a number of profound observations for combining personal interests with those of society as a whole, i.e., the state (cf. Petrosyan, 1972: p. 32).

Machiavelli, at the outset of the sixteenth century, had also sought to develop a rational theory of the state and of government, but he had done so on the assumption that intriguing self-interest and insatiable desires constituted the mainsprings of human activity, a fitting enough reflection, say Soviet historians, of the earliest period of capitalist expansion before the notions of class, class-interest, and class conflicts of interest, had become fully developed, and had shown that exploitation lay at the root of the evils to which mankind was subject.

The emergence of bourgeois relations carried great calamities for ordinary people, argue Soviet historians, but those who saw this later in the sixteenth and seventeenth centuries reasoned on very different lines to Machiavelli, in that they saw private property as the root of the evils which beset men, rather than anything innate in human nature. They failed, however, to fully understand the workings of capitalist society, and so could offer little but utopian dreams as a corrective to the ills they so accurately described. Such, for instance, were Thomas More and Tommazo Campanella, two thinkers to whom Soviet studies of the history of 'progressive' thought pay great attention.[15] Still, however, a just and equitable social system remained but a dream, as did a true humanism.

Yet the notion of regularity in mankind's historical development began to emerge in the seventeenth and in the eighteenth centuries, superseding the theological notion of predestination, which had lain at the heart of early Protestantism. By the seventeenth century a considerable body of knowledge relating to world cultures had come into being and what Soviet historians continue – inaccurately – to refer to as the 'English materialists of the seventeenth century', by which they mean Hobbes and Locke, utilised this body of knowledge in their writings.[16] Locke, in whom we can first trace the notion of the 'innocent savage', in raising the question as to the happiness of those who knew neither government nor wealth, also raised a question which was to trouble humanism from his time to ours – the question whether men were good by nature or whether they were in need of the harsh bridle of strong government. Whatever the answer to this question – and Hobbes' answer is something of an embarrassment to Soviet historians – from the notion of a primitive happiness and from the dreams of the utopians, men were at last in possession of the idea that society need not *per se* be exploitive. We are thus on the threshold of the development of a true humanism.

It is, however, the French Enlightenment of the eighteenth century which, for Soviet scholars, more fully represents the growing intensity of the antagonistic contradictions between the feudal system and the new capitalistic system of relations than any other movement in European thought, for nowhere was the struggle between feudalism and capitalism so direct and so un-compromising as in pre-revolutionary France.[17] Thus the criticism of the 'feudal-clerical' outlook, as Soviet scholars term it – religious, political, economic, philosophical, ethical and aesthetic – was more intense and more militant in France than anywhere else – certainly more so than in England. There was the same emphasis on man, as the highest of all values, as in the English and Dutch 'bourgeois' revolutionary thinkers, but the rejection of the established institutions of religion, and even of God himself, was much more openly and much more violently expressed.

Man, claim Soviet historians, was at the centre of the thought of the French *philosophes* for he alone, in the whole of nature, possessed self-awareness – awareness of joy and of grief, of what is just and what is unjust and of life and death. Rejecting all religious explanations of the origin of man, the French materialists – d'Holbach and La Mettrie, in particular – laid special emphasis – in a way in which English philosophers did not – on the fact that man is part of nature and that there is nothing supernatural about him. The standards for moral and social conduct should, therefore, argued d'Holbach, be established from nature and not from any 'divine principle'. The humanism of the French Enlightenment was based on the assertion of man's natural right to pleasure and happiness – a happiness which they interpreted in extremely terrestial terms. Thus, when defining 'happiness', the 'ideologists of the French bourgeois' – as they are for Soviet historians – from Montesquieu to d'Holbach, wrote of material well-being, political freedom, and of individual and social equality. Yet neither Helvétius, Diderot nor d'Holbach associated material well-being with property equality, nor with the abolition of private ownership. Like their earlier English and Dutch counterparts they went no further than the utopian demand for limitations on the excessive use of the power derived from the private ownership of estates, and argued vigorously against the demands of the early upholders of a communist ideal, such as Meslier, and later Morelly and Mably.

Meslier – like Gerard Winstanley somewhat earlier in England – set out in his posthumously published *Testament* a version of a communist society without oppressors or oppressed and he, again like Winstanley, insisted that revolutionary struggle was the only way to bring this about, for only thus could private property be abolished. Although a rural priest, Meslier rejected – in the most violent language yet written in Europe – both God and the Church. Man was alone in the world and must take his destiny into his own hands, if necessary – and Meslier believed that it would be necessary – in violent conflict with the entrenched powers of Church and State.

It is with the thinkers of the French Enlightenment that Soviet historians begin their critique of previous forms of 'progressive' thought and of humanism in particular. Helvétius and d'Holbach, for instance, are criticised for believing that the mere abolition of feudal relationships would bring plenty for everyone in its wake. Yet feudalism gave way to capitalism, and not to the hoped for age of peace and prosperity.

While opposing the feudal order of things, the French Enlightenment put forward, according to Soviet historians, only a restricted bourgeois conception of freedom. This was the spirit in which they formulated the basic principles of the bourgeois democratic freedoms and the theoretical case for the freedom of the press, of speech, of religion, and of conscience. What, in reality, the ideologists of the French Enlightenment were defending was the bourgeois-democratic state – the 'enlightened monarchy' of Helvétius, Diderot and d'Holbach and of which the English constitutional settlement was regarded as the ideal.

Yet it is hard, Soviet historians are agreed, to overestimate the historical significance of the French Enlightenment's defence of the principle of individual freedom, because in defending this principle to the limit, the thinkers of the French (and earlier English) Enlightenment also defended the principle of private property, and so ruled out the possibility of real human freedom, freedom from all forms of exploitation and, consequently, from political oppression.

The bourgeois ideal of equality is similarly criticised. Whilst this idea expressed a quite proper desire to put an end to feudal privileges and to make all men equal before the law and so represented a step forward in the attempt to transform social life on the basis of humanist principles, founded as it was on privately owned, capitalist enterprise, it could not prevent the rise of new, legally protected, privileges for the few and new forms of legal deprivation for the many.

Finally, whilst the ethical views of the *philosophes* are indeed subjected to criticism by Soviet historians, much space is also taken up in Soviet studies defending such thinkers as Diderot, La Mettrie, Helvétius and d'Holbach, from the crude representation of their views as being but a crass, materialistic egoism. It is true, Soviet scholars admit, that the French materialists regarded men as selfish by nature and true that they (wrongly) assumed that egoism had always been, and would continue to be, an essential feature of human psychology and so of human behaviour, but in so doing they were simply absolutising the characteristic features of the property-owning bourgeoisie, and seeing these as 'eternal' features of human nature as such. As one Soviet historian writes:

Having no faith in the possibility or expediency of a communist organisation of society, they naturally ruled out the possibility of overcoming individualism and self-love. (Petrosyan, 1972: p. 36)

In defence of the French materialists, Soviet historians point out that their stress on egoism was not intended to justify the 'war of all against all' not to justify immorality, indifference or cruelty to one's fellow men; rather was it an attempt to find a natural basis for a new ethic to offset the hitherto theologically undergirded ethic which sought support in divine revelation, or in supposed innate ideas of justice and goodness and which ruled out the need for social reform to make men more humane. All the French materialists believed that it was possible to combine personal and public interests, that the two could work harmoniously together. From an examination of the writings of Helvétius and d'Holbach in particular, it is possible to see that the French materialists believed that ideal human relationships could be achieved not through abstract religious teachings (and threats) but through legal reforms which would promote the formation of individuals with philanthropic moral conceptions who would work for the good of society as a whole.

But from a Marxist-Leninist point of view, the humanism of the French Enlightenment was essentially class biased. This is revealed in the fact that whilst pursuing the aiming of combining private and public interest they in one way or another always placed the logical emphasis on private interest. It is for the sake of personal interest that, according to their argument, public interests are to be observed. Their belief that the society that was to supersede feudalism would bring about the triumph of humanist relations and humanist morality, was utopian. The capitalism which eventually superseded feudalism was unrelentingly individualistic and self-centred.

Yet despite their obvious class limitations, the thinkers of the French Enlightenment made an outstanding contribution, in Marxist eyes, to the development of humanism. Their doctrine of the decisive role of the social environment in the formation of man's intellectual and moral nature served later as one of the ideological sources of the utopian socialism of the nineteenth century. Indeed, it is still very much alive in 'progressive' circles today.[18]

Two further groups of people continue to attract Soviet scholarly attention in the period of pre-scientific humanism and atheism – the German and the Russian 'progressive' traditions.

The German bourgeois Enlightenment,[19] which includes such notable figures as Lessing, Herder, Schiller, Goethe and Kant, was one with the English and the French Enlightenment in its proclamation of humanist ideals and in its opposition to feudalism in all spheres – particularly in art. Soviet scholarship has paid particular attention to Herder's idea that the history of man is a united, consistently developing process of the activity of the various peoples. Herder's devotion to folk-art, and his extolling of its humane spirit is also commended by Marxist-Leninist historians. But whilst the contribution of Lessing, Herder and others of the German Enlightenment – particularly their condemnation of colonial wars, national oppression and the enslavement of backward peoples – is a significant one, it is generally held to be less sharp than the French, the more so in its later stages. German 'progressive' thought broke less easily with religion and with idealism. This is particularly so in the philosophy of Kant. The explanation of this fact is held to lie in the feeble development of capitalist relations in Germany, and in the weakness and half-heartedness of the German bourgeoisie which made concession after concession to feudalism and to the feudal-religious ideology. The outcome was that, up to the time of Feuerbach, German philosophy was predominantly idealist and closely linked to religion and to religious notions of morality. It is, however, in their critique of German bourgeois idealism, with its overt adherence to humanistic values, that Marxism-Leninism – following, of course, the lead given by Marx and Engels themselves – seeks to bring out the essential weakness of all forms of humanism and atheism which are not Marxist-Leninist, including Western 'bourgeois humanism' today.

Before turning to this criticism, we must look briefly at the way in which Soviet historians have sought to explore their own indigenous atheistic and humanistic tradition – that of the revolutionary democrats of the nineteenth century – whose influence on Lenin and, therefore, on Marxism-Leninism was, as we saw earlier, so pronounced. All expositions of 'scientific atheism' today, without exception, contain at least one section on the Russian democratic, revolutionary, atheistic tradition (*IiTA:* pp. 286-297; *NA:* pp. 144-147; *ONA:* pp. 87-88).

The study of pre-Marxist social thought in Russia shows, Soviet 'scientific atheists' claim, that the ideals of the mass of the people were profoundly expressed in the revolutionary-democratic and atheistic ideology of such thinkers as Belinsky, Herzen, Chernyshevsky, Dobrolyubov and their followers.[20]

The views developed by these revolutionary democrats reflected the interests of the masses oppressed by serfdom and Tsarist despotism and, although, as is recognised, they were profoundly influenced in their thinking by the French materialists of the eighteenth century and, to a lesser extent, by Feuerbach and the 'left-wing' Hegelians, it is held that they developed certain important and distinctive features of their own, features which in Maria Petrosyan's words make the humanism of the Russian revolutionary democrats 'the highest form of pre-Marxist humanism' (op. cit., p. 64). Foremost among these distinctive traits is the emphasis which the revolutionary democrats placed on the organic unity of man and his environment and their recognition that human society is divided into classes with different aspirations and interests. Furthermore, while acknowledging the part played by environment, they also stressed the active role of the subject of historical action – that is, the role of the people in creating hisotry. Some of them, such as Dobrolyubov, even saw that historical development is subject to laws.

But the chief glory of the Russian revolutionary democrats in Soviet eyes is that they championed not man in general, but the essential rights of the workers – the freedom of the serf, and the creation of truly human conditions for his existence and development. 'The Russian people', wrote Herzen, 'are for us more than our native land. We see in them the soil in which a new system of state will develop, soil that far from being stale and exhausted holds all the seeds of renewal, all the conditions of development' (Herzen, *Soch.*, vol. 16, p. 9). Thus, not surprisingly, most of them championed – in some form or other – the newly developing outlook of socialism not, however, in its utopian form put forward by Fourier, Saint-Simon and Owen, which denied the class struggle and placed its hope in obtaining the cooperation of the ruling classes to establish a just social order, but in a more militant form which did not rule out the necessity for using force to bring in the new order. Russia, they recognised, must 'take up the axe'.

But Soviet 'scientific atheism' is not content simply to tell the story of the progress of mankind towards the truly atheistic and truly humanistic world-view of Marxism-Leninism. It must also point to the failings in the pre-Marxist tradition — failings which continue in the various forms of 'bourgeois humanism' current in Western countries today. The history of atheism is thus also part of the ongoing ideological struggle with the West (cf. *Nauchnyy ateizm:* ch. 10 *'Ateizm i sovremennaya ideologicheskaya bor'ba'* (Atheism and the Contemporary Ideological Struggle)).

6.2   BOURGEOIS ATHEISM AND HUMANISM CONTRASTED WITH MARXIST-LENINIST 'SCIENTIFIC ATHEISM'

The Western atheistic and humanistic tradition comes to fruition, that is, to full scientific expression, according to Soviet 'scientific atheism', only in the world outlook of Marxism-Leninism. The achievement of Marx and Engels was, it is argued, to transfer the problem of humanism from idealist and 'abstract-ethical' heights to the real ground of social relations, and to have offered a practical, scientific programme for the implementation of a truly humanistic society. This was the criticism which Marx had brought against the German humanism of his own day in his early writings, and in his *Theses on Feuerbach* in particular, and which had started him on his own quest for a more realistic and practical solution to the ills which he had diagnosed as lying at the root of the 'alienation' of man from himself and his society. Marxism-Leninism, in that it claims, in the Soviet Union, to be in the process of implementing Marx's solution, claims at the same time to be the only true humanism. In so far as it makes that claim, it offers, and knows that it offers, the social scientist — and others — an empirical yardstick by which to measure that claim. Hence, perhaps, the stridency of Maria Petrosyan's (and others) defence of the Soviet mode of life at the close of her book. Thus, the fundamental criticism which Marxism-Leninism levels at all previous forms of atheism and humanism — where it was historically excusable — and at all contemporary 'bourgeois' forms of atheism and humanism — where it is not — is that it is an 'abstract' humanism. 'Communism', on the other hand, as was argued by

Marx in the *Economic and Philosophic Manuscripts of 1844*, 'marks the advent of practical humanism' (*MEBW:* pp. 296-298). Contemporary Soviet 'scientific atheism' puts it like this:

> Long before the victory of socialist revolution, in the period when Marxist theory was being evolved, it was realised that the full achievement of humanist ideals meant creating certain objective social conditions for people to live in — above all material conditions. (Petrosyan, 1972: p. 237)

Or alternatively:

> The main question of history has been put before people for over a century now; it is the question of how to proceed from the *abstract* man to the *concrete* man, how to see to it that all human beings of all countries are able to make *real* use of human rights, and satisfy and develop their needs, how to guarantee for *every single* representative of the human race respect for his personal dignity, and a life without wars, without hunger, poverty or disease. (Fedoseyev, 1964: p. 9)

Marxism-Leninism's claim is that only a society founded on the 'scientific' principles enunciated by Marx, Engels and Lenin can solve the real problem of humanism and atheism.

Once again we see that in Soviet 'scientific atheism' theory and practice go hand in hand. The history of atheism and humanism, like the history of religion, is meaningful, and to the point, only when it is told in such a way as to lead to practical activity designed to solve in practice the problems which, at the theoretical level, such a study has presented. The history of atheism and humanism, no less than the history of religion, is, for Soviet 'scientific atheism', an ideological activity. From the Marxist-Leninist point of view, as we have seen earlier, there can be no such thing as a history of *ideas*, and therefore, whenever possible — as Soviet histories of atheism and humanism illustrate — the story of man's emerging consciousness of himself and of the possibilities open to him must be interwoven with the more fundamental history of the society of which it is part, and which it 'reflects'. That this leaves many of the essential problems of man untouched is a criticism to which we shall return in the final part of this study:

'Scientific Atheism' and the 'Concrete' Sociological Study of Religion and Atheism in the USSR

7.1 SOCIOLOGICAL STUDY OF RELIGION

As Soviet 'scientific atheism' has increasingly had to acknowledge and come to terms with the fact of the persistence of religion in the USSR, it has, of late, as a way of seeking to find out why this should be so in a society which − according to its own estimation of itself − is rapidly approaching full Communism, initiated what it terms 'concrete' (*konkretnye*) sociological studies to determine both the actual extent of religiosity among its citizens and the effectiveness of its own anti-religious propaganda. These studies provide important sociological information about religion in the Soviet Union today − and indeed about religion generally − which would not otherwise be available.[1]

The *Problematik* of such study is, of course, Marxist-Leninist and such study issues therefore, not, as does much Western socio-logical study of religion, from an interest in religion as such, but only as necessary preliminary step towards the eventual overcom-ing of religion. As a Western sociologist who has made a particular study of Soviet sociology of religion puts it: 'In the Soviet Union. . . .understanding is still sought to further the eradication of religion from the life of a socialist society' and whilst, as she claims, Soviet sociologists subscribe, on the whole, to the same methods as Western scholars and like them aspire to 'scientific objectivity', she admits that Soviet sociological study of religion is 'hampered by the dictates of the fairly rigid ideological and methodological framework given by Marxism-Leninism, which cannot be ignored'. 'This', she says, 'restricts the number of ques-tions raised in any enquiry' (Lane, 1978: p. 15). In the light of what we have ourselves said so far, this is what we would expect. We must also note that many Western students of religion ques-tion not only the limitations inherent in the particularly Marxist-

Leninist methodological presuppositions of Soviet study, but the inherent limitations of sociological study as such. Christopher Read for instance, criticises Dr. Lane's study on the grounds that whilst, as she claims, 'part of the predisposition' for her work — that of testing sociological models and of seeking to confirm or refute a 'particular typology of religious collectivities' — is 'to have a relatively value-free approach and scientific language', her own, somewhat limited, sociological values come through: 'Churches', she says, 'cater for' their adherents; some people require 'a minimum of religious need satisfaction'; the survival of Orthodox 'religiosity' can be explained by considering what 'cultural and/or psychological rewards are gained by Orthodox Christians', and so on. 'These statements' Read holds, 'reveal the problem of trying to study, in value-free, quantitative terms, what is an essentially qualitative and value-based aspect of human life'. Read's point is that much in religion is excluded by such an approach — 'the pride of any church ', 'its saints and martyrs who are a statistically insignificant aberration' etc. Further 'social disillusionment' is assumed by Dr. Lane to underlie many of the phenomena about which she writes, Read claims, without 'any reference to the question of why. . .disillusionment should be expressed through religion and not through drunkenness, hooliganism or any other channel' (Read, 1979: p. 183).[2]

That this is a problem with regard to the methodology not only Soviet sociology, with its avowedly naturalistic understanding of religion, but for any sociological study of religion, has long been recognised by students of religion, and the use of the phenomenological method by scholars working in the field of *Religionswissenschaft* was espoused specifically to overcome it (cf. Hultkrantz, 1970; Pye, 1974; Sharpe, 1977). In the study of religion much obviously depends on a scholar's own ontological committment, on whether he regards religion as a 'primary' datum — if only, as in phenomenology, as a methodological device for 'getting at' the complexity and subjectivity of much that is regarded as 'religious' by religious believers themselves — or, if religion is to be quantified at all, it must be regarded, as a 'secondary' datum, to be understood in terms of concepts derived from the disciplines of psychology and sociology.[3]

But the worries which Western students of religion – including Dr. Lane, voice, with regard to Soviet sociological study of religion, go beyond this general methodological problem in at least two respects and are concerned with: (1) the ideological rigidity of the Marxist-Leninist understanding of religion and the limitations which this imposes on Soviet study, and (2) the reliability of such data as Soviet sociological study collects. The two, as Lane recognises, are not unconnected (op. cit., p. 15). We will deal with each in turn.

1. For Soviet 'scientific atheism', as we have seen, religion is nothing but an ideological 'reflection' of physical and social reality in the mind of man. In class society, religion serves as an ideology of specific groups, and seeks to justify the groups own estimation of its place in society. It follows from this analysis of religion that in a society, such as is claimed has been brought into being in the Soviet Union, and where classes have been abolished, that religion can only exist as a 'survival', for whatever reasons, of earlier social conditions. The ultimate aim, therefore, of Soviet sociology is to see why this is so. But if religion is what Soviet 'scientific atheism' understands it to be, then the range of possible answers to the question, 'Why does religion persist in Soviet society?' will be severely restricted. This is not to say that the answers given to this question by 'scientific atheism' may not be true – it is simply to point out that certain possible answers – for example, that religion 'survives' because a religious attitude to life is innate in man, or that it fulfils personal needs which it alone can fulfil, and which are not always methodologically excluded in Western study of religion, are excluded from the outset in Soviet study. It also means, and this is more damaging, that what believers themselves say about the reasons for their belief must often be either ignored, or re-interpreted, to fit the methodological presuppositions of Soviet study. This, as Christel Lane has pointed out, can be the case even in contexts where those reasons are not particularly 'religious' – for example, where they spring from a general dis-

illusionment with life in the Soviet Union (cf. Lane, 1978: pp. 158-159). No Marxist-Leninist could write at length on *that* theme — even were he to claim to be simply reporting what was said to him — and hope to be published!

The restrictive nature of Soviet society itself also hampers research into religiosity in other ways, among which must be numbered the fact that many religious believers — particularly the more educated — often do not declare themselves as such — usually because of the fear of reprisals — and so fall outside any and all surveys of religiosity in the Soviet Union. There is, however, some evidence to support the view that it is among just such people that religious belief in the Soviet Union is growing.[4] If I might intrude my own impression at this point, it is that — as in Western Europe — at a time when adherence to institutional religion is in decline, a genuine *personal* interest in religion is high — not least, in the Soviet Union, among many of the younger personnel professionally involved in the study and, therefore, in the combatting, of religion. The amount of Western religious literature — some of it of a quite bizarre nature, — which circulates among young intellectuals in Leningrad is, as I can testify from personal experience, considerable.

2. So far as the question of bias in Soviet sociological study of religion is concerned, and hence of the reliability of Soviet studies of religiosity in contemporary Soviet society, it should be noted that Soviet scholars are themselves aware of the danger of this and strive, in a number of ways to overcome it (cf. Pivovarov, 1974; Alekseyev, 1967). Not only do they try to be non-polemical in their interviews with believers, but they also try to compensate for any ideological bias that remains by checking their results with key informants and by reference to documentary evidence from the religious groups themselves. Lane also thinks that Soviet researchers are helped by the 'low level of sophistication' among large sections of believers who are often, she says, 'unaware of the purpose of the research in which they are participating' (op. cit., p. 16). This, I myself doubt, but it is not this group of believers in whom Soviet researchers are primarily interested. With more

educated believers, and with those who belong to illegal or anti-Soviet sects, the pretence of ideological neutrality is harder to maintain. As Lane writes: 'In these latter cases [the illegal sects] the methods outlined above probably cannot overcome the ideological bias and some socially vulnerable or politically hostile respondents will probably give a false response or no response at all' (ibid.). This can, however, be partially overcome, as Lane recognises, by researchers supplementing their results by again consulting with key informants and by prolonged observation of religious life. The social scientist himself is often a member of the local community, or will have lived and worked, often as an *antirelioznik* (a militant atheist) in the community − or be in close touch with such − and will thus have a knowledge of what is going on in the community which is not dependent solely on his formal interviews and questionnaires. Living in the community and reporting on its religious activities, even in the interests of sociological research, can however, as Dr. Lane fails to notice, bring him close, however unintentionally, to becoming an 'informer'. Of this fact, I know, many sociologists are extremely aware.

Whilst these considerations go some way towards mitigating the effects of ideological bias in Soviet sociological study of religion,[5] and whilst, as Lane says, actual manipulation of results is rare, we should also be aware of what, from the point of view of Western students of *Religionswissenschaft*, are other limiting factors in Soviet sociological study of religion − although, again, we must note that many of these are factors which the student of religion would hold to be limiting in any claimed exhaustive sociological study of religion. These concern the indices of religiosity.

Soviet research workers in sociology of religion spend much of their time today collecting data on the incidence of religiosity, seeking answers to such questions as, 'how much religious behaviour is exhibited?', 'what is its nature?', 'who is involved?' and 'what are the conditions?'. The most obvious symptoms of religiosity, for them, are the presence of icons in the home, overtly expressed belief in God, attendance at places of worship, and – a symptom of extreme religiosity – giving religious instruction to the young. Recently, however, on the basis of statistical material already gathered, A.A. Lebedev has put forward a rather more sophisticated schema for measuring religious behaviour (Lebedev, 1970).

Lebedev distinguishes seven types of religious believer, extending the concept into the negative range. They are B 1. The convinced believer, who asserts belief in God and the immortality of the soul, claims that man's goals are God-given, engages in religious practices and diseminates his views; B2. The second-rank believer, who exhibits all the traits of B1 with the exception of the last; W1. The 'waverer' who yet proclaims his belief in the supernatural and occasionally indulges in religious practices; W2. The 'waverer' – what in the West would be called an 'Agnostic' – who neither asserts, nor denies, belief in God, but usually does not believe in the immortality of the soul and pursues material goals as ardently as non-believers; I. The totally indifferent, who may sometimes indulge in religious practices for non-religious reasons; AI. The atheist who does not engage in religious practices and reacts negatively to all forms of religion, and A2. The atheist who also disseminates his views (Lebedev, 1970: pp. 138-139).

An obvious comment on these indices of religiosity is, of course, that they only apply within a Christian (or theistic) frame of reference, but it is easy to see how they might be adapted for research into other religions conditions. The limitation, from the point of view of the student of religion who may be interested in the quality of religious belief, and in the reasons given by believers for their belief, will be obvious. But this, as I have already pointed out, is a limitation appertaining to sociological study of religion in general and is not peculiar to Marxist-Leninist study. The limitation of Marxist-Leninist study lies, overall, in the realm of explanation rather than of research, and is linked perhaps to an over-emphasis on the views of religious sectarians – a failing that many have seen in Western sociological studies of religion also.

With these provisos in mind we can now turn to Soviet 'concrete' sociological study of religion. The Western student of religion is fortunate in that some of the material relating to this area of Soviet study has been translated (a great deal of it in the journal *Soviet Sociology*) and much of it has been analysed — particularly studies relating to the Christian religion — by Christel Lane, in her book, *Christian Religion in the Soviet Union — A Sociological Study*, to which reference has already been made, and by Ethel and Stephen Dunn (1975 etc.).

The current model for Soviet empirical sociological study of religion was first put forward by A.I. Klibanov, in an article published in 1961 (translated as 'The Dissident Denominations in the Past and Today' and published in *Soviet Sociology*, 1965, Vol. III, No. 4, pp. 44-60), and although he has written extensively on religious sectarianism in both Tsarist Russia and the Soviet Union since, any modification of the position he set out in 1961, both on his own part, and on the part of those who have followed his approach, has been slight. Klibanov's achievement was to base the study of religious sectarianism not, as had previously, in the pre-war period, been the case, on the ideologically dictated assumption that all sectarians are hostile to Soviet power and, therefore, dangerous, but on the attitude of believers themselves, as established by empirical study, and 'scientific atheism' has overall, followed him in this, not only in the study of religious sectarianism, but in the study of religiosity in the Soviet Union as a whole.

The basic division of all history in the Soviet Union is, of course, a division which centres on the 'Great October Revolution' of 1917. Thus the study of the history of religion in Russia is similarly divided into religion before 1917, when society was divided into classes, and religion after 1917, when classes began to be eradicated. It is assumed that different forces were at work during these two periods, though the history of the various religions is treated as a whole. Thus, when Klibanov is discussing religious dissent in pre-revolutionary Russia, he points out that this 'falls into the category of socio-historical movements' which, he says, 'it is customary to term those of religious reformation'. He continues:

Religious dissidence was a sharp protest against the church, the clergy and the entire organisation and system of Orthodoxy, which gave its blessing to the system of serfdom. . .

and after describing how the Russian sectarians contrasted the reverence for icons, the belief in the letter of Holy Writ, and the luxurious ceremonial of the established church — which they called the worship of the 'God of the dead' — with a faith based on 'internal conviction' and service to God 'in spirit and in truth', and with the belief that man is his own church, he comments:

This ideology of anti-feudal protest contained a positive ideological elements. The . . . appeal to individual freedom, to a man's inner conviction, and the expressed confidence in man's intellectual and moral strength. . . represented the founding in the peasant environment of the ideology of bourgeois individualism, clothed in religious disguise.

Yet, despite this 'positive ideological element', for the rest, the peasant was, he says,

. . .striving for the bourgeois order of things, in which peasants hoped to take their place as free community producers.

This is why, he continues:

. . .the world view of the modern religious dissidents is a bourgeois ideological survival in the most exact sense of those words. The world view of religious dissidence thus differs from that of Orthodoxy which, while it pays tribute to bourgeois ideology, also bore, and still bears, an enormous burden of ideological carry-overs from feudalism. It must not be forgotten that the Orthodox Church made its appearance in Russia many centuries before religious dissidence and unswervingly served the feudal lords and serf-owners throughout its history. (Klibanov, 1965: pp. 47-48)

Religious dissidence in Tsarist Russia, he says further, was a 'profoundly contradictory phenomenon', which was 'not adapted to active participation in the social struggle' and which by 1905 had become profoundly reactionary. As he said in an article written in 1967:

As is well known, religious sectarianism is a social movement, arising out of and set in motion by the struggle of the working masses, and particularly the peasantry, against the exploitation of serfdom and, later, against the survivals of serfdom in the economic and socio-political structure of Tsarist Russia. Religious in form only, sectarianism is, in reality, a democratic movement which changes its form according to the various stages in the development of the situation of the peasantry – on the one hand, towards increasing pauperisation; on the other, towards the formation of a peasant bourgeoisie. In approaching the study of sectarianism it is, therefore, necessary to different-iate between sectarianism as a broad, democratic religio-social movement and bourgeois sectarianism, noting the historical origin of groups and the contradictory tendencies – democratic or bourgeois – which developed in them. (Klibanov, 1967: p. 352)

On the whole, however, for Klibanov, it is the bourgeois aspects of sectarian revolt which have prevailed.

Klibanov rejects the kind of classification of sects which has dominated Western study of sectarianism, and he sees the frag-mentation of religious groups into new sects simply as manifesta-tions of the class struggle, pointing out in the third volume of his monumental study of sectarianism in Tsarist Russia and the USSR, entitled *Religioznoye sektantstvo i sovremennost'* (Religious Sectarianism Today), and published in 1965, that whilst, by the end of the 1920's, sects of Western origin – Baptists, Adventists, Pentecostalists and Jehovah's Witnesses – were in decline, as were indigenous Russian sects such as the Molokans, Dukhobors and Khlysts, 'no new forms of sectarianism arose to replace them' (op. cit. p. 5). He thus has to consider such modern breakaway movements from the Orthodox church as 'The True Ortho-dox Christians' and 'The True Orthodox Church' not as sects, but as Orthodox movements outside the Church. He writes:

In the 20th century, parallel to bourgeois-reactionary orientation, the prin-ciple of religious individualism has taken on a directly anti-social meaning . . . The counterposing of the 'inner man' to social man is what is distinctive in the 'philosophy' of late dissidence. . .

The sects, he says, have become 'a historical anachronism' and although during the second world war, and into the middle 1950's in Central Russia, and into the late 1950's and early 1960's in Kazakhstan, sectarian movements experienced some growth, the trend, Klibanov asserts, was downward, because sectarian movements have been abandoned by working people and have become the preserve of the elderly, of females and of alienated segments of Soviet society (Klibanov, 1965: p. 52; 1971: pp. 505-566). Theological preoccupations, he further asserts, have now become greatly intensified.

Central to this ideology [he writes] is the concept of man entirely absorbed by his relationship to God and, on that basis, condemnatory of any active attitude towards society. . . Religious dissidence is thus profoundly reactionary. . .a distorted survival of capitalist society. (Klibanov, 1965: pp. 57-59)

Here it seems to me, we have a good example of the way in which Marxist-Leninist ideology predetermines the way in which religious phenomena is interpreted − and this in the face of the evidence, for not only is Klibanov wrong in his statement that no new sects have arisen in the Soviet Union and that all have gone into decline, − the activities of the Muslim Brotherhood in many of the southern 'autonomous' republics of the Soviet Union would alone repudiate this assertion − but there seems no good reason − other than ideological necessity − to treat the 'New Orthodox Christians', and other breakaway groups, as other than sectarian.

Soviet answers to the question, 'why does religion 'survive' under socialism?', fall under five major headings: (1) Public and family pressure; (2) Nationality; (3) Social situation; (4) The Sexual and Age differential, and (5) Education.

-   1. Community pressure for conformity − a factor obviously linked to the second factor outlined above − nationality − is regarded by many Soviet sociologists as being of more significance than family pressures. For example, data collected by L.N. Ulyanov indicate that conformity to longstanding communal traditions, rather than immediate family pressure, were of overriding importance in the decision of 42% of those who had had their children baptised in the sample Ulyanov studied (Ulyanov, 1970:

p. 180). It is often difficult, of course, as Ethel and Stephen Dunn have pointed out in their analysis of Soviet material relating to this factor, to establish where community pressure leaves off and family pressure begins (op. cit., p. 136). This, I would think, would be particularly difficult in certain Moslem, and in Christian national areas such as the Ukraine and the Baltic republics.

Soviet research has also paid considerable attention to religious upbringing within the family and it sees this as playing an extremely important part – particularly among sectarians (cf. A.F. Yery-shev, 1967: pp. 138-144) – in the survival of religion (cf. Klibanov, 1969: p. 110). An interesting, if rather sinister, method used in Soviet research to find out from children themselves if they are receiving a religious upbringing is described by a Latvian '*antireligioznik*', D.A. Meykshane, in volume 11 of *Voprosy nauchnogo ateizma* (1971), pp. 264-275. It involves the use of 'flash-cards' relating to religious themes and the child's recognition or otherwise of them.

2. Nationality (and nationalism) is without doubt – particularly, but by no means exclusively in Moslem areas – a factor in religious adherence, though not many Soviet sociologists have paid much attention to this. The exception, as we might expect, is Klibanov, who has shown, to give but one example from his study of contemporary sectarianism, that 30% of the Evangelical Christian Baptists in Voronezh *oblast* are Ukrainian (43% in the city of Voronezh itself). According to the 1959 census Ukrainians were 7.6% of the population as a whole (Klibanov, 1969: p. 77). Few, however, have followed his example and taken nationality seriously as a factor affecting religious belief, yet in the Moslem areas, to ignore nationality as a factor making for the continuance of religion is surely to put the dictates of the prevailing orthodoxy – the official line is that there is no nationalities question[6] – above the serious study of religion to the extent of ignoring what is, in the opinion of many – including Moslems themselves in these areas – the primary and overriding factor behind the observance of religious practices. In these areas – the Azerbaydzhan, Uzbekistan, Kazakhstan republics – nationality and religion are

intertwined to the extent that the leading Western authority on Islam in the Soviet Union can ask the question, whether the expression 'Moslem' when used of those who live in them still has a religious, or only cultural and political meaning? (Bennigsen, 1975: p. 91). Before 1917, certainly, any distinction between religion and culture would have been meaningless. The Moslem peoples of Tsarist Russia – 80% of whom were Turks – were not fully aware of belonging to any nation and the current expressions of nationality were never used by them. The masses rarely went beyond tribal or a religious consciousness – tribal if they were sedentaries, religious if they were nomads – and to this day it makes sense to speak of a 'Moslem way of life' when referring to the way of life of the vast majority of inhabitants of these areas (Bennigsen, op. cit., pp. 91-98). The effect of this on religious observances – as research by Soviet sociologists cannot ignore, though it can play it down – is incalculable. As Bennigsen says, whilst it is virtually impossible to measure private belief, and whilst the number of those attending mosques for regular worship has declined, the great (and sometimes local) Moslem festivals are still extremely important 'national' occasions (op. cit., p. 94).

Communal pressures to observe certain religious practices – circumcision, marriage and burial customs, – is still overwhelming in Moslem areas; much more so, in fact, than in traditionally Christian areas. What is more, such pressure shows little sign of diminishing, and can even be said to be growing, to the extent that anti-religious workers in Uzbekistan stated, in *Uzbekistan Kommunist* in June 1970, that Islam was making considerable inroads into both the Komsomol and, indeed, into the Party itself. If in the Moslem areas nationality cannot be ignored as a factor making for the 'survival' of religion, it cannot be ignored when the religion is Judaism, Roman Catholicism, or certain forms of Protestantism. The Ukraine and the Baltic Republics might be instanced as areas where the relationship between religion and nationality would bear much more investigation than Soviet sociologists can, in the present political climate, give them.

3. That the social circumstances of many workers represent a

factor making for religion is another area where Soviet sociologists, whilst they are aware that this is so, are unable, in the present state of things, to gove it the attention which – on a Marxian analysis alone – it would deserve. Some pioneering who has, however, been done by Zdravomyslov (1970), Shubkin (1970) and Zaslavskaya (1970), but the sociology of work is not a topic upon which Soviet sociologists are encouraged to concentrate. There is some evidence, however, in the works cited above, that some workers, alienated in their work, turn to religion – in classical Marxian fashion – to seek for a fulfilment denied them under present conditions.[7] This is not, however, emphasised, and this is an area where further research is needed.

4. The sexual and age differential is a factor which Soviet sociologists take very much into account in endeavouring to explore religiosity in Soviet society. What they seem to have established in this respect is that whilst religious groups are overwhelmingly female, religiosity in men can be high in youth – particularly in the countryside – and when men are actively raising a family (cf. Kolbanovsky, 1970: pp. 230-231). Further, Soviet sociologists have established that the leadership in almost all religious groups is male. They also appear to have established that the oft quoted thesis that pensioners automatically turn towards religion is a thesis which needs considerable refinement, since much depends on what the pensioner did before retirement and what his or her opportunities are for continuing such interests after retirement (Saprykhin, 1970: p. 130). Baykov has also shown that in a secular environment women seeking self-expression often do so in secular, rather than religious activities (Baykov, 1970: pp. 228-230). My own impression is that so far as sex and age are concerned in religion, Soviet findings do not differ in any significant respect from the findings of Western sociologists, though an area in which further research is needed is into the attitudes to religion of young people. Here again, however, is an area where, in present conditions, it would be difficult to get honest answers to straightforward questions.

5. The last factor in current Soviet studies of religiosity in

Soviet society that we must mention is education. We mentioned earlier L.N. Mitrokhin's statement to the effect that religion and semi-literacy are often found together and we saw how he sought to account for this socially (cf. p. 210 above), and Soviet sociologists have in fact, more and more of late, directed their research towards establishing the educational level of believers — especially as this relates to technological skills and job qualifications. For an example of the results of this research the reader is referred to the statistics given in Ethel and Stephen Dunn's article 'Religious Behaviour and Socio-Cultural Change in the Soviet Union' (in Bociurkiw and Strong, 1975: pp. 135 and 137). Unfortunately, to date, such research has been conducted, for the most part, among members of the more extreme sects — Seventh Day Adventists, Jehovah's Witnesses etc., — and thus, the results published so far in Soviet sociological journals and in *Voprosy nauchnogo ateizma* tend to confirm Mitrokhin's lowly estimate of the educational level of the majority of believers. Much more extensive research in this area is obviously needed, although, again in present conditions, it is doubtful if much of interest would be revealed.

These then, are the main factors taken into consideration by Soviet sociologists seeking to account for the persistence of religion in the face of the fundamental changes which have taken place in the 'base' of society in the Soviet Union over the last sixty years. All of them are social and all are based on the assumption — overtly expressed in Soviet writing on religion and adopted as a conscious methodological procedure in Soviet sociology of religion — that religion is not only a wholly social phenomenon, but is, in particular, an expression of social pathology.

One further factor, however, needs to be mentioned, although it does not affect the overall judgement of Soviet theory that religion is a pathological phenomenon, and that is the attention which is beginning to be paid in Soviet study to the personal, psychological (subjective) factors making for belief. This, as a Soviet sociologist has recently pointed out, is a complex business. He writes:

Sometimes in our literature this fact is either underestimated or entirely ignored. There is a widespread view that in general people come to religion who have experienced personal misfortune – illness, the death of loved ones, etc . . . or who are materially insecure – pensioners, those who have left their jobs, etc. Undoubtedly such assertions have some truth in them, but one should not absolutise this. We know that by no means everyone who has suffered becomes a believer. We have, apparently, here to deal with a whole complex of reasons, motives and various circumstances of an objective and subjective nature in which this or that man finds himself. (Saprykhin, 1970: p. 117)

The increased willingness of Soviet 'scientific atheists' to consider individual psychology as a factor in religious belief is one to which we have already called attention. Thus Klibanov ends a recent survey of Soviet research into religious sectarianism by emphasising the role which psychology of religion has to play in explaining the persistence of religion in the Soviet Union. He writes:

To them (contemporary researchers into religious sectarianism) it is necessary to get the hang of psychology – and this is especially important so that they can establish a way into the spiritual world of believers, and establish scientific ideas and facts about it, which will aid the working out of the philosophical and historical problems connected with religious sectarianism. Systematic study of the psychological aspects of religious sectarianism is, however, a task for the future. (Klibanov, 1967: p. 383)

This being so, Soviet studies of religious behaviour in the Soviet Union still tend to follow the model layed down earlier by Klibanov and to interpret religiosity, therefore, almost wholly in socio-economic terms. The inadequacy of the actual socio-economic explanation put forward in contemporary Soviet sociology of religion – in which religion is held to be maintained in Soviet society today by the force of tradition within individual face-to-face communities (including the family), and in which it does not arise from any objective factors in contemporary Soviet society, with the consequence that religion will eventually die out – has been thoroughly examined by the American sociologists

Ethel and Stephen Dunn and found wanting (1975: pp. 130-145). There are many objective factors in Soviet society itself which, in their opinion, make for religion; a view shared by a few Soviet philosophers and sociologists themselves (cf. P.P. Cherkashin, 1958: pp. 29-51). Their own conclusion is that 'the most obvious threat to the believers today is not so much a particular political system. . .as an inexorable process taking place in the world over − secularisation' (op. cit., pp. 142-143) − a view which I myself put forward in an earlier publication (Thrower, 1975: p. 14). Whether this process is indeed inexorable is, of course, another and a wider question.

7.2   THE SOCIOLOGY OF ATHEISM

If Soviet research into contemporary religiosity in the USSR is carried on − as I believe it is − within the context of a general nervousness that all is not well in the progress towards a society which will be free of religion, a similar nervousness characterises research into the effectiveness of the campaign against religion and into the progress towards the creation of a positive, atheistic society − that is into *ateistichieskoye vospitaniye* − atheistic upbringing. The implications of this research are wider than their immediate objective, in that *ateistichieskoye vospitaniye* is but one aspect − though an important one − of the attempt of the Communist Party of the Soviet Union to refashion the consciousness and the culture of an entire people. It is for this reason that an American sociologist, David Powell, who has made a special study of Soviet anti-religious propaganda, subtitles his book on the subject 'a study of mass persuasion' (Powell, 1975).

As we have seen earlier, the study of religion in the Soviet Union is but the negative side of the more important task of education in atheism. This is the true objective of Marxist-Leninist 'scientific atheism' and it is not surprising, therefore, that the Communist Party of the Soviet Union, which has invested vast resources in the development of this aspect of its ideology, should initiate 'concrete' research in an endeavour to establish the success or otherwise of this important enterprise. Two areas in particular stand at the forefront of Soviet endeavour and, therefore, of Soviet sociological research: (1) The educational system (including clubs, and museums devoted to atheism) and (2) the new 'Soviet Rites' and ceremonies designed to replace religious festivals and ceremonies.[8]

Though the school system is potentially the Party's most powerful weapon in the struggle against religion, its influence has not been nearly so persuasive and profound as might have been expected. Working against success in this area is the prior socialising influence of the family and the lack of interest and skill of many of the teachers dealing with religion. Many children grow up in families where at least one member is a believer and many children are exposed to the influence of believing grandparents. Such children are said to lack 'atheistic immunity' (Smirnov, 1971), and may have difficulty in assimilating the teachers message. Suggestions that pre-school education should also be orientated towards atheism (Shelikhanov, 1971) have been largely ignored. Resourceful teachers can and do weave anti-religious messages into the most diverse topics, but this is by no means uniformly so throughout the Soviet Union. Pupils in upper grades receive some formal instruction in 'scientific atheism' — often in courses in social studies and civic training — but these are still offered on an elective basis and are, in fact, taught in very few schools (Lensu, 1970: p. 147).

The most distinctive extra-curricula activity in atheistic upbringing involves 'atheist clubs' and visits to city 'atheist museums'. However, despite the elaborateness of some of the programmes and activities of the atheist clubs, their contribution to the atheist effort is limited. Only a small number of pupils are involved and the remaining pupils in the school are hardly touched at all (Filippova, 1971: p. 20). Many pupils, it has been found, master their school lesson well, but retain their religious beliefs (Kozhemyako, 1964: p. 3). The problem is compounded by the fact that few teachers share the enthusiam of the professional *antireligionzniki*

(Okunev, 1961: pp. 79-80). Many teachers are conscious of their own lack of training and so of expertise in this area — in 1972, for example, only a third of all schoolteachers had actually taken courses in 'scientific atheism' (Lagov, 1964: p. 2; Ramm, 1972: p. 2; Gorelov, 1971: p. 48) — and many consider that their role is to inculcate academic expertise into their pupils and not to insult or abuse whatever private beliefs children may have acquired at home (*Prepodavaniye istorii v shkole,* No. 1, 1972, p. 4). Further, the avialable text-books help but little should a teacher wish to aid *ateisticheskoye vospitaniye*. Neither the *Programme of Instruction* nor the *Teacher's Commentary* — used in all Soviet nurseries and kindergartens — make any reference whatever to religion or atheism (Chauncey, 1969) and the various teachers' manuals are little better, giving only general exhoration, and little practical advice (Lagov, op. cit., p. 2; *NKA:* p. 502). Recently, however, there have been serious and sustained attempts to remedy this situation and in 1975 the journal *Narodnoye obrazo-vaniye* (Public Education) carried special directions for teachers in secondary schools, giving them methodological instructions in the atheistic education of pupils approved by the Ministry of Education's Central Board for Schools (*Narodnoye obrazovaniye*, No. 3, 1975: pp. 122-125). Whilst some attempt is made to give practical advice, as for instance when it is suggested that pupils may be led to atheistic conclusions by acquainting them with works of art which emphasise, 'the joy of life and man's active role as fighter and creator' and which will, it is claimed, 'in the long run negate a religious outlook which belittles man and earthly values' (op. cit., p. 125), the document is largely taken up with exhortation and the statement of broad principles. For example, the document's opening sentence reads as follows:

It is imperative, in the schools, to prove logically the essence and nature of the centuries—old, irreconcilable conflict between science and religion, to reveal the social and epistemological roots of idealism and materialism and to help pupils to understand the Marxist-Leninist teaching in the development of nature, society and thought. (op. cit., p. 122)

The document also urges that the central place in all atheistic teaching be assigned to the unmasking of the pretentions of religious morality, of what it terms 'the abstract humanism of religion, which is divorced from real life'. It says:

The problems of unmasking religious morality and asserting the moral principles of those who are building Communism should occupy the central place in atheist education in schools. Teachers should start by showing the worldly origins of morality and prove that human beings eventually derive their moral views, be it consciously or unconsciously, from social relationships on which their class position is based. (op. cit., p. 124)

How this is to be done in the class-room situation is not stated.

Conditions for the propogation of atheism in institutions of higher education are little better, despite the fact, as we had occasion to mention earlier, that the study of 'scientific atheism' has been compulsory since 1964, and by the inclusion of 'practical work' in atheistic agitation as part of the course. Anti-religious work in Soviet institutions suffers from a number of factors, among which we should mention the fact that departments of 'scientific atheism', have actually been set up in very few universities and institutes, and anti-religious training in other universities is extremely superficial. Textbooks and other resources are hard to come by – particularly in the non-Russian republics – and those that are available are extremely dated. Further, and this has been my own experience in the Soviet Union, students, as well as other members of the teaching staff in institutes of higher learning, resent the time spent on instruction in 'scientific atheism' (and indeed in other 'political' subjects also) and its teachers do not command the respect that teachers in the more academic and practical departments command (cf. Solokov and Belous, 1966: p. 3). Few persons register for graduate work in 'scientific atheism' – in fact, in the period 1957–1963, only three doctoral dissertations and some sixty 'candidates' theses in 'scientific atheism' were defended in the entire USSR (*Nir*, No. 1, 1964, p. 32). The situation has improved considerably since that time, but 'scientific atheism' still lags behind the other philosophical subjects in popularity (Afana-

siev and Petrov, 1969a: pp. 147, 149; 1969b: pp. 140-142). However, Powell's judgement, made in 1975, that 'lack of scholarly
research and interest, combined with faculty and student indifference to atheistic themes in their regular classwork, suggests that
the effectiveness of university-based programs is likely to be quite
limited' (Powell, 1975), is one that today needs some modification. The increasing inclusion of the detailed study of religion has,
I believe done much to revive interest in the discipline of 'scientific atheism'. Formerly critics of the syllabus of 'scientific atheism'
had, quite justifiably, argued that graduates were 'often ignorant
of the most elementary questions of religion and often totally
unfamiliar with the scriptures' (Sokolov and Belous, 1966: p. 3)
and until recently Soviet ideologists tended to assume that the
success of atheistic work depended primarily on the conviction,
perseverance and tenacity of the atheistic worker rather than on
his knowledge of religion. As one critic expressed it, most university graduates were better equipped to challenge a neo-Kantian
than an ordinary believer (Khudyakov, 1962: p. 15). This situation is now changing and the period since the November 1954
resolution of the Central Committee of the Communist Party of
the USSR on 'scientific atheism' has witnessed both a revival of
interest in the study of religion and a considerable rise in the
number of students pursuing further research into it. This has
also − if Soviet sociological surveys are accepted as accurate − not
been without its effect on the formation of an atheistic outlook
among students as the results of a survey conducted among
students in two higher education institutes in 1971 show (Lebedev,
in V.N.A. Vol. 15 (1973) pp. 199-213).

Since the end of the 1950's, when the Party renewed its concern with the atheistic upbringing of Soviet people, it set up a
number of new organisations in individual cities and districts to
co-ordinate anti-religious activities. These 'clubs' or 'houses of
atheism' − membership of which is drawn, for the most part, from
the local intelligentsia − organise lectures and show films on
religion and atheism and often possess a library and reading room
stocked with anti-religious literature. Like the *Znaniye* (Know-

ledge) society – with whom these 'clubs' are urged to co-operate – membership is voluntary and membership of these organisations, in fact, often overlaps. In addition to educating their membership in atheism, these clubs also engage in active anti-religious propaganda in their local area. Often members are assigned to work on particular local religious groups and as a consequence of this not a few activists acquire, as part of their training for this task, some knowledge of the actual religious beliefs of the groups with which they are concerned. Such activists are also urged to show forth in their personal behaviour the moral values of 'atheist man' (cf. NiR, No. 5, 1960: pp. 75-76).

Perhaps the most distinctive feature of Soviet anti-religious propaganda are the 'museums of atheism' housed in former churches and cathedrals – of which the most impressive is the Museum of the History of Religion and Atheism housed in the former Kazan Cathedral in Leningrad.[9] Whilst the exhibits of such museums are there to impress on the visitor the more negative aspects of the religious life of the past, many of them have an intrinsic religious interest which undermines the purpose for which they were originally set up. (I have myself, for instance, seen peasant women praying before the icons exhibited in the Leningrad museum!). Moreover some house important collections of documents and artifacts which a serious student of religion can use to further his knowledge of religion.[10]

When Soviet sociologists produce the results of 'concrete' research into education in atheism, more often than not what they do is simply produce comparative annual statistics regarding the number of lectures given at the 'clubs' and 'houses of atheism' and the number of visitors to atheistic museums.[11] These, however, I feel, tell us more about the level of intensity of the Party's activities against religion than they do about the effectiveness of the propaganda put out.

One of the more interesting areas of atheistic activity in the USSR – and one which has fascinated Western sociologists[12] – is the attempt now being made by the Soviet authorities – in the wake of the belated recognition of the emotional roots of religion

− to provide substitute secular ceremonies for the age old rituals of religion.[13] The aim here is not simply the negative one of seeking to counteract the influence of religion, for the network of secular holidays and ceremonies also seeks to propagate positive Communist ideals and so contribute to 'the ideological, ethical and aesthetic upbringing of the builders of Communism' and 'the rearing of citizens. . .devoted to the ideals of the Party' (Filatov, 1967: pp. 20, 42). It is difficult, as yet, to assess their effectiveness, but the evidence from sociological surveys conducted so far suggests that this is by far the most effective of the measures so far taken by the Soviet authorities to counteract the influence of religion (cf. Powell, 1975: pp. 79-83). All the available statistics, for instance, show a dramatic decline in the last decade in the number of religious marriage ceremonies and in religious funerals. Religious holidays, for reasons which, perhaps, have little to do with religion itself, have however, proved harder to combat!

These then are the areas which most concern 'concrete' Soviet sociological research into the development of an atheistic mentality among Soviet citizens. The only conclusion that can at present be drawn is that whilst, on the evidence available from Soviet sources, religion appears to be decline, it is not declining at anything like the rate that either the classical Marxist analysis of the sources of religion would suggest for a socialist society rapidly approaching Communism, nor in proportion to the enormous outlay in manpower and resources which the Soviet government has invested in combatting it. Whether what is needed is more and better anti-religious activity − as almost all internal criticism of the ineffectiveness of present anti-religious activity suggests − or whether the conclusion to be drawn is that among certain sections of the community religion will continue to flourish irrespective of what the Soviet authorities do, is a matter upon which I do not myself feel able to prophesy. All I would suggest is that the persistence of religion in the USSR should make 'scientific atheists' more aware than they have been inclined to be of the extreme complexity, subtelty, and even perversity, of the religious consciousness, and aware also of some of the fundamental differences in motivation between believers and Marxist-Leninists which they have so far ignored and to which I shall call attention in the final section of this work.

PART THREE

Critique of the Marxist-Leninist Approach to the
Study of Religion

The Marxist-Leninist Understanding of 'Religion'

8.1 RELIGION AS A FALSE VIEW OF THE WORLD

Marxism-Leninism, as we have seen, is not simply a body of social doctrine but a total world-view — a *mirovozzreniye* (world-outlook) to use the current Soviet expression — and one which is fundamentally opposed to any and every religious understanding of the world. Whatever may be the case with other philosophical systems opposed to religion, opposition to religious belief — at least at the present stage of world-development — is not marginal to Marxism-Leninism, but belongs to its very core. Unless we understand this, we shall fail to understand the significance which Marxism-Leninism attaches to the study of religion and atheism. Marxism-Leninism takes its own, and a religious approach to the world, with a seriousness which has all but disappeared from the tolerant, pragmatic, pluralistic milieu inhabited by the majority of intellectuals in the Western world today. It is this which explains the vast resources and the fiercely partisan spirit which is brought both to the study of religion and to the propagation of atheism in the Soviet Union today. For Marxism-Leninism ideas matter, for it believes that only action informed by a 'correct' theoretical understanding of reality can ultimately be effective. Here, of course, there is a formal similarity with traditional Christianity which has also laid great emphasis on the salvic value of correct belief.[1] This 'correct' understanding of reality, Marxism-Leninism believes, is found only in the philosophy of dialectical materialism — a philosophy, it believes, which can in no way be reconciled to a religious understanding of reality. However much, of late, Soviet students of religion have come to appreciate the emotional aspects of religion, religion remains, for Marxism-Leninism, as the place accorded to education in combatting religion shows, essentially a set of beliefs about the workings of the world. From this perspective it appears, of course, as a false, obsolete, even absurd sort of outlook and one which stands refuted by modern empirical science.

This way of regarding religion, whilst it can be found in the writings of Marx and Engels — though more often than not there it is implicit rather than explicit, assumed rather than argued — is, as we have seen, of the essence of the Marxist-Leninist 'scientific atheist' understanding of religion (cf. Section 4.1 above). The draft of the new programme for the Communist Party of the Soviet Union — adopted at the XXII Congress of the Party in 1961 — makes this clear. It reads:

The Party uses ideological media to educate people in the spirit of a scientific materialist world conception. To overcome religious prejudices . . . It is necessary to conduct regularly broad atheistic propaganda on a scientific basis, to explain patiently the untenability of religious beliefs, which were engendered in the past when people were overawed by elemental forces and social oppression and did not know the real causes of natural and social phenomena. This can be done by making use of the achievements of modern science, which is steadily solving the mysteries of the universe and extending man's power over nature, leaving no room for religious inventions about supernatural forces. (*Pravda,* 31 Oct. 1961, KPSS v Rezolyutsiyakh, VIII.)

This understanding of religion — making as it does no distinction between religion and superstition — appears to many Western students of religion to constitute the fundamental weakness in the Marxist-Leninist understanding of that phenomenon — something taken over from the Enlightenment and long since refuted by theology and the science of religion. The German theologian Helmut Gollwitzer, for instance, in his penetrating study, *The Christian Faith and the Marxist Criticism of Religion* (1970), describes the Marxist understanding of religion as 'antediluvian' and says of it, that it is 'much more inadequate than the inadequacy of religious faith' of which it speaks (Gollwitzer, 1970: p. 84). Similarly, the Dominican theologian, J.M. Bocheński, who is head of the University of Fribourg's Institute of the U.S.S.R., and one of the leading interpreters of Soviet philosophy to the West, puts this criticism even for forcefully. He writes:

When the Marxist-Leninist doctrine concerning religion is considered from the point of view of research done over the past century, its antiquarian character is striking. Its basic tenets are simply taken over from the Enlightenment with all the usual misunderstandings which have long since been exposed . . . The central point, herein, is that religion is a type of human reaction to worldly evils . . . the basic element is fear: Man's fear of natural and, above all, social forces.

Now it is certain that in most cases religion does serve the function of providing answers to worldly pains and evils. However, since the Enlightenment, this has not been its essence. Religion, in its most authentic sense, is not concerned with worldly evils. It is, rather, an answer to the so-called 'limiting situations': the necessary failure in communication, in love, in death — in short, the essential fragility and hopelessness of human existence. Suppose a man to be completely free of all worldly evils and still he will have to face these limiting existential situations. Religion, in its essence, is precisely a reaction to such situations. Philosophers throughout the last one hundred years have taught that if religion is founded on fear, then the term 'fear' refers to something radically different than what is contained in expressions such as 'fear of lightning', 'fear of imprisonment' and even 'fear of death'. The religious fear has a peculiar object called 'the divine', or the 'tremendous mystery' known to St. Augustine and Otto. As long as a man has not experienced that fear, this peculiar relation to the Holy, he is not a religious man. Here again, the Marxist-Leninist doctrines conerning religion seem to be based on a total misunderstanding of the phenomenon in hand. (Bocheński, 1975: pp. 13-14)

But we must ask, can the Marxist-Leninist account of religion as a false view of the workings of the world be so cursorily dismissed? Has Marxism-Leninism misunderstood religion to the extent that Gollwitzer, Bocheński and others maintain? Has the criticism of religion which came to the fore in the European Enlightenment been so decisively refuted that it is no longer worthy of serious attention? Or might it not rather be the case that Soviet 'scientific atheism', in concentrating as it does, on the actual, substantial beliefs and practices of the vast mass of ordinary religious people — in the Soviet Union and elsewhere — gains an insight into living religion denied, or ignored, by those to whom such an insight might, to say the least, be an embarrassment? Does Fr. Bocheński, I wonder, seriously believe that the religious outlook of the vast mass of ordinary believers in the West — to say nothing of believers in other parts of the world — has changed all that radically in the two hundred years or so following upon the European *Aufklärung*? If the invocation of God, the saints, the Blessed Virgin, prayers for the healing of the sick, for fruitful harvests, for rain (or fair weather as the case may be), for protection against accident, disease and death, as enshrined in the immemorial, and still unchanged, rituals of Christendom mean anything, then they mean, surely, that those who subscribe to these rituals (or aid and abet them) believe that the world does, at times, operate other than as described in the text-books of physics, chemistry, agriculture, meterology, medicine and the like. Studies of the religious outlook in cultures other than that of Western Europe — in India and Africa, for example — serve but to confirm this.[2] This criticism of religion made manifest at the time of the European Enlightenment certainly constituted a crisis for Christian theologians, a crisis to which they have responded in a variety of ways — the nebulous belief in 'the transcendent', to which Bocheński refers, being but one of them; but to write, as Bocheński does, as if either the issues then raised had been definitively resolved, or as if the religious outlook of the vast majority of ordinary religious believers, even within the Christian tradition, had changed radically as a result, is surely to substitute the wish for the reality and to write, further, as if 'philosophers throughout the last hundred years', or those engaged in the study of religion, have been of one mind as to what constitutes the reality of religion, is to put forward a view which the most elementary reading in the history of philosophy and religion over the last century would quickly dispel. Rudolf Otto's analysis of religion, for instance, whilst widely influential, is certainly not as universally, nor as uncritically, accepted within the discipline of *Religionswissenschaft* as Bocheński appears to suggest.[3] The truth is that there is no agreement within the discipline of religious studies in the Western world as to what constitutes the reality of religion — the simple test suggested by Bocheński at the close of his remarks given above would be vigorously rejected by many religious believers themselves, who would object to their relationship to the household of their faith being dependent on so subjective, problematical and imprecise a criterion as the quality of their sense of 'the numin-ous'.[4]

By concentrating on the substantial beliefs of ordinary religious people, as well as on the doctrines of official religious institutions, Marxist-Leninist study of religion forcibly reminds us that religious people do, as a matter of fact, believe certain things to be true about the world, and the workings of the world, which non-religious people (whether Marxist or not) do not believe to be true. It also reminds us that religious people differ widely among themselves over the content of religious belief. By highlighting these differences, Marxism-Leninism not only enters into the day to day realities of religion, but calls attention to what is still – the world over – an important aspect of religious belief and of re-ligious motivation – namely, the fact that religious belief and practice does indeed serve, at times, as an alternative, or at the very least, as a compliment to scientific explanations of the world. For many in the world today the 'limit situations' occur sooner rather than later and, as Fr. Bocheński well knows, 'impotence', in Marxist-Leninist theory, plays as large, if not a larger part, than does 'fear' in producing religion. Many non-Marxist, Western socio-anthropologists have come to a similar conclusion. Half a century ago Malinowski, for example, noted that the Trobriand islanders utilised, in their cultivation of crops, both rudimentary scientific knowledge and magico-religious rituals to ensure success – activi-ties which, whilst they were not confused, were both held to be a necessary part of the total agricultural enterprise. As Malinowski put it:

He (the Trobriander) knows as well as you do that there are natural condi-tions and causes, and by his observations he knows that he is able to control these natural forces by mental and physical effort . . . (But) his experience has also taught him, on the other hand, that in spite of all his forethought and beyond all his efforts there are agencies and forces which one year be-stow unwonted and unearned benefits of fertility, making everything run smooth and well, rain and sun appear at the right moment, noxious insects remain in abeyance, the harvest yields a superabundant crop; another year again the same agencies bring ill luck and bad chance, pursue him from beginning till end and thwart all his most strenuous efforts and his best found knowledge. To control these influences and these only he employs magic. (Malinowski, 1954: pp. 28-29)

An examination of the liturgical material used in contemporary Christian, and other, religions would, I think, substantiate the fact that the 'attitude' to the world of 'modern' religious man is not so very different from that of the Trobriander. This, we should recall, is essentially what Ugrinovich was concerned to point out in his paper on 'The Religious Consciousness' which we considered in Section 4.1 above. In the religious mentality, as I have argued elsewhere, there is room for neither chance, tragedy, nor futility (Thrower, 1980: ch. 1).

A contemporary Western anthropologist writes in a similar vein. Basically, he says, religion:

. . . expresses man's fundamental dependence on the natural world which he occupies and of which he is part. We have seen that much ritual and religious behaviour translates uncontrollable natural forces into symbolic entities which, through the performance of ritual, can be manipulated and dealt with. Ritual is a language for saying things which are felt to be true and important but which are not susceptible of statement in scientific terms. Even if sophisticated modern man is less inclined to attach instrumental efficacy to the symbols which he has created to express his apprehension of the universe and of its ultimate meaning, he still feels the need to express this awareness. And in the areas beyond science there is no way of expressing it except symbolically. (Beattie, 1966: p. 239)

But symbols, as Beattie hastens to add, are held by religious people to have an objective referent. There can be no religion without ontology (cf. Thrower, 1960). Thus, even Bocheński's espousal of Otto's notion of 'The Holy' involves a minimal ontological commitment to the *reality* of 'The Holy', and to the possibility of Its entering into relationship with men. This was certainly a claim that Otto himself made for It (cf. Otto, 1924: pp. 60-61). It is this ontology that Marxism-Leninism is concerned to refute. That it conducts its discussion in terms of a rather naïve 'scientism', which is neither as subtle nor as open as the issues, perhaps, warrant, should not detract from our appreciation of the fact that Soviet 'scientific atheism', in calling our attention to the para-scientific character of religious belief and practice, calls attention to issues far too frequently glossed over in the philosophy of religion and in discussion between believers and unbelievers in the Western world today.

Alasdair Macintyre, in the first of his American Bampton Lectures entitled 'The Fate of Theism', and delivered at Columbia University in 1966, noted that many Christian theologians, in reacting to the crisis of faith brought about by the rise of modern empirical science, have sought to preserve their faith by doing one of two things: either they have retreated into a theistic enclave, and have there sought immunity from the cognitive standards of contemporary scientific culture, or they have settled for a form of latter day Deism in which secular standards in all areas of life and thought are accepted to the point where theism has no place at all. Either way, Macintyre contended, theism, and the religion associated with it, becomes irrelevant as an issue in contemporary culture. He wrote:

The role of theism in Victorian life was conflict-creating; that role is lost now. One key reason why contemporary theism is not a live issue is that its apologetic efforts have been oversuccessful. The decrease in tension between Christianity and the secular disciplines is often greeted by theologians as a sign of a more favourable climate for Christianity. They perhaps ought to ask themselves whether theism has lost a cultural role which lent it importance and relevance; whether theism in participating in the disputes over biological evolution and the historical criticism of the New Testament, did not for the last time claim for itself the authority to sit in judgement upon secular culture. (Macintyre and Ricoeur, 1969: pp. 19-20)

Can theism, Macintyre asks, survive the renunciation of all such claims? He himself thinks not, and in an extremely subtle analysis of the state of religion in the Western world today, he maintains that Western religion, in ceasing to affront us culturally, has reverted to a state akin to those primitive, pre-theistic religions in which, according to Durkheim, society in worshipping its gods is in fact worshipping itself. 'When religion is only thus able to retain its hold on society', Macintyre says, 'religious belief tends to become not so much belief in God as belief in belief' (ibid., p. 21). The theism of those theologians who have renounced all claims on the part of theology to have anything to say in those areas of our understanding covered by science – Bonhoeffer, Bultmann, Tillich, Van Buren – is one which, in Macintyre's words, has 'undergone a transformation which has evacuated it entirely of its theistic content' and produced a situation where 'religious formulae tend increasingly to be used . . . for purposes other than that of expressing the theological statements for which they were originally framed' (ibid., p. 22). Marxist-Leninists refuse to have anything much to do with such sophistry. Whether this is to their credit is for the religious believer to judge.

Macintyre's point is also relevant to a distinction which some writers on Marxism and religion make between questions of methodology and questions of ontology, a distinction which allows them to at least contemplate the possibility of a synthesis of religion and Marxism. Helmut Gollwitzer, for example, writes:

The decision to exclude the question of God and recourse to supernatural powers from the scientific explanation of the world does not commit one to an avowal of the atheistic position; this theory shares that decision with the whole of modern science; this is . . . the 'atheism' of method. (Gollwitzer, 1970: p. 86)

Thus, for Gollwitzer, as for many Latin American Christians, so long as dialectical materialism is thought of as a scientific theory which seeks simply to explain the development of nature and of society – and not as a metaphysical theory – Christians are free to regard it as they would today regard any other scientific theory and to evaluate it accordingly. (Gollwitzer, 1970: p. 87). Of late some Christians have claimed to find support for this view in the writings of the French Marxist, Louis Althusser, although Althusser's attempt to set up Marxism as a strictly 'scientific', 'structural' enterprise, was explicitly designed to rule out what

Althusser regarded as the contamination of Marxism by existential-ism phenomenology and Christianity (cf. Kołakowski, 1978: vol. III, p. 486).

We shall be returning to the question of the relationship between ontology and methodology in our next section, suffice it to say at the moment that if dialectical materialism is accepted as a correct, because scientific, account of the development of nature and society, then it is hard to see where specifically Christian claims with regard to man and his destiny could find a place. For Goll-witzer, as for Bonhoeffer, 'faith in God', which Gollwitzer, follow-ing Bonhoeffer and Barth, distinguishes from 'religion', seems to function as little more than a call to moral responsibility to our fellow men (cf. Gollwitzer, 1970: pp. 150-173). Marxist-Leninists believe that our responsibility to our fellow men requires no such 'backing'.

I would suggest, therefore, that in understanding religious belief in the way that it does, and thus continuing to take seriously the factual claims inherent in religion, Marxism-Leninism is not only in touch with the way in which many, perhaps the majority of ordinary religious believers, understand their religion, but does orthodox Christianity, and indeed religion in general, the service of making it culturally relevant. This is not to say that Soviet 'scientific atheism' is not aware of the pantheistic developments in contemporary Christian theology, nor that it does not seek to refute them as 'idealistic', for this would not be true. It is simply to say that in terms of the objective which it sets itself – that of changing the consciousness of ordinary people, and particularly the consciousness of Soviet people, it is with the religious outlook of the masses that it is primarily concerned. The student of religion, I would maintain, cannot but be similarly concerned.[5]

The conclusion to be drawn is that whatever individual (and far from representative) Marxists and Christians may say, norma-tive, orthodox Marxism – 'institutional Marxism' as some prefer to call it – and normative orthodox, Christianity are disjunctive belief systems. This, as a recent commentator on Marxist-Christian dialogue has pointed out, is more often realised by Marxists than by Christians, and he quotes in support the answer given by Kazimierz Kakol, the minister responsible for religious affairs in Poland, to the question whether a man could be at the same time a member of the Communist Party and of the Roman Catholic Church. Kakol replied:

> I think not. Membership in the Party does not merely consist in paying dues: it is an ideological commitment. If the basis of the Party is dialectical materialism, then one cannot be both a materialist and a believer in God . . . but there are some situations that the Party doesn't look at in rigid terms. For instance, a peasant who enters the Party but who has not looked into its entire philosophical base and remains a churchgoer might be judged differently from an intellectual. But a person of a certain level of intellectual development must make a choice. (Interview in *Newsweek*, 10 February 1975, Quoted Hebblethwaite, 1977, pp. 105-106)

The issue is complicated, of course, by the fact that there are in the world today a number of conflicting interpretations of Marxism, just as there are a number of conflicting interpretations of Christianity, and indeed of other religions also. If, however, we look dispassionately and analytically, as an American philosopher, Dale Vree, has recently sought to do, at what the majority of Marxists and the majority of Christians have believed, and continue to believe to this day, then the incompatibility of Marxism as such, and of Marxism-Leninism in particular, with Christianity becomes plain (Dale Vree, 1976).

This is not to say that there are not areas of mutual concern where Marxists, even Marxist-Leninists, and Christians cannot cooperate, but it is to say that, at the ontological level, Marxism and Christianity are expressive of two very different understandings of the world and of man and his destiny. Of this, as we have seen, Marxism-Leninism is in no doubt. Attempts at rapprochement — with a few notable exceptions — have come almost entirely from the Christian side. But even a Christian as deeply committed to a Marxian analysis of the social situation in his own country, and to a Marxist strategy for overcoming it, as José Miguez Bonino of Argentina recognises that:

Most Marxists . . . have claimed for materialism a totality and exclusiveness which negates in principle all reality which is not reduced in imminent terms. Such a claim Christians must reject, not because they speculatively pose the existence of a realm of the 'spirit' but because they have been grasped by the reality of the living God who is beyond history and the universe *as well as active in history and the universe,* the living God who in faith they know to be true, nay, to be the true and ultimate reality in which everything has meaning and existence. At this point no compromise is possible. Actually, such a compromise would void the engagement of the Christian as such of all authenticity and meaning. A Christian cannot be a Marxist in this sense, unless the claims of Marxist philosophy are considered as relative rather than absolute. (Bonino, 1976: p. 125) (my italics)

That a few individual Marxists have been prepared to leave the ontological question open, or to play it down, is irrelevant to our present concern, for it can be stated quite categorically that Marxism-Leninism makes no such concession; that its materialism is absolute, is beyond question, and this, before all else today, as we saw in Section 4, is the premise of its ongoing argument with religion. That they sought a compromise with religion, it will be recalled, was the burden of Novikov's and Shakhnovich's criticism of the Marxist 'revisionists' Garaudy and Fischer (cf. Section 2 above).

But although Marxism-Leninism regards religion, in whatever form, as an alternative, and a rival, to its own, claimed, 'scientific' materialist way of looking at the world, this is only part of its total understanding of religion. As important as the actual content of religious belief, for Marxism-Leninism, is the function which it holds religion to have served — and to continue to serve — in pre-socialist society. Religion, for Marxism-Leninism, as for classical Marxism, is a form of ideology, even if, overall, as I shall argue, it understands this in a rather simpler way than did Marx and Engels in their early writings.

8.2   RELIGION AS CLASS IDEOLOGY

We thus come to what Marxism-Leninism regards as Marxism's

distinctive contribution to the understanding of religion. Many thinkers before Marx, and many non-Marxists since, have criticised religion in the name of science, but none, so Marxists claim, have penetrated to the true source of religion, and none have analysed, as clearly as did Marx and Engels, the way in which religion subserves the interests of reactionary classes.

Religion, argues Marxism-Leninism, is false but, as experience in the struggle with religion in the Soviet Union has shown, it is not sufficient simply to demonstrate this, it must also be shown why, in spite of its evident falsity, religion has had, and continues to have, such a tenacious hold over people; only then can it be said that religion has been fully understood. That Marxism-Leninism faces this problem squarely, in a way in which the majority of contemporary intellectual non-believers in the West do not is, I want to argue, one of its strengths, for to abandon a religious outlook on the world, without explaining the reasons for its past cultural predominance, is not only to leave a major area of human experience unexplained, it is to betray one's essential humanity with the past.

It was not until the eighteenth century that philosophers in Western Europe began to enquire seriously into the secular origins of religion. Until that time they had confined themselves to examining the doctrines of religion, accepting some and amending or rejecting others. Only when doubts began to be cast on the claims of religion to be the outcome of a divine revelation, in large measure due to a growing awareness of the variety and conflicting nature of such claims, did it occur to men to enquire into the worldly origins of religion and to put forward theories to account for both its origin and its persistence.

A similar questioning of religion can be found in that crisis of faith which we can discern in the sixth century before the beginning of the Christian era in Ancient Greece, evidence, of which can be found recorded in Plato's dialogues with the Sophists. The Sophists took up and sought to answer a question which was not to be asked again in Europe until the eighteenth and nineteenth centuries when, through increasing contact with cultures other than its own, Europe was again made aware of its own particularity. It was contact with cultures other than their own which had made the Greeks aware that their own culture was not unique, even though it might to them appear to be superior to other cultures. There were, in the world, cultures with very different views to their own with regard to law, morality and religion. Reflecting on the diversity of beliefs in the world, the Sophists were led to ask whether such things as religion, morality, law and social structure were part of nature, so that there was but one true form of them valid for all men and all times, or whether they were the result of custom and were, therefore, relative and subject to change. As the Sophists put it − were these things of nature or of law? They themselves chose the latter alternative; for them, religion, morality and social structures were man made. That by subjecting religion, morality and even society itself to criticism the Sophists irritated their contemporaries is evident from Plato's treatment of them.

Among the more interesting theories put forward by the Sophists were the theories put forward to account for religion. Prodicus of Ceos, for example, put forward the view, to which both Europides and the Stoic writer Lucilus Balbus later refer, that the idea of gods arose as an act of gratitude and adoration on man's part towards the beneficient powers of nature. The gods were, therefore, the personification of those things which were necessary to man. Thus, bread became Demeter, wine Dionysius, water Poseidon, and so on. He also postulated that, at a later stage in the development of religion, the inventors of the various arts − of agriculture, metal work, and so on − were elevated to divine stature and became the object of cults devoted to them. He concluded that this being the origin of the gods, prayer to them was superfluous. A rather different theory − but one which anticipates certain aspects of Marxist-Leninist theory − was that put forward by the Sophist Critias. For him the gods were invented to put an end to lawlessness − to act as hidden and omnipresent witnesses to acts done in secret. Religion was for him, a political invention to ensure acceptable behaviour on the part of the masses (Sextus

Empiricus, *Against the Physicists:* 1,54). For both of these Sophists religion was a human invention.[6]

When in the eighteenth century in Europe philosophers again raised the question of the secular origins of religion, the answers which they gave were initially every bit as speculatively intell-ectualistic as had been the answers put forward by the Sophists in ancient Greece. Religion, they surmised, was the result of ignor-ance, of speculative but undisciplined curiosity, of fear — surmis-ings which they bequeathed to the anthropology of the nineteenth century.

It is a measure of Marx's insight into the nature of man and society that, unlike the rationalists of the eighteenth century, he saw that a phenomenon as widespread and as entrenched in human cultures as religion could not be accounted for simply in terms of ignorance of the workings of the world alone although, as we saw in the first part of our study, in their writings on the origin of religion, Marx and Engels did, at times, give some credence to this view. Building on Hegel's, rather than the Enlightenment's, view that the history of religion and philosophy is the history of the self-externalisation of Spirit at the levels of self-consciousness and reason, but rejecting entirely Hegel's notion of Spirit, Marx, for whom it was man alone who was alienated and not anything mani-fested in him, put forward the view that religion is a fantasy of socially alienated man, a form of false-consciousness, and an 'ideology' in the restricted meaning which, we saw, he and Engels gave to that term. He thus believed that when man overcomes alienation there will be no place left for religion, for religion ex-presses, above all else, man's sense that he is not his own master and that he is the victim of circumstances which are beyond his control. Yet, it also, and at the same time, for Marx, expresses man's desire to be his own master and to take control of his destiny.

Religion was thus, for Marx, more than the explanations of the origin of religion found in the philosophers of the Enlightenment, for, it 'reflected', for him, the human condition at a stage in the historical process when man was still incapable of understanding that condition. (If he had understood it, he would not have given religious expression to it). But man cannot understand his condition, for Marx, except in the process of overcoming it. Thus the paradox as we have it in the early writings of Marx is that, whilst, for Marx, it is a condition of man's overcoming his present alienated condition that he get rid of the religious illusion, he cannot get rid of the religious illusion until he has got rid of the state of affairs which produces it. Later, as his early interest in religion waned, he resolved the paradox, almost exclusively, in terms of remedying the alienated condition out of which religion draws sustenance. Soviet Marxist-Leninists, on the other hand, under the influence of Lenin, and later under the influence of Stalin's emphasis on the vanguard role of the Party in creating 'correct consciousness' in the masses, have tended to resolve the paradox more and more in terms of the religious illusion itself – the more so as religion has shown itself resilient to changes in the socio-economic and political structures out of which, according to Marxist theory, it arises. In this Marxism-Leninism has been aided by some of the things that Marx, Engels and, above all, Lenin, had to say about religion as the ideology of a class.

If, however, what we have said about the way in which Marx saw religion as a fantasy of alienated man is correct, then it will be clear that, for Marx himself, religion was more than the ideology of a particular class – which is the way in which Soviet Marxism-Leninism had tended to interpret the relationship between religion and class. Yet Marx's own analysis of religion does have a good deal in common with class ideology as Marxism-Leninism understands it, and it is thus easy to see why – in the absence of many of Marx's early writings during its formative period – Soviet 'scientific atheism' has found it tempting to speak as if religion was nothing but the ideology of the ruling classes. Just as, for Marx, religion expresses man's attitude to himself in the form of beliefs about the world as a whole so, for Marxism-Leninism, class ideology expresses the attitude of a class to itself in the form of a system of beliefs about the world as a whole. Bourgeois ideology, for example, is more than just a set of beliefs that promote the interests of the bourgeois class by legitimating its claims; it is also an image of society that expresses the bourgeois conception of man. This can take the form of a particular philosophy, a legal system, or, of course, of a religion. But whereas, for Marx and Engels, religion related to different classes in different ways – it could, for instance, as Engels' claimed in his writings on the Peasant Wars in sixteenth century Germany, be a form of ideological protest on the part of the oppressed – Soviet Marxism-Leninism has, certainly so far as concerns its analysis of religion in pre-revolutionary Russia – which, I would claim, has unduly coloured its analyis of all religion – seen religion as essentially a tool of the ruling class – as 'opium' *for* (as Lenin mistranslated Marx) rather than *of* the people.[7]

It is in offering an analysis of religion's role in society in this attenuated way that the real weakness of Soviet 'scientific atheism', in my opinion, lies – both as concerns its understanding of religion in general, and as concerns its understanding of religion in contemporary Soviet society in particular.

For Marx and Engels themselves, religion was certainly more than the ideology of a class. It will be recalled for instance, that Marx did not exempt for his general verdict on religion as a fantasy of alienated man the religions of primitive people, even though what he took to be a major cause of alienation – the extensive division of labour – it is not found among them. We saw also, when we were considering what Marx and Engels had to say about the sources of 'natural religion', that although there was a certain ambiguity in what they said about the continuance of these sources of natural religion into civil society, the balance on the whole – certainly in Engels' later writings – was that such sources did contribute towards the 'upkeep' of religion in civil society. If religion is simply the ideology of alienated classes, then the question arises, why did the non-alienated subscribe to it? That they simply used it to exploit the masses, whilst not themselves believing, is surely not only naïve, but false.

To summarise the argument so far: for Marx and Engels religion was more than the ideology of a particular class, whether that class be the proletariat class or ruling class. It was, in fact, in the sense in which Marx and Engels understood ideology, the ideology of pre-socialist man as such, and arose from factors which were wider than those of social alienation − although this was, for them, the greatest single and most important source of religion.

Further, even where Marx and Engels did conceive of religion as the ideology of a class, religion thus conceived was, as we saw, held to subserve two different, though related, ideological functions. On the one hand, it served the oppressed as an expression of and, at the same time, as a protest against their oppression, and there is, of course, a sense in which, in pre-scientific and pre-technological society, all men are oppressed by, or at least, are subservient to nature; on the other hand, religion served the exploiting classes as an instrument of exploitation, both by seeking to justify the existing order of things and by seeking to divert attention away from present ills to the joys which awaited men hereafter. Soviet 'scientific atheism', in that it tends, as we have seen, to see in religion only the ideology of the ruling class, thus attenuates the original Marxian analysis of religion on two counts: in the first place, it ignores the more general analysis of Marx and Engels to the effect that religion is a fantasy of alienated man irrespective of the class to which he belongs and secondly, it reduces what Marx and Engels had to say about religion's serving as the ideology of both exploiters and exploited to the more simple thesis that religion is the ideology of the exploiting class alone. In this ignoring the rich, complicated, though admittedly ambiguous, analysis of religion as set forward by Marx and Engels themselves, Soviet 'scientific atheism' is less than true to the full Marxist tradition which it claims to inherit.

It is a measure of the accuracy of Marx's own analysis of the human condition that many religious thinkers have recognised in it much that is akin to their own reading of that condition. The French Jesuit, Jean Yves Calvez, for instance, whilst he cannot, of course, accept Marx's understanding of religion as a fantasy of alienated man in its entirety, does not dismiss it as absurd or wide of the mark; in fact, he finds implicit in it ideas about the human condition which seem to him to be largely true (Calvez, 1956). Calvez' objections to Marxism are quite different from those of its earlier religious critics. He does not, for example, concentrate on its rejection of God, nor on its supposedly crude materialistic outlook on life. The burden of his argument against it is that the remedy which it offers for the ills which it so acutely describes is ultimately unsatisfying. In the end Marxism, argues Calvez, will not do, for it cannot give man what man — being the creature which for Calvez, as a Christian believer, he believes man to be — needs to enable him to deal adequately with the problems that face him. Only the Christian religion, argues Calvez, can provide man with this. Thus Calvez' objection to Marxism is, in the final resort, an objection to its doctrine of man — that is, to its anthropology.

A similar criticism has been voiced by the Czech theologian Jan Lochman. Whilst recognising that Marx 'widened and deepened' the anthropological debate of his time by placing new emphasis upon the dimensions of history, society and labour — an emphasis which, according to Lochman, had not been present in Judeo-European civilization since Biblical times — Lochman is critical of Marx's eventual restriction of alienation to the socio-economic realm — a restriction which, as we will see, is further emphasised by Soviet philosophers who have written about that phenomenon (cf. pp. 357f below). Lochman writes:

I take this doctrinaire statement (of the overriding significance of 'private property' in the Marxist analysis of alienation) to be an anthropological simplification of the complexity of relationships in the world of alienated man. It has very serious consequences. The 'localizing' of evil . . . arouses the expectation that a revolutionary change in this area — the radical socialization of the means of production — would lead to the overcoming of alienation in general. That is a dangerous illusion. It leads to underestimating the power of evil in the new society . . . The Christian conception of sin would greatly clarify the situation. (Lochman, 1977: p. 72)

The debate between a Christian and a Marxist view of society is, as I have argued elsewhere (Thrower, 1965, 1966), essentially a debate concerning very different conceptions of man and of human fulfilment, and it is no accident that it was this issue which was at the centre of the Marxist-Christian dialogue of the last decade. 'Scientific atheism', by restricting its understanding of alienation in the way that it does can, of course, look forward to the day when alienation will be wholly overcome. It is here that it differs, not only from the Christian view of things, but from the new anthropology which is beginning to emerge today — despite periodic setbacks — in the thought of many Eastern European and many Western Marxists, and which centres around that storm-centre of contemporary Marxian interpretation — the relationship of Marx's early and, so it is claimed, more humanistic writings, to his later, more socio-economic, and hence, so it is also claimed, more 'scientific' works.

But whatever the outcome of the debate within international Marxism with regard to this issue, the universal Communist ideal is well described in the following extract from Leszek Kołakowski's *Main Currents of Marxism:*

Communism puts an end to the division of life into public and private spheres, and to the difference between civil society and the state; it does away with the need for political institutions, political authority and governments, private property and its source in the division of labour. It destroys the class system and exploitation; it heals the split in man's nature and the crippled, one-sided development of the individual . . . The individual will absorb society into himself: thanks to de-alienation, he will recognise humanity as his own internalized nature. Voluntary solidarity, not compulsion or the legal regulation of interests, will ensure the smooth harmony of human relations. The species can then realise itself in the individual. Communism destroys the power of objectified relations over human beings, gives him control again over his own works, restores the social operation of his mind and senses and bridges the gulf between humanity and nature. It is the fulfilment of the human calling, the reconciliation of essence and existence in human life. It also stands for the consciousness of the practical, humane and social character that belongs to all intellectual activity, and repudiates the false independence of existing forms of social thought: philosophy, law, religion. Communism turns philosophy into reality, and by so doing abolishes it. Communism does not deprive man of individuality or reduce personal aspirations and abilities to a dead level of mediocrity. On the contrary, the powers of the individual can only flourish when he regards them as social forces, valuable and effective within a human community and not in isolation. Communism alone makes possible the proper use of human abilities: thanks to the variety of technical progress it ensures that specifically human activity is freed from the constraints of physical need and the pressure of hunger and is thus truly creative. It is the realization of freedom, not only from exploitation and political power but from immediate bodily needs. It is the solution to the problem of history and is also the end of history as we have known it, in which individual and collective life are subject to contingency. Henceforth man can determine his own development in freedom, instead of being enslaved by material forces which he has created but can no longer control. Man, under communism, is not a prey to chance but is the captain of his fate, the conscious moulder of his own destiny. (Kołakowski, 1978: vol. I, pp. 179-80)

I have quoted this highly eloquent portrayal of the Communist eschatological ideal at length, not only because it shows what, to a Communist, the overcoming of alienation would be, but also because it shows what I think is the near religious appeal which Communism has and the near religious commitment which it evokes from its adherents. It is, however, for Marxist-Leninists, as Kołakowski is careful to point out, more than an ideal in opposition to the real world, more than a theory which might have been invented and put into practice at any point in history, for when history is 'scientifically' understood, as Marxist-Leninists claim to have understood it, then it is seen as nothing less than the inevitable end to which history is working and in terms of which man must, if he is to live in accord with the 'imperative of history', and not fight against it, place himself and his activities today. The truth of this 'scientific' understanding of history is, of course, another matter and one which I do not propose to enter into at this point. Instead, I want to raise, in the light of what I said earlier, the question whether the implementation of the ideal described above would, in fact, result in men not only overcoming alienation but, as is claimed, achieving total self-realisation? This, as Calvez claims, is the true test of the Marxist understanding of religion.

The religions of the world, even where they might today accept something of the kind described above as a description of their own social ideal, say not, for they see man as having within him that which is more than material and which nothing in this world can ever ultimately satisfy. Man's destiny, for them, transcends the temporal order of things. It is for this reason that thinkers in many of the world's religions have sought to emphasise, in the face of both Marxism and of the triumphs of the science and technology in which Marxists, as well as many non-Marxists, place their faith, the enduring impotence of man before what the German existential philosopher Karl Jaspers has called 'the limit situations' and the German émigré theologian, Paul Tillich, 'radical contingency'. It is Marxism-Leninism's inability to acknowledge this aspect of human existence that for many critics lies at the root of its lack of a true and full understanding of religion. Yet if these critics are right, it is the need to adapt to the non-social existential problems, of hostility, frustration, defeat, despair and death, that have been among the more potent factors in human life making for religion, and there is no reason to think that such factors will ever disappear (cf. Bocheński, 1975: pp. 13-14; Yinger, 1970: pp. 6-8).

It is difficult, from a naturalistic point of view, to know quite what to make of this. Certainly Marxism-Leninism plays down — where it does not ignore — those aspects of human experience to which both Existentialists and religious men call our attention. Thus, for example, Academician M.B. Mitin of Moscow State University wrote, in a paper contributed to the Soviet Delegation Reports to the XIIIth World Congress of Philosophy held in Mexico City in 1963, that:

Whilst many modern philosophical trends go in for the so-called 'marginal situations', by which they mean the fear of death, dependence on change, conflict, suffering, guilt, etc., Marxist philosophy opens up real prospects and favourable conditions, forms and opportunities for the development of man's spiritual potential. Marxist philosophy teaches and encourages men to think not of death, but of life, of remaking and improving life; to dwell not on loneliness but to think of the collective of people, of the good of society and of the whole of mankind. Men who adhere to the Marxist outlook do not feel, nor have any reason to feel, alone, doomed, condemned to a vegetable existence. Marxist philosophy provides a scientific substantiation of the fact that man is a member of society, a collective, that he is the master of nature, who perfects it according to the requirements of the objective laws of the development of matter. (Mitin, 1963: pp. 48-49)

And the leader of the Soviet delegation to this Congress, Academician P.N. Fedoseyev, head of the Institute of Philosophy of the U.S.S.R. Academy of Science, Deputy Director of that Academy, and perhaps the most prestigious figure in Soviet philosophy today, taking up the question of 'alienation' in his own contribution to the *Congress Report,* wrote:

The problem of 'alienation' in the theory of Marxism is treated above all primarily as the task of *eliminating alienation.* The solution of this problem consists in the revolutionary transformation of the world, in changing social relations by man and consequently in changing man himself. Only this approach makes it possible to treat the problem in a vigorous way. This problem is the more important since it is extremely involved and though it is frequently referred to by Western authors, the latter, essentially speaking, do not comprehend it and even distort it. (Fedoseyev, 1963: p. 17)

Fedoseyev then gives a summary of the now standard Marxist-Leninist analysis of 'alienation' in terms of alienated labour, and the consequent distortion of personal relations in capitalist society, before concluding that:

No theory, unless it takes this real, socio-economic — and not only philosophical, ethical and aesthetic — stand, is capable of pointing the way out from the alienation which is characteristic of bourgeois society. Therefore, both the theological and the existentialist attempts at solving this problem must invariably prove futile. (ibid., p. 17)

That there are urgent problems of social alienation in society today, few today would wish to deny; that the religions of the world have, over the greater part of their history, either sought to bypass these problems — to the extent at times of even seeking to justify social injustice as being the will of God for man — or have proved themselves, where they have recognised the problem, singularly inept at dealing with it, must be admitted, and often is admitted by religious people themselves (cf. Gollwitzer, 1970;

Bockmuehl, 1980: pp. 63-81). But that the problem of man and of his alienation can be entirely reduced to a solution to the problem of the correct organisation of social relations is something which not only religious people, but many non-religious people who are not Marxists, would also deny, and to assert, as Soviet propagandists assert, that alienation has all but disappeared in socialist societies as they advance towards communism is to become the victim of one's own propaganda to an extent to which only the pen of a Zamyatin, a Zinovyev or a Voinovitch can do justice.[8] Neither the religious man nor the Marxist, of course, contemplates that man might live in an 'absurd' and tragic universe of the kind that Albert Camus so poignantly and so courageously described, nor that a possible response to the world might be that noble pessimism that was so characteristic a feature of many of the best minds of Antiquity, and which I sought to trace in my book *The Alternative Tradition* (1980). I shall be returning to this problem in Section 9.2 of this study.

A greater challenge to the Marxist-Leninist claim that religion derives almost entirely from social alienation is the fact that, as is now beginning to be recognised by 'scientific-atheists' themselves, in countries where, so it is claimed, the major sources of social alienation have all but disappeared, religion not only persists, but appears to be gaining ground. To this problem there are for the Marxist but two solutions: either to admit that social alienation has not been entirely abolished in socialist society − or even that it is increasing − or to radically backtrack on the view that the sources of religion are to be found wholly in perverse social conditions. Soviet 'scientific atheism' has, as we have seen, inclined to the latter of these solutions and has sought an answer in the realms of psycho-pathology. Either way it has not, as yet, or is only beginning to be prepared to consider that religion might answer to something more fundamental and more enduring in the human personality than any and every structure of social relations − something to which Marxism-Leninism must find its own answers. This reluctance to move beyond the now firmly established Marxist-Leninist analysis of 'alienation' is a striking illustration of the closed nature of Soviet study of religion.

Our conclusion must, therefore, be that Soviet Marxism-Leninism, in concentrating almost exclusively on the social sources of religion, severely limits its understanding of religion. Conceiving of religion simply as a 'reflection' of the real world of socio-economic relationships, Marxism-Leninism not only confuses the medium which does the 'reflecting' with that which is 'reflect-ed' — a point made by Paul Radin against Marxist interpretations of primitive religion as long ago as 1937 (Radin, 1937: pp. 310-311) — but fails to get at many of the sources of religion which have seemed so obvious to anthropologists, philosophers, psycho-logists and indeed some theologians. To say this, however, is not to deny that materialist variables of the kind to which Marxists draw our attention do not at all contribute to the growth and persistence of religion; it is simply to deny that they account for it completely. Religion is not a single thing but, as Wittgenstein pointed out in his analysis of religious language, is more akin to a family or a cluster of related phenomena (Wittgenstein, 1966: pp. 53-72). A Marxist analysis of religion which took into account the factors we have mentioned could still be — what essentially Marxism is searching for — a naturalistic account of religion. Soviet study of religion, working within the rigid presuppositions that we have described, is unlikely, however, to provide such an analysis. Whether, on the other hand, the original Marxist analysis of religion might form the basis of such an enterprise is another matter and one which I shall consider in the conclusion to this present work.

Marxist-Leninist 'Scientific Atheism' as the Science of Religion

9.1 MARXISM-LENINISM AS SCIENCE

Many of Marxism's severest critics have recognised some value in approaching the study of history in the way in which Marx suggested. Thus Leszek Kołakowski writes that:

No reasonable person would deny that the doctrine of historical materialism has been a valuable addition to our intellectual equipment and has enriched our understanding of the past. True, it has been argued that in the strict form the doctrine is nonsense and in a loose form it is a commonplace; if it has become a commonplace, this is largely thanks to Marx's originality. (Kołakowski, 1978: vol. III, p. 524)

Certainly Western history of religions has not been immune to its influence, and thus, today, historians of religion pay far more attention than was once fashionable to the social and economic circumstances in which the religions which they study are found. The German Marxist, Karl Kautsky's strictures on Renan's *The Life of Jesus* (1863) are perhaps worth quoting at this point. He wrote:

Renan based his conception, not on the social conditions of that time, but on the picturesque impressions the modern tourist of Galilee receives. Hence Renan is able to assure us in his romance about Jesus that in Jesus' time this fair land 'abounded in plenty, joy and well-being' so that 'every history of the origin of Christianity becomes a charming idyll'. (Kautsky, 1953: p. 258)

Marx and Engels' placing of religion firmly within the context of the real lives, hopes, and aspirations of ordinary people, as well as their calling our attention to the social and economic circumstances by which religions have been influenced and which they themselves in turn have influenced, is something for which all who seek for a full and true understanding of religion cannot but be grateful; not withstanding the fact that it has always been notorious that men's religious, moral and political beliefs often suit their interests. But it is one thing to acknowledge that religions owe much to the social and economic conditions in which they arose, developed and sometimes decayed, and quite another thing to hold that these factors 'determine' all the rest. If this latter claim is meaningful, that is if it is a coherent, empirical hypothesis, as it is claimed to be, then it should be possible to test it. The materialist understanding of history should be of value, as one noted philosopher of history has put it, 'as a sort of recipe for producing empirical hypotheses' (Walsh, 1951: p. 162). This we have seen reason to doubt (Section 5.1, 5.2, above).

That much religion has subserved, and still subserves, socio-economic and, indeed, narrow class interests, few students of religion today would wish to deny. The persistence of the religiously legitimated caste-system in India, the Koranic legitimated feudal chiefdoms of the Southern Arabian peninsula, and, in South Africa, the Dutch Reformed Church's religious justification of *apartheid,* are but three extreme examples brought almost daily to our attention. The Christian claims of the established social structures in Germany and Russia at the time of Marxism's inception have already been mentioned. This, again, today few Christians would seek to deny. As one of them, Helmut Gollwitzer, writes:

Where in his wanderings could the tailor's apprentice Weitling, or the turner's apprentice Bebel, have found a manse in the Germany of that day in which a sermon would not have been preached to him on submission to his fate and humble acknowledgement of the divinely decreed order as the bearing which God required of him? . . . Where was there any sign that the church did not identify itself with the programme of a 'Christian State' under Friedrich Wilhelm IV, and did not gratefully profit from it? (Gollwitzer, 1970: pp. 90-91)

Similarly, Pope Leo XIII in an encyclical entitled *Rerum Novarum* issued in 1891 — an encyclical which is a classic of anti-Marxism — not only reasserted the rights of private property, no matter how extensive, which his predecessor Pius IX had asserted in the Roman Catholic Church's first condemnation of Communism – the encyclical *Qui Pluribus* of 1846 – but proclaimed that poverty was a condition ordained by God for the edification of his children and as such to be willingly and joyfully espoused (Adolfs, 1969: pp. 29-30, 37-38).

Examples of the religious legitimation of the *status quo* could be multiplied almost indefinitely. This today is not at issue, though many would deny that this is all – or even that it is the major part – of what there is to be said about religion's relationship to secular power.[1] What is at issue is the stronger, peculiarly Marxist-Leninist thesis, that religion is *nothing but* a counter in the ongoing struggle between classes for the satisfaction of material self-interest – that, in the words of Johannes Fabian, it is but 'the spirits of fighting social classes' (Fabian, 1965: p. 2). We have seen how Soviet 'scientific atheism' tells the story of the rise and growth of Buddhism, Christianity and Islam in this way, and we made some preliminary comments on it (Section 5.3). The time has now come for us to look somewhat more closely at the Marxist-Leninist thesis of the socio-economic 'determination' of religion, and at the claim which follows from it that Soviet 'scientific atheism', in that it alone fully understands this, is the only true science of religion.

That this understanding of religion is a simplified version of the original Marxian analysis of religion as a fantasy of alienated man we have already argued, but that this is the form in which the thesis is presented today in Soviet 'scientific atheism' has, I hope, been shown. It is, however, put forward in such a highly generalised way – in fact not so much put forward as dogmatically asserted as an established fact – that it is difficult to comment on it, and some words of John Plamenatz are apposite at this point. He wrote:

Marxists attracted to the doctrine that ideas and beliefs are socially determined have for the most part thought it enough to repeat it without explaining just what they understood by it . . . Marxists who say that ideas and beliefs are socially determined claim to be saying something more than that the creatures who have them are social beings and that there are social conditions of their having them. They claim to be saying more than what nobody has ever wanted to deny. Unfortunately, they do not explain what this something more is. (Plamenatz, 1970: pp. 54-55)

This, of course, is something of an exaggeration for Marxists do, in fact, specify some instances where religious beliefs — for example, belief in a hierarchical social order being ordained by God, in the sanctity of private property, and so on — appear to be little more than rationalisations of material self-interest, and in that sense they might be said to be socio-economically determined. When, however, it comes to putting forward more meaningful equations between the socio-economic base and the religious superstructure of a society, Soviet 'scientific atheism' tends to fudge the issue in the way that Plamenatz describes. We saw, in our discussion of Tokarev's paper 'Periodisation in the History of Religion' (Section 5.1 above), how a leading Soviet historian of religion shied away from any attempt to link his account of the development of religion at all closely to the more fundamental development of the socio-economic base of society and no Soviet scholar with whom I have discussed this question has been much more forthcoming. We saw also how Semenov, in his discussion of 'The Evolution of the Socio-Economic Stages of Development and the Objective Logic of the Evolution of Religion', similarly ignored this issue. It will also be recalled that the burden of the Soviet ethnographer, B.F. Porshnev's criticism of Tokarev's attempted 'explanation' of the development of religion was that he used the term 'determine' without in the least suggesting *why* or *how* this took place (p. 270f above). Thus, until Marxist historians offer something more substantial, both by way of articulating and by way of substantiating a thesis of the socio-economic 'determination' of religion, that thesis remains not only unproven but unintelligible. This was the conclusion we came to earlier when we examined Marx's own attempt in his *Preface to the Critique of Political Economy* to formulate a coherent doctrine of historical materialism, and Soviet Marxism-Leninism has advanced not one step beyond this original and difficult Marxist thesis. It has, in fact, simply rested content with the constant and near incantational reiteration of Marx and Engels' own phrases, seeking neither to explain, illustrate, or pass beyond them.

The issue between Marxist historians of religion and other historians of religion — not necessarily themselves religious believers — is, to a large extent, I believe, one regarding the motivation behind the religious quest. Few historians who are not Marxists have sought to explain religion wholly in terms of its socio-economic roots and Soviet study of religion itself has, as we have seen, come, of late, and somewhat reluctantly, to the conclusion that religion draws strength from sources other than social alienation, however much it seeks to denigrate these sources as pathological. The persistence of religion in Soviet society has of itself forced this conclusion upon it. Further, as Engels saw towards the end of his life, and as we have seen Soviet 'scientific atheism' also insisting, the religious superstructure of society possesses a life of its own and attracts, for a variety of reasons, which it is the business of the student of religion to analyse, deep and enduring emotional attachments to it on the part of its adherents — attachments which cut across the social divisions in any society. What the particular beliefs which move men at any particular point in time, or in any particular place, actually are is for the historian of religion to establish. Why they do so is probably beyond his or anyone's competence to explain. Certainly the capability of any theory of socio-economic 'determination' to explain just why, for example, in the India of the sixth century B.C. the belief in *samsara*, and not some other belief, should come to the fore, or why Christians should have developed the specific doctrines with regard to the Trinity which they did in the fourth and fifth centuries A.D., must be severely limited, and no Marxist historian of religion, so far as I know, has attempted to do so. Yet attempting to trace the growth of just such beliefs is a major part of the task of any historian of religion, just as comparing and contrasting them with beliefs in a variety of religions is the concern of the phenomenologist of religion. Marxism, as Marxism, has little to offer such students of religion, for whilst it is easy to see the relevance of certain socio-economic conditions to some religious beliefs — as in the examples referred to earlier in this section — it is extremely hard to see any connection at all between socio-economic conditions and religious beliefs of the kind we have referred to above.

What, then, are we to say about the claim that the Marxist-Leninist approach to the understanding of religion, and in particular that the Marxist-Leninist approach to the understanding of the history of religion as embodied in 'historical materialism', is the only approach that can truly be called 'scientific' — a claim which is part of the wider claim that Marxism-Leninism constitutes the only true science of society? In the light of what we have just said, such a claim looks bogus in the extreme. Without discussing in detail the wider claim of Marxism-Leninism to be the science of society, which would take us far beyond our present concerns, and which has, in any case, been adequately discussed by Karl Popper in the second volume of his *The Open Society and Its Enemies,* there are, I would suggest, at least two reasons why we must reject the claim of Soviet Marxist-Leninist 'scientific atheism' to be the only true science of religion. These are: (1) its inability to formulate any but the most obvious — where they are not meaningless — empirically verifiable (or falsifiable) hypotheses about religion, and the consequent abuse of the term 'science', and (2) its inability to account for at least one important area of religion that I shall call that of the 'personal religious quest'.

(1) We saw earlier — in the first part of this study — how loosely the term *Wissenschaft* was used in nineteenth century Germany, and how Marx and Engels probably understood the term in their early writings. We saw, also, how, in the later writings of Engels, under the impact of the growing prestige of natural science, the term 'science' began to take on the severer connotations attaching to the English term 'science' today. Much of the prestige of Marxism-Leninism — certainly in its homeland — derives from the exclusive abrogation of the term 'science' and its cognates to itself,

with all the overtones of objectivity, precision, and authority that, in the nineteenth century, the term then possessed. Following Engels, Soviet Marxism-Leninism maintains that the Marxist understanding of society is 'scientific' in exactly the same way that the understanding of nature is 'scientific'. Both cognise the world as it really is, and both have the same ultimate goal of finding the objective laws of the development of reality in order to transform it in the interests of man. Both imply discovery and not invention. As one leading Soviet philosopher has put it 'Dialectical materialism is:

. . . a method *discovered* on the basis of the deepest and most thorough study of the objective world, which takes shape as a result of the data of science and is a product of the critical and careful comprehension of all the history of mankind, of all achievements of human knowledge. The force of dialectical method consists in its truthfulness, in the fact that it truly reflects the objective laws of development of reality, the objective dialectics of the material world, that it is in a state of constant improvement in connection with discoveries in natural and social sciences and in social practice.

And with reference to historical materialism, he writes:

In order to secure the objective foundation of scientific method it was necessary to make fundamental social discoveries, and such discoveries were made. I shall briefly dwell on one of them, the materialist conception of history. The chaos and arbitrariness that had been dominant in pre-Marxist sociological and historical theories were replaced by a scientific approach to social processes. The material unity of the world was confirmed on a new ground. Also confirmed were the interrelation and interconditionality of all the processes of nature, society, and man's consciousness. (Mshvenieradze, 1974: p. 28)

Marx himself, in a letter to Kowalewski, wrote that 'it is impossible to think logically except on the basis of the dialectical method' (quoted, Garaudy, 1964: p. 184) and had thus implied that only dialectical thinking can fully comprehend the changing, developing nature of reality, and Engels, in *Anti-Dühring,* had tried to show that Marxism is not, properly speaking, a philosophy, but rather a dialectical method which alone permits science to be 'scientific', in the sense that a mode of thinking which is other than dialectical must inevitably fail to see that the truths which science discovers are not eternal truths, whose validity was always there to be discovered, but are rather historical truths which are not true until they become true in history (*Anti-Dühring:* pp. 19-22). There was, for Engels, no philosophy distinct from or embracing the particular sciences: there is only the dialectical method, which is what gives a scientific character to any investigation. 'Reality in process' can only be grasped in thought if thought, like reality itself, is dialectical. There is thus only one law to which all conforms: the law of dialectical development. To work out the 'science' of the development of society in 'all its details and connections', as Engels put it, is not a matter of deduction but a matter of determining the (derivative) laws of the socio-economic process on the basis of the observed process of history (*Anti-Dühring:* p. 40).

What comes out of this — whether as expressed by Engels himself or by his latter day Soviet interpreters, such as Mshvenieradze, is not, of course, science as such, or any particular science, but rather a criterion for determining whether what is called 'science' is truly so called. Only if what purports to be a science traces the real connections whereby reality becomes the reality it is, can it be said, on this criterion, to really be a science.

As has often been pointed out, what the Marxist scientist does in no way differs from what the non-Marxist scientist does, nor, today at any rate, except in the case of 'the science of history and of society', is his conception of this or that science noticeably different from non-Marxist science. His conception of what it is to be scientific is, however, very different from the views concerning this prevalent in Western science, for the Marxist scientist feels constrained, as his Western counterpart does not feel constrained, to show that what he does is subsumable under dialectical laws or he fails to be scientific. The 'laws of dialectic', however, are so general, so wide and all-embracing, so cognitively valueless, in fact, that this is a relatively easy, if somewhat otiose, exercise. It is easy because, as a number of non-Marxist philosophers have pointed out the cognitive status of the so-called 'laws of dialectic' is that of truisms dressed up as profound revelations.

Among the truisms of dialectical materialism (writes the former Marxist Leszek Kołakowski) are such 'laws of dialectic' as the statement that everything on the universe is somehow related, or that everything changes. No one denies these propositions, but they are of very little cognitive or scientific value . . . Everyone knows that phenomena are interconnected, but the problem of scientific analysis is not how to take account of the universal interconnection, since this is what we cannot do, but how to determine which connections are important and which can be disregarded. All that Marxism-Leninism can tell us here is that in the chain of phenomena there is always a 'main link' to be grasped. This seems to mean only that in practice certain connections are important in view of the end pursued, and others less important or negligible. But this is a commonplace of no cognitive value, as we cannot derive from it any rule for establishing the hierarchy of importance in any particular case. The same is true of the proposition that 'everything changes': cognitive value attaches only to empirical descriptions of particular changes, their nature, tempo, etc. (Kołakowski, 1978: vol. III, p. 152)

The fact that truisms like these are 'represented as profound discoveries known from no other source', led the adherents of Marxism-Leninism, Kołakowski concludes, to proclaim that Marxism was confirmed by 'science', and he adds:

Since the empirical and historical sciences are concerned generally with the fact that something changes or that it is connected with something else, it is safe to assume that each new scientific discovery will confirm the truth of 'Marxism' as thus understood. (ibid.)

A leading Western philosopher of science, Herbert Feigl, is equally blunt. Of the so-called 'laws of dialectic', he writes:

These alleged principles are not at all helpful in either their ontological or their methodological significance . . . it is my impression that once one replaces the dialectical formulae . . . by straightforward modern scientific language, nothing of their intended scientific significance would be lost, and an enormous gain in conceptual clarity would be achieved. (Feigl, 1974: pp. 114-115)

Our conclusion must be that the dialectical method has but little to offer students of religion who would seek to make their discipline more 'scientific'.

It is, however, what Marxism-Leninism claims for historical materialism that impinges most closely upon the concerns of the student of religion. Like Marx himself, who had no interest in showing that his conception of science was true of physics or biology, historical materialism seeks to trace the development of social forms – including religious forms – and socio-economic structures, which are what they are through the working out of history's discoverable 'necessary laws'. Here, certainly, there are no fixed natures of which a static science could claim to offer knowledge, and Marxism-Leninism's dialectical method does service in making students of religion perhaps more aware than hitherto of the dynamism of history. What there is, for Marx and for Marxism-Leninism, is 'historical necessity' and this, it claims, only its own 'dialectical' understanding of history can either understand or explicate (*Theses on Feuerbach: VI; Preface to the First Edition of Capital*).

Marx, of course, as we saw earlier, was no fatalist, nor was he a believer in Hegel's notion of the 'cunning of reason', which carries out its preconceived plans despite man's illusion that he acts in freedom. There must then, if the Marxist hypothesis is to have meaning, be a way in which history can be read such that it reveals not merely what does take place, but also, what must take place not, as Engels pointed out in the preface to his *The End of Philosophy,* in the sense of making moral judgements on history, but in the sense that some developments can be said to be in accord with the overall development of history – 'historical' developments – and some can be said to be deviations or retarded forms of 'historical' developments – 'unhistorical' developments.

Marx and Engels inherited from Hegel – whether they recognised it or not – an immense confidence in the rationality of history. Nowhere is this more evident than in Engels' interpretation of Hegel's dictum that 'the real is the rational and the rational is the real'. This proposition, Engels claims, implies that there is neither reality nor rationality without necessity. The real is the rational only when it is historically necessary that it be, or come to be; and the reality of the rational is the historical necessity of its coming into being. According to the laws of dialectic, this means that the real as given contains within itself the very irrationality (contradiction) which necessarily demands that it be superseded by what is truly rational and, thus, historically real (*Ludwig Feuerbach*; *MEBW:* pp. 238-242). The problem, of course – and it is this which makes the whole enterprise suspect as science – is that, without an in-built teleology, it is difficult to see what can be meant by speaking of 'historical necessity' or, as Soviet Marxist-Leninists do, of 'the scientific laws of history'. The notion of history as moving, or developing, or unfolding in a linear direction toward a goal is, as many non-Soviet Marxists are more and more realising, but a radically secularised version of the Judeo-Christian conception of *Heilsgeschichte* – of 'salvation history'.[2] This is the more noticeable today, placed as we are in a better position than were Marx and Engels, to compare the Judeo-Christian-Marxist understanding of history with that enshrined in other alien cultures. Kołakowski, for instance, at a time when he still considered himself a Marxist, called attention to the fact that what was common to both the Judeo-Christian and the Marxist traditions was 'the possibility of eschatology'. He wrote:

We (i.e., Marxists) put it (eschatology) otherwise, to all appearance non-theologically: Can the human values which we accept attain complete realisation? Does history evolve in a definite direction that promises ultimate equalisation and universal justice? . . . This secular eschatology, this belief in the future elimination of the disparity between man's essence and his existence (in the de-ification of man), presupposes, obviously, that 'essence' is a value, that its realisation is desirable, and that the wisdom of history will bring about its realisation. Secular eschatology trusts the final judgement of history.

And a little later he comments:

Once historical eschatology had demonstrated its possibilites, human history became a cogent argument for atheism, for it had become known that another force could take the burden of God upon itself and lull with a vision of a happy ending its unfortunate subjects toward which their torment and efforts tend. (Kołakowski, 1971: pp. 31-32)

The point that I wish to make is that the eschatological dimension of history — as Kołakowski's remarks indicate — is fundamental to Jew, Christian and Marxist in a way that it is not fundamental, for example, to the Hindu or the Chinese. Marxism inherits from the Judeo-Christian tradition a notion of history as moving forward to an *eschaton* even if, for the Marxist, this will take place within rather than beyond secular history.

The recognition of a basic affinity between Jewish, Christian and Marxist understandings of history has led a number of non-Soviet Marxists in recent years to a fundamental re-examination of the Biblical/Jewish sources of their world-view. The interesting thing, of course, is that they have found theologians also exploring the same territory. Foremost among Marxists who have been exploring this territory (and often simultaneously engaging in dialogue with Christians) are the German, Ernst Bloch, whose book *Controversy over the Biblical Heritage* is seminal to this discussion, the Czechoslovaks, Milan Machoveč and Vitězslav Gardavský, and the Swiss Konrad Farner.

Gardavský is in no doubt that Marxism takes over its basic historical outlook from the Judeo-Christian tradition. The point at issue in *Genesis,* he says — contrasting the Hebraic understanding of history with that of the Greeks — is:

Man in a time system, not in the cosmic system; in a three-dimensional temporal scheme, within which everything becomes fluctuating and uncertain, and in which man must fight all the time, over and over again, to defend his existence, must make up his mind between various possibilities, choosing and rejecting, erring and being punished . . . This open-mindedness, devoid of any degree of certainty, is the exact opposite of the self-contained and well-rounded image of man held by classical antiquity.

And he urges his readers to look anew at *Genesis* and to grasp the point that not only *Genesis* but, as he says:

The Old Testament as a whole contains something which is exceedingly important for the whole of European thought in general and for contemporary socialist and Marxist thought in particular: this is the first appearance of the idea of transcendence, of a step beyond all that has been achieved — although it is revealed here (he adds) in a pre-scientific and mythological form, it is nonetheless perfectly clear; the dream of a personal identity in the midst of time begins to show itself for the first time. (Gardavský, 1973: p. 28)

The Czech theologian, Jan Lochman, agrees. He argues that the fundamental attitudes of Marxism 'would be quite unthinkable without the Biblical background', and in support of this statement he instances 'the serious consideration of history as having meaning and purpose', 'the high value placed on labour and its constitutive importance for all that is human', 'the care for the poor and oppressed' and 'the assurance of freedom for the heavy laden' and, finally, 'the "Messianic" component: hope for the undoubted coming of redemption and deliverance from human alienation in the post-revolutionary "kingdom of the free"' (Lochman, 1977: p. 95).

The point that I want to make is that, as some Marxists now openly admit, the Marxist understanding of history — like its Biblical original — is not a 'science' but a hope, a vision, a faith in, and an invitation to, the future. Thus Kołakowski writes of communism as a 'horizon', and says of it that 'there is no place where this horizon exists, although every day can prepare us for it' (1964: p. 237). Similarly, another Polish Marxist Adam Schaff has written that: 'Communism is an ideal, a model, a limit towards which we strive through an unending process' (1965: p. 258).

As we have seen (Section 3), such radical reinterpretations of the traditional Marxist understanding of the historical process have been roundly condemned by Soviet Marxism-Leninism, and Soviet theoreticians see such a reinterpretation (rightly, from their point of view) not only as a threat to their own 'scientific' understanding of Marxism, but as a concession to religion. Thus S.A. Popov describes Kołakowski's views as 'a kind of pseudo-religion', and reminds his readers of Lenin's condemnation of 'God-building' with which he links these 'revisionist' interpretations. But Popov's reply to those who would abandon Marxism's claims to be a 'science', and to offer a scientific understanding of history, is simply to reiterate those claims. His reply is instructive, however, in that it demonstrates the reason why Marxism-Leninism clings so resolutely to the 'myth' — as I hold it to be — that it offers the proletariat a 'scientific' understanding of his condition and a 'scientific' way forward from that condition. He wrote:

In Marxism there is not a grain of Utopianism. Its strength lies in its ability not only to express the vital interests of the working class . . . but also to give them a scientific theory of the struggle against Capitalism, a theory of building Socialism and Communism. The root of any utopia, including religious utopia, is in the weakness, passiveness and lack of independence of the masses. 'Day-dreaming', as Lenin said, 'is the lot of the weak'. (Popov, 1977: pp. 145-146)

It is because Marxism-Leninism believes that all that religion offers is dreams, that it saps the vital energies of the proletariat by directing them away from truly revolutionary activities, that Soviet 'scientific atheism' opposes both religion, and what it believes to be 'revisionist' rewritings of religion, with so much vigour. In the light of what we said earlier about the attitudes of the Orthodox Church in nineteenth century Russia we should not find this surprising. That religion can be more than what it was, by and large, in nineteenth century Germany and Russia is something that Soviet 'scientific atheism' has yet to discover. Its continuing to read into all forms of religion an understanding derived largely from Marx, Engels and Lenin's somewhat limited and unfortunate historical experience of religion, is one of the weaknesses in the Soviet understanding of religious phenomena, and the present and unfortunate condition of Orthodoxy in the Soviet Union today but reinforces these prejudices.

Popov also attacks Roger Garaudy's book, *The Alternative Future* for — among other things — describing Marxism as a 'perspective' and Bloch's — which he names only by implication — for speaking of Marxism as 'a hope which arises in the sea of the possible'. Not so, says Popov; these interpretations of Marxism are but dreams, divorced alike from the realities of capitalist exploitation and scientific Communism. Marxism, he insists, is a science, and just because it is a science it can confidently predict not only the final victory of Communism, but also the eventual disappearance of religion as a phenomenon in human culture, for religion, 'scientifically' understood, is but an 'ideological reflection' of contradictory (and, therefore, ultimately 'unreal') socio-economic structures, destined to disappear by being superseded. When that occurs, religion will then have nothing left to 'reflect' (Popov, 1977: p. 153). It is this latter claim, presupposing as it does that religion is but a variable of more fundamental socio-economic processes, which for Soviet 'scientific atheism' constitutes the 'scientific' aspect of its approach to the understanding of religion. It is this claim which, for the reasons set out earlier in this chapter, it is difficult for non-Marxist students of religion to either understand or accept.

(2) It is, however, in the second criticism which I want to bring against the claim of Marxist-Leninist 'scientific atheism' to be the only possible science of religion that the fundamental weakness of Marxist-Leninist methodological presuppositions for the study of religion are most evident. It is the inability of 'scientific atheism' – on its own avowed presuppositions – to offer anything approaching a satisfactory appreciation of many of the motives underlying the personal religious quest, as these are articulated in the writings of the great religious personages in the world's religious traditions.

As an example of what I mean, I shall take as an example, not one of the acknowledged leaders of the spiritual life, such as Śankara or St. Augustine, but the seventeenth century French scientist Blaise Pascal, for Pascal's analysis of the human condition bears some resemblance to the condition of 'alienation' described in Marx's early writings. It is, however, an analysis – at least as Pascal conceives it – which has little or nothing to do with *class*. It is intended, by Pascal, to be an analysis of *the human condition as such*, but should it reveal no more than Pascal's reading of his own condition, it is sufficiently like the reading of that condition as found in other masters of the spiritual life – in Christianity,

Islam, Judaism, Buddhism, etc., − for it to be of concern to those who truly seek to understand religion. It is the inability of Marxist-Leninist 'scientific atheism' to come to terms with this reading of the human condition that, in my opinion, vitiates its claim to offer a complete, or even an adequate, understanding of religion.

Pascal's analysis of the human condition rests on a categorical statement to the effect that man is 'wretched' − not because of any particular material circumstances in which he finds himself that could be altered by revolutionary political activity, but 'wretched as such', as man. That such 'wretchedness' as Pascal describes is an essential feature of the human condition is a claim vigorously denied, as Alban Krailsheimer, in a recent study of Pascal, has pointed out, even by those who are most discontented (Krailsheimer, 1980: p. 50). The right to happiness, Krailsheimer says, is obscurely felt to be so much a part of the human lot that the search, however vain, is unremitting. 'Even those who feel that they are happy', he writes, 'fail to recognise that the loss of health prosperity, or loved ones could instantly plunge them into misery' (op. cit., p. 50). If security and fulfilment are accepted as components of happiness, insecurity and frustration, a burning dissatisfaction with all that this world has to offer − actually or potentially − clearly belongs to what Pascal calls 'wretchedness'. Man's condition is, says Pascal, 'inconstancy, boredom, anxiety' (*Pensées,* 24) and much of the time he is led astray by the 'deceptive powers' of the imagination, vanity, and so on, masquerading as reality. Yet, whilst man, for Pascal, is 'only a reed, the weakest in nature', he is also 'a thinking reed' (ibid., 200), and man's 'wretchedness' arises out of just this capacity for self-awareness − a self-awareness which is at once the reminder of his 'wretchedness' and the proof of greatness lost (ibid., 116). What Pascal means by 'wretchedness' is explained by means of reference to *Ecclesiastes:*

Any one is unhappy who wills but cannot do. Now he wants to be happy and assured of some truth, and yet he is incapable of knowing and not desiring to know. He cannot even doubt. (*Pensées, 75*)

Elsewhere in his analysis, Pascal adds the physical dimension, showing man as a being subject to disease, death and destruction, but unable to do anything about it, while striving incessantly against the inevitable.

Man's instinctive response to these unpalatable truths, says Pascal, is 'diversion' yet, as he points out, 'if man were happy, the less he was diverted the happier he would be' (ibid., 132), and Pascal further points out that the happiness gained from diversion is illusory, since it depends on something outside, merely distracting us momentarily from the painful truth: 'the sole cause of man's unhappiness is that he does not know how to stay quietly in his room' (ibid., 136). Man, therefore, seeks 'diversion', but for Pascal and for those who think like him, these 'diversions' are ultimately unsatisfying for man has that within him which nothing in the world can ultimately satisfy. We are reminded of St. Augustine's *'cor inquietum'* and of Śankara's description of the world of everyday reality as *maya* – 'play' or illusion.[3]

Krailsheimer sums up Pascal's understanding of himself and of man as follows:

Man is a paradoxical creature, split into two parts variously described as wretchedness and greatness, instinct and reason, the origin of his fruitless search for happiness lies in the past history of mankind, and not in that of the individual; all human values and justice are relative, human life provisional and diversions futile. The only positive pointer is that one should listen to God and recognise that our present state represents a fall from our true and original nature, which was grace . . . so long as we fail to admit that man must transcend man, Pascal says, we shall be locked in the prison of human limitations. Worse than that, the natural selfishness of each man left to himself means that this is solitary confinement . . . even those philosophers who preach and practice brotherly love and human solidarity are still hemmed in by man's radical inability to change his human condition and are pinning such faith as they have on a species as fallible collectively as they themselves are individually. (Krailsheimer, 1980: pp. 53-54)

Without going into Pascal's positive Christian solution to the situation he has outlined, we can see that there is a reading of the human condition – of which Pascal's analysis in the *Pensées* is typical – which we find in all the major religious traditions and which concerns man as such, which cuts across the class-structures and class ambitions of society and which is the ultimate motivation – however differently it works itself out in various religions – of much in religion that Soviet 'scientific atheism' ignores, and which it neither understands nor is able, as yet, to counteract. It is Marxism-Leninism's inability to understand this aspect of the motivation behind much that is greatest in religion that constitutes its failure to be considered the only true *Religionswissenschaft.*

Our conclusion must be that whilst Soviet 'scientific atheism' calls attention to some of the motives underlying religion – motives which certainly at the time when the Marxist anlaysis was first propounded were either grossly neglected or completely ignored – and so imparts to the study of religion a much needed sense of the material realities in the context of which all religious activity is played out, it fails as an exhaustive empirical explanation, not only of the particular features of religions, but certainly of religion as such and is not, therefore, the 'science of religion' it claims to be. Those who cannot accept a religion's own explanation for its existence and so must look for some other explanation – or set of explanations – must look elsewhere. This is not to say the Marxian analysis of religion – particularly in the form put forward by Marx and Engels in their early writings – might not provide a partial explanation of religious phenomena, might not, indeed form the basis for a more acceptable, naturalistic theory of religion; it is simply to say that, as put forward in Soviet writing about religion, it fails to offer anything like an overall, exhaustive explanation of the empirical phenomenon of religion. This is, unfortunately, the claim so often made for it in Soviet study of religion.

9.2   MARXIST-LENINIST PARTISANSHIP AND THE STUDY OF RELIGION

If, as we have suggested earlier, an ontological commitment is of necessity presupposed in every study of religion, then partisanship in the study of religion is not only unavoidable, but is a virtue to be cultivated that the clarity of our vision be unimpaired and that the seriousness of our concern with the questions raised by religious claims be made manifest. On this both religious men and Marxists are agreed. To be and to seek to remain ultimately non-partisan on the issues with which both Marxism and religion seek to engage our concern is to abrogate our responsibility as human beings for ourselves and for others. In these matters we cannot escape a decision, since to seek to remain agnostic would in effect be to take a decision against the world-view concerned. The maxim 'He who is not with us is against us' is as important for the Marxist as it has been for the religious man. As the German existential philosopher Karl Jaspers has written:

It is typical of every faith that it rejects unbelief. Believing that he was in possession of a total system of knowledge, Marx, like the theologians, was the enemy of agnosticism and scepticism. (Jaspers, 1952: p. 16)

And in point of fact the study of religion has but rarely sought to be non-partisan, and even where it has, it has but rarely succeeded. Basic ontological presuppositions will without.

Thus if we look at the history of *Religionswissenschaft* as an autonomous, non-theological discipline, we see that its protagonists themselves were quite explicit about their own ontological commitment and about the ultimately Christian (or religious) objectives which they saw the new discipline subserving. Friedrich Max Müller, for example, in a paper entitled 'Plea for a Science of Religion' (1867) claimed that the 'science of religion' would 'give a new life to Christianity', that it 'would assign to Christianity its rightful place among the religions of the world' by showing what was truly meant by 'the fulness of time' and by 'restoring to the whole history of the world, in its unconscious progress towards Christianity, its true and sacred character' (Müller, 1867: pp. xviii-xxviii). Joachim Wach, half a century later, was equally explicit when, in a paper entitled 'The Meaning and Task of the History of Religions', he maintained that the 'practical significance of *Religionswissenschaft*' is that:

It broadens and deepens the *sensus numinis,* the religious feeling and under-standing; it prepares one for a deeper conception of one's own faith; it allows a new and comprehensive experience of what religion is and means. This is as true of the religious experience as such as it is of the doctrinal and dogmatic aspect of religion. The effectiveness of the religious genius, the power and the formation of the religious community, the shaping of culture by religion − all these are experienced in new and manifold ways which do not paralyse but rahter strengthen and fortify religious impulses. (Wach, 1967: p. 4)

And a contemporary practitioner of *Religionswissenschaft,* Mirčea Eliade, whom many regard as the discipline's most illus-trious Western representative, is in no doubt that 'the sacred' and its manifestations, unreduced to any other phenomena, is the proper object of the study of religion. He writes:

For the historian of religions, *every* manifestation of the sacred is important: every rite, every myth, every belief or divine figure reflects the experience of the sacred and hence implies notions of *being,* of *meaning,* and of *truth.* (Eliade, 1979: p. xiii)

In one way or another Western practitioners of *Religions--wissenschaft* are as committed to 'religion', as an irreducible reality, as Marxists are to reducing it to some other, more material form of reality. It is here, it seems to me, that we meet the great divide between Western and Soviet study of religion today. Western 'phenomenological' approaches to the study of religious phenomena implicitly, and sometimes explicitly, assume the irreducibility of the reality of religion; Soviet students explicitly deny any reality to religion over and above its being an ideological 'reflection' of material circumstances − an assumption which they share, of course, with many Western sociologists of religion who are not Marxist. As the Swedish historian and phenomenologist of religion, Åke Hultkrantz has noted in a historical survey of the rise of Western phenomenology of religion, a characteristic of the phenomenological approach, discernible, for instance, in one of its earliest protagonists, the Dutch scholar Gerardus van der Leeuw, is that in an intuitive way it wants to 'gain knowledge about the (immanent) import and intention of religious phenomena — to become acquainted with its essence' (Hultkrantz, 1970: p. 71). Gerardus van der Leeuw and his Dutch colleagues consciously cultivated the thesis, Hultkrantz maintains 'that the true "essence" of religion and religious phenomena must be sought for behind the disturbing labour which historical, psychological, and sociological models of investigation pursue . . . In the foreground (of their work) stands the demand for the subjective empathy into the phenomenon of religion, an empathy which in the final round, is carried by the researcher's own religious belief' (Hultkrantz, 1970: p. 72). Today, as Hultkrantz' own position makes clear, this is still the motivation behind Western historical and phenomenological study of religion — as a discipline ultimately independent of psychology, sociology and secular history.

But although both Soviet Marxist-Leninist and Western *Religionswissenschaft* bring very different ontological commitments to the study of religion, Soviet 'scientific atheism' is more than a point of view with an overt ontological commitment — it is also a *Praxis* in the sense that, to it, the study of religion is more than an academic exercise, more than the study of religion for its own sake; it is for Soviet scholars but a necessary preliminary to the abolition of religion as a phenomenon in human culture. Here again I think it is important — despite an abhorence of Soviet administrative measures against religious institutions — that we do not magnify this difference. Western study of religion has had, and continues to have, extra-academic, practical objectives, only in its case it is, more often than not, the furtherance of a religious view of the world. In so important an area of human concern as the study of religion, what the scholar must guard against is not partisanship, but the uncritical acceptance of established positions and blind prejudice. Against these, neither religious study of religion, nor Marxist study of religion, have shown themselves to be particularly immune.

The issue is, however, in my opinion, somewhat more complicated than this last remark would suggest, for in the Soviet Union a situation obtains which in many ways resembles the situation in

Europe in the late eleventh and early twelfth centuries (cf. Thrower, 1973: pp. 58-61) where philosophy – as the free and critical exercise of the reasoning faculty – had to contend, not just with deeply held prejudices, but with institutionalised prejudice. Let me explain what I mean.

In contemporary Soviet thought no distinction is drawn between philosophy and ideology. Ideology, as we saw in the first part of this study, is a much abused term. For Marx and Engels, at least in their early writings, and in *The German Ideology,* it referred primarily to rationalisations used to express and justify, by those whose interests they serve, existing institutions and practices. This meaning has been preserved by Soviet philosophers, particularly when they are referring to bourgeois forms of philosophy, art, literature, law, etc. But they have also enlarged and changed the meaning of 'ideology' to include true conceptions and valid justifications of institutions and practices – at least when these originate with the Communist Party of the Soviet Union. Thus the Soviet *Filosofskiy Slovar'* (Philosophical Dictionary) defines ideology as:

> . . . a system of views and ideas: political, legal, moral, aesthetic, religious and philosophical. It is part of the superstructure and as such reflects in the final analysis economic relations. The struggle of class interests in a society with antagonistic classes corresponds to the ideological struggle. Ideology may be a true or a false, a scientific or an unscientific reflection of reality. (op. cit., p. 160)

Marxism-Leninism, in its own estimation, constitutes the only truly scientific reflection of reality, is the ideology of the working class and so of the overwhelming majority of mankind. In the present order of things it is engaged in a life and death struggle with bourgeois ideology on all fronts – not least with religion. This, as we have seen, constitutes the *raison d'être* for the study of religion in the Soviet Union today.

The thesis that I wish to advance, however, is that, contrary to what is maintained by Soviet 'scientific atheism', the study of religion and atheism in the Soviet Union, in that it is now inextricably tied to the Marxist-Leninist world outlook, is ideological, not in the broad sense used by Soviet philosophers today, but in the narrower, and much more acute sense, given to the term by Marx and Engels.

Philosophy, as traditionally understood in the West, can be defined as an attempt to understand the totality of reality on the basis of human experience and human reason alone. Its main functions are analysis — of presuppositions and terms — and synthesis, or the attempt to relate the diversity of experience into a coherent whole. It differs from theology in being based on reason and experience without recourse to any supposed revelation, and from the sciences in that its subject matter is both more general and more basic. It is a 'second-order discipline' analysing and synthesising the claims to knowledge put forward by the 'first order' disciplines whose task is to enquire into the nature of the world.

Ideology, I contend, whether it be religious or political, can be distinguished from philosophy in a number of ways. The component parts of an ideology are more often than not unanalysed and frequently not clarified and so are systematically ambiguous. They mean different things in different places within the ideology. In addition to their systematic ambiguity, ideological systems, and indeed statements within ideological systems, are not held on strictly rational grounds; that is, they are not primarily held because of the rational arguments which can be adduced in support of the system or statement, but on authority. Ideology is thus dogmatic and immune from critical analysis. A further difference between philosophy and ideology is that whereas the impetus behind philosophy is primarily the search for understanding, the aim of ideology is not primarily understanding but action. An ideology not only states how things are but also what is to be done. Its appeal, as a consequence, is not only to reason but also to the emotions, and its content is usually stated in language calculated to form attitudes and inculcate values leading to certain desired patterns of action.

If this distinction is valid, and I believe that it is, then the conclusion seems to me inescapable that Soviet study of religion is ideological in the way we have defined it, for Soviet statements about religion are not open to critical philosophical analysis, do not move far from the positions adopted by the authorative founders – Marx, Engels and Lenin – whose writings are quoted incessantly – and are designed to further understanding of religion only as a prelude to activity designed to overcome it.

The Marxist-Leninist understanding of religion, though amenable to critical analysis when formulated by Marx, Engels and Lenin, quickly became dogmatised and was accepted as proven, not because of any inherent rationality it might be held to possess, but on the authority of the Party alone. In this it was, of course, no different from any other aspect of the Soviet Marxist-Leninist *Weltanschauung*. It simply became part of a process that began in the 1930's under Stalin and from which neither it, nor Soviet thought in general, has since been able to recover. Stalin's repressive policy, as Leszek Kołakowski has demonstrated, was not simply a matter of destroying only actual or potential rivals to himself, but was one of 'wiping out the sole organism in which there were still any remnants, however faint and impotent, of loyalty to any cause other than the state and its leader – in particular, remnants of a belief in Communist ideology as a frame of reference and object of worship, independent of the leader and the party's current directives' (Kołakowski, 1978: vol. III, p. 85). All forms of revolt against the ruler had appealed to the ideology of which the Party was the custodian. Consequently, argues Kołakowski, that ideology had to be revised so as to make it clear to all that such an appeal was inadmissable – just as in mediaeval Europe unauthorised persons were not allowed to comment on the Scriptures or the doctrines of the established church. Stalin and later, in the post-Stalin period, the Leader and his inner circle of advisers' interpretation of Marxism-Leninism became unquestionably obligatory on all.[4] The general nervousness with regard to even the slightest suggestion of independent thought, which grew up among intellectuals in the Stalinist era, is one which in almost all areas of Soviet thought, including Soviet thought about religion, has not yet been outgrown. For ongoing, creative Marxist thinking

about religion, we must, alas, for the time being, at least, look elsewhere than to the Soviet Union.

Conclusion

Atheism, as we demonstrated in the first part of this study, was a fundamental presupposition of Marx and Engels' outlook on the world. Initially no more than the necessary converse of the positive assertion of the autonomy of man proclaimed in the German critical philosophy, Marx and Engels' atheism took on clearer political overtones as their analysis of the alienation inherent in the human condition became more defined. Religion was seen not just as a fantasy of alienated man, but as the legitimating ideology of a perverse social order — an ideology which had to be opposed by an atheism which would be one with the more practical, revolutionary struggle which Marx and Engels believed to be necessary before the final emancipation of the alienated classes in society could be accomplished. Such atheism was reinforced, and given the philosophical support it had hitherto lacked, when Engels, towards the end of his life, sought to establish a 'scientific Marxism' on the ontological and cosmological foundations of an absolute materialistic monism — a process which Plekhanov, Lenin, and the Soviet tradition of Marxism-Leninism was to complete.[1] Henceforth any rapprochement with religion would be impossible, and Soviet Marxism, drawing both on the later work of Engels and on the indigenous Russian tradition of political atheism and anticlericalism, was early led to declare 'militant materialism' an integral aspect of its total world view. It is only recently, however — since about 1954 — that 'scientific atheism', as it is now called, was proclaimed an essential component part of Marxism-Leninism and developed accordingly.

'Scientific atheism', as we saw in the second part of this study, has a twofold role to perform within the structure of the overall objectives of the Communist Party of the Soviet Union. It must: (a) continue to criticise religion, both in theory and in practice, and (b) set forth the positive atheist ideals of the new (Soviet) humanity and of the society which it is seeking to create. All study of religion and atheism in the Soviet Union today subserves — and is intended to subserve — these overriding objectives. Soviet study of religion and atheism is an intensely practical enterprise. This we also sought to show in the second part of our study, whilst in the third part we pointed to some of the limitations which this rigid ideological framework places on the Soviet understanding of religion. Marxism-Leninism's claim that 'scientific atheism' constitutes the only true 'science of religion' (*Religions-wissenschaft*) — in that it, and it alone, truly understands the nature and historical role of religion — was a claim which we found wanting. We did not, however, conclude, on that account, that it could be summarily dismissed in the manner of some Western commentators (Bocheński, 1975; Blakeley, 1964) for 'scientific atheism', we also claimed, offers some vital insights into the nature of religion — and particularly into the nature of popular, ordinary, everyday religion — which are often overlooked, or deliberately ignored, by Western students of religion. We concluded that even if the account of religion found in Soviet 'scientific atheism' did not exhaust our understanding of religion, 'scientific atheism' must be taken seriously — certainly by those seeking for a naturalistic understanding of religion — as the most thorough and consistent naturalistic account yet offered of the phenomenon of religion.

But where, if I may now drop — as I have argued earlier any serious commentator on religion must eventually drop — the convention of neutrality, does this leave the naturalistically inclined student of religion who, whilst unable to accept the claims made upon him by the religions of the world, is yet predisposed to try to make some sense of this important aspect of his cultural heritage? Must he seek to go beyond Marx and try to substitute for the Marxist theory of religion a superior one of his own or should he, on the basis provided by Marx, perhaps seek for a revised form of Marxist theory which will take into account the criticism which has been brought against that theory, but which yet remains faithful to many of its basic insights? This is the approach adopted, for instance, by the American sociologist of religion, Norman Birn-baum (in Glock and Hammonds, 1973: pp. 3-70), and it is the position to which I am myself most inclined. As Birnbaum says, such an approach will 'manifest . . . jaggedness and contradictori-ness', but, as he also adds, 'this will, perhaps, be compensated for by a certain metaphysical openness' (op. cit., p. 5). Whilst my own search is somewhat different from Birnbaum's (in that I am not a sociologist but a student of *Religionswissenschaft* who does not believe that his discipline can be reduced to the sociology of religion) like Birnbaum, I believe that the search for a new historical-philosophical location from which to examine the com-plex phenomena of religion involves 'moving from within the Marxist system to its boundaries and then outside them' (Birn-baum, ibid., p. 5).

The conclusion to a study of Soviet 'scientific atheism', how-ever, is not the place to present in detail a new theoretical frame-work for the study of religion — even were I fortunate enough to have one to present, which I have not — and I can conclude, there-fore, only by stating, in the light of the study of both Marxist theory of religion, and of Soviet 'scientific atheism', just some of the considerations which seem to me important to take into account in the formulation of such a theory. All scholarly work is, alas, work in progress.

Marx's original insight into religion as a fantasy of alienated man, found in his earliest writing on religion and never later repu-diated or denied by him (cf. Section 1.3 above), seems to me an insight that is both profound and enduring. The publication of the full corpus of Marx's early writings has produced a flood of exegesis and critical comment of which not the least interesting aspect has been the reaction of theologians, many of whom have been led by these writings — and by the revitalisation of Marxist philosophy which they have produced in both Eastern and Western Europe — to a creative re-examination of their own tradition.[2] The publication of these early manuscripts has also initiated consider-able controversy within the Marxist tradition itself. Without at all going into this — which would be beyond the scope of this present study – we can say that the relationship of 'material' to 'ideal' factors in the Marxist analysis of ideology – including religious ideology – now appears to be much more subtle and complex than schematic representations of an unequivocal and unilinear 'determination' of 'superstructure' by 'material base'. We saw how Soviet 'scientific atheism' ran into difficulties when it sought to move from general assertion of principle to particular and precise statements of fact regarding this relationship in the history of religions (Section 5 above), and it will be obvious that much work will be needed, by those who hold that this fundamental aspect of the Marxist understanding of the history of ideas remains an important one, before much of value for the history of particular religious traditions is forthcoming.

Yet something of general value does, I believe, emerge from working with a Marxist approach to the history of religions. Three major themes, as we saw, characterised the original Marxian theory of religion – those of impotence, alienation and ideology.

That much religion arises from impotence in the face of the frustrations of the natural and social environment of man seems to me obvious. It is a theme which has, of late, been emphasised by a number of contemporary Western anthropologists, most notably by Weston La Barre (1970) and by John Beattie (1966). Beattie puts it like this:

Why should human beings everywhere people their world with such multiplicities of non-natural agents, often fearsome and terrifying? The answer lies partly in the human condition, especially that of members of simpler, technologically under-developed communities. Although life in the conditions of such societies may offer rewards unavailable to civilised man, everyday existence is surrounded by unpredictable and sometimes terrifying hazards of which mortal illness is not the least. As there exists no adequate body of empirical knowledge which might enable men to cope with these hazards, or even to cope with them, by means of practical scientifically proven or provable techniques. So they must cope with them symbolically and expressively instead. (Beattie, 1966: p. 227)

But Marx and Engels' analysis of the origins of religion goes beyond, whilst, of course, recognising this fact, particularly with regard to religion in 'civil society'. Here the concept of alienation rather than that of impotence is central. Working from within the German critical tradition, Marx and Engels, on the basis of the work done by Bauer, Strauss and Feuerbach, recovered what they took to be the human aspirations at the root of the Christian religion and sought, on the basis of this, to put forward a new humanistic philosophy. Their ultimate dissatisfaction with this form of humanism arose from their relaisation that it was a philosophy of humanity no less abstract, no less remote from the concrete, than that of Hegel which it had sought to replace. The 'left-wing' Hegelians had replaced the worship of God by a religion of an abstract humanity which did little or nothing to solve the enduring human problems of poverty, oppression and exploitation. Feuerbach and the 'left' Hegelians had depicted a humanity alienated from itself because it was subject to the creations of its own mind and in particular to religious images of itself. Feuerbach's answer to this subjugation was to correct the images by reinterpreting them in terms of man's highest aspirations for himself. Yet this reinterpretation remined, for Marx and Engels, ideal and remote from the sufferings of humanity in its concrete setting. Men needed religion because they could not confront their own reality as human beings. Here, as I tried to show in Section 9.1 above, is a real point of issue between Marxist naturalist humanism and some of the deepest religious readings of the human situation, for many religious men − Pascal was the example we took − even when they have confronted both themselves and the human situation, not just in terms of their concrete reality but in terms of all human possibilities, remain incapable of being reconciled to it. Here we are confronted by a fundamentally different response to the human condition and one which in my opinion will for ever remain. It is for that reason that I do not believe that religion will ever 'wither away', no matter what changes take place in the human condition. Marx and Engels' answer to the question, which they felt Feuerbach and the 'left' Hegelians had failed to ask, namely, why men needed religion, was to be found in the misery and degradation of the human condition as they saw it and their belief that the ultimate solution to the problem of religion would be found in a post-revolutionary reorganisation of human society in terms of communism is, as is now being realised in the Soviet Union itself, only a partial one. Much religion remains excluded in such an analysis. There are, and will remain, forms of alienation which lie entirely outwith the purview of any and every Marxist social analysis of the sources of religion. The inability of Soviet 'scientific atheism' to come to terms with these forms of aliena-tion was part of the criticism we brought against it in Ch. 9 above. Part, but by no means the whole, of this inability lies in the fact that, as yet, Soviet 'scientific atheism' has not fully come to terms with the early writings of Marx, dismissing all attempted 'creative' interpretations of Marxism in terms of them as 'revisionary'. But this, I repeat, is only part of 'scientific atheism's' inability to fully comprehend the motivation of religious men.

Marxist sociology of religion is inseparable from the radical humanism of Marx and Engels. That humanism – so different from the humanism of contemporary Western Humanist associa-tions, of which, as we have seen, Marxist-Leninists are particularly critical[3] – opposed a true and fulfilled humanity to an inauthen-tic, or injured and subjugated one. Where the religious man parts company with the Marxist – and indeed with all forms of secular humanism – is over the interpretation of what, in the last resort, constitutes true human fulfilment. An adequate theory of religion must, I would suggest, take this into account, in that it must at least describe, even if it cannot explain, the need on the part of some men for a transcendence of themselves and a fulfilment which is not of this world.

With regard to the history of religion Marxist theory has in fact been much more specific than the theory outlined above would suggest, for it has sought to ascribe religious forms of alienation to the specific forms of production, productive relations and man's relationship to nature, found in the successive stages of human history. Whilst we were extremely critical of Soviet 'scien-tific atheism's' reluctance to be quite as specific as the claims which it makes require, we cannot doubt that there are insights here which it would be foolish to overlook. For Marx and Engels, the precise mode by which religion was produced was a replica of the prevailing mode of production in human society. In particular, Marx and Engels held that the division of labour had immensely significant consequences for the creation of spiritual and philosophical world-views. Under very primitive conditions individuals, and the societies to which they belonged, produced their own spiritual worlds. When those societies were closely and immediately dependent on nature, natural religions developed. With the growth of forces of production and the occurrence of the division of labour, religious specialists appeared who concentrated on the production of codified systems of belief. They performed what were, at the time, indispensable social functions — but if history records a progression towards a market system in commodities it does not do so in the realm of the spirit. What was produced, by whom, and for whom, were matters of jealous interest to those in power. The general Marxist proposition that those who owned the means of production also owned ideological production was particularly true in religion (as the eighth century Prophets of Israel recognised). Natural religions — or in the peculiar case of Israel (a claimed) revealed religion — were transformed into state religions, legitimated by (and in turn legitimating) the state itself. With the consolidation of larger societies, polytheism based on fusions of regional sub-groups — each with its own gods — gave way to monotheism, proclaiming a strong and uniform discipline.

So much, of course, as we pointed out earlier, can be found in the anthropology of the nineteenth century. What distinguished the work of Marx and Engels — and still distinguishes Marxist analysis of religion — was their account of the inner structure of religion and its relationship to society. Religion, for Marx and Engels, as we have seen, was part of the general process of the production of what they termed ideology. Here again, we have an insight into religion which, whilst not in any sense exhaustive of religion's relationship to secular power, let alone of religion as such, is one that few today would deny. As a mode of ideology religion has shared, throughout the greater part of, certainly,

European history, ideology's most distinguishing characteristic: that of legitimating the *status quo*. But ideology was not, for Marx and Engels, a totally false account of the human condition; rather was it a partial one, 'determined' by the imperfect development of humanity. Ideology was, as Marx himself expressed it, the truth of a false condition (Marx: *Contribution to a Critique of Hegel's Philosophy of Law, MECW:* 3; 175-187). Marx and Engels − certainly in their early writings − had an acute sense of the spiritual dimension of human existence, as well as considerable knowledge of the Western, Christian religious tradition. It was unfortunately not an exhaustive one and it lacked what was only to be recovered in the twentieth century, any appreciation of the revolutionary religious role of the religion of Israel. Only today − and that, unfortunately outwith the Soviet Union − are Marxists seeking to come to terms with this vital aspect of the Western Judeo-Christian tradition. Thus, for Marx and Engels, religious interpretations of human existence, as they understood them, were solely the outcome of the misery and degradation of the human condition. Thus religion, as a derivative of alienation, would disappear when alienation was overcome. That religion − or to be precise the Christian religion − could so recover its revolutionary roots in the Judaic tradition so as to move to a vigorous critique of old and new forms of alienation − in East and West − was something that Marx and Engels' reading of religion's performance in the past and the present, could not have contemplated. Here, again, we are confronted by a dimension of religion − or at least of the Christian tradition − which falls outwith all and every Marxist analysis. Marx and Engels' appreciation of the 'protest role' of religion comes close to recognising this dimension of religion, but is not identical with it, for an essential aspect of it is an appeal to a superhuman, divine standard where all − rich and the poor, oppressor and oppressed − stand under judgement. The human need for such a superhuman standard − and the support which in trial and tribulation it gives to the oppressed − is to my mind one of the most difficult issues that the secular humanist has to face and I do not know where the naturalistic answer to this need lies − if, indeed, there is one.[4]

The impulses which produce religion were, for Marx and Engels, profoundly human: a demand at once for dignity and consolation, for explanation and for moral coherence. Marxism, if it is to satisfy this demand — and not reimpose new and hitherto undreamed of alienations of its own — must, as Soviet 'scientific atheism' at its best recognises, satisfy these demands, or fail to be what on the whole it claims to be, namely, the natural secular successor to religion in the ongoing development of human society. Whether or not a socialist society can so satisfy these great and enduring demands of human nature remains to be seen. The alternative, for the naturalist, however, is not necessarily a return to religion, but a profound and uncompromising reconciliation to the tragedy of existence. The problem with Soviet 'scientific atheism' is that it has to a large extent forgotten just what these enduring demands of human nature are. Only thus could 'scientific atheists' write as facilely as did Mitin and Feodoseyev about the inherent tragedy of the man in a godless world, where death brings to nought all and every human endeavour (pp. 355-356 above). Soviet 'scientific atheism' — and indeed any form of secular humanism — has, as yet, much to learn from the study of religion.

I would like to make one last point and it concerns the attitude of the secular scholar engaged upon the study of religion. Soviet 'scientific atheism' has been criticised on a number of counts, but one criticism that needs to be put more strongly than hitherto is that the virulent hatred (there is no other word) of religion — derived say some from the peculiar Russian experience of the institutions or religion and, perhaps, also from the personal animosity of Lenin to religion — which characterises much of its writing on religion, must give way, not just to a more objective attitude, but to an attitude of positive empathy, if it is to come to a truer and more just understanding of religion than hitherto. Such an attitude certainly characterised Marx's own writing on religion and such still characterises the best Marxist writing on religion as exemplified, for example, in Milan Machoveč's recent book *A Marxist Looks at Jesus* (1973). I would like, however, to end by quoting some words of the French Marxist, Maxime Rodinson —

from his book *Mohammed* (1961) — which I find relevant, significant and moving in this respect:

I am concerned (he writes) with a religious founder, a man who, during most
of his life at least, was profoundly and sincerely religious, with a keen sense
of the direct presence of the divine. It may be objected that I, as an atheist,
cannot possibly understand such a man. That may be so; after all, what
actually constitutes understanding? However, I am convinced that, provided
he takes enough trouble, and totally excludes any contempt, pharisaism or
sense of superiority, an atheist can in fact understand a religious outlook —
certainly as well as an art critic can understand a painter, an adult a child, a
man of robust health an invalid (and vice versa) or a scholarly recluse a
businessman. Certainly a religious man would understand my subject differently, but better? I am not so sure.

And he continues:

Founders of ideologies have given men reasons for living, and personal and
social tasks to fulfil. When the ideologies are religious they have declared
(and generally believed) that their message came from beyond our world, and
that what they themselves represented was something more than merely
human. The atheist can only say that this extra-human origin remains un-
proved. But that gives him no reason for denigrating the message itself;
indeed, he may even place a higher value on it, as being an admirable effort
to surpass the human condition. Ultimately he may be forced to admit that
it may be rooted in functions of the human mind that we do not yet understand. I believe that he can sometimes capture the original excitement of it,
and feel more at one with it than many of its conformist believers for whom
the message has developed into something taken for granted; consoling,
perhaps, or justificatory, but doing no more than cheaply enabling them to
lead an unadventurous life with a clear conscience. To repeat the admirable
words of Epicurus to Menoeceus: 'The impious man is not the man who
rejects the gods of the multitude, but the man who adheres to the conception
that the multitude has of the gods'.

— a remark, incidentally, of which Marx himself was particularly
fond, quoting it, for instance, in the 'Preface' to his doctoral dissertation. Rodinson concludes:

One critic . . . objects that I display too calm an attitude towards mystery.

I remain calm, though I do not reject mystery. What we know is quite disturbing enough to make us require more proof than we yet have, before we declare that what we do not know is any more so. (Rodinson, 1961: pp. xiii-xiv)

What naturalist but could not concur?

Appendix I

A. THE 10TH NOVEMBER 1954 RESOLUTION OF THE COMMUNIST PARTY OF THE SOVIET UNION 'ON ERRORS IN THE CONDUCT OF SCIENTIFIC AND ATHEISTIC PROPAGANDA AMONG THE POPULACE'

In accordance with its Programme, the Communist Party is conducting scientific and educational propaganda of the materialist world view, aimed at a constant increase of the consciousness of the labouring masses and toward their gradual liberation from religious prejudices. In so doing the Party has always considered it necessary to avoid offending the feelings of believers in any way.

The Central Committee has information at its disposal that attests that in recent times gross errors have been committed in scientific and atheistic propaganda among the populace in a number of places.

Instead of developing regular, painstaking work in propagating natural-scientific knowledge and instead of waging an ideological struggle against religion, certain central and local newspapers, as well as speeches of certain lecturers and reports, are permitting offensive attacks against clergy and believers participating in religious observances. There are cases of the ministers of religious cults and believers being represented — without any basis in fact — in the press and in propagandist' speeches as people who are not politically trustworthy. In a number of 'rayons' [an administrative district] there have been cases of administrative interference in the activities of religious associations and groups, as well as coarseness towards the clergy on the part of local organisations and certain individuals.

Such errors in anti-religious propaganda are fundamentally contrary to the Programme and policy of the Communist Party with respect to religion and believers and are a violation of repeated instructions by the Party concerning the inadmissability of offending the feelings of believers.

The Central Committee considers it incorrect that many Party organisations have divested themselves of day to day leadership of scientific and atheistic propaganda and do not concern themselves with the careful selection of propaganda personnel. Frequently people who are ignorant of science and questions of atheistic propaganda, and at times even hacks, knowing mainly anecdotes and stories about the clergy, are permitted to publish in the press and give lectures and reports. Such an irresponsible approach to the selection of authors of articles and lecturers and reporters and the absence of appropriate supervision by party organisations of the correct trend of scientific and atheistic propaganda is doing serious harm to cultural and educational work among the population.

The Central Committee of the CPSU resolves:

That it is incumbent upon 'oblast' and 'kray' (Provincial and Regional) Party committees, the Central Committees of Communist Parties of the Union Republics and upon all Party organisations resolutely to eliminate errors in atheistic propaganda and in no case to permit in the future any offences whatsoever against the feelings of believers and clergy or to permit administrative interference in the activities of the church. It is necessary to keep in mind that offensive actions with regard to the church, the clergy, and citizens who are believers are incompatible with the line of the party and state on the conducting of scientific and atheistic propaganda and are contrary to the Constitution of the USSR, which accords freedom of conscience to Soviet citizens.

As a result of the profound changes in the socio-economic conditions of life, the liquidation of the exploiting classes, and the victory of socialism in the USSR, and as a result of the successful development of science and the overall growth in the country's cultural level, the majority of the Soviet Union's population has long since freed itself of religious carry-overs from the past; the consciousness of the workers has grown immeasurably. However, one must not fail to keep in mind that there are also citizens who, while actively participating in the life of the country and honestly fulfilling their civic duty to the homeland, are still under the influence of various types of religious beliefs. The Party has always demanded, and will continue to demand, a tactful and attentive attitude toward such believers. It is all the more stupid and harmful to consider certain Soviet citizens politically suspect because of their religious convictions. Profound, patient and properly conceived scientific and atheistic propaganda among believers will help them ultimately to free themselves from their religious errors. On the contrary, all manner of administrative measures and offensive attacks against believers and clergy can only do harm and result in a consolidation and even reinforcement of their religious prejudices.

In conducting scientific and atheistic propaganda, it should be kept in mind that one cannot equate the situation of the church in a socialist country with the situation of the church in an exploitative society. In bourgeois society the church is a support and weapon of the ruling classes, which utilises it for the purpose of enslaving the workers. This does not rule out the possibility that individual clergymen in capitalist society are also capable of going over to, and do go over to, the viewpoint of the workers on a number of basic political questions. However, these clergymen are usually subjected to all manner of persecution on the part of the church and government circles of the capitalist countries because of their behaviour contrary to the interests of the exploiting classes.

In Tsarist Russia the church faithfully served the autocracy, the land-owners, and the capitalists, justified the harsh exploitation of the masses and supported the exploiters in their struggle against the toilers. It is a known fact too that immediately after the victory of the October Socialist Revolution, during the years of the civil war and afterward, many religious organisations and groups of the clergy maintained a hostile attitude toward the Soviet government. In this connection certain ministers of religious cults were called to account by the state not for their religious activities, but for their anti-government activities directed against the interests of the Soviet people and designed to please internal counter-revolution and international imperial-ism. It is natural, therefore, that the struggle of the Soviet people against the enemies of the socialist state also included struggle against those reactionary church representatives who conducted activities hostile to the Soviet people. At the present time, as the result of the victory of socialism and the liquida-tion of the exploitative classes in the USSR, the social roots of religion have been sapped and the base on which the church supported itself has been destroyed. Today, the majority of the clergy, as facts testify, also take a loyal stand with regard to the Soviet government. Therefore, the struggle against religious prejudices today must be regarded as an ideological struggle of the scientific, materialist world view against the anti-scientific, religious world view.

Righting of the mistakes committed in anti-religious propaganda must not lead to a weakening of scientific and atheistic propaganda, which is an integral part of the communist education of the working people and has as its aim the dissemination of scientific, materialistic knowledge among the masses and the liberation of believers from the influence of religious prejudices.

(*Pravda,* 11 November 1954   *KPSS v rezolyutsiyakh* vi, 516-20)

B. EXTRACT FROM THE PROGRAMME OF THE CPSU ADOPTED AT THE XXII CONGRESS, OCTOBER 1963

f. *Elimination of the survivals of capitalism in the minds and behaviour of people*

The party considers it an integral part of its communist educational work to combat manifestations of bourgeois ideology and morality, and the remnants of private-owner psychology, superstitions and prejudices.

The general public, public opinion, and extensive criticism and self-criticism must play a big role in combatting survivals of the past and mani-festations of individualism and selfishness. Comradely censure of anti-social behaviour will gradually become the principal means of doing away with manifestations of bourgeois views, customs and habits. The power of example in public affairs and in private life, in the performance of one's public duty, acquires tremendous educational significance.

The party uses ideological media to educate people in the spirit of a scientific materialist world conception, to overcome religious prejudices without insulting the sentiments of believers. It is necessary to conduct regularly broad atheistic propaganda on a scientific basis, to explain patiently the untenability of religious beliefs, which were engendered in the past when people were overawed by the elemental forces and social oppression and did not know the real causes of natural and social phenomena. This can be done by making use of the achievements of modern science which is steadily solving the mysteries of the universe and extending man's power over nature, leaving no room for religious inventions about supernatural forces.

g. *The exposure of bourgeois ideology*

The peaceful coexistence of states with different social systems does not imply an easing of the ideological struggle. The Communist Party will go on exposing the anti-popular, reactionary nature of capitalism and all attempts to paint bright pictures of the capitalist system.

The party will steadfastly propagate the great advantages of socialism and communism over the declining capitalist system.

The Party advances the scientific ideology of communism in contrast to reactionary bourgeois ideology. . .

Labour and everyday life are the indivisible components of the communist way of life. The plenum orders all party committees, local soviets of workers' deputies, trade unions, and the Komsomol to unleash a struggle to strengthen communist everyday life, to elevate its cultural level, to drive all relics of the past out of our everyday life and family relations.

A stubborn struggle must be waged against religious survivals, scientific atheism must be more broadly propagated. The movement for communist labour must be genuinely unified with the movement for communist relationships in everyday life.

The training of the whole Soviet people in the spirit of communist consciousness, the formation of a scientific-materialistic world-view in all Soviet people demands a general expansion of the study of Marxist-Leninist theory by Communists and non-Party people. Marxist-Leninist theory must be studied in intimate connection with life so that the knowledge acquired will help the toilers to achieve better results in production, will promote the consolidation of communist social relations and communist morality in the life of the Soviet people.

The plenum considers it necessary to heighten the role of science in the formation of a communist worldview, in the ideological and scientific education of the people. Soviet science must occupy a pre-eminent position in all areas of world science; science must serve to acquaint the toilers with scientific and technical creations. Instilling knowledge in the masses is the honoured duty of Soviet scientists.

(*Pravda* 31 Oct 1963   *KPSS v rezolyutsiyakh viii*)

Appendix II

CONTENTS OF COURSE IN 'SCIENTIFIC ATHEISM'

The following is a translation of the Section, Chapter and Sub-Chapter headings in the official text-book for university courses in 'Scientific Atheism': *Istoriya i teoriya ateizma* (The History and Theory of Atheism'), Moscow, 1974.

Introduction: Atheism as the System of Views Opposed to Religion (in three sections: Atheism as the Essential Component of the Scientific, Materialist *Weltanschauung;* Religion and Philosophic Idealism; The History of Atheism and Religion as the Expression of the Fight of the Inimical *Weltanschauungen,* Materialism and Idealism).

Section 1. Origins of Religion, Origins and Development of the Great Religions: Ch. 1. The Origins of Religion in Primitive Society (The Pre-Religious Era; The Origins of Religion and its Early Forms; Religion in the Era of the Downfall of Primitive Society and the Formation of Class-Society; Shamanism). Ch. 2. The Great Religions and their Particularities. Ch. 3. Buddhism and Lamaism. Ch. 4. Judaism. Ch. 5. Christianity (Social, Economic and Ideological Premises of the Formation of Christianity; Early Christian Communities. The Appearance of the Church and Dogmatic Theology; Roman Catholicism; Protestantism; Orthodoxy; Russian Orthodoxy). Ch. 6. Islam (The Origins of Islam and its Social Role; Islamic Theology. The Koran; Basic Tendencies and Sects in Islam; Moslem Theology. Halam. Mysticism in Islam; Rites and Feasts of Islam. Saints; Pan-Islamism, its Sociological Base and Political Role).

Section 2. Pre-Marxist Atheism: Ch. 7. Rudimentary Atheism in the Ancient East. Ch. 8. Atheism in Antiquity (Ancient Mythology. Rudimentary Atheism During the Rise of the Ancient Greek Slave-Owning Democracies; Development of Atheism During the Flowering of Ancient Greek Democracy; The Fight Between Atheism and Religion During the Decline of Ancient Greek Slave-Owning Democracy; Atheism in the Hellinistic World and in Rome). Ch. 9. Heresies as Ideological Expression of Anti-Feudalism in the Middle Ages. Ch. 10. Elements of Atheism in the Philosophy of the Byzantine Renaissance. Ch. 11. Elements of Free-Thinking in Mediaeval Scholasticism (Realism and Nominalism; Conflict Between Realism and Nominalism in the Eleventh and Twelfth Centuries; Elements of Free-Thinking in Late Scholasticism). Ch. 12. Atheism During the Renaissance and Reformation (Humanism and the Reformation; Counter-Reformation; Italian Philosophy of Nature; The Struggle Between the Church and Science). Ch. 13. Free-Thinking and Atheism in English Philosophy of the Seventeenth and Eighteenth Centuries (Elements of Atheism in the *Weltanschauung* of Francis Bacon; The Anti-Clericalism and Atheism of Thomas Hobbes; English Deists and the Cambridge Platonists; John Locke's Position of Compromise; Bishop Berkeley's Attempt to Defend Religion; English Free-Thinkers of the Beginning of the Eighteenth Century). Ch. 14. The Atheism of Benedict Spinoza (Spinoza's Doctrine on Substance-God; Criticism of Religion). Ch. 15. The Development of Atheist Thought in France from the Sixteenth to the Eighteenth Centuries (Criticism of Religion and the Church in the Sixteenth and Seventeenth Centuries; Jean Meslier; French Deists; The Atheism of the French Materialists of the Eighteenth Century; Anti-Religious Ideas in the Works of the Minor Lights of the French Enlightenment). Ch. 16. German Enlighteners of the Eighteenth Century in Conflict with Religion and the Church (Predecessors of the German Enlighteners; The Anti-Clericalism of the German Democrats of the Eighteenth Century; Elements of Atheism in the *Weltanschauung* and Works of Lessing, Herder, Schiller and Goethe). Ch. 17. Problems of Religion and Atheism in German Classical Philosophy (Kant's Defence of Religion; Hegel's 'Philosophy of Religion'; Feuerbach's Atheism). Ch.18. Atheist Tendencies in the Social Thought of Russia in the Eighteenth Century (Free-Thinkers Among Peter's 'Brigade of Scholars'; M.V. Lomonosov's Fight with Religion and the Church; The Atheism of A.N. Radishchev). Ch. 19. Atheism in Nineteenth Century Russia (The Atheist and Anti-Clerical Views of the Decembrists; The Atheism of the Petrashevists; The Atheism of the Russian Revolutionary Democrats; Criticism by the Revolutionary Democrats of Religious Conceptions of the Soul and Morality.

Section 3. Marxist-Leninist Atheism: Ch. 20. Marxism-Leninism on the Class Roots and Epistemological Roots of Religion. Ch. 21. Religion and Science (The Opposition Between Science and Religion; On the History of the Struggle Between Science and Religion; Particularities of the Fight Between Science and Religion Today; The Irreconcilability of Science and Religion in Conceiving Social Life). Ch. 22. Religion and Morals (The Class-Historical Conditioning of the Norms of Religious Morality; The Anti-Scientific and Anti-Humanistic Character of Religious Morality; The Incompatibility of Religious and Communist Morality). Ch. 23. Religion and Art (Art in Conflict with Religion; The Rapprochement of Contemporary Bourgeois Art and

Idealist Philosophy and Religion; The Role of Art in Scientific-Atheist propaganda). Ch. 24. The Relation of the CPSU to Religion and Church. Ch. 25. The Guarantee of Genuine Freedom of Conscience in the USSR (Religious Freedom of Conscience in Capitalist Countries; Realisation of Genuine Freedom of Conscience in the USSR). Ch. 26. Causes of the Existence of Religious Survivals Under Socialism.

Section 4. The Reactionary Essence of Contemporary Religious Ideology: Ch. 27. Causes for the Adaptation of Religious Organisations to the new Historical Conditions. Ch. 28. Efforts to find a new 'Rational' Foundation for Religion. Ch. 29. Neo-Thomism as the Reactionary Ideology of Contemporary Catholicism (The 'Union' of Reason and Faith, and Science and Religion, According to the Neo-Thomists; Neo-Thomism's Social Doctrine, Neo-Thomist Ethics). Ch. 30. Irrationalism in the Service of Religion. Ch. 31. The Ideology and Politics of Catholicism; The Ideology and Politics of Catholic Parties; Catholicism in the USSR). Ch. 32. Ideological Currents in Contemporary Protestantism. Ch. 33. Missionaries and Colonialism. Ch. 34. Zionist Organisations and their Activities. Ch. 35. The Ideology of Contemporary Orthodoxy (Efforts at Adaptation of the Russian Orthodox Church to the new Historical Conditions in the USSR; Feeling and Rites in Contemporary Orthodoxy). Ch. 36. Christian Sects in the USSR and their Ideology (General Description of the Activity and Ideology of Contemporary Christian Sects; Baptists; Adventists; Old Believers; True-Orthodox; *Pyatidesyatniki;* Jehovah's Witnesses; Khlystovist Sects). Ch. 37. Communism and Religion.

Appendix III

The following is a translation of the CONCLUSION to Tokarev's major study in the history of religion: *Religiya v istorii narodov mira* (Religion in the History of the Peoples of the World), Moscow, 1964. This translation is taken from the 3rd edition, 1976: pp. 539-558. I have translated it *verbatim* so as to given readers some idea of both the style and content of serious Soviet writing in the history of religion. Both Tokarev's style of writing and the views which he expressed provide further evidence, I believe, to support many of the statements I have made in the body of my study regarding the contemporary Soviet understanding of religion.

What can the history of religion teach us? What role has religion played in the past, and what role does it play today in the life of people?

Religion is not just ideas

The first and most obvious conclusion to be drawn is that the history of religion is not simply a history of the errors of the human mind. If religion was simply a collection of mistaken ideas about the world, it would have played a very minor role indeed in the history of mankind. Humanity has overcome many false ideas in the course of its history. These false ideas slowed down progress, but were eventually swept away by progress. The fate of religion has been different. It is indeed a collection of false and fantastic ideas, but of ideas so well established in the human mind that they cannot be divorced from human experience of the world. Let us take, as an example, the case of Christianity. Simple common sense, to say nothing of scientific research, can easily prove that the Old and New Testaments, and other religious books, are full of naive fantasies; but millions of people, some of them well educated, believe in them. Thus, there is something in religion that supports all these incomprehensible ideas.

Religion is not just a set of fantastic images fixed in the minds of people; religion also consists of particular ceremonies, sacrifices and taboos, as well as of moral precepts and rules appertaining to family and social life. Religion is also sometiems part of a legal system and even influences international relations. It is also material things, such as icons, churches, monasteries, etc. It is also groups of people devoted to it — from witches, among primitive peoples, to modern churchmen and believers. It also includes church organisations, such as schools run by the church, divinity faculties in universities, political parties and trade unions.

One can say, therefore, that religion is not only a human attitude to god or the gods, but also relations between people — or to be more precise, relations between people in relationship to a god or gods.

Social Carriers of Religion

The strength of religion lies in the fact that so many people, and influential groups of people, are connected with it, and are sometimes materially dependent on it, and also on the fact that many of these people are members of the ruling classes. This does not mean, however, that religion was invented by priests, as some writers have claimed. The roots of religion are deeper than this. In primitive societies, in the later stages of their development, there were many people who were 'knowledgeable' in different cults and were the guardians of religious secrets. This marked a general tendency to differentiate between manual and intellectual labour. These 'professionals' were not just the guardians of religious secrets, they were also *creating* religion. Even the most primitive of beliefs were not created in one day and shared at once by all the people. This would have been the greatest of all miracles. The conditions of the origins of religious beliefs in each tribe were similar, but these beliefs originated, first of all, in the heads of one or of a few people, and were then spread among children and the younger generation. One has reason to believe that these 'specialists' were the first to discover, then change and modify, these beliefs and only later to pass them on to the rest of the tribe. Usually it is witches and priests themselves who give ethnographers the information necessary for them to describe the religion of certain peoples.

This does not, however, prove the theory that religion is but the 'lies of priests', since witches and the like, in most cases, actually believe themselves what they teach to others. But they, more than anyone else, are firstly, capable of 'inventing' beliefs, and secondly, more than any others, they are interested in the preservation of these beliefs.

In class-society religion is in a true sense a weapon of social oppression, and it could not have played such a role if it was simply a mistaken view of the world, since mistakes can easily be corrected by experience. The main problem is not that of mistaken ideas, as bourgeois atheists have sometimes imagined, but lies in the fact of centuries of tradition, and in the rituals and ceremonies that support these beliefs. These traditions are, in their turn, supported by well organised church hierarchies. Church organisations are the social force which is the basis and support of religion. In class society religion is also part of the ruling class and acts as its ideological weapon.

One should also not forget about the psychological (and ideological) influences of religion on people, who look to religion for support and solace — especially in times of crisis. This tradition is, in fact, so deeply rooted in the human consciousness that even in our own day, in both our own and other socialist countries, where the social roots of religion have been broken, and its authority shaken, many people still, in times of crisis, turn to religion for solace.

Thus we see that religion serves a conservative function, not only in the lives of people, but also in the spheres of politics, and economics.

The Evil Nature of Religion

This is a sad conclusion. People have inherited from the earliest days of their history a whole load of useless and even harmful ideas. Religion has wasted and destroyed so much human effort. How many people, for instance, have given their lives and all their strength to serve non-existent gods? How many people have been killed in religious wars or because they were suspected of witchcraft or heresy? Although the real causes of such wars were material interest, religious motivation made them even more cruel. 'Death to the heretics' has been a catchword in the history of religion. Today there are no religious wars, but animosity between different religions remains. Thus we must conclude that religion, far from uniting people, actually disunities them.

Finally, religion is a heavy financial burden on the shoulders of many people. To get the protection of supernatural forces a man will make sacrifices in the literal sense of the word; peasants will give away their last cow, fishermen their dog — their main treasure. Tradition and superstition have forced men to give away their last pennies, thinking that they will be rewarded for it. In the ancient East, slaves, peasants, and artisans, who lived on the lands of temples, worked all their lives fo the benefit of these temples and their personnel. In Europe, in the Middle Ages, almost half the serfs belonged to monasteries and were feeding lazy churchmen who did not work because they were serving God. Indian peasants today are still giving away their last penny on religious ceremonies and sacrficies. Russian peasants, in the past, had to pay for every church ceremony — from weddings to funerals. In capitalist countries this is so even today.

The Roots of Religion

Religion is a social phenomenon. It is not the product of abstract thinking on the part of 'primitive philsophers', as Edward Tylor thought, nor is it a 'disease of language' as Max Müller thought. Religion, throughout its history, has been closely connected with public life — from social psychology to economics.

This connection is two-fold: on the one hand, religion is connected with material life by being a distorted image of it; on the other, it has influenced both material factors and, indeed, all spheres of social life.

Let us look at the first aspect of this: it was proved by science long ago that religious beliefs are a distorted image of reality in the minds of people. Not only Marxists agree upon this, but many liberally minded bourgeois scientists as well. But to acknowledge this truth is not sufficient. It is far more difficult to get at the roots of religious beliefs. This is the main task of the history of religions, and is certainly a more important task than that of simply describing in detail religious beliefs and ceremonies. Such descriptions are only of use to future researchers; they do not explain the roots of such beliefs as they describe. The details of the different religious traditions, given in previous chapters (of his book) are of interest only when related to real life.

Against a Simplified Understanding of the Roots of Religion

One should not simplify the task of searching for the roots of religion: these are never lying close to the surface. Further, one should not think that each particular religious beliefs and ceremony is directly related to real life. The situation is far more complicated than that. One should never forget that every ideology is relatively independent and that religion is no exception. Religious ideas are very stable and can survive even under very changed conditions. They can also react on each other and become extremely complex. Individual parts of the whole sometimes cannot, on that account, be explained in isolation. We shall give some examples to prove this point. What, for example, is the origin of baptism by water in the Christian religion? One can say that the belief in the purifying power of water — washing away sin — is based on the real character of water to wash away dirt; but we cannot be wholly satisfied with such an explanation, since only Christians have this ritual of baptism by water. We must, therefore, look to the direct roots of this Christian custom. When we do this, we see that Christians borrowed this custom from a sect called the 'Mandey' in Asia Minor. This sect must have borrowed it, in turn, from the Babylonians, who had a cult of a water god. In this case, it should be noted, to get at the roots of a religious custom, we have to go through serveral historical links of a chain.

As a second example, let us take the case of juvenile circumcision as practised by Moslems and Jews and which plays the same role vis-a-vis those religions as does baptism by water in Christianity. There have been attempts to explain this custom from the point of view of hygiene, but to get at its real roots we must recognise that it also exists among very primitive peoples as well. There it is done, not at birth or at the age of seven, but much later during puberty; the explanation of this being that it was a way of retarding sexual life. This is the real root of the custom.

Our third and final example concerns the Christian myth of Mary, the Mother of Christ. One could explain this myth by the desire to present the 'Saviour of the World', as other than a mere human being — even to the extent of his being born differently to others. The very similar beliefs concerning miraculous births that we encounter in other religions — Egyptians, Indians and Chinese peoples had them — does not, however, explain the myth of a woman conceiving without having known a man. This particular myth originated, in fact, in ancient times in a period of group marriage, when people could not understand the male role in procreation.

From these examples one must draw the conclusion that it is not always easy to get at the real roots of certain religious beliefs and cutoms; sometimes it is, in fact, impossible to do so, not because there are not such roots, but because they are buried in the distant past. Very often it is the absence of facts, and the presence of unreliable information that prevents us getting at the real roots of certain religious beliefs. In such instances we must be satisfied with theory, or leave the question open. To give but one example: it is difficult to explain at present why certain people of Eastern Asia — Chinese, Mongolians and others — worship the sky, whilst the Japanese worship the sun. But our inability to find the roots of this difference means only that our present knowledge is insufficient. There are many similar cases. Specialists in the history of religion have much work ahead of them.

The Influence of Religion on Social Life

Let us examine another side of the problem of religion — the influence of religion on human life and, in particular, its influence on the material side of life. Here the influence is great, but it is always secondary. Bourgeois scholars have attempted to explain certain aspects of social life by reference to religious beliefs — Kühn, for instance, attempted to prove the religious roots of art, Fustel de Coulages the religious origin of marriage and the family, Frazer the religious origin of the state, Preuss the religious origin of primitive machinery and Marr of language itself. But today no-one can be found to defend these fantastic theories. Only burial customs are yet being considered the product of religious thinking, although these are no more likely to have arisen originally from religion than marriage or the state. One cannot look for the real roots of social institutions in religion, though we must not deny that these have been influenced by religion, and the study of such influences on the arts, and on morality, law, social life, economics, politics, etc., is the second most important task of the historian of religion. Here is a field still open to research, though certain firm conclusions can be drawn from the material mentioned above.

Religion and Art

Let us now examine the influence of religion on the arts, something which can be seen clearly in all stages of human development — from cave murals to modern religious paintings. Does this mean that art has religious roots? Certainly not! It is the business of art scholars to decide to what extent artists are influenced by religion, but what is already known from their works proves that religion had no positive influence on art; quite the opposite, in fact! Religion limits the imagination of the artist. To take a few examples: in caves, we see beautifully realistic murals of animals side by side with ugly and fantastic figures illustrative of some religious belief or other. We see the same thing in the art of ancient Egypt and in contemporary Australian Aboriginal art. In the art of ancient Egypt a truly artistic style is observed in such secular works of art as the bust of Nepher and others. In the course of the development of art in ancient Greece, to take another example, we see art gradually freeing itself from religious influences, and a similar development can be seen in the European Renaissance where religious motifs were used to describe ideas far from religion (in Rafael, Titian, Michelangelo, etc.). The same development can be seen in the development of European music — in Bach and in Mozart. The fact that for centuries artists, architects, musicians and poets were creating works of art on religious themes, and that churchmen used these to create an air of glamour around their religion, simply proves the power of the church. In our own time, however, the situation is changing and even in the capitalist world there are more artistis working outside of than in the sphere of religion and the church.

Religion, Morality and Law

With regard to the relationship of religion to law and morality we are confronted by a vast area for research. In the opinion of its supporters, religion provides the only possible basis of morality, an opinion which is shared even by some non-religious, liberally-minded, authors. There are yet others who share Plekhanov's opinion that religion and morality only became connected at a late stage in the development of human culture and that in the more primitive stages of social development that it had nothing to do with it. Both views are, however, incorrect. The roots of morality do not lie in religion, but in the real conditions of human beings as social animals, though even in primitive societies religion was utilised in the service of morality, thus sanctifying it. Taboos, for example, were used with such a purpose in mind. So in class society, morality and law became sanctified by religion in the interests of the ruling classes. Here, however, relations between morality and religion are more complex and become even more complex as class society develops. In India, China and Japan, the oppression of the lower classes was always sanctified by religion. The same is true in the ancient states of Asia

Minor. But in Classical Antiquity (Greece and Rome), slaves were made to submit by force alone and not by religion. Only with the advent of Christianity did submission to masters become a religious duty on the part of slaves. In the Middle Ages religious propaganda in support of obedience to the the rich and powerful was continued, though the ruling classes themselves often treated religious laws with contempt. As a result, the demands of the oppressed during their periodic revolts, were often expressed religiously – as a demand for the restoration of divine justice. In contemporary capitalist states the use of force is often justified by an appeal to religion and, according to Lenin, 'executioners' and 'priests' are both equally useful to the ruling classes. What I have said does not cover all that might be said about the relationship of religion to law and morality – for this sphere is not limited to class relations in that it also touches on private, family and on other relationships as well.

The 'Positive' Role of Religion

One may wonder why people did not see the uselessness and harmfulness of religion – particularly as they were oppressed for so long by it. Why, one may ask, despite the progress of science, are there still so many religious believers today? Perhaps this signifies that religion does indeed play a positive role in the history of mankind? This certainly is a question put by some bourgeois scholars. Many of them – and not all of them believers – have tried to prove that religion, despite all its drawbacks, does help people in their struggle for existence in that it helps organise them, gives them a morality and ideal goals in life. Is this really so? Was there any positive influence on the part of religion? Religious customs and beliefs did certainly satisfy some material needs of people and we gave (in our book) many examples of this. People certainly expected something from religion – whether it was the curing of the sick, or success in hunting and farming. But did they get what they wanted? Certainly not! The skills of industrious hunters, farmers and artisans produced the results which were mistakenly attributed to divine intervention. And in the sphere of morality, whilst people sometimes think that they act in accordance with the laws of god they are, in reality, obeying human laws without which society could not exist. One should not forget that religion sanctifies not only useful norms of behaviour, but that some of its laws are unfair and unwise.

The history of religions is full of examples of occasions when religious customs and laws, which originated in the needs of people, did not really answer to such needs and even worked against them. For example, most religions have dietary prohibitions. These originated as an attempt to regulate food consumption. But what was the result? – useless taboos, different ways of slaughtering animals (in Judaism) and fast-days (in Christianity and Islam).

Have such customs really any purpose? To take another example: burial ceremonies and the beliefs surrounding them. Some of these were dictated by common sense — such as isolating a decaying corpse, etc . . . but under the influence of religion many of these ceremonies became ugly and macabre — for instance, the sacrificing at funerals of animals and even of people. To give one final example: religious medicine. Witchcraft originated in primitive folk medicine and so was meant to fight illness; but later it developed into the useless slaughter of animals, trade in 'sacred relics' and cisits to sacred places (e.g., in Kiev The Pochaev monastery and in France, Lourdes) — yet very few people are healed and many feel deceived and are disillusioned.

The Variety of Beliefs and Customs

One of the most important observations that one can make when studying the history of religions concerns the variety of beliefs and ceremonies which one finds in different times and places. Such variety cannot be explained wholly in terms of the development of society and religion. This, of course, had something to do with it, but not all, for different people at the same stage of social development have had a variety of religions. What should be stressed most of all is that such variations do not only concern particular beliefs, but the style and spirit of a religion. When we speak of difference in the 'style' of a religion, we mean the attitude to life itself and to its various sides.

Let us take a few examples: Confucianism and Buddhism are two religions which originated at about the same time under similar conditions; more than that, both religions were at one time practised in the same country (China), yet Buddhism alone became a world religion and spread to different countries. One cannot imagine two more different religions — almost completely opposite in spirit! Confucianism sanctified the existing socio-political order, idealised feudal monarchy, and supported the tribal traditions under which the eldest in a family had all the rights. Further, Confucianism had strict rules and ceremonies, but without any 'mysticism'. Buddhism, however, rejected the pleasures of earthly life, saying that it is all lies and suffering, and proclaimed an ideal of passivity and non-existence (*nirvana*). This is what these two religions taught. But in reality the differences between these two — as practised — were not as great as their teachings would suggest. Indeed, some people even managed to combine adherence to both.

We can also compare religion in China with religion in India. The Chinese were very diligent in their performance of religious ceremonies, but their rituals were easy and simple. Indians, however, followed a life of asceticism, self-torture, mystical relations with god, and the common people were tied to a routine of religious taboos and had also to offer costly sacrifices. The Chinese were more practical — they gave the minimum to their religion, while Indians were wholly controlled by it.

Different religions have different attitudes to everyday life. The religion of ancient Greece originated about the same time as that of the Jews, but Greek religion did not concern itself with everyday life and its trifles; the Jewish religion, on the other hand, limited everyday life in a variety of ways – dress, food, and so on.

Different religions have different attitudes towards death and dead people. In ancient Egypt the cult of the dead was developed to its greatest extent. Egyptians took care of their own funerals well in advance of their death – arranging for mummification and, if well-to-do, building pyramids. On the other hand, the ancient Iranians considered dead bodies unclean and the bodies of the most honoured people were given to the wild beasts; the beasts; the kingdom of death was the kingdom of evil.

Different religions also treat human beings differently. Here, of course, we can see a direct connection with general social development. That is why the 'correlations' of 'collective' and 'individual' trends in religion change in favour of the second. This process began a long time ago in the earliest days of human history, so we cannot explain this trend by reference to one stage of development alone. There are also cases when this process was reversed: Buddhism, for instance, was highly individualistic in its earliest period and one could achieve *nirvana* only by relying on one's own strength, but later human personality came to be regarded as secondary and rituals became more important. In other religions relations between 'the collective' and 'the individual' are different. In ancient Oriental and in the religions of Classical Antiquity, the collective trend was obvious, but the Greeks had many individual sects. Judaism followed the 'collective' trend, though Hasidism, which matured inside it, had strong individual tendencies. The religions of Japan and China were purely 'collective': they were concerned only with the observation of ritual. Hinduism has both trends in equilibrium. Catholic Christianity has a strong 'collective' trend – as the salvation of mankind can only be found within the church – which takes care of all sins, but various Protestant churches shifted the emphasis towards the individual. Islam is 'collective', but the sect of the 'Sufis' emphasises individual communion with god.

Such a variety of religious customs and beliefs need not surprise us, since the history of two nations is never the same. Religion is influenced not only by the material life of a people, but also by politics, culture and other influences. One must study individual conditions in each country in order to understand the differences between the religious of India and China, Egypt and Iran, Greece and Rome, etc.

Whilst we are speaking about religious differences among differing peoples, we must not forget that, despite all this, the substance of religion is the same – it is a multilated image of the real world, it expresses human impotence, but in different ways and, just as the world itself is colourful and varied, we cannot expect religion to be less so.

Differences in Religious Influences on the Life of Peoples

Religion has always played a very important role in the history of mankind. But this has varied from place to place and from time to time. There are many examples in the history of mankind when religion played a more and sometimes less important role. Sometimes this role was extremely modest — the Romans are good examples; their sacrifices to their gods were very modest indeed.

Free-thinking Against Religion

Can we speak of a gradual diminishing of the role of religion? Yes, we can, although we cannot describe it as a continuous and even process, for there were ups and downs in this process. Whenever religion got weaker, freethinking throve. So one cannot describe the history of human development as an internal struggle of religion with freethinking.

We can see traces of freethinking in some primitive societies — in Polynesia, Africa and in America before Columbus, as well as in ancient Egypt and Mesopotamia. In ancient India and China a materialistic outlook on life became enshrined in philosophical systems, and in ancient Greece and Rome we find the cradle of European atheism. In these peoples there was no struggle between religion and freethinking as such, but sometimes atheists were expelled. In these cases the ruling classes felt instinctively that an attack on religion was an attack on their interests. But the struggle between religion and freethinking began in earnest in Europe at the end of the Middle Ages. It was connected with the anti-fedual movement. The Church was at the height of its power and would not stand for any opposition or criticism. But the new class of the bourgeoisie demanded more freedom for scientific research and experiment. This paved the way for the development of free-thinking, although until the eighteenth century only very few courageous people stood out against the Church in defence of such views — such were Bacon, Hobbes and Spinoza. The first major struggle between church ideologists and bourgeois freethinkers began in France in the eighteenth century. This marked the beginning of the French Revolution. After enormous struggles, and after a number of important discoveries in the natural sciences in the eighteenth and nineteenth centuries, religious ideology finally had to give up many of its positions, and although bourgeois atheism continued to struggle with religion, religions' chief enemy from the nineteenth century was proletarian socialist atheism. From this period onwards we observe a sudden drop in religious interest, despite some desperate attempts to secure the old positions.

One should not consider the decline in religion from the 19th century onwards to be the result of the development of freethinking, as something which occurred as the outcome of rational thought. Politics and economics played the major part in this decline. The economic position of the church was undermined and its political power weakened. This is particularly obvious in socialist countries where the church has lost its old position of power and prestige. This old position is, however, still maintained in capitalist countries, but even here we must take note of changes. Thus the church generally is declining in authority today.

To prove this point we do not need to refer to either anti-religious writers or Marxists. There is another proof. The most conservative of all European countries is England, and most conservative of all are the English middle-classes. The mirror of this class is English literature. If we compare the works of Charles Dickens (mid-nineteenth century) with John Galsworthy's novel *The Forsyte Saga*, we cannot but notice the difference. Dickens' characters are all religious people, speaking of god in both happiness and grief; but Galworthy's characters — all middle-class and conservative — never mention god. Indeed, they joke about religion and the church.

Today, even the clergy are acknowleding the fact that they have lost their hold over people — especially in the sphere of morality where the church was always strong. Evidence of this can be found, not only in English, but in French, German and American literature.

Thus the authority of the church is gradually being undermined even in the sphere of morality. Statistics prove the same point: people, and especially workers, in capitalist countries rarely today go to church, or read religious publications, whilst in socialist countries, most people have nothing whatever to do with religion. This proves that the masses have reached a high stage of consciousness — that their living and cultural standards are high. Religion, therefore, is doomed.

Appendix IV

BIBLIOGRAPHICAL SURVEY OF SOVIET WORK RELATING TO BUDDHISM, CHRISTIANITY, AND ISLAM

A. *Buddhism*

Buddhist studies in Russia go back to a time well before the Revolution of 1917. By the end of the nineteenth century and well into the early years of the present century, the names of scholars such as V.V. Vasel'ev, I.P. Minayev, O.O. Rozenberg and P.I. Shcherbatsky were internationally known in the community of learning. Some continued their work well into the period of Soviet power, establishing a tradition which — if at times severely interrrupted — has continued to the present day. The Indian historian D.N. Shastri said of Shcherbatsky's book *Buddhist Logic* (1930-1932) that it was 'the most eminent work on Buddhist philosophy to appear in the last 250 years' (quoted, A.N. Anikeyev, 1957: p. 134), and the same authors' study of *Buddhist Ethics* (1935) was equally well received. Today, however, his writings are hardly mentioned in Soviet writing on Buddhism — not a single one of his books, for instance, is mentioned in Tokarev's bibliography on Buddhism in *Religiya v istorii narodov mira* — yet he was, perhaps, the last student of Buddhism in the Soviet Union to be known to any great extent beyond its frontiers.

An aspect of contemporary Soviet study of Buddhism which had its origins well before the 1917 Revolution and which continues to this day is the collecting and editing of ancient Buddhist texts — particularly those appertaining to norther (*Mahayana*) Buddhism. The Imperial Russian Academy began in 1897 to publish the now well-known series *Bibliotheca Buddhica*, and the Academy of Sciences of the USSR has continued — albeit intermittently — to bring out further volumes in this series. In 1959 The Soviet Academy established a further series, *Pamyatniki literatury narodov Vostoka* (Literary Texts of the Peoples of the East). Prominent among recent editions to the earlier series, *Bibliotheca Buddhica*, have been V.N. Toporvo's edition of the *Dhammapada* (vol. XXXI, 1960) and A.I. Vostrikov's *Tibetskaya istoricheskaya literatura* (Tibetan Historical Literature) (vol. XXXII, 1962). Vostrikov had been a pupil of Shcherbatsky, as had E.E. Obermiller who, in 1963, brought out a facsimile edition of the now famous Sanskrit manuscript, the *Bhavanakrama*. This manuscript, which relates to the renewal of Buddhism in Tibet in the seventh century AD, and which was written by Kamalashina, was brought to the Soviet Union from Tibet in the 1930's by the famous Soviet Lamaist Agvan Dorshiev as a gift from the then Dalai Lama.

In 1965, V.S. and M.I. Vorob'ev-Desyatovsky brought out an edition of a previously unknown fragment of Khotan poetry — the so-called fragment 'E' — under the title *Skazaniye o Bkhadre* (Tales about Bhadra), as a volume in the series *Pamyatniki pis'mennosti vostoka*. Written by an unknown author in Khotan in the seventh to eighth centuries AD this poetical fragment expounded the fundamental tenets of Buddhism in a series of Buddhist stories, thus providing invaluable information about Buddhism in Khotan at that time.

Also in the 1960's L.N. Men'shikov brought out two important items relating to Chinese Buddhism in the series *Pamyatniki literatury narodov vostoka: Kitayskiye rukopisi iz Dun'khuana* (Chinese Manuscripts from Tunhuang) (1963) and *Bya'ven' o Veymotsze* (1963). In 1962, A.P. Barannikov and O.F. Volkov brought out an important edition of the *Girlyanda dzhatak, ili Skazaniye o podvigakh Boddhisattvy* (The Garland or Tales about the Exploits of the Boddhisattvas) of Ar'ya Shura in the same series.

The task of collecting, editing and publishing the works of northern Buddhism — and particularly works relating to the Buddhism of Tibet — continues. A major study of Tibetan iconography, for example, is in the process of being published by A.A. Terent'ev of the Leningrad Museum of the History of Religion and Atheism. (The same scholar has already published an important contribution to Jain scholarship: '*Nekotoryye osnovy dzhaynskoy mifologii*' (Some Principles of Jain Mythology) in *Problemy izucheniya i kritiki religiy vostoka: Sbornik trudov* (Problems in the Study and Criticism of the Religions of the East: a Collection of Work), Leningrad, 1979).

The advent of Soviet power, and with it ever-increasing pressure towards ideological conformity and towards a distinctive Marxist approach to religious studies, introduced new methods and new interests into Buddhist studies in the USSR. Whereas the older generation of Russian buddhologists had been interested in Buddhist metaphysics, logic and ethics — as a system of philosophy, if not as a religion — the newer generation of Soviet buddhologists — when not engaged in textual studies — turned increasingly to study the socio-economic and political situation at the time of Buddhism's inception and of Buddhism's role in it.

The politicisation of Buddhist studies in the Soviet Union began with Lenin, who is reported, towards the end of 1917, as having addressed C.F. Ol'denburg, one of the leading buddhologists of the day and a fervent supporter of the Bolshevik revolution, as follows:

As for your subject . . . although it seems far from our concerns, it is, in fact, quite close to them. Go to the masses, to the workers, and tell them about the history of India, about all the centuries of suffering of these unfortunate, enslaved masses, oppressed (now) by the English, and you will see how our proletariat responds. This will inspire you to new researches, to new work of the highest scientific importance. (Bonch-Bruyevich, 1966: pp. 32-33)

In August 1919, Ol'denburg, Shcherbatsky and others, organised a massive display in Petersburg of Buddhist exhibits, and leading buddhologists delivered lectures. Soviet as opposed to Russian study of Buddhism had begun. They were characterised from the beginning by a self-conscious attempt to 'scientifically' explain both the origin and the growth of Buddhism in Marxist terms: that is, in terms of the socio-economic forces which, so they held, underlay it.

Foremost among those who sought to explain Buddhism in this way was M. Reysner. In his book, *Ideologii Vostoka: Ocherki vostochnoy teokratii* (Ideologies of the East: Studies of Eastern Theocracy), published in 1927, Reysner argued that Buddhism arose during the transitionary period in Indian society between feudalism and the advent of commercial capitalism. He put forward the view that Buddhism was originally the ideology of young aristocrats who 'disgusted with the dissipation of their luxurious lives, turned their pessimism into a philosophical system and, renouncing the world, freely embraced moral precepts within the context of the twilight world of monasticism' (Reysner, 1927: p. 226). In particular, he argued, that original Buddhism 'was not a religion but a distinctive half-mystical, half-rationalistic system of philosophy which was distinguished by its atheistic character' (ibid., p. 219).

Reysner's views were first criticised and then abandoned by Soviet scholars as being the outcome of an inadequate analysis of the socio-economic and political circumstances in which Buddhism arose, although they were perpetuated for some time in that Reysner had put them forward in the article which he wrote on 'Buddhism' for the first edition of the *Bol'shaya sovetskaya entsiklopediya* (Great Soviet Encyclopaedia) (1932), and traces of them can be found in S. Ursynovich's book *Buddizm i lamaizm*, which was published in 1935. Ursynovich, however, offered a better analysis, in Soviet eyes, of the socio-economic situation out of which Buddhism arose by concentrating on the crisis among the 'slave-owners' of the sixth century BC in North India and on the failure of the caste system — a line of analysis which was continued by V.V. Struve, B.A. Turaev and P.K. Kokovtsev — scholars whose careers had begun well before the 1917 Revolution. Struve suggested a schema for writing the history of ancient Eastern societies which, in Soviet eyes, 'combined a Marxist analysis with the facts of the case' (Kochetov, 1967: p. 433). In particular he criticised previous views, such as those associated with Reysner, for their obsession with what he termed 'everlasting oriental feudalism'. Indian society of the sixth century BC was not 'feudal', he argued, but 'slave-owning'. He does not appear to have himself published his views, but the school which he founded included such noted Soviet scholars as A.P. Barannikov, G.G. Il'in, V.I. Avdiev, D.A. Suleykin, N.A. Sholpo, V.I. Kal'yanov, A.M. Osipov and V.S. Vorob'ev-Desyatovsky. Other works which such scholars drew on were G.F. Il'in's article *'Osnovnyye problemy rabstva v drevney Indii'* (Major Problems of Slavery in Ancient India) and G.M. Bongard-Levin's *'Nekotoryye osobennosti gosudarstvennogo ustroystva imperii Maur'ev (istochniki i problematika)* (Some Particular State Arrangements of the Empire of Maurya [Sources and Problematic]), published in a collection of work of the Higher Institute for the Study of the Peoples of Asia of the Academy of Sciences of the USSR and produced for the XXVI International Congress of Orientalists (*vostokovedy*) in 1963 and entitled *Istoriya i kul'tura drevney Indii* (History and Culture in Ancient India), Moscow, 1963.

In recent years Soviet scholars have moved somewhat away from the problem of the origin of Buddhism to discuss its 'ideological development'. The Soviet painter Rerikh who died in 1961, is held to have done important work on this topics, or at least to have inspired others to publication in this field. Many of Rerikh's disciplines are (or were) to be found in the various institutes of the USSR Academy of Sciences working on Buddhist themes; for example, G.M. Bongard-Levin, whose work we have mentioned,[1] O.F. Volkov, A.M. Pyatigorsky[2] — now working in exile at the School of Oriental and African Studies in London — M.I. Vorob'ev-Desyatovsky, whose work we have also mentioned, E.S. Semerkoy,[3] B.I. Bogoslovsky,[4] and E.I. Kychanov[5] in the Institute of the Peoples of Asia, G.G. Statanovich[6] and N. Zhukovsky[7] in the Institute of Ethnography and A.T. Yakimov[8] in the Institute of History. Some interesting work was also produced on Indian philosophy by Rerikh's pupil, I.M. Kutasov.[9]

Serious research work on Buddhism in Mongolia began in the post-war period with the publication of manuscripts from the national archives of the Mongolian Peoples' Republic. Thus S. Purebzhav was enabled to present a doctoral thesis on the Lamaist monk Gandan-Dkhun-khure at the Institute for the Study of Peoples of Asia in 1959.

In the 1960's Soviet scholars also began to study the contemporary situation of Buddhism in countries outwith the Soviet Union. Thus Yuri Kuznetsov in an article for the journal *Aziya i Afrika segodnya* entitled, *'Buddizm i politika'* (Buddhism and Politics), 1965, no. 6, looked at the political role of Buddhism in present day Japan, a theme also taken up by E.Y. Batalov in *'Buddizm "Dzen" i burzhuaznaya ideologiya'* (Buddhism, 'Zen' and Bourgeois Ideology), in *Filosofskiye problemy ateizma*, (Philosophical Problems of Atheism), Moscow, 1963.

Soviet study of Buddhism in the autonomous republic of Buryatiya — which Soviet 'scientific atheism' tends to distinguish from Buddhism itself and call 'Lamaism' — began, under the exigences of the imperative to propagate atheism there in the 1930's, with the establishment of a special secretariat for the propagation of atheism and the setting up of an antireligious museum under the auspices of the Buryat Academy of Sciences. Both, however, under the direction of A.I. Gerasimov, did valuable work in collecting and editing manuscript materials relating to Buddhism in Buryatiya. Much of this work was also inspired by B.D. Togmitov who, in 1932, had published his *Sovremennyy lamaizm v Buryatii i zadachi dal'neyshey bor'by s nim* (Contemporary Lamaism in Buryatiya and the Problem of the Ongoing Struggle with It). But the serious study of 'Lamaism' in the Soviet Union can really only be said to have begun in 1938, when the central Museum for the History of Religion and Atheism in Moscow sent N.A. Pupyshev to conduct field work in the monasteries of Buryatiya. Unfortunately, Pupyshev was killed in the 1941-45 war before he could publish the results of this work. After the war the Buryat Academy of Sciences continued to support research into Lamaism — though the 'working' monasteries had by that time been reduced, as today, to two — and in 1959 the state publishing house, under the editorship of G.N. Rumyantsev, began to publish works from the archives of the chief Lama, Laksan Gombaev — particularly works relating to Lamaism in the second half of the eighteenth century and the early part of the nineteenth century (G.N. Rumyantsev, *Arkhiv zasak-lamy Laksana Gombaeva*, Ulan-Ude, 1959).

As is the case with all study of religion in the Soviet Union, serious scholarship and sometimes crude anti-religious propaganda go hand in hand and the study of Buddhism is no exception. Thus much valuable material relating to Buddhism in Buryat must be distilled from what are overtly anti-Buddhist tracts. Such, for instance, is F.M. Shulunov's *Proiskhozhdeniye i reaktsionnaya sushchnost' lamaizma* (The Origin and Reactionary Essence of Lamaism) published in Ulan-Ude in 1950. Shulunov, in the course of this violently antagonistic study, presents many valuable descriptions of contemporary practices in the monasteris of Buryat. The same is true of A. Atarkhanov's article with the same title as Shulunov's book, published in 1952 in the anthology *Nekotoryye voprosy nauchnogo ateizma* (Some Problems of Scientific Atheism), Ulan-Ude, 1952. Other professional *antireligiozniki* who have published materials relating to Lamaism are: R.E. Rubaev,[10] S.A. Arutyunov[11] and K.M. Gerasimov.[12]

In line with a growing insistence in the post-1954 period of the study of religion and atheism in the USSR, that those engaged in combatting religion should be better informed as to the nature of what they were combatting, a number of valuable collections of materials relating to 'Lamaism' in Buryat were published. Thus, in 1965, there was published in Moscow the collected works of the great nineteenth century Russian Lamaist, Dorzh Banzarov, a collection of essays on the rites and ceremonies of Buddhism in Buryat. At the same time the *antireligiozniki* strove to make sense of some of the more esoteric rituals of Lamaism.[13] Foremost among these was K.M. Gerasimov, whose first publication *Materialy o dokhodakh datsanskikh kaznacheystv* had been published in 1955 as Volume XX of the series *Zapiski Bur.-Mong. NII kul'tury*. Between 1957 and 1964 he published two important monographs on various aspects of Lamaism in Buryatiya.[14] Both of these monographs were heavily ideologically orientated — and were particularly critical of the role of Lamaism in perpetuating the 'petty-bourgeois' nationalism of this area, often, as was claimed, with the support of outside influences.

Not only Buryatiya, but other areas of the Soviet Union where Buddhism still flourishes have attracted the attention of the professional *antireligiozhiki* — Kalmykiya and the Uryankhaysky district of the Tuvins autonomous republic in particular. Works of note in this area of study are Kh.B. Kanukov's *Buddolamaizm i ego posledstviya* (Buddho-Lamaism and its Legacy), Astrakhan, 1928; V.M. Iesuitov, *Ot Tuvy feodal'noy k Tuve sotsialisticheskoy* (From Feudalism to Socialism in Tuva), Kyzyl, 1956. Much remains to be done in these areas, however. Only one work so far, for instance, has explored the peculiarities of the religious beliefs and ceremonies of Buddhism in this area and that is M.Kh. Mannay-oola's *K voprosu o reaktsionnoy sushchnosti lamaizma* (On the Problem of the Reactionary Nature of Lamaism), published in Kyzyl in 1965.

One area of study which has been little researched as yet relates to the vast holdings of Buddhist manuscript and other materials in the museums of the USSR — particularly in the Hermitage Museum in Leningrad. Various projects have been started in this respect, but so far have borne little fruit, although N.V. D'yakonova published an interesting article, *'Buddiyskiye pamyatniki Dun'khuana'* (Buddhist monuments from Tunhuanng), in the *Trudy otdela vostoka Gosudarstvennogo Ermitazha* (Work of the Department of the East in the State Hermitage), vol. 4, 1947, pp. 445-470, and we should also mention: S.M. Zuber (Kochetova), *'Muzykal'niye instrumenty v Khara-Khoto'*, ibid., vol. III, 1940, pp. 325-338 and *'Bozhestva svetil v zhivopisi Khara-Khoto'*, ibid., vol. IV, 1947, pp. 471-502; K.V. Trever, *Pamyatniki greko-baktriyskogo iskusstva* (Monuments of Greco-Bactrian Art), Moscow, 1940.

Apart from the Hermitage collections many other state museums in the Soviet Union have important holdings relating to Buddhism, and in the 1920's some attempt was made to catalogue them, though work in this respect has been sadly neglected and it is only today that Soviet Buddhologists are beginning to explore the vast riches which some of these museums — including the Museum of the History of Religion and Atheism in Leningrad — contain. For early work on these collections see: B.A. Kuftin's *Kratkiy*

*obzor panteona severnogo buddizma i lamaizma v svyazi s istoriey po kollek-
tsii, vystavlennoy v Tsentral'nom muzee narodovedeniya* (A Short Survey of
the Pantheon of Northern Buddhism and Lamaism and its connection with
history in the Collections, exhibited in the Central Museums of Ethnology),
Moscow, 1927; A. Strelkov, *Vystavka kollektsii po lamaizmu: Kratkiy pute-
voditel'. Muzey vostochnikh kul'tur* (Collections of Exhibits on Lamaism: A
Short Guide to the Museums of Eastern Culture), Moscow, 1927.

Finally, we must mention work related to the study of Buddhism conducted by art historians. Two works are particularly worthy of mention:
O.N. Glykhareva and B.P. Denike, *Kratkaya istoriya iskusstva Kitaya* (A
Short History of Art in China), Moscow-Leningrad, 1948 and N.A. Vino-
gradova, *Iskusstvo srednevekovogo Kitaya* (The Art of Medieval China)
Moscow, 1962. The connection of art with religious ideology in Buddhism is
discussed in V.N. Toporov's article '*K rekonstruktsii nekotorykh mifologi-
cheskikh predstavleniy (na materialakh buddiyskogo izobrazitel'nogo
iskusstva)'* (Towards the Reconstruction of Some Mythological Representations (Based on Materials of Buddhist Figurative Art)), *Narody Azii i Afrikii*,
1964, no. 3, pp. 101-110.

In all, Soviet Buddhist studies today, together with studies (as we shall see)
into Christian religious sectarianism, represent perhaps the healthiest (and
most scholarly) aspect of Soviet study of religion.

B. *Christianity*

Three areas of Christian religion have been of particular concern to Soviet
historians and students of religion: the early history of Christianity, the
history of Russian Orthodoxy and the history of Russian sectarianism. As
Soviet study of the history of the Russian Church is inextricably bound up
with Soviet History of Russia itself, I shall, unfortunately, have to ignore it
here, as to treat it would take us far from our central concerns.

The early history of Christianity has and has continued to exercise a
peculiar fascination for Soviet historians of religion, for, with Engels, they
believe that a secular account of the rise of the Christian religion is an
essential prerequisite to a successful campaign against its continuing influence
in the present.

Before the 1905 revolution, Russian historians were hampered in their
research into the history of the Christian religion, and particularly in their
research into its early history, by the consorship then obtaining in the
country which forbade the publication of anything which might be though to
cast doubt on the account of the rise and development of Christianity promulgated by the Russian Orthodox Church. After 1905, with the easing of
the censorship, and after the publication in 1908 of N.A. Morozov's
Otkroveniye v groze i bure (Revelation in Storm and Tempest), the Russian

intelligentsia at last became familiar with the opinions then being canvassed by liberal German theologians and early Marxist critics of religion, in particular, seized upon these opinions and utilised them in their criticism of Orthodox accounts of the beginnings of the Christian religion. Plekhanov, for example, made liberal use of the opinions of Otto Pfeiderer in his own writings on this topic (Plekhanov, *Soch.;* vol. XVII, pp. 314-320). After the revolution of 1917 Soviet historians of religion and anti-religious propagandists returned to the early history of Christianity and Lunacharsky, Skvortsov-Stepanov, N.M. Nikol'sky, R.Y. Vipper, and S.A. Zhebelev, all wrote extensively on it during the early years of Soviet power. But from espousing the opinions of the liberal German theologians, to the effect that Jesus was simply 'the good carpenter of Nazareth' who was crucified for political sedition, Soviet writers soon moved to espouse the very different view that Jesus had, in fact, never existed, that he was a myth.

This view, which had originally been put forward by the German, Arthur Drews, in his book *Die Christusmythe* (1909) was taken up by Soviet writers on the beginnings of Christianity largely on account of Lenin's apparent acceptance of it as an established fact in the course of his criticism of some of Drew's other opinions in his article 'On Militant Materialism' (*LCW:* vol. 33; p. 231), and this opinion dominated Soviet accounts of the rise of Christianity until well into the post-war period when, although not officially discarded (cf. KSNA, 1964: pp. 590-591), the question of the historicity or otherwise of Jesus was superceded by a more Marxist interest in the general history of early Christianity and by a return to the explanation of it offered by Engels in his *On the Early History of Christianity* – an explanation which is now the standard explanation in Soviet writing on this topic. It was this explanation which Academician Zhukov put forward and which we discussed in Section 5.2 of our study. But although the existence of Jesus is now generally accepted in Soviet study of the origin of Christianity, stress is still laid on the mythological prototypes of the picture of Jesus as it emerged in the developing Christian tradition, and on the debt owed by Christianity to movements in Judaism, Egypt and the Greco-Roman world of the first century BC.

The beginning of this more serious Marxist concern with the origins of Christianity is traced by Soviet scholars themselves to the discussion about the 'slave-owning' societies of antiquity which occurred in the Soviet Union following upon the publication in 1929 of Lenin's lecture 'On the State' (Lentsman, 1967: pp. 278-279). In this lecturer Lenin raised a number of questions about the 'slave-owning' character of ancient societies, at a time when most scholars were looking at what they termed the 'modernisation' of the ancient world, and were searching for the beginnings of capitalist relations in it. Renewed interest in the socio-economic and political structure of the world in which Christianity arose, and new factual material relating to the social character of early Christianity, gave impetus to the construction of the peculiarly Marxist-Leninist understanding of the rise of Christianity.

The foremost scholar in this enterprise was the classicist and historian of Judaism, A.B. Ranovich. His paper on the documentary evidence for the period of the growth of early Christianity in the Soviet Academy's publication *Istochniki po izucheniyu sotsial'nikh korney khristianstva* (Sources for the Study of the Social Roots of Christianity), (1933) and his *Pervoistochniki po istorii rannego khristianstva: Materialy i dokumenty* (Primary sources for the History of Early Christianity: Materials and Documents), published in the same year, together with his *Antichnyye kritiki khristianstva: fragmenty iz Lukiana, Tsel'sa, Porfiriya i dr.* (The Ancient Criticism of Christianity: Fragments from Lucian, Celsus, Porphiry and Others), which appeared in 1935, provided Soviet historians of early Christianity with the materials to go about their task. His final work, *O rannem khristianstve* (On Early Christianity), published in 1959, is still regarded in the Soviet Union as the major Soviet study of this important topic. In all his works Ranovich underlined the necessity of establishing that which was unique to Christianity and which set it apart from the related cultures of the day. There were three things specific to Christianity, he held, which contributed to its success: (1) its teaching about the incarnation of the Godhead in man; (2) the social richness (*nasyshchennost'*) of its eschatology; and (3) the international character of its preaching.

In 1934 the Soviet scholar, N. Rumyantsev, under the influence of Ranovich, published a study of the *Book of Revelation* with the title, *Apokalipsis – Otkroveniye Ionna: yego proiskhozhdeniye i klassovaya rol'* (The Apocalypse – The Revelation of John: Its Origin and Class Role). Rumyantsev had, in the 1920's, been one of the leading exponents of the 'mythological' school, as the titles of his publications during this period suggest – *Mifologicheskaya shkola po voprosu o sushchestvovanii Khrista* (The Mythological School on the Question of the Essence of Christ) (1926) and *Iosif Flaviy ob Iisuse i Ioanne Krestitele* (Joseph Flavious on Jesus and John Chrestitus) (1929). He had also, in *Smert' i voskreseniye spasitelya: Issledovaniye iz oblasti sravnitel'noy mifologii* (The Death and Resurrection of the Saviour: Researches in Comparative Mythology) (1925), and in *Dokhristianskiy Khristos* (The Pre-Christian Christ) (1926), drawn attention to the pagan elements in the cult which grew up around 'Christ'. Now, however, in 1934, in his study of *The Apocalypse,* and in the wake of the search for a more specifically Marxist explanation of the rise of Christianity, Rumyantsev, whilst not explicityly renouncing his earlier opinions, offered an analysis of early Christianity which stressed, not its derivation from ancient mythology, but its intrinsic relationship to revolutionary, messianic elements in contemporary Judaism – something which allowed him to see early

Christianity as a disguised protest against social and political oppression — an interpretation which has continued to dominate Soviet writing on the origins of Christianity, as we have seen, to the present day.

In the immediate post-war period Soviet scholars again returned to the question of the origin of Christianity and two important monographs were published by Academician R.Y. Vipper: *Vosniknoveniya khristianskoy literatury* (The Beginnings of Christian Literature) (1946) and *Rim i khristianstvo* (Rome and Christianity) (1954). In the former of these works Vipper analysed the various New Testament and Apocryphal writings. Here Vipper concentrated his attention not on the origin of the Christian religion as such, but on the provenance of Christian writings, and he put forward the hypothesis that the *Book of Revelation* consisted of two different parts. On the basis of a difference in the usage of the terms 'lamb' (*agnets*) and 'Christ' (*Khristos*), Vipper came to the conclusion that the central part of *Revelation* must be dated before the outbreak of the Jewish War of 70 AD, but that the opening and conclusion came from a much later time towards the close of the first century AD. In his second work, *Rim i Khristianstvo* he suggested that Christian writings were heavily influenced by contemporary Greco-Roman writings, and thus even later dates were assigned to the major writings of the New Testament, than in his earlier work.

As we would expect Soviet authors seized on the publication in the post-war period of the Qumran and Nag Hammadi (Henoboskion) discoveries as revealing, in their opinion, the ideological proximity of the Qumran and Gnostic sects to early Christianity. In particular Soviet scholars concentrated their attention on two questions: (1) the links between these sects and the Christians; 'Was', they asked, 'the Qumran sect the direct forebear of original Christianity?' Might, in fact, the Qumran sect actually have been an early Christian sect? and (2) Did community property exist in early Christianity, as it has been established that it did among the sect at Qumran? Both questions were regarded as having great significance for the history of the origin and early social character of Christianity.

Despite the wish of some investigators — including Marxists such as Donini[15] — to show that the sect at Qumran and the Christians were virtually the same, most Soviet scholars are inclined to think that the sect at Qumran was only one among other direct predecessors of Christianity and that only some features were held in common by the two.[16] Soviet scholars are also today inclined to minimise the resemblance between the two sects over the holding of all property in common.

The study of the Nag Hammadi Gnostic writings also stimulated new research into the early history of Christianity in the Soviet Union — researches which sought to build on, but go beyond, the work done in the 1920's and 1930's. The work of Lentsman, Kovalyov, Kublanov, Sventsitsky and Kazhdan is important in this respect. Lentsman, for instance, in a book published in 1958 entitled *Proiskhozhdeniye khristianstva,* after a survey of all the available sources, sought to re-date the New Testament writings, taking up a position between the earlier viewpoints of Ranovich and Vipper. Only by the end of the second century, he argues, can we discern the canon of Christian Scripture emerging as we have it today. Lentsman also published two other important articles: *'Kak utverzhdalas' svyatost' Novogo zaveta* (How the New Testament became Sacred), *NiR,* 1962, no. 8, and *'Bylo li rannee khristianstvo kommunisticheskim?* (Was Early Christianity Communist?), *NiR,* 1963, no. 7. These articles describe the long process of establishing a canon of the New Testament writings and discuss the presence of community property in early Christianity. Kovalyov is, however, the most important post-war writer on early Christianity, and in a book published in 1964, entitled *Osnovnyye voprosy proiskhozhdeniya khristiantstva* (Basic Problems of Early Christianity), Moscow, 1964, he posed a number of important questions for Soviet historians of early Christianity. He claimed, for instance, that the question of the historicity of Jesus, although still a matter of dispute among Soviet historians, did not belong among basic Marxist historiographical questions relating to early Christianity, and he also emphasised the danger of a total denial of the historicity of all early Christian leaders. Unfortunately, Kovalyov did not live to finish his projected two volume study of Early Christianity, but two chapters from it summarising the sources for such a work and an extended historiographical essay survived and are highly regarded by contemporary scholars (Lentsman, 1967: p. 285). Kovalyov, like Ranovich, dates the change in the social base of early Christianity to the mid-second century and connects it with the emergence of a clergy and the growth in the number of wealthy Christians. A small work of Kublanov's *Iisus Khristos – bog, chelovek, mif?* (Jesus Christ – God, Man, Myth?), Moscow, 1964, looks at one aspect of what, even in the Soviet Union, has now become something of a hoary question. Kublanov's view is that a compromise must be reached in which the historicity of Jesus is not denied, but in which it recognised that mythological accretions surrounded the historical figure from a very early date. In 1965 Sventsitsky produced a study of the Apocryphal Gospels entitled, *Zapreshchennyye evangeliya* (Forbidden Gospels) in which he divided the Apocryphal Gospels in two groups: Judeo-Christian and Gnostic. The former he considered earlier than the New Testament writings and the latter much later. Lentsman, whilst approving Sventsitsky's use of foreign material not used previously in Soviet study, rejects, for the lack of clear evidence, his view that the Judeo-Christian gospels were earlier than the canonical gospels. He himself dates both to about the same time. The Ebionite sects, he argues, had existed a long time and their gospels – which he takes the Judeo-Christian Apocryphal writings to be — could have easily emerged at about the same time as the synopitc gospels. In any case, he says, it is too early to come to firm conclusions on the development of 'the gospel myth'.

Reviewing Soviet work on the problem of early Christianity in the period since the Revolution of 1917, Lentsman, argued, in 1967, that whilst discussion about the historicity of Jesus should now be abandoned, socio-economic research into the conditions surrounding the rise of Christianity must continue, and that whilst questions regarding the dating of the writings of early Christianity was an important one, the major task ahead lay in producing major Marxist studies of the rise of early Christianity. Lentsman's hope remains, as yet, unfulfilled (Lentsman, 1967: p. 286).

The second area of the study of the Christian religion where Soviet scholars have been particularly active is in the study of Russian sectarianism — past and present, indigenous and imported. Once again — as in the study of early Christianity — the inspiration for such study is traced back to Lenin, who as early as the 1890's, published a number of pamphlets setting forth the socio-political significance of religious sectarianism in the struggle of democratic forces in Russia (cf. Klibanov, 1967: p. 349). These pamphlets, however, were primarily tactical, in that their main objective was to win sectarian support for the Bolshevik cause. Plekhanov, Bonch-Bruyevich and Pokrovsky wrote in a similar vein.

Here, as in all Soviet study of religion, theoretical and 'concrete' study is combined with the exigencies of Party policy. The study of religious sectarianism — 'a product of the social contradictions of the Russia of capitalists and landlords', as Klibanov maintains — began when sectarianism was seen to be assuming a new role as a 'survival' of the capitalist period. The task, therefore, as it presented itself to Soviet scholars was, according to Klibanov, that of

. . . studying the factors tending to maintain the existence of sectarianism under the new social conditions, the influence upon sectarianism of the separation of church from state and school from church, the relationships between sectarianism and Russian Orthodoxy, the distinctive characteristics of the ideology and tactics of particular sects under conditions of class struggle, the attitude of the sects and of various strata within them toward the Soviet government, and the international connections of sectarianism and other such problems. (Klibanov, 1967: p. 350)

Such study was needed for the Party to formulate — on a sound basis — its policy towards the sects. Thus did the study of religious sectarianism come into being. During the period from the October Revolution to an important conference of the Party on anti-religious propaganda which took place in 1926, when certain 'theses' regarding the approach to be taken towards sectarians were adopted, the fundamental theoretical principles of Marxist research came into being. Though the number of publications during this period is small — including articles in the violently partisan newspaper *Bezbozhnik* (The Godless), they number no more than thirty — what was published was, and remains, valuable evidence as to the state of religious sectarianism in the Soviet Union at the time. For Soviet scholars these early studies, of which the most important were by V.D. Bonch-Bruyevitch[17] and P.A. Krasikov,[18] posed not only political but important methodological questions as well. Politically, they sought to expose the political position of the upper strata of sectarian movements, the class content of their ideological programmes, and their role in aiding and abetting counter-revolution. Methodologically, these early students of Russian sectarianism tried to consider all aspects of the social differentiation and heterogeneity of religious sectarianism. They recognised the 'internal contradictions' within sects and the many and varied differences of opinion among sectarians themselves as to the place which they should occupy in society and in their attitude to Soviet power. These differences of opinion, argues a later writer, had in fact been inherent in sectarianism since its inception. He writes:

As is well known, religious sectarianism was a form of social movement which arose and developed in the course of the history of the class struggle of the working masses, particularly of the peasantry, against the exploitation of serfdom and latterly against the vestiges of serfdom in the economic and socio-political structure of Tsarist Russia. Religious in form only, but ranking in character and significance with the democratic movements, religious sectarianism embodied, in its successive forms, the various stages in the historical development of the peasantry, its social stratification and the diverse stages of the pauperisation of the countryside, on the one hand and, on the other, the appearance, within the peasantry of a capitalist class. A differentiated approach to religious sectarianism involved distinguishing, within this large religious and social movement, between groups of democratic and groups of bourgeois historical origin. It also involved taking account, within each group, of the contradictions between the interests of democratic and bourgeois elements. (Klibanov, 1967: pp. 351-352)

Establishing this as a methodological principle was, in Klibanov's opinion, the achievement of the Soviet students of religious sectarianism in the 1920's. Bonch-Bruyevich, in particular, did much to put across to the public and to the Soviet authorities the fact that sectarianism were not unilaterally opposed to Soviet power, as did A.T. Lukachevsky, who in 1925 delivered a lecture — *'Sektanstvo prezhde i teper'* (Sectarianism in the Past and Today) — which was to have considerable influence on the future study of this important aspect of religion in Russia. His was the first Soviet text which sought to explore the socio-economic roots of religious sectarianism in Tsarist Russia, its role in the past and its role under Soviet conditions. Lukachevsky also attempted the first Soviet classification of sects. He was also among the first Soviet scholars to attempt to explore the history of the sects and to point out the different ideological and socio-political roles which they had played at different stages of their development. His lecture was further characterised by a principled, scholarly approach which was not to become widespread in Soviet study of religious sectarianism until well into the post-war period. In particular he sought to do away with the traditional names of the indigenous Russian sects on the grounds that they were abusive of the beliefs which the sects actually held. He wrote:

We must now agree on names for the sects. Such designations as *Khlysty, Shtundisty, Molokane* are in common use. There are sects of 'Leapers' (*Skakuny*), 'Jumpers' (*Pryguny*) etc. '*Khlysty*' is an abusive word. It was invented by the clergy of the Orthodox Church. The same is true of the word '*Shtundisty*'. This word was also given in ridicule . . . and *Skakuny, Pryguny* — all these names were invented for ridicule by the Orthodox clergy. (Lukachevsky, 1925: p. 41)

During the period of the New Economic Policy (1921-1928) a concerted attempt was made to draw many of the sects, and particularly the indigenous Russian sects, such as the Dukhobors and the Molokans — who had a great deal of experience in running peasant communes — into the development of agriculture. This provided an opportunity for Soviet sociologists of religion to engage in 'concrete' research into an important aspect of sectarian life. The diversity of sectarian currents, the internal contradictions within sectarianism, which were, so Soviet sociologists maintained, in the final analysis class contradictions, were found to complicate the situation in sectarian production units, to influence the relationship between these sectarian bodies and the general population, and were often a source of misunderstanding between the sectarian bodies involved and Soviet agencies. Thus, for example, among Baptists, Evangelical Christians and Adventists, it was found that the idea of forming labour co-operatives was not generally popular, and also that the leaders of those sects — particularly within the Dukhobor and Molokan communities — whose rank and file members responded eagerly to the opportunities offered to participate in building a new life, understood perfectly well that this involvement would eventually undermine sectarianism as a religious current (so Klibanov, 1967: p. 359).

The problem of involving sectarians in participation in the reconstruction of agriculture was studied by a number of Soviet sociologists and in particular by F.M. Putintsev and I. Morozov. Putintsev's study entitled *Kabal'noye bratstvo sektantov* (The One-sided Brotherhood of the Sects), Moscow, 1931, was the less scholarly of the two and was based not on first-hand experience but on the uncritical acceptance of press and journal reports. Morozov's study *Sektantskiye kolkhozy* (The Collective Farms of the Sects), Moscow, 1931, is also regarded by contemporary sociologists as being heavily biased against the sects. Careful study of the lives and habits of the sectarian communes showed that they were not identical either in the character of their organisation of work and daily life, in degree of economic success, or in overall viability (Klibanov, op. cit., p. 360). The negative aspects of sectarian communes — emphasised by both Putintsev and Morozov — were: their religious self-isolation; their accessibility to capitalist and kulak elements among the sectarians themselves; a tendency to keep all jointly produced products for their own exclusive use; the organised boycotting of military service in a number of communes; and the undue influence exercised upon communes by the central agencies of given sects and by the United Council of Religious Communities and Groups, an influence which was largely anti-Soviet. These negative aspects — of which much was made in the popular press of the day — did much to prejudice the Soviet authorities against them, and a broad discussion of their role in the agricultural enterprise was begun with the publication in *Pravda* in May 1924 of M.I. Kalinin's report *'O rabote v derevne'* (On Work in the Countryside), in which the activities of the sectarian communes was particularly referred to (article 13). In the ensuing discussion both Skvortsev-Stepanov and Bonch-Bruyevich emphasised the need to differentiate between sects, and between the different social strata within them. Dubovsky made the point that many sectarians were now actively seeking 'enlightenment' and were modernising their outlook, and S. Mitin that 'for poor peasants sectarianism was often a transitional form between the church and atheism and for the kulaks it is a new and stable form of religion — a transition from feudal to bourgeois (Protestant) religion — and so a progressive force (*Pravda*, May 3, 5, 7 and 8, 1924). The one firm decision that emerged from this discussion was to intensify anti-religious propaganda among sectarians, a decision that was confirmed at the XIII Congress of the Russian Communist Party (Bolshevik) in August 1924 (*KPSS v rezolyutsiyakh* I, p. 858).

As a consequence of this resolution a beginning was made in concrete sociological research into religious sectarianism. It was conducted along the lines of the study of the class composition of the elite and of the rank-and-file of the sectarian movements, the territorial distribution of sectarian groups, ideological differences between and within groups, and the relationships of sectarian groups to each other. This work was conducted in Omsk, Irkutsk,

Akmolinsk, in the Far Eastern Territories, in Voronezh, Tver and in the Ukraine. For this project whole armies of research workers were trained, among them F.M. Putintsev, whose studies of religious sectarianism dominated Soviet study until the post-war period[19] when A.I. Klibanov rapidly established himself as the leading authority in this field. The results of this research were summed up at a Party conference organised by the Department of Agitation and Propaganda of the Central Committee of the CPSU in April 27-30, 1926, at which various 'theses' were adopted. These dealt with the questions of the size and social makeup of sectarianism, its growth and the reasons for it, and with 'incorrect' approaches to sectarians made by over-enthusiastic *Antireligiozniks*. The 'theses' pointed out that 'quantitatively, quite a number of sects are mass organisations, numbering millions of members', and that 'sectarianism is most prevalent in areas with abundance of land (the Ukraine, Siberia, the Volga, the Caucasus, and the 'black earth' agricultural regions)'. In terms of social composition the research pursued was held to have established that sectarianism was a petty-bourgeois, primarily peasant, movement in which poor peasants predominated 'only in those districts where the number of middle peasants in the countryside did not increase sufficiently during the Revolution'. It was noted that 'capitalist and kulak elements were in a minority both in rural and urban sectarian communities' but that 'nevertheless were the leaders for all practical purposes'. The 'theses' spelt out in concrete terms the fact that there had been no growth observed in the followers of either the Old Believers, the Molokans, the Dukhobors or the Skoptsy, though there had been growth in Tolstoyism and Adventism — although of insignificant proportions. The Baptists and Evangelical Christians revealed the greatest and most widespread growth.

The reasons given in the 'theses' for the growth of sectarianism during the period of 'War Communism' was the 'neutralist mood' among the peasants. The sectarian religious ideological explanation and justification was held to provide a basis for this neutral mood: 'Thou shalt not kill', 'All men are brothers' and so forth. In the period of the transition to the New Economic Policy, it was held that 'the growth of sectarianism was intensified among the middle peasants precisely in those areas where the economic position of the kulaks became more stable, and the kulak succeeded in gaining considerable influence upon . . . the middle peasantry (in the Kuban' and in the Ukraine). In some places (for example, in Smolensk and in Belorussiya generally), the growth of sectarianism among the middle peasants was based on their insufficiently stable economic position'.

The reasons that led representatives of the rural poor to sectarianism were the most distinctive. The 'theses' stated that 'in Siberia, where the poor did not receive sufficient additional land, where the NEP put an end to their opportunity to use the kulak's equipment, and where, in the first years of the NEP, much dissatisfaction with the NEP was to be seen among the poor, sectarianism grew among the poor during these first years of the NEP'. The text of the 1926 'theses' can be found in *Kommunisticheskoye prosvesh- cheniye*, 1926, no. 5.

Reading through the analysis of religious sectarianism contained in the 'Theses' of the 1926 conference, one is struck by the careful attention devoted to individual factors making for sectarianism — a fact of considerable methodological importance for later Soviet study, particularly in the post-war years. This is important because it goes beyond the mere listing of general causes, however 'concretely' these may have been characterised from the historical or socio-political stanpoint. Klibanov was to use this as one of his major methodological principles in his work on sectarianism to which we shall be referring.

As important, perhaps, as the positive analysis of sectarianism contained in the '1926 Theses' were the harmful trends which they pointed out among much anti-religious agitation. Two in particular were singled out for 'correction': the tendency to regard sectarianism as an integrated and revolutionary whole — thus glossing over class differentiation and class struggle among the sectarians, leading to a too idealised picture of their revolutionary potential: secondly, the tendency to classify all sectarians as being in the camp of capitalist and kulak counter-revolution. Both views grossly oversimplifed the actual 'concrete' situation.

The 1926 conference also discussed the attitude to be taken to the pre-revolutionary history of religious sectarianism and reached a concensus as to the attitude to be taken toward the methodological principles of the pre-revolutionary study of sectarianism.

Thus Putintsev, in a follow-up article to the 1926 conference, wrote:

The techniques of categorisation employed by the priesthood were theological ones — based on dogma, rituals and worship — and thus concealed political forms of classification of the sectarian movement. For example, there were classifications of sectarianism into Eastern and Western, rationalistic and mystical, ritualistic and non-ritualistic . . . etc.'

(And upon these distinctions, it should be pointed out, certain far-reaching political decisions were often taken: e.g., that 'Western' type sects were in the pay of German espionage). Putintsev pointed to the failure of the system of measures adopted in the past by the autocracy and the church to deal with sectarians in terms of such a system of classification. Such a system ignored, he claimed, the 'socio-political and the socio-economic conditions under whose influences sects had developed 'spontaneously', often without any organisers or founders (Putintsev, *Kommunisticheskoye prosveshcheniye*,

1926, no. 5, pp. 30-40). Pre-Revolutionary works on sectarianism had also tended, claimed Putintsev, to examine the phenomenon of sectarianism exclusively in terms of ideas, and in terms of a conflict between 'theological' and 'metaphysical' truths in which authoritative ecclesiastical judgement had provided the final world. Thus was the real significance of the sects obscured.

The methodological principles underlying the 'theses' of the 1926 Conference not only represent, in Soviet eyes, (and no doubt in other eyes too) a methodological advance on pre-Revolutionary study, but they were to become the established way of proceeding in all subsequent study of this topic.

The next phase in Soviet study of religious sectarianism runs from 1927-1936, and is characterised by an expansion of the range of scholarly interests and the development of the structure of the field itself. During this period many important monographs were produced on the history and present condition of particular sects, as well as general works embracing the most recent period of history, the development of methods for carrying out concrete research into sectarianism, and towards the organsiation of investigations of sectarianism in particular locales. All were based on the principles laid down in the 1926 'theses' The number of scholars working in this area of religious study also increased dramatically.

Foremost amongst the scholars working in the field of the study of religious sectarianism at this time was Professor N.M. Matorin of Leningrad University. At the University of Leningrad he organised an ongoing seminar on religious sectarianism, and among the works produced by its members must be mentioned are N.N. Volkov's study of the Skoptsy sect, *Sekta skoptsov*, Leningrad, 1930-1931; A.I. Klibanov's study of the Menonites, *Mennonity*, Moscow and Leningrad, 1931; the collective work, *Po ochagam sektantskogo mrakobesiya* (Foci of Sectarian Obscurantism), Moscow and Leningrad, 1931 — written on the basis of data collected by N.N. Volkov, V. Druzhinin and others in the Central Black-Soil region; the pamphlets by Druzhinin on the Dukhobors, *Dukhobory*, Leningrad, 1930 and the Molokans, *Molokane*, Leningrad, 1930; the same author's *Klassovoye litso sovremennogo sektantstva* (The Class Nature of Sectarianism), Leningrad, 1931; and I.A. Klibanov's study *Adventisty* (The Adventists), Leningrad, 1931.

The same period also saw the publication of F.M. Putintsev's *Dukhobory* (The Dukhobors), Moscow, 1928; A. Yatsev's *Sekta evangel'skikh khristian* (The Sect of the Evangelical Christians), Moscow, 1928; G. Frizen's *Mennonity* (The Mennonites), Moscow, 1930; A. Reinmarus' *Adventisty* (The Adventists), Moscow, 1930; B. Tikhomirov's *Baptizm i yego politicheskaya rol'* (Baptism and its Political Role), Moscow, 1929; and I. Morozov's *Molokane* (The Molokans), Moscow and Leningrad, 1931.

The publication of these works finally resolved the question of the differentiated nature of the sects, both as regards ideology and practice. What they had in common was the recourse to primary sources – sectarian periodical publication and very occasionally access to the archives of the sects themselves. All devoted major attention – as a methodological principle – to the socio-political role of sectarianism, to the phenomenon of social stratification within sects, and to the inherent class-struggle which Soviet authors saw in sectarianism, albeit in a religious guise. But these works also contained accounts of the teachings and practices of the sects which have not lost their value even today.

On the basis of the study of individual sects, a number of authors sought to discuss the most significant features of sectarianism as such, its social roots, ideology and tactics and its socio-political role at various points in history. Such, for instance, was Putintsev's study *Politicheskaya rol' sektantstva* (The Political Role of Sectarianism), Moscow, 1928, and B. Kandidov's *Sektantstvo i mirovaya voyna* (Sectarianism and the World War), Moscow, 1930. The former of these studies was the more significant. In it Putintsev offered an analysis of the political positions of the various sects over a long period of Russia's recent history, particularly the period of Russia's three Revolutions; he claimed to have revealed the connection between the leaders of the sectarians and the interests of reactionary and counter-revolutionary forces and claimed that the Revolution of 1905-1907 marked the end of sectarianism as a religious form of social protest. Seven years later Putintsev published a further work *Politicheskaya rol' i taktika sekt* (The Political Role and Tactics of the Sects), Moscow, 1935, which, though somewhat rambling and imprecise – there is, for example, far too much reliance on newspaper reports of sectarian doings which are accepted quite uncritically – brought together important material although this must, as Klibanov has pointed out, be separated out from the Stalinist ideology which constitutes the framework of Putintsev's study of the sects (Klibanov, 1967: p. 514).

As stated, the early 1920's witnessed the first steps in the direction of concrete Soviet research into religious sectarianism. By the second half of the 1920's some experience had been accumulated and the Party conference of 1926 was preceded by 'concrete' studies in a number of *guberniyas* (provinces). On the basis of these, Putintsev developed a *'voprosnik i metodicheskiye ukazaniya po sobiraniyu svedenii o sektakh'* (Questionnaire and Technical Instructions for the Collection of Information on the Sects) which he published in *Antireligioznik*, 1927, no. 6. He divided his programme for the empirical study of sectarianism into the following major categories: (1) name, location and brief history of the sect; (2) property status, ethnic, sex and age composition of the sect; (3) reasons for growth (or decline) of the sect; (4) past political attitudes and activities of the sect; (5) political activity and role of the sect at the present time; (6) sectarian collective farms and co-operatives; (7) sectarian theology, rituals, and everyday practices; (8) sectarianism and anti-religious propaganda. Each category in turn was subdivided into questions envisaging a most complete treatment of the given subject division. The questionnaire was designed not so much for specialists and scholarly expeditions as for local intelligentsia and Party activists and he actively sought to involve these in concrete sociological research.

Empirical research into sectarianism during the second half of the 1920's and the early 1930's was conducted by questionnaire, interview, and the collection of statistical and documentary materials. Unfortunately, the results of these investigations remain to this day in inaccessible archives − closed to Soviet and foreign scholars alike − but, among published works of this period, note should be taken of an anonymous article which appeared in *Antireligioznik*, 1927, no. 8, entitled '*Sektanty v dal'nevostochnom kraye*' (Sectarians in the Far Eastern Territory); of M.I. Shakhnovich article '*Mysli i dumy sovremennykh sektantov*' (Ideas and Thoughts of the Sectarians Today) in *Voinstvuyushchiy ateist*, 1931, nos. 2, 3 − a valuable source of information for the world-view-of certain sectarian groups, and of Gainstsev and Krivokhatsy's article '*Tri mesyatsa s sektantami*' (Three Months with the Sectarians) in *Antireligioznik*, 1928, no. 7. The collected papers *Foci of Sectarian Obscurantism* fits into this same group, as does a book by a participant in the Lower Volga Expedition to Study a Religious Way of Life − A. Tersky's *U sektantov* (Among the Sectarians), published in Moscow-Leningrad, 1930.[20]

The study of the history of Russian sectarianism − that is, according to Klibanov, the study of the succession of forms taken by it in the course of the class struggle in Russia, the evolution of its social significance, research into the social roots of sectarianism during the various periods of Russian history' (Klibanov, 1967: p. 375) − has only just begun, although certain questions relating to the history of sectarianism were dealt with by M.N. Pokrovsky in his *Russkaya istoriya s drevneyshikh vremen* (Russian History Since the Most Ancient Times), Moscow, 1905, and his collaborator, N.M. Nikol'sky, provided some useful information, but as this was a work published before the Revolution the early date is reflected, from the point of view of contemporary Soviet researches, in the mistaken theorectical framework and on the overemphasis on sectarianism which it contains. A.T. Lukachevsky in his lecture *Sectarianism in the Past and Today,* of 1925, sought to bring Nikol'sky's information up to date, and in 1930 Nikol'sky himself published a larger work than the one he had written in collaboration with Pokrovsky, entitled *Istoriya russkoy tserkvi* (A History of the Russian Church), which contained more up to date information on the history of Russian sectarianism. Nikol'sky observed in that work that 'for a more fundamental re-writing of the chapters pertaining to the Raskol (Old Believers) and sectarianism, it would have been necessary to make use of the exceedingly rich materials in archives now available for research, but which I was unable to use owing to the early deadline given to me by the publishers' (op. cit., p. 3). Latterly, I.A. Klibanov has sought to build on the work begun by Nikol'sky, his most important single contribution being his *Istoriya religioznogo sektantstva v Rossii (60 -e XIX v. - 1917g.)* (The History of Religious Sectarianism in Russia (from the 1860's to 1917) published in 1965.

In the post-1954 period of the renewal of 'scientific atheism', much work on religious sectarianism was pursued in a conscious endeavour to serve this aspect of the Party's work and it is sometimes difficult to distinguish between genuine scholarly endeavour, and critical studies of sectarianism more crudely related to the Party's directives on the necessity for anti-religious propaganda. The gap between these has, however, now narrowed, and the accusatory tone which characterised so much early writing on the sects in the 1950's has all but disappeared. As Klibanov claims – with some justification: 'The new period in Soviet study of religious sectarianism is characterised, above all, by the posing of the deepest problems in philosophical, historical, ethnographic, and psychological study of religious sectarianism, taking into consideration both the last achievements of the social sciences and the newest developments in religious sects. This is the origin of the empirical sociological study of sectarianism' (1967: p. 379). His own work stands as a model of such study.[21]

A group of extemely competent empirical researchers has now been formed. It includes such figures as A. Antonova, D. Aptekman, E. Bartoshevich, A. Belov, W. Borisoglebsky, F. Garkavenko, A. Garasimets, A.A. Eryshev, M. Kuts, V. Lentin, G. Lyalina, E. Liagushina, I. Malakhova, L. Mandrygin, E. Mayat, L. Mitrokhin, A. Moskalenko, R. Nadol'sky, L. Serdobol'skaya, E. Filiminov, V. Cherniak, V. Yakovlev and others. This group of researchers conducted empirical studies in 1959 in Tambov province, in 1960 in Lipetsk and Voronezh districts, in 1961 in Riazan' province, as well as in other districts in the Ukraine, Belorussia, and the Kasak SSR.[22] In most cases these studies were conducted by means of the 'basic mass' technique; sampling was used less frequently, and the monographic approach was least common, yet a good example of the latter is the study conducted by Mandrygin and Makarov in Ol'shany village in the Stolin region near Brest, and published in 1966 – L.V. Mandrygin and N.I. Makarov, *'O kharaktere i prichinakh sokhraneniya religioznykh verovanii u krest'yan zapadnykh oblastey Belorussii'* (On the Character and Reasons for the Continuance of Religious Belief Among the Peasants of the Western Regions of White Russia), VNA, no. 1, 1964.

Empirical studies so far conducted in the Soviet Union remain, in Soviet eyes, imperfect, particularly so far as the use of mathematical statistics is concerned (Klibanov, 1967: p. 380). Sociological experiments have not been used at all. The greatest and most successful research has, in fact, been in the area of interviews and personal observations and in gathering documentary material. An important feature of these studies is the fact that the phenomena constituting their subject matter was studied in the process of change by a broad use of sources describing the phenomena at the given place over a fair period of time, and then by means of re-study after an interval of time. Primary significance was attributed to questions of methodology, techniques of research, and to the internal processes occurring in the sectarian movement — i.e., change in its social and demographic structure, numbers of adherents, and the evolution of its ideology. Less attention was paid to socio-psychological study of relationships within the family and to the daily life of sectarians.

Of late much attention has been paid in the Soviet Union to the notions of man, nature and of the meaning and purpose of life, and to the ethical ideas of sectarians and to their attitude to 'science' — particularly of the Baptists; as, for example, in L.N. Mitrokhin's *Baptizm i sovremennost'* (Contemporary Baptism), Moscow, 1964.[23] Work has also begun on what are termed socio-psychological studies of sectarianism, as for instance L.V. Mandrygin's contribution *'Ideya "utesheniya" v baptizme'* (Ideas of 'Consolation' in Baptism) to the collected work *Nravstvennost' i religiya* (Morality and Religion), Moscow, 1964.

The history of sectarianism in both the pre-revolutionary and in the post-revolutionary period of Russian history proceeds apace. Work has begun on the publication of sources in the history of religious sectarianism — see *Sovremennoye sektantstvo i yego preodoleniye* (Contemporary Sectarianism and How to Overcome It), Moscow, 1961. New questions relating to the history of political currents in Baptism are raised in Lialina's article *'Liberal'no-burzhuaznoye techeniye v baptizme (1905-1917)'* (The Bourgeois-Liberal Trend in Baptism (1905-1917)), VNA, no. 1, 1967. Klibanov's major study of religious sectarianism, published in 1965, we have already mentioned, and Soviet study of Baptism abroad has now also begun (cf. A.A. Kisilova, *'K istorii vozniknoveniya amerikanskogo baptizma'* (The History of Development of American Baptism), *VIRA*, vol. XII, 1964.

One of the most notable features of recent Soviet research into religious sectarianism is that, whereas in the past it was almost exclusively the preserve of the professional *antireligiozniki*, today it is attracting the attention of students in the disciplines of sociology, philosophy, history and latterly, psychology as well.

Local studies — often today under the guidance of professional sociologists — continue, and material gathered in this way has been presented in the writings of V.A. Brianov, D.V. Gegeshidze, and I.A. Sosina, as well as in works devoted to the study of sects in Azerbaydjan, Armenia, Georgia, Turkmenia and Kursk and Tomsk regions.[24]

One notable event of recent years that I would like to record before closing this brief survey of Soviet research into sectarianism in the USSR was the brief return, after an absence of almost thirty years, of V.F. Krest'yanov to the study of the Mennonite Communities in the Soviet Union. His *O nekotorykh osobennostyakh i putyakh preodoleniya religioznoy ideologii sektantov-mennonitov* (Some Features and Points for the Overcoming of the Religious Ideology of the Sect of the Mennonites) was published in *Uchenyye zapiski Tomskogo gosudarstvennogo universiteta* (Proceedings of Tomsk State University), 1964, no. 2.

Soviet concrete sociological study of religious sectarianism is making great efforts today to bring its work up to the level of the social sciences generally. Soviet researchers in this area are, at last, beginning to master modern techniques of research and to supply other areas of research into religion – philosophical, sociological and historical – with materials which they can use. Although there are still what Klibanov calls 'half-baked' and 'superficial' (*poverkhnostnyy i skorospelyy*) works, both large and small, the tendency today is to write major researches of long-range theoretical influence (Klibanov, 1967: p. 383). Scholarly undertakings of this kind are more and more involving the combined efforts of sociologists, philosophers, and historians, and a welcome feature of recent years has been the increasing involvement of the discipline of psychology. This, says Klibanov, is particularly important for 'psychologists are called upon to blaze a trail by which the scientific areas arising from the treatment of the philosophical and historical problems associated with the study of religious sectarianism can penetrate the spiritual world of the religious believer'. 'But', he adds, 'systematic study of the psychological aspects of religious sectarianism is still ahead of us' (ibid., p. 383). Further, says Klibanov, 'ethnographic study of sectarianism – that is the study of daily life, the family, marriage, and the upbringing of children in religious sects – has not gained the place in Soviet research it deserves, although life is constantly pointing to the significance of this sphere of relationships in maintaining sectarianism and even in reproducing (on no matter how reduced a scale) its numbers (ibid., p. 383). Needless to add that, for Klibanov, as for all those engaged in the study of religious sectarianism, the ultimate aim is to provide the wherewithall for the ultimate overcoming of the phenomenon of religious sectarianism. That this is the *Problematik* of Soviet study Klibanov makes quite clear in an article, written jointly with Soviet Union's other authority on religious sectarianism, L. Mitrokhin, for the authoritative journal *Kommunist* entitled '*Kommunisticheskoye vospitaniye i bor'ba protiv religioznogo sektantstva*' (Communist Upbringing and the struggle with Religious Sectarianism), no. 2, 1961.

C. *Islam*

As was the case with Buddhist studies, the study of Islam in Russia goes back to a time well before the 1917 Revolution. It did not, however, as a recent writer on the study of Islam in the Soviet Union has pointed out, become part of Marxist-Leninist 'science' until well into the period of Soviet power (Smirnov, 1967: p. 407).

Early Soviet concern with Islam was with Islam as the extremely reactionary world-outlook of many of the subject peoples of the Empire which it had inherited from the Tsars and which it was now seeking to integrate into the Union of Soviet Socialist Republics (Smirnov, 1967: pp. 406-407). During this period Soviet 'agitators' sought to counteract the influence of Islam by portraying it as primitive, feudal and barbaric, and as destined to quickly give way before the advance of the new, 'scientific', understanding of the world proclaimed by Marxism-Leninism. The connection between religion and nationalism, in particular was ill understood in this early period of Soviet power.

The earliest Soviet studies of Islam are found in articles in the newspaper (later to become the journal) *Zhizn' natsional'nostey* (The Life of the Nationalities) which began publication in the early 1920's. Soon a stream of anti-Islamic brochures and books also appeared, among them Soloveychik's *Basmachestvo v Bukhare* (The Basmachestvo in Buchara), Moscow, 1923, in which the connection between Islam and activities of the *Basmachestvo* — on anti-Soviet movement in Central Asia — was illustrated, but little analysed. The *Basmachestvo,* it was claimed, were motivated simply by class interests — a thesis that time was to disprove.

But alongside this agitational literature the serious study of Islam was kept alive by a small group of Islamists working within the newly established Soviet Academy of Sciences. Whilst not, in the eyes of later Soviet theoreticians, entirely free from idealistic bias in their approach to the understanding of Islam, this group of scholars — the most well known of which was V.V. Bartol'd — provided much factual material relating to the beliefs and practice of Islam; material which later generations of Soviet Islamists were to use as the basis for their own understanding of Islam. Bartol'd's books *Islam: Obshchiy ocherk* (Islam: A General Study) (1918) and *Musul'manskiy mir* (The Muslim World) (1922) also introduced Soviet scholars to European studies of Islam. Later generations of Soviet Islamists were to be particularly critical of Bartol'd's view that the reason for the backwardness of Islamic countries was the growth of religious fanaticism, for them more fundamental socio-economic causes were at work. But it was on the broad research which Bartol'd conducted into Islam that the new generation of Soviet Islamists began their work.

Another important figure in the early years of Soviet study of Islam was the distinguished Arabist I.Yu. Krachkovsky, who concentrated his attention on the early manuscripts of the Koran and on the translation of these into Russian. The outcome of his researches was the first complete critical edition of the Koran in Russian, together with his own commentary on it which appeared post-humously in 1963, the consummation of a lifetime's work. Prior to the publication of this, Krachkovsky was known primarily for his study *Takha Khuseyn v doislamskoy poezii arabov i yego kritiki* (Taha Hussein in the Pre-Islamic Poetry of the Arabs and its Critics), published in 1931 in *Izvestiya AN SSSR Seriya*, VII, no. 5, in which he showed that an Egyptian scholar, who utilised the Koran as one of the sources of his Arab poetry, criticised it and was persecuted for this by the Moslem clergy. Although the poet's work was banned, Krachovsky showed that it played an important part in the early development of a critical approach to this important source for the study of early Islam.

Three other members of this group of early Soviet Islamists must be mentioned — V.A. Gordlevsky, the Ukrainian scholar A.E. Krymsky, and Academician A.A. Semenov, who worked in the Tadjik Academy of Sciences. Semenov, in particular, did outstanding work on the varieties of Islamic sectarianism. His articles *'Nasyri-Khosrov o mire dukhovnom i material'nom'* (Nasyri-Hosrov on the Material and Spiritual World), *'Protivorechiya v uchenii o pereselenii dushi u pamirskikh ismailitov'* (Contradictions in the Study of the Migration of the Soul among the Patmir Ismailites), and *'Izmailitskaya oda, posvyaschennaya voploshcheniyu Aliyaboga'* (The Ishmailite Ode, dedicated to the incarnation of Ali-God)[25] are still highly thought of among Soviet Islamists, as are Gordlevsky's articles *'Religioznoye dvizheniye sredi kizylbashev Maloy Azii'* (Religious Movements among the Kizylbash of Little Asia), *Dervishi Akhi — Evrana i tsekhi v Turtsii'* (The Dervishes of Akha-Evran and the Guilds in Turkey), *'Zhitiye Sadr ed-Dina Kuneva'* (The Life of Sadr ed-Dina Kuneva) and *'Bakha ud-Din Nakshbend Bukharskiy'* — all of which were published in various journals relating to the Soviet East in the 1930's.[26]

The work of these scholars — useful as it was in providing Soviet scholars with a basic knowledge of Islam as a religion — was destined to give way to more overtly Marxist-Leninist accounts of that religion; accounts which would concentrate not on Islam as of being of interest in and of itself, but on the socio-economic conditions which brought it into being, which have allowed it to continue and develop and, as important, on the changes necessary in the socio-economic structure of Islamic society if it is eventually to disappear. The older generation of Russian and early Soviet Islamists virtually ignored any connection between Islam and social problems and were therefore, says a contemporary Soviet Islamist, remiss in exposing the class role and social roots of Islam and failed to demonstrate 'the reactionary role of the Moslem clergy' (Smirnov, 1967: p. 409).

This task – fulfilled in the early years of Soviet power by the agitational literature of such anti-Islamic 'agitators' as G. Ibragimov, L.I. Klimovich, A. Arshaun, Adalisa and others – was put on a more scholarly footing by the work of M.A. Reysner and M.N. Pokrovsky – work to which we have already referred in our survey of the rise of Soviet study of Buddhism. Their work, whilst not in the opinion of later Soviet scholars entirely Marxist in approach, was an essential prelude to the development of such an approach. Thus, Reysner, on the basis of the theory put forward by Pokrovsky on the historical significance of 'trading capitalism' (*torgovogo kapitalizma*), sought to account for the origin and rise of Islam (cf. Reysner, 1927b). The demands of world trade, says Reysner, pushed the Arabs into a union, which was carried out by one of the small traders, Muhammed, who managed to exploit his teaching about the one God in the interests of organising trade. According to Reysner, the Koran reflects the interest of trading and even of military capitalism. Islam, according to Reysner, is the product of trade-capitalism, as a special socio-economic formation which dominated the Arabs in the seventh to twelfth centuries AD. His arguments in support of this are, however, based on speculation and are not backed by factual material. Nevertheless, Reysner's theory had considerable influence on Soviet Eastern experts and Islamists, who were blinded by its 'economism'. Thus, in his book *Soderzhaniye Korana* (The Content of the Koran), Moscow, 1928, L.I. Klimovich also came to the conclusion that there was a direct link between the interests of the powerful merchants of Mecca and the contents of the Koran.

Reysner's views are also noticeable in an early work of N.A. Smirnov – now generally recognised as the Soviet Union's leading 'scientific atheist' writer on Islam. This book, originally published in 1928 under the editorship of Reysner himself as *Islam i sovremennyy vostok* (Islam in the Contemporary East), was re-issued in 1930 under the more general title *Sovremennyy Islam* (Contemporary Islam). In it Smirnov sought to deal with a wide and complex range of problems relating to the Marxist-Leninist understanding of Islam and, especially, he sought to lay bare the political role which Islam had played, and continued to play, in the countries in which it had become established, particularly in countries outwith the Soviet Union. Needless to say this role was conceived of as always and everywhere reactionary.

In seeking to break with bourgeois-idealistic conceptions of Islam, Soviet scholars turned to Marx and Engels own writings on this topic – an approach initiated by V. Dityakin's article *'Marks i Engel's o proiskhozhdenii i sushchnosti islama'* (Marx and Engels on the Origin and Essence of Islam), published in the journal *Ateist* in 1927, nos. 22-23. In particular, by returning to Marx and Engels account of the rise of Islam, Dityakin tried to prove that these views could be fully supported by the work of the then fashionable bourgeois authors Caetani and Lammas, who explained the origin of Islam by the climate and geography of Arabia (cf. Caetani, 1912 and Lammens, 1921). Whilst disagreeing with this particular hypothesis, Dityakin, at the same time, considered that the vast amount of material collected by Caetani should be used to confirm the Marxist view of Islam which had been put forward by Reysner, although he also felt that Reysner had oversimplified Islamic ideology.

The first fully Marxist-Leninist account of the rise of Islam is found in the work of E.A. Belyaev. In his article *'Rol' mekkanskogo torgovogo kapitala v istorii proiskhozhdeniya islama'* (The Role of Meccan Trade Capital in the History of the Origin of Islam) published in 1930 in the journal *Ateist,* no. 58, Belyaev sought to explain the rise of Islam on the basis of a study of the Koran and of Arab sources telling of the political and economic situation in Mecca at the time that it began. What Belyaev argued was that Islam was born among the petty traders and bourgeoisie of Mecca, whom he claimed were dependent on the rich merchants and the hereditary aristocracy. In explaining Islam in this way Belyaev, whilst departing from the views of Reysner, is held by present day Soviet Islamists to have set the Marxist-Leninist understanding of Islam on a surer and more scientific footing (so Smirnov, 1967: p. 411). L.I. Klimovich, who also returned to the views of Marx and Engels on the origin of Islam, espoused this view in his article *'Marks i Engel's ob islame i problema yego proiskhozhdeniya v sovetskom islamovedenii* (Marx and Engels on Islam, and the Problem of the Origin of Islam in Soviet Islamics), *Revolyutsionnyy vostok,* 1933; nos. 2-3 and it gradually became the official view of the origin of Islam, the more so after the now famous discussion on the origin of Islam in the pages of the journal *Ateist* during the early years of the 1930's.

The discussion, in which such scholars as N.A. Rozhkov, M.L. Tomar, S. Asfendiarov and S.P. Tolstov took part — though Tolstov confined his contributions, as was befitting an ethnographer of his standing, to the pages of the more scholarly journal *Sovetskaya etnografiya* — opened with an attempt to establish the precise nature of the socio-economic and political situation in Arabia in the seventh century AD and of which Islam was now seen, for almost the first time, as the ideological superstructure, as Marx and Engels had defined that term. In their conclusions, the scholars who took part in this discussion used the works of Western Islamists, though at many points they were highly critical of them. They tried to give an independent, original solution to the problem of the rise of Islam, although as Smirnov recognises in his discussion of their proposed solution, they did not wholly succeed, and he confesses that even today Soviet study of Islam is still searching for a truly convincing Marxist-Leninist solution to the problem of the origin of Islam (op. cit., p. 412).

The theories put forward in this discussion can be divided into two groups. In the first group were theories akin to those we have already mentioned and which held, in some form or other, that the moving force in early Islam was the trading bourgeoise of Mecca and other towns, so that Islam was the ideology of trade-capitalism. In the second group were theories which held that Mohammed's teaching was connected with a feudal revolution. Advocates of this view were N.A. Rozhkov and M.L. Tomar (cf. Rozhkov, *Russkaya istoriya v sravnitel'no-istoricheskom osveshchenii* (Russian History in a Comparative-Historical Light), vol. I, Moscow-Leningrad, 1928, and Tomar, *'Proiskhozhdeniye islama i yego klassovoye obosnovaniye'* (The Origin of Islam and its Class Base), *Ateist*, 1930, no. 58). Both of these scholars held that Islam was born among the poverty-stricken people of Mecca, but found its economic base in agricultural Medina. It was thus the ideology of the weaker classes, that is, these scholars considered Islam to be the ideology of the Arabian peasantry rather than of the bourgeoisie. Here, comments Smirnov (op. cit., p. 412) we can discern a certain idealisation of Islam and a failure to understand its role in class society. Another contributor to this debate was S. Asfeniarov who concluded that early Islam was not a religion at all and that Mohammed's activity was in reality, but a weapon to bring about the unification of the nomadic tribes of Central Arabia in their struggle with the trade-capitalists of Mecca. The outcome was that he created a mass movement of nomads who settled outwith Arabia (*Ateist*, 1930). Again, contemporary Soviet Islamists argue that this view also fails to fully comprehend the true class character of early Islam.

A more substantial theory was put forward by S.P. Tolstov in the journal *Sovetskaya etnografiya* (1932, no. 2). Tolstov maintained that an ancient slave-owning formation and not a feudal one had developed on the base of the multiplication of the Arab tribal structure at the time of the rise of Islam. The social structure of Arab cities, however, had not managed to develop an antique formation but had done just the opposite and developed a feudal structure. In such conditions of class differentiation a socio-religious movement arose which eventually became Islam.

An important place in this discussion of the early 1930's must also be assigned to a paper by L.I. Klimovich which appeared in the journal *Voinstruyushchiy ateism* (Militant Atheism) — the successor to the journal *Ateist* — in 1931 (nos. 2 and 3) — a paper in which Klimovich expressed doubts about the pronouncements of Arab sources about Mohammed on the grounds that all of them were compiled a long time after the death of Mohammed. Historians, in Klimovich's opinion, knew nothing whatever about a historical Mohammed; in fact, for all they knew he might never have existed. It was, it will be recalled, at about this time that Soviet historians of early Christianity were maintaining similar views with regard to the historical Jesus. However, those who took part in the ensuing discussion pointed to the weakness of Klimovich's argument. S.P. Tolstov's article, to which we have already referred, originated, in fact, as a reply to points raised by Klimovich. Tolstov argued that a purely negative argument was still not a base for denying the historicity of Mohammed. Before asserting this a fuller study of the *Sira* (biography) of Mohammed would be needed, as well as some argument to show (a) the mythological sources for the biography and (b) the social roots out of which the myth of Mohammed — if indeed it was a myth — emerged. Klimovich had in the course of his argument pointed to the similarities between some of the things said about Mohammed and Shamanism and this theme was taken up by I.N. Viniakov in an article entitled *'Legenda o prizvanii Mukhammeda v svete etnografii'* (The Legend about the Call of Mohammed in the Light of Ethnography) in the *Festschrift, Sergeyu Fedorovichy Ol'denburgu*, published in Leningrad in 1934. Viniakov came to the conclusion that the 'Call' of Mohammed reflected the preservation, in the religious beliefs of the Arabs, beliefs from more ancient times. The roots of the account of the 'Call' of the Mohammed lay in primitive Shamanism which was prevalent in all ancient cultures. This is not, however, a view which Soviet Islamists today take very seriously.

The second period in Soviet study of Islam begins in the mid-1930's and lasts until the mid-1950's. It is a period of eventful historical happenings in Soviet society and this is reflected — at least in the early period — in the attention paid to religion in general and to Islam in particular. The resistance in parts of the Islamic republic of the Soviet Union to the drastic transformation of Soviet Society into a socialist economy meant that the criticism of Islam became not only more fierce, but more political as well. Soviet Islamists and *antireligiozniki* sought not only to refute Islam, but to unmask its 'reactionary' and 'counter-revolutionary' nature — particularly as this was expressed in nationalistic and pan-Turkish movements. This called for study of Islamic sectarianism and the demonstration of its connection with reactionary forms of nationalism — as they appeared to be to Soviet theoreticians — a task which Soviet Islamists saw themselves as fulfilling in the interest of the Islamic masses. Just how deep Islam and Islamic nationalism went in the consciousness of the masses was little realised at the time — indeed, it is only just being realised now. Thus, as Soviet Islamists today recognise, many mistakes were made (cf. Smirnov, 1967: p. 414). The dogmaticism which characterised what was, and was intended to be, a frontal attack on Islam served but to alienate the very masses whom it was intended to 'liberate' and today the Soviet approach to Islam — whilst still critical — is to let well alone and to treat it, for the most part, as an interesting folk cultural survival which will eventually pass away into the museum of history.

Some serious and important work on Islam was, however, produced during this period. In 1936, L.I. Klimovich published a study of Islam in Tsarist Russia (*Islam v tsarkoy Rossii*), in which he sought to show the role of Islam in both the internal and external politics of Tsarism and the role of the Muslim clergy in the ideological and religiously legitimated oppression of the masses. He also noted the existence in Islam of reforming tendencies and, more significantly, of pan-Islamic idealism. This latter he saw as a movement inspired, on the whole, by the clergy of foreign countries as a way of seeking to increase their influence and importance and as inspired also by imperialism.

During this period a number of works on Islam also appeared from the presses of the publishing houses in the Soviet (Islamic) republics. Among these we should note Nigmet Sabitov's *Mekteby i medrese u kazakhov* ('Mekteba' and 'Medresa' among the Cossacks) published in Alma-Ata in 1950, and O.A. Sukharev's article *'K voprosu o kul'te musul'manskikh svyatykh v Sredney Azii'* ('On the Cult of Muslim Sanctity in Central Asia') published in the yearbook of the Uzbekistan Historical and Archaeological Institute in the same year. In this article Sukharev called attention to the syncretistic aspects of Central Asian Islam, showing that much in the 'cult of sanctity' pre-dated the advent of Islam − a theme which is also found in the writings of S.P. Tolstov.

Soviet scholars also turned their attention to the study of Islam outwith the Soviet Union and a number of important historical studies were produced − among them M.S. Ivanov's study of the mid-nineteenth century uprising of the 'Babists' in Iran, *Babidskiye vosstaniya v Irane 1848-1852* (1939). In this work Ivanov argued − on the basis of a detailed study of archival material − that 'Babism' arose as a spontaneous ideology in peasant and lower class town circles. The teachings of the 'Bab' himself reflected not only the interests of the peasantry and their struggle with entrenched feudal power and domination, and with foreign capital, but also the struggle of the artisans and the petty bourgeois of the towns with more powerful forms of commerce. The 'Bab' also reflected the dreams of the peasantry and the poor of the towns about a future kingdom of happiness where all people would be equal and where all oppressors would be banished. This analysis, which owes much, of course, to Marx's early writings on religion (now available) and to Engels' own writings on the Peasant War in Germany, was one of the first attempts made by Soviet scholars at analysing 'religions of protest'. Others were to follow. Thus, in 1948 A.M. D''yakov, in a monograph entitled *Natsional'niy vopros i angliyskiy imperializm v Indii* (National Questions and British Imperialism in India), sought to analyse the role of Islam, and of Muslim organisations, in the growth of both the class and independence struggle in India. Similarly, S.R. Smirnov, in his book *Vosstaniye makhdistov v Sudane* (The Mhadi Uprising in the Sudan) (1950), saw a 'progressive' side to Islam in the role which it played in this uprising of 1881-1889 against

British Imperialism and Egyptian feudalism. Where, on the other hand, Islam resisted Soviet power, it was roundly condemned as 'reactionary', and seen as being inspired not from below but from outwith the masses — that is, by either the clergy or by foreign powers, or by both.

Marxist-Leninist principles for interpreting religion were also applied at this time to the analysis of the nineteenth century movement in the mountainous region of the Caucasus whose leader was Shamil' and which became known as Muridism — basically a social movement which sought to cover itself with the cloak of Islam, as one Soviet commentator puts it (Smirnov, op. cit., p. 415). Soviet researchers sought to get at the real roots of this movement by analysing its documents, dogma and the personal cult of Shamil'. Foremost in this endeavour were M.N. Pokrovsky who in his *Diplomatiya i voyny tsarskoy Rossii v XIX stoletii* (Diplomacy in the Wars of Tsarist Russia in the 19th century) sketched in the socio-economic and political background to the movement, S.K. Bushuev who published his *Bor'ba gortsev za nezavisimost' pod rukovodstvom Shamilya* (The Struggle of the Mountainous People for Independence under the Leadership of Shamil') in Moscow in 1939, R.M. Magomedov who published his own book under the same title in the same year as Bushuev, and N.I. Pokrovsky.[27] Their work, in Smirnov's opinion, applied a far too rigid and dogmatic approach to the understanding of Muridism, for they saw it simply as a reactionary movement without at all appreciating its positive features (Smirnov, op. cit., p. 416). A more substantial and fair-minded study of Muridism was that of A.V. Fadeyev who published his article *'O vnutrenney sotsial'noy baze myuridistskogo dvizheniya na Kavkaze'* (On the Internal Base of the Muridist Movement in the (Caucases), in *Voprosy istorii*, no. 6, 1955. Fadeyev held that under the reactionary cloak of Muridism there must be seen the genuine desires of the Mountain peasants of the Caucas religion for independence from feudal and colonial exploitation. The discussion over Muridism continued into 1956 in the Institute of History of the Academy of Sciences and the articles which appeared in its journal, *Voprosy istorii*, stressed the necessity for getting at the social roots of Muridism in the life of the peoples it attracted, and of ignoring its religious covering. This view prevailed and was published in a number of articles which appeared in the authoritative journal *Istoriya SSSR* (The History of the USSR) in 1960 (cf. for example Fadeyev's article, *'Vozniknoveniye myuridistskogo dvizheniya na Kavkaze i ego sotsial'nyye korni'* (The Rise of the Muridist Movement in the Caucasus and its Social Roots') no. 6, 1960). It was later incorporated into the textbook on Soviet History — *Istoriya SSSR* — used in higher education, where it was set forth in the chapter contributed by Kh.M. Khashev *'Obshchestvennyy stroy Dagestana v XIX v'* (The Social Order of Degestan in the 19th century) published in Moscow in 1961.

The third phase in Soviet study of Islam begins in the 1950's and continues to the present day. As with the study of religion generally, the study of Islam was given renewed emphasis in the wake of Khrushchev's proclamation of the building of Communism in the Soviet Union and the anti-religious activity associated with this. If Islam was to be finally eradicated from the consciousness of the new Soviet citizen then a necessary prelude to this was that roots of Islam in the consciousness of the ordinary believers be understood. To this task the new generation of Soviet Islamists, and more especially those engaged in promoting 'scientific atheism' in the autonomous 'Islamic' republics, addressed themselves. These included, among many others, such scholars as G. Abdullaev, M. Abdullaev, M. Aliev, A. Abilov, A. Artykov, M. Bagabov, S. Gadshiev, M. Kasumov, M. Makhotov, A. Salamov, K. Rakhmanov, B. Tsavkilov, and A. Shikhaidov. The themes which dominated their work were the unmasking of the real essence of the Koran, the study of religious survivals, rites, festivals and fasts, the cult of sanctity, and the position of women. Many of their writings were in the languages of the republics from which they came and many were never translated into Russian. They are thus, to a large extent, inacessible to the student of religion in the Soviet Union.

This restriction does not apply, however, to many of the voluminous monographical studies which have been produced since the mid-1950's, not all of them at all related to the immediate task — which produced many of the resources that made their publication possible — of the elimination of Islam in the USSR. E.A. Belyaev's fine study, *Araby, islam i arabskiy khalifat v ranneye srednevekov'ye* (Arabs, Islam and the Arab Caliphate in the Early Middle Ages), which was published in 1965, is a case in point, as is L.I. Klimovich's study, *Islam,* 2nd ed., 1965). Both of these works, however, seek for a Marxist-Leninist understanding of both the origin and the development of Islam. Belyaev, for instance, came to the conclusion that Islam arose in Arabia in the guise of a new ideology, reflecting the internal contradictions and changes in the Arab society of the time — prosperity and poverty, slavery and the growth of trade, which threw up the new ideology as a protest against the slave-owning structure then in the process of disintegration. L.I. Klimovich, however, laid less stress on this side of things — though he did not deny its part in the rise of Islam, but for him Islam quickly became the ideology of the ruling classes and of the early feudal Caliphate. Much work into the social and economic structure of early Islamic society will be needed before Soviet scholars are of one mind on this important issue.

Another area to which Soviet scholars turned their attention in the post-1954 period was to the history of the divisions in Islam and to the history of the development of Sh'ism in particular. Thus in 1958, in Leningrad, the Persian scholar N.D. Miklukho-Maklaya published an important historical article *'Shiizm i yego sotsial'noye litso v Irane na rubezhe XV-XVI vv'* (Shi'ism and its Social Face in Iran at the Turn of the fifteenth century) in *Pamyati akademika I. Yu. Krachkovskogo*. In this article the author argued that Sh'ism did not arise in Persian circles at all and that it was only much later, in the sixteenth century, that it was adopted as the state religion of Iran and became the religion of the Persian people. In the fifteenth century, he argued, many feudal lords had adopted Sh'ism as their ideology in their struggle with the central authorities. The fact that Sh'ism was at that time persecuted also drew to it many peasants and many of the lower classes of the towns, who enrolled under its sectarian flag. In the sixteenth century victory was achieved and from Iran Sh'ism spread, from the sixteenth to eighteenth centuries, to other countries in central Asia.

A notable event of the post-1954 period of the study of Islam was the appearance in 1963 of a translation with commentary of the entire Koran. This work which had been initiated by I.Yu. Krachkovsky, and largely produced by him, looked at the Koran, not as a religious document, but as a literary monument to a bygone culture. Krachkovsky, in his commentary, sought to get at the meaning of the Koran for its own time.

An area of much needed research which also developed rapidly during this period was the study of Islamic sectarianism, both in the past and in the present. The foremost scholar to work in this field was E.A. Belyaev whose *Musul'manskoye sektantstvo (istoricheskiy ocherk)* (Muslim Sectarianism (Historical Outline)) was published in Moscow in 1957. The author emphasised the role of sects as organs for the expression of peasant struggle against exploitation under fedual social structures. Not one sect, in Belyaev's opinion, was actually able to transform the essential social structure of any state, although this was the wish of the masses who supported them. Religious sectarianism was, thus, in his opinion, a somewhat forlorn spectacle.

Progress was also made in this period in the study of Ismailism in several of the republics of the USSR and in particular in areas of Tadjikstan. Foremost in this endeavour was A.A. Semenov, to whose earlier work in this respect we have already referred, and E.E. Bertel's, whose *'Nur-al-ulum: Zhizneopisaniye sheykha Aby-l-Khasana Kharakani'* (Nur-al-ulum: A Biography of Sheik Aby-l-Khasana Kharakani) was published in the third volume of *Iran* in 1929.

The problem of the origin of Muridism was discussed again and a major study of this important topic of Soviet Islamic studies, entitled *Myuridizm na Kavkaze* (Muridism in the Caucasus), was published by Smirnov in Moscow in 1963. In this work Smirnov reiterated the view which had emerged from earlier discussion of this topic to the effect that Muridism was not really a religious movement but was a social movement of protest on the part of the peasants of the mountainous regions of the Caucasus against feudal exploitation.

The study of the particularities of Islam in the various Soviet republics was also begun during this period (cf. O.A. Sukharev's fine study of *Islam v Uzbekistane* (Islam in Uzbekistan), published in Tashkent, 1960), as was the study of Islam as a world-wide religion. Important works on this latter topic were S.M. Gadzhiev's *Osnovnyye cherty sovremennogo islama* (The Fundamental Traits of Contemporary Islam), Makhachkala, 1962, and his more important study — in Soviet eyes — *Puti preodoleniya ideologii islama* (Ways of Overcoming the Ideology of Islam) published in Makhachkala in 1963. In this respect we should also mention Nadir Kuliev's *Antinauchnaya sushchnost' islama i zadachi ateisticheskogo vospitaniya trudyashchikhsya v usloviyakh sovetskogo Turkmenistana* (The Anti-Scientific Essence of Islam and the Problem of Atheistic Educational Work in the Conditions of Soviet Turkmenistan), published in Ashkabad in 1960.

Finally, during this period Soviet scholars turned their attention to the condition of Islam abroad and to 'Islamic nationalism', both of concern to a country which harboured many millions of Muslims within its frontiers and which bordered on a number of important Muslim states. The most notable study of these studies was L.R. Gordon-Polonskaya's *Musul'manskiye techeniya v obshchestvennoy mysli Indii i Pakistana (Kritika musul' manskogo natsionalizma* (Muslim Currents in the General Thought of India and Pakistan [A Critique of Muslim Nationalism]), published in Moscow, in 1963. The author's general line is that the phrase 'Muslim nationalism' arose in the period between the two world wars when the religiosity of the Eastern bourgeoisie intensified as a form of reaction to the revolt of the Muslim masses against exploitation and to their entertaining materialistic and socialist ideas. Further impetus was found in a general national reaction to colonial exploitation, particularly in India and Pakistan. Yet such nationalism, Gordon-Polonskaya argues, is essentially a relic from feudal times, for underlying it is a theological conception of Islamic society, which although feudal in origin, is well fitted to serve bourgeois interests in the present. Thus, it has become, as in Pakistan (and no doubt the author would have added in Iran today) the official ideology of the ruling classes. As the author writes: '"Muslin nationalism" prevents the formation of a bourgeois-democratic ideology, and gradually national groups of petty and middle bourgeoisie move away from it and seek to replace it with notions of a harmony of class interests without the established structures of exploitation' (quoted, Smirnov, 1967: pp. 422-423). Such at least was the author's hope!

Notes

FOREWORD

1. Thrower refers to the English translation of Wetter's book. The original German title is *Der dialektische Materialismus, seine Geschichte und sein System in der Sowjetunion,* Vienna, Herder, 1952 (4th ed. 1958). There is also a French translation: *Le matérialisme dialectique,* Paris, Désclée De Brouwer, 1962. Another important book along the same lines with penetrating philosophical analyses is that of Guy Planty-Bonjour, *Les catégories du matérialisme dialectique, l'ontologie soviétique contemporaine,* Paris, P.U.F., 1965. Several other works should be cited: the first volume of G.A. Wetter and W. Leonhard, *Sowjetideolgie heute,* Frankfurt am Main and Hamburg, Fischer, 1962 (French translation, *L'idéologie soviétique contemporaine,* Paris, Payot, 1965). The first volume, by Wetter, has as subtitle *Dialektischer und historischer Materialismus,* and the second volume, by Leonhard, is subtitled *Die politische Lehren.*
2. *Bibliographie der sowjetischen Philosophie,* Dordrecht, Reidel, 1959-1968, 7 vols. The passage quoted is from the preface to the first volume.

PREFACE

1. Useful surveys of Church-State relationships in the Soviet Union can be found in N.S. Timasheff, *Religion in Soviet Russia* 1917-1942, London, 1943; Paul Anderson, *People, Church and State in Modern Russia,* London, 1944; Walter Kolarz, *Religion in the Soviet Union,* London, 1961; R.H. Marshall (ed), *Aspects of Religion in the Soviet Union,* 1917-1967, Chicago, 1971; Bodhan Bociurkiw and John W. Strong (ed), *Religion and Atheism in the USSR and Eastern Europe,* London, 1975; Gerhard Simon, *Church, State and Opposition in the USSR,* London, 1974; Trevor Beeson, *Discretion and Valour,* London, 1974; Christel Lane, *Christian Religion in the Soviet Union: A Sociological Study,* London, 1978. More up to date information can be got from the journals *Religion in Communist Lands* (Keston College, England) and *Religion und Atheismus in der UdSSR: Monatlicher Informationsdienst* (Konigstein, GDFR).
2. e.g. David E. Powell, *Antireligious Propaganda in the Soviet Union: A Study in Mass Persuasion,* Cambridge, Mass., 1975.
3. Theological studies of Marxism are many, but the following stand out for the clarity of their understanding of Marxism: Helmut Golwitzer, *The Christian Faith and the Marxist Criticism of Religion,* Edinburgh, 1970; Giulio Giradi, *Marxism and Christianity;* New York, 1968; J. Lochman, *Encountering Marx,* Belfast, 1977; Yves Calvez, *La Pensée de Marx,* Paris, 1956; Dale Vree, *On Synthesising Marxism and Christianity,* New York, 1976.
4. A claim also made of late by Chinese 'scientific atheism'. Cf. Ren Jiyu, 'The Struggle to Develop a Marxist Science of Religion' in *Zhexueyanjiu,* no. 4, 1979; English translation in *Ching Feng,* 22 (2), 1979: pp. 75-89. Ren Jiyu is the director of the Research Institute for the Study of World Religions of the National Academy of Social Sciences in Peking.

5. Neither Jacques Waardenburg's *Classical Approaches to the Study of Religion* (1973) nor Eric Sharpe's *Comparative Religion* (1975) – two recent surveys of the development and current state of *Religionswissenschaft* – make any reference to Marxist study of religion, not even to any influence that Marx himself might be said to have exercised on the discipline.

6. The only other exception that comes to mind is R.C. Zaehner's short article 'Dialectical Materialism' in R.C. Zaehner (edit), *Concise Encyclopaedia of Living Faiths,* London, 1977.

CHAPTER 1

1. The Dutch theologian, Arend van Leeuwen, reminds us that the German term *Kritik* has overtones not adequately conveyed by the English translation 'critique', still less by the translation 'criticism'. In nineteenth century Germany, he contends, the term *Kritik* could not have been used in philosophical writing without some implied reference to its use in the critical philosophy of Kant. Marx's use of the term must, therefore, he claims, be understood in terms of this tradition. In particular, he claims that there is a parallel between the succession of Kant's *Critique of Pure Reason* and his *Critique of Practical Reason* and Marx's transition from theory to practice. He writes: 'The critique of religion and philosophy which preoccupied Marx's mind during his early period and the critique of political economy which absorbed the rest of his life are rooted in a joint apperception of the essence and meaning of critique' (1972: pp. 12-13). For David McLellan, however, *Kritik* signifies no more than the working over of other people's ideas and adding comments of one's own (1976: p. 69). A much more substantial point with regard to Marx's critique of religion has been put to me by Professor Trevor Ling of Manchester University and it is that it would be incorrect to take what Marx says about religion – as Marx himself did – and assume, without further argument, that it applies, without exception, to all the religions of the world. Marx's acquaintance with religion was extremely limited and Ling doubts if it was such as to provide a general critique of religion as such. Marx's reply, I think, would be that whatever the differences that exist between the religions of the world all, if his general theory of the social origin of the ideational super-structure of society (which includes religion) is correct, spring from the same social roots, whatever the particular form they assume at any given historical time or geographical place. This is, however, a point that I shall be returning to when I come to look at Soviet attempts to apply general Marxist-Leninist methodology to the study of world religions.

2. The second volume of Franz Schnabel's *Deutsche Geschichte im neunzehnten Jahrundert,* Freiburg, 1964 contains detailed evidence in support of this.

3. For the meaning of *praxis* in both Fichte and Marx, cf. Kostas Axelos, *Alienation, Praxis and Techné in the Thought of Karl Marx,* London, 1976: passim. Cf. also, Tom W. Goff, *Marx and Mead: Contributions to the Sociology of Knowledge,* London, 1980. As Goff points out, *praxis,* in Marx's writings, refers to material reality as the active, conscious relationship of people with physical nature, and thus unifies the material world and consciousness of it with practical activity.

4. Both of these early essays of Hegel can be found in T.M. Knox and R. Kroner's edition of Hegel's *Early Theological Writings* (1948).

5. It is interesting to note that Leszek Kołakowski begins his recently published history of Marxism (*Main Currents of Marxism,* three volumes, 1979) by tracing the background to Marxist thought about the world to the problem of theodicy

as this was raised in the writings of Plotinus and the early Christian Fathers (cf. vol. 1, pp. 9-80).

6. One should not, however, under-estimate the influence of Bauer, to whom Marx was extremely close during his student years in Berlin and for two or three years afterwards. It was Bauer who convinced Marx that orthodox religion was the chief illusion standing in the way of human self-understanding and it was Bauer who first reinterpreted Hegel's self-alienation of Spirit as being more applicable to human beings. It was humans, he claimed, who had created the God who now stood in the way of man himself as 'the highest divinity' (cf. Singer, 1980: pp. 14-15).

7. The phrase 'religion of humanity' was the invention of the French Positivist, Auguste Comte, but its use spread far beyond Positivist ranks. It was certainly used by the Young Hegelians — David Friedrich Strauss for example, wrote of *Humanitätsreligion* — and although Feuerbach himself never used the term, that it is implied in his expressed intention of transforming theology into anthropology is plain.

8. The evidence for Marx's early religious beliefs is presented by David McLellan in his book *Marx Before Marxism,* Chapter 2.

9. Thus in his brief spell as editor of the *Rheinische Zeitung* (1841-1842) Marx had descended from the rarified atmosphere of Hegelian philosophy to discuss such mundane issues as divorce, censorship, a Prussian law prohibiting the gathering of dead wood from the forests, and the economic distress of the Mosselle winegrowers.

10. For a summary of the social, economic and political situation in Germany at the beginning of Marx's career, cf. Quentin Lauer, 'Marx's Science of History' in *Dialogues in the Philosophy of Marxism,* ed. John Somerville and Howard L. Parsons (1974), pp. 144-145.

11. It must be pointed out that Marx did not at all countenance those who during his lifetime urged an even stronger line against religion. Both he and Engels vehemently denounced attempts on the part of anarchists, Blanquists, Dühring and others who suggested the use of coercive measures against religion. As Marx somewhat crudely put it in his *Critique of the Gotha Programme:* 'Everyone should be able to attend to his religious as well as his bodily needs without the police sticking their noses in . . . the workers' party . . . endeavours rather to liberate the conscience from the witchery of religion' (*MEOR:* p. 128). Engels went further and, in an article published in 1874, claimed that 'the only servive which one can still render to God is to declare atheism a compulsory article of faith' (*Emigrant Literature; MEOR:* p. 127); and in *Anti-Dühring* he wrote: 'Herr Dühring . . . incites his gendarmes of the future against religion, and thereby helps it to martyrdom and a prolonged lease of life' (*MEOR:* p. 440).

12. The story of the fate of Marx's early writings is a fascinating one and is told in Chapter XI of Robert Tucker's *Philosophy and Myth in Karl Marx,* Cambridge, 1964.

13. It may also be the case that the conception of religion as a form of alienated life owes something to the writings of Robert Owen and the German socio-religious thinker Weitling, for both these had put forward the notion of a humanity come into possession of its religious heritage by the realisation of the religious vision of humanity in new social forms. Whilst Marx and Engels would have denied that humanity needed a religious legitimation for its search for a true community, their views on religion may well have been clarified by their contact with these thinkers in that both had demonstrated the close connection between religious ideals and a defective social reality. Both had seen religion as a response to earthly

misery and both had sought to heal the split in the actual human community
between reality and religion by seeking to create on earth a community hitherto
reserved for heaven.

14.   Cf. Basil Willey, *The Seventeenth Century Background*, Harmondsworth, 1962,
       pp. 29-43.

15.   Thus Lenin wrote: 'Socialism in so far as it is the ideology of the struggle of the
       proletarian class, undergoes the general conditions of birth, development and
       consolidation of an ideology, that is to say, it is founded on all the material of
       human knowledge, it presupposes a high level of science, demands scientific
       work, etc. . .' 'Letter to the Federation of the North'; *LCW:* 39;403. In accord-
       ance with this usage – which is now the normal one in the Soviet Union – Stalin,
       at the seventh Congress of the Communist Party of the Soviet Union in 1934
       referred to: 'our tasks in the sphere of ideological work' (Quoted in *Handbook
       of Marxism:* p. 945) and the Soviet press today calls continually for an 'intensi-
       fication of ideological work among the masses' and speaks frequently of 'the
       ideological struggle' with the Western democracies. That this is not the way Marx
       and Engels understood the term should now be plain.

16.   Cf. Those anthropologists who, following Malinowski, see religion as a response
       to such uncertain and uncontrollable areas of life as accident, disease and death.
       The English anthropologist John Beattie, for example. sees both magic and
       religion as ways of coping – symbolically – with situations which lie beyond
       rational, scientific control. He writes: 'Basically it (religion) expresses (man's)
       fundamental dependence on the natural world which he occupies and of which
       he is part . . . much ritual and religious behaviour translates uncontrollable natural
       forces into symbolic entities which, through the performance of ritual, can be
       manipulated and dealt with' (*Other Cultures:* p. 239). Delos B. McKown makes
       a similar point *vis-a-vis* Lenin's analysis of religion in his book *The Classical
       Marxist Critiques of Religion:* p. 100.

17.   As, for example, at *Capital* I; 72, 79, 372, 672 *et al.*

18.   Cf. Engels' letters of August 9 and September 1, 1871 to P.L. Lavrov; *MEW:*
       XXXVIII; pp. 261 and 265.

19.   For criticism of nineteenth century 'intellectualist' accounts of the origin of
       religion, cf. E. Evans-Pritchard, *Theories of Primitive Religion:* pp. 20-47.

20.   For Western phenomenological approaches to religion, cf. Eric Sharpe, *Compara-
       tive Religion:* pp. 220-250; Å. Hultkranz, 'Phenomenology of Religion: Aims and
       Methods' in *Temenos,* Vol. 6, 1970: pp. 68-88; M. Pye, 'Problems of Method in
       the Interpretation of Religion' in *Japanese Journal of Religious Studies,* 1/2-3,
       June-September, 1974: pp. 107-123.

21.   Cf. Jacques Waardenburg, *Classical Approaches to the Study of Religion:* pp. 85-
       113.

22.   So Fischer, *Marx in His Own Words:* pp. 90f.

23.   Cf. Feuerbach, *Wider dem Dualismus von Leib und Seele, Fleische und Geist:*
       p. 362.

24.   More often than not in the writings of Marx and Engels what constitutes member-
       ship of a class is ownership or non-ownership of the means of production – a
       criterion which in *The Communist Manifesto* and in *Capital* allows them to
       identify two major classes – the bourgeois and the proletariat – directly facing
       each other. At other times, however, Marx and Engels use the term 'class' of a
       wide variety of social groups. In writing of Britain, for instance, Marx wrote of
       'the ruling classes' and proceeded to identify two sub-groups within this class
       – the finance capitalists and the landowners – and describes them as 'two distinct
       classes'. A further problem in the identification of classes is caused by the

existence of the peasantry and by what Marx termed 'the *Lumpen-proletariat*'. The former – even though he be a small landowner – Marx usually, though not always, linked to the industrial proletariat: the latter, Marx regarded as being outwith the class structure of society altogether. A further problem arises with regard to the intelligentsia – doctors, teachers, musicians, writers, artists, etc. These, Marx and Engels proclaimed, did not constitute a class. Thus, in view of the loose way in which Marx and Engels spoke of classes, the most that can be said is that they did not regard classes as rigid and unchangeable, but as something thrown up in the course of history and which, by the middle of the nineteenth century, were beginning to crystallise into two major groupings related to the ownership or otherwise of the means of production and attaching to themselves a variety of sub-groups outwith this major division of society.

25. Marx wrote: 'Yet, from a social point of view, Hindustan is not the Italy, but the Ireland of the East. And this strange combination of Italy and of Ireland, of a world of voluptuousness and of a world of woes, is anticipated in the ancient traditions of the religion of Hindustan. That religion is at once a religion of sensual exuberance and a religion of self-torturing asceticism; a religion of the Ligam and the Juggernaut, the religion of the Monk, and of the Bayabere' ('The British Rule in India'; *MEOR:* pp. 31-32) and: 'We must not forget that this undignified, stagnatory, and vegetative life, that this passive sort of existence evoked on the other part, in contradistinction, wild, aimless, unbounded forces of destruction, and rendered murder a religious rite in Hindustan. We must not forget that these little communities were contaminated by distinctions of caste and slavery, that they subjected man to external circumstances instead of elevating man to be the sovereign of circumstances, that they transformed a self-developing social state into never changing natural destiny, and thus brought about a brutalising worship of nature, exhibiting its degradation in the fact that man, the sovereign of nature, fell down on his knees in adoration of Hanuman, the monkey, and Sabbala, the cow' (*ibid; MEOC:* pp. 36-37).

26. Engels, however, saw an important (ethnic) difference between reforming movements in Europe and reforming movements among the Arabs. After referring to the periodic 'cleansing' that frequently took place in Arabia, when the Bedouin from the desert would come to pillage the town – ostensibly for 'religious' reasons – he wrote: 'All these movements are clothed in religion but they have their source in economic causes; and yet, even when they are victorious, they allow the old economic conditions to persist untouched. So the old situation remains unchanged and the collision recurs periodically. In the popular risings of the Christian West, on the contrary, the religious disguise is only a flag and a mask for attacks on an economic order which is becoming antiquated. This is finally overthrown, a new one arises and the world progresses' (On the Early History of Christianity'; *MEOR:* p. 282).

27. A very recent, and stimulating, contribution to this discussion is the collection of papers contained in *Issues in Marxist Philosophy,* edited by John Mepham and D-H Ruben, Vol. 2, *Materialism,* Brighton, 1979.

28. Cf. the official Soviet publication, *The Fundamentals of Marxist-Leninist Philosophy,* 1974: pp. 54-62; 71-124.

CHAPTER 2

1. For more detailed study of the Russian background to Marxism, cf. J.M. Bocheński, 1963: pp. 20-27; Donald W. Treadgold, *The West in Russia and China,*

Vol. I *Russia 1472-1917*, Cambridge, 1973: pp. 152-242; Richard Pipes (1977); James H. Billington, 1970: pp. 359-472; George Vernadsky, *A History of Russia*, New Haven, 1969: pp. 218-276; Nicholas Riasanovsky, *A History of Russia*, New York, 1969: pp. 353-502; J. Plamenatz, *German Marxism and Russian Communism*, London, 1954.

2. i.e. immediately after 'The Time of Troubles' (*Smutnoye Vremya*). Cf. Riasanovsky, 1969, pp. 193-201; Billington, 1970: pp. 127-135.

3. See Billington, 1970: pp. 63-69.

4. Two extremely fine recent studies of the Russian intelligentsia are Philip Pomper, *The Russian Revolutionary Intelligentsia* (1970) and Isaiah Berlin, *Russian Thinkers* (1978). See Billington, 1970: pp. 232-242, 388-390 for the origins of the Russian *Intelligentsia*. As to the word itself, as Pipes has pointed out, although it is commonly believed to be of Russian origin, its etymological roots lie in Western Europe. It is, he writes, 'a latinized adaptation of the French *intelligence* and the German *Intelligenz* which in the first half of the nineteenth century came to be used in the west to designate the educated, enlightened, "progressive" elements in society . . . The word entered the Russian vocabulary in the 1860's, and by the 1870's became a household term . . .' (Pipes, 1977: p. 251).

5. Cf Dostoyevsky's early novel *Notes from Underground* (1864), Richard Peace has written: 'The chief target of *Notes from Underground* is Chernyshevsky – the then acknowledged leader of the younger generation, who the previous year (1863) had published *What is to be Done?* This work claimed to be more than a novel, it was offered as a 'textbook of life' for the author's younger contemporaries. In *Notes from Underground* we have Dostoyevsky's reply (Peace, 1971: p. 7). Chernyshevsky saw rational self-interest as the mainspring of human behaviour – what he termed 'rational egoism'. The 'underground man' jeers at this self-centred basis for morality:

If it is demonstrated that half an ounce of your fat ought essentially to be dearer to you than a hundred thousand of your fellow creatures and that this demonstration finally disposes of all so-called good deeds, duties and other lunacies and prejudices, simply accept it; there's nothing to be done about it, because twice two is mathematics. Just try to argue! (Dostoyevsky, *Notes from Underground*, Pelican, edit. 1971: p. 23)

The brunt of Dostoyevsky's attack falls on Chernyshevsky's attempt to link egoism and reason, and the 'underground man' argues that if the rational faculties constitute a mere twentieth part of man's makeup, how then can reason be equated with the whole of man's interest? There is, he maintains a greater self-interest which Chernyshevsky has left out of account, i.e., the freedom to do exactly as one chooses, even if it means acting against one's own interest – and in a passage prophetic of events to come in Russian society, the 'underground man' stresses that for man's happiness volitile urges are more important than rational motives, in so far as the mind seeks to impose restrictions on desires, it curtails man's freedom and prevents him from realising his full potential. The values of the advocates of 'rational egoism' strive towards what they take to be 'the perfect society'. This, in the estimation of 'the underground man', is nothing but the ideal of the ant-heap. The perfect symbol of the society which 'rational egoism' strives to bring about is, indeed, 'The Crystal Palace' – Chernyshevsky's own symbol.

The fact that the perfect society is encased in glass precludes any possibility of privacy (Zamyatin in his satirical novel *We* – a novel which presages Orwell's *1984* and Huxley's *Brave New World* – made similar play on this symbol). But, for the underground man, the very perfection of the 'crystal palace' is the mark of its non-human quality for, argues the 'underground man', human beings hate perfection and hate to achieve their goal. He says:

Perhaps I fear this edifice just because it is made of crystal and eternally inviolable, and it will not be possible even to put out one's tongue at it in secret. (ibid., p. 42)

But, as Peace points out, 'the crystal palace' is also, for Dostoyevsky, a symbol of man's hoped for ability to comprehend and codify the whole of creation (op. cit., p. 9). Human science, says the 'underground man' will end by destroying man himself; for it will reduce him to the function of a piano key or organ stop.

Yet this can never be, for man will choose to go mad, so that he might, in some fashion, live according to the dictates of his own non-rational will.

What the 'underground man' claims to do is to take to extremes what others dare to take only half-way – as Chernyshevsky's symbol of the palace of crystal. Similarly, he pushes the counter argument on man's will to its very limits; for the 'underground man' human desires reach out towards infinity. The 'god-seeking' which arises out of this fact – even when expressed in blasphemy – will be a major theme of Dostoyevsky's later novels and will stand as an indictment against all and every form of totalitarian society in which the 'infinite spirit', which Dostoyevsky discerns in man, is cramped or stifled.

6. Bakunin wrote:

If God is, man is a slave: now, man can and must be free; then, God does not exist . . . A jealous lover of human liberty, and deeming it the absolute condition of all that we admire and respect in humanity, I reverse the phrase of Voltaire, and say that *if God really existed, it would be necessary to abolish him.* (Cox and Steves, 1973: pp. 125, 128)

7. For extremely valuable accounts of the reception of Marxism in Russia see Donald W. Treadgold *The West in Russia and China*, Vol. 1. Russia 1472-1917, pp. 217-222, and David McLellan, *Marxism After Marx*, pp. 65-77.

8. Arthur Koestler, for example, has described his decision to join the Communist Party of Germany in December 1931 in the following terms:

To say that one had 'seen the light' is a poor description of the mental rapture which only the convert knows. The new light seems to pour from all directions across the skull; the whole universe falls into pattern like the stray pieces of a jigsaw puzzle assembled as if by magic at one stroke. There is now an answer to every question, doubts and conflicts are a matter of the tortured past – a past already remote, when one lived in dismal ignorance in the tasteless, colourless world of those who *don't know* (Richard Crossman, ed., *The God That Failed*, p. 19)

9. For an account of Lenin's youth and early intellectual development see David Shub, *Lenin:* pp. 13-46. A more controversial account is Leon Trotsky, *The Young Lenin.*

10. These early pamphlets are, in fact, marked more by anti-clericalism than atheism. In them Lenin takes up the cause of the persecuted sectarians and *inovertsy* (non-Orthodox) origin, in the name of 'an unlimited freedom of conscience', a 'complete separation of the church from the state and the state from the school' (*LCW:* vol. 46, pp. 9,472; vol. 2, pp. 85, 289-292; vol. 4, pp. 186, 224; vol. 5, pp. 338-339; vol. 6, p. 86). This demand, linked with a demand for the confiscation of 'monastic property', appears in Lenin's drafts of the Party programme prepared for the Second Congress of the RSDWP (Russian Social Democratic Worker's Party) in July-August 1903 (*LCW:* vol. 6, pp. 206, 209).

11. As, for instance, expressed by Lenin in his pamphlet *To the Village Poor* (1903), in which he elaborated, for the first time, the Party's 'minimum programme' for Church-State relations in Russia. He wrote:

> The social democrats demand . . . that everyone should have full rights to profess any faith absolutely freely . . . Every one should have full freedom not only to adhere to the faith of his choice, *but also to propagate any creed and change his confession* . . . There should be no 'ruling' confession or church. All creeds, all churches should be equal before the law. (*LCW:* 7;173)

12. April 1919, an administrative order of the Commissariat of Education of the RSFSR. See Sukhoplyuev, 1923: pp. 13-14. For the decree banning pornography, see *Leninskii sbornik*, vol. XXXVI, p. 319.

13. The constitutional provision with regard to religion reads: '*Article 124.* In order to ensure to citizens freedom of conscience, the church in the USSR is separated from the state and the school from the church. Freedom of religious worship and freedom of antireligious propaganda are recognised for all citizens'. For a full statement of the constitutional and legal rights of believers and for the way in which these have been interpreted (and violated) over the years cf. Michael Bourdeaux, Hans Hebly, Eugene Voss (ed.) *Religious Liberty in the Soviet Union* (1976), pp. 25-39. The new constitution proclaimed in 1977 in no way alters these earlier provisions regarding religion and atheism.

14. Cf. Nadezhda Mandelstam's penetrating comments on *The Short Course* in the first volume of her memoirs: *Hope Against Hope*, pp. 276-277.

15. One reason that has been suggested to account for this omission is that Stalin was well aware of the political connotations that the phrase 'the negation of the negation' had had for earlier revolutionary activists — a connotation that was not lost on those, such as Trotsky, who advocated a state of permanent revolution.

CHAPTER 3

1. Cf. Appendix I.

2. The reasons for Khrushchev's onslaught against religion remain something of a mystery to this day, but cf. Lowrie and Fletcher, 'Khrushchev's Religious Policy', in Marshall (ed.), 1971: pp. 131-155.

3. For detailed accounts of the anti-religious campaigns of the early period of Soviet power, cf. Edward A. Walsh, *The Last Stand,* Boston, 1931; Walter Kolarz,

Religion in the Soviet Union, London, 1961: pp. 1-35; N.S. Timasheff, *Religion in the Soviet Union, 1917-1942,* London, 1943: pp. 21-57. Soviet accounts of this period can be found in Y.M. Glan, *Antireligioznaya literatura dooktyabr'skogo perioda,* T.I. (1917-1929), Moscow, 1930; T.II (1929-1930), Moscow, 1930; T.III (iyul' 1930; noyabr' 1932), Moscow, 1932; Yu.A. Chukovenkov, '*Sovetskaya antireligioznaya pechat'*, v 1937-1941' (Soviet Anti-Religious Writing: 1937-1941), *YMIRA,* vol. V, 1961, pp. 76-90; B.L. Andrianova and S.G. Rutenburg, '*Antireligioznyy plakat pervikh let sovetskoy vlasti*', (Anti-Religious Posters During the First Years of Soviet Power), *YMIRA,* vol. 5, 1961, pp. 188-205.

4.   For further details of some of the serious writing relating to religion and atheism in the journals of this period cf. notes 1, 3, 4 to Chapter 6.

5.   For a detailed account of the debates over the interpretation of Marxist materialism in the Soviet Union during this period cf. Kołakowski, 1979, vol. III, ch. 2.

6.   An earlier Plenum of March 1930 had urged local Party organisations 'positively *to put an end to* the practice of closing churches forcibly, fictitiously disguising it as the public and voluntary wish of the population'. The same Plenum also urged local Party organisations 'to bring to the strictest accountability those guilty of mocking the religious feelings of peasant men and women' (*KPSS,* Part II, p. 641). The 1936 Plenum was simply verbally reinforcing these measures.

7.   An interesting statistical analysis of the subject matter of the journals *Voprosy istorii religii i ateizma* and *Yezhegodnik muzeya istorii religii i ateizma* can be found in an article by Kinga Nowicka entitled '*Voprosy istorii religii i ateizma*' (1950-1964) I '*Yezhegodnik muzeya istorii religii i ateizma (1957-1964): Zarys analizy statystycznej*' in the journal of the Polish society for the Study of Religion, *Euhemer,* 1975, no. 10, pp. 101-126. Among the more interesting statistics presented by Mrs. Nowicka is the fact that there were – taking both journals together – 194 items on the history of religion, and 163 on the history of atheism. Among the subjects touched on in the history of religion were the history of the Orthodox Church in Russia (39 items), the history of the Roman Catholic Church (53 items), the history of non-Christian religions (32 items), the history of the Christian religion – other than Orthodoxy and Catholicism – (25 items), and the history of sects and heresies (22 items). The theory of religion was also discussed in both journals (17 items) as was theology (6 items). Among topics in the history of atheism discussed in these journal are such subjects as the Marxist critique of religion (9 items), secularisation (26 items), atheist morality (3 items), the history of freethinking (72 items), anti-church movement (12 items) and atheism in the fine arts and in literature (17 items). Mrs Nowicka's conclusion is that 'In *VIRA* articles concerning the history of the church were predominant, while in *YMIRA* the history of atheism and the problems of socialist secularisation were more predominant. Overall, historical articles were predominant, and papers on the philosophy and sociology of religion were few' (op. cit., p. 125).

8.   The full text of the November resolution is given in Appendix I.

9.   At a conference held at the Institute of Scientific Atheism in 1966 to coordinate research work in areas of religion and atheism and at which there were representatives from academic and ideological institutions from throughout the Soviet Union, an ambitious programme of research was drawn up. It contained over 400 topics and eleven groups (or projects) were set up. They covered such topics as: 'The Leninist Legacy and the Present', 'The Degree and Character of Religiosity in the USSR', 'Peculiarities of the Struggle between Science and Religion under Present Conditions', 'Moral Progress and Religion', 'Religion and the Nationality Question', 'The System of Scientific-Atheist Education in the

USSR', 'Forms and Methods of Atheistic Propaganda', 'Atheist Education of the New Generation', 'The History of Religion and Atheism', 'New Tendencies in Religious Ideology and the Activities of Religious Organisations in Capitalist Countries', and 'Atheism and Freethinking Abroad at the Present Time'. Individual problems were allocated to specific academic institutions and 40 'bases' were established throughout the USSR to carry out 'concrete sociological research' and to discuss how the findings of this research might be applied to practical atheistic work. My respondents in the Soviet Union tell me that this programme has only 'intermittently' been carried out.

10. At the same time, and at a level intended not for specialists but for the ordinary intelligentsia, the *Znaniye* society began publishing from Moscow a monthly borchure, of about 100 pages in length, on some topic or other in the field of religion and atheism – *seriya nauchnyy ateizm*. This series still continues and the list for the period November 1979 to October 1980 was as follows:

11/79 M.A. Popova, Yu.Ya. Bondarenko, *Kritika liberal'no-gumanist i cheskikh kontseptsiy religii* (Criticism of Liberal-Humanist Conceptions of Religion).

12/79 A.B. Chertkov, *Kriticheskaya otsenka filosofskikh osnov religioznoy morali* (A Critical Evaluation of the Philosophical Foundations of Religious Morality)

1/80 P.K. Kurochkin, *Nauchno-ateisticheskoye vospitaniye v sisteme ideologicheskoy raboty* (Scientific-Atheist Upbringing in the System of Ideological Work)

2/80 G.L. Bakanursky, *Krizis i modernizatsiya iudaizma* (The Crisis and Modern Judaism)

3/80 A.N. Kochetov, *Kritika mirovozzrencheskikh osnov Buddizma* (Criticism of the Foundations of the Buddhist World-View)

4/80 A.D. Ursul, Yu.A. Shkolenko, *Chelovek i vselennaya* (man and the Universe)

5/80 V.E. Dolya, *Problema svobody v ateizme i religii* (The Problem of Freedom in Atheism and in Religion)

6/80 V.I. Garadzha, *Nauchnaya i khristianskaya interpretatsiya istorii* (Scientific and Christian Interpretation of History)

7/80 M.M. Skibitsky, *Sovremennoye yestestvoznaniye i religiya* (Contemporary Science and Religion)

8/80 R.N. Danil'chenko, *Problema lichnosti v sovremennom khristianstve* (The Problem of Personality in Contemporary Christianity)

9/80 V.Yu. Nyunka, *Sovremennyy vatikan* (The Contemporary Vatican)

10/80 I.M. Brechak, *Kritika religioznoy kontseptsii proiskhozhdeniya cheloveka* (Criticism of Religious Conceptions of the Origin of Man)

11. For further corroboration that philosophical materialism today constitutes the basis of Marxism-Leninism's argument with religion cf. O. Yakhot, *'Marksistsko-leninskaya filosofiya - nauchnaya osnova ateizma'* (Marxist-Leninist Philosophy as the Scientific Foundation of Atheism), *Propagandist i agitator*, vol. 21, 1955, pp. 45-51; M.I. Sidorov, *'Dialekticheskiy materializm - osnova nauchnogo ateizma'* (Dialectical Materialism as the Foundation of Scientific Atheism), *Nauka i zhizn'*, 1955, no. 10, pp. 35-37. See also Novikov's remarks below - pp. 287 ff.

12. A further example from this post-mortem was a letter from the editors of the popular anti-religious journal *Nauka i religiya* attacking one Alla Trubnikova, a veteran *antireligioznik,* whose numerous writings included an expose of convent life based upon her experiences there in the guise of a pilgrim. It was not just her method of obtaining information which the editors of *Nauka i religiya* criticised,

but her characterisation of religious believers as one and all scoundrels and vagrants, mental and moral cripples, and sworn enemies of Soviet society. Religion, proclaimed the editors, is a false and foolish ideology, but believers are loyal citizens and deserve respect. To win them to atheism demands patient dialogue rather than the slanderous charges of a Trubnikova – which, the editorial borad significantly added, 'are well adapted to encouraged those with a fondness for crude administrative measures' (*Nauka i religiya*, 1965, no. 3). This letter from the editorial board of *Nauka i religiya* produced an enormous response. One correspondent, an atheist lecturer from Minsk called Ivanov, openly admitted the self-defeating nature of vulgar representations of religion and of the intimidation of believers. 'There can be no doubt', he wrote, 'that the violations of the legislation on the cults and the offending of the religious sentiments of believers contributes to the existence of religious survivals' (*NiR*, 1965, no. 10). The whole debate is instructive and tells us much about those engaged in anti-religious propaganda – not least that there are a variety of approaches to atheistic work. This was very evident from the editorial summing up of the whole discussion in the October issue (*NiR*, 1965, no. 10) where criticism of misdirected anti-religious enthusiasm was broadened to include the official government newspaper *Izvestiya* – which unlike the newspaper of the Central Committee, *Pravda,* had not opened its columns to debate on the religious issue – and it was stated that at *Izvestiya* there were obviously some comrades who, forgetful of the ideological character of religion, still wished to combat it chiefly by means of the criminal code.

Finally, in 1967 a writer in *Voprosy nauchnogo ateizma* called for 'a scientific explanation of the nature of religion' writing that: 'Deviating from this principle is a subjectivist conception which ultimately reduces the essence of religion to the deception of simpletons by charlatans and finds the causes for the existence of religious survivals in our country in alien ideological influences and the resourcefulness of churchmen, on the one hand, and in the shortcomings of atheistic propaganda on the other. 'Such a conception', he continued, 'leads to erroneous conclusions, revives efforts to artificially speed up the overcoming of religion and encourages administrative methods in atheistic work'. 'A "scientific materialist" approach to religion', it claimed, 'must recognise that there are still objective social factors underlying religious survivals in Soviet society, such as essential differences between the city and the village, between intellectual and manual work and other remnants of the old way of life, as well as the alienation of individuals from the collective, weak social ties of housewives and the like' (V.I. Evokimov, 1967; *VNA.* p. 8). Cf. Cherkashin's not dissimilar point referred to in the footnote immediately below.

13. In this article Cherkashin argued the continued existence in the Soviet Union of certain epistemological and social roots of religion. Religious survivals in the Soviet Union were to be explained, he said, by certain shortcomings in that society itself – for instance, inequality of rewards, marginal injustices and coercion. 'Real contradictions and difficulties in our society', he wrote, 'may painfully affect the fate of the individual person, especially one not firmly tied to the collective', and he continued: 'In our circumstances there may be "failures" and "fortunates", not only in family life. Personal plans may be drastically changed or shattered by unforeseen circumstances, unexpected events in the life of the country, some shift or other in economic policy . . .' Moreover, he pointed out that 'certain features of our life which simply contradict socialist principles feed religious survivals', and he listed, among other things, 'errors in the direction of agriculture', 'a seemingly all-powerful bureaucracy which is isolated from the masses and which disregards their needs and interests', and in the recent past,

'the excesses of Stalinism with its noted crude violations of Soviet legality'. Finally, Cherkashin noted that Soviet society – especially in the countryside – had not yet 'fully overcome the dependence of man's activities on the play of the elemental forces of nature' (op. cit., pp. 29-41). Cherkashin's article came under immediate attack from the Central Committee of the CPSU in July 1959 for 'its incorrect conclusions that the same reasons which nourish religious prejudices in capitalist countries operate also in socialist society' (*Voprosy ideologicheskoy raboty*, 1961, pp. 280-281).

14. See, for example, M.B. Mitin, '*Marks, Lenin i problema cheloveka*' (Marx, Lenin and the Problem of Man) in *Karl Marks i sovremennaya filosofiya*, Moscow, 1968; cf. also pp. 534-551 of the 7th edition (1974) of *FMLP*, and M. Petrosyan, 1972: pp. 155-164.

15. For information on this important aspect of contemporary Soviet thinking, cf. Richard T. De George, *Soviet Ethics and Morality*, Ann Arbor, 1969 Cf. the same authors' 'The Soviet Concept of Man', *Studies in Soviet Thought*, IV (1964), pp. 261-276; 'Soviet Ethics and Soviet Society', *ibid.*, pp. 206-217; both the book and the articles contain extensive reference to Soviet material.

16. For a detailed analysis of the official Soviet attitude cf. Christopher Read, 'The Soviet Attitude to the Christian-Marxist Dialogue' in *RCL.*, Vol. 1, No. 6. 1973: p. 9.

17. For the Soviet attitude to Islam, cf. A.A. Abilov, S.M. Gadzhiev, '*Vserossiyskaya nauchnoteoreticheskaya konferentsiya o perezhitkakh religii islama i putyakh ikh preodoleniya*' (All-Russian Scientific-Theoretical Conference on the Remnants of the Islamic Religion and Paths for Eliminating Them', *FN*, 1961, no. 3, pp. 183-186.

18. The theme of Marxism-Leninism as a new secular Gnosticism is one that theologians and historians of religion would find it profitable, in my opinion, to explore.

CHAPTER 4

1. This theme is further developed in an article by Yu.A. Levada, '*Sovremennoye fideizm i nauka*' (Contemporary Fideism and Science), *VF*, 1957, no. 3, pp. 72-79.

2. Cf. K. Neilson, 'Wittgensteinian Fideism', *Philosophy*, vol. 42, 1967, pp. 206-226; D.Z. Phillips' position can be found in *Faith and Philosophical Enquiry*, London, 1970, Wittgenstein's in his later writings on language in general and in the posthumously published *Lectures and Conversations in Aesthetics, Psychology and Religious Belief* (ed., Cyril Barrett, Oxford, 1966) in particular.

3. See, for instance, Milton Yinger, *The Scientific Study of Religion*, London, 1970, pp. 1-40.

4. Cf. Frazer, *The Golden Bough*, 3rd ed., 1932, vol. I.

5. Soviet historians of Christianity are particularly fond of tracing 'parallels' to Christian beliefs in the ancient world and particularly in ancient Egypt; cf. *ITiA*: pp. 99-102; L.I. Yemeliyakh, *Proiskhozhdeniye khristianskogo kul'ta* (The Origin of the Christian Cult), Leningrad, 1971: pp. 12-36.

6. Cf. Plekhanov, *Fundamental Problems of Marxism*, 1969 ed., London: pp. 57-62.

7. The arguments given here are taken from such widely used text books as: *Kratkiy nauchno-ateisticheskiy slovar*' (Short Scientific - Atheist Dictionary) (SSAD); *Osnovy marksistko-leninskoy filosofii* (Fundamentals of Marxist-Leninist Philosophy) (EMLP). Cf. also: D.M. Ugrinovich, *Filosofskiye problemy kritiki religii*

(The Philosophical Criticism of Religion): P.P. Cherkashin, *'O sotsial'nykh kornyakh religii' VF*, 1958, no. 6, pp. 29-41; O. Yakhot, *'Marksistko-leninskaya filosofiya - nauchnaya osnova ateizma'* (Marxist-Leninist Philosophy as the Scientific Foundation of Atheism), *Propagandist i agitator*, 1955, vol. 21, pp. 45-51; S.V. Yarovsky, *'K voprosu o gnoseologicheskikh kornyakh religii* (On the Epistemological Roots of Religion) *Vestnik Leningradskogo Gos. Un.*, 1958, nos. 23, 53; V.N. Lentin, *'O dokazatel'stvakh bytiya bozhiya'* (On the Proofs of the Existence of God), *Nauka i zhizn'*, 1959, no. 12, pp. 53-57; I.K. Noskov, *'Kritika nekotorykh sovremennykh bogoslovskikh "Dokazatel'st" sushchestvovaniya boga* (Critique of Some Contemporary Theological Proofs for the Existence of God), *FN*, 1962, no. 1, pp. 114-121; A.D. Sukhov, *Sotsial'nye i gnoseologicheskiye korni religii* (Social and Epistemological Roots of Religion), Moscow, 1951; *'Gnoseologicheskiye korni religii'* (Epistemological Roots of Religion), FN, 1958, no. 4, pp. 102-112; N.I. Sherdakov, *'K voprosu o gnoseologicheskikh kornyakh religii'* (On the Epistemological Roots of Religion) in *Nauchnye Trudy, Lesotekhnicheskaya akademiya*, Leningrad, 1963; I.A. Kryvelev, *O dokazatel'stvakh bytiya bozhiya* (On the Proofs of the Existence of God), Moscow, 1960.

8. Some of the more recent Soviet publications in this area are: I.B. Inov and A.F. Pereturin, *'Nauka protiv religii'* (Science against Religion), *VF*, 1962, no. 2, pp. 172-176; F.Kh. Kessidi, *'Protivopolzhnost' nauchnogo znaniya religioznoy vere'* (Opposition of Scientific Knowledge to Religious Belief), *VF*, 1957, no. 1, pp. 200-212; O, Klor, *'Yestestvoznaniye i religiya'* (Natural Science and Religion), *VF*, 1960, no. 5, pp. 94-102; M.Ya. Koval'zon, *'Nauka vedet vpered, religiya otbrasyvayetsya nazad'* (Science Leads Forward: Religion Throws Back) *Nauka i zhizn*, 1956, no. 11, pp. 42-46; Yu.V. Kryanev, *'Mesto nauchno-populyarnoy literatury v sisteme antireligioznogo vospitaniya* (The Place of Anti-Religious Education, *VF*, 1962, no. 11, pp. 159-1962; Yu.A. Levada, *'Sovremenniy fideizm i nauka'* (Contemporary Fideism and Science), *VF*, 1957, no. 3, pp. 72-79; *Nauchnoye i religioznoye mirovozzreniye'* (Scientific and Religious World Views), *VF*, 1954, no. 4, pp. 20-27 (Editorial); S. Val'dgard, *Nauka protiv religii*, Moscow, 1952; S.N. Benkliev, *Nauka oprovergaet religiyu* (Science Refutes Religion), Voronesh, 1960; V.I. Ezersky, *Nauka i religiya o vselennoy* (Science and Religion on the Universe), Kharkov, 1960; K. Fadeyev, *'Nauka otvergaet religiyu* (Science Refutes Religion), Agitator, 1960, no. 4, pp. 23-25; V.I. Voytko, *Nauchnoye i religioznoye mirovozzreniye* (Scientific and Religious World Views), Kiev, 1960.

CHAPTER 5

1. This is the schema whereby society is held to have passed from primitive/communal through share-owning and feudal relationships to capitalism.
2. That is, the classical Marxist analysis of religion as interpreted by Lenin. That this was a simplified and attenuated version of the analysis of religion put forward by Marx and Engels themselves should be clear by reference to the first part of this study. One of the major points I am seeking to establish is that the Soviet understanding of religion, as we find it in 'scientific atheism', is less rich, in a number of important respects, than that put forward by Marx and Engels themselves.
3. That such an interest is still suspect in the Soviet Union is shown by the following remarks from the 'conclusion' to Tokarev's book, *Religiya v istorii narodov mira:* 'The main task of the history of religions is to get at the roots of religious belief and is certainly a more important task than that of simply describing . . . religious

beliefs and ceremonies. Such descriptions are only of use to future researchers' (1976b; p. 544; cf. Appendix III to present work, p.   ).

4. Pettazzoni, *Essays on the History of Religions,* Leiden, 1954.

5. The style and substance of Tokarev's 'conclusion' to his book *Religiya v istorii narodov mira* offers further evidence in support of this contention and is one reason why I have given it verbatim as an appendix to this study (Appendix III).

6. Once again, Tokarev hovers on the verge of admitting ideas intrinsic to religions as motivating factors in the development of religions but does not come out and say so explicitly.

7. Again I would refer the reader to Appendix III for further collaboration of these general criticisms of Soviet history of religion.

8. cf. Sharpe, 1975: p. 93.

9. Although Tokarev's *Religiya v istorii narodov mira* was originally published in 1964, references are given to the revised, 3rd edition of 1976 (1976b).

10. cf. James, 1949: pp. 9-11; 1957, p. 18. Koenigswald, *Spentocht in der Prehistorie,* Amsterdam, 1956.

11. But note Porshnev's attempt to revive, in a modified way, this position (Porshnev, 1965).

12. Cf. Kryvelev, 1975.

13. M.I. Shakhnovitch in private conversation with the author.

14. But understood in the crudest, materialistic way.

15. The distinction between 'lower' and 'higher' forms of religion, like the continued use of the term 'primitive', is not in Soviet study of religion indicative of any value judgement, but serves only to describe the development from simple to more complex forms of society and of religion.

16. Porshnev rejects the only attempt made so far at a formalisation of concepts of development by means of mathematical logic; that of the Polish philosopher O. Lange (Porshnev, op. cit., p. 137).

17. Cf. Ninian Smart, *The Religious Experience of Mankind* London, 1969; Collins, John B. Noss, *Man's Religions,* 5th ed.; New York and London, 1974, Collier-Macmillan; etc.

18. Cf. J.G. Frazer, *The Golden Bough,* 1960, Abridged edit., London, 1960; Macmillan; M. Eliade, *Patterns in Comparative Religion,* London, 1958; Sheed and Ward.

19. Birnbaum suggests two disparate reasons why Kautsky and Bernstein should have so reduced the original Marxist analysis of religion. The first is that both these German socialist thinkers took up with positivism as a method and proclaimed an almost total identification between the natural and the social sciences – a position which, in the history of thought, has frequently led to what Birnbaum calls a position 'external to religion' in which religious structures are reduced to their observable contexts and where the religious consciousness is regarded as wholly epiphenomenal. The second reason that Birnbaum advances for the 'religious insensitivity' of Kautsky and Bernstein's views on religion is that they held 'the curious view', as Birnbaum calls it, that if Marxism is a science, then Marxism's predictions as to the future had to be verified mechanically and inevitably. 'But no political movement', syas Birnbaum, 'can long maintain itself with a doctrine of inevitable triumph, however useful this may be for converting those outside it and for maintaining the morale of those within it'. Bernstein met this problem by appealing to Kantian morality; socialism will come about because it ought to come about – as an expression of humanity's actual moral characteristics. Such a view, Birnbaum argues, excludes the element of qualitative and historical trans-formation and works with a static view of human nature. In such a context,

religion seems at best arbitrary and at worst irrelevant or obscurantist – an element of history embarrassing to explain and most conveniently got rid of by treating it as a factor in pre-history not to be taken too seriously (Birnbaum, 1973: pp. 22-23). For a rather different, and somewhat more positive, assessment of Kautsky's contribution to Marxist theory of religion, cf. Delso McKown, 1975: pp. 122-157.

CHAPTER 6

1. See, for example, L.I. Aksel'rod, *Spinoza i materializm*, in *Krasnaya Nov'*, 1925, no. 7; A.I. Ardab'ev, *Ateizm Lyudviga Feyerbakha* (The Atheism of Ludwig Feuerbach), Moscow, 1963; M.S. Belen'ky, *'Ob ateizme Spinozy'* (On the Atheism of Spinoza), *FN*, 1959, no. 3; *Spinoza*, Moscow, 1964; B.M. Boguslavsky, *U istokov frantsuzkogo ateisma i materializma* (The Sources of French Atheism and Materialism), Moscow, 1964; B.E. Bykhovsky, *Byl li Spinoza materialistom?* (was Spinoza a Materialist?), Minsk, 1928; I. Baynshteyn, *'Spinoza i materializm, PZM*, 1926, no. 3; Y.P. Frantsev, *'Materialisty proshlogo o proiskhozhdenii religii'* (Materialists of the Past on the Origins of Religion), EMIRA, vol. I, 1957; I.A. Konikov, *Materializm Spinozy* (The Materialism of Spinoza), Moscow, 1971; M.T. Kocharyan, *Ateizm Gol'bakha* (The Atheism of d'Holbach), Moscow, 1957; P.S. Kudryavtsev, *Isaak N'yuton*, Moscow, 1963; G.M. Livshits, *Svobodomysliye i materialisticheskaya filosofiya v zapadnoy yevrope (vtoraya polovina XVII veka)* (Freethinking and Materialistic Philosophy in Western Europe (Second Half of the 17th century)), Minsk, 1975; A.V. Lunacharsky, *Ot Spinozy do Marksa* (From Spinoza to Marx), Moscow, 1925; A.D. Makarov, *Istoriko-filosofskoye vvedeniye k kursu marksistsko-leniniskoy filosofii* (Historico-Philosophical Materials for the Course on Marxsist-Leninist Philosophy), Moscow, 1972; M. Mitin, *'Spinoza i dialekticheskiy materializm'* (Spinoza and Dialectical Materialism), *PZM*, 1932, nos. 11-12; G. Obichkin, *'O materializme Spinozy'* (On the Materialism of Spinoza), *Antereligioznik*, 1932, nos. 23-24; V.I. Pekov, *P'er Beyl'*, Moscow, 1933; E. Sitkovsky, *'L. Feyerbakh ob ateizme Spinozy'* (L. Feuerbach on the Atheism of Spinoza), *PZM*, 1937, no. 9; V.V. Sokolov, *'Filosofiya Spinozy v kul'ture XVIIv'* (The Philosophy of Spinoza in the Culture of the 17th century), *Vestnik istorii mirovoy kul'tury*, 1959, no. 5; *Filosofiya Spinozy i sovremennost'* (The Philosophy of Spinoza Today), Moscow, 1964; *Dialektika i metafizika v istorii domarksistskoy filosofii* ('Dialects and metaphysics in pre-Marxist Philosophy') *Istoriya obshchestvennoy mysli*, Moscow, 1972; O.V. Trakhtenberg, *Razvitiye materializma i yego bor'ba protiv idealizma v period pervykh burzhuaznikh revolyutsiy (konets XVII – nachalo XVIII veka)* (The Development of Materialism and its Struggle with Idealism during the Period of the First Bourgeois Revolution (The End of the 17th-Beginning of the 18th century)), Moscow, 1956; I.P. Voronitsyn, *Istoriya ateizma*, Ryazan, 1930; V.I. Garadzha, *Istoriya ateizma – aktual'naya zadacha marksistskogo issledovaniya* (The History of Atheism – An Urgent Problem of Marxist Research), *VNA*, 1968, no. 5; N.I. Sherdakov, *Lektsii po istorii ateizma* (Lecturers on the History of Atheism), Leningrad, 1963. For works relating to the English 'materialist' and freethinking tradition, cf. below note 3.

2. See, for example I.L. Andreyev, *Voinstvuyushchiy ateizm velikikh russkikh revolyutsionerov-demokratkov N.G. Chernyshevskogo i N.A. Dobrolyubova* (The Militant Atheism of the Great Russian Revolutionary Democrats, N.G. Chernyshevsky and N.A. Dobrolyubov), Moscow, 1954; V.N. Ivanov, *Materializm i ateizm V.G. Belinskogo* (The Materialism and Atheism of V.G. Belinskogo), Moscow, 1954.

3.   See, for example, B.E. Bykovsky, *Materializm Tomasa Gobbsa* (The Materialism of Thomas Hobbes), *PZM*, 1938, no. 6; E.M. Beytsman, *T Gobbs – borets protiv religii* (T. Hobbes – Fighter Against Religion), in I.D. Pantskhav (ed.). *Materializm i religiya*, Moscow, 1958; L. German, *'Ucheniye Gobbsa ob obshchestve'* (Hobbes' Theories on Society), *PZM*, 1938, no. 6; V.F. Golosov, *Ocherki po istorii angliyskogo materializma XVII-XVIII vv*) (Essays on the History of English Materialism 17-18th centuries), Krasnoyarskk, 1958; I.S. Narsky, *'K voprosu ob osobennostyakh materializma Lokka'* (On the Problem of the Peculiar Materialism of Locke), *FN*, 1958, no. 3; *Filosofiya Dzhona Lokka*, Moscow, 1960; K. Pankratov, *'Dzhon Lokk i yego "Opyt o chelovecheskom razume"'* (John Locke and his "Essay on Human Understanding"), *PZM*, 1940, no. 2; M. Petrosova, *'Gobbs o religii'* (Hobbes on Religion), *PZM*, 1938, no. 6; V. Pozner, *'Tomas Gobbs – vydayushchiysya materialist i ateist'* (Thomas Hobbes – Outstanding Materialist and Atheist), *Kniga i proletarskaya revolutsiya*, 1938, no. 4; I. Razumovsky, *'Obshchestvenno-politicheskiye vozzreniya Tomasa Gobbsa'* (Socio-Political Views of Thomas Hobbes), *Vestnik kommunisticheskoy akademii*, vols. 37-38, 1930; P.G. Rakhubo, *'Ob osobennostyakh sensualizma Dzh. Lokka'* (On the Peculiar Sensualism of John Locke), *Iz istorii filosofii*, vol. II, ed. M.M. Grigor'yan, Moscow, 1958; V. Stal'nyy, *Utopiya Dzherarda Uinstenli* (The Utopia of Gerard Winstanley) *Istoricheskiy zhurnal*, 1942, nos. 3-4; B.A. Chagin, *'Kritika religii Tomasom Gobbs'* (Thomas Hobbes' Critique of Religion), *EMIRA*, vol. III, 1959; L.A. Chekin, *Tomas Hobbes – Rodonachal'nik sovremennogo materializma* (Thomas Hobbes – The Founder of Contemporary Materialism), Moscow, 1924; *Tomas Gobbs (yego zhizn' i ucheniye v svyazi s istoriyey obshchestvennoy zhizni Anglii kontsa XVI i pervoy poloviny XVII v.*) Thomas Hobbes [His Life and Studies in the Light of the History of Social Life in England at the End of the 16th and the first half of the 17th centuries]), Moscow, 1929; A.S. Kolesnikov, *Svobodomysliye Bertranda Rassela* (The Freethinking of Bertrand Russel), Moscow, 1978; A.S. Bogomolov, *Angliyskaya burzhuaznaya filosofiya XX veka* (English Bourgeois Philosophy in the 20th century), Moscow, 1978.

4.   See, for example, G.F. Aleksandrov, *Ocherk istorii sotsial'nykh idey v drevney Indii* (Outline of the History of Social Ideas in Ancient India), Minsk, 1959; N.P. Anikeyev, *O materialisticheskikh traditsiyakh v indiyskoy filosofii* (On the Materialistic Tradition in Indian Philosophy), Moscow, 1965; A.A. Avetis'yan, *Ocherki po istorii religii i ateizma (Drevniy mir)* (Essays on the History of Religion and Atheism (The Ancient World)), Kiev, 1960; B.F. Asmus, *Democrit* (Democritus), Moscow, 1960; A.M. Deborin, *Materializma: dialektika v drevneindiyskoy filosofii* (Materialism and Dialectic in Ancient India Philosophy), Moscow, 1956; T.B. Vasil'eva, *'Kontseptsiya prirody u Lukretsiya'* (Lucretius' Conception of Nature), *VF*, 1969, no. 7; V.V. Golovnya, *Aristofan*, Moscow, 1955; M.A. Dynnik, *Ocherk istorii filosofii klassicheskoy Gretsii* (Essays on the History of Philosophy in Classical Greece), Moscow, 1936; *'Bor'ba materializma i idealizma v antichnom obshchestve'* (The Struggle between Materialism and Idealism in Ancient Society), *PZM*, 1938, no. 5; *'Za marksistskoye izucheniye antichnogo materializma* (Towards a Marxist Study of Ancient Materialism), *VDI*, 1948, no. 4; A.P. Kazhdan, *Religiya i ateizm v drevnem mire* (Religion and Atheism in the Ancient World), Moscow, 1957; F.K. Kessidi, *'Religioznoye svobodomysliye i ateizm v drevney Gretsii'* (Religious Freethinking and Atheism in Ancient Greece), *FN*, 1962, no. 1; *'Gippokrat protiv religii'* (Hippocrates Against Religion), *Nauka i Zhizn'*, 1958, no. 1; A.H. Kochetov, *'O materializme i ateizme v drevney Indii'* (On Materialism and Atheism in Ancient India), *Anti-*

religioznik, 1940, no. 12; M.M. Kublanov, '*Ateisticheskiye vozzreniya Lukretsiya*' (The Atheistic Views of Lucretius), *YMIRA*, vol. III, 1959; G.M. Livshits, *Ateizm v drevnosti i sredniye veka* (Atheism in Antiquity and in the Middle Ages), Minsk, 1973; '*Materialisticheskiye i ateisticheskiye vozzreniya Lukretsiya*' (The Materialistic and Atheistic View of Lucretius) in *Vestnik Belorusskogo gosudarstvennogo universiteta*, Vol. III, 1970, no. 1; S.Y. Lur'e, *Teoriya beskonechno malykh y drevnikh atomistov* (The Theory of the Infinitely Small in the Ancient Atomists), Moscow, 1935; *Demokrit*, Moscow, 1937; *Arkhimed*, Moscow, 1945; *Ocherki po istorii antichnoy nauki* (Essays on the History of Ancient Science), Moscow, 1947; *Democrit, Epikur i Lukretsiy* (Democritus, Epicurus and Lucretius), Moscow, 1947; L.A. Lyakhovetsky, '*O materializme peredovikh mysliteley rabovladel'cheskogo obshchestva* (On the Materialism of the Progressive Thinkers of Slave-Owning Society), *FN*, 1960, no. 2; '*K voprosu o filosofskom materializme antichnogo obshchestva*' (On the Problem of Philosophical Materialism in Ancient Society), *Vestnik Moskovskogo universiteta, Seriya VIII*, 1961, no. 5; '*Neskol'ko slov o Geraklite* (Some Words on Heraclitus), *FN*, 1962, no. 4; A.O. Makovel'sky, *Drevnegrecheskiye atomisty* (The Ancient Greek Atomists), *Baku*, 1946; '*K voprosu ob ateizme Lukretsiya*' (On the Problem of the Atheism of Lucretius', *YMIRA*, vol. III, 1959; M.B. Mat'e, '*Iz istorii svobodomysliya v drevnem yegipte*' (The History of Freethinking in Ancient Egypt), *Voprosy istorii religii i ateizma*, 1956, no. 3; A.A. Petrov, *Van Chun – drevnekitayskiy materialist i prosvetitel*' (Wang-Chung – Ancient Chinese Materialist and Luminary), Moscow, 1954; Y.B. Radul'-Zatulovsky, '*Velikiy kitayskiy ateist Fan*' *Chzhen*'' (The Great Chinese Atheist Fang-Cheng), *YMIRA*, vol. 1, 1957; V.E. Timoshenko, *Materializm Demokrita* (The Materialism of Democritus), Moscow, 1959; Y.F. Shul'ts, *Epigramma Lukiana* (The Epigrams of Lucian), *VDI*, 1955, no. 1.

5.   Though it must be noted that Livshits concludes his study of atheism and materialism in antiquity by writing:

Almost all bourgeois historians of philosophy misrepresent the views of the materialists of the ancient world, glossing over their atheism, and interpreting them in the spirit of Idealism. Only Marxism-Leninism correctly interprets the significance of ancient materialism for the later development of science and philosophy. The materialistic and atheistic thought of the ancient peoples marks the beginning of the struggle with religion and idealism. This struggle reflected the interests of the most advanced state of the society of those days. Ancient materialistic philosophy even in its leading representatives – Wang Ch'ung, Democritus, Epicurus and Lucretius – was unable to reveal the social roots of religion and to show it in its true light. It put forward a mechanical materialism, but remained uninterested in social questions. The historical limitations of ancient materialism must be explained by the state of the science of its time and, above all else, by the fact that the materialists themselves belonged by right to the slave-owning class and were, therefore, not particularly concerned to overthrow religion. Yet the progressive ideas of these ancient thinkers was to become the foundation for the later development of materialistic thought. (Livshits, 1973: p. 171).

Livshits does not, unfortunately, state which bourgeois historians of philosophy he has in mind.

6. Chaddopadhyaya's book *Lokayata* was translated into Russian in 1961, his book on *The History of Indian Atheism* in 1966.

7. Cf. N.A. Bortnik, *Ereticheskiye sekty Italii pervoy poloviny* XIII v. (Italian Heretical Sects in the First Half of the 13th century), *Sb. Sredniye veka*, Moscow, 1957; G. Ley, *Ocherk istorii srednevekovogo materializma* (A History of Medieval Materialism), Moscow, 1962.

8. Cf. Livshits, 1973: pp. 369-371; Frantsov, 1975: pp. 14, 18, 20, 84, 115, 119, 274, 371.

9. See A.I. Klibanov, *'Samobytnaya yeres'* (*Iz istorii russkogo svobodomysliya kontsa XV – pervoy poloviny XVI v*) ("A Distinctive Heresy" – From the History of Russian Freethinking at the end of the 15th-first half of the 16th centuries), *VIRA*, vol. V, 1958; *'Svobodomysliye v Tveri v XIV - XV vv'* (Freethinking in Tver in the 14th-15th centuries), *VIRA*, vol. VI, 1958; *'K izucheniyu genezisa yereticheskikh dvizheniy v Rossii'* (The Study of the Beginning of Heretical Movements in Russia), *VIRA*, vol. VII, 1959; *Reformatsionnye dvizheniya v Rossii v XIV – pervoy polovine XVI v* (Reforming Movements in Russia in the 14th-First Half of the 16th centuries), Moscow, 1960; V.I. Koretsky, *'Bor'ba krest'yan s monastyryami v Rossii XVI·– nachala XVII v* (The Struggle of the Peasants with the Monasteries in Russia from the 16th to the beginning of the 17th centuries), *VIRA*, vol. VI, 1958; Cf. also I.U. Budovnits, *Russkaya publitsistika XIV veka* (Russian Publicist Writing of the 14th century), Moscow-Leningrad, 1947; *'Pervyye russkiye nestyazhateli'* (First Russian 'Nestyazhateli'), *VIRA*, vol. V, 1958; *Obshchestvenno-politicheskaya mysl' drevney Rusi (XI-XIV vv)* (Socio-political Thought in Ancient Russia (11th-14th centuries), Moscow, 1960; *Monastyri na Rusi i bor'ba s nimi krest'yan* (The Peasant Struggle with the Monasteries of Russia (14th-16th centuries), Moscow, 1966.

10. Cf. I.S. Braginsky, *Iz istorii tadzhikskoy narodnoy poezii (Elementy narodno-poeticheskogo tvorchestva v pamyatnikakh drevney i srednevekovoy pis'mennosti')* (From the History of the Tadjik Peoples' Poetry [Elements of folk-poetical creativity in Ancient and Medieval Writings]), Moscow, 1956.

11. Cf. Colin Morris, *The Discovery of the Individual 1050-1200*, London, 1972; R.W. Southern, *Medieval Humanism*, Oxford, 1970.

12. Cf. Livshits, 1973: pp. 195-258; B.E. Bykhovsky, *'Filosofskoye naslediye Ibn-Siny'* (Philosophical Heritage of Ibn Sin), *VF*, 1955, no. 5; G. Ley, *Ocherk istorii srednevekovogo materializma* (Outline of the History of Medieval Materialism), Moscow, 1962.

13. Cf. Livshits, 1973: pp. 172-427; Grigor'yan, 1974: pp. 42-53; O.V. Trakhtenberg, *Ocherki po istorii zapadnoyevropeyskoy sredenevekovoy filosofii* (Essays on the History of Western European Philosophy), Moscow, 1957.

14. For an almost complete bibliography of Soviet studies in this area, cf. Livshits, 1975: pp. 369-375.

15. Cf. B.F. Asmus, *'Tommazo Kampanella'*, *PZM*, 1937, no. 8; A.Kh. Gorfunkel', *Tommazo Kampanella*, Moscow, 1969; for the importance which Soviet historians of social thought ascribe to Thomas Moore, cf. Livshits, 1973: pp. 369-371.

16. Cf. bibliography contained in footnote 3 to present chapter.

17. Cf. V.I. Pikov, *P'er Beyl'*, Moscow, 1933; *Frantsuzskiye prosvetiteli XVII v o religii* (French Enlightenment of the 18th century on Religion), Moscow, 1960; Grigor'yan, 1974: pp. 119-154; Prantsov, 1972: pp. 50-61.

18. Cf. Frantsov, 1975: pp. 49-77.

19. Cf. Grigor'yan, 1974: pp. 153-168; G. Geyne, *K istorii religii i filosofii v Germanii*

(On the History of Religion and Philosophy in Germany), *Poln. sobr. soch.*, vol. VII, Moscow, 1936.

20. Cf. Frantsov, 1972: pp. 74-85; Grigor'yan, 1974: pp. 200-216. The major study in this area is Andreyev, *Voinstvuyushchiy ateizm velikikh russkikh revolyut-sionerov-demokratov N.G. Chernyshevskogo, i N.A. Dobrolyubova* (The Militant Atheism of the Great Russian Revolutionary-Democrats, N.G. Chernyshevsky and N.A. Dobrolyubov), Moscow, 1953.

CHAPTER 7

1. Western sociologists and students of religion, even when allowed to enter the Soviet Union in an official capacity, are not, of course, allowed to pursue field-work but are confined to studying the results of Soviet research in libraries, archives (and private conversations with Soviet colleagues).

2. The answer to this question is perhaps found in the early writings of Marx. Only 'the fantasy world of religion', I think Marx would have said, and not − except maybe momentarily − hooliganism and drunkenness, can satisfy the thwarted human needs for recognition and self-fulfilment.

3. I shall be returning to this question in Part III of this study and in the Conclusion.

4. Cf. Wassilij Alexeev and Keith Armes, *'German Intelligence: Religious Revival in Soviet Territory'*, RCL, vol. 5, Spring 1977, pp. 27-30; John Lawrence, *'Observations on Religion and Atheism in Soviet Society'*, RCL.

5. Two leading American students of Soviet research into religion in the Soviet Union wrote:

   In evaluating current Soviet research on the problem of the sociology of religion we are faced with a dilemma, in that we have no independent testimony concerning social phenomena which Soviet researcher's describe, and no means of getting any. All we can say, therefore, is that Soviet research in sociology of religion seems to us serious, scientific and worthy of study. It is not unbiased − far from it, but at least its bias is clearly, not to say, compulsively, stated, which is more than can be said for the work of many Western social scientists. (Ethel and Stephen Gunn, 1975: p. 130)

6. Cf. L.I. Breshnev, *Leninskim kursom* (On Lenin's Course), vol. 4, p. 50.

7. see V.A. Chernyak in *Formirovaniye nauchno-materialisticheskogo ateisticheskogo mirovozzreniya (Sotsiologicheskiye problemy)* (The Formation of a Scientific-Materialist Atheist World View (Social Problems), Alma, Ata, 1969.

8. The literature on this is vast, but see Powell, 1975: pp. 66-84; Binns, 1978; and articles in *RCL* passim.

9. This museum, a distinguishing feature of which is the vast library which it possesses on all aspects of religion and atheism, divides the scholarly work (and the displays which are constantly changed and brought up to date) pursued by scholars permanently attached to it, into eight departments: (1) Science and Religion; (2) The Origin of Religion; (3) Religion and Atheism in the Ancient World; (4) Religions of the East; (5) The Origin of Christianity; (6) Religion and Atheism in the West; (7) History of Russian Orthodoxy and Russian Atheism; (8) The Overcoming of Religious Survivals in the Period of the Expanded Con-

struction of Communism in the USSR (cf. Butinova, 1962). For more information on this museum, cf. *KNAS* pp. 382-383; *'25 let Muzeya istorii religii i
ateizma'* (25 years of the Museum of the History of Religion and Atheism) in
YMIRA vol. 1, 1957; M. Shakhnovich, *'25-letiye Muzeya istorii religii i ateizma'*
in *VIRiA*, no. 5, 1958; Shurygin, *Kazanskiy sobor* (Kazan Cathedral), Leningrad,
1961; *Kratkiye spravochniki-putevoditeli po muzeyu* (Short Guide for Tour-
Leaders around the Museum), *NiR*, 1961. It was in the library of this museum
that most of the research for this present study was undertaken.

10. Sir John Lawrence has pointed out to me that one other and rather subtle way in
which religious knowledge is conveyed to the public by Soviet scholars sympathetic to religion is by means of lengthy expositions of theological material which
are then followed by the ritual, critical concluding chapter and he instances, as
examples, Averintsev's book on early Byzantine literature *(Poetika rannevizantiy-
skoy literatury*, Minsk, 1970) and a book *Teyyardizm popytka sinteza nauki i
khristianstva (Teilhardism: An attempt to Synthesise Science and Christianity,*
published in Moscow in 1977.

11. Cf., for instance, the tables quoted by Powell, 1975: pp. 50, 60, 81, 88-90, 105.
12. Cf. Unger, 1974: pp. 188-203; Powell, 1955: pp. 63-84 and 1975b, in Bocurkiw
and Strong, 1975: pp. 151-170; Binns, 1978.
Nikita Struve, 'Pseudo-Religious Rites Introduced by the Party Authorities' in
Fletcher and Struve, 1967: pp. 44-48.
13. The Soviet literature on 'secular rites' is vast, but the following should be noted:
D.M. Ugrinovich, *Obryady: za i protiv,* (Rites: For and Against) Moscow, 1975;
N.S. Sausenbayev, *obucheniye traditsii i obshchestvennaya zhizn'* (The Teaching
of Tradition and Social Life), Alma-Ata, 1974: pp. 211f. A fuller bibliography is
contained in the footnotes to Binns, 1978. Cf. also articles in almost every
edition of *VNA.*

CHAPTER 8

1. Edwyn Bevan traces this emphasis in Western civilization on the salvic value of
correctly formulated belief to the Greeks, cf. Bevan, 1932: p. 110.
2. Cf. E. Bolaji Idowu, *African Traditional Religion,* London, SCM, 1973: pp. 137-
202; John S. Mbiti, *African Traditional Religions and Philosophy,* London,
Heinemann, 1969; esp. pp. 75-91; G. Parrinder, *African Traditional Religion,*
London, Sheldon Press, 1962: pp. 113-122 ('Spiritual Forces').
Cf. also B.I. Sharevskaya, *Starye i novyye religii afriki* (The Old and New Religions
of Africa), Moscow, Nauka, 1964.
3. For criticism of Otto, cf. H.J. Paton, *The Modern Predicament,* London, Allen
and Unwin, 1955: pp. 129-145; Ninian Smart, *Philosophers and Religious Truth,*
London, SCM, 1964: pp. 130-166; David Barstow, 'Otto and Numinous Experience', in *Religious Studies,* vol. 12, no. 2, 1976, A reading of Waardenburg's
Classical Approaches to the Study of Religion, The Hague, Mouton, 1973, vol. I,
or Eric Sharpe, *Comparative Religion: A History,* London, Duckworth, 1975,
will quickly dispel any impression that Western *Religionswissenschaft* constitutes
a unified disciple with 'assured results'.
4. So, for example, Eric Mascall in *He Who is,* London, Longmans, Green and Co.,
1954: pp. 16-26.
5. This is now being recognised, for instance, in the study of Indian religion where,
until quite recently, specialists tended to concentrate their attention on the highly
sophisticated beliefs of the Vedanta and to ignore the ordinary, everyday beliefs

of the average Indian — as, for example, did R.C. Zhaener in his study *Hinduism*, 2nd ed., Oxford, 1966. Today, the study of 'village Hinduism' represents a major step forward in our understanding of Indian religion; cf. Simon Weightman, *Hinduism in the village Setting*, Open University Press, 1978.

6. For a more detailed account of Greek 'naturalistic' theories of religion, cf. my *The Alternative Tradition*, pp. 162-168.
7. Cf. Lenin, 'Socialism and Religion', *LCW:* 15: 202.
8. Cf. Yevgeny Zamyatin, *We*, London, Penguin Modern Classics, 1977; Vladimir Voinovich, *The Life and Adventures of Private Ivan Chonkin*, London, Penguin Books, 1978; Zinov'yev, *The Commanding Heights*, London, 1979. Vladimir Bukovsky tells a beautifully sad little story in his recently published *To Build a Castle*, London, Andre Deutsch, 1978, which typifies that aspect of Soviet propaganda to which I am referring. He writes:

The teacher at a Soviet nursery school is giving a little talk. She hangs a map of the world on the wall and explains: 'look, children, here is America. The people there are very badly off. They have no money, therefore they never buy their children any sweets or ice-cream and never take them to the cinema. And here, children, is the Soviet Union. Everybody here is happy and well-off, and they buy their children sweets and ice-cream every day and take them to the pictures'. Suddenly one of the little girls bursts into tears, 'What is the matter, Tania, why are you crying?' 'I want to go to the Soviet Union', sobs the little girl. (op. cit., p. 53)

CHAPTER 9

1. Cf., for example, the story of early Christianity's struggle with the political ideology of the *Pax Augusta* as told in Cochrane's classic study *Christianity and Classical Culture*, New York, Harper Torch Books, 1968. Cf. also S.L. Greenslade, *The Church and the Social Order*, London, SCM, 1947.
2. It is for this reason, I think, that Soviet historians and philosophers pay far more attention than do Western historians and philosophers to the historical schemata put forward by thinkers such as Arnold Toynbee and Teilhard de Chardin.
3. Hellen Waddell brilliantly describes the development of this response to the world in the early Middle Ages in her book *The Wandering Scholars*, Harmondsworth, Penguin Books, 1954: pp. 31-88.
4. It is no accident that Soviet publishing houses are at present issuing Leonid Brezhnev's exposition and interpretation of Marxism-Leninism under the general title *Leninskim kursom* (Following Lenin's Course).

CONCLUSION

1. The development of Marx's thought about religion is traced in great detail in Charles Wachenheim's *La faillite de la religion d'après Karl Marx*, Paris, PUF, 1963. Wachenheim shows that Marx's atheism was in constant evolution, but he distinguishes three main periods in his thought about this subject, each of which was dominated by a specific conception of the nature and role of religion: (1) The

period 1835-1842 where Marx is trying to construct a philosophical critique of religion. Although Marx's thought during this period is basically Hegelian, he agrees with the 'left wing' Hegelians in rejecting Hegel's own effort at reconciling philosophy and religion, and in seeing that God and the Christian religion were but arbitrary appendages to the Hegelian synthesis. He therefore joins the Hegelian left in a return to the rationalistic atheism of the *Aufklärung* with its cult of reason and progress, though he was soon to pass far beyond this. (2) The second period extends from about 1842-1845. Here Marx is engaged on a fundamental criticism of the whole Hegelian synthesis and of all philosophy hitherto. The central theme of Marx's thought at this time was the fundamental unity of theory and practice. Religion is now rejected in the name of Marx's developing conception of the practical nature of man's condition. Religion is an alienation, but must be reduced to its socio-economic base. Of all forms of alienation religion is the most insidious in that it causes man to ignore what is essential to his liberation here on earth. (3) The third period, 1845-1848, is the period in which Marx becomes more and more involved in actual political activity (cf. Nicolaievsky and Otto Maenchen-Helfen, *Karl Marx: Man and Fighter,* Penguin Books, 1976: pp. 129f) and turned his attention from nature and man to historical materialism and the evolution of history and society. Applying the conception of alienation to society, Marx now sees religion as an ideology, and as an arm in the class struggle, used to prevent man's progress towards self-realisation. It is this latter aspect of Marx's views on religion, which, as Wachenheim points out, has been seized on by Marx's Marxist-Leninist heirs. Whilst, as will be obvious from my own treatment of Marx on religion, I think Wachenheim formalises Marx's concern with religion too rigidly, I am in basic agreement with what he says and in full agreement with his latter point regarding what Soviet 'scientific atheism' picks out of Marx's criticism.

2. The work of the *Paulusgesellschaft,* a group of German speaking theologicians and scientists meeting between 1965-1967 at Salzburg, Chiemsee and Marianske Lazné (Marienbad) was fundamental to this enterprise. Accounts of the recent theological response to Marxism can be found in Hebblethwaite, 1977; cf. Isham, 1972 and Dale Vree, 1976.

3. For a recent criticism of Western 'bourgeois' humanism by a 'Scientific Atheist' cf. Z.A. Tazhvrizima, *'Burzhuaznyy ateizm v proshlom i nastoyashchem* (Bourgeois Atheism in the Past and in the Present), Moscow, *Znaniye: seriya nauchnyy ateizm,* vol. 3, 1976.

4. I am comforted by the fact that Bertrand Russell has expressed a similar despair, cf. Russell, *Autobiography,* London, Allen & Unwin, vol. II, pp. 158-160.

APPENDIX IV

1. Other publications of his include: '*Novyye arkhivnyye issledovaniya v Indiyskoy respublike (1954-1955)* (New Archival Research in the Indian Republic (1954-1955) in *Sovetskaya arkheologiya,* 1957, no. 3; *'Kalingskaya voyna i ee zhacheniye v istorii pravleniya Ashoki'* (The Study of the Kaling War in the History of the Rule of Ashoka'), *VDI,* 1958, no. 3; *'Agrames-Ugrasena-Nanda i votsareniye Chandragupty',* *VDI,* 1962, no. 4; *'Istoricheskiye osnovy drevneindiyskikh avadan'* (Historical Foundations of Ancient Indian Avadan), *Narody Azii i Afriki,* 1963, no. 1; *K probleme istorichnosti III sobora v Pataliputre'* (On the Problem of the 3rd Council in Pataliputra' in *Indiya v drevnosti* (India in Antiquity), Moscow, 1965; and an edition of the *'Fragmenty sanskritskoy rukopisi*

iz Zang-te-pe' (Fragments of a Sanskrit Manuscript from Zang-Te-Pe', in collaboration with M.I. Vorob'ev-Desyatovsky and E.N. Temkinym, in *VDI,* 1965, no. 1.

2. Who together with Bongard-Levin produced an influential article *'Legenda o Mare i Upagupte'* for the book, *Ideologicheskiye techeniya sovremennoy Indii* (Ideological Tendencies in Contemporary India), Moscow, 1965.

3. His *kandidat* dissertation was on the theme of *'Sotsial'noeconomicheskaya i politicheskaya rol' buddiyskoy sankhi v drevnikh i srednevekovykh gosudarstvakh Tseylona'* (The Socio-Economic and Political Role of the Buddhist *Sanga* in Ancient and Medieval State of Ceylon), and he also published an important article *'Sistema upravleniya drevnimi monastyryami Tseylona po materialam singal'skoy epigrafiki'* (The System of Government in the Monasteries of Ceylon According to Singalese Epigraphical Material) in the anthology, *Indiya v drevnosti,* Moscow, 1965.

4. His major work includes: *Ocherk istorii tibetskogo naroda (stanovleniye klassovogo obschchestva)* (Essays on the History of the Tibetan People) (The Making of Class Society)), Moscow, 1962; *'Proniknoveniye buddizma v Tibet* (VII-IX vv' (The Penetration of Buddhism into Tibet (seventh to ninth centuries)) in *Trudy Buryatskogo kompleksnogo NII SO AN SSSR, Wy*p. 8, Ulan-Ude, 1962: pp. 68-81.

5. Cf. his *'Iz istorii buddizma v gosudarstve si Sya',* pp. 140-157 of *Daln'niy Vostok* (The Far East), Moscow, 1961.

6. Whose most well known publication was *'Narodnye verovaniya v buddizme'* (Buddhist Folk Beliefs), in *Buryatskogo kompleksnogo NII SO AN SSSR i buryatskoy organizatsii ob-va 'Znaniye',* Burknigizdat, 1965.

7. Cf. his article *'Iz istorii religioznogo sinkretizma v Zabaykal'* (The History of Religious Syncretism in Zabaykal), *SE,* 1965, no. 6.

8. Cf. his *Rol' buddizma v istorii Mongolii* (The Role of Buddhism in the History of Mongolia), Chita, 1945.

9. Cf. I.M. Kutasov, *'Buddiyskaya filosofiya i logika v trudakh akademika F.I. Shcherbatskogo'* (Buddhist Philosophy and Logic in the Work of Academician F.I. Shcherbatsky', *Sovetskoye vostokovedeniye,* 1958, no. 3.

10. Cf. *Kritika ideologii lamaizma i shamanizma* (Critique of the Ideology of Lamaism and Shamanism), Ulan-Ude, 1965, and the article which he contributed to a collection of essays, *O nekotorykh religioznikh kul'takh i ikh sushchnosti* (Some Religious Cults and their Essence), Ulan-Ude, 1961, and entitled *'Chto soboy predstavlyayut lamaistskiye molebstviya i prazdniki'* (What Lamaist Services and Holidays Mean to Me).

11. Cf. *'Sovremennoye sostoyaniye buddizma za rubezhom'* (Contemporary Fortunes of Buddhism Abroad) in *Kritika ideologii lamaizma i shamanizma,* Ulan-Ude, 1965.

12. Cf. his *'Sushchnost' izmeneniy buddizma'* (The Essence of Changing Buddhism) in the collected work cited in footnote 1.

13. Cf. the earlier attempts of the 1920's and 1930's as exemplified in G. Tsibikov, *'Tsagalgan',* Buryatievedeniye, 1927, nos. 3-4; S.L. Ursinov, *Tsam', Antireligioznik,* 1933, no. 6; N. Shastina, *'Tsam', Khozyaystvo Mongolii,* 1928, no. 6 (13); *'Religioznaya misteriya "Tsam" v monastyre Dzunkhure'* (The Religious Mystery of 'Tsam' in the Monastery of Dzunkhur), *Sovremennaya Mongoliya,* 1935, no. 1; R. Khaptaev, *'Khubiliganstvo v zapadnikh aymakakh Buryatii'. Antireligioznik,* 1935, no. 5.

14. Cf. *Lamaizm i natsional'no-kolonial'naya politika tsarizma v Zabaykal'e v XIX i nachale XX vekov* (Lamaism and National-Colonial Politics in Zabaikal in the Nineteenth Century and the Beginning of the Twentieth Century), Ulan-Ude,

1957; *obnovlencheskoye dvizheniye buryatskogo lamaistskogo dukhovenstva (1917-1930 gg)* (Renewal Movements of Buryat Lamaist Clergy (1917-1930), Ulan-Ude, 1964.

15.   Cf. Donini, *Rukopisi iz okrestnostey mertvogo morya i proiskhozhdeniye khristianstva'* (The Manuscripts from the Region of the Dead Sea and the Origin of Christianity), VDI, 1958, no. 2.

16.   Cf. I.D. Amusin, *Rukopisi mertvogo morya* (Manuscripts From the Dead Sea), Moscow, 1960; *Nakhodki y mertvogo morya* (The Dead Sea Finds), Moscow, 1964; S.I. Kovalev and M.M. Kublanov, *Nakhodki v Iudeyskoy pustyne* (Finds in the Jewish Desert), 2nd ed., Moscow, 1964.

17.   Cf. V.D. Bonch-Bruyevich, *'Krivoye zerkalo sektantsva'* (The Distorting Mirror of the Sects', *Izvestiya*; July 30, 1921.

18.   Cf. P.A. Krasikov, *'Vedayut li, chto tvoryat?'* (Do They See What They are Creating?), *Revolyutsiya i tserkov;* 1920, no. 9; *'I myt'em, i katan'em'* (By Hook and by Crook), in *Na Tserkovnom fronte* (On the Church Front), Moscow, 1923.

19.   Cf. *'Metody izucheniya i kritiki sektanstva'* (Techniques for the Study and Critique of Sectarianism) and *'Sektantsvo i antireligioznaya propaganda'* (Sectarianism and Antireligious Propaganda) in *Kommunisticheskoye prosveshcheniye*, 1926, nos. 5, 6; *'Sovremennoye sektanstvo'* (Contemporary Sectarianism), *Antireligioznik*, 1926, nos. 4, 6; *Klassovaya sushchnost' sektantskikh teorii i praktiki'* (The Class Nature of Sectarian Theory and Practice), AR, 1926, no. 1; *Rayony rasprostraneniya sektantstva prezhde i teper'* (Areas of Previous and Current Distribution of Sectarianism), AR, 1927, no. 1; and *Sektantstvo i antireligioznaya propaganda* (Sectarianism and Anti-religious Propaganda), Moscow, 1928.

20.   Cf. also: A. Dolotov, *Tserkov' i sektantstvo v Sibiri* (Churches and Sects in Siberia), Novosibirsk, 1930; N. Matorin, *Religiya i bor'ba s ney v severnom krae* (Religion and the Struggle with It in the Northern Territories), Leningrad, 1930; I. Shchepkin, *Sektanty na Urale* (Sects in the Urals), Sverdlovsk, 1928: *Ural'skoye sektantstvo prezhde i teper'* (Sects of the Urals, Past and Present), Sverdlovsk, 1930; P. Tikhomirov, *'Sektanty v Krymu'* (Sects in the Crimea), AR, 1931, no. 10; L. Klimovich, *Sektantstvo v Tatarskoy respublike'* (Sectarianism in the Tatar Republics), AR, 1928, no. 5; A.I. Golovkin, *Ryasniki i sektanty Ivanovskoy oblasti* ('Ryasniks' and Sects in the Ivanov Provinces), Ivanovo, 1930; M.V. Popov, *Sektanstvo Ivanovskoy promyshlennoy oblasti prezhde i teper'* (Sects of the Ivanov Industrial District in the Past and Today), Ivanov, 1931; P. Zarin, *'Rabota sektantov v voronezhskoy Gubernii'* (The Work of the Sects in the Voronezh Guberniya), AR, 1928, nos. 1-3; S. Vainshtein, *'Sektantskoye dvizhenie v gorode Vladivostoke'* (Sectarian Divisions in the City of Vladivostok), AR, 1932, no. 2; I. Medvedev, *Na beregu 'Svyashchennogo Baykala'* (On the Shores of Holy Baikal), Moscow, 1930; Z.O. Krainyuk, *'O setantskom dvizhenii v Muromskom uyezde'* (On Sectarian Movements in Murom District), AR, 1929, no. 4.

21.   Cf. apart from the major work mentioned above, his *Religioznoye sektantstvo i sovremennost' (sotsiologicheskiye i istoricheskiye ocherki)* (Religious Sectarianism and the Present (Sociological and Historical Essays)), Moscow, 1969; *Sovremennoye Sektantstvo* (Contemporary Sectarianism), *VIRA*, 1961, vol. IX.

22.   See *'Sovremennoye sektanstvo i yego preodoleniye (po materialiam ekspeditsii v tambovskuyu oblast'* (Contemporary Sectarianism and its Overcoming Accroding to Material from the Expedition to the Tambov Province), VIRA, 1961, vol. IX; I.A. Aleksandrovich, G.E. Kandaurov and A.M. Memirovsky, *'Sektantstvo v voronezhskoy oblasti i rabota po yego preodoleniyu'* (Sectarianism in the Voronezh Province and the Work Being Done to Overcome It), *YMIRA*, vol. 5,

1961; A.I. Klibanov, *'Sovremennoye sektantstvo v lipetskoy oblasti'* (Contemporary Sectarianism in the Lipetsk Province), *VIRA*, 1963, vol. XI; N.S. Zlobin, *'Sovremennyy baptizm i yego ideologiya'* (Contemporary Baptists and Their Ideology), *VIRA*, 1963, vol. XI; E.K. Dulman and V.K. Tancher, *'Opyt konkretnogo issledovaniya kharaktera religioznykh predstavlenii'* (Experience of Concrete Research into the Character of Religious Beliefs), VF, 1964, no. 10; *Prichiny sushchestvovaniya i puti preodoleniya religioznykh perezhitkov* (The Reason for the Existence and the Way to Overcome Religious Survivals), Minsk, 1966; V. Chernyak, *O preodolenii religioznykh perezhitkov* (On the Overcoming of Religious Survivals), Alma-Ata, 1965; D.M. Aptekman, *'Reaktsionaya sushchnost' sekty trezvennikov* (The Reactionary Essence of the Sects of Teetotalers), *Nauchnyye trudy lesotekhnicheskoy akademii*, no. 101, Leningrad.

23. Cf. also the same authors' *Khristianskaya nauka zhizni* (Christian Science of Life), Moscow, 1961; L.N. Mitrokhin and E.Ya. Liagushina, *Nekotoryye cherty sovremennogo baptizma'* (Some Aspects of Contemporary Baptism), *VF*, 1964, no. 2; E.G. Filimonov, *'Apologiya individualizma i dukhovnoy nishchety'* (The Apology for Individualism in Spiritual Misery), *VF*, 1964, no. 11; G. Yakovlev, *Formirovaniye nauchnogo mirovozzreniya i khristianskoye sektantsvo* (The Formation of a Scientific World-View and The Christian Sects), Alma-Ala, 1965; V. Lentin, *Adventism i nauka'* (Adventism and Science), *VNA*, no. 2, 1966.

24. Cf. P.A. Gladkov and G.Ya. Korytin, *Khristianskiye sekty, bytuyushchiye v Azerbaydzhane* (Christian Sects in Azerbaidian), Baku, 1961; K.I. Kozlova, *'Izmeneniya v religioznoy zhizni i deyatel'nosti molokanskikh obshchin'* (Changes in Religious Life and Activities of the Molokans), VNA, 1966, no. 2; A. Shamaro, *'U poslednikh prygunov'* (Among the Last 'Jumpers') *NiR*, 1964; no. 9; A.G. Zolotov, *'Reaktsionnyy kharakter molokanstva (po materialam, sobrannym v 1959-1960 gg. v Gruzinskoy SSR)'* (The Reactionary Character of the Molokans (From Material Collected 1959-1960 in the Georgian SSR), *YMIRA*, vol. VI, 1962; A.M. Chiperis, *'Sovremennoye sektantstvo v Turkmenskoy SSR'* (Contemporary Sectarianism in the Turkmen SSR), in *Izvestiya Akademii nauk Turkmenskoy SSR: Seriya obshchestvennykh nauk*, Ashkhabad, 1964; Yu.A. Solnyshko, *Nishchiye (pravda o sekte evangel'skikh khristian-baptistov)* (The Beggars (The Truth about the Sect of Evangelical Baptists)), Kursk, 1962; A.Z. Chernov, *O religioznykh sektakh Tomskoy oblasti'* (The Religious Sects of the tomsk Region), Tomsk, 1960.

25. In *Sbornik vostochnogo instituta v chest' A.E. Shmitt*, Moscow, 1923; *Byulleten' Sredneaziatskogo gosudarstvennogo universiteta*, 1925, no. 9; Cf. also his *K dogmatike pamirskogo ismailizma* (The Dogma of the Pamir Ismailites), Tashkent, 1926.

26. In *Novyy Vostok*, 1922, no. 1; *Izvestiya AN.SSSR*, 1927, nos. 15-17; *Izvestiya AN.SSSR*, 1929, *Seriya VII, and Sergeyu Fedorovichu Ol'denburgu*, Leningrad, 1934.

27. Cf. N.I. Pokrovsky, *'Myuridism u vlasti'* (Muridism in Power), *Istorik-marksist*, 1934, no. 2; 'Muridism' in *Uchenyye zapiski istoricheskogo fakul'teta Rostovskogo-na-Donu gosudarstvennogo pedagogicheskogo instituta*, Vol. I, 1941.

Select Bibliography

Short bibliographies of major Soviet (and occasionally Western) works in certain special-ised areas are contained in the notes to some chapters and in Appendix III. The following select bibliography refers only to works cited in the text and in extended footnotes outwith the bibliographical ones. For abbreviations used, cf. above p. xxv-xxvi; for a note on transliteration from Cyrillic cf. above p. xxvii-xxviii.

Acton, H.B. (1973), *The Illusion of the Epoch: Marxism-Leninism as a Philosophical Creed,* London, Routledge and Kegan Paul.

Administration of Teaching in the Social Sciences in the USSR (1960), Ann Arbor, University of Michigan Press.

Adolfs, Robert (1969), 'The Church and Communism' in *Destreicher.*

Afansiev, V.G. and Petrov, Ya.A. (1969), 'O dissertatsionnykh rabotakh po filosofii v 1967/68 uchebnom godu' (On Post-graduate Work in Philosophy during the Academic Year 1967/68), *VF,* no. 1., 1969.

— (1969b), 'O dissertatsionnykh rabotakh po filosofii i sotsiologii v 1968/69 uchebnom godu' (On Postgraduate work in Philosophy and Sociology during the Academic Year 1968/69), *VF,* no. 12., 1969.

Akselrod, L.I. (1926), *Etyudy i vospominaniya* (Sketches and Reminiscences), Moscow.

Alekseyev, N.P. (1967), 'Metodika i resul'taty izucheniya religioznosti sel'skogo naseleni-ya, na materialakh Orlovskoy oblasti' (Methodology and Results of a Study of the Religiosity of an Agricultural Population: Material from Orlov Province), *VNA.,* vol. 3, pp. 131-150, 1967.

Alexeiev, N.N. (1938), 'The Marxist Anthropology and the Christian Conception of Man', in Jessop, 1938.

Althusser, Louis (1969), *For Marx,* New York, Vintage.

Andreyev, G.L. et al. (1967), 'Nauchnyy ateizm za 50 let' (Fifty Years of Scientific Atheism), *VF,* no. 12, 1967. pp. 37-47.

Anikeyev, N.P. (1957), 'Ob istoriografii indiyskoy filosofii' (On the Historiography of Indian Philosophy), *VF,* no. 2, 1957.

Anisimov, A.F. (1936), *Rodovoye obshchestvo evenkov (tungus)* (The Tribal Society of the Evenks (Tungus), Moscow.

— (1958), *Religiya evenkov v istoriko-geneticheskom izuchenii i problemy proiskhozh-deniya pervobytnikh verovaniy* (The Religion of the Evenks in Historico-Genetic Studyies and the Problem of the Origin of Primitive Beliefs), Moscow.

— (1959) *Kosmologicheskie predstavleniya narodov Sibiri* (Cosmological Views of the Peoples of Siberia), Moscow.

— (1966), *Dukhovnaya zhizn' pervobytnogo obshchestva* (The Spiritual Life of Primi-tive Society), Moscow.

Antireligoznik (AR) (The Anti-religionist), Moscow, 1925-44.

Bakunin, Michael (1973), *Selected Writings* in A. Lehning, ed. Trans. Steven Cox and Olive Stevens, London, Jonathan Cape, 1973.

Barstow, David (1976), 'Otto and Numinous Experience' in *Religious Studies,* vol. 12, no. 2. 1976.

Barth, Karl (1957), Introduction to Feuerbach, *The Essence of Christianity;* trans. by George Eliot. Forward by H. Richard Niebuhr. Harper Torch Books, New York.

Bartol'd, V.V. (1918), *Kul'tura musul'manstva* (Muslim Culture), Petersburg.

– (1922), *Musul'manskiy mir* (The Muslim World), Petrograd.

Batunsky, M.A. (1961), 'Iz istorii zapadnoyevropeyskogo islamovedeniya perioda imperializma (From the History of Western European Islamic Studies during the Imperialistic Period) in *Nauchnye raboty i soobshcheniya (Otdeleniye obshchestvennykh nauk* AN.SSR. Kn.2).

– (1962), 'Kritika ideynykh osnov burzhuaznogo islamovedeniya kontsa XIX-nachala XX' v (Criticism of the Fundamental Ideas of Bourgeois Islamic Studies: End of the 19th century - beginning of 20th century), *VIRA.,* vol. 10. 1962.

Baykov, E.M. (1970), ' Izmeneniye sennostnykh orientatsii lichnosti' (Change in the Value Orientation of Personality), in Kurochkin, ed., 1970.

Beattie, John (1966), *Other Cultures: Aims, Methods and Achievements of Social Anthropology,* London, Routledge and Kegan Paul.

Belyaev, E.A. (1930), *Rol' mekkanskogo torgovogo kapitala v istorii proiskhozhdeniya islama* (Role of Meccan Trade-Capitalism in the History of the Rise of Islam), *Ateist,* no. 58, 1930.

– (1951), *Musul'manskoye sektanstsvo (istoricheskiy ocherk)* (Muslim Sects: Historical Outline), Moscow.

– (1965), *Araby, islam i arabskiy khalifat v rannee srednevekovye* (Arabia, Islam and the Arab Caliphate in the Early Middle Ages), Moscow.

Benningsen, Alexandre and Lemercier-Quelquejay, Chantal (1967), *Islam in the Soviet Union,* New York, Praeger.

Benningsen, Alexandre (1975), 'Islam in the Soviet Union', in Bociurkiw and Strong (1975), pp. 91-100.

Benningsen, A. and Wimbush, S.E. (1976), 'Muslim Religious Dissent in the USSR., in George, Richard T de and Scanlan, James P., 1976.

Berdyayev, N. (1933), *Problems du communisme,* Paris.

– (1938), *Les sources et le sens du communisme russe,* Paris.

Berger, Peter (ed.) (1969), *Marxism and Sociology: Views from Eastern Europe,* New York, Appleton-Century Crofts.

Berlin, Isaiah (1978), *Russian Thinkers,* London, The Hogarth Press.

Bernstein, Basil (1964), 'Social Class and Psycho-Therapy', in *British Journal of Sociology,* no. 15, 1964.

Bernstein, Edward (1907), *Die Vorlaufer das Neueren Sozialismus,* Stuttgart; Deitz.

Bevan, Edwyn (1932), *Christianity,* London, Thornton Butterworth.

Billington, James H. (1970), *The Icon and the Axe: An Interpretive History of Russian Culture,* New York' Vintage Books, Random House Pub. Co.

Binns, Christopher A.P. (1978), 'The Development and Significance of the Soviet Festal and Ritual System'; unpublished paper read to National Association for Soviet and East European Studies, Cambridge.

Birnbaum, N. (1968), 'Eastern Europe and the Death of God', in D.R. Cutler, ed., *The Religious Situation,* Beacon Press, pp. 917-930.

– (1973), 'Beyond Marx in the Sociology of Religion', in Glock, Charles Y. and Hannard, Phillip E., *Essays in the Scientific Study of Religion,* Harper and Row, New York, 1973.

Blakeley, Thomas J. (1962), 'Is Epistemology Possible in Diamat?', *Studies in Soviet Thought,* II, Dordrecht, Holland.

– (1964), 'Scientific Atheism: An Introduction', in *Studies in Soviet Thought* IV, 4 (December), 1964, Dordrecht, Holland, D. Reidel.

– (1967), 'Marxist-Leninist Scientific Atheism', in *Sovietica: Philosophy in the Soviet Union: A Survey of the Mid-Sixties,* in Ervin Lazlo, ed., Dordrecht, Holland.

Bloch, Ernst (1968), *Atheismus in Christendum,* Frankfurt/M. Suhrkomp Verlag.
Bocheński, J.M. (1962), 'The Three Components of Communist Ideology', *Studies in Soviet Thought* II, Dordrecht, Holland.
Bocheński (and Niemeyer) (edits.) (1962), *Handbook on Communism,* New York, Praeger.
- (1963), *Soviet Russian Dialectical Materialism, (Diamat),* Dordrecht-Holland, D. Reidel Pub. Co.
- (1975), 'Marxism-Leninism and Religion', in Bociutkiw and Strong (1975).
Bociurkiw, Bohdan (1967), 'Lenin and Religion', in Shapiro and Reddaway, pp. 107-134.
Bociurkiw and Strong, John W. (eds.) (1975), *Religion and Atheism in the USSR and Eastern Europe,* London, Macmillan.
- (1974), 'Soviet Research on Religion and Atheism since 1945', *RCL.,* vol. 1, pp. 11-16.
Bockmuehl, Klaus (1980), *The Challenge of Marxism,* Downers Grove, Illinois, IVP.
Bogdanov, A.A. (1906), 'Avtoritarnoye myshleniye' (Authoritative Thought) in *Iz psikhologii obshchestva,* St. Petersburg.
- (1914), *Nauka ob obshchestvennom soznanii* (Science on Social Consciousness), Moscow.
- (1920), *Filosofiya zhivogo opyta* (The Philosophy of Living Experience), Petrograd.
- (1924), *O proletarskoy kul'ture* (On Proletarian Culture), Petrograd, 1924.
Bogoraz-Tan, V.G. (1939), *Chukchi,* vol. I, 1934, vol. II, 1939, Leningrad.
Bol'shaya sovietskaya entsiklopediya (Great Soviet Encyclopaedia), 1st ed., 1932.
Bonch-Bruyevich, V.D. (1966), *V.I. Lenin v Petrograde i Moskve (1907-1928) Vospominaniya* (V.I. Lenin in Petersburg and Moscow (1907-1920) Reminiscences), Moscow.
Bonino, Jose Miguez (1976), *Christians and Marxists: The Mutual Challenge to Revolution,* London, Hodder and Stoughton.
Bourdeaux, Michael (ed.) (1978), *Religious Liberty in the Soviet Union,* Keston Books, no. 7, Rapid Reproductions, West Wickham.
Brandon, S.G.F. (ed.) (1970), *A Dictionary of Comparative Relgiion,* London, Weidengeld and Nicolson.
Breshnev, L.I. (1979), *Leninskim kursom* (Following Lenin's Course), 4 vols., Moscow, 1976.
Brown, Peter (1971), *World of Late Antiquity,* London, Thames and Hudson.
Buchholz, A. (1961), 'Problems of the Ideological East-West Conflict', *Studies in Soviet Thought* I, Dordrecht, Holland, 1961.
Bukin, V.R. and I.I. (1962), 'O prirode religioznogo chustva' (On the Nature of Religious Feeling), in *VF,* no. 2, 1962.
Bukin, V.R. (1963), 'Preodoleniye religioznykh chuvstv' (Overcoming Religious Feelings), *Kommunist,* no. 2.
Bukin, V.R. and I.I. (1964), 'Religioznaya psikhologiya i ateisticheskoye vospitaniye' (Religious Psychology and Atheist Education), *FN,* no. 1, 1964.

Caetani, L. (1912), *Chronographia Islamica,* 5 vols., Paris.
Calvez, J.Y. (1956), *La Pensée de Karl Marx,* Paris, editions du seuil.
Chattopodhaya, D. (1959), *Lokayata: A Study in Ancient Indian Materialism,* New Delhi, People's Pub. House.
Chauncey, Henry (ed.) (1969), *Soviet Preschool Education,* 2 vols., New York, Rinehart and Winston.
Cherkashin, P.P. (1958), 'O sotsial'nykh kornyakh religii' (On the Social Roots of Religion), *Voprosy filosofii* 1958, no. 6, pp. 29-41.

– (1964), *Gnoseologicheskie korni idealizma* (Epistemological Roots of Idealism), Moscow.

Chernyak, V.A. (1969), *Formirovaniye nauchno-materialisticheskogo ateisticheskogo mirovozzreniya (Sotsiologicheskiye problemy)* (Formation of a Scientific-Materialist Atheist World Outlook (Sociological Problems), Alma-Ata.

Conze, E., 'Buddhism in the Soviet Union', *The Middle Way*, vol. 35, no. 3, 1953.

Cornforth, Francis (1957), *From Religion to Philosophy*, New York, Harper Torch books.

Cracraft, James (1971), *The Church Reform of Peter the Great*, London.

Crossman, Richard (ed.) (1959), *The God That Failed*, New York, Bantam Books.

De George, Richard T. (1963), 'A Bibliography of Soviet Ethics' in *Studies in Soviet Thought*, III, (1968), pp. 83-103, Dordrecht.

– (1969), *Soviet Ethics and Morality*, Ann Arbor, University of Michigan Press.

– (1970), *Patterns of Soviet Thought*, Ann Arbor, University of Michigan Press.

– and Scanlan, James P. (ed.) (1974), *Marxism and Religion in Eastern Europe*, paper presented at the Banff International Slavic Conference, September 4-7 *Sovietica*, vol. 36, Dordrecht, Holland, D. Reidel Pub. Co.

Destutt de Tracy (1827), *Elements d'ideologie*, Paris, Chez Madam Lévi Libraire.

d'Holbach, P.H.Th. (1770), *Système de la Nature*, Paris.

Dityakin, V. (1927), 'Marks i Engel's o proiskhozhdenii i sushchnosti religii' (Marx and Engels on the Origin and Essence of Religion), *Ateist*, nos. 22-23, 1927.

Dodds, E.R. (1965), *Pagan and Christian in an Age of Anxiety* (Wiles Lectures, Queen's University, Belfast, 1963), Cambridge, C.U.P.

Donini, A. (1961), *Raffaele Pettazzoni e gli studi storico-religiosi in Italia*, Bologna.

Dostoyevsky, Fyodor (1884), *Notes from Underground*, trans. Jessie Coulson, Harmondsworth, Penguin Classics, 1972.

Douglas, Mary (1973), *Natural Symbols*, Harmondsworth, Pelican Books.

Eliade, Mircea (1958), *Patterns in the Comparative Study of Religion*, London, Sheed and Ward.

– (1979), *A History of Religious Ideas*, 3 vols., Chicago, Chicago University Press.

Empiricus, Sextus, *Against the Physicists* in *Works of Sextus Empiricus* (ed.), R.G. Bury, 4 vols., 1933-49, London, Heinemann.

Engels, Friedrich (1850), *The Peasant War in Germany*, Moscow, F.L.P.H. n.d.

– (1877), *Socialism: Utopian and Scientific* in *MEBW*.

– (1877-78), *Anti-Dühring*, Moscow, Foreign Languages Publishing House, 1954.

– (1886), *Ludwig Feuerbach and the End of Classical German Philosophy*, in *MEBW*.

– (1872-82), *Dialectics of Nature*, London, Lawrence and Wishart Ltd., 1946.

– (1894-1895), *On the Early History of Christianity*, in *MEOR*.

Evans-Pritchard, E. (1934), 'Levy-Bruhl's Theory of Primitive Mentality' in *Bulletin of the Faculty of Acts*, Egyptian University (Cairo), vol. II, 1934.

– (1940), 'Obituary: Lucien Lévy-Bruhl', *Man*, 1940, no. 27.

– (1965), *Theories of Primitive Religion*, Oxford, Clarendon Press.

Fabian, Johannes (1965), 'Ideology and Content', *Sociologus*, N.S. 16, 1965, pp. 1-18.

Fedoseyev, P.N. (1933), 'Lenin o sotsial'nykh i gnoseologicheskikh kornyakh religii' ('Lenin on the Social and Epistemological Roots of Religion'), *PZM*, 1933, no. 4, pp. 159-178.

– (1938), *O religii i bor'be s ney* ('On Religion and the Struggle with it), Moscow.

– (1939), 'Gnoseologicheskiye korni religioznikih verovaniy (Epistemological Roots of Religious Beliefs) *Antireligioznik*, 1939, no. 9.

- (1963), 'Humanism and the Modern World' in *Philosophy, Science and Man*, pp. 5-28.
Feigl, Herbert (1974), 'Critique of Dialectical Materialism' in Somerville Parsons (ed.), 1974, pp. 105-115.
Fetscher, Irving (1966), 'Developments in the Marxist Critique of Religion' in *Conciluim*, vol. 6, no. 2, June 1966: pp. 57-68.
Feuer, Lewis (1963), 'What is Alienation? The Career of a Concept' in Stein and Vidich, 1963.
Feuerbach, Ludwig, *The Essence of Christianity*, Trans. George Eliot, Intro. K. Barth, Foreword A. Richard Neibuhr, New York, Harper Torch Books, 1957.
- *Lectures on the Essence of Religion*, trans. Ralph Manheim, New York, Harper and Row, 1967.
- (1841), *Wider dern dualismus von Leib und Seele, Fleisch und Geist* in *Sämmtlicher Werke* (ed.), Bolin and Jodl, 1903-11, Berlin.
- (1842), *Verläufige Thesen zur Reform der Philosophie*, in *Sämmtlicher Werke* (ed.), Bolin and Jodl, Berlin, 1903-11.
- (1843), *Grundsätze der Philosophie der Zukunft*, in *Sämmtlicher Werke* (ed.), Bolin and Jodl, Berlin, 1903-11.
Fichte, J.G., *Sittenlehre*, in *Sämmtlicher Werke* (ed.), I.H. Fichte, 8 vols., Berlin, 1845-46.
Filatov, A. (1967), *O novykh i starykh obryadakh* (On Old and New Rites), Moscow.
Filippova, R.F. (1971), 'Ob effectivnosti ateisticheskogo vospitaniya uchashchikhsya' (On the Effectiveness of Atheistic Upbringing of Students) in *Sovetskaya pedigogika*, no. 11, 1971.
Filosofskiye nauki (FN) (The Philosophical Sciences), Moscow, 1958-.
Fischer, E. (1973), *Marx in his Own Words*, Harmondsworth, Penguin Books.
Fletcher, William C. and Strover, Antony J. (1967), *Religion and the Search for New Ideals in the USSR*, New York, Praeger.
Frantsov, G.P. (1940), *Fetishizm i problema proiskhozhdeniya religii* (Fetishism and the Problem of the Origin of Religion), Moscow.
- (1959), *U istokov religii i svobodomysliya* (At the Sources of Religion and Free Thinking), Moscow-Leningrad.
- (1972), *Nauchnyy ateizm*, Moscow, Nauka.
- (1975), Philosophy and Sociology, Progress Publishers, Moscow.
Fromm, Eric (1965), *The Sane Society*, Greenwich, Conn., A Fawcett Premier Book.
Fundamentals of Marxist-Leninist Philosophy, Moscow, Progress Publishers, 1974.

Garaudy, Roger (1964), *Karl Marx*, Paris, Seghers.
- (1967), *From Anathema to Dialogue*, London, Collins.
- (1970), *Marxism in the Twentieth Century*, Trans. by René Hague, London, Collins.
- (1975), *The Alternative Future*, Harmondsworth, Penguin Books.
Gardavský, Vitězslav (1973), *God is not Yet Dead*, Harmondsworth, Penguin Books.
Glock, Charles Y and Hammond, Phillip E. (ed.) (1973), *Beyond the Classics? Essays in the Scientific Study of Religion*, New York, Harper and Row.
Gollwitzer, Helmut (1970), *Die marxistiche Religionskritik und der christliche Glaube*, English trans. D. Cairns, *The Christian Faith and the Marxist Criticism of Religion*, Edinburgh, St. Andrews Press, 1970.
Gorbachev, N.A. (1966), 'K voprosu o predmete teorii nauchnogo ateizma (The Problem of the subject of Scientific Atheism), *VNA*, 1966, vol. 1.
Gordon-Polonskaya, L.R. (1963), *Musul'manskiye techeniya v obshchestvennoy mysli Indii i Pakistana (Kritika musul'manskogo natsionalizma)* (Muslim Tendencies in Social Thought in India and Pakistan (Criticism of Muslim Nationalism)), Moscow, 1963.

Gorelov, A. (1971), 'Dokhodit' do kazhdogo' (To Get Through to Everybody), *Partiinaya zhizn*, 1971, no. 12.

Goryacheva, A.I. (1963), 'O vzaimootnoshenii ideologii i obshchestvennoy psikhologii' (On the Mutual Relations of Ideology and Social Psychology), *VF*, 1963, no. 11.

Gregor, A. James (1974), 'The Concept of Alienation in the Philosophy of Karl Marx', in Somerville and Parsons, 1974.

Grigor'yan, M.M. (1974), *Kurs lektsiy po istorii ateizma* (Course of Lectures on the History of Atheism), Moscow.

Grimm, Jacob and William (1960), *Deutsches Wörterbuch*, vol. 15, pt. 2, Leipzig, Hirzel.

Gubanov, N.I. (1967), 'Razrabotka problem ateizma v sovetskoi filosofskoy nauke' (The Working-Out of the Problem of Atheism in Soviet Philosophical Science), VNA, 1967, vol. 4: pp. 183-204.

Hebblethwaite, Peter (1977), *The Christian-Marxist Dialogue and Beyond*, London, Darton, Longman and Todd.

Hegel, G.F. (1796), *The Positivity of the Christian Religion;* See Hegel: *Early Theological Writings.*

– (1800), *The Spirit of Christianity and its Fate*, See Hegel: *Early Theological Writings.*

– *Lectures in the Philosophy of History*, see Sibree.

– (1948), *Early Theological Writings*. trans. T.M. Knox with introduction and fragments, translated by Richard Kroner, Illinois, University of Chicago Press.

Herzen, Alexandre, *Sochineniya* (Works), 30 vols., 1954-64, Moscow, AN.SSSR.

Hook, Sidney (1962), *From Hegel to Marx*, Ann Arbor, Michigan, University of Michigan Press.

Hultkrantz, Åke (1970), 'The Phenomenology of Religion: Aims and Methods', *Temenos*, vol. 6, 1970.

Isham, George Fredrick (1972), *Messianism, Humanism and Atheism: Issues in Marxist-Christian Dialogue 1956-1971*, unpublished Ph.D. thesis, Columbia University.

Issledovaniya i materialy po voprosam pervobytnykh religioznykh verovaniy (Research Materials on Problems of Primitive Religious Beliefs), Moscow, 1959.

Istoriya i teoriya ateizma (IiTA), Mosocw, 1974, Mysl'.

Ivanov, I.G. (1967), 'Ateisticheskoye zhacheniye trudov sovietskikh yestestvoispytateley' (Atheistic Problems in the Work of Soviet Natural Scientists), *VNA*, vol. 4, 1967: pp. 205-241.

Izimbetov, T. (1961), 'Ob ideologii sovremennogo islama' (On the Ideology of Contemporary Islam) in *Kritika religioznoy ideologii*, Mosocw, 1961.

– (1964), 'Ob ispol'zovanii islama v kachestve ideologicheskogo oruzhiya antikommunizma' (On the Utilization of Islam as a Weapon Against Communism) *VIRA*, 1964, no. 12.

Izvestiya, passim.

James, E.O. (1949), *The Beginnings of Religion*, London, Hutchinson's Univ. Lib.

– (1957), *Prehistoric Religion*, New York.

Jaspers, Karl (1952), *Reason and Anti-Reason in Our Time*, London, S.C.M.

Jessop, T.E. et. al. (1938), *The Christian Understanding of Man*, London, George Allen and Unwin.

Jiyu, Ren (1979), 'The Struggle to Develop a Marxist Science of Religion', *Zhexueyanjiu*, no. 4, 1979. Eng. trans. Ching Feng, 22(2), 1979, pp. 35-89.

Jordan, Z.A. (1967), *The Evolution of Dialectical Materialism: A Philosophical and Sociological Analysis*, London, Macmillan.

- (1974), 'Contemporary Problems of Dialectical Materialism', in Richard T. de George and James. P. Scanlon (ed.), 1974.

Karl Marx i sovremennaya filosofiya (Karl Marx and Modern Philosophy) (1968), Progress Publishers, Moscow.
Kautsky, Karl (1908), *The Foundations of Christianity,* trans. Henry F. Mims, New York, 1953, Russell and Russell.
- (1910), *The Class Struggle,* Chicago, C.H. Kerr.
Kelt, G. (1965), 'Svyataya svatatykh-chelovek' (The Holy of Holies – Man), in *Komsomol'skaya pravda,* Aug. 15, 1965.
Khudyakov, S. (1962), 'Soderzhaniye i formy propagandy' (The Content and Forms of Propaganda), *NiR,* no. 3, 1962.
Kitagawa, J. (ed.) (1967), *The History of Religions: Essays on the Problem of Understanding,* Chicago, University of Chicago Press.
Klibanov, A.I. (1960), *Reformatsionnye dvizheniya v Rossii* (Movements of Reform in Russia), Moscow.
- (1965), *Istoriya religioznogo sektantsvtvya V Rossii* (A History of Religious Sectarianism in Russia), Moscow. (English translation, Ethel Dunn, 1982, Pergamon press, Oxford)
- (1965b), 'The Dissident Denominations in the Past and Today', in *Soviet Sociology* (1965), vol. III, no. 4, pp. 44-60.
- et. al. (1967), *Konkretnyye issledovaniya sovremennykh religioznykh verovanii* (Concrete Studies in Contemporary Religious Beliefs), Moscow.
- (1967b), 'Pyatdesyat' let nauchnogo issledovaniya religioznogo sektantstva' (Fifty Years of Scientific Study of Religious Sectarianism), *VNA,* no. 4, 1967: pp. 349-384.
- (1969), *Religioznoye sektantsvo i sovremennost' (sotsiologicheskye i istoricheskiye ocherki)* (Religious Sectarianism and the Present (Sociological and Historical Outline), Moscow.
- (1973), *Religioznoye sektantstvo v proshlom i nastoyashchem* (Religious Sectarianism in the Past and Today), Moscow.
Klimovich, L.I. (1923), 'Marks i Engel's ob islame i problema ego proiskhozhdeniya v sovetskom islamovedenii' (Marx and Engels on Islam and the Problem of its Origin in Soviet Islamics) in *Revolyutsionnyy Vostok,* 1933, nos. 2-3.
- (1936), *Islam v tsarskoy Rossii* (Islam in Tsarist Russia), Moscow.
- (1965), *Islam,* 2nd ed., 1965, Moscow.
Knox, T. and Kroner, R. (1961), *On Christianity: Early Theological Writings of Fredrich Hegel,* New York, Harper Torch Books.
Kochetov, A.N. (1967), 'Izucheniye buddizma v SSSR' (The Study of Buddhism in USSR), *VNA,* no. 4, 1967: pp. 427-444.
Kotakowski, Leszek (1971), *Marxism and Beyond,* London, Paladin Books.
- (1978), *Main Currents of Marxism,* Three Volumes vol. 1, The Founders; vol. 2, The Golden Age; vol. 3, The Breakdown; Oxford, Clarendon Press.
Kolbanovsky, V.N. (ed.) (1970), *Kollektiv kolkhoznikov: sotsial'no-psikhologicheskoye issledovaniye* (Collective of the Kolkhez Farmers: Social-Psychological Examination), Moscow.
Kolmogorov, A.N. et. al. (1964), *Vozmozhnoye i nevozmozhnoye v kibernetike* (Possibilities and Impossibilities in Cybernetics), Moscow.
Kommunist, passim.
Kommunisticheskaya Partiya Sovetskogo Soyuza v rezolyutsiyakh i resheniyakh s''ezdov, konferentsiy i plenumov TsK (Communist Party of the Soviet Union in Resolutions and Decisions of Congresses, Conferences and Plenums of the Central Committee) *(KPSS v resolyutsiyakh),* 8th ed., Moscow, 1970-72.

Kon, lgor S. (1969), 'The Concept of Alienation in Modern Sociology', in Berger (1969).
Kozhemyako, V (1964), 'Uchitel boretsya za cheloveka . . .' (Teachers Fight for Mankind), *Pravda,* July 12, 1964.
KPSS o kul'ture, prosveshchenii i nauke: (CPSU on Culture, Education and Science), Moscow, 1954.
Krachkovsky I.Ya. (1931), *Takha khuseyn v doislamskoy poezil arabov i yego kritiki* (Taka Hussein in the Pre-Islamic Poetry of the Arabs and the Criticism of Him), *Izvestiya AN SSSR, Seriya VII,* 1931, no. 5.
– (1934), 'V.V. Bartol'd v istorii islamovedeniya' (V.V. Bartol'd in the History of Islamics), in *Izvestiya AN.SSSR, 1934, Seriya VII,* no. 1.
– (1963), *Koran. Perevod i kommentarii* (The Koran: Translation and Commentary), Moscow, 1963.
Krailsheimer, Alban (1980), *Pascal,* Oxford, Oxford University Press.
Kratkiy filosofskiy slovar' (A Short Philosophical Dictionary), Moscow, 1954.
Kratkiy nauchnoateisticheskiya slova' (KNAS) (A Short Scientific-Atheist Dictionary), Moscow, 1964, Nauka.
Kritika religioznoy ideologii (The Criticism of Religious Ideology), Mosocw, 1961.
Kryvelev, I.A. (1956), 'Ob osnovnom opredelyayushchem priznake ponyatiya religii' (On the Fundamental Characteristics of Religion), *VRA,* 1956, vol. 4.
– (1975), *Istoriya religii* (The History of Religion), 2 vols., Moscow.
Kurochkin, P.K. et. al. (1970), *K obshchestvu, svobodnomu ot religii (Protsess sekulyarizatsii v usloviyakh sotsialisticheskogo obschshestva)* (Towards a Society Free of Religion (The Process of Secularisation in Conditions of Socialist Society), Moscow.
Kursanov, G.A. (1974), *Kritika teologicheskikh kontseptsiy istiny* (Critique of Theological Conceptions of Truth), *VNA,* vol. 16, 1974, pp. 125-144.
Kuznetsova, N.A. (1963), 'K istorii izucheniya babizma i bekhaizma v Rossii' (The History of the Study of 'Babism' and 'Bekhaizm' in Russia), *Ocherki po istorii russkogo vostokovedeniya, Sb. VI,* Moscow, 1963.

La Barre, Weston (1970), *The Ghost Dance: The Origins of Religion,* London, George Allen and Unwin.
Lagov, N. (1964), 'Rastit, voinstvuyushchikh ateistov' (Raising Militant Atheists), in *Pravda,* March 6, 1964, p. 2.
Lammens, H. (1921), *La Syrie. Precis Historique,* 2 vols., Beirut.
Lane, Christel (1974), 'Some Explanations for the Persistence of Christian Religion in the Soviet Union', *Sociology,* 2, 1974, pp. 233f.
– (1978), *Christian Religion in the Soviet Union: A Sociological Study,* London, George Allen and Unwin.
Larrain, Jorge (1979), *The Concept of Ideology,* London, Hutchinson.
Lauer, Quentin (1974), 'Marx's "Science" of History', in Somerville and Parsons (ed.), *Dialogues on the Philosophy of Marxism,* 1974, pp. 140-164.
Lazlow, Ervin (ed.) (1967), *Sovietica: Philosophy in the Soviet Union; A Survey of the Mid-Sixties,* Dordrecht, Holland, Reidel.
Lebedev, A.A. (1970), 'Sekulyarizatsiya naseleniya sotsialisticheskogo goroda' (Secularisation of the Population of a Socialist City) in P.K. Kurochin (ed.) (1970).
– (1973), 'Studencheskaya molodezh' i ateizm' (Nekotoryye itogi sotsialogicheskogo issledovaniya) (Student Youth and Atheism (Some Results of Sociological Research)), *VNA,* vol. 15, 1973, pp. 199-213.
Lenin, V.I., Collected Works (LCW), 38 vols., Foreign Languages Publishing House, *Leninskii sbornik,* 40 vols., Moscow n.d.
Moscow, 1962.
Lensu, M.I. et. al. (1970), 'Differentsirovannyy podkhod v ateisticheskom vospitanii' (Differing Approaches to Atheistic Upbringing), *VNA,* 1970, vol. 9, pp. 134-152.

Lentsman, L.A. (1967), 'Izucheniye sovetskimi uchenymi rannego khristianstva' (Studies by Soviet Scholars of Early Christianity), *VNA*, 1967, no. 4, pp. 267-286.
Leo XIII (Pope), *Rerum Novarum* (1891).
Leroy-Beaulieu, Anatole, *L'Empire des Tsars et les Russes*, 3 vols., Paris, 1889.
Levada, Y.A. (1965), *Sotsnial'naya priroda religii* (Social Nature of Religion), Moscow.
Lévi-Bruhl (1910), *Les Functions Mentales dans les sociétés inférieures.*
– (1922), *La Mentalité primitive.*
Ling, Trevor (1976), *The Buddha*, Harmondsworth, Penguin Books.
– (1979), *Buddha, Marx and God*, 2nd ed., London, Macmillan.
Livshits, G.M. (1973), *Svobodomysliye i ateizm v drevnosti i sredniye veka* (Freethinking and Atheism in Antiquity and the Middle Ages), Moscow.
– (1975), *Svobodomysliye i materialicheskaya filosofiya v zapadnoy yevrope (vtoraya polovina XVI veka)* (Freethinking and Materialist Philosophy in Western Europe (Second Half of the 17th Century)), Moscow.
Lobkowicz, Nicholas (1964), 'Karl Marx's Attitude to Religion', *The Review of Politics*, XXVI, July 1964, pp. 319-352.
Lochman, Jan Mileč (1972), *Christus oder Prometheus*? Hamburg, Furch Verlay.
– (1977), *Encountering Marx*, Belfast.
Lopatkin, R.A. (1968), 'Na opornykh punktakh instituta nauchnogo ateizma' (On the Strong Points of Scientific Atheism), *VNA*, vol. 5, 1968.
Lowith, Karl (1949), *Meaning in History*, Chicago, University of Chicago Press.
– (1954), 'Man's Self-Alienation in the Early Writings of Marx', *Social Research XXI*, Summer, 1954, pp. 204-230.
Lukachevsky, A.T. (1930), *Proiskhozhdenie religii* (The Origin of Religion), Moscow.
– (1932), *Marksizm-leninizm kak voinstvuyushchiy ateizm* (Marxism-Leninism as Militant Materialism), Moscow.
– (1934), *Vvedenie v istoriyu religii* (Introduction to the History of Religion), Moscow.
Lunarcharsky, A.V. (1908), *Religiya i sotsializma* (Religion and Socialism), Moscow.
– (1924), *Vvedenie v istoriyu religii* (Introduction to the History of Religion), Moscow.

Macintyre, Alasdair and Ricoeur, Paul (1969), *The Religious Significance of Atheism*, New York, Columbia University Press.
Macintyre, Alasdair (1971), *Marxism and Christianity*, Pelican Books, Harmondsworth, Middx.
McKown, Delos B. (1975), *Classical Marxist Critiques of Religion: Marx, Engels, Lenin, Kautsky*, The Hague, Martinus Nijhoff.
McLellan, David (1972), *Marx Before Marxism*, Harmondsworth, Pelican Books.
– (1975), *Marx*, London, Collins.
– (1976), *Karl Marx*, London, Paladin Books.
– (1979), *Marxism after Marx*, London, Macmillan.
– (1979b), *Engels*, London, Collins.
Malinowski, B. (1944), *A Scientific Theory of Culture*, Chapel Hill, University of North Carolina Press, 1944.
– (1954), *Magic, Science and Religion*, New York, Doubleday Anchor Books.
Mandelstam, Nadezhda (1970), *Hope Against Hope*, Harmondsworth, Penguin Books.
Marchoveč, Milan (1976), *A Marxist Looks at Jesus*, trans. Peter Hebblethwaite. London, Darton, Longman and Todd.
Marr, N.Y., *Izbrannyye raboty* (Selected Works), 4 vols., Leningrad, 1937.
Marshall, Richard H. (ed.) (1971), *Aspects of Religion in the Soviet Union 1917-1967*, Chicago, The University Press.
Matlaw, Ralph E. (ed.) (1976), *Belinsky, Chernyshersky and Dobrolyubov*, Bloomington, Indians U.P.

Marx and Engels, *Collected Works (MECW)*, Lawrence and Wishart, London, 1975-.
Karl Marx, Friedrich Engels: Werke (MEW), 39 vols., Berlin: Dietz Verlag, 1956-1970.
Marx and Engels, *Historisch-Kritische Gesamtavsgabe* (MEGA), Frankfurt, 1927-35 (incomplete).
Marx, *Selected Works* (MSW) (Includes selection of writings of Engels, Lenin and Stalin), two volumes, Moscow, Foreign Language Publishing House, 1946.
Marx and Engels, *Basic Writings on Politics and Philosophy* (MEBW), Lewis Feuer (ed.), London, Collins, 1974.
Marx and Engels (1948), *Communist Manifesto.*
Marx, Karl, *Capital*, vol. 1. trans. Ben Fowkes, 1976, Harmondsworth, Penguin Books.
Marx, Karl, *Capital*, vol. 3, Moscow, 1962, F.L.P.H.
Marx, Engels: *On Colonialism*, Moscow, F.L.P.H., n.d.
Marx and Engels, *On Religion (OR)*, Moscow, Progress Publishing House, 1972.
Mascall, Eric (1954), *He Who Is*, London, Longmans, Green and Co.
Mbiti, John (1969), *African Religions and Philosophy*, London, Heinemann.
Meerovsky, B.V. (1964), 'O predmete istorii ateizma' (On the Subject of the History of Atheism), *FN*, 1964, no. 5.
Menshing, G., *Die Religion: Erscheinungsformen, strukturtypen und Lebensgesetze*, Stuttgart, 1959.
Meykshane, D.A. (1978), *Metody izucheniya otnosheniya uchashchikhsya k religii (po materialism shkol Latviyskoy SSR)* (Methods of Studing the Attitudes of School-children to Religion (from School Material in the Latvian SSSR)), *VNA*, 1970, no. 11, pp. 224-275.
Mitin, M.B. (1934), *Dialekticheskiy materializm* (Dialectical Materialism), Moscow.
– (1963), 'Man as an object of Philosophical Investigations', in *Philosophy, Science and Man*, pp. 29-51.
– (1968), 'Marx, Lenin and the Problem of Man', in *Karl Marx and Modern Philosophy*, Moscow, Progress.
Mitrokhin, L.N. (1967), 'O metodologii issledovanii sovremennoy religioznosti' (On the Methodology of Research into Contemporary Religiosity) in Klibanov (ed.), 1967.
Moiseyev, Oleg (1963), 'Aktivneye nastupat' na perezhitki proshlogo' (More actively to Work on the Relics of the Past), *Agitator*, 1963, no. 15.
– (1966), 'Permskiye razdumya' (Permian Mood) in *NiR*, no. 10, 1966.
Moorey, P.R.S. (ed.) (1979), *The Origins of Civilization* (Wolfson College Lectures, 1978), Oxford, Clarendon Press.
Mshvenieradze, V.V. (1974), 'Objective Foundations of Scientific Method', in Somerville and Parsons, 1974.
Müller, F. Max (1867), *Chips from a German Workshop*, vol. 1, London, Longmans, Green and Co.
– (1888), *Natural Religion.*

Narodnoye obrazovaniye (Public Education), 1975, no. 3.
Nastol'naya kniga ateista (NKA) (Reference Book of Atheism), S.D. Skazkin et. al. (eds.), Moscow, 1968.
Nauchnyy ateizm (NA) (Scientific Atheism), Moscow, Politidat, 1974.
Nauka i Religiya (NiR) (Science and Religion), Moscow, 1965-.
Novikov, M.P. (1973), 'O predmete nauchnogo ateizma' (On the Subject of Scientific Atheism), *VNA*, vol. 15, pp. 25-36, 1973.
Nowicka, Kinga (1975), 'Voprosy istorii religii i ateizma' (1950-1964) I 'Yezegodnik muzeja istorii religii i ateizma' (1957-1964): Zarys analizy statystycznej, *Studia Religioznawcze*, 1975, no. 10, Warsaw.

Oestreicher, Paul (ed.) (1969), *The Christian-Marxist Dialogue*, New York, Macmillan.

Okulov, A.F. (1966), 'Za glubokuyu nauchnuyu razrabotku sovremennikh problem ateizma' (Towards a thorough Scientific Working Out of Contemporary Problems of Atheism), *VNA*, vol. I, 1966, pp. 1-35.

Okunev, I. (1961), 'Shkole pora nastupat' (It is Time to Begin in School), *NiR*, 1961, no. 12.

Osnovnye voprosy nauchnogo ateizma (Fundamental Problems of Scientific Atheism), Moscow, 1976.

Osnovy marksistko-leninskoy filosofii (OMLF) (The Fundamentals of Marxist-Leninist Philosophy), Moscow, revised ed., 1974.

Osnovy nauchnogo ateizma (ONA) (The Fundamentals of Scientific Atheism), Moscow, 1975, Vysshaya Shkola.

Otto, Rudolf (1924), *The Idea of the Holy*. trans. by John Harvey, Oxford, Clarendon Press.

Pantskhava, I.D. (1966), 'O predmete nauchnogo ateizma' (The Subject of Scientific Atheism), in *Osnovnye voprosy nauchnogo ateizma*, Moscow, 1966, ch. 1, sect. 1, pp. 5-18.

Parrinder, E.G. (1962), *African Traditional Religion*, London, Sheldon Press.

Pascal, Blaise, *Pensées*, Harmondsworth, Penguin Classics, ed., 1966.

Paton, H.J. (1955), *The Modern Predicament*, London, George Allen and Unwin.

Peace, Richard (1971), *Dostoyevsky: An Examination of the Major Novels*, Cambridge, Cambridge University Press.

Petrosyan, M. (1972), *Humanism*, Moscow, Progress.

Philosophy, Science and Man, Soviet Delegation Reports for XIII World Congress of Philosophy, Moscow, 1963, AN.SSSR.

Pipes, Richard (1977), *Russia Under the Old Regime*, Harmondsworth, Penguin Books.

Pius IX (Pope), *Qui Pluribus* (1846).

Pivovarov, V.G. (1974), 'The Methodology of Collecting and Processing of Primary Sociological Information in the Study of Problems of Religion and Atheism', *Social Compass*, 2, 1974, pp. 191-206 (translated from article in *K obshchestvu, svobodnomu ot religii*, Moscow, 1970.

Plamenatz, John (1954), *German Marxism and Russian Communism*, London, Longmans, Green and Co.

– (1970), *Ideology*, London, Macmillan.

– (1975), *Karl Marx's Philosophy of Man*, Oxford, Clarendon Press.

Plekhanov, G.V., *The Development of the Monist View of History*, Moscow, F.L.P.H., 1956.

– *Fundamental Problems of Marxism (with an Appendix of his essays: The Materialist Conception of History and the Role of the Individual in History*, London, Lawrence and Wishart, 1969.

– *Sochineniya* (Works), 26 vols., Moscow, 1922-27.

Poa znamenem marksizma (PZM) (Under the Banner of Marxism) Moscow, 1922-1944.

Pokrovsky, M.N. (1923a), 'Otvet tov. Stepanovu' ('Answer to Comrade Stepanov'), *PZM*, no. 1, 1923.

– (1923b), 'Istoriya religii na kholostom khodu' (Nechto vrode rezyuma) (The History of Religion Freewheeling), *PZM*, nos. 2-3, 1923.

Pomper, Philip (1970), *The Russian Revolutionary Intelligentsia*, Illinois, A.H.M. pub. co.

Popov, A.A. (1958), 'Perezhitki drevnikh doreligioznykh vozzreniy dolganov na prirodu' ('The Survivals of Ancient Pre-Religious Views of the Dolgans on Nature'), in *Sovetskaya etnografiya* (1958), no. 2.

Popov, S.A. (1977), *Socialism and Humanism,* Moscow, Progress.
Popper, Karl (1945), *The Open Society and its Enemies* vol. 2: *Hegel and Marx,* London, Routledge and Kegan Paul.
Porshnev, B.F. (1965), 'Poiski obobshcheniy v oblasti istorii religii' (Attempts at Synthesis in the Field of the History of Religion), *Voprosy istorii,* 1965, no. 7, pp. 137-149.
– (1966), *Sotsial'naya psikhologiya i istoriya* (Social Psychology and History), Moscow.
Powell, David E. (1975), *Antireligious Propaganda in the Soviet Union,* Cambridge, Mass., M.I.T. Press.
– (1975b), 'Rearing the New Soviet Man: Anti-Religious Propaganda and Political Socialisation in the USSR., in Bociurkiw and Strong, 1975, pp. 151-170.
Pravda, passim.
Pye, M. (1974), 'Problems of Method in the Interpretation of Religion', *Japanese Journal of Religious Studies,* 1/2-3 June-September, 1974.

Radin, Paul (1937), 'Economic Factors in Primitive Religion' in *Science and Society,* I (Spring, 1937), pp. 310-311.
– (1957), *Primitive Religion,* New York, Dover Paperback.
Raeff, Marx (ed.) (1966), *Russian Intellectual History: An Anthology,* New York, 1966.
Ramm, B., 'Vospityvat' voinstvuyushchikh ateistov' (Raising Militant Atheists), *Uchitel'skaya Gazeta,* Jan. 29, 1972, p. 2.
Ratner-Shternberg, S. (1928), *L.Y. Shternberg kak issledovatel' religii* (L.Y. Shternberg as Student of Religion), Moscow, 1928.
Read, Christopher (1979), Review of Lane (1978) in *Religion in Communist Lands,* vol. 7, no. 3, Autumn, 1979, pp. 182-183.
Religion in Communist Lands, 1973-, Keston College, England.
Religion und Atheismus in der UdSSR: Monatlicher Informationsdienst, 1975-, München.
Reysner, M. (1927a), *Ideologii vostoka: Ocherki vostochnoy teokratii* (Ideologies of the East: An Outline of Eastern Theocracy), M-L, 1927.
– (1927b), *Ideologiya Korana,* Moscow-Leningrad.
Riasanovsky, Nicholas V. (1969), *A History of Russia,* New York, OUP.
Richter, A., *Die Religion in Geschichte und Gegenwart,* Tubingen, 1961.
Rodinson, Maxime (1961), *Mahomet,* Paris, Club francais du livre. Eng. trans. by Anne Carter, Penguin Books, 1978.
Rosenthal, M. and Yudin, P. (eds.) (1967), *A Dictionary of Philosophy,* Moscow, Progress.
Rousseau, J.J. (1754), *Discourse on Inequality.*
– (1761), *Emile.*
– (1761), *La Novelle Héloise.*
Rumyantsev, N. (1925), *Smert' i voskreseniye spasitelya: Issledovaniya iz oblasti sranitel'noy mifologii* (The Death and Resurrection of the Saviour: Researches in the Area of Comparative Mythology), Moscow.
– (1926), *Dokhristianskiy Khristos* (The Pre-Christian Christ), Moscow.
– (1926b), 'Mifilogicheskaya shkola po voprosu o sushchestvovanii Khrista' (The Mythological School on the Problem of the Essence of Christ), *Ateist,* no. 12, 1926.
– (1929), 'Iosif Flaviy ob Iisuse i Ioanne krestitele' (Joseph Flavius on Jesus and John Krestitelos), *Ateist,* 1929, no. 36.

Sanders, N.K. (1979), 'The Religious Development of Some Early Societies', in Moorey (ed.), 1979, pp. 103-127.
Saprykhin, V.A. (1970), 'Rol' sub"yektivnogo faktora v preodolenii religii v usloviyakh

sotsializma' (The Role of the Subjective Factor in the Overcoming of Religion in Conditions of Socialism') in Kurochkin et. al., Moscow, 1970.

Schaff, Adam (1963), *A Philosophy of Man*, London, Lawrence and Wishart.

– (1965), *Marxismus und das menschliche individuum*, Vienna, Europa Verlag.

Schiller, J.C.F. von (1795), *Letters on the Aesthetic Education of Mankind*.

Schnabel, Franz (1964), *Deutsche Gesschichte im neunzehnlten Jahrhundet*, vol. I, *Die Grundlagen der Neueren geschichte*; vol. II, *Der Aufstieg der Nationen*, Freiburg, Herder, 1964.

Semenov, Yu.I. (1976), 'Razvitiye obshchestvenno-economicheskikh formatsiy i ob" yektivnaya logika evolyutsii religii (The Development of the Socio-Economic Stages (of Society) and the Objective Logic of the Evolution of Religion), *VNA*, vol. 20, 1976, pp. 43-61.

Shakhnovich, M.I. (1948), *Ot suyeveriy k nauke* (from Superstition to Science), Leningrad.

– (1961), *Lenin i problemy ateizma* (Lenin and the Problem of Atheism), Moscow-Leningrad, AN.SSSR.

– (1967), 'Issledovaniye sovetskoy naukoy problem proiskhozhdeniya religii i yeye rannikh form' (The Researches of Soviet Science into the Problem of the Origin of Religion and its Early Forms), *VNA* (1967), vol. 4, pp. 242-266.

Shapiro, Leonard and Reddaway, Peter (1967), *Lenin: The Man, The Theorist, The Leader*, London, Pall Mall Press.

Sharevskaya, B.I. (1959), 'Etnologiya i teologiya' (Ethnology and theology), *SE*, 1959, no. 6, pp. 188-201.

– (1964), *Staryye i novyye religii tropicheskoy i yuzhnoy Afriki* (Old and New Religions of Tropical and Southern Africa), Moscow, 'Nauka'.

Sharpe, Eric J. (1975), *Comparative Religion: A History*, London, Duckworth.

Shastri, D.N. (1956), *2,500 Years of Buddhism*, New Delhi, 1956.

Shelikhanov, M.A. (1971), 'Ateisticheskoye vospitaniye detey' (The Atheistic Upbringing of Children), *Nachal'naya shkola*, no. 10. 1971.

Shternberg, L.R. (1936), *Pervobytnaya religiya v svete ethnografii* (Primitive Religion in the Light of Ethnography), Leningrad, 1936.

Shub, David (1966), *Lenin*, Harmondsworth, Pelican Books.

Shubkin, V.N. (1970), *Sotsiologicheskiye opyty (Metodologicheskiya voprosy sotsial'nykh issledovaniy)* (Social Experiences (Methodological Questions of Social Research)), Moscow.

Sibree, J. (1900), trans. Hegel: *Lectures in the Philosophy of History*, London.

Singer, Peter (1980), *Marx*, Oxford (Past Masters Series), O.U.P.

Skolimovsky, H. (1967), 'Creative Developments in Polish Marxism', in *Cambridge Review*, 1967, pp. 255-260.

Skvortsov-Stepanov, I.I. (1922a), 'O zagrobnoy zhizni, o boge u bessmertii (On Life After Death, God and Immortality) in *Molodaya gvardiya* (Young Guard), 1922, nos. 4-5.

– (1922b), 'Strakh smerti protiv istoricheskogo materializma' (The Fear of Death against Historical Materialism), *PZM*, nos. 11-12, 1922.

– (1923), 'Smert' strakha smerti kak itog moyey polemiki' (The Death of the Fear of Death as the Sum of my Polemics), *PZM*, nos. 9-10, 1923.

– (1925), *Ocherk razvitiya religioznykh verovaniy* (Outline of the Growth of Religious Beliefs), Moscow.

Smart, Ninian (1964), *Philosophers and Religious Truth*, London, S.C.M.

Smirnov, I.A. (1928), *Islam i sovremennyy vostok* (Islam and the Contemporary East), Moscow.

Smirnov, N.A. (1954), *Ocherki istorii izucheniya islama v SSSR* (Outline of the History of Islamic Studies in the USSR), Moscow.

- (1963), *Myuridizm na Kavkaze* (Muridism in the Caucuses), Moscow.
- (1967), 'Pyat'desyat let sovetskogo islamovederuya' (Fifty Years of Soviet Study of Islam), *VNA*, vol. 4, 1967.
Smirnov, V. (1971), 'Voinstvuyushchiy neprimirimyy' (Unacceptable Militancy) in *Komsomol'skaya pravda*, Oct. 13, 1971, p.2.
Sokolov, N. and Belous, S. (1966), 'Chto znachit byt'ateistom' (What It means to be an Atheist), in *Sovetskaya Rossiya,* July 6, 1966.
Somerville, John and Parsons, Howard L. (ed.) (1974), *Dialogues on the Philosophy of Marxism,* Westport, Connecticut, Greenwood Press.
Sputnik ateista (The Atheists' Companion), 2nd ed., Moscow, 1961.
Stalin, J.V., *Sochineniya* (Works), vols. 1-13, Moscow, 1946- (not completed).
- *Collected Works* (SCW), Eng. trans. 13 vols., New York, 1954-.
- *History of the Communist Party of the Soviet Union (Bolsheviks):* Short Course, Moscow, F.L.P.H., 1951.
- *Problems of Leninism,* Moscow, F.L.P.H., 1951.
- *Marxism and Linguistics,* New York, 1951, International Pub.
Stein, M. and Vidich, A. (eds.) (1963), *Sociology on Trial,* New York.
Stetskevich, T.A. (1977), 'Nekotoryye aktual'nyye problemy istorii islama v sovremennoy sovetskoy istoriographii (Some Actual Problems of the History of Islam in Contemporary Soviet Historiography), in *Ateizm, religiya, sovremennost': sbornik trudov* (MIRA), L. 1977.
Strauss, David Friedrich (1835), *Life of Jesus.*
Studies in Soviet Thought, IV (1964), pp. 319-338 'Bibliography: Soviet Writings on Atheism and Religion'; V (1965), pp. 106-113 'Bibliography; Soviet Writing on Religion and Atheism: Supplement. Dordrecht, Holland, Reidel.
Sukharev, O.A. (1958), 'K voprosu o kul'te musul'manskykh svyatykh v Sredney Azii (The Problem of the Cult of Muslim Saints in Central Asia), *Trudy Instituta istorii i arkheologii A.N. Uzbekskogo SSR T.II.*
Sukhoplyuyev, I. (1923), *Vidokremlennya shkoly vid tserkvy,* Kharkiv-Kyiv.
Sykes, Gerald (ed.) (1964), *Alienation: The Cultural Climate of Our Time,* 2 vols., New York.

Thrower, James (1960), Religion Without Ontology?, unpublished MA thesis, University of Durham.
- (1965/1966), 'Karl Marx on Religion', in *Ghana Bulletin of Theology,* vol. 2; no. 8, June 1965, pp. 33-39; nos. 9 and 10, December 1965, June, 1966, pp. 44-49.
- (1975), 'Atheism and "Religious Survivals" in the Soviet Union with Particular Reference to the Anti-Religious Offensive of 1959-64', dept. of R/s, Aberdeen.
- (1976), 'Irreligia a ateizm' (Irreligion and Atheism), in *Euhemer,* 1976, no. 4 (102), Warsaw.
- (1980), *The Alternative Tradition: Religion and the Rejection of Religion in the Ancient World,* The Hague, Mouton.
Tiele, Cornelis, P. (1899), *Elements of the Science of Religion,* 2 vols., Edinburgh and London, Blackwood and Sons.
Tokarev, S.A. (1956), 'Problema proiskhozhdeniya i rannikh form religii' (Problems of the Origin and Early Forms of Religion), *VF,* 1956, no. 6, pp. 125-138.
- (1957), *Religioznye verovaniya vostochnoslavyanskikh narodov XIX-nachala XXv* (The Religious Beliefs of Eastern Slavic Peoples), AA.CCCP, 1957.
- (1962), 'Chto takoye mifologiya?' (What is Myth?) *VIRA,* vol. 10, 1962, pp. 338-375.
- (1964a), *Religiya v istorii narodov mira* (Religion in the History of the Peoples of the World), Politizdat, Moscow, 3rd revised ed., 1976.

– (1964b), *Ranniye formy religii i ikh razvitiye* (Early Forms of Religion and Their Development), Nauka, Moscow.
– (1976), 'Problemy periodizatsiya istorii religii' (Problems of 'Periodisation' in the History of Religion), *VNA*, vol. 16, 1976, pp. 62-87.
– (1976b), 3rd ed. of *Religiya v istorii narodov mira*. All refs (unless to 1964b) are to this edition.
Toncher, V.K. and Duluman, E.K. (1964), 'Opyt konkretnogo issledovaniya kharaktera religioznykh predstavleniy (The Experience of Concrete Research into Religious Conceptions), *VF*, 1964, no. 10.
Treadgold, Donald W. (1973), *The West in Russia and China* vol. I, *Russia 1472-1917*, Cambridge, C.U.P.
Trotsky, Leon (1974), *The Young Lenin*, Harmondsworth, Pelican Books.
Tucker, Robert (1961), *Philosophy and Myth in Karl Marx*, Cambridge, C.U.P.
Tugarinov, V.P. (1960), *O tsennostyakh zhizni i kul'tury* (On the Importance of Life and Culture), Leningrad, 1960.
Tylor, E.B. (1871), *Primitive Culture*, 2 vols., New York, Harper Torch Books, 1958.

Ugrinovich, D.M. (1965), *Filosofskiye problemy kritiki religii* (Philosophical Problems of the Criticism of Religion), Mosocw.
– (1966), 'Religiya kak predmet marksistskogo sotsiologicheskogo issledovaniya' (Religion as a Subject of Marxist Sociological Study), *VF*, 1966, no. 1.
– (1967), 'O spetsifike i structure religioznogo soznaniya' (On the Specific Features and Structure of the Religious Consciousness), *VNA*, no. 1, 1967.
Unger, A.L. (1974), *The Totalitarian Party*, Cambridge, CUP.
Ulyanov, L.N. (1970), 'Izmeneniye kharaktera religioznosti' (Change in the Characther of Religiosity) in *K obshchestvu, svobodnomu ot religii*, Moscow.

van Leeuwen, Arend Th. (1972), *Critique of Heaven*, London, Lutterworth Press.
Voprosy filosofii (VF) (Problems of Philosophy), Moscow, 1947- Pravda.
Voprosy ideologicheskoy raboty (Problems of Ideological Work), Moscow, 1961.
Voprosy istorii religiya i ateizma (Problems of the History of Religion and Atheism) (VIRA), Moscow, 1950-1964, AN SSSR.
Voprosy nauchnogo ateizma (Problems of Scientific Atheism) (VNA), Moscow, 1966-Mysl'.
Vree, Dale (1976), *On Synthesising Marxism and Christianity*, New York, Wiley-Interscience Publication.

Waardenburg, Jacques (1973), *Classical Approaches to the Study of Religion*, vol. 1, Introduction and Anthology, The Hague, Mouton.
Wach, Joachim (1935), 'The Meaning and Task of the History of Religions' in Kitagawa (ed.), 1967.
Wackenheim, Charles (1963), *La faillite de la religion d'après Karl Marx*, Paris, P.U.F.
Walsh, W.H. (1951), *An Introduction to Philosophy of History*, London, 1951.
Watt, W. Montgomery (1961), *Muhammad: Prophet and Statesman*, Oxford, Oxford University Press.
Wetter, Gustav (1963), *Dialectical Materialism: A Historical and Systematic Survey of Philosophy in the Soviet Union*, New York, Praeger.
Willey, Basil (1934), *The Seventeenth Century Background*, Harmondsworth, Penguin Books, 1962.
Wittgenstein, L. (1966), *Lectures and Conversations on Aesthetics, Psychology and Religious Belief*, Cyril Barrett (ed.), Oxford, Basil Blackwell.

Yablokov, I.N. (1965a), 'Isvrashcheniye religiey nravstvennykh chuvstv' (The Distortion in Religion of Moral Feelings), *FN,* 1965, no. 1.
– (1965b), 'Vliyaniye nekotorykh psikhologicheskikh faktorov na religioznost' (The Influence of Several Psychological Factors on Religiosity), *Vestnykh M.G.U.* seriya *Ekonomika, filosofiya,* 1965, no. 2.
Yaroslavsky, E. (1934), *Kommunisty i religiya* (Communists and Religion), Moscow.
Yastrebov, I.B. (1979), *Sotsial'nyy progress i razvitiye ateizma* (Social Progress and the Growth of Atheism), *Seriya nauchnyy ateizm,* no. 7, 1979, Znanie, Moscow.
Yeryshev, A.A. (1967), 'Opyt konkretno-sotsiologicheskikh issledovaniy religioznosti naseleniya na Ukraine' (Experiences of Concrete Sociological Research on Religiosity of the Population of the Ukraine), in Klibanov et. al., 1967.
Yezhegodnik muzeya istorii religii i ateizma (YMIRA), 7 vols., Moscow-Leningrad, 1957-1963.
Yinger, J. Milton, *The Science of Religion,* London, Macmillan, 1970.

Zaehner, R.C. (1966), *Hinduism,* Oxford, O.U.P.
– (ed.) (1971), *Concise Encyclopaedia of Living Faiths,* London, Hutchinson.
Zavlavskaya, T.I. (1970), *Migratsiya sel'skogo naseleniya* (Migration of a Rural Population), Moscow.
Zdravemyslov, A.G. et. al. (1970), *Man and His Work,* trans. Stephen P. Gunn, White Plains, New York.
Zhukov, E.M. (1976), 'Rol' religii v mirovoy istorii' (The Role of Religion in World History), *VNA,* vol. 20, 1976.
Zybkovels, V.F. (1958), *Doreligioznaya epokha: k istorii formirovaniya obshchestvennogo soznaniya* (The Pre-Religious Epoch: Towards the Formation of Social Consciousness), Moscow.

Index